CHILD DEVELOPMENT
CHANGE OVER TIME

▼

Eighth Edition

NORA NEWCOMBE
Temple University

Based on
CHILD DEVELOPMENT AND PERSONALITY
Seventh Edition

PAUL HENRY MUSSEN
University of California, Berkeley

JOHN JANEWAY CONGER
University of Colorado School of Medicine

JEROME KAGAN
Harvard University

ALETHA CAROL HUSTON
University of Kansas

■ HarperCollins*CollegePublishers*

Acquisitions Editor: Jill Lectka
Developmental Editor: Rebecca Kohn
Project Editor: Susan Goldfarb
Text Designer and Art Coordinator: Alice Fernandes-Brown
Cover Designer: Rubina Yeh
Art Studio: Network Graphics
Photo Researcher: Rosemary Hunter
Electronic Production Manager: Alexandra Odulak
Manufacturing Manager: Hilda Koparanian
Electronic Page Makeup: Americomp
Printer and Binder: R. R. Donnelley & Sons, Inc.
Cover Printer: New England Book Components

Cover: *Carousel* (1957) by Mary Flournoy Passailaigue/Morris Museum of Art, Augusta, Georgia.

Child Development: Change over Time, Eighth Edition
Based on *Child Development and Personality,* Seventh Edition

Library of Congress Cataloging-in-Publication Data
Newcombe, Nora.
    Child development : change over time / Nora Newcombe. — 8th ed.
        p.   cm.
    Rev. ed. of: Child development and personality / Paul Henry Mussen
    . . . et al. 7th ed. c1990.
    Includes bibliographical references and indexes.
    ISBN 0–673–99311–6
    1. Child psychology.   2. Child development.   I. Child development
and personality.   II. Title
BF721.N5146   1995
155.4–dc20   95–12721
                                                      CIP

95 96 97 98 9 8 7 6 5 4 3 2 1

For
Talia and Andrew

BRIEF CONTENTS

Contents vii
Preface xvii

CONTENTS

▼

PREFACE

▼

This text is both new and old. It is based on the seventh edition of *Child Development and Personality,* a classic textbook originally written by Paul Mussen and John Conger. Jerome Kagan joined Mussen and Conger as an author of subsequent editions, and this team later added Aletha Huston as a coauthor. When these four scholars were unable to continue with revision of the book, Jerry Kagan (and HarperCollins) invited me to assume authorship. So, retitled *Child Development: Change over Time* and with a single author, it's now both an eighth edition and a book with new information and a fresh "feel." This combination gives students a textbook containing the scholarly expertise of five well-known child development researchers but with an evenness of literary style and unity of approach not usually found in multiple-authored books. In short, students get the best of two worlds.

It's been interesting to work on a book from which I learned as an undergraduate (in Bob McCall's child development course at Antioch College) and from which I taught as a graduate student at Harvard. Pedagogy has changed a great deal since those days, I believe for the better. As a small example, the book I read at Antioch followed the practice of using superscript numbers in the body of the text to designate numbered references, so that students had to look up the corresponding notes at the back of the book to get a sense of the evidential base for the text's assertions. Simply from the fact that references are given as names in the text, the student today gets much more of a sense that knowledge is created by real people who may disagree with one another. Advances in critical thinking skills may flow even from simple changes.

✷ CHANGES IN COVERAGE

The field of developmental psychology has changed a great deal, too, since I used an early version of this text as an undergraduate. When one is bogged down in the day-to-day details of research, it's easy to lose sight of the progress we are making in understanding development. But progress there is, and one of the most personally gratifying aspects of working on this book has been to gain a full view of how much we've been learning and how fast the pace of that learning now is. More than 20 percent of the references in this book are new to this edition (that is, they date from 1989 or later), and around 40 percent of the text was rewritten to reflect changes in thinking about child development since the last edition was published.

Many topics have been specially updated or appear for the first time in this edition, and there have been changes in organization from the seventh edition. New or extensively updated topics include the following:

♦ Genetics and behavior genetics, now set off from prenatal development in a separate chapter (Chapter 2).

♦ Up-to-date treatment of prenatal testing and the birth process (Chapter 3).

♦ New material on brain development (Chapter 4).

♦ Integration of Piagetian approaches to cognitive development with other views (in both Chapter 5 and Chapter 9), a task that entailed integrating the seventh edition's separate chapters on Piagetian and information-processing approaches to childhood cognition.

♦ Treatment of the spate of new research on infant perceptual and cognitive development (Chapters 4 and 5).

♦ A discussion of attachment styles (Chapter 6).

♦ A contemporary approach to day care issues (Chapter 6).

♦ New data on the growth of symbolic representation such as delayed imitation and the use of models (Chapter 7).

♦ Integration of nativist and empiricist approaches to language development, still often presented as diametrically opposed (Chapter 8).

♦ A discussion of domain-specific and Vygotskyan approaches to cognition, as well as information-processing and Piagetian approaches (Chapter 9).

♦ Juxtaposition of the IQ controversy with a discussion of issues of schooling, so that students see the relationship between genetic and environmental influences more clearly (Chapter 10).

♦ A new treatment of ethnic identity (Chapters 11 and 15).

♦ A presentation of new research on gender and sex role (Chapter 11).

♦ A discussion of recent research on the female experience of puberty and adolescence (Chapter 14).

♦ A new chapter on developmental psychopathology (Chapter 16).

❁ KEY FEATURES

This text contains several distinctive features, many of them new to this edition.

Theoretical Foundations

As in previous editions, the book presents child development in the context of developmental theory rather than simply presenting isolated facts about child development. This is essential if students are to get a sense of developmental psychology as a science and are to be given the conceptual tools for thinking on their own about problems in development. However, the text does not isolate theory in separate history or theory sections of an introductory chapter. Rather, theories are introduced and explained in context, in order to enhance students' sense of how theory is related to the study of substantive issues. For example, Piaget's work is introduced and summarized in the discussion of infant cognition in Chapter 5, "Cognitive Development in Infancy." Piaget's theory is then reintroduced and used to structure a good deal of the discussion of childhood thought in Chapter 9, "Cognitive Development in Childhood," and of adolescent thought in Chapter 14, "Physical and Cognitive Development in Adolescence." This way of dealing with theory prevents students from viewing theory as a decontextualized subject of its own. When attempting to understand particular facts and problems, there is nothing so practical as a good theory.

Pedagogy

There are three pedagogical features new to this edition that are designed to engage students in thinking about the material.

♦ *"Critical Thinking About the Chapter."* Each chapter includes, along with detailed review questions, questions to encourage critical thinking about themes in the text. These questions are intended to provoke students into wrestling with controversial or unsolved issues and to relate the scholarly material to personal questions and concerns. Instructors may wish to use these questions as themes for brief essays or as topics for small-group discussions.

♦ *Boxes.* The boxes in this book are drawn from literature and are meant to add a personal and emotionally direct perspective on topics treated in the text, as well as to underline the diversity of human development across the boundaries of gender, ethnic group, and historical period. For example, novelist Zora Neale Hurston's account of how she used to believe as a child that the moon followed her around (in Chapter 9, "Cognitive Development in Childhood") is an amusing and beautifully written description of thought in early childhood, as well as a view of childhood in a time and place different from those experienced by most college students. As another example, Marjorie Shostak's account of childbearing by a !Kung woman in southern Africa (in Chapter 3) is both direct and gripping, and leads students to appreciate the diversity of human experience.

♦ *Vignettes.* Each chapter is introduced by a short vignette. These stories were written to focus students' attention on issues that are addressed in the chapter, again in a personal and emotionally direct way, emphasizing the diversity of human development. The vignettes are accompanied by photographs to form arresting chapter openers. Vignettes are also used within the text to relate factual information and theoretical themes to particular experiences.

Illustrations

This new edition contains an entirely new set of illustrations. Photographs in child development books increase students' interest in the subject if they are carefully tied to themes in the text. I have tried to select pictures that are visually appealing but also reinforce important intellectual points. In addition, the photographs help to emphasize the diversity of human development across gender, ethnicity, and social class.

Supplements

The publisher has prepared a comprehensive set of supplementary material to accompany this new edition.

The Study Guide (ISBN 0-673-99332-9) is written by Rebecca L. Slaton. Each chapter contains a chapter outline, key terms, learning objectives, study tips, and a practice test.

The Instructor's Manual (ISBN 0-673-55770-7), by Judith Semon Dubas, features chapter outlines, learning objectives, key words and concepts, teaching tips and classroom activities, lecture and discussion modules, lists of audiovisual suggestions, and references and suggested readings.

The Test Bank (ISBN 0-673-55772-3), written by Sharon Hawkins, contains approximately 1600 test questions. Each of the multiple choice, short answer, and essay questions are referenced to text page number, topic, and skill.

Two forms of software are available with the Test Bank. TestMaster Computerized Testing System is a flexible, easy-to-master computerized test bank that includes all the test items in the printed test bank. The TestMaster software allows instructors to edit existing questions and add their own items. It is available in IBM or Macintosh formats. Quizmaster is a new software program available to instructors that allows students to take TestMaster-generated tests on the computer. Quiz-Master gives the students their scores right away, along with a diagnostic report at the end of the test. This report lets the students know which topics or objectives they may need to review in order to improve their scores. Test scores can be saved on disk, allowing instructors to keep track of scores for individual students, class sections, or whole courses.

Supershell II Student Tutorial (ISBN 0-673-99332-9) is an interactive computerized tutorial for IBM and IBM-compatible computers, as well as for Macintosh. In addition to chapter outlines and glossary terms, it provides immediate correct answers to multiple choice, true-false, and short answer questions. All of the material is referenced to the corresponding text page. This tutorial contains material not found in the Study Guide and provides a running score for students. It is written by Pamela Griesler of the Columbia Medical School.

❂ ACKNOWLEDGMENTS

I would like to thank Carol Foltz and Eunhui Lie for their help with bibliographic research and organization, and my development editor at HarperCollins, Becky Kohn, for her patient and insightful guidance and suggestions. Jill Lectka, Art Pomponio, and Marcus Boggs of HarperCollins were also unfailingly supportive and helpful. My colleague at Temple, Kathy Hirsh-Pasek, was kind enough to comment on the chapter on language development. The following colleagues reviewed the book for HarperCollins and made many helpful suggestions:

Len J. Abbeduto, University of Wisconsin–Madison
Mark B. Alcorn, University of Northern Colorado
Alan C. Butler, University of Maine
Richard Clubb, University of Arkansas at Monticello
Shari Ellis, Carnegie–Mellon University
Daniel Fawaz, DeKalb College
Shirlee Fenwick, Augustana College
Gregory T. Fouts, University of Calgary
Harvey Ginsburg, Southwest Texas State University
Sydney Hans, University of Chicago
Rebecca Kriesel-Bigler, University of Texas at Austin
Frank Manis, University of Southern California
Shitala Mishra, University of Arizona
Barbara Moely, Tulane University
Lois Muir, University of Wisconsin–La Crosse
Charlotte Patterson, University of Virginia
Robert Shilkret, Mount Holyoke College
Peggy Skinner, South Plains College
Jerome Small, Youngstown State University
Bob Thompson, Shoreline Community College

Finally, I'd like to thank my family: my children, Talia and Andrew, who have taught me much about development one cannot learn from books; and my husband, Jeffrey Lerner, who believed I could do this project even when I didn't.

Nora Newcombe

PART

1

INTRODUCTION

▼

CHAPTER

1

THEORY AND METHOD IN THE STUDY OF CHILD DEVELOPMENT

Janice looked around unhappily at the group of four-year-olds at the birthday party. Everyone seemed happy and excited: everyone that is, except her daughter Molly. Molly sat alone, looking frightened. Despite repeated urging from Janice, she wouldn't join in the games, sing "Happy Birthday," or even watch her friend Sarah open her presents. She asked Janice again and again to take her home.

Janice wondered, as she had many times before, why Molly behaved this way and what she should do about it. Molly's older sister, Emma, was very outgoing, but Janice herself had been shy as a child. Was it inherited? Or did Molly's reluctance to join into group activities have to do with something Janice had done? Too much or too little love and attention? And, most important, what did this behavior mean for the future? Would Molly be able to adjust to school, make friends, and get along in the world? Would she just "grow out of it," as Janice's own mother always said when the topic came up?

Carl frowned as he walked away from the day care center holding his son's hand. He'd arrived to find Nicholas in "time out" yet again. Donna, the teacher, had spoken with him about Nicky. She said he just couldn't seem to remember not to hit children who made him mad. In fact, he always seemed to be nudging or shoving someone, and the teachers were at the end of their rope.

Carl tried to talk to Nicky about hitting in the car on the way home. But all he got in response was a long list of the complaints Nicky felt had justified his every action. Clearly, something had to be done. But what? Should they limit Nicky's TV-viewing? Should they take him out of day care for a while? Carl also wondered if anything really needed to be done. After all, wasn't this behavior just typical for boys of Nicky's age?

The kind of questions plaguing Janice and Carl exemplify the questions about children's development that come up again and again: for parents, for teachers, for therapists, and for people just plain curious about their lives and the lives of others. The answers to some questions are very clear, while others are tentative or hotly debated. This book explores how we ask and answer questions about children's development. It will examine both what we have learned and what we still do not know. The knowledge gained from research on child development is important for advising parents (or being a parent), forming educational programs, creating and defending government programs for children, making legal policies affecting children, and devising treatments for problem behavior.

✿ WHAT IS DEVELOPMENT?

Answers to questions like those that plagued Janice and Carl are usually sought first in common sense and introspection. For instance, Janice talked to her mother about Molly's problems and searched her own life for clues to their cause. But every time she seemed to find an answer, something came up to challenge it. The scientific investigation of children's development arose from the hope that these and other questions could best be answered by systematic investigation of larger groups of individuals.

The study of human development is the study of how and why the human organism grows and changes throughout life. **Development** is defined as orderly and relatively enduring changes over time in physical and neurological structures, in thought processes, in emotions, in forms of social interaction, and in many other behaviors. In the first 20 years of life, these changes usually result in new, improved ways of reacting—that is, in behavior that is better organized, more complex, more stable, more competent, or more efficient. Advances from creeping to walking, from babbling to talking, or from concrete to abstract thinking are all examples of development. In each case, the later-appearing state represents an improved way of functioning.

One goal of studying development is to understand changes that appear to be *universal.* These are changes that occur in all children regardless of the culture in which they grow up or the experiences they have. For example, children all over the world smile at human faces during the second or third month of life, utter their first word at around 12 months, and walk alone at around 13 months. We try first to describe these changes. Then we attempt to explain why they occur—to understand what biological variables and what experiences influence them. The knowledge we generate can be used to determine, among other things, what behaviors are normal or natural for different ages, or whether child-rearing practices have different effects at different ages.

A second goal of studying development is to explain *individual differences.* Some infants react by crying loudly when their mother leaves the room; others play happily. Some children are gregarious and extroverted; others (like Molly) have a hard time with strangers and with new situations. Some children learn mathematical concepts quickly; others find math more difficult. Information about individual differences can help answer questions about what characteristics of individual children should be considered in making decisions about schooling, custody, or discipline plans.

A third goal of studying development is to understand how children's behavior is influenced by the *environmental context* or situation. A child may be friendly and outgoing to adults who come to her home, but shy when she meets adults at school.

Children go through universal stages of motor development. Learning to walk occurs at very similar ages worldwide, although encouragement and opportunity for practice also make a difference.

An adolescent is more likely to use marijuana if he attends a school where many others use it than if marijuana use is uncommon among his peers.

Environmental context includes not only the immediate situation but also attributes of the larger settings in which people live—the family, neighborhood, cultural group, or socioeconomic group. Such settings are sometimes described as the **ecology** of the child's behavior. They can influence development by creating opportunities for different behaviors to occur or by affecting parents' behavior. For instance, children who live within walking distance of their school have more opportunity to play with classmates or participate in after-school activities than those who live at a distance and must leave immediately after school on a bus. Conscientious parents who live in dangerous urban neighborhoods often do not allow their children to play outdoors after school. Their priority is protecting their children. In a safer neighborhood, the same parents may encourage their children to go to a local park or to another child's home (Eccles & Harold, 1993).

Cultural and subcultural groups also value different behaviors. Modern American parents whose child talks back to them may view the child as articulate and assertive, but in other historical periods, parents saw such behavior as disobedient and insolent. In another context, a shanty town in Brazil where almost half the children born die before the age of 5 years, parents may value a child seen as a "fighter" because such a child is seen as likely to have the stamina to survive in a hostile environment (Scheper-Hughes, 1985).

These three aspects of children's development—universal patterns, individual differences, and contextual influences—are all necessary for a full understanding of development. The emphasis placed on any one of them depends on the theoretical orientation guiding the investigator and the types of questions being studied.

⊙ THEORETICAL ISSUES

Anyone who studies children, whether as a scientist or as a practitioner, must confront certain fundamental issues. There is no one "right" answer to most of them. Instead, different points of view represent different assumptions about human nature, about how to interpret existing information, and about which approaches to advancing knowledge are most promising. Integrating points of view and deciding among them is an ongoing process for scientists and for all individuals who deal with children. In this chapter, some of the key issues that need to be decided are outlined. We will return to them in more specific terms throughout the book. In reading this section, you should try to get a feel for the theories and the debates that you will encounter in more depth as you pursue the study of child development.

Environmental vs. Biological Determinants of Behavior

One of the most basic questions facing developmental psychologists is the relative importance of environmental and biological determinants of behavior. This issue is the well-known "nature versus nurture" controversy.

A dedicated biological determinist argues that much of human behavior is guided by genetic makeup, physiological maturation, and neurological functioning. According to this view, the universals of development, such as the emergence of walking, speaking, and responding to other people, are the result of inborn biological factors. Biological determinists also believe that individual differences are largely a result of genetic and physiological differences. Thus, in examining children's learning of language, a biological determinist would see language as an ability that emerges universally at about the same age, with minimal impact of environmental factors such as how adults speak to children. The fact that some children learn to talk a little earlier or later than other children would be seen as likely to be caused by differences in their genetic makeup and neurological maturity.

At the other end of the continuum, environmental determinists argue that the physical and social environments are the key influences shaping development. They believe that children respond to the people and objects around them and that developmental changes are largely the result of experience. In examining language learning, they would focus on the language children hear in their environments, emphasizing that the language addressed to children is often especially simple and thus well suited for beginners to language. The environmentalist would explain differences among children in when they learn to talk as related to whether they hear appropriately simplified speech or not.

Can we resolve this debate simply by acknowledging that both kinds of influence are important? For instance, one might recognize that language has both a biological basis (as shown by the fact that other species do not have a full language capacity) and an environmental basis (as shown by the fact that children not exposed to language do not learn to talk). But arguments still arise over which influence is *more* important. In part, this is because deciding how to intervene in order to correct a developmental problem depends on one's assessment of what the major determinants of the problem are. For example, in dealing with a group of people whose children tend to show language delay, a psychologist who believes in the importance of biological factors might recommend government-supported pre-natal care and periodic evaluation of the children by pediatricians and hearing experts. On the other hand, a psychologist who emphasizes environmental factors might argue for an intervention program that teaches parents the skills of interact-ing with and talking to their children in simple and interesting ways that would encourage their language development.

Many scientists contend that we cannot separate or assign weights to biological and environmental factors because the two interact from the moment of birth (and probably before). These scientists suggest that we should not be concerned with how much effect each influence has; rather, we should concentrate on how the influences work together to lead to outcomes (Anastasi, 1958). These scientists sometimes speak of *transactions* between the organism and the environment.

Imagine two children, Alex and Bob, both born with a biologically based ten-dency to be aggressive, and a third child, Cameron, born without this tendency. In rearing children, one generally wants to avoid having them show inappropriate or excessive levels of aggression. Alex has parents who, when he hits or bites another child, respond to him inconsistently—either coercively or by spanking him. As a result, his tendency to be aggressive increases over time. Bob, in contrast, has par-ents who use consistent and nonphysical forms of punishment. He learns to control his biologically based aggressive tendencies. Cameron, born with a lesser biological predisposition to aggression, is less likely to try hitting and pushing. The way his parents respond to aggression is not an important influence because his aggression occurs infrequently and is easy to discourage with mild reproof.

It is very difficult to say, in each of these cases, whether the outcome is the product of biology or of environment. Alex might not have turned out as aggressive with different parents, so it may seem that environment is crucial. But Alex's par-ents, had they been given Cameron as a son, would have reared a child low in aggression. In short, behavior is usually a product of repeated transactions between biological and environmental determinants.

We will return to the nature-nurture controversy at points throughout the book, as we analyze specific aspects of development. In fact, in Chapter 2 we dis-cuss in detail the impact of genetic and environmental influences on intelligence, personality, and psychopathology, as well as review continuing controversies regarding the role of genetics and environment in development.

Active vs. Passive Nature of the Child

Some theorists view children as passive receivers of experience; others consider them active in organizing, structuring, and in some sense creating their worlds. A scientist who considers children to be passive does not think they are unresponsive, just that they enter the world ready to absorb whatever knowledge is provided by the environ-ment. According to this view, children are molded by stimuli in the external environ-ment and driven by internal needs over which they have little control.

The most prominent theory of development taking this view of the child is what is called *learning theory*. Researchers in this tradition seek to analyze children's development in terms of *stimulus-response learning*. Such learning is the acquisition of connections or associations between environmental events (stimuli) and behav-iors of the child (responses). For example, a child may learn that seeing a moving car in the road should lead to his or her staying on the sidewalk. John B. Watson, an early leader in the learning theory movement, wrote:

> Give me a dozen healthy infants, well-formed, and my own specified world to bring them up in and I'll guarantee to take any one at random and train him to become any type of specialist I might select—doctor, lawyer, merchant, chief, and yes, even beggar-man and thief, regardless of his talents, penchants, abilities, vocations, and the race of his ancestors. (1930/1967, p. 104)

Clearly, Watson believed that the environment determines the nature of children's growth.

More recently, *social learning theory,* as delineated by psychologists such as Albert Bandura and Walter Mischel, has added a dimension to the learning theory of Watson: the recognition that children are shaped, not just by the rewards and punishments they receive, but also by their observation of what others do. Thus, a child may learn to eat food with utensils by observing family members use them. Rewarding a child for using them or punishing the child for eating with his or her fingers may not be necessary. This phenomenon, called *observational learning,* or sometimes *modeling,* adds another mechanism by which the environment affects the child. But the child is still seen as simply absorbing the knowledge made available.

Theorists and educators who view the child as essentially passive often favor direct and carefully structured teaching methods. For example, some methods for teaching children to play a musical instrument contain a series of highly specific steps. Chords and tunes must be learned in a prescribed order. The child must master each step before proceeding to the next one.

A very different view of the child is taken by theorists who believe that children actively interpret their environment. These theorists assume that human beings have an inborn tendency to be curious, to explore their environment, and to organize the resulting experience in their own mental frameworks. What children do and learn, then, depends mainly on interests that come from within and reflect their individual level of understanding. A music teacher who had this view of child development might allow children more freedom to explore the effects of different actions on their instrument, intervening to show what combinations produced pleasing sounds when children seemed ready for such information. The teacher might continue by encouraging children to make up tunes or select among different exercises.

The most prominent theorist taking this position on the nature of the child is Jean Piaget. A Swiss psychologist, he revolutionized our understanding of children's cognitive development. Particular aspects of his theory are reviewed in following chapters. His observations of development, including intensive studies of his three children, led him to argue that the way children interact with the environment is determined by their current level of understanding. An infant will have a very different understanding than an older child or an adult. The baby, for instance, may see something that shakes and makes a noise, whereas the older child sees a piggybank and the adult sees a priceless antique.

Continuity vs. Discontinuity in Development

Do developmental changes occur continuously in small, gradual, cumulative steps, or in discontinuous jumps that produce qualitatively new and different abilities and patterns of behavior? Consider an example from motor development. Babies typically begin to crawl sometime during the second six months of life. At first they

When teaching, an adult can follow a strict sequence of steps or can interact with the child in a way that builds on the child's interests and readiness to learn.

creep on their stomach, then rock on hands and knees, and finally lurch forward and start to crawl. Over time they become better coordinated, faster, and more skilled at crawling. These changes are continuous—that is, they show a gradual improvement in skill. To stand on two feet and walk across the room, however, requires a completely different set of movements. The change from crawling to walking is not just a simple extension of crawling skills; it represents a qualitatively different behavior pattern. It is a discontinuous change.

Examples of continuous and discontinuous developmental curves appear in Figure 1.1. Discontinuous changes are sometimes called **stages of development**. The term *stage* is used in everyday speech to describe almost any behavior that is related to age (for example, a parent might speak of a toddler as being in the "No" stage). But in developmental psychology the term *stage* has a more specific meaning. First, stages are qualitatively different from one another. The underlying structure of behavior or thought changes when a child moves from one stage to another. Stages of motor behavior include crawling and walking; stages of thought refer to different ways of thinking about the world. Second, stages occur in a fixed order. Crawling always precedes walking. Children may go through stages at different ages, but they all go through them in the same order.

All developmentalists agree that some changes occur continuously and gradually, but they do not agree about whether some changes are discontinuous. Some assert that all changes are cumulative, building on what went before. Learning the-

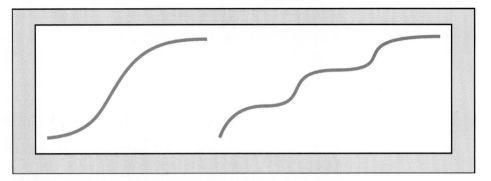

FIGURE 1.1 Examples of two types of growth curves. The curve on the left shows a continuous pattern of gradual change leveling off as the maximum level is reached. An example might be growth in vocabulary. The curve on the right shows discontinuous growth in which relatively sudden changes are interspersed with gradual change. An example might be the learning of grammar, where there are sudden changes as children acquire control of particular ways of putting sentences together.

orists and social learning theorists typically take this position. Other theorists argue that some aspects of development are best regarded as discontinuous. Piaget took this view of cognitive development. In the realm of social and emotional development, stage theories have been advanced by Sigmund Freud and Erik Erikson. Freud, the founder of psychoanalysis, argued that children progress through stages defined by the parts of the body where their energy is focused, beginning with the mouth in the oral stage of infancy and going through stages of anal and phallic focus as preschoolers. Elementary-school children are in a latency period, and adolescence leads the way to a final adult stage. Erikson, originally trained as a Freudian psychoanalyst, modified and broadened these stages to focus on their social as well as individual meaning, and he extended the model to cover the whole life span.

Stability over Time

Is an aggressive preschooler likely to be an aggressive adult? (This is one of the questions to which Carl, the father in one of our opening vignettes, would like an answer.) Does early separation from the family produce long-term feelings of anxiety about separation? Does early education produce lasting changes in intelligence? Affirmative answers to these questions would mean that children's behavior is reasonably stable over time—that is, that early-formed behaviors and personal characteristics predict later behavior.

Many developmental theorists have emphasized the importance of early experience. Sigmund Freud, for instance, thought that children's early experiences with satisfaction of their bodily urges—first oral, then anal, then phallic—had a very great influence on their adult personality. Another theorist, the English psychiatrist John Bowlby, emphasized different early experiences as determinative, focusing on social interaction with significant others in the first three years of life. By contrast, other theories see later experiences as at least as important as early ones in determining behavior. That is, children retain what can be called *plasticity*. Difficult early experiences can be overcome or compensated for. The other side of this coin, unfortunately, is that even an excellent start in life does not guarantee that later negative events will not have a negative effect, although a good start may increase a child's chance of coping with problems.

A considerable amount of research has been devoted to studying the stability of children's behavior. The results are open to different interpretations. One reason for these differing interpretations is that different writers focus on different behaviors and different developmental periods. In general, children's behavior becomes more stable as they grow older. For example, IQ scores in the first few years of life are not good predictors of later IQ, but IQ at age 7 is a reasonably good predictor of IQ in adolescence and adulthood. In addition, different behaviors show different patterns of stability. Aggression is a reasonably stable behavior pattern; children who are aggressive in early and middle childhood are likely to be aggressive in adolescence and adulthood. Altruism and helpfulness are less stable from one time to another (Mischel, 1968).

The question of stability over time is further complicated by the fact that the same characteristics may be expressed in different ways at different ages. In such cases we say that the different behaviors are functionally equivalent. An aggressive child who hits others in nursery school may use insults and subtle hostility at age 12. A sociable 4-year-old offers toys and asks other children to play; at age 12, this child may show the same characteristic by spending hours on the telephone. Because behavior changes with age, psychologists examine the question of stability by looking at how children compare with their peers at one age and then how they compare with their peers at a later age. That is, does a child high in a particular behavior relative to agemates stay high later, and does a child low in the behavior stay low? If a child who has a high rate of initiating play with others compared to other children in nursery school also ranks relatively high in the amount of time on the telephone at age 12, we infer that a trait such as sociability is stable over time.

Consistency Across Situations

Is a child who is highly aggressive at home also aggressive at school? Is a child who is shy with peers also shy with adults? In other words, is children's behavior specific to particular situations, or do children have traits that are manifested in a wide range of settings? Is it the person or the situation that primarily directs the individual's behavior?

Learning theorists, most notably Walter Mischel (1968), marshalled evidence that behavior is quite variable across situations. By contrast, theorists such as Freud, Erikson, or Bowlby would predict more consistency of personality across situations; their theories view personality structure as constant once it is developed. Another group of scientists who would emphasize cross-situation consistency are those who believe that personality traits are under substantial genetic control. (We discuss this further in Chapter 2.)

As you can see from this overview of five key theoretical issues confronted by investigators of child development, there are many different approaches to the issue of understanding development. Because theories of development are often constructed to explain behavior and behavioral change in particular domains, most of these theories are best understood in the context of discussing particular topics in development. Therefore, for example, we will discuss Piaget when we deal with cognitive development, and Erikson when we examine personality development. Similarly, many of the controversies we have outlined are more important and more clearly delineated in certain areas than in others. So, for instance, our discussion of language development will revolve around the relative emphases different researchers place on innate knowledge and on the role of the environment.

In taking this approach to theory, we are encouraging you to see theory as relevant to explanation rather than as an isolated body of assertions with little direct connection to phenomena. We are also encouraging you to see theories as evolving rather than as static, and controversies as leading to advances in knowledge and understanding rather than as polarities in need of immediate resolution. The philosophy behind this approach is articulated more fully (and more poetically) in Box 1.1.

⚙ RESEARCH ON CHILD DEVELOPMENT

Folk wisdom or informal experiences with children are often the beginning points for inquiry about children's development. But firmer answers to questions usually require systematic research and careful collection, analysis, and evaluation of evidence. Because we do not know the answers, research is challenging and exciting. The process has elements of creating new ideas, solving puzzles, and making the most telling and logical arguments in a debate. Scientific research is central to our knowledge of child development. In this section of the book, we examine what kinds of research developmentalists are engaged in and what methods they use in their inquiry.

Applied and Basic Research

Research is sometimes inspired by pressing social and practical issues concerning children. At other times it is inspired by curiosity about an intriguing observation or by a desire to test the predictions of some theory of development. An example of research inspired by practical concerns is the fact that, as divorce in families with young children has become increasingly common, psychologists and others have studied how children are affected by divorce, what helps children cope with divorce, and how different patterns of custody after divorce affect children's adjustment. Research designed to help parents, schools, and others who deal with children is called **applied research.**

Research intended to generate knowledge about the processes and sequences of development is called **basic research.** An example of such research is the study of infants' ability to recognize the differences among human speech sounds. This study was originally inspired simply by the desire to understand the origins of the complex process of speech perception. Investigators used infant sucking patterns to discover that infants seem to process speech sounds using the same distinctions as are present in adults. Later, clinicians began to use this technique to determine whether a child is hearing-impaired. Thus, basic research often gives rise to knowledge of practical importance.

The Research Process

"Just when I knew all of life's answers, they changed all the questions," proclaims a Hallmark poster. In science, as in many other areas of life, the answers we get are

BOX 1.1
HOW TO STUDY HUMAN DEVELOPMENT

There are many different views of child development, both informal and formal. If they are approached with the view that only one can be right, choosing among them will feel overwhelming and baffling. In this excerpt, Melvin Konner articulates a different attitude toward theory and research, similar to the one we will adopt in this book.

The great Welsh poet Dylan Thomas once wrote:

*The force that through the green fuse drives the
flower
Drives my green age . . .*

The force of life, he meant; the force of growth. Whatever magic wells up irrepressibly through the stem and then slowly breaks a blossom out of the bud, also presses the man up through the body and mind of the boy, the woman through the small frame of the girl. Thomas wrote, too, of a boy his age who'd moved into his neighborhood. They saw each other, and immediately were fighting. Then, having thrashed one another soundly, they strode off, arms around each other's shoulders, friends for life—love at first fight. Such a moment is charged with the mystery of development, with the strange wild incomprehensible independence of childhood: the force that through the green fuse drives the flower.

And yet we say, too, "As the twig is bent, so grows the tree," which seems to mean that we can make a child in our image, that we can gain control of the same growth forces. Or even more arrogantly in our grown-up delusion of power, "Give me a child till he's ten and he'll be mine forever"—in one form or another, a cherished belief of ideologues from the Jesuits to the Bolsheviks. The image is one of training,

drill, reward, punishment, setting examples, molding, shaping moist clay in our hands. In this view the life force seems almost incidental— something like, say, the consistency of the clay. So which vision of childhood is the right one?

Neither, of course—and both. That is the other part of the mystery—the unknown; which, increasingly, we are justified in calling the partly known. It is the vast unexplored sea of *potential* knowledge of just how children change and grow. It is the "science" part. For about a century we have been systematically studying child development with increasingly sophisticated methods. Although much of this research has been in the framework of child psychology, it is now deriving from a surprising array of other disciplines: neuropsychology, sociobiology, cognitive science, molecular genetics, psychological anthropology, computer-based training, behavioral pediatrics, neonatology, adolescent psychiatry. . . . We could go on, but we needn't detain ourselves with such jargon. The point is knowledge, new knowledge, based on really superb research. . . .

Erik Erikson, perhaps the most modest grand theorist, once said wisely: "The trouble with followers is, they repeat what the leader said fifty years ago and think they are following him, but they are not following him anymore." He meant, of course, that the leader would have moved, as he always did while he was living and thinking. To repeat without modification what he said long ago is unfairly to fossilize that thought, and to restrict our own freedom to discover what is true.

Source: From *Childhood* (pp. 6–7, 19), by Melvin Konner, 1991, Boston: Little, Brown. Copyright © 1991 by Melvin Konner. Reprinted by permission of Little, Brown and Company.

only as good as the questions we ask. The first step in scientific research is to identify a good question. How do developmental psychologists decide what to study? How do they choose among the many questions that interest them?

Applied researchers in child development tend to be sensitive to urgent social issues; they often choose questions that address "hot" issues on the public agenda. Moreover, if a social issue becomes a national concern, government funds may be made available to study it, encouraging further interest. For example, in the late 1960s the outbreak of riots in urban ghettos stimulated concern about violence in American society. As a result, government funds were appropriated for a coordinated set of studies to determine how viewing violence on television affects aggressive behavior.

Basic research questions sometimes arise from the need for descriptive information about what children can do at different ages (for example, how many words children usually know at ages 2 or 3). More often, such questions originate from prominent theories that generate testable hypotheses. A theory serves as a lens to help the researcher focus on particular aspects of development while ignoring others. For example, much of the research on child-rearing practices conducted during the 1950s and 1960s was based directly or indirectly on Freud's psychoanalytic theory, which holds that early feeding and toilet training play a significant role in personality development. Psychologists therefore studied the effects of feeding practices and toilet training. They could just as easily have studied children's play patterns or interests, but Freud's theory did not emphasize those domains of children's behavior.

Whatever the initial source of a research question, generating knowledge is a continuous and dynamic process. The diagram in Figure 1.2 illustrates how issues arising from basic theory or from social concerns may be the initial impetus for a

drive force

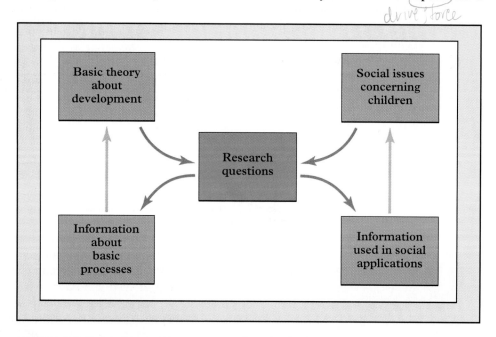

FIGURE 1.2 Research questions can come from basic theory and from social issues concerning children. The answers to each type of question, in turn, contribute to the formulation of additional research problems.

research question. As answers are provided, they feed back to stimulate further questions. Indeed, very often an applied social issue will lead to new theories and basic questions, or the results of basic research will suggest new ways of fostering children's development in the real world. For example, in the 1940s a psychiatrist named René Spitz wrote about severe intellectual and emotional problems among infants in orphanages. His observations led others to do careful basic research on the conditions that are important for the development of visual perception, cognition, and emotional health in infancy. That research, in turn, led institutions and hospitals that served infants to provide mobiles and varied visual stimuli, opportunities to play with toys, and social interactions with adults.

The selection of both basic and applied questions is inevitably affected by contemporary social and cultural values. This idea conflicts with the stereotype of science as the dispassionate pursuit of truth, but in fact, science is not insulated from value judgments. Ultimately, research is a part of a social and political discourse, not removed from it, and recognizing the impact of values on research is a vital part of assessing that research. The findings of research constrain and shape the social and political discourse, though, so that controversies can be informed and modified by data.

An example of the influence that values and theory can have on research is seen in the debate on appropriate child care for infants. Investigators who assume that infants should be cared for primarily by a single adult figure, based perhaps on their reading of Bowlby's theory of development, may investigate day care for infants by asking whether such care has harmful effects. Investigators who believe that receiving sensitive care is the key issue for infants—and who place less emphasis on that care needing to come from a single person—may study the beneficial effects of day care. In either case, the evidence uncovered might or might not support the investigator's views; thus, the data provide a corrective for mistaken theory. But the process of correction may be a drawn out one, because the findings will be interpreted, at least initially, through the lens of the investigator's theory of development. For instance, if no harmful effects of day care are found, someone who believed that they are likely might emphasize the deficiencies of the research and call for use of more sensitive methods of assessing the children.

Methods Used in Studying Children

Many of us observe children every day. For example, teachers and parents know a great deal about children from frequent contact. What is different about the way a researcher observes children? What is required for the scientific study of their behavior?

The methods described here are alike in one way: all of them call for controlled, systematic observation of behavior. In some investigations, behavior is observed as it occurs in real-life settings such as the home or school. In others, specific tasks or situations are created, often in laboratories, so that the reactions of different children can be observed in comparable circumstances. Sometimes children are interviewed; sometimes they are given tests; and sometimes observers use a prearranged set of categories and count the number of times each child displays behaviors in each category. In each case, however, the investigator tries to carry out similar procedures with all the children included in the study and tries to control or evaluate the situational variables that may affect each child's response.

Applied researchers are currently very interested in the effects of day care on infants.

Objectivity is another fundamental feature of scientific research. No matter how a study is designed, its measuring techniques must be as free from subjective bias as possible. For example, in studying aggressive behavior, a researcher must specify exactly and objectively what behaviors are to be called aggressive. Using such precise definitions, different observers can code the behavior of the same children. If these independent observers score a child's behavior similarly, the coding system is assumed to be objective. Objective measures are usually quantifiable—that is, they yield a set of numbers rather than just a verbal description of children's behavior. For example, the number of times a child hits other children might be counted and perhaps compared with the number of times other children hit the child being observed.

Different ways of measuring the same attribute may produce different results. For example, if you want to know how aggressive a group of children are, you might get three quite different answers depending on whether you asked teachers for ratings, asked peers to nominate aggressive children, or observed the children's behavior directly. In general, we feel most confident in drawing conclusions when the results obtained using different methods are *convergent*—that is, when they agree.

In the rest of this section we examine different methods of research in the context of two related research problems. First, does a particular behavior remain stable over age, or does it increase or decrease in frequency? For example, does aggression remain stable or does it change with age? Second, what factors are causally related to a particular behavior? For example, what is the effect of television violence on aggressive behavior? (As you may remember, these were two of the questions that preoccupied Carl after his talk with Nicky's teacher.)

Methods for Studying Change over Time. Because much of developmental psychology is concerned with stability and change in behaviors over time, researchers must have methods for studying children at different ages. They usually begin to study developmental changes with **cross-sectional investigations**, in which children of different ages are compared at one point in time. For example, if we compared groups of children aged 4, 8, 12, and 16, we might find that the amount of hitting and physical aggression is greater for younger children and the amount of verbal, insulting aggression is greater for older children.

Cross-sectional studies provide information about age differences, but they have two important problems. First, differences between different age groups at one point in time could reflect age changes, but they could also be a result of experiences associated with particular historical periods. For example, suppose that television violence had become much more frequent during the two years preceding the study. The 4-year-olds might be responding to the television violence; their behavior might be quite different from that of 4-year-old children ten years earlier who had not been exposed to as much television violence.

A second problem with cross-sectional studies is that they do not enable a researcher to determine whether individual children undergo a transition from physical to verbal aggression and thus maintain a propensity for some form of aggression. For Carl, that is a crucial question. It may be a relief to know that when Nicky is older he won't be hitting as much. However, if he has merely substituted verbal for physical aggression, he may continue to have problems.

Only by studying children over time can we examine whether those who show one kind of behavior at one age are more likely to show a different kind of behavior at another age. This method of study is called **longitudinal investigation**. In a longitudinal investigation, the same children are observed or tested at regular intervals over an extended period, sometimes a decade or longer. This approach overcomes some of the weaknesses of the cross-sectional method. It allows an investigator to study the stability of behavior over time. It is also useful for determining whether individual children undergo the developmental transitions suggested by cross-sectional investigations (e.g., from physical to verbal forms of aggression) and whether, if they do, they nevertheless maintain their relative level of the behavior, or whether they may undergo more profound change.

Longitudinal study, however, also has disadvantages. Clearly, it is time-consuming and expensive. In addition, if people drop out of the study and cannot be observed at older ages, this may introduce bias into the study. For instance, the more aggressive children may not come back to the study because their parents are embarrassed about their behavior. Repeated testing and observation may also change the results, as children gain practice on the tests given or become familiar with the testing environment.

Careful attention to potential problems of both longitudinal and cross-sectional studies may help to solve some of them. For instance, a researcher may work to keep contact with as many people as possible in a longitudinal study, to avoid bias from dropouts. But the best developmental work probably combines cross-sectional and longitudinal methods of investigation.

Methods for Studying Causal Relations. Very often, we not only wish to describe behavior but would also like to assess its causes. For instance, we may want to ask whether viewing violent television programs leads to aggressive behavior in children. Does the television viewing *cause* the aggressive behavior? Establishing causality turns out to be a very tricky enterprise in the study of development.

A first step in investigating the causes of behavior is often the **correlational** study. In the simplest version of a correlational study, an investigator measures two characteristics for a particular group of people and determines whether there is a statistical association (called a *correlation*) between them. For example, information about how much violent television a large sample of elementary schoolchildren watched at home could be obtained by asking the children to indicate which programs they viewed regularly. Their aggression at school could be measured by peer nominations—asking each member of a class to name the children in the class who pushed, shoved, and fought most often. Then the investigator could compute a correlation and see if the two characteristics are related to each other.

A positive correlation means that high levels on one variable tend to be associated with high levels on the other, as might be expected for watching aggressive TV and being aggressive at school. A negative correlation means that high levels on one variable tend to be associated with low levels on the other. For example, education is negatively correlated with the amount of television people watch. Highly educated people watch less television than people with little education. No correlation means that the two variables are not related. For example, height is not related to the amount of television people watch.

Correlations can range from +1.0 to −1.0. The + or − sign indicates the direction of the correlation (positive or negative), and the number describes the magnitude of the relationship. The greater the number, whether it is positive or negative, the more consistent the association. For example, the correlation between IQ at age 3 and age 10 might be +.36; the correlation between IQ at age 8 and age 10 might be +.88. This means we can predict IQ at age 10 with considerably greater accuracy and confidence from IQ at age 8 than from IQ at age 3.

Correlational data help determine whether or not a relationship exists between variables such as viewing violence and behaving aggressively, but they do not permit researchers to draw conclusions about causes. When the study of television violence that we have sketched was actually performed, the investigators found that watching television violence was indeed positively correlated with aggression—that is, children who watched more violence were more aggressive (Huesmann, Lagerspetz, & Eron, 1984). But this positive correlation could be accounted for in three ways. First, watching violent television may instigate aggression. Second, highly aggressive children may select violent programs—that is, the child's aggressive tendencies may cause the television viewing choices. Third, children's aggression and their preference for watching violent television may arise from a third variable associated with both, such as having an aggressive parent who turns on violent television programs often and whose aggression the child imitates.

Longitudinal investigations can sometimes help to answer questions about causal direction by enabling researchers to determine whether a possible cause appears earlier in development than a behavior thought to result from it, thus strengthening the argument for causation. However, longitudinal study may also show the viability of both directions of causation. For instance, the study of television violence and aggression previously mentioned not only collected measures for first- and third-graders, but it also measured the same children two years later, when they were in the third and fifth grades. The investigators found that children who watched heavy doses of television violence at a young age were more aggressive than their peers two years later. But the reverse was also true: children who were more aggressive at a young age watched more violence two years later. That is, viewing appeared to contribute to aggression, and aggressive personality characteristics appeared to contribute to a preference for TV violence (Huesmann, Lagerspetz, & Eron, 1984).

The most rigorous way to establish that a variable like watching violent TV shows has a causal effect on another variable is through the use of an **experiment**. The essence of the experimental method is that the investigator systematically changes one variable (called the **independent variable**) and collects objective measurements on another variable (called the **dependent variable**). Meanwhile, all other factors that might affect the dependent variable are held constant. For example, one experiment to test the effects of violent television on aggressive behavior was conducted by bringing individual children to a laboratory where they watched either a violent television program or a nonviolent travel film. Exposure to television violence was the independent variable; it was determined by the experimenter, not by the child. After viewing, the children were taken to a playroom containing toys that could be used for aggressive play, such as inflated punching dolls and toy guns. Aggressive behavior in this play setting was the dependent variable; the researchers measured differences in aggressive play between children who had watched violent or nonviolent shows (Liebert & Baron, 1972).

One of the most important features of the experimental method is that the experimenter controls what treatment the people in the experiment get. Because the children in the preceding example do not select the show they watch, their characteristics cannot be affecting the choice. Some more aggressive children will be watching both shows, and some less aggressive children will be watching both shows. One way of expressing this key fact about experiments is to say that the children were *randomly assigned* to the violent-TV group or the travel film group. That is, they were placed in one group or the other by chance (e.g., by flipping a coin). Random assignment is a critical feature of experiments because it is the means of controlling individual differences among children. With a sufficiently large number of children in each group, we can assume that children who initially differed in level of aggression are evenly distributed in the violent and nonviolent viewing groups. Therefore, differences between the two groups after viewing are not due to predispositions or personality differences among individual children.

The experimental method permits inferences about the causal direction of effects. Because viewing violent television was varied systematically and other variables were controlled by means of random assignment, we can conclude that the television viewing influenced the aggressive behavior. Because the control groups also watched television, we can also conclude that aggression is stimulated specifically by violent content and not simply by viewing television for a certain period. Thus, the experimental method enables the scientist to separate possibly important variables and to test hypotheses about the processes that account for the behavior of interest—in this case, aggression.

Although experiments provide an excellent tool for discovering causal links, the

In studying the effects of viewing violent television, researchers have examined reactions both at home and in the lab, with similar results.

experimental method also leaves some questions unanswered. First, most experiments are necessarily short-term. For example, in the study described earlier, the total time that the children watched television in the laboratory was about 10 minutes. We cannot be sure whether the many hours children spend watching television at home would have the same effect. A second problem with experiments is that they take place in the artificial environment of the lab. Researchers cannot be sure how well laboratory findings will generalize to natural settings such as home or school. For example, the aggressive behavior measured in the study described here was not very violent, for ethical reasons. Children in a laboratory cannot be allowed to hit, kick, or bite each other. Naturally occurring aggression, such as interactions between siblings in the home, might show more effects of watching violent television.

Experiments provide precise and unique information about human development, but must be considered in combination with observations of naturally occurring events. One kind of natural observation occurs in a correlational study, as we have already described. Another method of study can be called the **field experiment**. A field experiment is an attempt to combine the advantages of the correlational and experimental approaches. In a field experiment, children are randomly assigned to groups that undergo different experiences, as in a laboratory experiment. However, the groups are observed in naturally occurring situations and for a relatively long period. For example, in one study, adolescent males living in residential treatment facilities were randomly assigned to see violent or nonviolent movies every evening for a week (Parke, Berkowitz, Leyens, West, & Sebastian, 1977). Trained observers rated aggressive behavior in the residences before, during, and after the week of movies. The boys who had seen violent movies behaved more aggressively during and after the week of viewing than did those who had been shown nonviolent movies.

The field experiment shows causal direction and at the same time preserves the "real-life" quality of measurement in field settings. However, there is still the problem that the experimenter has assigned people to treatments; the effects of viewing something that someone has prescribed could be different from the effects of viewing one's own choices. No one method of study is perfect, but in combination, various methods allow researchers to converge on reasonable conclusions.

Cross-cultural and Multiethnic Studies. It is tempting to make generalizations about trends in development after studying children who share a common cultural background, such as middle-class American children from families of European descent. Comparative studies in other cultures or among other ethnic or social class groups can help researchers avoid unscientific overgeneralization. For example, observers in Western societies, particularly the United States, have often described adolescence as a period of "storm and stress" characterized by mood swings, rebellion, and conflict with parental authority. However, in many cultures adolescents become fully integrated members of their societies, doing adult work and starting families, without an extended period devoted to building identity and autonomy.

Sometimes information from different cultures extends the range of variables that can be observed. For example, virtually every American child is exposed to television from birth onward, and television programming in every part of the country contains a great deal of violence. Therefore, it would be difficult to find American children who have not seen a good deal of violence on television; there are almost no children who have grown up without it. However, television programming in many other countries is less violent. A group of investigators from Poland, Israel, Finland, and Australia conducted longitudinal studies that were parallel to the U.S. investigation of the relationship between television violence and aggressive behavior discussed earlier. Even though the rates of TV violence in the various countries were quite different, many of the results were similar (Huesmann & Eron, 1986).

"Universals" of development can also be evaluated in cross-cultural studies. For example, the first primitive sentences of English-speaking children contain names of concrete objects (e.g., *kitty*) and action words (e.g., *hit*). Is this due to certain characteristics of the English language and the language environments provided by English-speaking parents, or do infants learning to speak other languages also name concrete objects first? This question has been addressed by cross-cultural investigations of children's early speech in many languages. The results have shown that there are many common patterns among children in different cultures.

Cross-species Studies. Developmental questions are sometimes studied using animals instead of human beings because animals can be raised in highly controlled environments. For example, in a classic set of studies with monkeys, Harry Harlow investigated early deprivation of maternal care. Newborn monkeys were raised in isolation or with artificial mothers of various kinds, and the effects of the depriva-

A monkey being raised with an artificial mother.

tion on their later behavior was measured (Harlow & Suomi, 1970). Human children cannot be deprived of mothering, nor can they be kept in a laboratory for lifetime observation as the monkeys were.

Although we must exercise caution in generalizing from other species to humans, cross-species studies can provide valuable information about developmental processes that are comparable to those that occur in human beings. For instance, the infant monkeys in Harlow's studies seemed to prefer a soft terry-cloth "mother" that gave no food over a wire-mesh "mother" that dispensed food. This led Harlow to suggest that feeding was not the critical reason why human babies become emotionally attached to their mothers—an important developmental issue that is explored more fully in Chapter 6.

Summary of Research Methods. Each of the many methods used to study human development has strengths and weaknesses. Together, they complement and compensate for one another. We can feel more confident of conclusions obtained from studies using a variety of methods than of those obtained from only one type. In the case of television violence, the fact that correlational studies, laboratory experiments, and field experiments yield similar findings provides support for the conclusion that television violence contributes to aggressive behavior. Thus, Carl would be well advised to consider carefully his son Nicky's TV-viewing habits, and to work to reduce the number of violent shows that he watched.

Ethical Issues in Research

Scientific researchers follow ethical guidelines and monitor research procedures for ethical appropriateness. Gross violations of children's rights, such as deliberately depriving them of stimulation in early life, are recognized by everyone as unethical. But there are more subtle ethical problems with which we must also be concerned. For example, if investigators ask children questions about their parents' child-rearing practices, are they invading the family's right to privacy? Might the questions themselves lead to problems in parent-child relationships? Do parents have the right to be given information about things children have said in confidence? Is it ever morally justified to deceive children, for example, by misleading them about their performance on a test or telling them that they will be alone in a room when they are being observed through a one-way mirror? Is it ethical to subject a child to mild frustration or stress for experimental purposes? Is it permissible to observe people in public settings without their consent? These are difficult questions that have no absolute answers. The questions become even more difficult when research is conducted with high-risk children and adolescents (Fisher, 1993).

The Society for Research in Child Development has formulated written guidelines and principles for research, particularly research with children. Some of the principles taken from the report of the Committee on Ethics in Research with Children (Society for Research in Child Development) are summarized in Box 1.2.

Of course, ethical problems in research with children cannot be solved simply by applying a set of rules. Investigators must weigh the advantages and disadvantages of conducting a particular study. Can the investigator's judgment about possible harm to children or potential benefits of the research be trusted? Often it can be, but many feel that any one individual's decision about ethical problems needs to be evaluated or monitored by some sort of jury. Therefore, many universities and other research facilities—as well as the U.S. Public Health Service, which supports a great deal of research in child development—require that an ethics advisory committee review every research proposal that involves human subjects. This committee, consisting of other researchers representing several disciplines and also of community representatives, serves as a panel of judges. It considers the objectives and potential benefits of the study, weighs these against the possible harmful effects on the children, and most important, guarantees that all possible steps are taken to safeguard the welfare and integrity of participants.

In the final analysis, neither codes nor committees can substitute for the investigator's moral integrity, maturity, honesty, sensitivity, and respect for the rights of others. Ultimately, the investigator is responsible for the conduct of the study and for applying the highest ethical standards in research.

⊙ ORGANIZATION OF THIS BOOK

Having examined some of the basic theoretical issues in development and some of the methodology used in research on development, we are in a position to start to study the actual processes of development. Five age periods define the next five sections of this book: (1) prenatal development (before birth); (2) infancy (the first year); (3) toddler development (age 1 to about age 3); (4) early and middle childhood (about age 3 to age 12); and (5) adolescence (about age 12 to age 20). Of course, the content discussed for different ages overlaps because most features of human development are not perfectly correlated with age. For each of these five

Box 1.2
Ethical issues in research

Research with human beings entails many ethical issues and responsibilities. The researcher's primary obligation is to safeguard the welfare, dignity, and rights of all participants in research, children and adults alike. Some of the ethical dilemmas encountered in developmental research are easy to solve, but others are more subtle.

To help psychologists in making ethical decisions, professional organizations such as the American Psychological Association and the Society for Research in Child Development have formulated some broad principles for conducting research with children. Of course, ethical problems cannot be solved simply by applying a set of rules; investigators must continually weigh the advantages and potential contributions of research against the disadvantages that may be involved in conducting it.

The following are the principles formulated by a committee of the Society for Research in Child Development.

Principle 1. Nonharmful procedures: The investigator should use no research operation that may harm the child either physically or psychologically. The investigator is also obligated at all times to use the least stressful research operation whenever possible. . . . When the investigator is in doubt about the possible harmful effects of the research operations, consultation should be sought from others. When harm seems inevitable, the investigator is obligated to find other means of obtaining the information or to abandon the research. Instances may, nevertheless, arise in which exposing the child to stressful conditions may be necessary if diagnostic or therapeutic benefits to the child are associated with the research. In such instances careful deliberation by an Institutional Review Board should be sought.

Principle 2. Informed consent: Before seeking consent or assent from the child, the investigator should inform the child of all features of the research that may affect his or her willingness to participate and should answer the child's ques-

tions in terms appropriate to the child's comprehension. The investigator should respect the child's freedom to choose to participate in the research or not by giving the child the opportunity to give or not give assent to participation as well as to choose to discontinue participation at any time. Assent means that the child shows some form of agreement to participate without necessarily comprehending the full significance of the research necessary to give informed consent. Investigators working with infants should take special effort to explain the research procedures to the parents and be especially sensitive to any indicators of discomfort in the infant. . . .

Principle 3. Parental consent: The informed consent of parents, legal guardians or those who act in loco parentis (e.g., teachers, superintendents of institutions) similarly should be obtained, preferably in writing. Informed consent requires that parents or other responsible adults be informed of all the features of the research that may affect their willingness to allow the child to participate. . . . Not only should the right of the responsible adults to refuse consent be respected, but they should be informed that they may refuse to participate without incurring any penalty to them or to the child.

Principle 4. Additional consent: The informed consent of any persons, such as schoolteachers for example, whose interaction with the child is the subject of the study should also be obtained. As with the child and parents or guardians informed consent requires that the persons interacting with the child during the study be informed of all features of the research which may affect their willingness to participate. All questions posed by such persons should be answered and the persons should be free to choose to participate or not, and to discontinue participation at any time.

Principle 5. Incentives: Incentives to participate in a research project must be fair and must not unduly exceed the range of incentives that the child normally experiences. Whatever incentives are used, the investigator should always keep in mind that the greater the possible effects of the investigation on the child, the greater is the obligation to protect the child's welfare and freedom.

Principle 6. Deception: Although full disclosure of information during the procedure of obtaining consent is the ethical ideal, a particular study may necessitate withholding certain information or deception. Whenever withholding information or deception is judged to be essential to the conduct of the study, the investigator should satisfy research colleagues that such judgment is correct. If withholding information or deception is practiced, and there is reason to believe that the research participants will be negatively affected by it, adequate measures should be taken after the study to ensure the participants' understanding of the reasons for the deception. Investigators whose research is dependent upon deception should make an effort to employ deception methods that have no known negative effects on the child or the child's family.

Principle 7. Anonymity: To gain access to institutional records, the investigator should obtain permission from responsible authorities in charge of records. Anonymity of the information should be preserved and no information used other than that for which permission was obtained. It is the investigator's responsibility to ensure that responsible authorities do, in fact, have the confidence of the participant and that they bear some degree of responsibility in giving such permission.

Principle 8. Mutual responsibilities: From the beginning of each research investigation, there should be clear agreement between the investigator and the parents, guardians or those who act in loco parentis, and the child, when appropriate, that defines the responsibilities of each. The investigator has the obligation to honor all promises and commitments of the agreement.

Principle 9. Jeopardy: When, in the course of research, information comes to the investigator's attention that may jeopardize the child's well-being, the investigator has a responsibility to discuss the information with the parents or guardians and with those expert in the field in order that they may arrange the necessary assistance for the child.

Principle 10. Unforeseen consequences: When research procedures result in undesirable consequences for the participant that were previously unforeseen, the investigator should immediately employ appropriate measures to correct these consequences, and should redesign the procedures if they are to be included in subsequent studies.

Principle 11. Confidentiality: The investigator should keep in confidence all information obtained about research participants. The participants' identities should be concealed in written and verbal reports of the results, as well as in informal discussion with students and colleagues. When a possibility exists that others may gain access to such information, this possibility, together with the plans for protecting confidentiality, should be explained to the participants as part of the procedure of obtaining informed consent.

Principle 12. Informing participants: Immediately after the data are collected, the investigator should clarify for the research participant any misconceptions that may have arisen. The investigator also recognizes a duty to a report general findings to participants in terms appropriate to their understanding. Where scientific or humane values justify withholding information, every effort should be made so that withholding the information has no damaging consequences for the participant.

Principle 13. Reporting results: Because the investigator's words may carry unintended weight with parents and children, caution should be exercised in reporting results, making evaluative statements, or giving advice.

Principle 14. Implications of findings: Investigators should be mindful of the social, political and human implications of their research and should be especially careful in the presentation of findings from the research. . . .

periods, we discuss development in the domains of physical and biological growth, cognitive functioning, and social-emotional behavior. We consider the universals of human development, as well as the bases for individual differences. Central influences—the family, school, peer group, and mass media—are considered as they apply to different age periods. We discuss major theories and applied social issues as they become relevant at particular time periods. Finally, we provide a concluding section on development psychopathology.

When you have read some or all of the following chapters, it may be advisable to return to the introduction. The theoretical issues about the nature of development presented here will take on added meaning as you apply them to the specific knowledge presented in later chapters. Similarly, you will be in a better position to appreciate the contributions different methodologies can make to answering questions about development, once you consider some particular questions and know more about how scientists have gone about studying them to date.

✸ SUMMARY

[handwritten margin notes: development - orderly ongoing changes over time 1. universal 2. ind. diff 3. behavior → context]

Development is defined as orderly and relatively enduring changes over time in physical and neurological structures, thought processes, and behavior. One goal of studying development is to understand changes that appear to be universal. Another is to explain individual differences among children, and a third is to understand how children's behavior is influenced by the context or situation.

A number of theoretical issues must be addressed when studying children's development. One of the most basic of these is the relative importance of environmental and biological determinants of behavior ("nature versus nurture"). Few scientists may be found at either extreme of the nature-nurture controversy. Most believe that behavior is a product of repeated transactions between biological and environmental determinants.

Another basic issue is the active versus passive nature of the child. Some theorists view children as passive receivers of experience; others consider them active in organizing, structuring, and in some sense creating their worlds. Theorists also disagree on whether developmental changes occur continuously or discontinuously. Although all developmentalists agree that some changes occur continuously and gradually, they disagree on whether some changes are qualitative, that is, not extensions of previous development.

Still another issue on which researchers disagree is the stability of behavior over time. One reason for differing interpretations is that some behaviors and some periods of development are more stable than others. Another is the fact that the same characteristics may be expressed in different ways at different ages. In addition to stability over time, researchers study consistency of behavior across situations. There is evidence that both individual traits and situational variables influence behavior.

Research on child development may be either applied or basic. Applied research is designed to help parents, schools, and others who deal with children. Basic research is intended to generate knowledge about the processes and sequences of development, even when there is no immediate social need for that knowledge. Basic research questions usually originate from prominent theories that generate testable hypotheses. The selection of both basic and applied questions is inevitably affected by contemporary social and cultural values.

A variety of methods are used to study children. Cross-sectional investigations compare children of different ages at one point in time. In a longitudinal study, the same children are observed or tested at regular intervals over an extended period. Correlational methods are used to test hypotheses about what variables may contribute to individual differences in development. In experimental investigations the experimenter systematically changes one variable and collects objective measurements on another variable. Field experiments differ from laboratory experiments in that groups who are given different experiences are observed in naturally occurring situations over a relatively long period.

Comparative studies in other cultures can serve as an antidote to overgeneralization from studies of children who share a common cultural background. In addition, developmental questions are sometimes studied using animals instead of human beings.

Each of the many methods used to study human development has strengths and weaknesses. Together, they complement and compensate for one another. Researchers feel more confident of conclusions obtained from studies using a variety of methods than of those obtained from only one type.

Research in child development raises complex ethical dilemmas. Both the American Psychological Association and the Society for Research in Child Development have formulated written guidelines and principles for research. In addition to applying these rules, investigators must weigh the advantages and disadvantages of conducting a particular study. Many universities and other research facilities require that an ethics advisory committee review every research proposal that involves human subjects.

REVIEW QUESTIONS

1. What is meant by development? What are the goals of studying development?
2. Briefly discuss the nature versus nurture controversy.
3. List four other theoretical issues that must be addressed in the study of child development.
4. Distinguish between applied and basic research.
5. How do investigators select the questions on which they focus their research efforts?
6. Briefly describe several methods that are used in studying children's development.
7. What is a correlation? How is correlation related to causation?
8. What are some ethical issues that must be resolved by scientists who do research on child development?

CRITICAL THINKING ABOUT THE CHAPTER

1. Think about some important aspect of yourself as you are at present, for example, how easy or hard you find it to get to know people. How do you explain it? Were you always this way? What experiences contributed to your development? As much as possible, relate your thinking on this issue to the themes explored in the chapter.

2. Suppose you were asked to gather evidence on one of the conclusions you reached in thinking about question 1. What methods might you use for your study? What would be the advantages and disadvantages of these methods?

KEY TERMS

applied research

basic research

correlation

cross-sectional investigation

dependent variable

development

ecology

experiment

field experiment

independent variable

longitudinal investigation

stages of development

SUGGESTED READINGS

Fisher, C. B., & Lerner, R. M. (Eds.). (1994). *Applied developmental psychology.* New York: McGraw-Hill. Chapters in this book are written by leading researchers in each area. They draw together basic research and show its implications for applied problems in diverse areas, including investigation of child sexual abuse, the effects of ear infections on development, and the prevention of adolescent drug abuse.

Salkind, N. J. (1985). *Theories of human development* (2nd ed.). New York: Van Nostrand. A student who is interested in theory will find it useful to read a supplementary text devoted to a discussion of theory. This book organizes theories around the major issues discussed in the chapter, such as the passive versus active view of the child.

P A R T

II

THE PRENATAL PERIOD

▼

CHAPTER

2

GENETICS AND BEHAVIOR GENETICS

THE MECHANISMS OF HEREDITARY TRANSMISSION

GENES AND BEHAVIOR

FINDINGS OF BEHAVIOR GENETICS

Ellis and Edward were identical twins. That fact was apparent to any casual observer: they looked alike, moved in a similar way, liked the same activities. But their mother, Janet, was quite tired of finding a smile and a bright comment for every person who passed them, did a double take, and stopped to say, "Oh goodness, they are as alike as peas in a pod!" And—more than tired—she was exasperated with the fact that these same strangers often felt free to ask, "Oh, they're not yours, are they? Where did you get them from?" That they had been born in Korea of Korean parents was not anyone's business but hers and her husband's, she felt, and she resented the idea that they weren't "hers." She had cared for them from earliest infancy and she loved them with all her heart. She thought they reflected the effort and love she had put into their care, as much as if they had been biologically related to her.

Ellis and Edward are very much alike, a fact that seems natural for identical twins, who share exactly the same genetic material. In addition, since they have also been raised in the same circumstances by the same loving parents, it seems equally natural to think that their family environment has been important in their development. In this chapter, we examine the role of heredity in development. We begin in the first section by presenting the basic facts about mechanisms of hereditary transmission, including a discussion of the genetic defects that create specific syndromes such as Down syndrome. We then go on to examine the field known as **behavior genetics**, which is the study of the extent to which and the ways in which genes affect complex human behaviors, and how genetic effects interact with effects of the environment. In this discussion of recent findings of behavior genetics, we will be examining in greater depth one of the themes outlined in Chapter 1: the "nature versus nurture" question.

✦ THE MECHANISMS OF HEREDITARY TRANSMISSION

When Charles Darwin published *The Origin of Species* (1859), which proposed his theory of evolution, he did not know *how* physical or behavioral characteristics were transmitted or how variation among individuals might arise. Since its beginning in the last century, the science of genetics has made dramatic progress. During the past few decades, new discoveries have been announced with accelerating frequency. We are now in the midst of a massive project to map the whole human genome. Still, at present, there are many medical conditions and aspects of human behavior whose genetic basis has not been established. Nevertheless, understanding the basic facts of hereditary transmission is vital for understanding many aspects of human development.

The development of every individual begins when a sperm cell from the father penetrates the wall of an ovum, or egg, from the mother. At the moment that the tiny, tadpole-shaped sperm penetrates the wall of the ovum, it releases 23 minute particles called **chromosomes**. At approximately the same time, the nucleus of the ovum breaks up, releasing 23 chromosomes of its own, so that the new individual begins life with 46 chromosomes.

This process is of great interest because the chromosomes, which are further subdivided into even smaller particles called **genes**, are the carriers of the child's heredity. There are about 1 million genes in a human cell—an average of about 20,000 genes per chromosome. The child's entire biological heritage is contained in these 23 pairs of chromosomes. Of these pairs, 22 are called **autosomes** and are possessed equally by males and females. The twenty-third pair, the **sex chromosomes**, differ in males and females. Normal females have two X chromosomes (XX), while normal males have an X and a Y chromosome (XY) (see Figure 2.1).

The critical component of genes is **DNA** (deoxyribonucleic acid). James Watson and Francis Crick (later winners of the Nobel prize in medicine) deduced in 1953 that DNA is composed of two molecular chains, which are coiled around each other to form a double-stranded helix. Perhaps the simplest way to visualize this is to imagine a rubber ladder twisted around its long axis as shown in Figure 2.2. Alternating sugar and phosphate molecules form the legs of the ladder. The cross steps are made up of the nitrogenous bases adenine, thymine, cytosine, and guanine. The nitrogenous bases, which are held together by hydrogen bonds, are always paired in a special way to form distinctive strands. By knowing the order of the

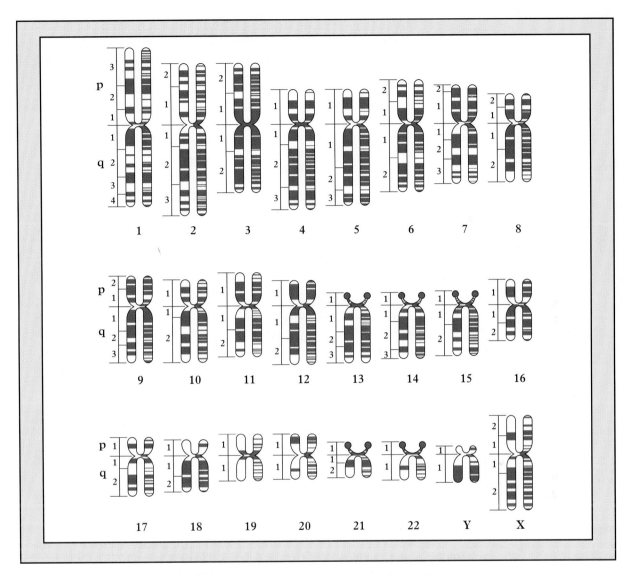

FIGURE 2.1 Chromosomes of a human male, showing light and dark bands that help identify the chromosome. Upper arms of a chromosome are marked *p* and the lower arms are marked *q*. From "High Resolution of Human Chromosomes," by J. J. Yunis, 1976, *Science, 191,* p. 1269. Copyright © 1976 by the American Association for the Advancement of Science. Reprinted by permission.

nitrogenous bases in one strand of the helix, we can determine their order in the other (Fraser & Nora, 1986; K. L. Moore, 1982).

When a cell divides to reproduce itself, in a process called **mitosis**, the original strands of DNA separate at the hydrogen bonds in the manner of a zipper. Bases from a pool of nucleotides in the cell nucleus attach themselves to the appropriate bases in the chain to form a complementary chain. The result is that two chains are constructed along the original chains to form two new helixes, each one chemically identical to the helix from which it was derived (see Figure 2.3). When cells divide in this way, the genetic information they contain is preserved and transmitted

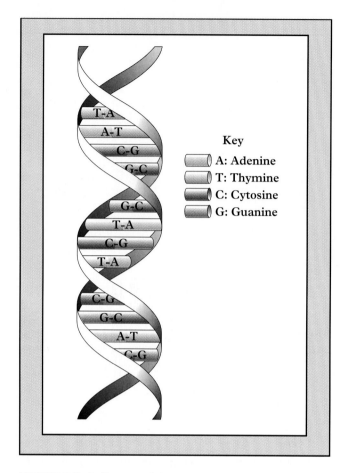

Key
A: Adenine
T: Thymine
C: Cytosine
G: Guanine

FIGURE 2.2 A diagram of the structure of DNA.

unchanged to the daughter cells (Fraser & Nora, 1986; Whaley, 1974). Cell division through mitosis is how growth and renewal take place in all the kinds of body cells that people possess, including bones, muscle, skin, and so on. However, there is one important exception.

The exception is germ cells—the cells from which the sperm and ova are derived. Germ cells divide into sperm or ova by a process called **meiosis** (from the Greek word meaning "to make smaller"). Meiosis results in cells whose nuclei contain only half the number of chromosomes present in the parent cell (see Figure 2.4). When meiosis occurs, except for the fact that half of each of the 23 pairs goes to one sperm or ovum and the other half to the other, the pattern of division is random. In other words, the way one pair of chromosomes separates does not influence the way another pair will split. This fact results in an extremely large range of variation in the genetic makeup of ova and sperm, even from the same individual.

Moreover, in meiosis, a process called **crossing-over** increases the likelihood that each sperm or ovum will be unique and, therefore, that each individual will be unique (Scarr & Kidd, 1983). When the 23 pairs of chromosomes line up during meiosis, they can exchange blocks of corresponding genetic material much as if

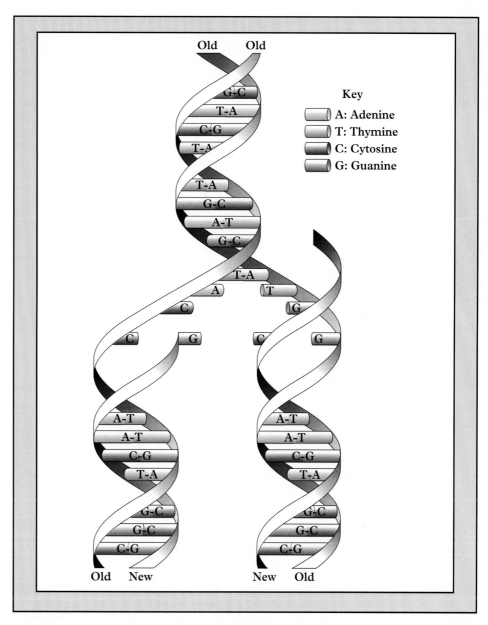

FIGURE 2.3 How DNA replicates. When the double helix divides and unwinds, the free "rungs of the ladder" (shown in the middle) attract their complements, and two identical DNA molecules result.

human beings facing each other were to exchange parts of their fingers. The likelihood that two particular genes will be exchanged together depends on how close to each other the gene sites are along the length of a chromosome. Genes that are located close to each other will usually be inherited together, while those located at opposite ends of one of the larger chromosomes are likely to be inherited independently (Scarr & Kidd, 1983).

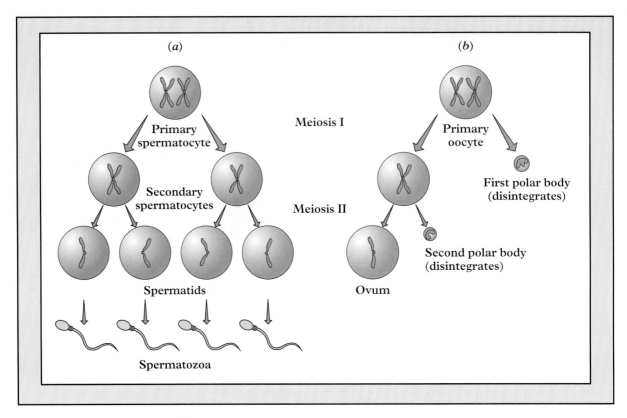

FIGURE 2.4 How germ cells are produced. On the left are the steps in production of sperm and on the right steps in production of an ovum. From *Understanding Inherited Disorders* (p. 14), by L. F. Whaley, 1974, St. Louis: C. V. Mosby Company. Copyright © 1974 by L. F. Whaley. Reprinted by permission of C. V. Mosby Company.

Further variation arises at conception. A single ovum can unite with only one of the approximately 350 million sperm cells released in a single male ejaculation. The new individual will possess a different set of chromosomes, depending on which of these many cells wins the race for fertilization.

If crossing-over did not occur, the total number of different combinations of sperm and ovum from one mother and father would be approximately 64 billion. Thus, one pair of parents could produce many more different kinds of children than the total number of people on the earth today. With crossing-over, the number of possible different offspring is many, many times that number. Except for identical twins, then, each human being is genetically unique and biologically different from every other person on earth.

As we saw in Figure 2.1, one of the 23 pairs of chromosomes consists of the sex chromosomes and determines the sex of the child. In the normal female, both members of this pair are large and are called X chromosomes. In the normal male, one member of the pair is an X chromosome; the second is smaller and is called the Y chromosome. Thus, the body cells of males contain one X chromosome and one Y chromosome. Half of the sperm cells contain an X chromosome; the remaining half contain a Y chromosome. When a female ovum (which contains an X chromosome) unites with a sperm containing a Y chromosome, a male child is produced; when it unites with a sperm containing an X chromosome, a female child is produced.

Recent research (Page et al., 1987) has identified a single gene on the Y chromosome that appears to determine sex. When an ovum unites with a sperm carrying an X chromosome, a female child develops. Since half of the sperm cells contain X chromosomes and half contain Y chromosomes, theoretically the odds are 50:50 that a boy or a girl will be conceived. In actuality, there is a slight excess of male over female births (approximately 106 boys to 100 girls), and this may mean that Y sperm are more likely than X sperm to penetrate the ovum (Falkner & Tanner, 1978a; K. L. Moore, 1982).

Genes affect development in ways both direct and indirect. The simplest kind of genetic effect occurs when a single gene codes for a single characteristic and different versions of that gene are either **dominant** or **recessive**. The usual illustration is eye color. The gene for brown eyes is dominant, and the gene for blue eyes is recessive, which means that, if the two genes are paired, the individual will have brown eyes and the presence of the gene for blue eyes will be masked. Thus, if a brown-eyed man with two brown-eyed genes and a blue-eyed woman have children, all of the children will have brown eyes, as shown at the top left of Table 2.1. If, however, the brown-eyed father has one blue eye-color gene whose effect is masked, half of the children will have blue eyes, as shown at the top right of Table 2.1.

In actuality, the genetics of eye color are somewhat more complex than the traditional illustration assumes. More than one pair of genes may be involved in determining eye color, and there are more than two varieties of eye-color genes, not all of which are dominant or recessive with respect to each other. Sometimes, there is a blending, as in gray, green, or hazel eyes, or different shades of blue and brown. Generally, however, the genes for darker eye colors tend to be dominant over those for lighter colors (Fraser & Nora, 1986).

The example of eye color allows for a good explanation of two terms often used in discussions of genetics: **genotype** and **phenotype**. The term *genotype* refers to the underlying genetic makeup of an individual, which may or may not be manifest in outward appearance and behavior. The term *phenotype* refers to observed appear-

TABLE 2.1 The (Simplified) Genetics of Eye Color

		Brown-Eyed Father (BB Genes)		Brown-Eyed Father (Bb Genes)	
Brown-eyed genes are represented by B, and blue-eyed genes are represented by b. Because of dominance, individuals with a Bb pairing have brown eyes.					
		B	B	B	b
Blue-Eyed Mother (bb Genes)	b	Bb	Bb	Bb	bb
Brown-Eyed Mother (BB Genes)	B	BB	BB	BB	Bb

ance and behavior, which may be the product of multiple influences, both biological and environmental. Thus, there is no one-to-one mapping between genes and what a person actually becomes. In the case of eye color, we see that people with the same phenotype (brown eyes) may have a different genotype (BB or Bb). It is also possible for people with the same genotype to have different phenotypes, because of other genetic, biological, or environmental factors. For instance, in the case of the genetically-based disease *phenylketonuria,* discussed in detail in the next section, infants with the same pair of recessive genes may develop very differently, depending on their diet.

Genetically Caused Problems in Development

As we have mentioned, not all of the problems in development that we know to have genetic origins have specific genetic bases that have been identified. However, this situation has been rapidly changing. In 1993, for instance, a collaborative group involving 56 researchers from ten institutions announced the discovery of the genetic basis of Huntington's disease, a condition involving progressive neural deterioration. Discoveries of the genetic bases of disease may pave the way for deeper understanding of the biological and chemical effects of the deleterious genes, and for the invention of new therapies and cures. The discoveries also facilitate the identification of people who carry deleterious genes but who will not manifest problems themselves. The individuals can then consider **genetic counseling**, in which they will be given detailed information about their situation, the probabilities of their children being affected, and what steps they may want to consider in terms of prenatal diagnosis of any children they conceive.

Here we consider four genetically based problems whose bases are understood. There are more than 150 known gene defects that may result in mental retardation and other developmental disabilities, though fortunately most of these occur rarely (Scarr & Kidd, 1983; Vandenberg, Singer, & Pauls, 1986). In some instances, pairing of recessive genes leads to failure to give the cells the proper instructions to produce enzymes needed for normal development, or to giving incorrect instructions. We shall discuss an example of one problem of this type, phenylketonuria. In other instances, the problem is the result of abnormalities in the overall structure of the chromosomes. These abnormalities may occur in either the autosomes or the sex chromosomes. We shall discuss one autosomal abnormality, Down syndrome, and two sex-chromosome abnormalities.

Phenylketonuria. The disease *phenylketonuria* (PKU) is a disorder that is caused by the presence of a particular pair of recessive genes. Many of the foods we eat contain a chemical called phenylalanine. Most people possess an enzyme that converts phenylalanine into a harmless by-product. However, a small number of children are born without the enzyme that converts the phenylalanine because they lack the gene that produces it. As a result, the concentration of phenylalanine rises above the normal level and the chemical is converted into phenylpyruvic acid. This substance damages the cells of the central nervous system and results in mental retardation. Once scientists learned the nature of the specific metabolic disorder in PKU, they were able to devise a diet that is nutritious but contains very low levels of phenylalanine. When children with PKU follow this diet, the toxic acid does not accumulate and their mental development is almost normal. Even more recently, work on the cognitive development of children with PKU has shown that traditional dietary con-

A leading figure in the effort to identify the genetic basis of Huntington's disease is Dr. Nancy Wexler, seen here with a victim of the disease.

trol is often not strict enough to prevent damage to the frontal portion of the brain (Diamond, 1994). More stringent control can result in diminishing this remaining effect of PKU and bringing functioning even closer to normal.

Autosomal abnormality

Down Syndrome. A good example of abnormalities in the structure of the autosomes is *Down syndrome,* a form of mental retardation that results, in the vast majority of cases, from the presence of an extra (third) copy of chromosome 21 (a normal pair is shown in Figure 2.1). Down syndrome affects approximately 1 of every 600 live births (Hook, 1982). Children with this disorder are born with a distinctive facial appearance and may have eye, heart, and other developmental defects. Many adults with Down syndrome have been found to develop brain pathology resembling that occurring in elderly individuals affected by Alzheimer's disease (Thase, 1988).

Most children affected by Down syndrome who are reared at home have IQs in what is called the moderately retarded range. A few have higher IQs, in the mildly retarded range, and a very select few can read and write (see Box 2.1). They generally develop through the same stages as normal children, but at a slower rate, and one that may slow increasingly as development progresses (Hodapp & Zigler, 1990). Stereotypes of children with Down syndrome as especially cheerful and sociable seem to have little basis in fact, although their social development may proceed at a pace a little faster than their cognitive development (Serafica, 1990). There is some evidence that language development in Down syndrome children, especially the ability to combine words into complex sentences, may be more delayed than overall development (Fowler, 1990).

18

A stimulating environment and careful instruction help children with Down syndrome achieve their full potential.

BOX 2.1
THE AUTOBIOGRAPHY OF A DOWN SYNDROME CHILD

Down syndrome children suffer from varying degrees of mental retardation and may have particular difficulties with language. Some of them are able, however, to learn to read and write, often with the help of extraordinarily dedicated teachers and parents. One such individual was Nigel Hunt, a British boy whose mother, Grace, began spelling short words to him phonetically almost as soon as he could talk. Following is the introduction to his autobiography.

It gives me great pleasure to write this, my very first book. I hope it will do well in America and England.

Now I had better introduce myself.

I am Nigel Hunt and I live at 26 Church Avenue, Pinner, England with my parents. They are very nice indeed. I was born in England in 1947. I have never been to America yet. The lady who advised me to write this was Mrs. Eileen J. Garrett and she says that I shall be very busy.

So it's hallo! Welcome to my first good attempt in making this book and Douglas Hunt [his father] is assisting me. I had a royal honour in coming to London to see Mrs. Garrett at Claridges Hotel and the flags were carried out for me and I saluted my own colour. I was educated at many places; at Longfield Primary School, Inellan School, Pinner, and at my father's school, Atholl School.

I have my own typewriter and I taught myself to type. When I went to London many years ago I made a film with Prof. Penrose looking at my palms. I also smiled at the camera, and he says it will go to America, and I hope you have seen it.

Source: From *The World Of Nigel Hunt* (pp. 45–46), 1967. Reprinted by permission of Garrett Publications.

Sex-Chromosome Abnormalities. Other structural abnormalities occur in the sex chromosomes rather than the autosomes. For example, one sex-chromosome abnormality, the *fragile-X syndrome* (Bregman, Dykens, Watson, Ort, & Leckman, 1987; Vandenberg et al., 1986), ranks second to Down syndrome as the most prevalent chromosomal defect that may cause mental retardation, particularly in boys (Webb, Bundey, Thake, & Todd, 1986). In this condition an X chromosome has a pinched or constricted area near the lower tips that may result in breakage. About 80 percent of boys who inherit this genetic condition have mental impairment, which may range from severe retardation to low-normal intelligence (Bishop, 1986; Bregman et al., 1987; de la Cruz, 1985). Many also have behavioral problems such as hyperactivity and emotional outbursts and, in some cases, infantile autism—a severe disorder characterized by rigid, ritualistic behavior, serious learning problems, and inability to communicate or form social and emotional relationships (W. T. Brown, Jenkins, & Friedman, et al, 1982; Chudley, 1984; Largo & Schinzel, 1985). Girls with a fragile-X chromosome are less likely than boys to show problems; about a third of all girls with a fragile-X chromosome have some degree of retardation or learning disability. Perhaps a girl's other X chromosome (which boys lack) may be able in some instances to mitigate or negate the damaging effects of the defective X chromosome.

Another sex-chromosome abnormality is *Klinefelter's syndrome,* which results from the presence of two X chromosomes in males (i.e., XXY rather than XY). Boys affected by Klinefelter's fail to develop secondary masculine characteristics such as facial hair at puberty and may have breast enlargement. Administration of the male hormone androgen promotes the development of male secondary sex characteristics, but the boy remains sterile. Boys with Klinefelter's syndrome are more likely than their peers to have behavioral problems and retarded intellectual development (Reed, 1975; Scarr & Kidd, 1983).

The study of children with sex-chromosome abnormalities (SCA) provides an opportunity to observe the interplay of genetic and environmental influences. One recent research project followed 46 infants born with SCA, together with a control group of non-SCA siblings, studying them annually to adolescence (Bender, Linden & Robinson, 1987). The SCA infants were identified through screening of 40,000 consecutive births in Denver, and included individuals with less extreme forms of SCA than Klinefelter's. The data indicated that a nurturant home environment can reduce the effects of these forms of SCA on development, eliminating them altogether in the case of school problems and interpersonal functioning (top right and bottom left panels of Figure 2.5). A stressful, nonsupportive home environment can increase these effects, in some instances dramatically.

GENES AND BEHAVIOR

What Is Behavior Genetics?

Most behavioral traits are **multifactorial**; that is, they depend on more than one genetic or environmental factor (Scarr & Kidd, 1983; Vandenberg et al., 1986). At the genetic level, a particular characteristic often is affected by more than one gene,

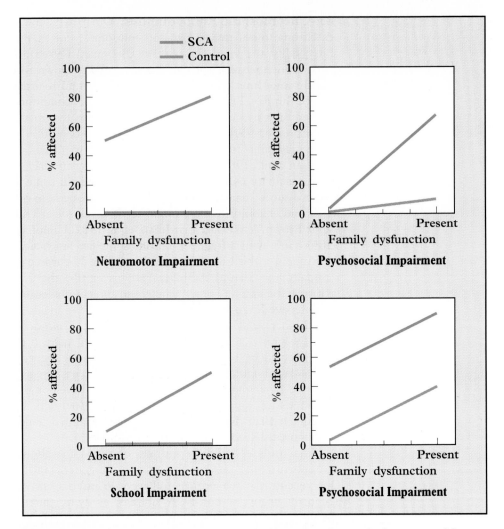

FIGURE 2.5 Percentages of children showing significant impairment in four areas of functioning, as related to whether or not they have sex-chromosome abnormalities and whether they come from functional homes. After "Environmental and Developmental Risk in Children with Sex Chromosome Abnormalities," by B. G. Bender, M. G. Linden, and A. Robinson, from *Journal of the American Academy of Child and Adolescent Psychiatry, 26,* pp. 499–503. Copyright © 1987 by the American Academy of Child and Adolescent Psychiatry. Adapted with permission.

a situation that is termed **polygenetic inheritance**. As we have seen, even eye color is not strictly the product of a single gene, but rather is subject to polygenetic inheritance. In investigating multifactorial traits subject to polygenetic inheritance, we can almost never identify a set of genes that underlie the trait. Instead, investigators interested in the genetics of behavior rely largely on studying incidence patterns among individuals who are genetically related in varying degrees and have been exposed to similar or different environmental influences. This kind of investigation is called *behavior genetics.* As we shall see, a variety of techniques have been employed in studying the degree to which behaviors "run in families," including "pedigree" studies of incidence within individual families, adoption studies, and studies comparing **monozygotic (identical) twins,** who are genetically identical, and **dizygotic (fraternal) twins,** who are only as genetically alike as are any two siblings, with about 50 percent overlap on average.

FINDINGS OF BEHAVIOR GENETICS

Modern behavior genetics goes beyond the question of attempting to ascertain how much of the variation among people in some trait is due to heredity; it also examines evidence regarding what kinds of environmental factors have an impact on behavior and how genetics may affect environmental input, leading to correlations between particular genetic endowments and particular environmental inputs. In the sections that follow, we shall examine behavior geneticists' conclusions about how heredity and environment affect three major classes of behavior: intelligence, personality, and psychopathology.

Intelligence

To what extent are the kinds of abilities measured by intelligence tests (see Chapter 10 for discussion of the tests) influenced by heredity? As a first step, we might predict that, if genetic factors do play a significant role in determining scores on IQ tests, we would expect to find that a child's or adolescent's IQ is more highly correlated with the IQs of his or her parents and other immediate relatives than with those of randomly selected nonrelatives. This is indeed the case. Unfortunately for investigators, however, the matter is not so easily resoved by "pedigree" studies. Parents have not only provided their children with their genetic endowment; they have also helped to determine their environment. Advantages that are related to intellectual ability, such as good health, a stimulating home environment, and superior educational opportunities, might account for the family resemblances, rather than genetics. Thus, if we are to isolate the potential contributions of heredity, we must find a way to control the potential effects of other variables.

Investigation of the effects of heredity on intellectual ability is greatly aided by various kinds of **twin study**. In one kind of twin study, monozygotic (MZ) twins are compared with dizygotic (DZ) twins, usually of the same sex, who are no more alike genetically than ordinary siblings. If genetic influences play an important role in the determination of intellectual ability, we would expect the IQs of monozygotic twins to be more highly correlated than those of dizygotic twins or nontwin siblings.

This turns out to be true. A review of a large number of studies comparing the intelligence and abilities of monozygotic and dizygotic twins found an average correlation of .86 for monozygotic twins and .62 for dizygotic twins of the same sex (Bouchard & McGue, 1981). (Recall from Chapter 1 that correlations range in the positive direction from 0, or no relation, to +1.00, or a perfect correspondence.)

In addition, a second kind of twin study involves looking at MZ twins who are reared together (the usual situation) and MZ twins who are reared apart (usually because the pair were broken up when an adoption was necessary). The correlation

The study of identical twins is one of the techniques used in behavior genetics.

in IQ for MZ twins reared apart is .72 (Bouchard & McGue, 1981). This value is lower than the .86 observed when twins are reared together, indicating a role of the environment, but still quite high.

Although twin studies can be extremely valuable in the search for genetic influences, some qualifications should be kept in mind. First, comparisons of MZ and DZ twins depend on the assumption that the environmental influences to which DZ twins are exposed are as similar as those to which MZ twins are exposed (Plomin, 1986). However, several studies have found that compared to fraternal twins, identical twins spend more time together, have more similar reputations, and are more likely to be in the same classrooms, have similar health records, and in many other respects share a nearly identical physical and social environment (Jones, H. E., 1946). MZ twins may also be treated in more similar ways by parents, siblings, peers, and others than DZ twins are, partly because they look alike and partly because their behavior is more similar to begin with (Loehlin & Nichols, 1976; Lytton, 1977; Plomin, Willerman, & Loehlin, 1976; Scarr & Carter-Saltzman, 1979; Willerman, 1979). Second, studies of MZ twins reared apart depend on the assumption that the environments to which the twins are sent are not similar to each other. This may often not be the case, as when one relative takes over the care of one twin and another relative the other. Thus, even in twin studies, environmental effects cannot be fully controlled.

Another useful way to investigate genetic influences on intelligence is the **adoption study**. In a study of this kind, a researcher looks at children and adolescents who have been raised by adoptive parents from a very early age and compare their IQs with those of their biological and adoptive parents (Plomin, 1986; Plomin & DeFries, 1985). Because these children have had little or no contact with their biological parents, any similarity to those parents is assumed to reflect genetic influences. The correlation between the IQs of children and their adopted parents is assumed to indicate environmental influences. Munsinger (1975) reported a correlation of .19 between the averaged intelligence test scores of two adopting parents and the scores of their adopted children, a value confirmed by Bouchard and McGue (1981). In contrast, the correlation between these children's scores and those of their biological parents was .48. Children raised by their biological parents showed a correlation of .58 with their parents.

The fact that there was a substantial correlation between biological parents' intelligence and that of the children they did not raise suggests genetic influence. However, the fact that there was a significant, if smaller, correlation of adoptive parents' intelligence with that of their adopted children suggests environmental influence, as does the fact that correlations are higher when biological parents raise children themselves than when they give them up for adoption. This conclusion is supported by more recent studies (Horn, 1983; Plomin, 1986). Additional support for a role of environment comes from the finding that adoptive siblings, biologically unrelated but reared in the same family, show correlations of about .30 (Bouchard & McGue, 1981).

In summary, the data indicate a powerful role of biology in creating familial resemblances in IQ scores. At the same time, an important role of the environment is also indicated. There are two important qualifications to keep in mind, however, about what these data do and do not show.

First, it is important to distinguish between studies that examine correlations and those that also take a look at mean levels. Genetic effects may appear substantial when we examine the rank order of intelligence scores, with the highest-scoring biological parents more likely to have the highest-scoring children, and so on, as seen in the preceding correlations. But this fact tells us nothing about how the groups as a whole score. A common finding is that the overall score of the adopted children is substantially higher than the overall score of their biological parents (Horn, 1983; Huston, 1984; Scarr & Weinberg, 1976; Skodak & Skeels, 1949; Walker & Emory, 1985). In a French adoption study, for instance, where children born to unskilled parents were reared by upper-income professional families (Schiff, Duyme, Dumaret, & Tomkiewicz, 1982), it was found that the IQs of the adopted children were similar to those of natural children from the same socioeconomically advantaged group, and 14 points higher than those of children of unskilled workers in general. In this sense, the environment of the adoptive home has had an important effect, even though there may be more limited similarity in the rank orders of the adopted children and their adopting parents.

A second point to remember about studies of genetic and environmental influence on IQ is that IQ scores, while correlated with academic achievement (see Chapter 10), are not identical with it. School achievement, an outcome with far greater real-world consequences than IQ, might show different patterns of genetic and environmental influence. Indeed, a recent study of 146 MZ twin pairs and 132 DZ twin pairs suggests that genetic effects on academic achievement may be much less pronounced than those for IQ (Thompson, Detterman & Plomin, 1991). As Figure 2.6 shows, the analyses suggested that only about 20 percent of the differences among the children in achievement could be attributed to genetic influences, whereas about 60 percent of the differences in IQ were attributed to environment. (We shall discuss very shortly the distinction drawn in these figures between common and specific environment.)

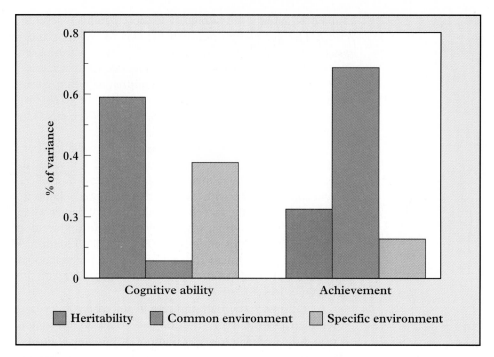

FIGURE 2.6 Estimates of genetic and environmental influence on cognitive ability (left side of figure) and on scholastic achievement (right side of figure). After "Associations Between Cognitive Abilities and Scholastic Achievement: Genetic Overlap but Environmental Differences," by L. E. Thompson, D. K. Detterman, and R. Plomin, 1991, *Psychological Science, 2,* p. 162. Copyright © 1991 by the American Psychological Society. Adapted with permission.

In summary, similarities in IQ are highest between people who are most closely related genetically (i.e., monozygotic twins) and lowest between those who are unrelated. It seems clear that an individual's genetic inheritance is an important determinant of individual differences in IQ. However, there are also similarities between adoptive parents and their adopted children, which indicate the importance of environment, and other indications of the role of environment as well, such as the fact that biological parents who raise their children have IQs more closely correlated with the children's than is the case when biological parents give up their children for adoption. Environmental factors may be especially important in raising (or lowering) children's overall IQ level, as well as in affecting academic achievement. Thus, Janet, the mother in our opening vignette, was right: the love and care she and her husband have invested in the twins will bear fruit in their overall level of intellectual functioning, even though their intelligence may also be correlated with that of their birth parents.

Personality

Studies using twin methods and adoption methods have also suggested that genetics has an important effect on personality (Plomin, 1986; Scarr & Kidd, 1983). In general, it appears that genetic influences are strongest for basic temperamental

Babies differ substantially in their temperaments.

characteristics (e.g., calm–easily distressed, passive–active, reflective–impulsive, shy–gregarious) that tend to be relatively stable during development, and weakest for characteristics that are highly dependent on learning and social experience, such as ethical and social values (Buss & Plomin, 1984; Goldsmith & Campos, 1982; Kagan, Reznick, & Snidman, 1988; Matheny, 1983).

Studies of infants reveal that MZ twins are more alike than DZ twins in their responses to strangers, including smiling, playing, cuddling, and expressions of fear (Goldsmith & Campos, 1982; Matheny, Wilson, Dolan, & Krantz, 1981; Plomin, 1986; Scarr & Kidd, 1983). Identical twin babies also appear to be more alike in frequency of displays of temper, demands for attention, and amount of crying (Plomin, 1986; Wilson & Harpring, 1972). From infancy to adolescence, MZ twins resemble each other significantly more than DZ twins do in many temperamental traits, including activity, attention, task persistence, irritability, emotionality, sociability, and impulsiveness (Buss & Plomin, 1984; Cohen, Dibble, & Grawe, 1977; H. H. Goldsmith, 1983, 1984; Matheny, 1983; Torgersen & Kringlen, 1978). At later ages, significant differences between MZ and DZ twins have also been found in such characteristics as introversion-extraversion and neuroticism (Floderus-Myrhed, Pederson, & Rasmuson, 1980; Matheny, 1983; Plomin, 1986; Scarr & Kidd, 1983). A study of MZ and DZ twins separated and reared apart showed greater similarity for the MZ pairs (Tellegen et al., 1988), confirming that genetic effects rather than shared environment accounted for the findings of previous studies.

Although these studies suggest that genetic factors significantly affect temperament, it should be kept in mind that virtually all personality characteristics are influenced by both genes and environment. Further, genetic predispositions can frequently be "overridden" by environmental influences. Naturally shy individuals can often be helped to become more assertive, and punitive experiences can cause exuberant extraverts to become hesitant or withdrawn.

Psychopathology

The role of genetic factors in causing mental disorders has been a source of much controversy. Many investigators have conducted a search for specific genetic mechanisms that might predispose afflicted individuals to mental illness. For instance, J. E. Egeland et al. (1987) announced discovery of a specific genetic marker, located on chromosome 11, coding for at least one form of bipolar (manic-depressive) disorder. But subsequent studies showed that the supposed marker does not correlate with bipolar disorder after all (Kelsoe et al., 1989). Thus, most broadbased investigations of the potential role of genetic factors in major mental disorders are still dependent on studies of familial incidence.

Schizophrenia. Schizophrenia, the most common form of major mental disorder, is characterized by severe defects in logical thinking and emotional responsiveness. Several generations ago, it was believed that traumatic experiences in childhood or poor family communication styles were the primary determinants of schizophrenia. However, recent research suggests that hereditary factors frequently play a significant role (Gottesman & Shields, 1982; Plomin, 1986; Vandenberg et al., 1986). In a number of studies, the incidence of this disorder (or, perhaps, set of disorders with similar symptoms) among the relatives of schizophrenics has been shown to vary according to how closely they are related biologically (Gottesman & Shields, 1982; Plomin, 1986; Rosenthal, Wender, Kety, Welner, & Schulsinger, 1971). For example, several well-controlled investigations have found that if one identical twin has schizophrenia, the chances are about 1 in 2 that the other twin will also develop it; among nonidentical twins the ratio is less than 1 in 10 (Kessler, 1975, 1980; O'Rourke et al, 1982; D. Rosenthal, 1970). In an extensive study carried out in Denmark, schizophrenia occurred far more often among the biological relatives of adoptees who developed schizophrenia than among the relatives of those who did not. There were no differences in incidence among the adoptive parents of the two groups (Kendler, Gruenberg, & Strauss, 1981; Kety, Rosenthal, Wender, Schulsinger, & Jacobsen, 1975, 1978).

It may be more correct, however, to speak of inheriting greater vulnerability to schizophrenia than to speak of inheriting schizophrenia per se (Freedman, Adler, Baker, Waldo, & Mizner, 1987). Otherwise, similarity between identical twins would be far higher than the 50 percent overlap that is actually found. Whether or not the disorder actually occurs seems to depend on two factors: how vulnerable a particular individual is and how much or what kind of stress he or she is subjected to. Certain life experiences may increase the chances that a person with a genetic susceptibility to schizophrenia will actually develop the disorder (M. J. Goldstein, 1987; Mednick, Parnas, & Schulsinger, 1987; Tienari et al., 1987).

Depression. In many forms of depression, particularly those that are relatively minor and transient, psychological and social factors play the principal causative role. In such conditions the depressed feelings may be expected to recede when the problems that have brought them about—such as loss of a job, disappointment in love, or the death of a friend—are somehow resolved or worked through. In the case of severe depressive disorders, however, genetic factors—mediated by biochemical processes—appear to play a significant role (Klerman, 1988; Puig-Antich, 1986; Rutter, Izard, & Read, 1986; Weissman et al., 1984; Winokur, 1975).

Of the major mental disorders, bipolar or manic-depressive appears to have the strongest genetic component. This disorder is characterized by periods of excessive euphoria, grandiosity, hyperactivity, and poor judgment, alternating with periods of normality and periods of severe depression, loss of energy, and feelings of worthlessness (American Psychiatric Association, 1987). If one identical twin has bipolar disorder, the chances are about 2 out of 3 that the other twin will also suffer from this disorder (Klerman, 1988; Nurnberger & Gershon, 1981; Plomin, 1986). In the case of nonidentical twins, the chances of the other twin also developing bipolar disorder are less than 1 in 6 (14 percent).

Do Children Select Their Environments?

The research we have examined shows that some important aspects of development are affected by genetics. One way of thinking about genetic influence is to conceptualize it as setting a **reaction range** for development. This term refers to the idea that each individual's genotype (or genetic makeup) sets a limit on the phenotype (or actuality) that can arise for that individual in development. The implication is that human beings are changeable, but not infinitely changeable.

Is it true then that genetics sets the reaction range, or creates a set of possibilities for what a particular infant may become, and that the environment determines where in the reaction range a person ends up? Scarr and McCartney (1983) suggest that genes do not only set a certain reaction range. They argue that genetic characteristics also affect the kinds of experience a person has in life. Thus, apparently environmental effects on behavior may have a genetic basis.

Scarr and McCartney identified three specific ways in which this could happen. The first is through *passive* effects of the child's genotype. They call these

Sandra Scarr.

effects passive because the children themselves do nothing to produce the environment; it is imposed on them by parents, who are typically genetically related. This kind of effect is important to keep in mind because it means that studies of correlations between aspects of the environment and child outcome using samples of biological families are not easy to interpret. Parents who rear their own children provide both genes and environment. Hence, a correlation between, for instance, the amount of time parents read to their children and the children's reading abilities may merely mean that the common genetic background of parents and children leads to a common love of reading. Scarr and McCartney argued, however, that the effect of this kind of parentally imposed environment becomes less important as children grow up, based on studies suggesting that resemblance between adopted children growing up in the same family decreases as the children reach adolescence (Scarr & Weinberg, 1976; Teasdale & Owen, 1985).

The second way in which a genotype can affect development is through *evocative* effects. Thus, a musically talented child may arouse in an adult the idea of giving music lessons, or an aggressive child may evoke from an adult a coercive style of interaction that exacerbates the problem. Sometimes, the characteristic evoking a certain kind of treatment may not be logically related to the treatment. For instance, genetic sex often evokes very different handling of children by adults, as when they give toy guns and cars to boys and dolls and dress-up clothes to girls. This treatment is based on genetics, in a sense, because being an XY or an XX individual is a genetic matter.

The third way in which a genotype can affect the environment is *active*, based on individuals selecting their own environment. For instance, two children may both have access to art materials and to sports equipment, but one may choose to spend much more time on art and the other much more time on sports. Scarr and McCartney (1983) suggest that these kinds of choices become increasingly common and important as children grow up and have more control over their environment.

Scarr (1992) has very forcefully argued that these ideas lead to the conclusion that, for the kinds of "average, expectable" environments that children participating in psychological studies are usually in, environment has surprisingly little effect on children's outcome. A "good enough" parent (and school, and so on) is all children need. Given basic environmental support, children develop in ways largely determined by their genotype.

Several criticisms of this argument have been raised (Baumrind, 1993; Jackson, 1993). Perhaps the most important is that the limits of the acceptable environment are very vague. Scarr recognizes that abuse and neglect are not "good enough," while arguing that minor variation in just what toys or books or extracurricular activities a child has are unimportant. But between these extremes lies a large uncharted territory. Research may be necessary to clarify just where to draw the line between the crucial and the trivial.

A second important criticism has to do with the fact that all of the effects Scarr discusses can be said to depend on environment at least as much as on genetics. Evocative effects of genes depend on cultural beliefs. In a culture with different beliefs about gender, the fact of genetic sex would not lead to differential rearing. Similarly, active effects of genes are limited by what a child's environment offers. A child cannot seek something the environment does not contain. For instance, at the beginning of the twentieth century, when very few children went to school for more than a few years, economic pressures may have prevented many very intelligent children from developing their intellectual abilities. For everyone who managed to read a book by candlelight after a day in the factory, there may have been many who were too poor to afford the book or the candle. Thus, in summary, it may be misleading to think of gene-environment transactions as mainly genetic.

Why Are Siblings So Different?

Behavior geneticists generally distinguish between two kinds of environmental effects: **shared environment** and **nonshared environment**. Shared environment is everything in the environment that would be shared among siblings growing up in the same household, such as parents' personality, neighborhood of residence, books in the home, religious affiliation, and so on. Nonshared, or specific, environment is everything in siblings' environments that they do not share. For instance, siblings—because they are different ages—typically have different sets of friends.

From studies of twins and adopted relatives, there is evidence that the environmental influence on characteristics such as intelligence, personality, and psychopathology comes almost entirely from the nonshared environment. Specifically, Robert Plomin and his colleagues (Dunn & Plomin, 1990; Plomin & Daniels, 1987) have summarized evidence that 35 to 45 percent of the differences among people on these dimensions are due to nonshared environment, with only 5 percent of the differences explainable by shared environment (see Figure 2.7). It is interesting to compare these estimates to those in Figure 2.6 for school achievement. Note the much higher influence of shared environment for achievement. These findings suggest that aspects of rearing often emphasized by both developmentalists and parents, such as discipline practices, may be much less influential in development than we have thought.

One commonsense way to think about the importance of nonshared environment is to reflect on how different siblings often are from each other. Plomin has raised the question: Why should siblings not be very similar indeed, if they share about half their genes and also share a common environment, and if these influences on development are the most important ones?

Robert Plomin.

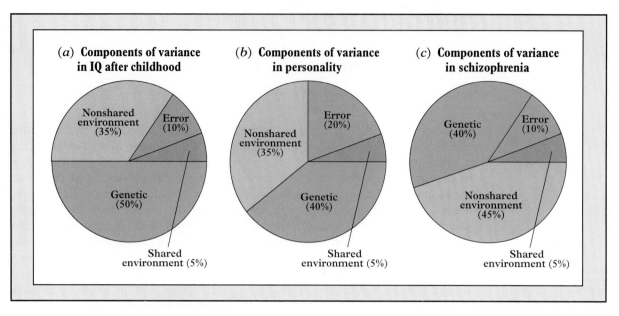

FIGURE 2.7 Estimates of genetic and environmental influence on cognitive ability after childhood (*a*), on personality (*b*), and on schizophrenia (*c*). From *Separate Lives: Why Siblings Are So Different* (pp. 50–52) by J. Dunn and R. Plomin, 1990, New York: Basic Books. Copyright © 1990 by Basic Books. Reprinted by permission.

To answer this question, we need to specify what important nonshared influences might be. One important environmental influence is certainly parents, and, while parents are often assumed to be the same for all their children, they may not be. Despite the cultural prescription to treat siblings equally, parents may prefer one or dislike another. In addition, parents are different ages when their children are born, and their life circumstances may change enough to cause them to treat their children differently. A parent's unemployment may cause different effects on a 3-year-old child and on a 10-year-old sibling. Finally, the child's *observation* of apparently differential treatment may be key. The parent who ties a 3-year-old's shoes while asking the 6-year-old to do it herself may be seen by the 6-year-old as favoring the sibling, even though the parent tied the 6-year-old's shoes three years ago. That argument doesn't go far with an angry or hurt child!

Siblings also affect each other, sometimes in very different ways. Even when they are engaged in interacting with each other, what they get out of the experience can be very different, if their roles in the interaction are quite different. For instance, when an older sibling teaches a younger one, the younger one may learn the skill taught, while the older one learns how to teach and learns the virtues of patience and care in structuring an experience for a less mature person.

The differences between how siblings see their relationship and what they get out of it can be very striking. It's hard to believe that the following accounts of sibling relations come from siblings in the same family.

> Well, he's nice to me. And he sneaks into my bed at night time from Mummy. I think I'd be very lonely without Carl. I play with him a lot and he thinks up lots of ideas and it's very exciting. He comes and meets me at the gate after school and I think that's very friendly. . . . He's very kind. . . . Don't

This older sister is showing her 1-year-old brother how to kick a ball. They will each learn something different from this experience.

really know what I'd do without a brother. [Nancy, 10 years old, talks about her 6-year-old brother Carl]

    She's pretty disgusting and we don't talk to each other much. I don't really know about her. [Interviewer: What is it you particularly like about her?] Nothing. Sometimes when I do something wrong she tells me off quite cruelly. [Carl talks about Nancy]

    (Dunn & Plomin, 1990, p. 88)

In addition to these factors, siblings may have different experiences. We already mentioned they are likely to have different friends, but they may also join different clubs, have different periods of sickness, and so on. Even the same experience may affect them differently depending on their age when it happens and other factors. McCall (1983) offers the hypothetical case of a family visiting the Kennedy Space Center. The 16-year-old is already very interested in basketball and dating, and the visit has little effect. But the 9-year-old, who has mathematical ability but has never been interested in school, is fascinated. Returning home, he discovers his neighbor is a pilot, strikes up a friendship, and goes up on some flights. (Note that the older

The development of special interests depends on gene–environment interactions.

brother also has this man for a neighbor, but the fact has no impact on his life.) This interest in aviation causes the 9-year-old to become very engaged in science and math classes and to blossom academically.

Not all researchers accept that shared environment is unimportant, however (Hoffman, 1991). A commonsense way of expressing doubt about the idea that shared environment has few effects would be to note that shared and specific environmental factors are not different in kind from each other. The general way a parent interacts with children is very similar to the way that parent interacts with a particular child. Nevertheless, even if shared environment turns out to also play a vital role, the data Plomin discusses certainly suggest that specific factors are important. This perspective enriches our understanding of the important processes in development.

✹ SUMMARY

The development of every individual begins when a sperm cell from the father penetrates the wall of an ovum from the mother. At that time both the sperm and the ovum release 23 chromosomes, each of which is subdivided into many thousands of genes. The genes contain the child's biological heritage.

The basic mechanism of hereditary transmission is the replication of deoxyribonucleic acid (DNA). DNA is composed of two molecular chains coiled around each other to form a double-stranded helix. When DNA replicates itself the strands separate and reconstitute themselves to form two new helixes, each of which is chemically identical to the one from which it was derived. The process by which the original fertilized ovum multiples to form new cells is called mitosis.

The reason children of the same parents are not identical is that the germ cells, from which sperm and ova are derived, differ from other cells in the process by which they divide. That process, meiosis, results in cells whose nuclei contain only half the number of chromosomes present in the parent cell. This means that different sperm and ova contain different sets of chromosomes. In addition, a process called crossing-over, in which pairs of chromosomes exchange genetic material, increases the likelihood that each sperm or ovum will be unique.

One of the 23 pairs of chromosomes contains the sex chromosomes and determines the sex of the child. In females both members of the pair are X chromosomes; male body cells contain one X and one Y chromosome. However, as a result of meiosis, sperm cells may contain either an X or a Y chromosome. When a sperm containing a Y chromosome unites with an ovum, which contains an X chromosome, a male child is produced.

Genes may be either dominant or recessive; if a dominant gene is present, the effect of a recessive gene for the same trait (e.g., eye color) will be masked. Numerous known gene defects may result in mental retardation and other developmental disabilities. In some instances, as in the case of phenylketonuria, genes fail to give the cells the proper instructions to produce enzymes needed for normal development; in others, abnormalities in the structure of the chromosomes may be responsible for mental retardation. Studies of children with sex chromosome abnormalities (SCA) indicate that a nurturant home environment can reduce the effects of less extreme forms of SCA on development.

Most behavioral traits are multifactorial, meaning that they depend on more than one genetic or environmental factor. A particular characteristic may require the presence of a number of genes, a situation that is termed polygenetic inheritance. The extent to which intelligence (as measured by intelligence tests) is influenced by heredity is a subject of controversy. It is difficult to isolate the potential effects of heredity from those of other variables such as good health and superior educational opportunities. Twin studies have found a higher correlation between the IQs of monozygotic ("identical") twins than between those of dizygotic ("fraternal") twins or nontwin siblings. Even twin studies are not entirely definitive, though, since the environmental influences to which dizygotic twins are exposed may be less similar than those to which monozygotic twins are exposed. Moreover, there are similarities between adoptive parents and their adopted children, suggesting that environmental as well as genetic factors play an important role in a child's intellectual performance.

Certain personality characteristics also may be affected by genetic factors; in general, genetic influences are strongest on basic temperamental characteristics (e.g., activity-passivity). However, genetic predispositions can be overridden by environmental influences. Certain mental disorders, such as schizophrenia and affective disorders, appear to be caused at least partially by genetic factors. It may be more correct to speak of inheriting vulnerability to these disorders than to speak of inheriting the disorders themselves.

Sandra Scarr has recently argued that the genetic makeup of an individual plays an increasingly strong role as children get older in guiding selection of environments that will foster the growth of inherited characteristics. These effects, however, are in some sense as environmental as they are genetic, an argument which reminds us that ultimately the two influences are interactive. Further, with extreme environmental variation, the environment will be seen to have a stronger effect.

Robert Plomin has concentrated on a different piece of this puzzle, focusing on the fact that many environmental factors serve to make children from the same family different rather than the same. Study of the specific (or nonshared) environment should lead to an enrichment in our understanding of development.

REVIEW QUESTIONS

1. What is the basic unit of hereditary transmission? By what means does hereditary transmission occur?

2. Why is each human being genetically unique?

3. What is meant by the terms *dominant* and *recessive*? What is polygenetic inheritance?

4. Briefly describe the current state of research concerning the influence of heredity on intelligence.

5. What role do genetic factors play in the occurrence of mental disorders such as schizophrenia and bipolar (manic-depressive) disorders?

6. Describe the difficulties encountered in investigating the role of genetic factors in the development of personality. Is there evidence that they play any role at all?

7. Summarize how Scarr believes that children "select" their own environments.

8. What aspects of siblings' lives might work to make them different from each other?

CRITICAL THINKING ABOUT THE CHAPTER

1. Table 2.1 does not show what eye colors would be shown by children of two individuals, each of whom had Bb genes. What are the odds that a child born to this brown-eyed couple would have blue eyes?

2. Consider you and your siblings (or a family you know well, if you are an only child). How are the siblings different from each other? Can you think of specific experiences (nonshared environment) that help account for these differences?

KEY TERMS

adoption study	mitosis
autosomes	monozygotic (identical) twins
behavior genetics	multifactorial
chromosomes	nonshared environment
crossing-over	phenotype
dizygotic (fraternal) twins	polygenetic inheritance
DNA	reaction range
dominant	recessive
genes	sex chromosomes
genetic counseling	shared environment
genotype	twin study
meiosis	

SUGGESTED READINGS

Dunn, J., & Plomin, R. (1990). *Separate lives: Why siblings are so different.* New York: Basic Books. A very readable introduction to behavior genetics and to the study of family life.

Watson, James D. (1986). *The double helix.* New York: New American Library. A suspense-filled story of the competition to discover the structure of DNA, told by one of the discoverers.

CHAPTER 3

PRENATAL DEVELOPMENT AND BIRTH

STAGES OF PRENATAL DEVELOPMENT

Conception
The Germinal Period
The Embryonic Period
The Fetal Period

PRENATAL ENVIRONMENTAL INFLUENCES

Age of the Mother
Maternal Nutrition
Drugs and Radiation
    Alcohol
    Nicotine
    Caffeine
    Cocaine
    Radiation
Maternal Diseases and Disorders During Pregnancy
The Rh Factor
Maternal Stress
Paternal Effects

PRENATAL TESTING

THE BIRTH PROCESS

Vaginal Delivery
Caesarean Section
Drugs Taken During Labor and Delivery
Anoxia and Other Complications
Prematurity

Celia woke up with the curious mixture of positive and negative feelings, both physical and mental, which she was getting used to as she approached the last weeks of her first pregnancy. She looked down at her enormous belly with feelings both of pride and of real amazement: it didn't seem that it could possibly belong to her. In fact, she sometimes bumped into people in crowded restaurants or buses, because she literally forgot how far she now extended. As she watched, she felt the curious tingle as her baby stretched, and some limb or other moved across her insides. The baby seemed so real now, no longer an idea or a hope but a very tangible physical being. It was odd that she knew nothing about it, though, really. Her doctor said it looked healthy, and she had taken every step possible to ensure its growth. She had given up her morning cup of coffee, refused all alcoholic drinks, and eaten a very carefully planned diet. But who knew? As she approached her due date, Celia felt she was headed for an unknown land. What would labor be like? Would the baby be OK? What would the baby be like? And what would she be like as a mother?

It is a curious fact that even though we recognize that development begins at conception, we reckon a person's age from the moment of birth. Yet the environment in which unborn children grow has a tremendous influence on their later development, both physical and psychological. In this chapter, we gain an overview of the stages of prenatal development, study the environmental influences that can affect development at this time, and examine the process of birth.

STAGES OF PRENATAL DEVELOPMENT

Prenatal development can be divided into several periods. First, there is conception. Then, the time from conception to birth is usually divided into three phases. The first phase, the **germinal stage,** lasts from conception until implantation, when the developing organism becomes firmly attached to the wall of the uterus. This period is about 10 to 14 days long. The second phase, which extends from the second to the eighth week, is the **embryonic stage.** It is characterized by cell differentiation as the major organs begin to develop. The last phase, from 8 weeks until delivery, is the **fetal stage.** It is characterized mainly by growth rather than by the formation of new organs. Delivery normally occurs at around 38 weeks after conception, or 40 weeks from the last menstrual period. (Pregnancy is often dated from the last menstrual period, even though the woman was not pregnant for about the first two weeks of that time, simply because the date of the last menstrual period is usually known with more certainty than the date of conception.)

Conception

Conception occurs when a sperm from the male penetrates the cell wall of an ovum, or egg, from the female. Once every 28 days on the average (usually around the middle of the menstrual cycle), an ovum ripens in one of the two ovaries, is discharged into the corresponding *fallopian tube,* or oviduct, and begins its slow journey toward the uterus, propelled by the small, hairlike *cilia* that line the tube. In most cases it takes from 3 to 7 days for the ovum to reach the uterus (see Figure 3.1). If the ovum has not been fertilized in the course of this journey, it disintegrates in the uterus after a few days. If, on the other hand, a mating has taken place, one of the many millions of sperm released by the male may find its way into the oviduct during the time that the ovum is making its descent. There, if it unites with the ovum, a new individual is conceived.

As noted in Chapter 2, each sperm is a single cell that resembles a tadpole. The oval head of the sperm is packed with the 23 chromosomes. Behind the head are special structures that supply the energy required for the sperm to reach the ovum. It is estimated that the sperm travels at a velocity of about $1/10$ of an inch per minute.

At the moment of conception, the ovum, the largest cell in the human body, is still only about $1/175$ of an inch in diameter. When the sperm enters the ovum, the nucleus of the sperm becomes fused with the nucleus of the ovum. The fertilized ovum, or **zygote,** immediately begins to grow and subdivide. The elapsed time from the sperm's penetration of the ovum to the first subdivision is usually from 24 to 36 hours.

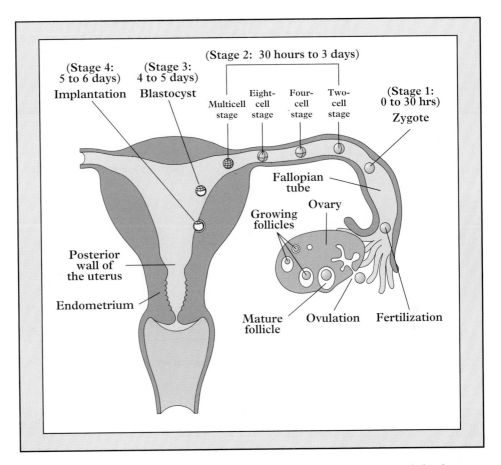

FIGURE 3.1 Diagrammatic summary of the ovarian cycle, fertilization, and development before implantation. After *The Developing Human: Clinically Oriented Embryology* (3rd ed.), by K. L. Moore, 1982, Philadelphia: W. B. Saunders. Copyright © 1982 by W. B. Saunders & Company. Adapted with permission.

The Germinal Period

The fertilized ovum continues to divide during its journey from the oviduct to the uterus. By the time the fertilized ovum reaches the uterus, it is about the size of a pinhead and contains several dozen cells. A small cavity is formed within the mass of cells, resulting in an outer cluster of cells and a separate inner cluster (see Figure 3.2). The outer layer, called the **trophoblast,** will ultimately develop into accessory tissues that protect and nourish the embryo. The inner cluster, gathered at the *embryonic pole* in Figure 3.2, will become the embryo itself.

While these developments are taking place, small burrlike tendrils have begun to grow around the outside of the trophoblast. In a few more days these tendrils will attach the ovum to the uterine wall. In the meantime the uterus itself has begun to undergo changes in preparation for receiving the fertilized ovum. At the time of implantation, extensions of the tendrils from the trophoblast reach into blood spaces that have formed within the maternal tissue. At this point the period of the ovum comes to an end and the second phase of prenatal development, the embryonic period, begins.

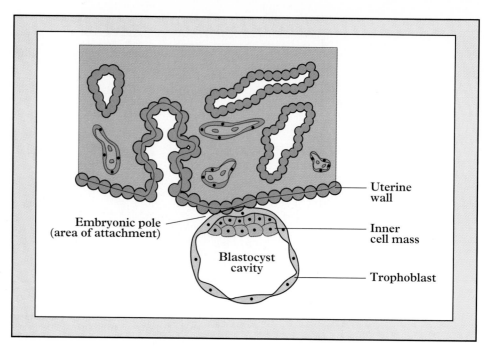

FIGURE 3.2 Schematic representation of the ovum at an early stage of implantation in the uterine wall.

The Embryonic Period

When it enters the embryonic stage the new individual has ceased to be an independent, free-floating organism and has established a dependent relationship with the mother. Once the growing egg is successfully lodged in its new home, development is rapid. The inner cell mass, which will become a recognizable embryo, begins to differentiate into three distinct layers: (1) the **ectoderm** (outer layer), from which will develop the epidermis (the outer layer of the skin), the hair, the nails, parts of the teeth, skin glands, sensory cells, and the nervous system; (2) the **mesoderm** (middle layer), from which will develop the dermis (the inner skin layer), the muscles, the skeleton, and the circulatory and excretory organs; and (3) the **endoderm** (inner layer), from which will develop the lining of the entire gastrointestinal tract and the eustachian tubes, trachea, bronchia, lungs, liver, pancreas, salivary glands, thyroid glands, and thymus (K.L. Moore, 1982; Nilsson, Furuhjelm, Ingelman-Sundberg, & Wirsen, 1981; Rugh & Shettles, 1971).

While the inner cell mass is being differentiated into a recognizable embryo, the outer layers of cells are giving rise to two fetal membranes: the **chorion** and the **amnion**. These, together with a third membrane derived from the uterine wall, extend from the wall of the uterus and enclose the developing embryo (see Figure 3.3). They form a sac filled with a watery fluid (called **amniotic fluid**) that acts as a buffer to protect the embryo from shocks experienced by the mother and helps maintain an even temperature for the embryo.

Simultaneously, other fetal sacs are formed; the most important of these becomes the **umbilical cord.** It extends from the embryo to the section of the uterine wall where the uterus and the chorion are joined. This area is called the

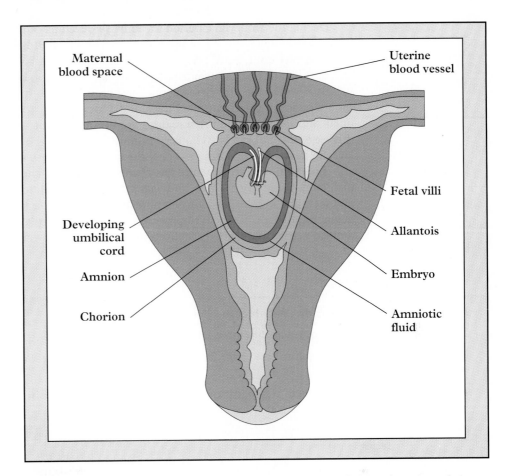

FIGURE 3.3 Diagram showing the uterus, the membrane, and the embryo in early pregnancy. After "Origins and Prenatal Growth of Behavior," by L. Carmichael, in *A Handbook of Child Psychology* (2nd ed., p. 50) edited by C. Murchinson, 1983, Worcester, MA: Clark University Press. Copyright © 1983 by Clark University Press. Adapted with permission.

placenta. The umbilical cord is the lifeline of the embryo. Through it, two arteries carry blood from the embryo to the placenta and a vein carries blood to the embryo from the placenta. However, the relationship between the child's bloodstream and the mother's is indirect. Both the child's and the mother's bloodstreams open into the placenta. But the two systems are always separated by semipermeable membranes that function as extremely fine screens, large enough to permit the passage of gases, salts, and other substances but too small to allow blood cells to get through. This is called the **placental barrier.**

Various nutrient substances from the mother's blood—sugars, fats, and some protein elements—permeate the placenta and can reach the child. Waste products from the infant, primarily carbon dioxide and other metabolites, can also pass through the placenta and be disposed of by the mother. In addition, some vitamins, drugs (including nicotine and alcohol), vaccines, and disease germs (e.g., diphtheria, typhoid, influenza, and rubella) may get through the placental barrier from the mother's system and affect the embryo's development. Thus, the health of the mother directly affects the health of the fetus, as we shall see in more detail shortly.

During the embryonic period the embryo develops extremely rapidly (see Table 3.1). By the eighteenth day it has begun to take shape. It has established a longitudinal axis; its front, back, left and right sides, head, and tail are discernible. By the end of the third week a primitive heart has developed and begun to beat.

By 4 weeks the embryo is about ⅕ of an inch long. It has the beginnings of a mouth region, a gastrointestinal tract, and a liver. The heart is becoming well developed, and the head and brain regions are becoming more clearly differentiated. At this stage the embryo is still a very primitive organism, however. It has no arms or legs, no developed features, and only the most elementary of body systems.

By 8 to 9 weeks the picture has changed markedly. The embryo is now about 1 inch long. Face, mouth, eyes, and ears are fairly well defined. Arms and legs, hands and feet, and even stubby fingers and toes have appeared; the sex organs are just beginning to form. The development of muscle and cartilage also begins, but well-defined neuromotor activity (activation of the muscles by impulses from the nerves)

TABLE 3.1 Steps in Prenatal Development

1 week	Fertilized ovum descends through fallopian tube toward uterus.
2 weeks	Embryo has attached itself to uterine lining and is developing rapidly.
3 weeks	Embryo has begun to take shape; head and tail regions discernible. Primitive heart begins to beat.
4 weeks	Beginnings of mouth region, gastrointestinal tract, and liver. Heart is developing rapidly, and head and brain regions are becoming more clearly differentiated.
6 weeks	Hands and feet begin developing, but arms are still too short and stubby to meet. Liver is producing blood cells.
8 weeks	Embryo is about 1 inch long. Face, mouth, eyes, and ears have begun taking on fairly defined form. Development of muscle and cartilage has begun.
12 weeks	Fetus is about 3 inches long. It has begun to resemble a human being, though the head is disproportionately large. Face has babylike profile. Eyelids and nails have begun to form, and sex can be distinguished easily. Nervous system still very primitive.
16 weeks	Fetus is about 4½ inches long. The mother may be able to feel the fetus's movements. Extremities, head, and internal organs are developing rapidly. Body proportions are becoming more baby-like.
5 months	Pregnancy half completed. Fetus is about 6 inches long and is able to hear and move about quite freely. Hands and feet are complete.
6 months	Fetus is about 10 inches long. Eyes are completely formed; taste buds appear on tongue. Fetus is capable of inhaling and exhaling and of making a thin crying noise should birth occur prematurely.
7 months	An important age. The fetus has reached the "zone of viability" (having a chance to live if born prematurely). It is physiologically capable of distinguishing basic tastes and odors. Pain sensitivity appears to be relatively absent. Breathing is shallow and irregular, and sucking and swallowing are weak.
7 months to birth	Fetus becomes increasingly ready for independent life outside the womb. Muscle tone increases; movement becomes sustained and positive; breathing, swallowing, sucking, and hunger cry become strong. Visual and auditory reactions are firmly established.

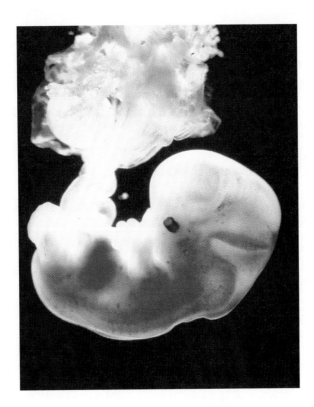

Human fetus at about four weeks.

is still absent (Nilsson et al., 1981; Rugh & Shettles, 1971). The internal organs—intestines, liver, pancreas, lungs, kidneys—take on a definite shape and assume some degree of function. The liver, for example, begins to manufacture red blood cells. During this period the head is large in relation to other parts of the body.

The embryonic period is characterized by extremely rapid development of the nervous system. This suggests that the first 8 weeks constitute a sensitive period with respect to the integrity of the nervous system (see Figure 3.4). If there is any mechanical or chemical interference with development at this time (e.g., if the mother falls down stairs or takes an overdose of a drug), it is more likely to cause permanent damage to the nervous system than would be caused by a similar disruption at a later date. For example, if the mother contracts rubella (German measles) during this period, the child is more likely to be mentally deficient than if she were to have the illness during the last 8 weeks of pregnancy (Lubchenco, 1976).

The Fetal Period

The third period of prenatal development, the fetal period, extends from the end of the second month until birth. During this time the various body systems, which were laid down in rudimentary form earlier, become quite well developed and begin to function. Up until about 8 weeks the fetus has led a relatively passive existence, floating quiescently in the amniotic fluid. At this time, however, it becomes capable of responding to tactile stimulation. From this point on, motor functions become increasingly differentiated and complex.

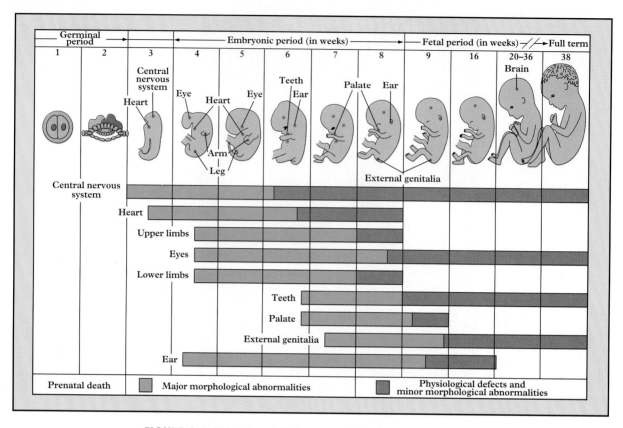

FIGURE 3.4 Critical periods in prenatal development. The risk of abnormalities is greater when organs are being formed. From *The Developing Human: Clinically Oriented Embryology* (4th ed.), by K. L. Moore, 1988, Philadelphia: W. B. Saunders. Copyright © 1988 by W. B. Saunders & Company. Reprinted by permission.

Toward the end of the eighth week, the reproductive system begins to develop. In both sexes the gonads (ovaries and testes) initially appear as a pair of blocks of tissue. It appears that the hormones manufactured by the male's testes are necessary to stimulate the development of a male reproductive system. If the testes are removed or fail to perform properly, the baby will possess a primarily female reproductive system. Evidence from rabbits indicates that if the ovary is removed immediately after its formation, the female fetus develops normally. The anatomy of the female reproductive system thus can be considered basic; it is the form that will develop if either testes or ovaries are removed or do not function.

By the end of 12 weeks the fetus is about 3 inches long and weighs about ¾ of an ounce. It has begun to resemble a human being, though the head is disproportionately large. The muscles are becoming well developed, and spontaneous movements of the arms and legs may be observed. The eyelids and nails have begun to form, and the fetus's sex can be distinguished easily. The nervous system is still very incomplete, however.

During the next 4 weeks the fetus's motor behavior becomes more complex. By the end of 16 weeks the mother can feel the fetus's movements. (In popular language this is known as "quickening.") At this point the fetus is about 4½ inches

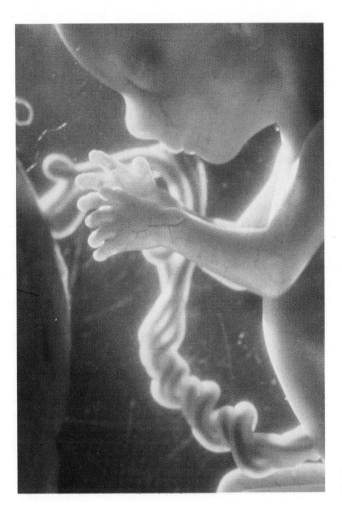

Human fetus at about four months.

long. In the period from 16 to 20 weeks, the fetus grows to about 10 inches in length and 8 or 9 ounces in weight. It becomes more human in appearance, and hair appears on the head and body. The mouth becomes capable of protrusion as well as opening and closing, and blinking of the eyes occurs, although the lids are still tightly fused. The hands become capable of gripping in addition to closing.

After 20 weeks the skin begins to assume adult form, hair and nails appear, and sweat glands develop. By 24 weeks the eyes are completely formed and taste buds appear on the tongue. The fetus is now capable of taking air into the lungs and exhaling it, and of a thin crying noise if born prematurely. However, the organs, especially the lungs, are still not well developed enough to sustain independent life, and children born this premature almost always die shortly after birth.

The fetal age of 28 weeks (dated from the last menstrual period) is an important time. It demarcates the zone between **viability** (ability to live if born) and nonviability. By this age the child's nervous, circulatory, and other bodily systems have become sufficiently mature to stand a chance of functioning adequately outside of the uterus, although special care is required, and children born this premature have a significant risk of death or of suffering permanent effects of premature birth. At this point, however, the fetus's reactions to temperature changes approximate those of the full-term infant. Experimental studies of infants born at this age indicate that the fetus can differentiate among the basic tastes—sweet, salt, sour, and bitter—and among basic odors. Visual and auditory reactions occur, though not as clearly as in the full-term infant. On the other hand, sensitivity to pain seems to be slight or absent in the premature infant.

The period from 28 weeks to birth at full term (38 to 42 weeks from the last menstrual period) is marked by further development of the basic body structures and functions. Gains in body weight and height continue to be rapid. By 7 months the average unborn baby weighs about 4 pounds and is 16 inches long. During the eighth month another pound and 2 inches will be added. Much of the weight gain during these last 3 months comes from a padding of fat beneath the skin that will help to insulate the newborn baby from changes in temperature after birth.

Each additional week that the fetus remains within the mother's uterus increases the likelihood of survival and normal development. As muscle tone improves, a good hunger cry and a strong sucking reflex develop, and mental alertness and perceptual and motor development increase. Most important, the fetal lungs mature and become more capable of supporting independent breathing. By the time the unborn infant weighs 3 pounds, the chances of successful postnatal development are markedly improved; a baby born weighing at least 5 pounds will probably not need to be placed in an incubator (Apgar & Beck, 1974; Korones, 1986; Lubchenco, 1976).

By the beginning of the ninth month, the unborn baby, who once floated in weightless ease in the fluid of the amniotic sac, has grown so large that movement inside the uterus is quite constricted. Usually the fetus settles into a head-down position because this gives it the most room in the uterus, which is shaped like an inverted pear. Consequently, most babies are born head first, the easiest and safest way. However, about 10 percent of babies assume a feet-first position, which leads to a *breech* delivery or, in modern American obstetric practice, to a Caesarean section (discussed in "The Birth Process"). A few babies maintain a crosswise position and also require delivery by means of a Caesarean section. The average full-term baby is 20 to 21 inches long and weighs 7 pounds, but a wide range of heights and weights are considered normal.

✦ PRENATAL ENVIRONMENTAL INFLUENCES

There are many variations in prenatal environment, and the pressures to which one fetus is subjected may differ greatly from those exerted on another. Recent research suggests that the mother's physical and emotional state—and, consequently, the prenatal environment she provides—have important influences on fetal development and the subsequent health and adjustment of the child. In addition, a father's physical state may affect the development of the children he helps conceive. Some of the more important prenatal environmental factors that have been investigated are discussed in the following sections.

To place our discussion of prenatal risk factors in perspective, it should be noted that morbidity (disease or illness) and mortality risks for infants have declined markedly in recent years. For example, in the United States the infant mortality rate has declined from 140 per 1000 live births at the turn of the century to 11 per 1000 today (U.S. Bureau of the Census, 1987). However, despite our wealth as a nation, approximately 14 countries have lower infant mortality rates. This is probably due to greater availability in these countries of proper health care and nutritional assistance for infants and their mothers (Conger, 1988; Schorr, 1988).

Age of the Mother

With increasing numbers of adolescents becoming pregnant and many women in their thirties having children for the first time, there has been growing interest in the effects of age on fertility and on the health of both the infant and the mother. With good medical care, proper health practices, and adequate nutrition, most women of all ages will have healthy babies and will remain healthy themselves. Nevertheless, the years between ages 20 and 35 remain the most favorable for childbearing.

The pregnancies of adolescents—particularly younger adolescents—are more likely than those of women in their twenties to endanger the health of both mother and child, although the risks are substantially reduced by adequate prenatal and postnatal care and good nutrition (C. D. Hayes, 1987; Menken, 1980). Currently, babies of teenage mothers are more likely to have low birth weights (a major cause of infant mortality) as well as neurological defects and childhood illnesses. The mothers themselves are more likely to have complications of pregnancy such as toxemia and anemia. Among very young teenagers (those under 15), pregnancy tends to inhibit the mother's growth as well as the child's (Gunter & LaBarba, 1980; Hayes, 1987).

Women over 30 have a lower fertility rate than those in their twenties, and fertility continues to decline with age (Guttmacher & Kaiser, 1986). They are also more likely than younger women to experience illnesses during pregnancy and to have longer and more difficult labor. Mothers over 40 run a sharply increased risk of having a child with a chromosomal abnormality, particularly Down syndrome. The average incidence of this disorder increases from less than 1 per 1000 through age 29 to 1.5 at ages 30 to 34, 6 at ages 35 to 39, 20 at ages 40 to 44, and 30 at ages over 45 (Guttmacher & Kaiser, 1986). Women over 35 are also more likely to have miscarriages and to give birth to underweight or stillborn babies (Kopp & Parmelee, 1979; Korones, 1986; Lubchenco, 1976). The older the woman, the greater the likelihood that these problems will arise; nevertheless, the absolute incidence of serious complications remains relatively small, especially for women who engage in good health practices and receive appropriate medical care. In cases in which there is reason to suspect the presence of a chromosomal or other abnormality, procedures such as chorionic villus sampling (CVS), ultrasound scans, and amniocentesis may be recommended (see section on prenatal testing).

Maternal Nutrition

An expectant mother should have an adequate diet if she is to maintain her own health during pregnancy and deliver a healthy infant. This appears entirely reasonable when we remember that the growing fetus's food supply comes from the mother's bloodstream via the semipermeable membranes of the placenta and the umbilical cord. The diet should include from 2000 to 2800 calories daily, obtained from foods that give adequate amounts of protein, vitamins and minerals, in addition to calories (National Academy of Sciences, 1989).

Some aspects of diet are especially important in the first few weeks of pregnancy, before many women know they are pregnant at all. For instance, not having adequate levels of folic acid, a B vitamin found in green leafy vegetables, asparagus, and liver, is a risk factor for having a baby with *spina bifida,* a condition in which the spine is not well-formed and the spinal cord is exposed. Adequate levels are vital in the first few weeks after conception and are difficult to get from diet alone. Hence, women of child-bearing age should continue taking on a routine basis a multivitamin supplement that, together with diet, would provide from 0.4 milligrams to not more than 1.0 milligrams of folic acid daily.

Babies born to mothers with nutritionally deficient diets are more likely to have low birth weights, to suffer from impaired brain development, to be less resistant to illnesses such as pneumonia and bronchitis, and to have a higher risk of mortality in the first year of life (Dobbing, 1976; Katz, Keusch, & Mata, 1975; Knoblock & Pasaminick, 1966; Kopp & Parmelee, 1979; Metcoff, 1978). Information about the effects of deficient diet comes from studies that have included careful controls for other potentially harmful effects that may co-occur with poor diet, such as disease. For instance, in one well-controlled study in Guatemala, the residents of several villages received nourishing supplemental diets for several years while the residents of other similar villages received soda pop supplements. Infant mortality and morbidity were lower and birth weight higher in the first two villages. In another controlled study of the effectiveness of a federally funded nutritional supplement program for needy, high-risk pregnant women, mothers, and infants in Massachusetts, it was found that participation by pregnant women for at least four months resulted in infants with significantly higher birth weight, less prematurity, and decreased neonatal mortality (Kotelchuck, Schwartz, Anderka, & Finison, 1983). Moreover, the longer the subjects participated in the program, the more impressive the results were (see Figure 3.5). Thus, inadequate diet has a clear association with physical effects on developing fetuses.

In addition, data suggest that prenatal malnutrition can affect cognitive development. In the Guatemalan project, children from those villages receiving supplements scored somewhat better on mental tests at the end of seven years, and showed definite advantages in adolescence. The effects were especially marked in children from the poorest groups, who presumably had the worst diets and the least cognitively stimulating environments. While some of the effects may be due to children receiving supplements in the first two years of life as well as prenatally, these findings suggest that severe maternal malnutrition may impair the child's intellectual development in addition to having adverse effects on physical development (Bhatia, Katiyar, & Apaswol, 1979; Cravioto & DeLicardie, 1978; Katz et al., 1975; Metcoff, 1978; Pollitt, Gorman, Engle, Martorell & Rivera, 1993).

The relatively modest cost of adequate health care and nutritional programs for mothers and infants is clearly a good investment; it saves later medical and educational costs that are required for children who have birth defects, mental retardation, or other problems as a result of poor prenatal nutrition. Nevertheless, funding for prenatal and postnatal medical care, disease prevention, counseling, and nutrition for poor families declined steadily in the 1980s (Conger, 1988; Edelman, 1987). The United States' progress toward reducing infant mortality came to a halt in 1985; among black infants, neonatal mortality (death in the first 28 days of life) rose for the first time in twenty years (CDF Reports, 1988).

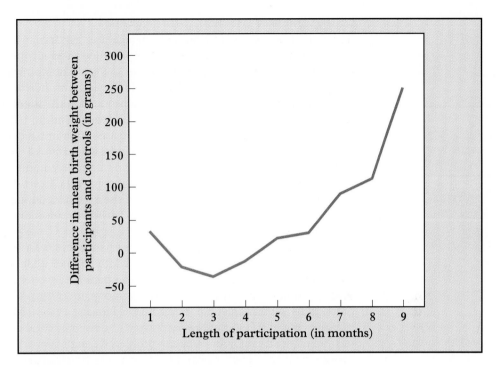

FIGURE 3.5 Mean differences in birth weight between participants in a federal nutrition program and controls. After *Massachusetts Special Supplemental Food Program for Women, Infants and Children Evaluation Project,* by M. Kotelchuck, J. Schwartz, M. Anderka, K. Finison, 1983, Boston: Dept. of Public Health. Copyright 1983 by Boston Department of Public Health. Adapted with permission.

Drugs and Radiation

Physicians and parents have become increasingly concerned about the potentially harmful effects of drugs on the developing embryo and fetus. One of the most dramatic reasons for this concern was the discovery around 1960 of the gross anatomical defects caused by a drug, thalidomide, that many women had taken during pregnancy. Thalidomide was introduced as a medication to control nausea in pregnant women, but it turned out to cause severe malformations in the legs and/or arms of the developing child.

Many other drugs are suspected of producing birth defects when taken during pregnancy; substances that produce such effects are called **teratogens**, from Greek words meaning "something that can produce monsters." There is a long list of substances known or suspected to be teratogens, including legal drugs (alcohol, nicotine, caffeine), prescription drugs (some antibiotics, hormones, steroids, anticoagulants, anticonvulsants, tranquilizers, methadone), illegal drugs (cocaine, heroin, marijuana), and environmental pollutants (including lead, methylmercury, and polychlorinated biphenyls, or PCBs) (Apgar & Beck, 1974; Behrman & Vaughn, 1987; Catz & Yaffe, 1978; Madden, Payne, & Miller, 1986; K. L. Moore, 1982). Here we review the known and suspected effects of some of these substances.

Alcohol. We begin with alcohol for two reasons. First, it is a known teratogen, firmly established to have behavioral as well as physical effects on the developing fetus (Vorhees & Mollnow, 1987). Second, it is a very common substance for women to use who are of child-bearing age. For instance, 61 percent of a representative U.S. sample of women aged 15 to 44 had used alcohol in the month before the survey (Adams, Gfroerer, & Rouse, 1989). The combination of danger and widespread use is clearly one threatening to children's health.

Drinking by pregnant women can produce **fetal alcohol syndrome** (Abel, 1980; Behrman & Vaughn, 1987; K. L. Jones, Smith, Ulleland, & Streissguth, 1973). It is estimated that each year at least 6000 infants born in the United States suffer from fetal alcohol syndrome. The symptoms of this condition include retarded prenatal and postnatal growth, premature birth, mental retardation, physical malformations, sleep disturbances, and congenital heart disease. The heavier the pregnant woman's drinking, the greater the risk of fetal alcohol syndrome. One-third or more of the babies of heavy drinkers are born with this syndrome (Behrman & Vaughn, 1987).

Although the incidence of fetal alcohol syndrome is far lower among the babies of moderate drinkers, it is still significantly higher than among the babies of abstainers. In one study, 12 percent of the babies of moderate drinkers (i.e., those who consume the equivalent of 2 ounces a day of 100-proof liquor) showed one or more signs of fetal alcohol syndrome (Hanson, 1977). Moderate drinking also increases the likelihood of low birth weight, developmental delays, physical difficulties (e.g., breathing and sucking problems), and spontaneous abortion (K. L. Moore, 1982; Streissguth, Barr, & Martin, 1983; Streissguth et al., 1984).

It is important to know that studies relating prenatal alcohol exposure to later deficits typically report what is called a *dose-response relation* between the amount of alcohol consumed and the likelihood and probability of effects on the fetus. That is, higher amounts and frequencies of drinking are systematically related to larger numbers of affected babies and to more severe symptoms. The shape of the graph showing this relation is such that there is no known safe exposure level to alcohol (Barr, Streissguth, Darby, & Sampson, 1990). It is best for pregnant women not to drink at all.

Social policy for dealing with pregnant women who abuse alcohol or other drugs is a currently controversial topic. Some people think that women who do so should be subject to legal sanctions and, if necessary, jailed during their pregnancy to prevent them from injuring the fetus. (In Box 3.1, we can read such an opinion from the adoptive mother of an FAS child, an excerpt that also gives a keen awareness of the suffering that FAS engenders.) However, other experts argue that legal sanctions will not work, that they will simply deter pregnant women from seeking any social or prenatal services whatsoever. Meanwhile, alcoholic beverage containers and bars are now required to carry signs warning against drinking while pregnant.

Nicotine. Cigarettes are the second most common drug used in the representative sample of women of child-bearing age mentioned previously; 33 percent of the women had smoked in the month before the survey (Adams et al., 1989). Smoking by a pregnant woman retards the growth of the fetus by limiting the amount of oxygen it receives, and it lowers the newborn's birth weight and resistance to illness (Korones, 1986; K. L. Moore, 1982; Page, Villee, & Villee, 1981). It also increases the chances of spontaneous abortion and premature birth.

Long-term effects of smoking during pregnancy on physical and intellectual development are less clear. The reduced capacity of the mother's blood to transport oxygen to the fetus is, however, suggestive of the potential for such problems

BOX 3.1
HOW CAN WE PREVENT FETAL ALCOHOL SYNDROME?

Fetal Alcohol Syndrome is a devastating lifelong condition. Before the problem was known and labeled, Michael Dorris, then a single man beginning his first university position teaching anthropology, adopted an American Indian boy whose mother drank heavily during her pregnancy. He eventually wrote a book about his struggle to understand his son Adam's physical, mental, and emotional difficulties. The following passage is taken from a foreword to the book written by Louise Erdrich, a well-known American Indian novelist who became Adam's adoptive mother.

I drank hard in my twenties, and eventually got hepatitis. I was lucky. Beyond an occasional glass of wine, I can't tolerate liquor anymore. But from those early days, I understand the urge for alcohol, its physical pull. I had formed an emotional bond with a special configuration of chemicals, and I realize to this day the attraction of the relationship and the immense difficulty in abandoning it.

Adam's mother never did let go. She died of alcohol poisoning, and I'd feel sorrier for her, if we didn't have Adam. As it is, I only hope that she died before she had a chance to produce another child with his problems. I can't help but wish, too, that during her pregnancy, if she couldn't be counseled or helped, she had been forced to abstain for those crucial nine months. On some American Indian reservations, the situation has grown so desperate that a jail internment during pregnancy has been the only answer possible in some cases. Some people, whose views you will read in these pages, have taken more drastic stands and even called for the forced sterilization of women who, after having previously blunted the lives of several children like Adam, refuse to stop drinking while they're pregnant. This will outrage some women, and men, people who believe it is the right of individuals to put themselves in harm's way, that drinking is a choice we make, that a person's liberty to court either happiness or despair is sacrosanct. I believed this, too, and yet the poignancy and frustration of Adam's life has fed my doubts, has convinced me that some of my principles were smug, untested. After all, where is the measure of responsibility here? Where, exactly, is the demarcation between self-harm and child abuse? Gross negligence is nearly equal to intentional wrong, goes a legal maxim. Where do we draw the line?

The people who advocate forcing pregnant women to abstain from drinking come from within the communities dealing with a problem of nightmarish proportions. Still, this is very shaky ground. Once a woman decides to carry a child to term, to produce another human being, has she also the right to inflict on that person Adam's life? Because his mother drank, Adam is one of the earth's damaged. Did she have the right to take away Adam's curiosity, the right to take away the joy he could have felt at receiving a high math score, in reading a book, in wondering about the complexity and quirks of nature? Did she have the right to make him an outcast among children, to make him friendless, to make of his sexuality a problem more than a pleasure, to slit his brain, to give him violent seizures?

It seems to me, in the end, that she had no right to inflict such harm, even from the depth of her own ignorance. Roman Catholicism defines two kinds of ignorance, vincible and invincible. Invincible ignorance is that state in which a person is unexposed to certain forms of knowledge. The other type of ignorance, vincible, is willed. It is a conscious turning away from truth. In either case, I don't think Adam's mother had the right to harm her, and our, son.

Knowing what I know now, I am sure that even when I drank hard, I would rather have been incarcerated for nine months and produce a normal child than bear a human being who would, for the rest of his or her life, be imprisoned by what I had done.

Source: From *The Broken Cord* by Michael Dorris, Foreword by Louise Erdrich, 1989, New York: Harper & Row. Copyright © 1989 by Louise Erdich. Reprinted by permission of HarperCollins Publishers, Inc..

(Behrman & Vaughn, 1987; Moore, K. L., 1982; Page, Villee, & Villee, 1981; *Smoking and Health*, 1979). It has been reported that 6-year-olds whose mothers smoked while pregnant showed more impulsive behavior, poorer attention, and poorer memory (Fried, Watkinson, & Gray, 1992). Not all studies have found such effects, however, and the contribution of prenatal smoking as opposed to postnatal exposure to smoke, or other lifestyle differences between smoking and nonsmoking mothers, has not been clearly established.

Caffeine. There has been contradictory research on the possible effects of another commonly-ingested substance, namely caffeine, as found most notably in coffee, but also in tea, chocolate, and cola drinks. Infante-Rivard, Fernandez, Gauthier, David, & Rivard (1993) reported that women who drank 1 to 3 cups of coffee per day while pregnant had about double the risk of miscarriage of those who drank no coffee at all. While other studies have not found this association, holding caffeine consumption to a minimum during pregnancy is probably the wisest course (Eskenzai, 1993).

Cocaine. Adams et al. (1989) found that 3.5 percent of women aged 15 to 44 had used cocaine in the previous month. The number of babies born whose mothers have used cocaine or crack during pregnancy is hard to estimate because interviews with the mothers may result in unreliable reports, and urine tests can detect cocaine use only in the preceding five days. A conservative estimate coming from the President's National Drug Control Office suggests that 100,000 babies whose mothers have used cocaine are born each year in the United States, about 3 percent of births (Hawley & Disney, 1992). Percentages at large urban hospitals sometimes range as high as 31 percent (Ostrea, Brady, Gause, Raymundo, & Stevens, 1992).

Babies born to users of cocaine or crack cocaine are often portrayed as severely damaged and aberrant children who pose a severe threat to themselves and to society: unconsolable, inattentive, lacking in the capacity to form relationships. Cocaine use is indeed associated with prematurity (rates as high as 35 percent), low birth weight even in infants not born prematurely, and reduced head circumference (Hawley & Disney, 1992). As newborns, babies of cocaine users may have difficulty regulating sleep and may show abnormal reflexes (see Chapter 4 for discussion of reflexes). They may also cry in an abnormal fashion (Lester et al., 1991). Later in life, these children may show disorganized play and insecure attachment to the mother (that is, lack of emotional security, as discussed more fully in Chapter 6) (Rodning, Beckwith, & Howard, 1989, 1991).

Some of the problems of "crack babies," especially in later childhood, may not depend only (or even primarily) on their prenatal drug exposure, however. Another important factor may well be the neglectful homes in which the children are often raised, by parents who may continue to be consumed by their need for the drug. A vivid taste of the nature of these households comes from the following statement from a mother who still used cocaine as she attempted to care for a baby.

> You know, it was just like, damn, I done had a baby. "Go fix this bottle." "Okay, I'll fix it in a minute; let me get this other hit," you know? "Your baby wet!" "Oh, damn, I got to get this baby some diapers. I got ten dollars. Well, I just buy me a rock and I try to get him some diapers later on, ask some girl if I can borrow a couple diapers." That's how I wasn't being a Mom. Instead of me sayin', "I got ten dollars, I got to go buy my baby some diapers," I didn't. (Lawton, 1992, p. 44)

There are important practical implications of determining whether some of the problems of babies exposed to cocaine prenatally come from their later home environments. Public perception of these infants is often that they are doomed, but, actually, postnatal intervention efforts may have quite profound effects on their development. Currently, it is estimated that about 90 percent of drug-exposed children receive no intervention before they reach kindergarten age (Treaster, 1993).

Radiation. Another potential source of birth defects is radiation (X-ray) of the mother during pregnancy. This can result from treatment of pelvic cancer, from diagnostic testing, or from exposure to atomic energy sources, occupational hazards, or fallout (Brent & Harris, 1976; Illingworth, 1987; Kliegman & King, 1983). Although the hazards of radiation are not fully understood, it is clear that radiation can have a wide range of effects on unborn children, including death, malformation, brain damage, increased susceptibility to certain forms of cancer, shortened life span, and various mutations. Radiation that occurs between the time of fertilization and the time when the ovum becomes implanted in the uterus is thought to destroy the fertilized ovum in almost every case. The greatest danger of malformations comes between the second and sixth weeks after conception. Although the effects of X-rays may be less dramatic later in pregnancy, there is still some risk of damage, particularly to the brain and other body systems.

Maternal Diseases and Disorders During Pregnancy

In early pregnancy the placenta acts as a barrier against some harmful agents (e.g., larger organisms, such as syphilitic spirochetes and some bacteria). But even at this stage it allows many substances to reach the unborn child, and more can permeate it later. Some of these substances have positive effects. Antibodies produced by the mother to combat infectious diseases are transmitted to the fetus, usually producing immunity at birth and for some months thereafter. Other substances, including viruses, microorganisms, and various chemicals, may have extremely negative effects.

Viral diseases such as cytomegalovirus disease (which affects 5 to 6 percent of pregnant women), rubella (German measles), chicken pox, and hepatitis are particularly dangerous during the embryonic and early fetal periods (Behrman & Vaughn, 1987; Little, 1987). One of the most serious viral diseases during the first three months of pregnancy is rubella, which may produce heart malformations, deafness, blindness, or mental retardation. About 50 percent of babies whose mothers had German measles in the first month of pregnancy suffer birth defects; this figure falls to 22 percent in the second month, 6 percent in the third month, and only a small number thereafter (Babson, Pernoll, & Benda, 1980; Lubchenco, 1976; K. L. Moore, 1982). A pregnant woman can be tested to see whether she has already had rubella, but if she has not, she cannot be given vaccine for rubella because it contains the live virus. Thus, it is best for a woman who is considering pregnancy to ascertain whether she has had rubella before she becomes pregnant, and to receive vaccine at that time if she has not had it.

The rapid spread of the genital herpes virus among young adults poses another danger. Infection of the fetus with this virus usually occurs late in pregnancy—probably during delivery—and can result in severe neurological damage. When infection occurs several weeks prior to birth, a variety of congenital abnormalities can result. Prompt medical intervention is necessary if the presence of herpes during pregnancy is suspected (Dudgeon, 1976; K. L. Moore, 1982).

Acquired immune deficiency syndrome (AIDS) currently threatens the lives of a growing number of unborn and newborn babies. The percentage of pregnant women who have developed AIDS or ARC (AIDS-related complex)—principally through intravenous drug use or from a bisexual or drug-using partner—is rising rapidly, especially among poverty-stricken inner-city blacks and Hispanics. Mothers with AIDS can pass the virus to their babies, either across the placental barrier during pregnancy, during birth, or by breast feeding (Curran et al., 1988; Koop, 1986). Not all HIV-infected women infect their children, however. Estimates of transmission vary from 10 to 40 percent. Ongoing work is being done to determine if there are risk factors that influence the likelihood of transmission. For instance, Semba et al. (1994) recently found that mothers who transmitted HIV to their children had lower levels of Vitamin A (low enough to constitute a deficiency) than mothers who did not. If this finding holds up, or other risk factors are identified over which mothers have some control, it might be possible to reduce the number of babies born infected.

Infection of the fetus with syphilis is not infrequent. Fortunately, however, the placental barrier does not permit passage of the spirochetes that cause syphilis until after the fourth or fifth month of pregnancy. Consequently, transmission of the spirochetes (which otherwise would take place in about 24 percent of cases) may be prevented if treatment of a mother with syphilis begins early in pregnancy. When infection does occur, the spirochetes may produce miscarriage or a weak, deformed, or mentally deficient newborn. In some cases the child may not manifest symptoms of syphilis for several years.

Some general disturbances of the mother during pregnancy may also affect the fetus. One of the most common of these is *toxemia,* a disorder of unknown cause that affects about 5 percent of pregnant women in the United States. In its mildest form, toxemia is characterized by high blood pressure, rapid and excessive weight gain, and retention of fluid in the tissues. Prompt treatment usually ends danger to the fetus. However, if the disorder continues to progress, it can lead to convulsions and coma, resulting in death in about 13 percent of mothers and about 50 percent of their unborn infants. Children whose mothers had severe toxemia during pregnancy run a risk of lowered intelligence (Lubchenco, 1976).

The Rh Factor

The term *Rh factor* refers to a chemical factor that is present in the blood of approximately 85 percent of the population of the United States. In itself, the presence or absence of this factor makes no difference to a person's health. But when an Rh-positive man and an Rh-negative woman have children together, there can sometimes be adverse consequences for their offspring. If their baby has Rh-positive blood, the mother's blood may begin to form antibodies against the "foreign" positive Rh factor. During the next pregnancy the antibodies in the mother's blood may attack the Rh-positive blood of the unborn infant. The resulting destruction may be limited—causing only mild anemia—or extensive, causing cerebral palsy, deafness, mental retardation, or even death.

Fortunately, a way of preventing these consequences has been developed. The blood of the newborn infant is tested immediately after birth, using a blood sample from the umbilical cord. If an Rh-positive child has been born to an Rh-negative mother, the mother is given a vaccine that will seek out and destroy the baby's Rh-positive blood cells before the mother's body begins producing many antibodies.

The red cells of later children will not be attacked because the blood of the mother was never allowed to develop the antibodies (Apgar & Beck, 1974; Lubchenco, 1976).

Maternal Stress

Even though there are no direct connections between the maternal and fetal nervous systems, the mother's emotional state can influence the fetus's reactions and development. This is true because emotions like rage, fear, and anxiety bring the mother's autonomic nervous system into action, liberating certain chemicals (e.g., acetylcholine and epinephrine) into the bloodstream. In addition, under such conditions the endocrine glands, particularly the adrenals, secrete different kinds and amounts of hormones. As the composition of the blood changes, new substances are transmitted through the placenta, producing changes in the fetus's circulatory system.

These changes may be irritating to the fetus. One study noted that bodily movements of fetuses increased by several hundred percent while their mothers were undergoing emotional stress (Sontag, 1944). If the mother's emotional upset lasted several weeks, fetal activity continued at an exaggerated level throughout the entire period. When the upset was brief, heightened irritability usually lasted several hours.

Prolonged emotional stress during pregnancy may have lasting consequences for the child. Infants born to upset, unhappy mothers are more likely to be premature or have low birth weights; to be hyperactive and irritable; and to manifest difficulties such as irregular eating, excessive bowel movements, gas pains, sleep disturbances, excessive crying, and excessive need to be held (David, DeVault, & Talmadge, 1961; Joffe, 1969; Sameroff & Zax, 1973; Sontag, 1944).

In humans, this work is necessarily correlational; that is, maternal stress and various child outcomes are found to co-occur. However, mothers under stress may also fail to eat well, may smoke or drink, get poorer medical care, and so on, and these risk factors may be the causes of problems in their infants, rather than stress itself. (Recall from Chapter 1 our discussion of why finding two variables correlated does not allow one to conclude that one has a causal effect on the other.) The causal effect of stress on development is supported, however, by an experiment conducted with rhesus monkeys. A group of pregnant monkeys was randomly assigned to receive mild stress: removal from their cages for 10 minutes a day, and three episodes of unpredictable noise. Their infants had lower birth weights, were delayed in self-feeding, were more distractible, and had poorer motor development than infants born to unstressed mothers (Schneider, 1992).

Paternal Effects

There has been relatively little research and concern on the effects the health and habits of fathers can have on the babies they help conceive, but such effects are known to exist (Gunderson & Sackett, 1982). The risk of genetic disorders appears to increase with paternal as well as maternal age. For instance, it has been found that older fathers have an increased risk of having children who suffer from genetic disorders caused by dominant genes, but where there is no history of the disease in the family. Such deviant genes may arise in the process of cell division leading to spermatogenesis. The overall genetic mutation rate in sperm cells may be six times

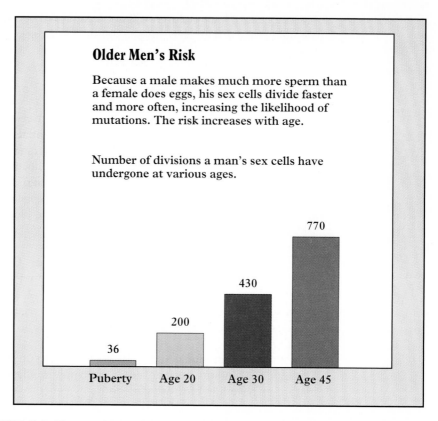

FIGURE 3.6 Characteristics of fathers, including age, affect the health of infants. From "Genetic Mutations Tied to Father in Most Cases," by Natalie Angier, *New York Times,* May 17, 1994, p. C12. From research by Dr. James F. Crow, University of Wisconsin. Copyright © 1994 by The New York Times. Reprinted by permission.

higher than it is in eggs (Angier, 1994). As a man's age increases, the number of times his sperm cells have gone through cell division also rises (see Figure 3.6).

Fathers can cause problems in infants in nongenetic ways as well. They may transmit viruses to mothers along with semen, including sexually-transmitted diseases such as herpes, gonorrhea, syphilis, chlamydia, and AIDS. Furthermore, fathers' exposures to alcohol, nicotine, radiation, and pollutants such as lead have all been associated with risks to offspring (Gunderson & Sackett, 1982).

It is important to keep in mind that the great majority of babies are born healthy. Moreover, infants and young children have an immense capacity for recovering from all but severe prenatal and perinatal stress. Yet there can be no doubt that future mothers and fathers would be well advised to do everything they reasonably can to foster their baby's optimal development.

✿ PRENATAL TESTING

Today, expectant parents have more and more choices to make concerning prenatal procedures that can help to diagnose the health and status of the developing fetus.

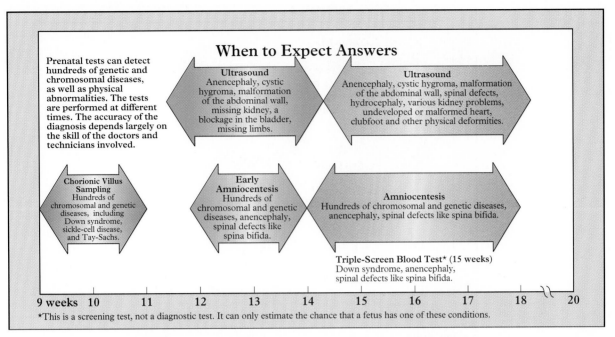

FIGURE 3.7 Prenatal tests: When can they be done and what can they diagnose? From "Waiting Game," by Susan Gilbert, *New York Times Magazine,* April 25, 1993, p. 70. Copyright © 1994 by The New York Times. Reprinted by permission.

These techniques include **chorionic villus sampling** (CVS), **amniocentesis,** and **ultrasound scans.** In addition, the mother's blood can be screened when she is about 15 weeks pregnant, to determine whether the child she is carrying may be at risk for Down syndrome or for neural tube defects (including spina bifida and anencephaly). If the blood test shows abnormal values, parents may wish to proceed with amniocentesis. Figure 3.7 summarizes when these procedures are done and what conditions they can detect.

In amniocentesis, a fine, hollow needle is inserted through the lower part of the abdominal wall into the amniotic sac that surrounds and protects the fetus, and a small amount of amniotic fluid (about two-thirds of an ounce) is removed (see Figure 3.8). The procedure is usually carried out 16 to 18 weeks after pregnancy has begun, but it is increasingly being done as early as 12 to 14 weeks. Amniotic fluid contains fetal cells that have been sloughed off in the normal course of events, just as we shed cells when we peel after a sunburn. These cells are cultured in a cytogenetics laboratory, and a chromosome analysis is performed.

To date, over 75 different genetically based diseases—many of them extremely rare—can be detected by means of amniocentesis, and the number is growing. Included are abnormalities in the autosomal chromosomes—as in Down syndrome—and sex-chromosome abnormalities, where there is an excess number of X or Y chromosomes. Amniocentesis can also detect a number of metabolic diseases (inborn errors of body chemistry that result in faulty production of enzymes) through excretions that appear in the amniotic fluid. Some of these metabolic diseases are concentrated in particular races, religions, or geographic areas because of selective mating over long periods. Examples include Tay-Sachs disease—which leads to mental retardation and early death at age 2 or 3 and is especially prevalent

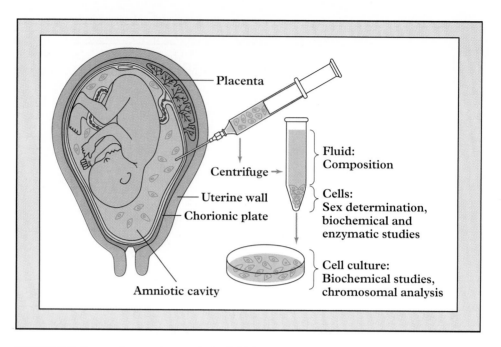

FIGURE 3.8 In amniocentesis, amniotic fluid is removed from the amniotic sac and analyzed. After "Prenatal Diagnosis of Genetic Disease," by T. Friedman, November 1971, *Scientific American, 225,* pp. 34–42. Copyright © 1971 by Scientific American. Adapted with permission.

in Ashkenazic Jewish families—and sickle-cell anemia, an abnormality of the red blood cells that can cause painful and disabling symptoms and is especially prevalent in African and African-American families.

A number of genetic disorders are sex-linked—that is, their genes are carried on a sex chromosome. For example, hemophilia, a defect in the ability of the blood to clot properly, is carried on the X chromosome. The daughter of a woman who is a carrier of this disease will almost never have the disease, because it will be masked by the presence of a normal gene on her other X chromosome. Any sons, however, will have a 50 percent chance of developing the disease because they do not have a second X chromosome that can carry a normal gene to protect them. Because amniocentesis reveals the sex of the fetus, a mother who may be a carrier for hemophilia or another X-linked disorder can normally feel reassured if her unborn baby is a girl.

The risk from amniocentesis to mother and fetus is small, although miscarriages can occasionally be induced by the procedure. Nevertheless, the test is not indicated for every pregnant woman. It should be done only where there is a good medical reason for such prenatal diagnosis—not, for example, merely to determine the sex of the baby out of curiosity. In general, amniocentesis is recommended when the family history of either the mother or father indicates that the fetus might have a genetic disease that can be detected—or ruled out—by this procedure. It is also useful for older women, over 35 and particularly after age 40, largely because of the increased risk of Down syndrome (K. L. Moore, 1982; S. Rubin, 1980; Rugh & Shettles, 1971).

Chorionic villus sampling involves gathering cells from the placenta (not from the amniotic fluid as in amniocentesis), either through a catheter inserted in the cervix or a needle inserted in the abdomen. This procedure can be done earlier in the pregnancy than even early amniocentesis, which is an advantage if the possibility of aborting the pregnancy is being considered. The cells obtained are examined for chromosomal defects or other problems, as are the cells obtained with amniocentesis. As with amniocentesis, the procedure should not be done on everyone, because there is a slight but real chance of inducing a miscarriage. There are also some reports, although the evidence is still debated, that the procedure can elevate the incidence of malformations of the fingers and toes.

Ultrasound scans do not involve obtaining cells. Rather, waves of ultrasound (that is, sound at frequencies humans can't hear) are aimed at the fetus, and the waves that bounce back are analyzed to obtain a "picture" of the fetus. Ultrasound is used to diagnose the existence of twins or triplets, as well as to search for structural abnormalities.

⊙ THE BIRTH PROCESS

Once the baby has developed in the uterus, it needs to be born. This process is far more difficult for humans than for other animals, even other primates. As Figure 3.9 shows, the size of the head of an average full-term infant makes it very difficult for it to fit through the birth canal. Evolutionary pressures toward larger brains (and hence, bigger heads) and toward erect locomotion (and hence, narrower hips) have combined to create a situation in which human birth can be hazardous both for mothers and for babies. Anthropologists are fascinated by what has been called the human "obstetrical dilemma," and ongoing research and theory-building are directed toward understanding how and when this apparently nonadaptive situation arose in evolution (Fischman, 1994). Here we examine the steps in the normal human birthing process.

Vaginal Delivery

In the last weeks of pregnancy, women's bodies prepare for labor. The cervix often (but not always) begins the processes of **effacement** (thinning and drawing up) and **dilation** (opening). The occasional contractions of the uterus that have occurred earlier in the pregnancy may become more frequent and more intense. Contractions may be strong enough to suggest that labor has started, but, unlike real labor, in "false labor" the intervals between contractions do not become progressively shorter.

The beginning of labor may be indicated by "bloody show," the ejection of the mucus plug that has blocked the cervix during pregnancy; by "breaking waters," the leakage (occasionally, flooding) of amniotic fluid from a ruptured amniotic sac; or by contractions that grow steadily stronger and closer together. In the contractions of active labor, the muscles of the upper uterus pull the cervical muscles upward (effacement) and outward (dilation).

The part of labor leading up to full effacement and dilation is sometimes called the **first stage of labor.** When the cervix is almost completely effaced and dilated, women enter a period sometimes called **transition,** as the process is completed.

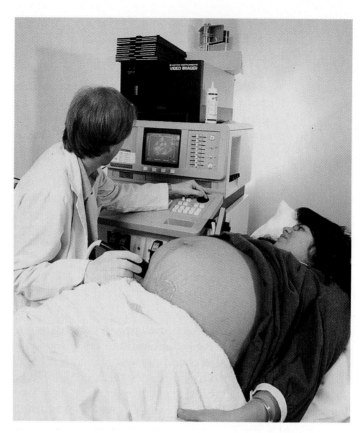

Pregnant women may be examined using an ultrasound scan to look for structural abnormalities in the fetus, to determine if they are carrying more than one fetus, or to assess size and positioning of the fetus.

For many women, this is the most difficult part of labor, as contractions are especially powerful and close together.

The **second stage of labor** is the phase of pushing the baby out. Women often feel a strong urge to push at the beginning of the second stage, which can last for minutes or hours. In North American hospitals, birth traditionally takes place with women on their back, often with their feet in stirrups, but a wide variety of other positions are possible, for example, sitting or squatting. Birth in other cultures may be quite different from that in modern industrialized nations (see Box 3.2). After the baby is born, the **third stage of labor** consists of the delivery of the placenta.

Caesarean Section

Vaginal delivery may not always be possible or may threaten the life or health of mother or infant. In this case, a doctor may deliver the baby through **Caesarean section,** a surgical procedure involving an incision in the uterus. This can often be conducted with spinal anesthesia, so that the woman is awake for the birth. A Caesarean section may be considered if labor has continued without evident progress in cervical effacement and dilation for a considerable time, including if more than 24 hours has elapsed since the waters breaking (due to the rising risk of infection).

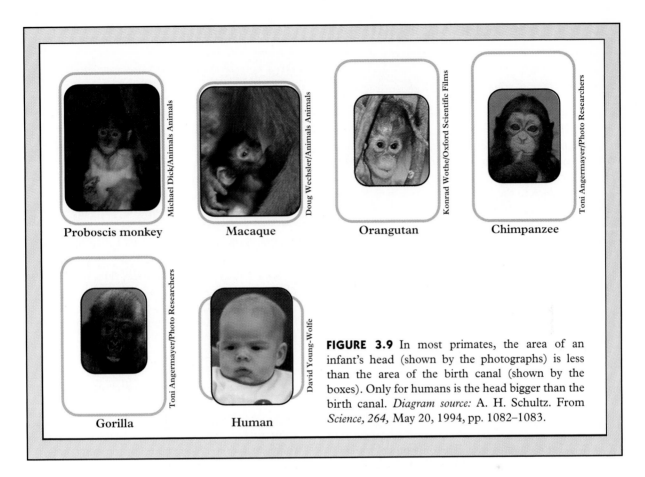

Proboscis monkey — Michael Dick/Animals Animals

Macaque — Doug Wechsler/Animals Animals

Orangutan — Konrad Wothe/Oxford Scientific Films

Chimpanzee — Toni Angermayer/Photo Researchers

Gorilla — Toni Angermayer/Photo Researchers

Human — David Young-Wolfe

FIGURE 3.9 In most primates, the area of an infant's head (shown by the photographs) is less than the area of the birth canal (shown by the boxes). Only for humans is the head bigger than the birth canal. *Diagram source:* A. H. Schultz. From *Science, 264,* May 20, 1994, pp. 1082–1083.

Multiple births are often delivered in this way, as are babies who do not present in the head-down position and who do not turn during labor.

Drugs Taken During Labor and Delivery

Because birth can be a painful process for women, various approaches have been devised to help deal with the pain. Perhaps the safest methods for both mothers and babies are methods for controlling pain through breathing, meditation, showers, appropriate movement, and support from a partner. Giving birth in this way is sometimes termed *natural childbirth*. However, other women feel they benefit from the use of medical intervention for pain control during delivery.

Drugs such as pentobarbital or meperidine (Demerol) are one method of pain control. If taken just prior to delivery of a baby, however, they may make the infant less attentive, at least temporarily. Another medical method of pain control is anesthesia through *epidural* injection of painkillers into the mother's spinal cord. If administered too close to delivery, however, such anesthesia can make it difficult for birthing mothers to push effectively in the second stage of labor.

One study of the effects of anesthetic drugs on sensorimotor functions in newborns found lags in muscular, visual, and neural functioning (Brackbill, 1979; Conway & Brackbill, 1970). While most such effects were greatest in the first few days of life, longer-term effects on cognitive functioning and gross motor

BOX 3.2
CHILDBIRTH AMONG THE !KUNG

The !Kung San are people who live in remote regions of the Kalahari Desert. Until very recently, they have lived in the traditional way, by hunting and gathering, in a fashion that may bear some resemblance to the lifestyle of human beings living millennia ago. Marjorie Shostak is an American anthropologist who lived among the !Kung for almost two years. Her relationship with a 50-year-old woman called Nisa was the basis for her writing a book about Nisa's life, largely in Nisa's own words. The following is Nisa's account of the birth of her first child.

I lay there and felt the pains as they came, over and over again. Then I felt something wet, the beginning of the childbirth. I thought, "Eh hey, maybe it is the child." I got up, took a blanket and covered Tashay [her husband] with it; he was still sleeping. Then I took another blanket and my smaller duiker skin covering and I left. Was I not the only one? The only other woman was Tashay's grandmother, and she was asleep in her hut. So, just as I was, I left.

I walked a short distance from the village and sat down beside a tree. I sat there and waited; she wasn't ready to be born. I lay down, but she still didn't come out. I sat up again. I leaned against the tree and began to feel the labor. The pains came over and over, again and again. It felt as though the baby was trying to jump right out! Then the pains stopped. I said,

"Why doesn't it hurry up and come out? Why doesn't it come out so I can rest? What does it want inside me that it just stays in there? Won't God help me to have it come out quickly?"

As I said that, the baby started to be born. I thought, "I won't cry out. I'll just sit here. Look, it's already being born and I'll be fine." But it really hurt! I cried out, but only to myself. I thought, "Oh, I almost cried out in my in-laws' village." Then I thought, "Has my child already been born?" Because I wasn't really sure; I thought I might only have been sick. That's why I hadn't told anyone when I left the village.

After she was born, I sat there; I didn't know what to do. I had no sense. She lay there, moving her arms about, trying to suck on her fingers. She started to cry. I just sat there, looking at her. I thought, "Is this my child? Who gave birth to this child?" Then I thought, "A big thing like that? How could it possibly have come out from my genitals?" I sat there and looked at her, looked and looked and looked.

The cold started to grab me. I covered her with my duiker skin that had been covering my stomach and pulled the larger kaross over myself. Soon, the afterbirth came down and I buried it. I started to shiver. I just sat there, trembling with the cold. I still hadn't tied the umbilical cord. I looked at her and thought, "She's no longer crying, I'll leave her here and

abilities, particularly with heavy drug dosages, have been found at 1 year of age (Brackbill, 1979; K. M. Goldstein, Caputo, & Taub, 1976; Standley, 1979).

Anoxia and Other Complications

The ease or difficulty with which a baby is born and how quickly it begins to breathe can affect its well-being. One major danger associated with birth is hemorrhaging, which is caused when very strong pressure on the head of the fetus breaks blood vessels in the brain. Another danger is failure of the infant to begin breathing soon after being separated from the maternal source of oxygen. Both hemorrhaging go to the village to bring back some coals for a fire."

I left her, covered with leather skins. (What did I know about how to do things?) I took a small skin covering, tied it around my stomach, and went back to the village. While I was on the way, she started to cry, then she stopped. I was rushing and was out of breath. Wasn't my genital area hurting? I told myself to run, but my judgement was gone; my senses had left me.

My heart was pounding and throbbing when I arrived. I sat down by the fire outside my hut to rest and to warm myself. Tashay woke up. He saw me with my little stomach, and he saw the blood on my legs. He asked how I was. I told him everything was all right. He asked, "Where is that which I thought I heard crying?" I told him the baby was lying covered where I had given birth. He asked if it was a boy. I said she was a girl. He said, "Oh! Does a little girl like you give birth to a baby all alone? There wasn't even another woman to help?"

He called to his grandmother, still asleep, and yelled, "What happened to you that you stayed here while a little girl went out by herself to give birth? What if that childbirth had killed her? Would you have just left her there for her mother to help, her mother who isn't even here? You don't know that the pain of childbirth is fire and that a child's birth is like an anger so great that it sometimes kills? Yet, you didn't help! She's just a little girl. She could have been so afraid that the childbirth might have killed her or the child. You, an adult, what were you asking of her?"

Just then, the baby started to cry. I was afraid that maybe a jackal had come and hurt her. I grabbed some burning wood and ran back to her. I made a fire and sat. Tashay continued to yell, "Find her. Go over there and cut the baby's umbilical cord. What happened to you that you let my wife give birth by herself?"

His grandmother got up and followed Tashay to where I was sitting with the baby. She arrived and called out softly to me, "My daughter-in-law . . . my daughter-in-law. . . ." She talked to the infant and greeted her with lovely names. She cut her umbilical cord, picked her up, and carried her as we all walked back to the village. Then they laid me down inside the hut.

The next day, my husband went gathering and came back with sha roots and mongongo nuts, which he cracked for me to eat. But my insides were still sore and I was in pain. He went out again and killed a springhare. When he came back, he cooked it and I drank the gravy. That was supposed to help the milk come into my breasts, but my milk didn't come down.

We lived in the bush and there was no one else to help feed her. She just lay there and didn't eat for three nights. Then milk started to fill one breast, and the same night the other one filled. I spilled out the colostrum, the bad thing, and when my chest filled with good milk, she nursed and nursed and nursed. When she was full, she went to sleep.

Source: From *Nisa: The Life and Words of a !Kung Woman* (pp. 1–3), by Marjorie Shostak, 1983, Cambridge, MA: Harvard University Press.. Copyright © 1983 by Marjorie Shostak. Reprinted by permission of Vintage Books..

and failure to breathe affect the supply of oxygen to the nerve cells of the brain and produce a state called **anoxia.** The neurons of the central nervous system require oxygen; if they are deprived of it, some cells may die, and this can cause physical and psychological defects. If too many neurons die, the infant may suffer serious brain damage or, in extreme cases, may die.

Anoxia in a newborn is more likely to damage the cells of the brain stem than those of the cortex, and to result in motor defects. The child may experience paralysis of the legs or arms, a tremor of the face or fingers, or inability to use the vocal muscles. In this last case, the child may have difficulty learning to speak. The term *cerebral palsy* describes a variety of motor defects associated with damage to the brain cells, possibly as a result of lack of oxygen during the birth process. It is estimated that about 30 percent of cerebral palsy cases involve problems that occurred during birth or immediately afterward (Apgar & Beck, 1974; Kopp & Parmelee, 1979; Lubchenco, 1976).

Anoxic infants are more irritable and show more muscular tension and rigidity than normal infants do during the first week (F. K. Graham, Matarazzo, & Caldwell, 1956; Korones, 1986; Voorhies & Vanucci, 1984). Infants with mild anoxia score lower on tests of motor development and attention during the first year and are more distractible (Corah, Anthony, Painter, Stern, & Thurston, 1965; Ernhart, Graham, & Thurston, 1960; Lubchenco, 1976). At age 3, they perform less well on tests of conceptualization. By age 7 or 8, behavioral differences between normal and mildly anoxic children are generally small, and their IQ scores are equal. In brief, the differences between mildly anoxic and normal children become smaller with age, and there is at present no firm evidence of serious and permanent intellectual damage.

Prematurity

Infants born earlier than the thirty-eighth week of gestation and weighing less than 5 pounds are referred to as premature. Prematurity is more frequent among economically disadvantaged mothers than among the affluent. In addition, as we have already noted, smoking, alcohol, and various drugs increase the likelihood that a baby will be born prematurely. Multiple births (twins, triplets, etc.) also tend to be premature.

There is a significant correlation between the birth weights of infants and the birth weights of their mothers, and there are also ethnic differences (even after controlling for the effects of such factors as maternal nutrition, smoking, and alcohol and drug use). This suggests that genetic factors play a role in determining birth weight (Klebanoff, Gronbard, Kessel, & Berendes, 1984; Shiono, Klebanoff, Gronbard, Berendes, & Rhoades, 1986).

The long-term effects of prematurity on development depend on how early the infant is born (gestational age), its birth weight, the type of postnatal care it receives, and the quality of its environment during early and middle childhood. Infants with gestation periods of less than 28 weeks ("extreme prematurity") or weights of less than 3.3 pounds have a reduced chance of survival. In contrast, those who are only slightly premature (34 to 38 weeks) and whose weight is appropriate for their gestational age resemble full-term babies in many ways. They are generally healthy, though they are less mature, more vulnerable to illness, and slower to gain weight, and they must be monitored carefully (Hack, 1983; Kopp & Parmelee, 1979; Korones, 1986; Lubchenco, 1976; Lubchenco, Searls, & Brazie, 1972).

Neonatal risk of mortality or handicap is related to both gestational age and birth weight. An infant who is significantly premature and has a low birth weight for its gestational age faces a more serious risk than an infant of the same gestational age whose birth weight is age-appropriate. In general, risks appear highest for the small minority of infants who weigh less than 1500 grams (3.3 pounds) at birth (Allen, 1984; Battaglia & Simmons, 1978; Lubchenco, 1976).

Recently, considerable progress has been made in caring for extremely premature infants and for "intermediate-term" infants, those that fall in the middle

Premature infants receive a variety of interventions in the modern neonatal intensive care nursery. They also need gentle stimulation and body contact.

range of prematurity. These babies' gestational ages range between 30 and 33 weeks, and their birth weights are at least average for their age—around 1500 grams (3.3 pounds) or more at 30 weeks and 2000 grams (4.4 pounds) or more at 33 weeks. Premature babies that have received intensive, highly specialized care in university medical centers and major community hospitals have not only survived but gone on to develop normally (Allen, 1984; Battaglia & Simmons, 1978; Brandt, 1978).

A special problem for premature babies is *respiratory distress syndrome,* or breathing problems. This syndrome affects 65,000 premature infants each year in the United States (Travis, 1993). It is typically caused by a lack of a substance called surfactant, a foamy material lining the inside of the lungs that helps the lungs to expand and draw in air. Some progress is currently being reported in manufacturing substitute surfactant. Another difficult problem for premature babies is the occurrence of *intracranial hemorrhage,* or bleeding in the brain, which can cause permanent damage.

Premature infants need more than just medical care. Psychologists have worked on various kinds of programs to provide sensory and tactile stimulation and encourage parents to participate in the child's care while the child is hospitalized (Korner, 1987). Some investigators have thought that children would benefit from rocking (as on water beds) and gentle tactile stimulation (as from lying on sheep skins), interventions aimed at simulating the conditions in the uterus. Others have provided visual, tactile, and auditory stimuli (such as mobiles, massage, and music) that are thought to facilitate development in newborn infants. Both kinds of programs appear to produce short-term benefits for premature children, including greater weight gain, less irritability and more quiet sleep, and better sensory responsiveness. The differences that can be attributed to the interventions typically decrease with age, as time since the interventions increases.

Like children who experience anoxia or complications during birth, premature children are particularly vulnerable to the effects of their environment. Premature children who are born into loving, nurturing homes where they receive competent physical and psychological care usually show little long-range impairment unless they were very premature or did not receive appropriate neonatal or postnatal care (Apgar & Beck, 1974; Battaglia & Simmons, 1978; Werner & Smith, 1982; R. S. Wilson, 1985). In homes with poor parental care and living conditions, premature babies are far more likely than full-term children to have both physical and psychological difficulties. Because prematurity and perinatal complications are more frequent among economically disadvantaged families than among middle-class families, poor children are more likely than richer ones to have to deal both with impairment at birth and a less favorable environment (Lubchenco, 1976; Richmond, 1982; R. S. Wilson, 1985).

A recent study evaluated the effects of providing educational, medical, and family support services to premature infants from disadvantaged families over the first three years of life. As you can see in Figure 3.10, the intervention group did better than the control group on cognitive tests at 2 and 3 years (Brooks-Gunn, Klebanov, Liaw, & Spiker, 1993). The study also found that the intervention group was less likely to develop behavior problems.

⚙ SUMMARY

The time from conception to birth is usually divided into three phases: the germinal period, which lasts from fertilization until implantation; the embryonic period, in which the major organs begin to develop; and the fetal period, which is characterized mainly by growth. Throughout prenatal development the bloodstreams of the mother and child are separated by the placental barrier, but certain substances, including nutrients from the mother and waste products from the infant, pass through the barrier. Some vitamins, drugs, vaccines, and disease germs may also get through and affect the embryo's development. The fetus becomes viable (able to live if born) at 28 weeks.

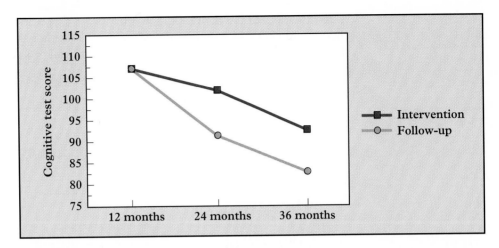

FIGURE 3.10 The cognitive status of premature infants at three ages in an intervention group and a control group. The intervention group did better at 24 and 36 months. After "Enhancing the Development of Low-Birthweight, Premature Infants: Changes in Cognition and Behavior over the First Three Years," by J. Brooks-Gunn, P. K. Klebanov, F. Liaw, and D. Spiker, 1993, *Child Development, 64*, p. 741. Copyright © 1993 by Child Development. Adapted with permission.

Prenatal environmental influences can significantly affect the individual's development. These influences include the age of the mother (the years between ages 20 and 35 appear most favorable); maternal nutrition; drugs, including alcohol, nicotine, certain antibiotics, hormones, steroids, and narcotics, all of which can adversely affect fetal development; X-rays; maternal diseases and disorders, such as rubella and AIDS, chicken pox, genital herpes, and toxemia of pregnancy; and a negative Rh factor in the blood. The mother's emotional state and the age and physical state of the father also affect the fetus.

Prenatal testing can be done to evaluate the normality of the developing fetus. Techniques include screening of the mother's blood, amniocentesis, chorionic villus sampling, and ultrasound scanning.

The normal birth process involves a first stage of labor in which uterine contractions lead to effacement and dilation of the cervix, a second stage of pushing the baby out, and a third stage of ejecting the placenta. Sometimes a Caesarean section may be necessary.

The ease or difficulty with which a baby is born and how quickly it begins to breathe can affect its well-being. Interruptions in the supply of oxygen to the nerve cells of the brain produce anoxia, which can cause serious brain damage or death. Another cause of problems for newborns is premature birth. Premature babies usually have low birth weights and, therefore, a higher risk of mortality. Considerable progress has been made in caring for extremely premature and "intermediate-term" infants. Premature children raised in favorable home environments usually show little long-range impairment.

Fortunately, the vast majority of all babies born in this country do not experience any of the problems discussed in this chapter. Most infants begin life well within the normal range. In addition, infants are surprisingly malleable, and many children apparently recover from early deficits, whether they are due to prematurity, anoxia, or other mild to moderate developmental problems.

REVIEW QUESTIONS

1. Briefly describe the three major periods of development between conception and birth.

2. What aspects of the prenatal environment influence fetal development and the subsequent health and adjustment of the child?

3. What are the available techniques for prenatal testing?

4. What features of the birth process may affect the well-being of the infant?

5. What is meant by prematurity? What are its implications?

CRITICAL THINKING ABOUT THE CHAPTER

1. Society has an interest in ensuring the health and well-being of future generations, and babies may be seen as having a right to be born with a chance for a good life (see Box 3.1). However, individuals also have a right, at least within the tradition of some countries including the United States, to individual liberty. Consider your position on whether or not pregnant women can have some of their liberties restricted, in order to ensure that they bear healthy children.

2. Make a summary of a plan for maximizing a woman's chances of having a healthy baby. Using yourself or a woman you know as an example, describe which aspects of the plan would be most challenging, and explain why.

KEY TERMS

amniocentesis
amnion
amniotic fluid
anoxia
Caesarean section
chorion
chorionic villus sampling
dilation
ectoderm
effacement
embryonic stage
endoderm
fetal alcohol syndrome
fetal stage

first stage of labor
germinal stage
mesoderm
placenta
placental barrier
second stage of labor
teratogen
third stage of labor
transition
trophoblast
ultrasound scans
umbilical cord
viability
zygote

SUGGESTED READINGS

Guttmacher, Alan F., revised by I. H. Kaiser (1986). *Pregnancy, birth, and family planning.* New York: New American Library (paperback).

Macfarlane, Aidan (1977). *The psychology of childbirth.* Cambridge, MA: Harvard University Press. A sensitive account of birthing and of the first moments with a newborn.

Nilsson, Lennart (1986). *A child is born.* New York: Dell. An exciting account of development from conception to birth, beautifully illustrated with original color photographs by a prizewinning photographer.

PART III

INFANCY

▼

CHAPTER 4

PHYSICAL AND PERCEPTUAL DEVELOPMENT IN INFANCY

THEORIES AND ASSUMPTIONS

PHYSICAL DEVELOPMENT

Physical Growth
Maturation
Reflexes
Motor Development
    Sitting
    Crawling
    Standing and Walking
    The Role of Experience
    The Socioemotional Consequences of Motor Development
Sleep
Maturation of the Brain

LEARNING AND CONDITIONING

Classical Conditioning
Instrumental Conditioning

PERCEPTUAL DEVELOPMENT

Vision
Hearing
Touch, Taste, and Smell
Cross-Modal Perception

APPLICATIONS

Neonatal Assessment
Sudden Infant Death Syndrome

July 9

Dear Grandmama:

So tomorrow is your birthday! My oh my, how old you are compared to me! This is the first chance I have had to write and wish you a HAPPY BIRTHDAY. I expect that this will arrive a wee bit late but I hope you will excuse me. I am so busy these days! I'm up bright and early about 6 in the morning but my two servants don't get up till later on; this servant problem is a bit of a nuisance. When they finally get up they serve me my cereal (which I hate but don't tell them that for fear of hurting their feelings) and milk. Then I'm changed several times during the day and get my beauty sleep and practice my language lessons. This language is so difficult; I must say I haven't said a word of it yet.

I've been practicing sitting up. One of my servants holds out his/her fingers and I hold onto them and pull myself to a sitting position. Then if I hold onto the bar of my bed I can sit up all by myself for a while. My manservant gets great delight out of this. You know, I rarely see that man during the day. I don't know what he does with himself all day long.

Will you be coming down to see me this coming Saturday or Sunday? Please let me know which of the two if you are coming.

I am so busy that I really can barely find time to sign my letters, so excuse me if I just leave my footprint. Bye for now and Happy Birthday again.

Your grandaughter,

Stephanie

(Written by a new father to his mother, when his daughter was five months old)

The first two years of a child's life are a special time. The father writing the preceding letter was clearly delighting in his infant daughter's capabilities and unfolding growth, for instance, her developing ability to sit. Yet the father also attributed to his daughter (in a playful way) many thoughts and feelings that clearly would not be likely for an infant (such as fear of hurting her parents' feelings). And he was commenting ruefully on one of the most commonly felt negative aspects of caring for new babies, at least in Western countries—their sleep habits.

What is the world of the infant really like? And how does this world change over the first two years? The child grows from a neonate who seems to do little besides sleep, cry, and wave his limbs to a two-year-old who can walk and communicate, who has special relationships and a very definite mind of his own. Delineating the nature of the infant's world and the ways in which it changes has been the focus of some of the most fascinating developmental work of the past few decades. We review it in this section of the book (Chapters 4, 5, and 6). Chapter 4 examines physical and perceptual development, Chapter 5 looks at cognitive development, and Chapter 6 looks at infants' feelings and relationships with others. But before we begin to study any of these topics, we look at the theoretical lenses through which it is possible to view infant development.

☼ THEORIES AND ASSUMPTIONS

In all societies, the period of infancy is recognized as a special time and given a special name to distinguish it from later stages of life. Infancy is often defined in terms of the absence of qualities that characterize the school-age child, such as the ability to speak, to reason, and to experience the emotions of guilt, empathy, and pride. But infants can also be described positively as well. Infants have definite physical, perceptual, cognitive, and emotional capabilities.

The terms that psychologists use to describe infants are influenced by deep, often unconscious, beliefs. These beliefs, which are usually shared by the larger society, change over time. For example, nineteenth-century observers compared the human infant with infant calves and foals, which are born in a more mature state than humans and can walk immediately after birth. Because the human infant appeared so helpless compared with most other newborn mammals, these observers called the infant incompetent. Now that recent research has demonstrated the impressive, though less obvious, psychological capacities of the human newborn, contemporary psychologists describe the infant as competent.

Each scholar approaches the study of the infant with certain biases about what qualities are important, and puts his or her observational "lens" closest to those qualities. Consider as an analogy two people visiting Los Angeles for the first time. One comes from a rural village in Indonesia, the second from London. To the Indonesian, the crowds of people, traffic, and tall buildings are the most unusual aspects of the city. After returning home, this traveler describes Los Angeles as a place with many people, cars, and buildings. But because these qualities are not unusual to the visitor from London, she ignores them and concentrates on the inadequacy of public transportation and the high rate of street crime, both of which distinguish Los Angeles from London. The two visitors conceptualize Los Angeles in different ways because each came with different ideas of what cities are like.

The influence of a theorist's suppositions on the selection of descriptive terms is nicely illustrated by comparing four important theorists: Sigmund Freud, Erik Erikson, John Bowlby, and Jean Piaget. Each highlighted a different aspect of the infant because each was loyal to assumptions that were part of the larger cultural context in which he lived.

When Freud was thinking and writing about the human infant, soon after the turn of the century, Darwinian evolutionary theory and the physical concept of energy were major metaphors used in thinking about human development and functioning. Scholars promoting Darwinian theory believed that the human infant was a link between apes and human adults; hence, infants should have the same basic biological drives as animals. Because hunger and sexuality were regarded as the two most important drives of animals, Freud assumed that they were also central to human psychological development. In a brilliant set of essays he suggested that each child is born with a fixed amount of energy—which he called *libido*—that, in time, becomes the basis for adult sexual motives. During the period of infancy, the libido's energy is bound up with the mouth, tongue, and lips and the activities of nursing. For this reason, Freud called this first period of development the **oral stage**. Although this bold hypothesis may sound a little odd today, it was much more credible at the turn of the century because it was closely related to major ideas in the respected disciplines of evolutionary biology, physiology, and physics.

A half-century later, many American social scientists had come to believe that social experience, not biology, is responsible for the emergence of significant human qualities and for the obvious variations in adult talent, economic success, and character. Theorists looking at the infant during the period between the two world wars (the 1920s and 1930s) focused on social interaction between mother and infant. In their view, Freud's hungry, nursing baby became a social being who is cared for by an adult. Erik Erikson (1963) adapted Freud's conception of development to give more room to social interaction and influence. Erikson regarded the first phase of development as one in which the baby learns whether adults can be relied on for care, love, and emotional security. Erikson called this first period the **stage of trust**. This idea had the same ring of validity in the 1950s that Freud's concept of the oral stage had a half-century earlier.

John Bowlby also built on and adapted psychoanalytic thinking to place a more central emphasis on social interaction. In 1969, he published an important book in which he argued that human infants and their parents each have biological adaptations that function together over the first three years of life to enable the formation of an **attachment**, or a deep emotional bond, between them. This conception is similar to Erikson's emphasis on trust, but Bowlby's infant is a much more active seeker of interaction and processor of information than is Erikson's.

Like Freud and Bowlby, Piaget was influenced by evolutionary theory. But he differed from these thinkers in that he focused on changes in thought that permit successful adaptation rather than on emotions or on neurotic symptoms of maladaptation. Piaget believed that the first structures of an infant's mind are created through the active manipulation of objects rather than through repeated cycles of frustration and gratification of the hunger drive. Thus, when Piaget looked at the infant he saw a baby playing with her mother's face, hair, and fingers, and learning about the world. He termed infancy the **sensorimotor period**.

Nursing, receiving love and nurture, sending and receiving attachment signals, and exploring the caregiver's fingers and face are all characteristics of the human infant. It is not obvious that one of these functions is more central than the other; only a theory awards one class of events greater status than another. Together, the theories can give us a more complete picture of the starting points of development. Each generates predictions about development and generates distinct studies of questions generated by the theoretical point of view. Without theory, we would have no idea of what to describe when we observed children, or even of what we wanted to explain.

Theories sometimes conflict with each other, of course. This conflict is one of the centrally important attributes of theories. Experiments and discussion generated by the conflict can help either to decide between the approaches or to lead to new theories that are more complete. In the chapters that follow, we discuss and use each of the theories mentioned in this introductory section.

PHYSICAL DEVELOPMENT

Physical Growth

The average newborn infant weighs about 7.5 pounds and is about 20 inches long; boys are slightly larger and a little heavier than girls. The first year of life is characterized by rapid growth of the body and brain. Between birth and 1 year of age, healthy, well-fed children undergo a 50 percent increase in length and an almost 200 percent increase in weight. However, not all parts of the body grow at the same rate (see Figure 4.1), and there is no necessary correlation between the growth of one part (e.g., the head) and another (e.g., the muscles) (F. E. Johnston, 1978).

After 6 months, infants from economically advantaged homes grow faster than those from poorer families because of better nutrition, fewer illnesses, and higher standards of health. After the first birthday the growth rate slows, to be followed by

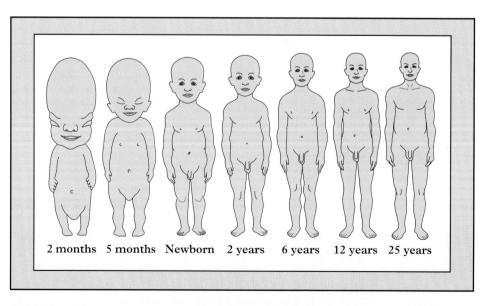

FIGURE 4.1 Changes in form and proportions during human growth. After "Some Aspects of Form and Growth," by C. M. Jackson, in *Growth* (p. 118), edited by W. J. Robbins, S. Brody, A. F. Hogan, C. M. Jackson, and C. W. Green, 1929, New Haven, CT: Yale University Press. Copyright 1929 by Yale University Press. Adapted with permission.

Different theorists would emphasize different aspects of this situation. Freud would see an infant receiving oral gratification, Erikson an infant building a sense of basic trust, Bowlby an infant and mother forming an attachment bond, and Piaget an infant exploring the world visually.

a steady, almost linear increase in height and weight until adolescence. It is not until 3 years of age that a child's height becomes a good predictor of his or her height at maturity.

Maturation

To understand some of the changes that occur in reflexes, motor development, sleep, and many other domains during the first two years of life, it is necessary to understand the concept of **maturation**. Maturation refers to a universal sequence of biological events occurring in the body and the brain. These events permit a psychological function to appear, provided that the infant is healthy and lives in an environment containing people and objects. The appearance of speech between 1 and 3 years of age in almost all children who are exposed to adult language is one of the best illustrations of this concept. The brain of a 5-month-old is not sufficiently developed to permit the infant to understand or speak a language (despite Stephanie's father's joking belief that his daughter was taking language lessons). The brain of a 2-year-old is sufficiently mature, and by that age the child will normally have learned quite a lot of language. However, a child will not speak if he or she has not been exposed to the speech of others. Thus, maturation alone cannot cause a psychological function to appear. It only serves to establish the earliest possible time of appearance of that function.

Maturation can have another effect as well. For some psychological functions, it appears that there are periods in early life, sometimes called **critical periods**, during which particular experiences are crucial for normal development. Experience during this time has an impact that cannot be duplicated if only provided later in life. For instance, there may be a critical period for language acquisition, such that language learning in adolescents and adults has a different character than that occurring in childhood. The beginning and end of critical periods is likely to be set by maturational events.

Reflexes

On the day they are born, normal infants display a set of inherited reflexes, many of which are present in other primates such as monkeys and chimpanzees. For instance, if you stroke a baby on the cheek, she will turn her head in the direction of the touch, open her mouth, and try to suck. This is called the **rooting reflex**. The **Moro reflex**, another example of an early reflex, is a startle response in which an infant's arms spread wide and then slowly come together at the midline while the legs are brought up in a similar fashion. It is usually elicited by a loud noise, by letting the infant's head drop a few inches, or by banging the side of the baby's crib while it is lying on its back. Table 4.1 lists the major reflexes that are present during the opening days of life.

Some of the reflexes listed in Table 4.1, such as rooting, sucking, and grasping, are useful as the infant adjusts to a new environment and must nurse and, later, start to grasp objects. Others, which are not obviously adaptive, are present because the cerebral cortex is not yet mature enough to control or monitor them. The Moro

TABLE 4.1 Reflexes Present in the Newborn Infant

Reflex	*Procedure Used to Elicit Reflex*	*Description*
Babinski reflex	The examiner gently strokes the side of the infant's foot from heel to toe.	The infant flexes its big toe while extending the four smaller toes.
Moro reflex	The examiner either produces a sudden loud noise (e.g., popping a balloon) or holds the infant and drops its head a few inches. If the baby is lying on its back in a crib, the examiner strikes the crib simultaneously on each side of the infant's head.	The infant throws its arms out and then brings them together in the midline.
Blink reflex	A bright flash of light.	The infant closes both eyelids.
Grasp reflex	The examiner puts a finger or pencil against the infant's palm.	The infant grasps the object.
Stepping reflex	The infant is held upright and the examiner moves it forward and tilts it to one side.	The infant makes movements as if it were walking.
Rooting reflex	The examiner stimulates the infant at the corner of the mouth or on the cheek.	The infant turns its head toward the finger, opens its mouth, and tries to suck.
Sucking reflex	The examiner inserts an index finger into the infant's mouth.	The infant begins to suck.
Withdrawal reflex	The examiner pricks the sole of the infant's foot with a pin.	The infant flexes the leg and withdraws from the pin.
Licking reflex	The examiner puts sugar water on the infant's tongue.	The infant licks its lips and may suck.
Pursing reflex	The examiner puts a sour substance on the infant's tongue.	The infant purses its lips and may blink.

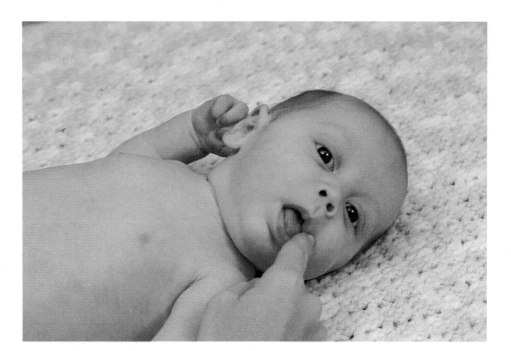

rooting

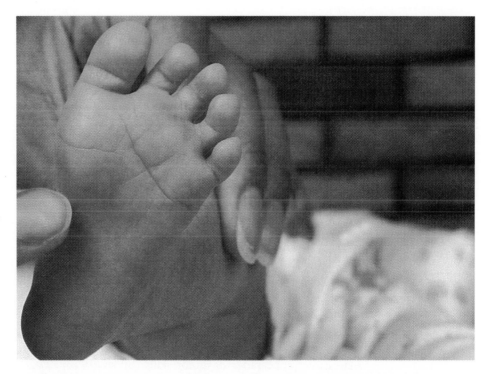

Babinski

These photographs show two early reflexes, the rooting reflex and the Babinski reflex.

reflex is a good example, for it does not seem to have an obvious advantage in human infants. (It may be useful for monkeys, who are carried upside down on their mother's bellies for most of the day, and must hold tightly onto her hair as she moves in response to an alarm.) However, by three months of age the cortex is more mature, and it inhibits the Moro response to a sudden loud noise.

Motor Development

Human infants are born with very little ability to move around their environment, or even to position their own bodies. Once laid on their stomachs or backs, they initially can't even roll over. (But beware taking advantage of this fact to put them down on an ordinary bed or a table; that moment may be the one in which they first succeed in turning!) Maturation of the brain and the establishment of neural connections between the brain and motor circuits in the spinal cord eventually permit the child to sit, crawl, and walk.

Progress in motor development through the first year is illustrated in Figure 4.2. In looking at this material, it is important to remember that individual children may not conform exactly to this schedule. A child may be a few months early or late in reaching these motor milestones without being abnormal. Serious deviations, however, should be evaluated by a pediatrician.

Sitting. Although the newborn cannot sit even with support, this ability develops early (Gesell & Amatruda, 1941). Four-month-old babies are able to sit with support for a minute. (Stephanie, at 5 months, could do a bit better than this.) By 7 months most babies can sit without support, and by 9 months most can sit without support for 10 minutes or longer.

Crawling. Although there are individual differences in the age at which infants begin to crawl and creep, all who are allowed to locomote on the ground tend to go through the same sequence. The average age for crawling (moving with the abdomen in contact with the floor) is about 9 months; creeping on hands and knees occurs at about 10 months. An infant may skip one or two stages in development, but most children progress through most of the stages (Ames, 1937).

Standing and Walking. The ability to walk is built on a series of earlier achievements. As in other aspects of development, the ages at which these achievements occur cover a wide range. The median age for pulling up to a standing position and standing while holding on to furniture is between 9 and 10 months. The average child stands alone at about 11 months, walks when led by one hand at 1 year, and can walk alone, although awkwardly, at about 13 months. By 18 months, the child can get up and down stairs without help (and usually without falling) and can pull a toy along the ground. By the second birthday, the child can pick up an object from the floor without falling down and can run and walk backward (Gesell & Amatruda, 1941; Gesell et al., 1940).

The Role of Experience. Exactly when a child sits, stands, or walks depends in large part on the maturation of the neural and muscular systems. But opportunities to practice emerging motor skills have an effect as well. Specific training seems to lead to earlier appearance of motor skills (Super, 1976; Zelazo, Zelazo, & Kolb, 1972). African babies are often ahead of Caucasians in sitting, standing, and walking—and

FIGURE 4.2 The development of posture and locomotion in the infant.

these are precisely the motor acts that African parents encourage in their infants. There are no differences between African and Caucasian infants in the time of appearance of responses that are not taught, such as rolling over or crawling (Super, 1976). By contrast, children growing up among the Ache in Paraguay are delayed in walking because adults restrain them from exploring their environment (Kaplan & Dove, 1987). Thus, the opportunity—or lack of it—to use motor skills as they emerge can speed up or slow down the development of universal skills in motor coordination.

Another influence on motor development is the presence of useful vision. Blind children are typically delayed in crawling and walking, and they take longer to begin to reach toward a sounding object than sighted infants do to reach for a seen object (Fraiberg, 1977). They eventually develop normal motor capabilities, however, and their delays do not seem to have a physical cause. Vision seems to impel children to work to explore their world.

The Socioemotional Consequences of Motor Development.   The changes infants undergo in their motor abilities are dramatic. The advent of each new skill is typically noted with great pride by parents. Learning to sit, crawl, and walk transforms the child's ability to do things in the world. Thus, it is not surprising that motor changes are associated with changes in how children interact with people and how they explore. In one controlled study of this phenomenon, Gustafson (1984) compared the behaviors of noncrawling infants in two situations: in walkers and seated on the floor. She found the infants were much more social with adults when they were in the walkers. They also looked around the room more. Same-aged infants who had already begun to crawl had similar high levels of social interaction and visual exploration as the noncrawlers in the walkers. (A word of caution: while this study indicates some apparently positive effects of infant walkers, great care must be taken in using them. Serious accidents can occur when infants manipulate walkers on stairs or inclines.)

Infants' motor abilities (and lack thereof) also have important consequences for parents. One at least partly humorous insight into how and why this is true can be seen in Box 4.1.

Sleep

Psychologists classify infants as being in one of six states: (1) a state of regular sleep in which the eyes are closed and respiration is regular; (2) a state of irregular sleep in which one sees limb movement and facial grimaces; (3) a state of drowsiness characterized by open eyes but general inactivity; (4) a state of alert inactivity in which the infant's eyes have a bright quality and pursue moving objects; (5) a state of waking activity in which the infant engages in diffuse motor activity involving the whole body; and (6) a state of distress characterized by crying. Of these, state 4 is optimal for learning and interacting with others.

Although newborns sleep a great deal, their periods of sleep and wakefulness are distributed quite evenly through a 24-hour period, rather than following the night-day cycle of most adults. The total amount of time spent sleeping decreases dramatically across infancy: from about 18 hours a day during the first month of life to about 12 hours a day by the time the child is 2 years old. These early changes in sleep and other basic life functions occur because the infant's brain is immature at birth and much growth occurs during the initial years.

The consequences of brain growth can be observed in changes in the states of sleep. One sleep state is called rapid eye movement, or REM, because it is accom-

Babies who can maintain an upright posture (or who are helped to do so by a walker) are free to engage in more social interaction and visual exploration.

panied by eye movements that can be observed under the eyelids. As the individual matures, there is a dramatic decrease in the proportion of time spent in REM sleep, from 50 percent of a sleep bout in the newborn to about 20 percent in an adult (see Figure 4.3). By 6 months, most infants follow the adult pattern, in which the first phase of sleep is non-REM and only after sleep becomes deep does REM sleep occur (Kligman, Smyrl, & Emde, 1975; Roffwarg, Muzio, & Dement, 1966).

Cultures differ dramatically in how they manage infant sleep and in how much of a problem the typical infant's sleep habits pose for adults. In Western countries, where adults often have strong prescribed daylight work hours, irregular or fitful sleep at night often cannot be made up during the day, and hence infants' sleep habits can be a major stressor for parents. Furthermore, in many Western families, it is considered most appropriate for infants to sleep alone, at least after they reach a few months of age. This practice is considered important for fostering independence, and for protecting the parents' privacy. Infants are often encouraged to use objects such as teddy bears to help them get to sleep alone at night. By contrast, in many other cultures, for instance among the Highland Maya people of Guatemala, children sleep with their mothers into toddlerhood, and with others (e.g., siblings) thereafter. Sleeping alone is considered a hardship. The Maya see these arrangements as facilitating mother-child closeness. As one Guatemalan woman said:

> In our community the babies are always with the mother, but with North Americans you keep the babies apart. Maybe that's why the children here understand their mothers more; they feel close. Maybe U.S. children feel the distance more. (Morelli, Rogoff, Oppenheim, & Goldsmith, 1992, p. 610)

BOX 4.1
INFANT MOTOR ABILITIES AND PARENTAL WELL-BEING

When infants are born, they are quite helpless motorically. As a consequence, the adults who care for them have to adapt to their abilities and be vigilant as they develop. Insight into this process (for nonparents) and humorous reflection on it (for parents) can be gained from this excerpt from a column called "Baby Gear," written by former *New York Times* columnist Anna Quindlen.

Well, another year has gone by and still the Nobel Prize has not been awarded to the inventors of the Snugli baby carrier. I can't figure it. Here you have someone (I prefer to think it's a woman) who has come up with an invention that takes literally hundreds of thousands of people who have lost the use of their hands and gives them a new lease on life. They can pick up oranges in the supermarket, they can flip through magazines, they can smear lipsticks on the backs of their hands in a test try, and all this despite the fact that they have babies.

That this kind of achievement could go unrecognized is beyond me. The only people who have come close in the circles of civilization in which I currently mingle are the folks who developed the baby backpack and who took young impressionable people who heretofore thought the world consisted of knees, cuffs, and running shoes and enabled them to see at adult eye level. I say bravo.

These are exciting times in which to live. My mother-in-law gasped at her first sight of a collapsible stroller. It was not the miracle of engineering, the sleek design; it was the bittersweet (in that order) memory of pushing perambulators the size of sanitation trucks up steps. My father, who had five children and yet whose experience at holding babies was basically confined to the baptismal font, was mesmerized by the sight of an infant confined to its mother's chest in a blue corduroy Snugli. "They didn't have anything like that when you were kids," he said. Actually they did, but my mother owned the contraption; it was called arms, and it had no warranty and a limited life span.

Source: From *Living Out Loud* (pp. 113–114), by Anna Quindlen, 1988, New York: Random House. Copyright © 1988 by Anna Quindlen. Reprinted by permission of Random House.

Maturation of the Brain

The nervous system is composed of nerve cells, or **neurons** (see Figure 4.4). Neurons consist of a cell body and two types of projections: **dendrites** and **axons**. Dendrites receive impulses from other cells, while axons are the long projections that carry "outgoing" messages. The axon of one neuron may transmit information to the dendrite of another. This is done by chemical changes occurring in the small space between the axon and dendrite, called a **synapse**.

The initial formation of neurons and their migration to appropriate regions of the brain are events that take place almost entirely during prenatal development. In fact, almost all of the neurons we will ever have are in place in the 7-month-old fetus (Rakic, 1977). Interestingly, the newborn infant actually has many more neurons than are typical for an adult.

There are several lines of postnatal neural development. They can be placed in two broad classes. One kind of changes are additive events in which something is built or added to the nervous system. The other kind of changes are subtractive

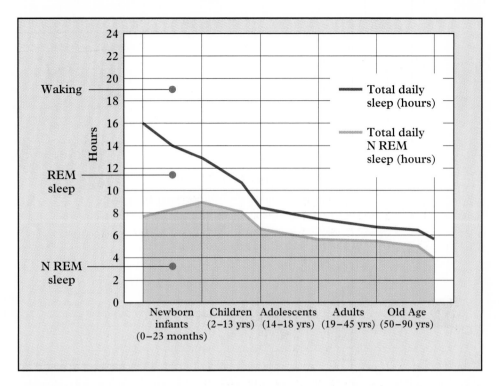

FIGURE 4.3 Age changes in the total amounts of daily sleep and daily N REM and REM sleep. The percentage of sleep that is REM sleep drops from 50 percent in newborns to 25 percent in the 2- to 3-year-old child. After "Ontogenic Development of the Human Sleep Dream Cycle," by H. P. Roffwarg, J. N. Muzio, and W. C. Dement, 1966, *Science, 152,* pp. 604–619, as revised since publication by Dr. Roffwarg. Adapted with permission of the senior author.

events in which something dies and is lost. Evidence is mounting that both of these kinds of changes are vital to neural development. Subtractive events are not necessarily negative, as one might think at first. Instead, the nervous system seems to begin with an overabundance of cells and connections. It develops by the selective elimination of some of them. Subtractive events seem to play a vital role in "tuning" the nervous system to operate in an adaptive fashion.

Additive events include three kinds of changes. First, there is the formation of long-range connections among the major brain regions, through the growth of axons. Axon growth seems to be completed by 9 or 10 months postnatally (Conel, 1939–1963). Second, the fatty sheaths surrounding neuronal paths are either laid down or increase in size, a process called **myelination**. Myelination increases the efficiency and speed of neural transmission. It is a process that takes place gradually over the age range from birth to 18 years. Third, there is an increase in the number of short-range connections (synapses) among neurons in the cortex. This process is called *synaptogenesis*. Very large increases in the density of synapses occur between the ages of 9 and 24 months, with peak levels reached at somewhat different times in different areas of cortex (P.R. Huttenlocher, 1990).

All of the additive changes, except for myelination, have their subtractive counterparts. Cell formation, occurring prenatally, is followed by gradual cell deaths. In

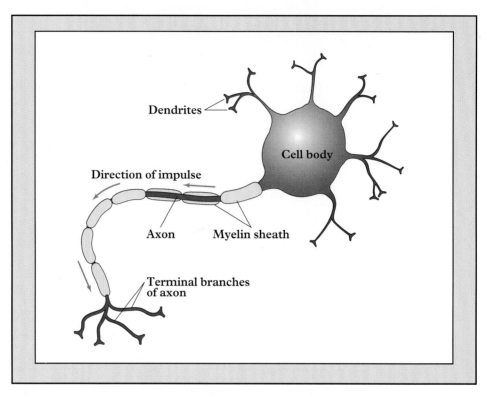

FIGURE 4.4 A schematic illustration of a neuron.

fact, elimination of neurons begins during gestation and is quite rapid in the cortex of the brain in the first 6 months of life (Huttenlocher, 1984). Still, even by 2 years of age, the density of neurons in the frontal cortex of the brain is still 55 percent above adult levels. Some axonal connections are later withdrawn or retracted, and some synaptic connections later degenerate. In fact, following the peak in synaptic connections at 24 months, the numbers gradually decline, with adult levels not reached until somewhere between 11 and 16 years (P. R. Huttenlocher, 1990). However, in later childhood and adolescence the acquisition of new knowledge may still be accompanied by the addition of synapses (Greenough, Black, & Wallace, 1987).

The very marked changes in the nervous system during development, and especially during infancy, may well be one of the maturational constraints on acquisition of motor skills, of language, and of cognitive abilities. Sometimes it is less well recognized, however, that experience can also affect nervous system development. A classic demonstration of the effects of environment on neural development is an experiment by Hirsch and Spinelli (1971). They equipped kittens with special lenses that focused horizontal lines (only) for one eye and vertical lines (only) for the other eye. Even after the lenses were removed, each eye responded only to stimuli oriented in the way that the early stimulation of that eye had been oriented. The neural connections needed to respond to stimuli of the nonexperienced orientation had degenerated from lack of use. Experiments like these have shown that normal environmental exposure is crucial to normal development of the nervous system during a *critical period* in early development.

✺ LEARNING AND CONDITIONING

In order to adapt to their environment and survive, organisms must learn. There are many ways to learn about the environment, including relatively complex mechanisms such as forming and evaluating hypotheses, processes that we look at in later chapters. Organisms, including humans, also have available simple mechanisms for learning what events go together in their environment, what sights, sounds, smells, and tastes signal danger, and which ones signal the availability of valued commodities such as food or shelter. **Conditioning** is the term psychologists use to refer to the learning of the relations between events (Rescorla, 1988). Psychologists have intensively studied two types of conditioning, known as *classical conditioning* and *instrumental conditioning.* Developmentally oriented psychologists have further studied whether these mechanisms are operative from the beginning of life or whether they themselves develop.

Classical Conditioning

In **classical conditioning**, a particular event that occurs frequently in conjunction with another event that automatically produces a response also acquires the ability to evoke that response. For instance, when a puff of air is directed at the eye, the eyes automatically blink. If a tone occurs in conjunction with the air puff or predictably a short time in advance of the puff, then, after a time, the tone alone will lead to an eye blink. Thus, in classical conditioning, new stimuli acquire control over behavior. This can have adaptive value, in preparing organisms to respond to environmental events.

A newborn only 2 hours old is able to learn a classically conditioned response. In one study demonstrating this phenomenon, the unconditioned stimulus was a sugar solution delivered to the infant's mouth with a pipette. The sugar solution elicited an unconditioned response consisting of orienting the head, puckering the lips, and making sucking movements when the sugar solution was delivered (Blass, Ganchrow, & Steiner, 1984). The conditioned stimulus was stroking of the infant's forehead. One group of infants received the sugar solution immediately after their foreheads were stroked. A second group received the sugar solution, but only after a much longer and more variable delay following the stroking. A third group received only the sugar solution and never received any stroking. After many trials, the stroking was administered without giving the baby any sugar solution. Only the first group of babies showed puckering of the lips and sucking movements when the examiner stroked their forehead, suggesting that these mouth responses had become classically conditioned to the tactile stimulus.

Infants (and older people as well) are prepared by their biological makeup to associate certain events with certain internal reactions or overt responses. Not all stimuli are capable of becoming conditioned stimuli for a particular response, and conditioned associations do not occur every time one event predicts another. A nursing baby, for example, is prepared to associate the fragrance of the mother's perfume with the feeling state that accompanies feeding, but is less prepared to associate the temperature of the room or the color of the walls with that feeling state.

Conditioning is not dependent on explicit memory of the pairings or of the events. Monkeys who have lost their amygdala and hippocampus (structures in the brain essential for retrieving memories of past events) nevertheless can learn over many trials to reach for a particular object that always leads to a reward (Mishkin &

An example of classical conditioning. Physical restraint can cause emotional distress in some infants at some ages. In this case, the sight and feel of the car seat have come to elicit distress, even in the absence of physical restraint. (Remember, though, even if a baby cries, placement in a car seat is an essential safety measure.)

Appenzeller, 1987). Newborn infants also learn to turn their head toward a particular stimulus over many trials, even though their working memory of a schema for a particular stimulus may be very fragile.

Instrumental Conditioning

A second set of relations that may be learned, called **instrumental conditioning**, is between a response and an event that alerts, surprises, or gratifies the child. If a psychologist arranged a situation so that an infant had to turn his head to the right to get the sugar water, the infant would increase his right head turning to obtain the pleasure of the sweetness. The infant would have learned the relation between the head turning and receiving a sweet taste. Instrumental conditioning, like classical conditioning, can be demonstrated from the start of life.

Instrumental (also called *operant*) conditioning differs from classical conditioning in many respects. A 1-year-old cries when his mother tucks him into bed, turns out the light, and begins to leave the room. The child's cry provokes the mother to reenter the room, turn on the light, and return to the infant's side. This sequence increases the probability that the child will cry when put to bed the next day, because the mother's return is a reinforcing event. Another 1-year-old picks up her glass of milk by the top, causing it to spill. When she picks up the second glass and holds it by the side, it does not spill, and she drinks the contents. The successful outcome is referred to as the *reinforcing event*. Because the reinforcement—the return of the mother or being able to drink the milk—was attained by crying or by holding the glass by the side, these responses have a higher probability of occurring again in response to these specific conditions.

Infants can do more than just learn which of their responses lead to reinforcement. They also learn to discriminate cues in the environment that signal when they will be reinforced or which of several behaviors will be reinforced. One scientist (Papousek, 1967) presented 6-week-old infants with either a bell or a buzzer. When the bell sounded, the baby would receive milk only from the nipple on the left. When the buzzer sounded, milk was available only on the right. After about 30 days of such experiences, the infants learned to turn to the left when they heard the bell and to the right when they heard the buzzer. Papousek was even able to condition 4-month-old infants to make two consecutive turns to one side or to alternate turns to the left with turns to the right.

Infants can also learn what response will be reinforced, based on an internally coded rule, with no external stimulation specifying what will happen. For instance, by 14 weeks infants are able to learn when an interesting stimulus will appear at a particular location, and they will turn their eyes to anticipate the onset of that stimulus. Infants were shown a screen above them, on which they saw a picture (e.g., a checkerboard) on one side of the screen. It moved up and down for 0.7 second and then went off. After an interval of 1 second, a different picture appeared on the other side of the screen. After only 1 minute of this alternation of pictures, some infants began to anticipate the appearance of the next picture and would move their eyes to the place where a picture was about to appear (Haith, 1987). They had learned the relation between the appearance of a picture on one side and the later appearance of a different picture on the other.

Reinforcement increases the probability of recurrence of the instrumentally conditioned response in a particular context. When the reinforcing event reduces a biological drive like hunger or thirst, it is called a *primary reinforcer*. Any objects or people that were present when the biological drive was reduced may acquire reinforcing value and are called *secondary reinforcers*.

With repetition, an event that is initially reinforcing may lose its reinforcing qualities. Consider the example of a baby who strikes a balloon full of plastic beads, causing it to move and make a noise. The baby laughs and repeats the action. The movement and interesting noise appear to be reinforcing, implying that the baby should repeat the act again and again. But after a few minutes the baby stops as if bored. This common phenomenon—boredom following attainment of a desirable goal—suggests that the child's state changes after he or she experiences reinforcements, and that the motivation for the reinforcing event is altered as a result.

The process of instrumental conditioning is extremely useful in changing human behavior. It has been used to help retarded children learn basic skills such as how to tie their shoes or eat with silverware. It can also be used to help children overcome specific fears such as fear of large dogs.

✿ PERCEPTUAL DEVELOPMENT

Not too long ago, many people believed that newborn infants could barely see, and thought that they possessed very few abilities to sort out their perceptual world into objects or events. In a famous phrase, William James, one of the founders of modern psychology, suggested that the infant's life must initially be one of "blooming, buzzing confusion." A good deal of research has now been done to show that this view is wrong. Infants have very surprising abilities to divide up the world into meaningful stimuli and to process them. At the same time, their perceptual systems do undergo development. In this section, we get an overview of development during infancy in the major perceptual systems.

However, before discussing the specifics of infant perception, it is important to consider the methods by which it is investigated. How do we know what babies perceive? It is obviously not possible to ask them to report verbally on what they see, hear, or smell. Developmental psychologists have invented several methods for looking at what infants can perceive.

One very important method is known as **habituation-dishabituation**. This procedure is based on the assumption that when infants become bored with a particular event because of repeated presentation or prolonged exposure, they will look at it for shorter and shorter intervals before looking away. When a changed stimulus appears, they will show increased attention (show longer looks) if they detect the change. The decreased interest or boredom that accompanies the repeated presentation is called *habituation;* the recovery of interest in response to the new event is called *dishabituation.*

The increase in attention is important because it implies that the infant recognizes the new event as different from the original one. For instance, if infants are shown a picture of two identical red spheres until they look away out of boredom, and then are shown a picture of a red sphere alongside a red cube, most will look longer at the cube, implying that they detect the difference between the shapes of the two objects.

But we must be cautious in concluding that infants do not detect a difference between an old event and a new one simply because they do not look longer at the new stimulus. For example, when infants were shown a picture of a circle containing two dots, those who had become habituated to this stimulus did not look longer at a picture of two dots outside a circle, even though they should have been capable of perceiving the differences between the two stimuli (Linn, Reznick, Kagan, & Hans, 1982). Because children do not always reveal their discrimination of a new stimulus by increased looking, it has proved valuable to record other behaviors besides fixation time when a dishabituation stimulus is presented. Changes in facial expression or heart rate and increases or decreases in vocalization or motor movements often occur.

Another method for assessing visual perception in infants is through **visual preference** techniques. If infants are shown two patterns and systematically look at one of them more than at the other, we can draw the conclusion that they perceive the difference between the two. A variant of this procedure is to show one of the patterns to the infants first, by itself. Then, when the pair of patterns is shown, infants will generally spend longer looking at the novel pattern, again, if they can see the difference. Even if they look longer at the familiar pattern (a phenomenon occasionally observed), we can still infer that they see the difference.

Psychologists who are interested in the discrimination of auditory stimuli cannot use visual fixation time. If the baby is young, they use a method involving **high-amplitude sucking** to assess hearing. A rubber nipple is placed in the baby's mouth, and every time the infant sucks with a specific pressure he hears a particular syllable—for instance, the syllable "pa." When the baby becomes bored, as indicated by less frequent and less intense sucking pressure, the stimulus is changed,

Infants look at what interests them. Timing visual fixation is an important part of two methods of studying infants: habituation-dishabituation studies and visual preference studies.

say, to "ba." If the infant increases the rate and pressure of sucking, the psychologist concludes that the child detected a difference between the syllables "pa" and "ba." Each of these changes in behavior—looking time, vocalization, sucking, heart rate—is a valid indicator that the child has detected a new stimulus.

Vision

Newborn infants inherit a number of perceptual abilities and preferences that lead them to pay attention to some objects and events in their surroundings while ignoring others. These abilities, in many cases, seem adapted to permit children to enter their physical world in a well-graduated way, in which they can learn easily and effectively. This state of affairs is hardly surprising; evolutionary forces have shaped abilities to ensure the acquisition of knowledge.

One of the most important perceptual tendencies infants have is their tendency to attend to stimuli that change in some way or that exhibit a great deal of visual variety. Thus, objects that move or objects that have black-white contrast are most likely to attract and hold an infant's attention.

Motion picture recordings reveal that when newborns are placed in a dark room, they open their eyes and look around for shadows or edges. For example, if

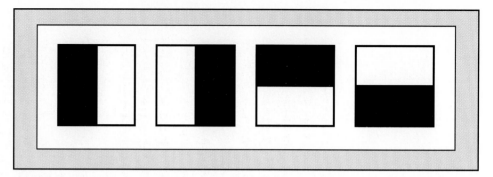

FIGURE 4.5 Newborn infants concentrate their visual scanning on the black-white borders of these stimuli. After *Rules That Babies Look By* (p. 59), by M. M. Haith, 1980, Hillsdale, NJ: Erlbaum. Copyright © 1980 by M. M. Haith. Reprinted by permission of the publisher, Lawrence Erlbaum Associates, Inc.

an alert infant is shown a thick black bar on a white background, such as those in Figure 4.5, the infant's eyes dart to the black contour and hover near it rather than wandering randomly across the visual field. Haith (1980) has suggested that newborns' attention seems to be guided by the following set of rules:

- *Rule 1:* If awake and alert, open your eyes.
- *Rule 2:* If you find darkness, search the environment.
- *Rule 3:* If you find light but no edges, engage in a broad, uncontrolled search of the environment.
- *Rule 4:* If you find an edge, look near the edge and try to cross it.
- *Rule 5:* Stay near areas that have lots of contour; scan broadly near areas of low contour and narrowly near areas of high contour.

The infant's preference for contrast can be used in a practical application: to test visual acuity, charting its development and allowing for identification of babies with visual problems. In one procedure, a baby is presented with two stimuli alongside each other. One stimulus is a set of vertical black lines separated by only a few centimeters; the other is a blank field of equal brightness. Infants who can discriminate the stimulus with closely spaced lines from the stimulus without lines will look at the former stimulus longer because they prefer to look at the contrast created by the dark lines. Infants who cannot detect the lines as separate will look at both stimuli equally long.

Using this procedure, psychologists have found that visual acuity increases dramatically in the first months of life. A 1-week-old baby can detect the difference between a pattern composed of stripes as wide as those shown in Figure 4.6 and a patch that is completely gray, from a distance of 1 foot. But finer stripes are not discriminated from gray. There is sharp improvement, however, in the first few months of life, and by 8 months, babies can see about as well as adults who, while they might need glasses, would often not bother to wear them. Visual acuity equals that of normal adults by 5 years of age.

As well as acuity changes in the first months, babies also improve in their ability to see depth. In particular, one of the most powerful cues to depth perception used by adults is called **stereopsis**, which is the ability of the brain to use information derived from the fact that the right and left eye generate (because they are

FIGURE 4.6 The finest stripes that newborns can discriminate from a gray patch. After *The World of the Newborn*, by D. Maurer and C. Maurer, 1988, New York: Basic Books. Copyright © 1988 by D. Maurer and C. Maurer. Adapted with permission of Basic Books.

separated) two slightly different images of an object that a person is looking at. The degree of difference between the retinal images is a good guide to how far away the object is. The ability to use stereopsis seems to appear dramatically quickly, with babies going from clearly not having it to having it within a week or two, generally between the ages of 15 and 20 weeks (Shimojo, Bauer, O'Connell, & Held, 1986).

The acquisition of stereopsis seems to occur within a *critical period*. When binocular disparity information is not input to the nervous system (as when children are cross-eyed and their eyes focus on different objects), surgical correction of the problem does not lead to stereopsis unless it is performed before the age of 3 years (Banks, Aslin, & Letson, 1975). For children aged 4 months to 3 years at the time of surgery, some stereopsis was achieved, but progressively less as time passed from the period when the nervous system ordinarily begins to receive binocular input.

Infants also perceive colors as belonging to discrete categories, just as adults do. The visible color spectrum (from red to purple) results from continuous differences in the wavelength of light, but we perceive the colors as if they belonged to separate categories. Thus, even though the differences in wavelength between two shades of blue, on the one hand, and a blue and a green, on the other, are equal, infants show a greater increase in attention to a change from blue to green than to a change from one shade of blue to another (Bornstein, Kessen, & Weiskopf, 1976).

Perhaps an even more surprising discovery about infant vision is that babies as young as 3 months are able to create a schema for a perceptual pattern as complex as that created by a person walking (Bertenthal, Proffitt, & Cutting, 1984; Bertenthal, Proffitt, Kramer, & Spetner, 1987). Infants 3 and 5 months old saw a moving

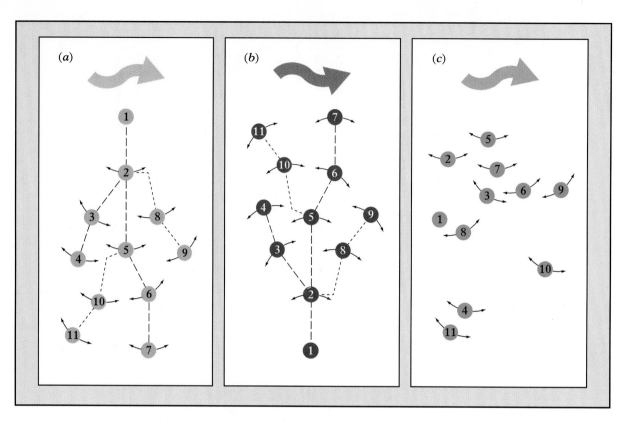

FIGURE 4.7 Babies seem able to see form from movement. Shown only dots moving as shown by the arrows (the dotted lines are included only to help in a static illustration), babies see the motion pattern on the left as different from both the motion pattern in the middle and the motion pattern on the right. After "Infant Sensitivity to Figural Coherence and Biomechanical Motions," by B. I. Bertenthal, D. R. Profitt, and J. E. Cutting, 1984, *Developmental Psychology, 23*, pp. 171–178. Copyright © 1984 by Academic Press. Adapted with permission.

pattern of 11 different lights on a screen (see Figure 4.7). The infants could tell the difference between the pattern of lights that corresponded to a person walking (stimulus A) and a random version of those lights (stimulus C). They could also tell the difference between the pattern of lights in stimulus A and an upside-down version (stimulus B).

In sum, young infants are prepared to orient themselves to particular aspects of the external world. The infant's attention is attracted and held by contrast, movement, curvilinearity, color, symmetry, and many other qualities, especially when they indicate a change in the immediate perceptual field. On the other hand, there is rapid change over the first few months of life in the acuity of visual perception and in infants' ability to see depth. These changes are likely to be related to maturation of the brain.

The biases to pay attention to qualities like symmetry and curvature, which appear to be inborn, might form the basis for our attraction to what are generally considered pretty, in contrast to plain or unattractive, female faces. The former tend to be curved rather than angular, and more symmetrical. Infants as young as two months look longer at female faces that both men and women judge to be attractive than at female faces that are judged unattractive—a fact that suggests that some criteria for attractive faces may be inborn (Langlois et al., 1987).

Hearing

At birth, infants hear quite well. Although noises need to be louder to elicit responses from a newborn than they would need to be to elicit responses from an adult, the differences are not as large as those that exist for visual acuity. As we saw with vision, there are also perceptual biases in hearing. The newborn is more responsive to low-frequency (e.g., throaty) sounds than to high-frequency sounds such as whistles, and reacts more to sounds with a great deal of variety than to simple sounds. Therefore, it appears that the sounds adults make when they talk to babies are precisely those that are most likely to get their attention (Colombo, 1986).

Infants have also shown a truly remarkable ability to remember particular voices. DeCasper and Fifer (1980) found that infants as young as 3 days would suck to hear a recording of their mother's voice more than to hear a recording of a female stranger. This preference could have been based on their exposure to their mother after birth, but a second study showed that it was due to memories for sounds heard while the babies were in utero. DeCasper and Spence (1986) showed that babies preferred to listen to their mothers reading a story that she had read several times while pregnant, over listening to their mothers reading a story she had not previously read.

An important ability in hearing is **auditory localization**. That is, when you hear something, you generally know where the sound came from, and can turn toward the direction from which it came. Newborns show good auditory localization, but this ability actually diminishes somewhat through the second and third month, coming back to newborn levels by the fourth month (Muir, Abraham, Forbes, & Harris, 1979).

This pattern of decline and revival may seem odd, but it has a good explanation. Early on, auditory localization may be effected by subcortical regions of the brain. As the cortex matures, it suppresses the subcortical mechanisms, but it is not yet itself able to perform as well. By 4 months, cortical maturation has proceeded to the point that auditory localization is again effective.

Touch, Taste, and Smell

Vision and hearing are extremely important human senses and have been more comprehensively studied, in adults as well as infants, than the other senses. We do know, however, that the other senses seem quite well developed at birth.

Newborns are sensitive to changes in temperature and are affected by being touched. As we mentioned in Chapter 3, premature infants seem to grow better when massaged or otherwise tactually stimulated. In fact, even before birth, the fetus is sensitive to touch (Carmichael, 1970).

Newborns have also been shown to be sensitive to taste and smell (Steiner, 1979). For instance, they will show distinctive facial expressions and tongue movements when sweet, sour, salty and bitter substances are placed in their mouths. They prefer sweet to sour tastes (Lipsitt, 1977). They also prefer smells associated with pleasant situations (an example of *instrumental conditioning*). Macfarlane (1975) found that, at 6 days of age, babies who were nursing preferred the smell of breast pads taken from their mothers' bras to those taken from other nursing mothers.

Cross-Modal Perception

As well as investigating infants' abilities to see, hear, touch, taste, and smell, developmental psychologists have been interested in the question of **cross-modal perception**. That is, can infants anticipate what something will look like after having felt it or know what it will feel like from looking at it? Or know what sound it might make if shaken from looking at it? and so on. There is some evidence that infants can in fact detect a similarity between two events when the events originate in different sense modalities, such as vision and hearing or vision and touch. If a 6-month-old baby is given a smooth or nubby nipple to suck on (see Figure 4.8) without being able to see the object, and later is shown both a smooth and a nubby nipple, the infant looks longer at the nipple she explored with her tongue. This surprising fact suggests that the infant may have created a schema for "nubbiness" when sucking the nipple and used that schema in her visual search (Meltzoff & Borton, 1979).

In a related experiment, babies first heard either a pulsing or a continuous tone and subsequently were shown a set of short, discontinuous line segments and a continuous line. The infants looked longer at the broken line after they had heard the intermittent tone, and they looked longer at the continuous line after they had heard the continuous tone (Wagner, Winner, Cicchetti, & Gardner, 1981). These findings suggest that the infants were able to extract the dimension of "discontinuity" in both the auditory and visual modes; in other words, they had constructed a cross-modal schema.

Infants only 5 months old are able to detect the relation between the shape of a

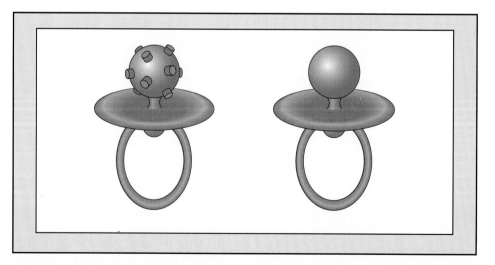

FIGURE 4.8 After sucking (but not seeing) one of these forms, infants looked longer at the one they had sucked, thus demonstrating cross-modal perception. After "Intermodal Matching by Human Neonates," by A. N. Meltzoff and R. W. Borton, 1979, *Nature, 282,* pp. 403–404. Copyright © 1979 by Macmillan Journals Limited. Adapted with permission of Macmillan Journals.

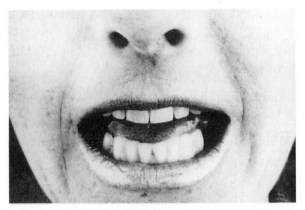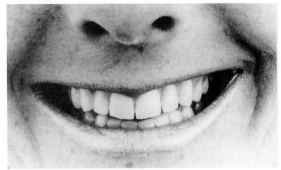

FIGURE 4.9 Photos of women saying "A" (left) and "E" (right). Copyright Jack Deutsch.

person's mouth and the sound uttered (Kuhl & Meltzoff, 1982). Infants first saw two silent films, each ten seconds long, one film right after the other. One film depicted a woman's mouth with the shape it assumes when she repeats the sound "A." The second film showed the shape of a woman's mouth as she repeats the sound "E" (see Figure 4.9). After the infants had seen the films in succession, they saw the same two films simultaneously but heard only the sound track corresponding to one of the films (either the "A" sound or the "E" sound). The infants looked longer at the face that matched the sound they were hearing. Thus, these 5-month-olds had created an association between the shape of a person's mouth and the vocal sound it produces.

In this case, the association between the shape of the person's mouth and the sound produced—a cross-modal schema—was learned. But some psychologists believe that infants can create cross-modal schemata when there is no possibility that they could have learned an association between the events in two different sensory modalities. We do not know whether the similarity between the two modalities is based on some shared quality of different modalities or on the degree of arousal generated by the events. For example, because an intermittent sound contains a great deal of change, it might produce greater physiological arousal than a continuous sound. Similarly, a discontinuous line with more contour would generate more arousal than a continuous line. As a result, the infant might match the discontinuous tone with the discontinuous line because both produced equivalent degrees of internal arousal, not because the infant generated an abstract schema of "interruptedness."

✿ APPLICATIONS

Neonatal Assessment

Although the vast majority of babies are born with no defects, a small proportion, no more than 10 percent, are born either prematurely or with some difficulty and, hence, may suffer minor brain damage. For these reasons, parents often wish to have a pediatrician, neurologist, or psychologist test the baby to determine that it is normal. Several such tests have been devised, including a neurological test that checks the baby's reflexes. The presence of the Moro reflex in the first two months has long been regarded as useful in assessing the state of the infant's central nervous system. If a 1-month-old infant does not exhibit the Moro reflex, the examiner may apply further tests.

Doctors, nurses, and psychologists often evaluate the state of the newborn by means of test procedures developed by pediatrician T. Berry Brazelton, and called the Neonatal Behavior Assessment Scale (NBAS). For example, in one procedure, the examiner moves a small, attractive object in front of the infant's face to see if the baby will attend to it and follow it as it passes from one side to the other. Healthy newborns will track the moving object. In another procedure, the examiner holds the baby's hands and attempts to pull the infant to a sitting position from lying down. The examiner also records behaviors—such as cuddliness, how easy the baby is to console if upset, how alert the baby is, and whether the baby trembles a lot—and assesses the baby's reflexes.

The NBAS has been found to be of some use in predicting later development (Brazelton, Nugent, & Lester, 1987) and is clearly effective in identifying subgroups of infants who are at risk for problems. One of the most interesting uses of the NBAS, however, is as a tool for helping parents to "get acquainted" with their infant. Parents may think initially of their newborn as not capable of doing much, but going through the NBAS with a trained examiner and doing some of the exercises themselves often reveals to them how much these little beings can already do and take in. Furthermore, in the course of this interaction, they have an opportunity to discuss the specific characteristics of their infant, and their own hopes and fears, with an experienced person. Parents who have had this opportunity have been found to be more responsive to their babies and more knowledgeable about them later on (Myers, 1982; Worobey & Belsky, 1982).

Sudden Infant Death Syndrome

Sudden infant death syndrome (SIDS) refers to the unexplained death of an infant, usually while sleeping, in the first full year of life. It is estimated that about 2 of every 1000 births ends in crib death. SIDS is, in fact, the most common cause of death in American infants between the ages of 1 month and 1 year. The highest incidence of SIDS is between 2 and 4 months of age. Our understanding of physical devlopment, learning, and perception in early infancy has been important in formulating hypotheses concerning the possible causes of SIDS, although no hypothesis has definitive support at present.

We know something about the circumstances and the babies with elevated risk of SIDS. SIDS deaths are most common during the winter months, often during or following a mild cold. SIDS is somewhat more common in males than females and more common in children whose mothers have smoked cigarettes or used cocaine. SIDS also appears to be more common in babies put to sleep on their stomachs, the position often recommended by American pediatricians, especially if the babies are not on a firm, smooth mattress without pillows. Preterm, low-birth-weight babies are at higher risk. Surviving twins have a 10 percent greater risk than the population at large of suffering from SIDS, while siblings have a 2 percent greater risk (Leibold, 1988).

Despite knowledge of these risk factors, pediatricians cannot predict in any precise way what babies are at risk, nor do scientists know the exact cause of SIDS. Typically, risk is revealed only when an infant is found either dead or suffering from anoxia. As one mother told her story:

On October 28, our family got their wish: a beautiful baby girl was born. On the evening of May 15, Joe and I went out to celebrate our anniversary and rejoice. Everything seemed so perfect, until later that evening, when we were en route home, an ambulance passed our car and stopped directly in front of our house. We ran into the house to find our two sons and the babysitter hysterical. Our precious baby girl was gray and her eyes were dull. We went from our local hospital to Massachusetts General Hospital. (Culbertson, Krous, & Bendell, 1988, pp. 202–203)

Anoxic infants who are revived are generally placed on an apnea monitor when sleeping. The monitor is a device that registers when the child is suffering from a period of no respirations (called apnea). If apnea occurs, the monitor sounds an alarm to summon someone to perform cardio-pulmonary resuscitation. Monitoring is a procedure which, while it may be beneficial, is also stressful for parents and siblings of the at-risk baby, due to the constant vigilance that it requires.

Because the brain centers that monitor breathing mature during the first half-year, theories of SIDS have focused on possible deficiencies in this maturational sequence. At birth, primitive relexes produce responses to respiratory obstruction, mediated at the subcortical level. Such reflexes are replaced over the first 6 months with learned responses requiring the cortex of the brain. Some investigators have stressed that the learning mechanisms necessary for takeover of responses to obstruction of breathing may be impaired in SIDS, and that they can be behaviorally taught (Burns & Lipsitt, 1991). Others argue that SIDS is due to abnormalities in the original subcortical control of cardiorespiratory mechanisms (C. E. Hunt, 1991), citing evidence of a chronic lack of oxygen found in infants who die of SIDS. Until the riddle of SIDS is answered, however, general health precautions (such as not smoking during pregnancy), putting infants to sleep on their backs on a firm mattress, and monitoring babies judged to be at risk, will be the best responses we can mount to the problem.

✷ SUMMARY

In all societies the period of infancy is recognized as a special time and distinguished from later stages of life. However, the terms that psychologists use to describe infants change over time as the fundamental beliefs of the larger society change. Freud, Erikson, Bowlby, and Piaget have all emphasized different aspects of infants' development.

Infants change a great deal in the first year of life. Their physical growth is rapid. Maturation (or universal sequences of biological events occurring in the body and the brain) are seen in many realms. One is the appearance and disappearance of reflexes. The normal infant displays a set of inherited reflexes, some of which are useful as it adjusts to its new environment; others are present because the cerebral cortex is not yet mature enough to control them. A second realm in which maturation is apparent is motor development; however, practice (or lack of it) can also accelerate or decelerate change in this area. A third realm of maturation is sleep. Sleep changes dramatically in the first year, decreasing in amount and approaching more adult patterns of distribution of sleep periods with and without rapid eye movements (REM sleep).

The infant's brain is immature at birth, and many changes in the infant's behavior are probably a result of brain growth. Brain changes are both additive and subtractive. Additive events include the growth of axons, myelination of neuronal paths, and synaptogenesis. Subtractive changes include elimination of neurons, withdrawal of axons, and decline in synaptic connections. Both kinds of processes are important in development.

Conditioning refers to the learning of a relationship between two events or between an action and an external stimulus event. In classical conditioning, the child learns that a neutral stimulus predicts a biologically salient event that automatically produces a response. After repeated presentations of the neutral stimulus before the biologically salient one, the former is able to elicit the biological response.

In instrumental or operant conditioning, a response is modified by presenting or withholding reinforcers (rewards and punishments). A reinforcing event that reduces a biological drive is a primary reinforcer; objects or people that were present when the biological drive was reduced may become secondary reinforcers. An event that is initially reinforcing can lose its reinforcing qualities with repetition.

The newborn inherits certain perceptual abilities. These can be studied using techniques called habituation-dishabituation, visual preference, and high-amplitude sucking. One of the most important of infant perceptual abilities is the tendency to attend to stimuli that change in some way or exhibit a great deal of variety. Infants appear to be especially interested in visual events characterized by contrast, movement, curvilinearity, and symmetry. They can see in color. Infants' vision increases greatly in acuity in the first months, and their ability to see depth improves as well. By at least 3 months, they can differentiate patterns of natural biological motion from random movements of points of light, indicating considerable knowledge of their visual world.

Hearing is better developed at birth than vision. Newborns prefer high-frequency sounds with a good deal of variety (such as their mother's voice). Indeed, they can recognize their mother's voice, apparently based on in-utero exposure. They can also use sound to turn their eyes to the sounding object.

Cross-modal perception is the ability to know what something will feel like from visual examination, to know what something will sound like from looking at a person's lips, and so on. Infants have shown remarkable abilities in tasks of this type.

Developmental infancy research has important practical applications. One area of application is in devising instruments for assessing newborns, including the Neonatal Behavior Assessment Scale developed by T. Berry Brazelton. Another area of application is research on Sudden Infant Death Syndrome (SIDS). SIDS is not currently understood, but several hypotheses are under active investigation, and risk factors are known.

REVIEW QUESTIONS

1. Define maturation. Give an example and explain it.

2. Describe the Moro reflex. To what use is it put in neonatal assessment?

3. Discuss the roles of maturation and practice in motor development.

4. Describe newborn sleep and compare it to adult sleep.

5. Define additive and subtractive events in brain development.

6. Define conditioning and distinguish between classical and instrumental conditioning.

7. What perceptual tendencies in the newborn lead it to pay attention to some objects and events in its surroundings while ignoring others?

8. What perceptual abilities does a newborn have? Which undergo change and which are similar to the adult state?

9. Infants appear to be able to relate different sensory modes. What are some implications of this ability?

10. What risk factors are known to exist for SIDS?

CRITICAL THINKING ABOUT THE CHAPTER

1. Suppose you were asked to talk about infant development to a group of adults expecting the birth of a first baby. What facts do you think they would most want to know about infants? Most need to know? How do you think knowledge about infant development would help them in adjusting to the arrival of the infant?

2. We have seen that blind infants have slower motor development, on average, than sighted ones. What other differences might you expect in the development of blind and sighted infants? How might knowledge of normal infant development assist in the planning of interventions to support the development of blind infants?

KEY TERMS

attachment
auditory localization
axon
classical conditioning
conditioning
critical period
cross-modal perception
dendrites
habituation-dishabituation
high-amplitude sucking
instrumental (operant) conditioning

maturation
Moro reflex
myelination
neuron
oral stage
rooting reflex
sensorimotor period
stage of trust
stereopsis
synapses
visual preference

SUGGESTED READINGS

Ferber, R. (1985). *Solve your child's sleep problems.* New York: Simon & Schuster. Presents basic information on the development of sleep cycles. Also gives advice on how to help children adjust to typical Western sleeping practices.

Maurer, D., & Maurer, C. (1988). *The world of the newborn.* New York: Basic Books. Presents in a highly readable style what psychologists have learned about the prenatal and early postnatal periods. Also presents an exceptionally good summary of the infant's visual and auditory capacities.

Osofsky, J. D. (Ed.). (1987). *Handbook of infant development* (2nd ed.). New York: Wiley. A professional overview of the literature, with chapters written by individual experts.

Rosenblith, J. F., & Sims-Knight, J. E. (1985). *In the beginning: Development in the first two years.* Monterey, CA: Brooks Cole. Covers all the basic research on infancy, including excellent discussions of conditioning and memory in infants, sensory and perceptual abilities, Piaget's theory, and early communicative behavior.

CHAPTER

5

COGNITIVE DEVELOPMENT IN INFANCY

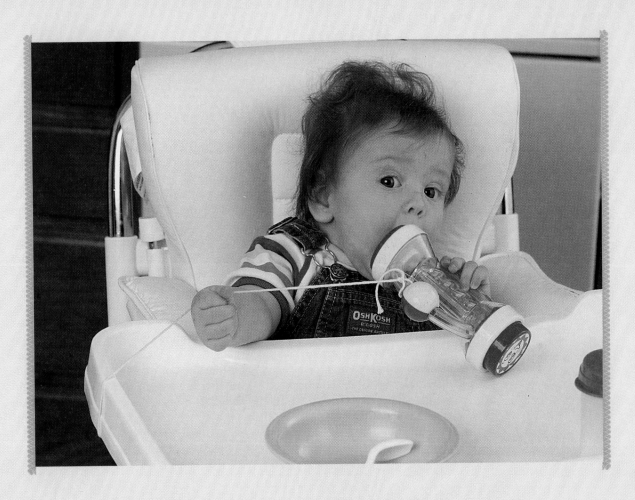

Sandra put her 6-month-old, Seth, into his high chair, fastened the strap around him, and snapped the tray in place. To keep him occupied while she prepared his breakfast, she handed him a clear plastic rattle with colored shapes inside it. This morning, she had attached it by a string to the high chair, so that when he dropped it, he could retrieve it rather than crying. (And besides, that way she wouldn't have to wash it so often!) But she had no sooner turned to the kitchen cabinets than she heard a wail. "What's wrong, Seth?" she said as she saw the rattle dangling from its string. "Pull it up, honey. Look, you can get it." But, after many demonstrations, Seth still didn't seem to understand. Every time he dropped his rattle, he started to cry.

An observer of this scene might draw various conclusions about Seth's behavior. One might be that, once the object is out of sight, Seth forgets that it still exists. On this account, he cries because he has nothing to do. Another interpretation might be that Seth remembers his rattle but doesn't know where it is. Thus he cries because it's missing. Yet another conclusion might be that Seth, while he remembers his rattle and knows where it is, lacks the ability to construct a means-ends sequence for getting it. In other words, he cries because he doesn't know how to bring the rattle back (and has trouble learning that pulling the string will do it).

Which of these arguments is correct? What do babies know about their world? Developmental psychologists are concerned with answering questions such as these. The aim of research on infant cognitive development is to describe how babies think and how and why thought changes with age. To achieve this goal, psychologists must find ways to observe and measure cognitive processes in babies before the acquisition of language. Some of these methods, such as habituation-dishabituation techniques, have already been discussed in Chapter 4.

When discussing cognitive development, however, we must confront two problems that go beyond the level of methodology. One problem is how we can draw conclusions about thought at all, when there is nothing directly observable about what goes on in someone else's head. A second issue is what we should conclude when someone fails to do a task we set. Is it that the task truly exceeds the individual's abilities, or could the failure be due to other factors? In this chapter, we begin by discussing these questions. We then present an overview of the thinking of Jean Piaget and look in a detailed way at his hypotheses about infancy. Finally we examine recent research and theorizing on infant cognitive development.

⚙ TWO ISSUES IN STUDYING COGNITIVE DEVELOPMENT

Inferring Thought from Behavior

Obviously, we cannot observe thought processes directly. We can only observe overt behavior or performance on a task. While some theorists have argued that observable behavior is psychologists' only legitimate concern (Bijou & Baer, 1961; Skinner, 1938), most developmental psychologists today are comfortable making inferences about thought from behavior, as long as those inferences are based on careful observations of what children do. They constantly refine their ideas and test them by predicting particular behaviors as precisely as possible.

Consider the case of children's attention. The simplest and most frequently used way of measuring attention, especially in infancy, is to observe where children are looking. If they are looking at something, they could be said to be "attending," and if they look away, they could be said to be "inattentive." But it is possible to stare blankly at a scene while thinking about something else, and it is also possible to attend to a stimulus without watching it—for instance, by listening. Hence, inferring attention from looking behavior might be argued to be excessively imprecise.

Investigators therefore must sometimes conduct research to test whether the behaviors they observe really tap the ideas they want to draw inferences about, such as attention. For instance, a researcher who believes that visual fixation indicates attention might test this idea by obtaining physiological measures that also index attention. If the physiological measures correspond to eye fixations, the researcher may conclude that visual fixation is a good measure of attention. In short, observable behavior is the criterion for testing theories, but the researcher's inferences about what each behavior means must themselves be tested.

Competence and Performance

A second, related issue is the distinction between the knowledge and skills that a child possesses, which is often called **competence**, and the demonstration of knowledge and skills in observable problem-solving situations, which is often called **performance**. People may possess knowledge that they do not use, even when the occasion calls for it. For example, although on a particular occasion a person may forget the name of an old friend, we would not necessarily conclude that the person does not know the friend's name or that he or she lacks the ability to recall people's names.

Consider a 2-year-old girl who was playing with some plastic rods that were brown, red, and orange. She and her mother met an adult friend, who asked her what colors her toys were. She looked a little blank and then said, "I don't know." A few minutes later she and her mother encountered another adult friend. The child spontaneously said, "Look what I've got. This one's brown, and this one's red, and this one's orange."

This example shows that one cannot conclude a child does not know something (i.e., lacks a particular competence) simply because she does not demonstrate her knowledge (performance). If individuals perform or demonstrate a skill, we can conclude with reasonable confidence that they possess that particular competence. However, the reverse is not true. If they fail to perform the skill, we do not know whether they have the competence or not.

⚙ PIAGET'S THEORY OF COGNITIVE DEVELOPMENT

Jean Piaget is regarded as the most significant theorist of cognitive development in this century. When he died in 1980 at the age of 84, he had published over 40 books and more than 200 articles. Piaget's theory is discussed in several parts of this book in association with various developmental stages (see Chapters 7, 9, and 14). In this section, we begin by presenting an overview of his theory so that you can grasp the main points that he made about development. We then deal in more detail with Piaget's view of cognitive development in infancy.

Piaget initially approached the study of children from the point of view of a biological scientist with an interest in describing naturally occurring processes of growth and change. His childhood interests had been in animal observation (at the age of 10, he published a one-page scientific note on an albino sparrow he had observed in a public park) and his graduate education was as a specialist in the study of mollusks. However, his reading and interests covered philosophy, religion, sociology, and psychology in addition to biology, and after obtaining his degree in 1918, Piaget spent some time in the laboratory of Binet, the founder of the modern intelligence test. He was assigned to give test items to schoolchildren in Paris, and soon he found himself more interested in the reasoning they used to obtain their answers than in whether the answers were right or wrong. The "clinical method" of asking children about their thinking became a hallmark of his later studies of children.

This little girl may be able to match shapes when playing with her shape-sorting toy, but it might be harder for her to display this competence in a formal shape-matching task. Situations such as these form the basis for the distinction between competence and performance.

Piaget was a meticulous and careful observer. His observations of his own three children, which formed the basis for many elements of his theory, were not simply the pastime of a doting father but a systematic, detailed record of children's spontaneous behavior. Here is an example of his daughter's early symbolic play (that is, play in which children let one object stand for or symbolize another):

> At 21 months, Jacqueline saw a shell and said "cup." After saying this, she picked it up and pretended to drink. . . . The next day, seeing the same shell, she said "glass," then "cup," then "hat," and finally "boat in the water." Three days later she took an empty box and moved it to and fro saying "motycar." . . . At 24 months and 22 days, she moved her finger along the table and said: "finger walking . . . horse trotting." (Piaget, 1951, p. 124)

Major Themes

Although Piaget began writing early in the twentieth century, his work was rediscovered in the United States in the early 1960s. His ideas radically changed the direction of developmental psychology in this country. In 1960 the dominant view, based on learning theory, was strongly environmentalist; little attention was given to maturation or heredity. Children were viewed as passive recipients of environmental stim-

Jean Piaget.

uli. Developmental change, when it was discussed at all, was described as gradual and continuous, and learning was thought to be specific to particular tasks or situations. Piaget's theory thus was not just another theory but a challenge to prevailing opinions on each of the fundamental issues described in Chapter 1. He saw development as the interactive product of biology and experience, he saw children as active in constructing their worlds, he saw change as discontinuous, and he saw children as having competences that were generally available across situations.

Maturation and Experience. Piaget's natural-science orientation led him to assume that the biological characteristics of the human child place some limits on the order and speed at which particular cognitive competences emerge. At the same time, he believed that active experience with the world is critical to cognitive growth. That is, he was a strong interactionist. He believed that maturation and experience are both important and cannot be assigned separate roles in development.

Piaget insisted that some cognitive ideas, operations, and structures are universal, not because they are inherited but because all children's ordinary experiences in the world of objects and people force them to come to the same conclusions. For instance, all children eventually learn to group categories like "dog" and "cat" together into more abstract categories such as "pets" or "mammals." Similarly, all children come to realize that events can be ordered by their magnitude, from smallest to largest or lightest to heaviest. These rules as well as a great many others develop, Piaget thought, as a result of the everyday interactions that occur between children and other people and between children and objects.

The Active, Constructive Child. Piaget's central thesis is that people are active, curious, and inventive throughout life. Moreover, knowledge is assumed to have a specific goal: to aid the individual in adapting to the environment. Human beings spontaneously seek contact and interaction with the environment and actively look for challenge. When left to their own devices, children explore, learn, and discover.

According to Piaget, children construct their world by imposing order on the raw material provided by sights, sounds, and smells. The major focus of Piaget's theory is to understand the transformations that humans impose on the information they receive through the senses. "It is the interpretation, not the event itself, which affects behavior" (Ginsburg & Opper, 1979, p. 67). Children and adults continually construct and reconstruct their knowledge of the world, trying to make sense of their experience and attempting to organize their knowledge more efficiently and coherently. This effort is apparent in one of Piaget's observations:

> At 25 months and 13 days, Jacqueline wanted to see a little hunchbacked neighbor whom she used to meet on her walks. A few days earlier she had asked why he had a hump, and after I had explained she said: "Poor boy, he's ill, he has a hump." The day before Jacqueline had also wanted to go and see him, but he had influenza, which Jacqueline called "being ill in bed." We started out for our walk and on the way Jacqueline said: "Is he still ill in bed?"—[I replied] "No. I saw him this morning, he isn't in bed now." [To which Jacqueline said]—"He hasn't a big hump now." (Piaget, 1951, p. 231)

In this example, Jacqueline draws her own conclusions from the conversation, given her current knowledge and understanding. When knowledge is limited, such conclusions may seem odd to an adult.

The idea of activity and constructivism implies that everyone, whether young or grown, will see the world in somewhat different terms. This idea was expressed by the African-American writer Zora Neale Hurston in her writing about her childhood:

> Nothing that God ever made is the same to more than one person. That is natural. There is no single face in nature, because every eye that looks upon it, sees it from its own angle. So every man's spice-box seasons his own food. . . . Naturally, I picked up reflections of life around me with my own instruments, and absorbed what I gathered according to my inside juices. (Hurston, 1942/1991, p. 45)

The assumption that children are active constructivists has important implications for education, especially in early childhood. Piagetians assume that cognitive growth will occur best when children are allowed to explore and act on their environment. They sometimes argue that when you teach children specific skills, you remove the opportunity for them to invent knowledge on their own.

Organization and Adaptation. The two basic principles guiding human development, in Piaget's view, are organization and adaptation. In order to appreciate the human capacity for organization, consider the drawing shown in Figure 5.1. Many people see a vase or a goblet, but you can also see profiles of two people. What you see depends on how you organize the stimulus.

Piaget proposed that the tendency to organize experience is a basic human

FIGURE 5.1 This figure can be seen as a vase or as two people facing each other.

characteristic. Not only do people organize their perceptual experience into figures that are important or meaningful to them; they also organize categories into more abstract categories, facts into explanations, and seemingly contradictory beliefs into more integrated ones. The most important effect of this overall tendency to mental organization, according to Piaget, is that human thought becomes more powerfully adapted to the environment as it becomes more organized. In using the concept of adaptation, Piaget was speaking from his biological training and emphasizing that intelligence should be seen as one of the most distinctive and important characteristics of the human species, an aspect of our biological endowment that has helped to ensure survival.

Cognitive Structures. Piaget argued that children form cognitive "structures" as a result of the interaction between maturation and experience. As we see in greater detail shortly, the sensorimotor schemes formed in infancy are the child's initial organizational structures. But after about age 2, according to Piaget, the child's cognitive structures are internal—or mental—structures. One important cognitive structure is the **operation**, an action that the child performs mentally and that is *reversible*, that is, that can be performed in reverse, allowing the person to return mentally to the beginning of the thought sequence. Planning a series of moves in a game of checkers or chess and then mentally retracing one's steps to the beginning of the sequence is an operation. Squaring the number 2 to get 4 is an operation; so is extracting the square root of 4 to obtain 2. Similarly, 8 stones can be divided into subgroups of various sizes—for example, 4 and 4, 7 and 1, or 6 and 2—and recombined into a single set.

Assimilation and Accommodation. As we have seen, Piaget viewed human cognition as a specific form of biological adaptation in which a complex organism adapts to a complex environment. Humans continuously interact with the environment, organizing what they experience and forming new organizational structures in response to new experiences. This process of adaptation occurs through two complementary processes: *assimilation* and *accommodation*.

Assimilation refers to the individual's "efforts to deal with the environment by making it fit into the organism's own existing structures—by incorporating it" (Donaldson, 1978, p. 140). New objects or ideas are understood by interpreting them using ideas or concepts that were previously acquired. A 5-year-old who has a concept of birds as living things that fly and have beaks and wings will assimilate an ostrich that she sees at the zoo to her concept of bird. She may, however, be a little bothered by the size of the ostrich (larger than her concept of bird) and by learning that the ostrich does not fly. Her discomfort about whether or not the ostrich is a bird puts her in what Piaget termed a state of *disequilibrium.*

Accommodation, the complement of assimilation, occurs when the qualities of the environment do not fit existing concepts well. Through accommodation, concepts are changed in response to environmental demands. The 5-year-old may accommodate to her new information about the ostrich by changing her concept of bird—for instance, she may decide that not all birds fly. She may also form a new concept, ostrich, that is different from her concept of bird.

As a result of accommodation, our 5-year-old will be in a temporary state of **equilibrium** or cognitive balance. Her concepts and her experience match reasonably well. Piaget assumed that all organisms strive for equilibrium. When cognitive balance is disturbed—for example, when something new is encountered—the processes of assimilation and accommodation function to reestablish it. Establishing equilibrium is sometimes called **equilibration**.

Assimilation and accommodation almost always occur together. The child first attempts to understand a new experience by using old ideas and solutions (assimilation); when these do not work, the child is forced to change his or her structure or understanding of the world (accommodation).

Although all adaptive behavior contains some elements of assimilation and accommodation, the proportions of each vary from one activity to another. The make-believe play of young children is an example of behavior that is almost entirely assimilative because the children are not very much concerned with the objective characteristics of their playthings. A piece of wood may be used as a doll, a ship, or a wall, depending on the game being played. By contrast, imitation is mainly accommodation; children shape actions to fit a model in their environment.

The extremes of disequilibrium become less frequent over time because people have more concepts and structures in their repertoires and confront completely new situations less often. Adults are unlikely to encounter a zoo animal that does not fit into some category they already know. An unfamiliar animal will be similar to some familiar ones; only minor modifications of the existing categories for animals are required. However, the processes of equilibration and adaptation function throughout our lives as we adapt our behavior to changing circumstances.

Developmental Stages

Piaget proposed that development proceeds discontinuously in a sequence of four qualitatively distinct stages: (1) the *sensorimotor stage* (0 to 18 months); (2) the *preoperational stage* (18 months to 7 years); (3) the *concrete operational stage* (7 to 12 years); and (4) the *formal operational stage* (12 years and over). The transition from one stage to the next entails a fundamental reorganization of the way the individual constructs (or reconstructs) and interprets the world. That is, when children pass from one stage to another they acquire qualitatively new ways of understanding their world. For example, an infant in the sensorimotor stage is said to have a sensorimotor scheme as a concept for balls—they are round objects that you can hold,

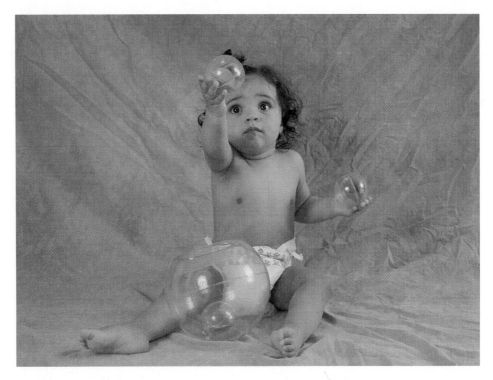

Piaget sees the infant as in a sensorimotor stage, in which, for example, balls are thought of in terms of their ability to be held, thrown, and bounced.

throw, and bounce. By 5 or 6 years, children may conceive of balls as part of a game, such as baseball, or pretend that a ball is some other object, such as an airplane. They can arrange six balls in order from small to large or from light to dark.

Piaget believed that the sequence of stages is invariant; that is, all normal children go through the stages in the same order. No child skips from the preoperational stage to the formal operational stage without going through the stage of concrete operations. This is because each stage builds on and derives from the accomplishments of the previous one. At each stage new, different, more adaptive cognitive capabilities are added to what has previously been achieved.

Although the order in which the stages emerge does not vary, there are wide individual differences in the speed with which children pass through them. Hence, the ages associated with the various stages are approximations or averages. Some children reach a particular stage early, others considerably later.

The Sensorimotor Stage. Cognitive growth during the sensorimotor stage is based primarily on sensory experiences and motor actions. Beginning with actions that are primarily reflexes, the infant advances through six substages in which behavior becomes increasingly flexible and goal oriented. We describe the characteristics of this stage more fully in the next section, after describing the remaining stages in development.

The Preoperational Stage. Between about 18 months and 2 years, the transition from the sensorimotor stage to the preoperational stage occurs. The hallmark of this transition is mental representation: the child acquires the ability to think about objects and events that are not present in the immediate environment—to represent them in mental pictures, sound, images, words, or other forms. The new ability allows children to move beyond the here and now—for example, to understand fully that objects still exist when you cannot see them.

Piaget saw several behaviors beginning between 18 and 24 months as evidence for the newly formed capacity for mental representation. Children begin to show delayed imitation, that is, the ability to imitate a behavior they observed some time ago. They begin to be able to search for objects even after a delay, thus showing mental representation of location. They begin to play symbolically, that is, to let one object stand for another, as for example, a block for a person. Perhaps most important, the increasing acquisition of words represents a very powerful use of symbols. The preoperational stage is discussed more fully in Chapter 7.

Concrete Operations. Some time between 6 and 8 years of age, children enter the stage of concrete operations. (You will recall that an *operation* is a basic cognitive structure that is used to transform information, or "operate" on it.) One achievement that is characteristic of this stage is the ability to engage in mental operations that are flexible and fully reversible. For example, children understand that subtracting a few pennies from a jar of pennies can be reversed by adding the same number of pennies to the jar.

Piaget believed that a wide variety of cognitive tasks require thinking at the level of concrete operations. These tasks include: (1) the ability to understand when quantities remain unchanged after something is done to them, as for example, the ability to understand that the amount of material in a ball of clay stays the same when the ball is rolled out; (2) the ability to arrange a group of objects in order along a dimension, as for example, to arrange a set of sticks in order from shortest to longest; (3) the ability to understand the relation between a set of objects and the larger category to which that set belongs. A full discussion of concrete operations can be found in Chapter 9.

Formal Operations. Concrete operational children are restricted to the here and now. They can reason well about things that are physically present but have difficulty with abstractions or hypothetical propositions. In the most advanced stage of cognitive development, which begins at about age 12 and extends through adulthood, the limitations of the concrete operational stage are overcome. The child develops the ability to reason about hypothetical problems—about what might be—as well as about real problems, and to think about possibilities as well as actualities. Adolescents' cognitive development is discussed more fully in Chapter 14.

The Sensorimotor Period

Sensorimotor Schemes. In Piaget's view, the central way of knowing in infancy is in terms of the **sensorimotor scheme**. This is a representation of a class of sensory or motor actions used to attain a goal. For example, the actions of holding, touching, and throwing are the child's scheme for balls or perhaps for round objects. Some important sensorimotor schemes are grasping, throwing, sucking, banging, and kicking.

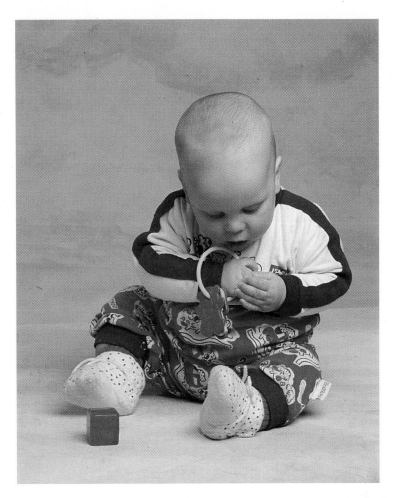

Another example of sensorimotor intelligence. This baby is learning about his toy by putting his hand through it. Later, he may see what happens if he shakes it, throws it, or puts it in his mouth.

Piaget claimed that infants acquire knowledge about objects through their actions with them. For example, children learn about their fingers by clasping and sucking them, and they learn about mobiles by tracking and kicking them. This knowledge is acquired through a sequence of stages, which together make up what Piaget termed the **sensorimotor period**.

According to Piaget, this first major stage of intellectual development occupies the first 18 to 24 months of life. Throughout this period, intelligence is manifested in action, but there are also important changes in infants' intelligence that take place during these stages. We trace two sequences of development to illustrate the nature of the theory.

Problem Solving. During the first two years, infants progress from automatic reflexes to inventing new ways to solve problems. They begin with reflexes, including crying, sucking, and orienting themselves toward sounds. Soon they go beyond these reflexes and develop *primary circular reactions,* in which they repeat actions that initially occur accidentally. For example, a hungry baby may accidentally brush his fingers against his lips and then repeat the action, a pattern that is not an inborn reflex. Around 6 months of age infants develop *secondary circular reactions,* in which they repeat actions that create interesting sights and sounds—making bells ring on a crib, for example. At this point they become interested in the effects of their actions on their environment rather than focusing just on their own bodily responses.

Near the end of the first year, children show increased ability to coordinate schemes to reach a goal. For instance, they will set aside an obstacle in order to reach a desired object, rather than picking up whatever they come to first. After about 12 months they form *tertiary circular reactions,* in which they vary their actions rather than repeating them, while observing their effects on the environment—almost as if they were systematically exploring the properties of objects. A 15-month-old will throw a ball, then push on it, then bang it on a surface—each time observing the sounds it makes or how soft it is.

In the last stage, children invent new schemes through a kind of mental exploration in which they imagine certain events and outcomes. An 18-month-old who wants to reach a light switch that is too high will look back and forth between the light switch and a chair, then suddenly pull the chair over to the light switch, stand on it, and turn on the light. Behavior of this kind, which occurs later during the second year, represents the final stage of the sensorimotor period. By this point, infants do not solve problems through trial-and-error explorations; instead they engage in "internal experimentation, an inner exploration of ways and means" (from Flavell, 1963). Piaget gives a vivid illustration:

> At one year, six months, for the first time Lucienne plays with a doll carriage whose handle comes to the height of her face. She rolls it over the carpet by pushing it. When she comes against a wall, she pulls, walking backward. But as this position is not convenient for her, she pauses and without hesitation goes to the other side to push the carriage again. She therefore found the procedure in one attempt, apparently through analogy to other situations but without training, apprenticeship, or chance. (Quoted in Flavell, 1963)

Object Permanence. Piaget made some ingenious observations of the development of what he called the concept of **object permanence**—the belief that objects continue to exist even when they are out of sight. During the first 2 or 3 months of life, children will follow an object visually until it passes out of their line of sight and then abandon their search for it. From 3 to 6 months, vision and movement of arms and hands become coordinated. At this age infants grab for objects they can see, but they do not reach for objects outside their immediate visual field. Piaget interprets the failure to search for hidden objects as indicating that children do not realize that the hidden objects still exist.

At about 9 months of age, children advance a step further. They reach for an object that is hidden from view if they have watched it being hidden. Thus, a child who watches an adult place a toy under a blanket will search for the toy there. Piaget argued, however, that a 9-month-old's knowledge of the location of an object is contained in the actions (or sensorimotor schemes) used in reaching for it previously. He based this conclusion on a very interesting error he observed infants of about this age make in hiding tasks, called the *A–not B error.* When an object has been hidden several times at one location (called location A) and it is then hidden at a second location (called location B), infants at this stage look for the object at location A (not B). They act as if the object and its location are defined by the motoric actions they have associated with obtaining it.

Piaget argued that it is not until infants no longer display the A–not B error that they truly have a conception of a permanent object independent of their own action. By 18 months or so, they do have such a conception of the permanent object. Not only can they avoid the A–not B error; they can even track where an object must be after a series of moves during which the object is never in view, as when a hand reaches under a cover and, closed, moves to several hiding places in succession before emerging open and visibly empty. This requires mental representation of the nonvisible object and its movements.

Piaget's theory of cognitive development is a monumental achievement. Nevertheless, it should not be regarded as the definitive word on cognitive development. Subsequent research has modified or called into question some of Piaget's hypotheses. For instance, his focus on infant action, on the "motor" part of the sensorimotor world of the infant, may have been overdone. Infants learn as much through their senses and by observation as they do through action. In the next section, we examine recent research on infant abilities.

✪ NEW EVIDENCE ON INFANT COGNITION

In the past 20 or 25 years, some very exciting work has been done on infant cognitive development. Developmental psychologists have been inspired, partly by Piaget, to look closely at the capabilities of babies. In doing so, they have uncovered some observations that challenge Piaget or that give new interpretations to his observations. They have studied phenomena he was not able to consider, given his methodology of relatively unstructured observation of infant behavior. The purpose of this section is to present some of the evidence gathered to date on the basic cognitive abilities of infants, on what babies know and how they think.

Object Permanence

The A–not B error and the whole concept of object permanence, discussed at the end of the section on Piaget, have been the focus of considerable research and controversy. Many investigators of infant behavior have thought that infants have a conception of objects as permanent considerably earlier than Piaget argued, and that their problems on tasks such as A–not B stem from other problems.

Evidence that infants do remember the existence of hidden objects has come, in particular, from experiments by Renee Baillargeon. For instance, Baillargeon, Spelke, and Wasserman (1985) showed infants of 5 months a display in which a screen moved back and forth, lying flat on a table at one end of its repeated motion. Once the infants had habituated to this (that is, had stopped looking at it as much as they had at first), a box was inserted into the path of the rotating screen (see Figure 5.2). Babies then saw one of two events. In one event, the screen continued to move as before, lying flat on the table as it moved back. Such an event is physically impossible if one continues to remember the existence of the box, because the screen would hit the box. In the other event, the screen stopped moving where it would hit the box, the natural and expected event if one remembers the continued existence of the box. The babies seeing the impossible event looked at the display much more than the group seeing the possible event. These data suggest that children as young as 5 months *do* in fact continue to remember the existence of hidden objects.

FIGURE 5.2 A diagram showing the procedure in Baillargeon, Spelke, and Wasserman's study. At the left, the baby habituates to a screen moving back and forth in an arc. Following habituation, babies look more at an impossible event (middle) in which a box is placed on the table and the screen then appears to move through it than they do at a possible event (right) in which a box is placed on the table and the screen stops when it reaches the box.

If babies do remember the continued existence of hidden objects, one may reasonably ask why they make mistakes on the A–not B task. Recent findings suggest that the error has more to do with the limited (but gradually increasing) ability of infants in the second half of the first year of life to resist acting on a habit (the habit of reaching to A) than with their conceptions of the nature of objects and their locations. Diamond (1985) reported that infants in this age range showed a very regular relation between likelihood of producing the A–not B error and the delay the experimenter imposed between hiding the object and allowing the infant to look for it. Infants of 7.5 months showed the error with about 2-second delays; by 12 months, delays of over 10 seconds were needed to produce the error (see Figure 5.3). At each age, shorter delays resulted in correct performance, while longer delays resulted in random or frustrated behavior.

Diamond's interpretation of this pattern is that infants in this age range have a memory for the object and its location, but they also have difficulty inhibiting action based on habit. When memory is strong relative to habit (as is true at short delays), correct performance results. When habit is strong relative to memory (as delay lengthens), one sees the A–not B error. The ability to inhibit habits increases with age, and hence the delay that can be tolerated in the A–not B task lengthens. This change in inhibition may be linked to maturation of the frontal lobes of the brain (see Diamond, 1990).

The work by Baillargeon and by Diamond suggests an answer for the riddle of Seth's behavior with the rattle, which we considered at the beginning of the chapter. It seems likely that Seth does know that his rattle exists and that he even knows where it is. What may well pose a problem at his age is understanding and remembering the means of retrieving it (i.e., pulling on the string). In fact, Piaget was one of the first to note that infants have difficulty with constructing means-ends sequences, as we have seen in discussing his analysis of changes in infants' problem solving.

Memory and Representation

Memory processes are vital to thought. To appreciate this fact, imagine that every few seconds your mind went completely blank and whatever train of thought you were following was lost and you had to begin again. It would hardly be possible to deal

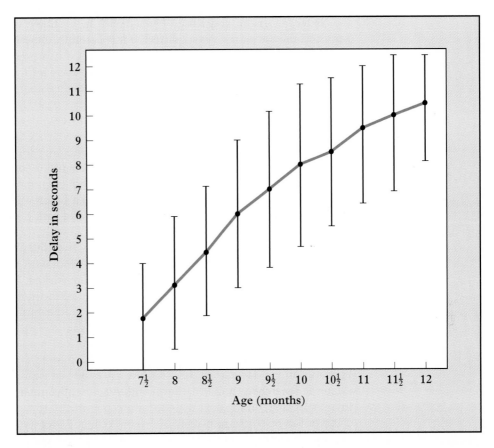

FIGURE 5.3 Delay at which the A–not B error occurs at different ages. With increasing age, longer delays are needed to show the error. After "Development of the Ability to Use Recall to Guide Action, As Indicated by Infants' Performance, on AB," by A. Diamond, 1985, *Child Development, 56*, p. 876. Copyright © 1985 by Child Development. Adapted by permission.

very adaptively with problems! Or imagine that you had no long-term memory for information and couldn't recall people's names and faces, or how to perform arithmetic operations, or the like. Again, the degree of impairment would be profound.

In considering whether or not infants can remember things, it is useful to distinguish different kinds of memory. One difference psychologists have emphasized is that between **recognition memory** and **recall memory**. In recognition, a person remembers that a present stimulus was experienced in the past. For instance, when you see a person, you remember that you met him before. In recall, no relevant stimulus is present and the person must retrieve the memory (e.g., bring to mind the image of a face). Thus, true-false questions on an examination require recognition, whereas essays require recall memory.

Infants appear to have fairly impressive recognition memory abilities from early in life. This ability is generally assessed in visual comparison tasks, where infants are shown a stimulus and then shown two stimuli, one old and the other new. The stimuli are carefully chosen so that, when both are new, babies don't prefer one to the other. If a preference is shown when one stimulus has been seen before, psychologists conclude that the preference is based on recognition memory for the previously presented pattern.

Slater, Morison, and Rose (1983, 1984) have shown that even newborns will acquire a memory for a visual pattern if it is carefully chosen to be visually discriminable from another pattern (see Chapter 4) and if it is presented for long enough. By the age of 3 months, infants' visual capacities have improved and they are easier to test, and many studies have shown that immediate recognition memory for visual patterns is quite robust (J. S. Werner & Perlmutter, 1979). Recognition memory can be demonstrated for some stimuli even after two weeks have passed (Fagan, 1973).

Another kind of memory that has been extensively studied in infants, especially by Carolyn Rovee-Collier and her associates, is memory for conditioned responses. Such memories go a bit beyond standard recognition paradigms because they involve presenting infants with a stimulus (a mobile hanging above their crib) that must not only be recognized as having been seen before but in response to which the infant must retrieve a response (the fact that a kick of the foot will cause this particular mobile to move).

In one experiment, 3-month-old infants saw two different mobiles (at different times). One of the mobiles was tied to the infant's foot with a satin string. When that mobile was present, it moved whenever the infant kicked. But if the infant kicked when the other mobile was present, no movement of the mobile occurred. Gradually the infants learned to kick in the presence of one mobile but not the other.

Three weeks later the babies were visited again to see if they remembered the difference between the two mobiles. If an infant had not seen the mobiles during the three-week delay, it forgot that kicking made mobile 1 move but not mobile 2. However, if one day earlier (i.e., 20 days after the last exposure to the mobiles) the infant had watched mobile 1 move, without the movement being produced by the infant's kicking, on the next day the baby remembered to kick in response to mobile 1 but not in response to mobile 2 (Fagen, Yengo, Rovee-Collier, & Enright, 1981). A series of similar experiments suggests that the association between the stimulus of a mobile and the act of kicking is forgotten after one or two weeks. However, if the infant sees the mobile prior to being tested, the association appears to be reactivated and there is less forgetting (see Davis & Rovee-Collier, 1983; Rovee-Collier, Sullivan, Enright, Lucas, & Fagen, 1980).

The capacity for recall is much more difficult to study in infants than recognition memory. It appears to be enhanced after 6 or 8 months of age. As we have seen, for instance, the ability to remember the location of an object appears to increase steadily in the second half of the first year (Diamond, 1985). This is also the age when infants begin to anticipate their mother's positive reaction when the two are in close, face-to-face interaction, and to act so as to invite the mother to respond (Cohn & Tronick, 1987).

One method of studying recall in infants is through *delayed imitation*. That is, an infant is shown an action or a series of actions not in his or her existing repertoire of actions and, after a delay, is presented with the materials or the situation in which the actions can be performed. If the child imitates the actions, it can be argued that the child has brought to mind, or recalled, a representation of the actions modeled. In fact, delayed imitation was first analyzed in this way by Piaget, who thought that it did not appear until around 18 months of age. He used this observation to argue that representation did not occur until that age.

As we have already seen with object permanence, however, Piaget may have underestimated children's abilities. The following vignette illustrates the point:

> It was during the blustery days of last March that 10-month-old Russell Ruud taught the other babies in his day-care group a lesson their parents

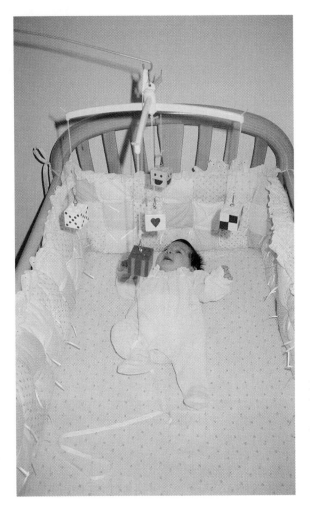

Infants will look with great attention at crib mobiles. Carolyn Rovee-Collier has shown that they will also remember if they are able to control the mobile's motion and will distinguish the mobile they can control from ones that they can't control.

may have wished he hadn't: how to unzip the Velcro chin straps of their winter hats. "One day I went to pick Russell up and his teacher told me that the other mothers were complaining that their children had learned from him how to take off their hats," said Dr. Judith Ruud, Russell's mother. . . . "I never showed Russell how to unzip the Velcro. . . . He learned it by trial and error, and the other kids saw him do it one day when they were getting dressed for an outing." (Goleman, 1993, p. C10)

Systematic research confirms this anecdote. In one study, Meltzoff (1988) showed 9-month-olds three novel actions. Even after 24 hours, they showed evidence of delayed imitation of these actions.

Thus current research indicates that infants can recognize stimuli well, probably from birth and certainly from 3 months. They also retain memory for how to achieve desired ends in the world (and the situations in which these responses will work) from a very early age. The ability to recall information may not be present initially, but it does seem to be available by the second 6 months of life. The overall picture of the infant's world gained from this research is one in which infants are less bound to their immediate perceptual and motoric world than Piaget thought.

Categories

The ability to group things in the world into categories is another vital aspect of human cognition. A **category** is usually defined as a mental representation of the dimensions that are shared by a set of similar, but not identical, stimuli or events. The shared dimensions can be physical features like size and color or actions like eating and throwing. Later in development the shared dimensions can be ideas like good, bad, justice, and beauty.

Categorization allows us to make predictions and generalizations, to anticipate what properties a new thing will have. Again, to appreciate the importance of this aspect of cognition, imagine for an instant a world in which everything you saw was new, an entity unto itself. When you saw a cat, you could observe its size, color, furriness, and so on, but you would have no way of knowing (without experimentation) what it might do, what it might eat, where it might live, and so on. It would be almost impossible to function in a world like this.

Given the importance of categorization to human thought, developmental psychologists have been very interested in the questions of when children begin to form categories and what their early categories are like. From the age of 2 or 3 months, infants show increased attention to things and events that are "somewhat different" from those encountered in the past, and less attention to things and events that are either very familiar or very novel. These "somewhat different" events can be called *discrepant events.* The recruitment of attention to such discrepant events implies that infants can create categories.

One process that may be involved in the formation of concepts by young infants is *prototype formation.* A prototype is the most representative member of a concept. For instance, sparrows and robins are prototypical birds, while ostriches and penguins are not.

When adults see a series of patterns, all based on a prototypical pattern, they regard the prototype as something they have seen before (even when they haven't). This shows that they have formed a prototype. A study by Bomba and Siqueland (1983) shows that infants as young as 3 months do the same. The infants were shown dot patterns based on distortions of a prototype. (In Figure 5.4, the three patterns on the right are distortions of the patterns on the left.) After they had habituated to the patterns, they remained bored by the prototype, even though they had never seen it before.

Another important process in category formation is attending to the *correlations* among particular characteristics. For instance, a beaver has a flat tail and also strong teeth, and these two attributes are strongly correlated and part of what adults use in categorizing beavers. Again, there is some evidence that infants attend to correlations among attributes, at least by the age of 10 months. This is shown by a study by Younger and Cohen (1983). They showed babies imaginary animals in which a particular kind of body always went with a particular kind of tail. Following habituation, the infants were shown an animal that had a body and a tail not previously combined. Even though both the body and the tail were familiar (and boring), the infants showed dishabituation to the novel combination.

Particular controversy has raged around the question of whether young children (and especially, infants) categorize objects in the world simply by co-occurrence (what are sometimes called *thematic* relations). For instance, a monkey and a banana are linked thematically. Adults prefer, of course, to group objects *taxonomically,* that is, by conceptual similarities. A monkey and a bear are related taxonomically. To examine this question, Bauer and Mandler (1989) asked children 1 year in age to

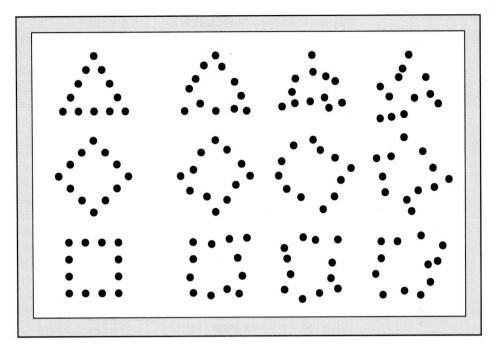

FIGURE 5.4 The figures at the left are prototypical triangles, diamonds, and squares. The other figures are, from left to right, increasingly large distortions of the prototypes. From "The Nature and Structure of Infant Form Categories," by P. C. Bomba and E. R. Siqueland, 1983, *Journal of Experimental Child Psychology, 35,* p. 302. Copyright © 1983 by Journal of Experimental Child Psychology. Reprinted by permission.

look at three objects. They pointed to one (e.g., a monkey) and asked the child to point to the one that was like that one. The children were more likely to point to the taxonomically related object (e.g., a bear) than to the thematically related one (e.g., a banana).

In summary, infants show surprising abilities to categorize. They abstract prototypes as early as 3 months, they notice correlated attributes as early as 10 months, and they make taxonomic groupings rather than thematic ones as early as 12 months. However, we should not leave the impression that infant concepts resemble adult ones exactly. For instance, children of 12 months may consider "balls" to be "things that can roll," and include round candles or round coin banks in this category (Mervis, 1987). Or they may deny that a child who is the brother of your mother could possibly be an "uncle" because he is not an adult, as uncles usually are (Keil, 1989). Nevertheless, by the end of the first year, children do have a firm initial grasp on the category structure of the world.

The picture of the infant's world coming from recent research differs from that advocated by Piaget. The child is now seen as engaging in more perceptual analysis and internal representation than Piaget imagined and as less dominated by action-defined categories.

Perception of Objects

What is an object? To an adult, the answer is so self-evident as to be almost unanswerable. But consider for a moment what the world might look like to an infant.

We saw in the previous chapter that infants can see in color, scan areas of high contrast, and improve in visual acuity and ability to see depth. But such information does not do a complete job of telling us what the infant's visual experience is like. For us as adults, to see is to see a world divided into objects, apparently without effort. We do not pause to consider whether the coffee cup is or is not attached to the desk on which it rests; we see the objects as naturally and obviously distinct. But do infants have the same experience? It might be that familiarity with cups and desks would be required to see them as distinct objects. Piaget's description of infant cognition as action-based would certainly suggest that young infants, who have difficulty grasping and interacting with the world of objects, would not see the world as composed of distinct objects in the absence of experience.

Recent research suggests, however, that infants too young to grasp with their hands do nevertheless see the world as organized into objects. Their grouping of their visual experience into objects derives from seeing objects as having parts that move together (Kellman & Spelke, 1983). Infants were shown a rod moving back and forth behind a block (see Figure 5.5). After habituating to this display, they were shown either a complete rod moving back and forth or two parts of the rod moving back and forth. They looked more at the two rods, suggesting that they were expecting to see a single rod. Surprisingly, however, infants do *not* seem to perceive connected objects when the separated parts share color—with edges aligned—and have a simple and regular shape. Common movement seemed absolutely necessary for object grouping.

BOX 5.1
WHAT IS A BABY'S WORLD REALLY LIKE?

Much of the research in this chapter is dedicated to answering the question of what the baby's world is like. It turns out that, in many ways, the baby's world is more like the world of an adult than one might have imagined. But it also must be different, in ways that researchers do not typically examine . . . such as scale!

Here is a whimsical look at this issue. These are the lyrics to a song called "In My World," written by Kathy Hirsh-Pasek, a researcher interested in language and infant auditory processing who is also one of two leading figures in Kamotion, a children's music group.

In my world, the
Paddington Bear is bigger,
Than anyone else I know of.
'Cept my mommy and my daddy,
And the crib that I sleep in,
And the floor that I play on,
And my chest of drawers.

All bigger than me.
All bigger than I.
All bigger than me, than I, than me,
Than I, than me,
So there.

In my house, the
Mickey Mouse is bigger,
Than anyone else I know of.
'Cept my mommy and my daddy,
And the crib that I sleep in,
And the floor that I play on,
And my chest of drawers.

All bigger than me.
All bigger than I.
All bigger than me, than I, than me,
Than I, than me,
So there. . . .

Source: "What Is a Baby's World Really Like?" by Kathy Hirsh-Pasek and Mona Goldman Zakheim. Copyright © 1987 by Kathy Hirsh-Pasek and Mona Goldman Zakheim. Reprinted by permission of the authors.

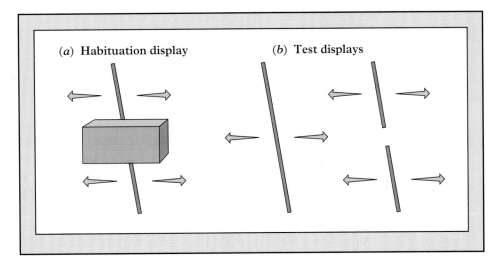

FIGURE 5.5 The displays used by Kellman and Spelke (1983). Babies are habituated to a rod moving back and forth behind a block (left). Looking times are then observed for one of two test displays (right). From "Perception of Partly Occluded Objects in Infancy," by P. J. Kellman and E. S. Spelke, 1983, *Cognitive Psychology, 15,* pp. 483–524. Copyright © 1983 by P. J. Kellman and E. S. Spelke. Reprinted by permission.

This research suggests that infants start out their task of learning about the world equipped to perceive separate coherent objects that move as units independently of each other. They do not need to act on these entities to perceive them in this way. However, they do need to learn through observation that continuous color and texture, simple form, and the like are also good indicators of objecthood.

An Emerging New View

We have discussed several ways in which current research has indicated that Piaget was "wrong" about such matters as whether young infants have a concept of a permanent object, mentally represent their world, and have a system of categories or an ability to perceive objects independent of physical action. It would be a mistake, however, to conclude that Piaget's theory as a whole is "wrong" and that some entirely new theory is therefore "right." Rather, several core insights of Piaget's are still valid, while others need modification.

Let us reconsider the major themes in Piaget's work we discussed at the beginning of the chapter, in light of the research we have reviewed. Nothing in the new work compels us to abandon a view of cognitive development as the interactive product of biology and experience, of the child as an active constructor of her world, or of human beings as having organized adaptations in which cognitive equilibrium is sought. Rather, the new work has questioned a particular account of the early stages of life, in which the infant is endowed with very little initially except reflexes and in which development is heavily dependent on physical interaction with the world. Infants seem to come equipped with capabilities considerably more sophisticated than reflexes and to learn through internal processing of sensory and perceptual information, as well as through physical interaction.

⚙ ASSESSING INFANT INTELLIGENCE

People have long been interested in how to determine the cognitive capacities of infants. Parents want to know, "How smart is my baby?" and anxiously monitor the baby's behavior for signs. Applied developmentalists and pediatricians would like a way to identify which babies are at risk for later intellectual problems, in the hope that early intervention would help avert those problems. Theoretically oriented psychologists would like to know what aspects of infant behavior relate to later intelligence because such knowledge might help to clarify what intelligence is and how it develops.

The first attempts to measure infant intelligence involved tests that measure infants' relative progress on behaviors such as vocalizing, making a stack of blocks, and imitating an adult. One well-known scale of this type is called the Bayley Scale of Infant Development, after Nancy Bayley, the psychologist who developed it. The Bayley Scale is the most fully standardized and widely used instrument for assessing infants' developmental status. It contains separate scales to measure mental and psychomotor development. The mental scales include vocalizing and imitating the action of an adult; the motor scales include grasping objects and rolling a ball. This is because, for many children, development proceeds at different rates in different domains. Thus, a child who is advanced in motor development may not be advanced in language development.

However, scores on tests such as the Bayley Scales have not been found to relate very highly to intelligence as measured on standard intelligence tests given in childhood or adulthood (Kopp & McCall, 1982). The low correlation may be because the time when behaviors such as vocalizing appear is basically maturationally determined. Nevertheless, while very few people still describe these scales as measures of intelligence, infant development scales remain useful for identifying potential developmental delays, particularly among high-risk infants. For example, among a group of premature and full-term infants, scores on the Bayley Scale were modestly related to later performance on intelligence and language tests in the preschool years (Siegel, 1979). Although children with serious mental retardation and delays in motor development would probably be identified without the test, it may detect less obvious problems and detect them earlier than a physician or parent might. If helpful interventions are begun early, they often are more effective than they can be later, when a problem has already become serious.

Recently, new tests have been developed that seem to be more successful at predicting later intelligence. One new kind of assessment involves examining individual differences in *habituation*. That is, when shown a repeated stimulus, some babies become bored with it much more quickly than others. Rapid habituation may be related to speed and efficiency of information processing. A second new kind of assessment, developed and standardized as an infant test by Joseph Fagan (1990), involves *recognition memory*. Infants are tested to see whether they look longer at a novel stimulus after being exposed to a familiar one, and differences among babies in the strength of this novelty preference are observed. Such tests may tap the infants' memory, their ability to analyze differences between stimuli, and their preference for novel information. There is now a substantial literature on these two procedures, which shows that both are successful in predicting scores on IQ tests in childhood. That is, infants who rapidly habituate to a repeated stimulus, or who show long periods of fixation to the novel member of a pair of stimuli, have higher IQs several years later (McCall & Carriger, 1993). These provocative findings are attracting many investigators and are being used with increasing frequency to predict children's future IQs.

⚙ SUMMARY

Scientists who wish to measure and conceptualize cognitive processes face three basic dilemmas: the extent to which thought can be inferred from behavior, the distinction between competence and performance, and broad versus narrow definitions of competence. Theorists disagree on whether and to what extent we can infer unobservable thoughts from observed behavior. Strict behaviorists assert that observable behavior is psychologists' only legitimate concern. On the other hand, many psychologists want to know about the events that take place inside children's heads. Most researchers use observable behavior as the main criterion for testing theories.

Competence refers to the knowledge and skills that a child possesses; the demonstration of knowledge and skills in observable problem-solving situations is called performance. Children may possess knowledge that they do not use, even when the occasion calls for it. Sometimes children's performance does not reveal their actual competence because they misunderstand the problems they are asked to solve. Most psychologists favor defining competences somewhat narrowly, partly because this approach permits more precise comparisons between different groups of children.

Piaget assumed that the biological characteristics of the child place some limits on the order and speed at which particular cognitive competences emerge. At the same time, he believed that active experience with the world is critical to cognitive growth. His central thesis is that people are active, curious, and inventive throughout life. Thus children construct their world by imposing order on the information they receive through their senses.

The two basic principles guiding human development, according to Piaget, are organization and adaptation. Children organize their experience into cognitive structures such as the operation, a manipulation of ideas that can be performed in reverse. In interacting with the environment, they adapt those structures in response to new experiences. The process of adaptation occurs through the processes of assimilation (using previously acquired ideas or concepts to understand new ones) and accommodation (modifying existing concepts in response to environmental demands). The result of these processes is a temporary state of equilibrium or cognitive balance.

Piaget proposed that development proceeds discontinuously in a sequence of four stages. The transition from one stage to the next entails a fundamental reorganization of the way the individual constructs and interprets the world. The sequence of stages is invariant because each stage builds on the accomplishments of the previous one. There are, however, individual differences in the speed with which children pass through the stages.

During the sensorimotor stage, cognitive growth is based primarily on sensory experiences and motor actions. Between about 18 months and 2 years, the transition to the preoperational stage occurs. The hallmark of this transition is mental representation, or the ability to think about objects and events that are not present in the immediate environment. The preoperational stage also marks the beginning of the ability to use and manipulate symbols.

Sometime between 6 and 8 years of age, children enter the stage of concrete operations. They become able to engage in mental operations that are flexible and fully reversible, and they can decenter; that is, they can focus on several attributes of an object or event simultaneously. In addition, they shift from relying on perceptual information to using logical principles such as the identity principle and the equivalence principle.

Upon reaching the stage of formal operations, the child uses a wider variety of cognitive operations and strategies in solving problems, is highly versatile and flexible in thought and reasoning, and can see things from a number of perspectives. The child can now manipulate ideas about hypothetical situations and engage in a systematic search for solutions.

Jean Piaget suggested the existence of a mental structure—sensorimotor coordination—that combines a scheme with action. A sensorimotor scheme is a representation of a class of motor actions that is used to attain a goal. According to Piaget, infants acquire knowledge about objects through their actions with them, and this occurs through a sequence of stages that make up the sensorimotor period.

Early in the first year infants progress from automatic reflexes to primary circular reactions, in which they repeat actions that initially occur accidentally. Later they develop secondary circular reactions, in which they repeat actions that create interesting sights and sounds. After about 12 months they form tertiary circular reactions, in which they vary their actions rather than repeating them, while observing their effects on the environment. In the final stage of the sensorimotor period, children invent new schemes by imagining events and outcomes.

Piaget also observed the development of the concept of object permanence—the belief that objects continue to exist even when they are out of sight. He believed that this concept develops as a result of the child's prior interactions with objects. Subsequent research has shown, however, that infants do expect objects to continue to exist when out of sight. Some of infants' difficulties with object-search tasks may derive from their problems inhibiting learned motor responses.

Infants seem to show excellent recognition memory and memory for conditioned responses from quite early in life. Recall may develop later, but by the second 6 months of life, children show an ability to recall stimuli and represent experience. Similarly, while their grouping of the world into categories undergoes considerable change during childhood, some fundamentals are present. In particular, infants abstract prototypes, correlate attributes, and see taxonomic relations by the end of the first year at the latest.

Infants see the world as divided into objects before they can grasp and manipulate objects. However, these groupings are determined by common movement of parts of an object, with color and coherence not leading to object perception, as they do later on.

Traditional tests of infant intelligence, examining simple sensory and motor development, do not predict later intelligence, although they remain useful as screening devices. Recently, individual differences among babies in rapidity of habituation and in preference for novelty have been shown to predict later intelligence.

REVIEW QUESTIONS

1. Briefly describe two basic dilemmas facing scientists who wish to measure and conceptualize cognitive processes.

2. According to Piaget, how do biological maturation and active experience influence cognitive development?

3. What is meant by organization and adaptation? By assimilation and accommodation?

4. Briefly describe the four stages of Piaget's theory of cognitive development.

5. What is an operation?

6. What is meant by object permanence? What does recent research show about the development of object permanence?

7. Describe the development of memory in the infant. Distinguish between recognition memory and recall memory.

8. Describe the nature of infant categorization abilities.

9. What methods have been developed to assess infant intelligence?

CRITICAL THINKING ABOUT THE CHAPTER

1. We have said that there is an emerging new view of cognitive development in infancy. Going back to the themes outlined in Chapter 1, consider to what extent this new view maintains or changes Piaget's position on these questions.

2. Many psychologists feel uneasy about efforts to accelerate infant cognitive development, and they believe that parents, at least middle-class parents in industrialized countries, are often unduly concerned to buy exactly the right mobile or toy for their baby to develop intelligence. Consider how the information about cognitive development presented in this chapter would help you to take a position on this issue.

KEY TERMS

accommodation
assimilation
category
competence
equilibration
equilibrium
object permanence

operation
performance
recall memory
recognition memory
sensorimotor period
sensorimotor scheme

SUGGESTED READINGS

Bremner, J.G. (1994). *Infancy* (2nd ed.). New York: Oxford University Press. A textbook on infant development. Contains current information on topics including cognitive development and also perceptual and socioemotional development.

Mehler, J., & Dupoux, E. (1994). *What infants know: The new cognitive science of early development.* New York: Oxford University Press. An up-to-date treatment of recent experiments, emphasizing the competence of infants to perceive and think about their world.

Siegler, R.S. (1991). *Children's thinking* (2nd ed.). Englewood Cliffs, NJ: Prentice-Hall. Covers theories of cognitive development, including Piaget, and also covers aspects of infant cognition.

Small, M.Y. (1990). *Cognitive development.* San Diego: Harcourt Brace Jovanovich. Covers theories and issues in cognitive development and includes two chapters specifically on infancy.

CHAPTER

6

EMOTIONAL AND SOCIAL DEVELOPMENT IN INFANCY

Betsy and Laurie were shopping with their daughters, both of whom had recently celebrated their first birthdays. The little girls were in strollers festooned with shopping bags as the group proceeded on their way. In the distance, Betsy spotted a strolling figure of the Easter Bunny waving at children and shaking hands. "Look!" she said to Laurie. "What a treat for the girls!" Laurie looked a bit dubious but went on in that direction, following her friend. As the costumed figure loomed closer, Betsy's daughter, Hannah, laughed and waved. "Bunny! Bunny!" she called. Laurie's daughter, Olivia, had a rather uncertain expression, though, and looked rapidly back and forth at the Easter Bunny and her mother. In the end, she burst into tears and struggled to get out of the stroller and into her mother's arms. Hannah, on the other hand, reached out eagerly. When she managed to shake the Easter Bunny's hand, she looked over at her mother with an expression of triumph.

In the last two chapters, we dealt with the physical, perceptual, and cognitive abilities of infants. In this chapter, we go on to consider infants' emotional life and their social ties. Three points illustrated in the opening story form the basis of the three major sections of this chapter. The first point is that infants clearly *have* emotions, although the stimuli that elicit them are sometimes different from those that affect adults. We consider the nature of the infant's feelings, including some of the special fears that can afflict infants. A second theme of the story is that infants differ from each other in their approach to the world. These temperamental differences can be very important to their social interactions and their emotional growth, and the second major section of this chapter considers temperament. Finally, the importance of social relationships and of the special tie that children have with family members is an ingredient of the anecdote. Both Olivia, who looked to her mother for comfort when distressed, and Hannah, who shared with her mother her positive feelings on meeting the Easter Bunny, were showing clearly the importance of the relationship that they had formed with their mothers. The third part of this chapter is devoted to discussing attachment relationships in infancy.

✸ EMOTION IN INFANCY

The Meaning of Emotion

In everyday conversation the word **emotion** refers to conscious awareness of a specific change in internal feeling tone. There are at least three elements to this awareness: a specific set of bodily changes, thoughts about what is happening, and thoughts about the events that produced the feeling. For example, a person might have a perception of an increased heart rate, might anticipate being hurt, and might attribute this feeling to the sight of a charging dog. Most people would call the resulting emotional state *fear*.

With young infants, especially those under a year old, it is not possible to assess all components of the emotions we know in adulthood. Lack of language in infancy makes it difficult to know if they are aware of bodily changes such as increased heart rate or if they have thoughts regarding such things as the possibility of being hurt. Thus, developmental psychologists have concentrated on studying the changes in the brain and body of the infant that follow encounters with situations that would lead to an emotion in an adult, such as stimuli that would elicit pain (e.g., an inoculation) or happiness (e.g., social interaction). They have also coded the facial expressions shown by infants in such situations.

Inferring Emotions in Infancy

Changes in facial expression in response to emotionally charged events are universal and are accompanied by changes in the brain and autonomic nervous system (Fox, 1991). Therefore, some scientists use these physiological indicators to infer the existence of specific emotions in infants. For example, 3-month-old infants usually smile when an adult looks down and vocalizes to them; 8-month-olds display a facial expression resembling anger if an adult takes a cookie from them when they

This 4-month-old is watching an interesting visual display while wearing a cap containing leads to monitor brain waves. Infants, like adults, show different patterns of activation in the brain when in different emotional states. Courtesy of Dr. Nathan Fox.

are about to eat it (Stenberg & Campos, 1983). Infants display a range of facial expressions during the opening weeks of life, many of them seemingly similar to adult expressions (W. F. Johnson, Emde, Pannabecker, Stenberg, & Davis, 1982).

One psychologist (Izard, 1982) devised a coding scheme to measure brief changes in infants' facial expressions. Using this scheme, he found that the expressions corresponding to surprise and sadness are present by 4 months of age; the expressions of fear or anger do not appear until 5 to 7 months; and those reflecting shame and shyness do not emerge until 6 to 8 months. Expressions of contempt and guilt are not present until the second year of life.

Emotions displayed in response to the same situation can change over age as the infant begins to interpret the situation differently. Infants between 2 and 19 months old were videotaped as they received a painful (but necessary) inoculation that usually made them cry (Izard, Hembree, Dougherty, & Spizzirri, 1983). Two-to 8-month-olds showed a facial expression of distress, characterized by a round mouth and closed eyes while they were crying. But 8-month-olds showed a facial expression of anger, characterized by a square mouth and open eyes while they were crying.

The smile is the infant's most welcome facial expression. Newborns will smile, but this reaction is sometimes a reflex, often elicited by stroking of the lips or cheeks. Smiling will occur, however, in response to certain sounds even during the first month of age (Wolff, 1987). By 2 months, the smile occurs in response to a wide range of stimuli, especially human faces and voices. The face of a person moving and speaking in front of a 6-week-old is the best way to generate a smile. During the first two months the mother's voice is much more effective than a high-pitched male voice (Wolff, 1987), and after 6 weeks the face is more effective than the voice.

Smiling may occur when the infant recognizes that an event resembles a previously acquired schema. At 3 months, children may smile in response to most human faces because they recognize that the face is similar to a familiar face, perhaps that of a parent. About one month later, at 4 to 5 months, infants begin to laugh (Sroufe & Wunsch, 1972), especially in response to social interaction, visual surprises, and tickling. During the first year, infants are likely to laugh at events imposed upon them—for example, a mother playing peek-a-boo or tickling the child. But after the first birthday infants will smile and laugh at events that they themselves have caused. An 18-month-old puts on an animal costume and laughs, or acts in a mischievous manner and smiles. These reactions appear to be products of a sense of mastery.

Research on adults has distinguished two kinds of smiles: the *felt* smile and the *unfelt* smile (Ekman & Friesen, 1982). The first kind of smile includes movement of a muscle around the eyes, as well as muscles around the mouth. Only the first kind of smile is accompanied by self reports of happiness. Research on 10-month-olds has supported the validity of this distinction in infants. When children were producing felt smiles, they were much more likely to have a pattern of brain activity associated with positive emotion, in which there is more activity in the left frontal part of the brain than in the right frontal part (Fox & Davidson, 1988).

Although cognitive changes account for the onset of smiling and laughing, once children begin to smile, environmental contingencies and reinforcements influence the frequency of smiling. Gewirtz (1965) studied patterns of smiling in infants raised in three different environments in Israel. Institutionalized infants living in residential buildings rarely saw their parents and received routine institutional care. Kibbutz infants were raised in large houses with professional caregivers but were frequently fed and cared for by their mothers during the first year. Family-reared children were raised in apartments by their mothers. Figure 6.1 graphs the frequency of smiling in response to a strange woman's face by infants in these three groups. Frequency of smiling reached a peak a few weeks earlier in the kibbutz- and family-reared infants than in the infants raised in the institution. But for all infants, smiling was most frequent at about 4 months of age. During the following year, however, the children in the institution smiled less frequently, while those in family care maintained a high rate of smiling. The difference is probably due to the fact that family-reared children received more social feedback than those reared in institutions. The similarity in the development of emotions in infants raised in different environments suggests that maturational factors are at work in onset, while later differences in smiling show that emotional expression is also influenced by learning.

As children mature, they begin to interpret and label their feeling states, often using concepts taught by other people. For example, suppose two children are fighting over a toy; a parent takes the toy away, and the children scream loudly. One parent might tell the children they are angry, another might say they are afraid of the punishment that is imminent, and a third might tell them they feel shame for doing something wrong. The children might learn to associate their feelings and the situation with the label "anger," "fear," or "shame." The next time they have the

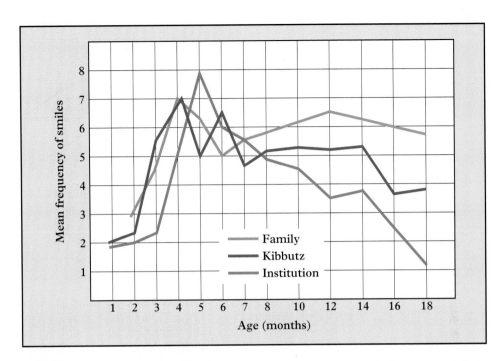

FIGURE 6.1 Frequency of smiling in response to a strange woman's face among infants raised in three different environments in Israel. Smiling begins at about the same time in all settings, but over time, infants in institutions begin to smile less frequently. After "The Cause of Infant Smiling in Four Child-Rearing Environments in Israel," by J. L. Gewirtz, in *Determinants of Infant Behavior, Vol. 3*, edited by B. M. Foss, London: Methuen, 1965. Adapted with permission of the publisher and the Tavistock Institute of Human Relations.

same or similar feelings in a similar situation, they may apply the label they learned earlier.

Fears of Infancy

During the period from about 7 to 12 months, infants develop several distinct fears. While a moderately unfamiliar event usually produces increased interest and, occasionally, excited babbling and smiling, a more discrepant event can lead to uncertainty and fear. For example, an infant may cry if the mother is wearing a hat that makes her look different or if he hears for the first time a human voice coming from the speaker in a tape recorder. The sight of a human figure looking like a large rabbit was enough to cause distress in Olivia in our opening story.

Fear is more likely to occur if an event is unpredictable than if it can be anticipated. Megan Gunnar and her associates demonstrated this in a study in which they varied the predictability of two noise-making mechanical toys (a cymbal-clapping monkey that produced a loud noise and a gun-shooting robot that lit up and made sounds). The predictable toys were active for 4 seconds and then inactive for 4 seconds on a regular schedule. When the toys were unpredictable, they could be on or off for 1 to 7 seconds. Each mother held her 1-year-old infant on her lap facing the toy until the toy had run through one cycle. After that the infants were free to move about the room. The infants who saw the predictable toys were much less fearful than those who were exposed to the unpredictable toys (see Figure 6.2).

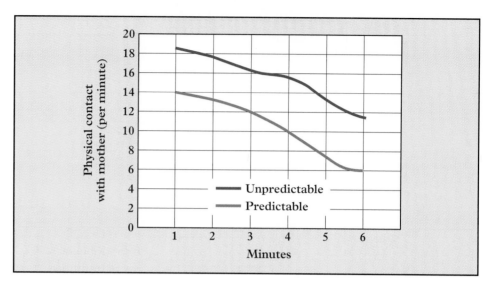

FIGURE 6.2 Infants given an unpredictable toy stayed closer to their mothers than those playing with a predictable one. After "The Effect of Temporal Predictability on the Reactions of One-Year-Olds to Potentially Frightening Toys," by M. R. Gunnar, K. Leighton, and R. Peleaux, 1984, in *Developmental Psychology, 20*, pp. 449–458. Adapted with permission.

Fear of Strangers. One of the most common fears of the last part of the first year is stranger anxiety. An 8-month-old is showing stranger anxiety when she wrinkles her face as a stranger approaches, looks back and forth between the stranger and her mother, and after a few seconds begins to cry. Children do not always react to a stranger with fear. The fear is least likely to occur if the stranger approaches slowly, talks gently, and initiates play with the child; it is most likely if the stranger walks toward the child quickly, is quiet or very loud, and attempts to pick up the child. Although some children are more fearful than others, almost all infants show a fear reaction to a stranger on some occasion between 7 and 12 months of age.

Separation Fear. The fear of temporary separation from a familiar caregiver usually appears between 7 and 12 months of age, peaks between 15 and 18 months, and then gradually declines. Separation fear shows up most clearly when the infant is left in an unfamiliar room or in the presence of an unfamiliar person. It is less likely to occur if the child is left at home or with a familiar relative or baby-sitter. In a typical instance of separation anxiety, a mother tells her 1-year-old, who is playing happily, that she is leaving but will return shortly, and then departs. The child gazes at the door where the mother was last seen and a few seconds later begins to cry.

Separation anxiety is seen in a wide variety of circumstances. Blind 1-year-olds, who cannot see the mother leave, are not protected against it; they cry when they hear the mother leave the room (Fraiberg, 1975). Infants all over the world show signs of separation anxiety somewhere between 8 and 12 months of age (see Figure 6.3). The age at which separation distress appears is very similar for children raised in nuclear families, kibbutzim in Israel, barrios in Guatemala, Indian villages in Central America, and American day-care centers. Although these settings provide different degrees and types of contact with the mother, separation anxiety appears at remarkably similar times in all of them. This fact suggests that separation anxiety is likely to depend on maturation. In particular, it may be that, once infants are

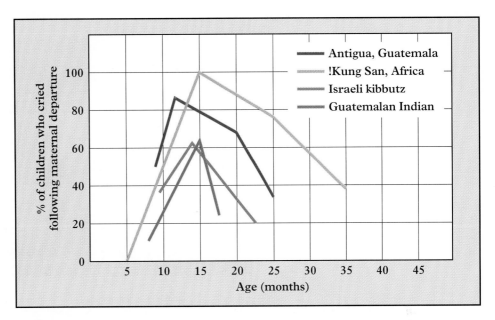

FIGURE 6.3 Separation anxiety appears in a similar way in very different cultures. After *Infancy: Its Place in Human Development*, by J. Kagan, R. Kearsley, and P. Zelazo, 1978, Cambridge, MA: Harvard University Press. Adapted with permission.

capable of recall memory, they may begin to think about where the mother is going, and wonder what will happen while she is gone and when she will return. This uncertainty could create fear. Separation distress recedes, at varying rates, after 2 years of age, probably because the older child is able to understand the event or predict the return of the mother. The child's experiences during the second year have created knowledge that makes it possible to solve the problem that engendered the anxiety in the younger child.

Fear on the Visual Cliff. Another fear that emerges in the second 6 months of life is fear of sudden drops in height. This fear has been measured by infants' avoidance of heights, as shown on an apparatus called the **visual cliff**, originally developed by Eleanor Gibson (Gibson & Walk, 1960) to assess early depth perception. An infant is placed on a narrow runway that rests on a large sheet of glass. On one side of the runway is a checkerboard pattern placed directly under the glass; on the other, the checkerboard pattern is placed 1 to 2 feet below the glass, giving the appearance of depth on that side—hence the term visual cliff. Prior to 7 months, and before the onset of anxiety, most infants do not avoid the deep side of the glass. If their mother calls them from the deep side, they will cross to her. But after 8 months most infants avoid the side that has the appearance of a cliff and will cry if they are placed on that side.

Avoidance of the apparently deep side of the visual cliff is not due to a new ability to perceive depth. Younger infants perceive the difference between the deep and shallow sides, as evidenced by the fact that they show a distinct cardiac reaction when lowered face down on the deep side (Campos, Langer, & Krawitz, 1970). But only when infants begin to crawl or creep, usually around 8 months of age, do they begin to avoid the deep side of the visual cliff (Campos, Hiatt, Ramsey, Henderson, & Svejda, 1978). This self-produced locomotion is important. If babies who

The visual cliff.

are unable to crawl on their own are given a "walker" so they can move around, they will also begin to avoid the deep side of the cliff. When infants begin to crawl, they encounter a broad range of new visual experiences and are confronted with continuous change in their visual perspective. These experiences may lead the infant to pay increased attention to the environment and its dangers.

An infant placed on the visual cliff will also look to a parent for guidance on how to proceed. If a 1-year-old is placed on the shallow side of the visual cliff while the mother is smiling and standing on the deep side, the child is likely to cross the deep side and approach her. But if the mother shows a fearful face the child is unlikely to approach her and may cry (Klinnert, Campos, Sorce, Emde, & Svejda, 1983). This phenomenon, called **social referencing**, is one sign that the infant has developed an attachment to an adult, a topic we discuss later in this chapter.

✿ TEMPERAMENTAL DIFFERENCES IN INFANTS

Any mother, father, or nurse in a newborn ward will tell you that there are obvious differences among infants that can be seen even from the first days of life. Some babies cry a lot, some are quiet; some sleep on a fairly regular schedule, others wake at irregular hours; some are constantly wriggling, others lie in their cribs quietly for long periods. It is possible, of course, to create excessively irritable or active babies through certain handling regimens. Nevertheless, there is good reason to believe that some babies are born with a bias toward certain moods and reaction styles. These inborn biases are called **temperament**.

Psychologists are interested in temperamental qualities for two reasons. First, if some qualities are based on inherited or prenatally acquired dispositions, these patterns might be resistant to change as the child grows. Second, children influence their parents and vice versa; thus, babies with different temperaments provoke different parental reactions and—even when they encounter similar experiences or child-rearing practices—react in different ways.

Experiments with animals support the idea of temperament. For instance, three species of monkeys show markedly different effects of traumatic events on infants. Rhesus monkeys that are totally isolated during the first 6 months of life emerge from isolation with seriously deviant social behavior; crab eater monkeys show minimal disruption; and pigtail monkeys display intermediate levels of disturbed social behavior (Sackett, Ruppenthal, Fahrenbruch, Holm, & Greenough, 1981). Similar findings have been recorded for different species of dogs. The social behavior of beagles is seriously affected by 12 weeks of isolation, while terriers show little reaction to the same experience (Fuller & Clark, 1968). These findings on other mammalian species have led many psychologists to search for analogous temperamental differences in our own species.

Infants vary in a large number of physiological and psychological characteristics. Two criteria have been used to assess which temperamental dimensions are most important: whether they are stable over time and whether they are based on inherited factors or on prenatal physiological factors. The pioneering studies of temperament were carried out by Alexander Thomas and Stella Chess (1977), and their work remains very influential. They conducted detailed interviews with a sample of mothers every three months for the first two years of their infants' lives and less frequently until the children were 7 years old. The dimensions of temperament that emerged from the interviews were qualities that were most salient for the parents. These were activity level, rhythmicity (regularity of sleep and eating), fussiness, distractibility, attention span, intensity, response threshold, and readiness to adapt to new foods, new people, and changes in routine (A. Thomas & Chess, 1977).

Rating the infants on these temperamental qualities, the researchers classified the babies as easy, difficult, or slow to warm up. The easy children, about 75 percent of the sample, were happy, adaptable infants who were not easily upset. The difficult children (about 10 percent) were often fussy, fearful of new people and situations, and intense in their reactions. The slow-to-warm-up babies (about 15 percent) were relatively inactive and fussy and tended to withdraw or to react negatively to novelty, but their reactions in new situations gradually became more positive with experience. By age 7, more of those children who were "difficult" infants had developed serious emotional problems than had children in the other two groups. It is likely that the parents of these hard-to-manage children sometimes

Some infants seem shy, inhibited, or "slow to warm up." Others have a much more outgoing and exuberant temperament.

responded to their behavior with frustration and hostility, thereby increasing the irritability that was an original characteristic of the infants' temperament.

It is not surprising that over time parents come to react in special ways to children with difficult temperaments. One group of mothers were asked to describe how difficult it was to take care of their infants. Later they were observed twice, once when their children were 12 months old and again at 18 months. On the first assessment, each mother was given various assignments; for example, to get her child to give her an object when she named it (a set of keys or a spoon) and to get the child to manipulate toys in a desired manner without touching them (pounding a single peg). When the infants were 18 months old, the mothers were given different tasks; for example, to help the child place puzzle pieces correctly or stack a set of rings in the proper order.

When the infants were 12 months old, the mothers behaved very similarly toward difficult and easy children. But six months later the mothers who had children (especially sons) with difficult temperaments exerted far less effort during the tasks, as if they had developed a low expectation of success. The children with difficult temperaments apparently had influenced their mother's attitudes (Maccoby, Snow, & Jacklin, 1984). Should such difficult children continue to frustrate their parents' standards and the parents continue to expect less of them, in time a spiral of self-defeating behavior could become established (see Box 6.1).

Activity Level

Squirmy, wiggly babies do not necessarily grow up to be the terrors of the schoolyard who run full tilt everywhere they go. Although very active newborns tend to be more active than most other children during the first year, there is only modest preservation of this quality in later childhood (Moss & Susman, 1980; Rothbart & Derryberry, 1981). Studies of identical and fraternal twins have suggested a moderate genetic contribution to activity level at 8 months, but by 4 or 7 years the difference between identical and fraternal twins disappears (H. H. Goldsmith & Gottes-

BOX 6.1
LIVING WITH A DIFFICULT BABY

When parents realize that an infant's behavior is determined partly by the child's temperament rather than wholly by what the parents do, they can work more effectively toward a positive outcome for the child. One of the most difficult babies in A. Thomas and Chess's (1977) sample typically showed intense irritability and withdrawal when faced with new situations and was slow to adapt to anything unfamiliar. He showed this tendency with his first bath and his first solid foods. He also reacted negatively to the first days in nursery and elementary school and on his first shopping trip with his parents. Each of these experiences evoked stormy responses and much crying and struggling. However, his parents learned to anticipate his reactions. They learned that if they were patient and presented new situations gradually and repeatedly, eventually the boy adapted to them. The parents did not interpret their son's difficulties as reflecting on their effectiveness as parents. As a result, the boy never became a behavior problem, even though

many children with this temperamental style are at risk for psychological problems.

During later childhood and adolescence, this boy was fortunate in being able to avoid many radically new situations. He lived in the same community and went through high school with the same friends. However, when he went to a college away from home he was confronted with new situations, new friends, and a complex relationship with a female student with whom he was living. In these circumstances his earlier temperamental tendencies to withdraw and show intense negative reactions were expressed once again. However, after a discussion with Dr. Thomas, who explained to the young man his temperamental history and some techniques he might use to adapt to college, the young man's difficulties disappeared, and by the end of the year he had adjusted again. When he was told that similar negative reactions might occur in the future, he said, "That's all right. I know how to handle them now" (A. Thomas & Chess, 1977, pp. 165–167).

man, 1981; Plomin & Foch, 1980), suggesting that activity level shows heritability only in infancy but not in later life.

Irritability

Differences among infants in crying, fussiness, and general irritability during the first 6 months do not always predict that these differences will persist in older children, even though extreme irritability in infants over 7 months old is modestly preserved for the next year or two (Rothbart & Derryberry, 1981; A. Thomas & Chess, 1977). However, there is some evidence that extremely irritable newborns are a little less likely to become sociable 2-year-olds, for such infants are less likely to laugh and smile than typical infants are (Riese, 1987).

Reaction to Unfamiliarity

Two of the most stable temperamental qualities are the tendency to be shy, timid, and quiet in unfamiliar situations and the contrasting tendency to be sociable, bold, and spontaneous. These two qualities are obvious to parents: when several thousand mothers of infants 4 to 8 months old filled out questionnaires about their infants' behavior, they named the tendency to approach or avoid unfamiliar people

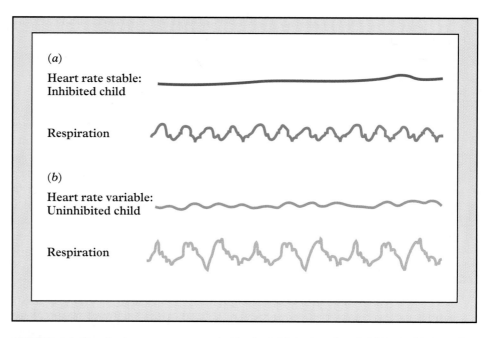

FIGURE 6.4 Respiration patterns are similar in inhibited and uninhibited children. But inhibited children show stable heart rates (top pattern) and uninhibited children show variable heart rates in which the peaks correspond to peaks in the respiration cycle (bottom pattern). After "Behavioral Inhibition in Young Children," by C. Garcia Coll, J. Kagan, and S. J. Reznick, 1984, *Child Development, 55*, pp. 1005–1019. Copyright © 1984 by Society for Research in Child Development. Adapted by permission.

and toys as the most striking quality (Sanson, Prior, Garino, Oberkaid, & Sewell, 1987).

About 10 percent of 2-year-olds are extremely quiet and shy and remain close to the caregiver for 10 or 15 minutes whenever they are in an unfamiliar place or with a stranger. These children are described as **inhibited**. A larger number of children, described as **uninhibited**, begin to play immediately and show no signs of initial timidity. Children in the former group resemble the prototypical adult introvert, while those in the latter group have the features of the future extravert.

These qualities were the most stable in a longitudinal study of children observed from birth through 25 years of age (Kagan & Moss, 1962). The children who were extremely shy, timid, and fearful during the first 3 years of life displayed a coherent cluster during the early school years. They avoided dangerous activities, were minimally aggressive, conformed to parental requests, and avoided unfamiliar peer groups. When they were adolescents they avoided contact sports. The four boys who were most inhibited chose relatively solitary careers as adults (one music teacher and three university scientists). The four boys who had been least inhibited during the first six years chose traditionally masculine vocations that involved more social interaction with others (one athletic coach, one salesman, and two engineers). In another longitudinal study, two groups of children who showed these qualities to an extreme extent were observed regularly from the second or third year of life through the eighth year. About half of the children who were very shy and timid on the first assessment retained that quality; at 7.5 years of age they had difficulty initiating play with unfamiliar children and were quiet and subdued when tested by adults or when playing with groups of nine or ten unfamiliar children.

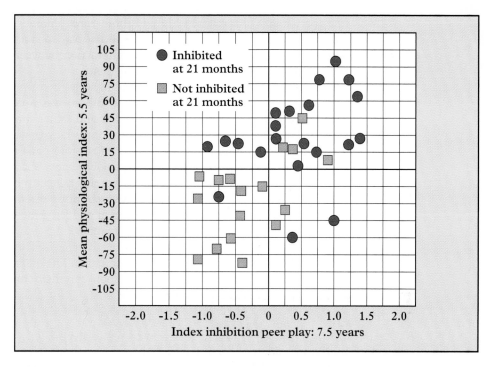

FIGURE 6.5 Children selected as extremely inhibited at 21 months showed higher levels of physiological arousal at 5 years of age and more timidity with peers at 7 years of age, compared with children who were uninhibited at 21 months. Courtesy of J. Kagan.

Moreover, persistently inhibited children had distinctive psychophysiological profiles: higher and more stable heart rates (see Figure 6.4), higher levels of cortisol (an indication of stress), and greater muscle tension. Figure 6.5 shows that the children who had the highest level of physiological arousal when they were 5.5 years old were the most inhibited two years later, when they were 7.5.

Variations along the dimension of inhibition can be observed as early as 4 months of age. Babies who are highly reactive to stimuli are more likely to become inhibited, while less reactive babies are more likely to become uninhibited (Kagan & Snidman, 1991). Child-rearing conditions can influence the degree to which a tendency to become inhibited will be actualized. If a child with this tendency is raised in an unusually benevolent environment that gently promotes an outgoing coping style, he or she will not develop into a shy, timid youngster. On the other hand, an overly stressful environment can create timid behavior even in children born with a temperamental disposition that favors spontaneous sociable behavior. The presence of a biological predisposition toward shyness does not guarantee that the child will become shy, and in fact only a small proportion of infants who are born with a temperamental disposition for shy behavior will become timid 3-year-olds.

The Principle of Bidirectionality

The reciprocal influence of parental behavior and infant temperament forms the basis for the principle of **bidirectionality** in development. This principle states that the parent-child relationship goes both ways: Parents influence children, and children influence parental behaviors. Another way to state this is to say that children's development is a product of the interaction between their own characteristics and those of the people who socialize them.

As an example, consider a family that includes two children born a little over a year apart. The older child, a boy named Elliott, was a cuddly baby who smiled readily and was very responsive. His mother and father smiled and talked to him a great deal. He was also very active. By 9 months he was walking, and soon he was getting into everything. He required a lot of attention just to ensure his safety. His younger sister, Susan, was a quieter, more sober baby. She watched people intently but did not smile readily. As a result, her parents talked to her less than they had to Elliott. Susan also was relatively inactive, apparently content to sit and watch others much of the time. She received less attention and less practice in social interaction, which may have contributed to her quiet manner.

Elliott and Susan had different patterns of behavior from the beginning, and as a result their parents treated them differently. The parents' behavior, in turn, encouraged different patterns of social response in their children.

EMOTIONAL AND SOCIAL RELATIONSHIPS WITH ADULTS

Theoretical Perspectives

The temperamental qualities of the infant combine with the practices, attitudes, and personality of the parents to produce a characteristic pattern of social interaction between the infant and each parent. Almost every theorist has assumed that this pattern of interaction influences the infant's psychological growth in important ways. During most of this century, psychologists have regarded children's relationships with people who care for them as the major bases for emotional and cognitive development (Bowlby, 1969; Freud, 1964; J. B. Watson, 1928).

Traditional psychological theories emphasized the significance of pleasure and pain in the development of behavior. They assumed that human beings are motivated by the desire to obtain pleasure and to avoid pain. As a result, they awarded the greatest significance to the actions of caregivers who provide pleasure. Infants were thought to develop positive feelings and close attachments to people who are frequent sources of pleasure, either because these people soothe and play with them or because they reduce the discomfort caused by pain, cold, hunger, or psychological distress. Recently, however, this approach has been challenged and largely replaced by a perspective that regards attachments as the product of social interactions governed by their adaptive value and hence created directly by the very nature of what it means to be human. In this section, we examine the various theories within which the tie between human adults and their infants has been conceptualized.

Psychoanalytic Theory. Sigmund Freud's conception of social and emotional development was based on the assumption that social ties derive from the satisfaction of more basic physiological drives. Freud assumed that infants are born with biological instincts that demand satisfaction. A child's need for food, warmth, and reduction of pain represents a "striving for sensory pleasure." Freud postulated a biological basis for this striving: a kind of physical energy, which he termed **libido**.

As Freud saw it, the activities, people, and objects in which children invest biological energy change in predictable ways as the child grows older. During infancy, Freud argued, the events surrounding feeding are the most important sources of gratification; as we have mentioned already, he called the period of infancy the **oral stage**. When children are being fed and cared for, their energy (or libido) becomes focused on the person providing the gratification. Freud suggested that too much or too little gratification of oral needs could slow the child's progress into the next developmental stage; that is, a fixation—or resistance to transferring the libidinal energy to a new set of objects and activities—might occur. Freud proposed the bold hypothesis that a fixation at the oral stage, caused by excessive or insufficient gratification, could predispose an adult toward specific psychological symptoms. For example, infants who were undergratified might develop serious depression or schizophrenia, and those who were overly gratified might be excessively dependent on others.

Freud suggested that the anal area and the activities surrounding defecation become important sources of libidinal gratification during the second year of life. Interactions with parents over toilet training assume special significance at this stage. Freud called this stage of development the **anal stage**. Fixation at this stage supposedly would produce either adults who are very neat, orderly, and concerned with their property, or else adults with the opposite qualities.

Other psychoanalytic theories derived from Freud's retain the assumption that early mother-child interactions have a special quality that is necessary for the infant's development, but these theories emphasize the psychological consequences of being cared for in an affectionate, consistent, reliable, and gentle manner, rather than the biological functions of feeding and toileting. Erik Erikson, as we have seen, proposed that the critical developmental event during infancy is the establishment of a sense of trust in another person. Infants who have consistently satisfying experiences of nurturance traverse this stage successfully. Those who do not will lack a basic sense of trust in others as they grow older.

In the second year, Erikson suggested, children attempt to establish a sense of autonomy and independence from their parents. Children who fail to gain a sense of autonomy may be vulnerable to feelings of shame and doubt about their ability to function independently. In discussing these and later stages in the life cycle, Erikson retained the essence of the Freudian idea of fixation: he believed that failure to progress through one stage satisfactorily would interfere with progression through subsequent stages. His theory differed from Freud's because it emphasized psychosocial stages in contrast to psychosexual stages. In fact, his approach has points in common with attachment theory, a perspective we consider shortly.

Social Learning Theory. Behaviorists, like psychoanalysts, assumed that hunger, thirst, and pain are basic drive states that propel infants to action. But the behaviorists rejected the Freudian concept of libido because it cannot be measured. The impetus for behavior, they believed, is not invisible feelings but biological drives and other measurable responses. An event that satisfies a child's biological needs (that is, reduces a drive) was called a **primary reinforcer**. For example, for a hungry infant, food is a primary reinforcer. People or objects that are present when a drive is reduced become **secondary reinforcers** through their association with the primary reinforcer. As a frequent source of food and comfort, an infant's mother is an important secondary reinforcer. The child therefore approaches her not only when hungry or in pain but on a variety of other occasions, displaying a generalized dependency on her. Social learning theorists assumed that the strength of the child's dependency is determined by how rewarding the mother is, that is, by how often she has been associated with pleasure and the reduction of pain and discomfort (Sears, Maccoby, & Levin, 1957).

The idea that infants' emotional ties and approach behaviors to the mother are based on the fact that she is associated with the satisfaction of biological drives dominated American theories of infancy from World War I until the early 1960s. Because feeding was considered so important, child development experts as well as parents devoted a great deal of attention to whether a child was breast-fed or bottle-fed, whether it was fed on a schedule or on demand, and when and how the child should be weaned from breast to bottle or from bottle to cup. These questions were investigated extensively, but no consistent relations between feeding patterns and the child's subsequent social and emotional development were discovered. The results of this research cast some doubt on the utility of the concept of the oral stage. More recent evidence also indicates that the strength of a child's attachment to either parent is not related in any simple way to the frequency with which that parent feeds, changes, or cares for the physical needs of the child (Ainsworth, Blehar, Waters, & Wall, 1978).

Psychologists' faith in theories emphasizing biological drive reduction was also challenged by a series of experiments with infant monkeys conducted by Harry Harlow and his colleagues. These researchers identified a new source of the mother-infant bond: contact comfort. In some of their experiments, young monkeys were raised in a cage with two different kinds of inanimate "mothers" (Harlow & Harlow, 1966). One mother was made of wire, and the infant could nurse from a nipple mounted on this mother's chest. The other mother was covered with soft terry cloth but did not provide the infant with any food. Contrary to the predictions of both psychoanalytic and behavioral theories, the infant monkeys spent most of their time resting on the terry-cloth mother. They went to the wire monkey only when they were hungry. When an infant monkey was frightened by an unfamiliar object, such as a large wooden spider, it ran to the cloth mother and clung to it as though it felt more secure there than clinging to the wire mother. At least for these primates, the pleasure associated with feeding seemed not to be the foundation for the attachment bond between parent and infant.

Ethology. At about the time that Harlow began his experiments with monkeys, the field of **ethology** was being created by a group of European naturalists, notably Konrad Lorenz (1981) and Nikko Tinbergen (1951). These scientists emphasized the need to study animals in their natural environments. In part, they were rebelling against the behaviorists' stress on conditioning and on research under strictly controlled laboratory conditions.

According to the ethologists, each species of animal is born with a set of **fixed action patterns**. A fixed action pattern is a stereotyped behavioral sequence that is set in motion when the proper environmental stimulus, called a **releaser**, occurs. Some fixed action patterns can be triggered only during a limited time span during the animal's development, called a critical period. Releasers that occur before or after the critical period have little or no effect on the animal's behavior.

Imprinting is a fixed action pattern that takes place shortly after birth in ducks, geese, chickens, and some other species. A newly hatched duckling is innately prepared to follow the first moving object it sees. If that object is its biological mother, the duckling learns to follow the mother and to approach her when in distress. But if the moving object that the duckling sees during the critical period for imprinting

Wire and cloth "mothers" used in Harlow's studies. Infants spent more time on the padded and soft cloth figure. They only visited the wire figure to feed.

is something else, such as a human being or an electric train, the young bird will follow that object instead of the mother duck.

The phenomena of imprinting are not seen in humans. But the ethologists had clearly demonstrated that it was possible to find strong ties between the adults and the young of a species, based on biological preparedness for the formation of this tie and not on any satisfaction of needs such as hunger. This demonstration prepared the way for a reconsideration of the nature of the tie between human infants and their caretakers.

Attachment Theory. The idea, derived from ethology, that human infants might be born into the world prepared to exhibit certain behaviors that are neither a result of prior learning nor based on drive reduction was attractive to a British psychiatrist named John Bowlby. Bowlby was trained in psychoanalytic theory but was receptive to the new ethological findings. He may also have been sensitized to the importance of emotional relationships by developments in British psychiatry after the First World War. The widespread deaths of young men in that war—and the need to deal

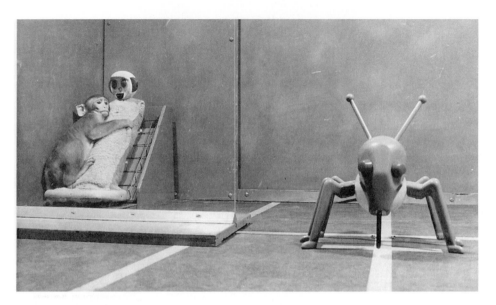

Infant monkeys in Harlow's studies ran to the cloth figure when frightened.

with what was called "shell shock" in survivors—led to an appreciation of emotional bonds and an understanding of what could happen when they were severed (Newcombe & Lerner, 1982).

Bowlby proposed that human infants are programmed to emit certain behaviors that will elicit caregiving from people around them and will keep adults nearby. These behaviors include crying, smiling, cooing, and crawling toward someone. From an evolutionary standpoint, these patterns have adaptive value because they help ensure that infants will receive the care necessary for their survival (Bowlby, 1969).

A major result of mother-infant interactions, according to Bowlby, is the infant's development of an emotional **attachment** to the mother. The function of the infant's attachment, from the infant's point of view, is to provide psychological security. The signs of an infant's attachment to a caregiver are evident in three phenomena. First, a target of attachment is better able than anyone else to placate and soothe the baby. (When Olivia became afraid of the person costumed as the Easter Bunny, she immediately sought the safety of her mother's arms.) Second, infants are much more likely to approach attachment targets for play or consolation than to approach others. (Hannah's mother could not have provided equivalent comfort to Olivia as could her own mother.) Finally, infants are less likely to become afraid when in the presence of attachment targets than when these people are absent. If Hannah had been alone or with a new baby-sitter when she met the Easter Bunny, she too might have reacted with fear.

The attachment system and its set of specific responses are aroused by novelty, danger, or distress and are muted by the perception of safety. Infants display attachment behaviors—such as orienting toward or remaining near the parent—when they are anxious, tired, hungry, or otherwise distressed. The purpose of the attachment behavior is to reduce unpleasant feelings through interaction with the target of attachment. It has been suggested that after the first birthday, children construct an internal working model of the self and its relationship to its targets of attach-

John Bowlby.

ment. This schema permits the infant to feel more secure, for the child knows that the target of attachment is potentially available even if he or she is not actually present.

Young children will ignore their parents and even prefer to play with a stranger as long as the target of attachment is present. But when infants feel threatened or experience uncertainty, they will turn quickly to the mother, father, or other attachment figure, often to seek information about the degree of safety or danger in a particular situation.

All infants seem to form attachments, but these can vary in their security. Attachment theorists propose that a secure attachment provides a basis for healthy emotional and social development during later childhood. Children with secure attachments are expected to become socially outgoing and curious about their environment, to be willing to explore, and to develop the ability to cope with stress. Serious disruptions in the attachment process are thought to produce problems in the child's later social development.

As well as varying in security, infants differ in how many attachment relationships they form. In some families—where there is a primary caretaker (usually the mother) and other adults are present much more infrequently—infants may be attached to only one adult. In other situations—where fathers, grandparents, or other relatives share caretaking responsibilities or where there is a babysitter, nanny, or day care teachers—there may be several attachment relationships. Worldwide, there is very marked variation in the extent to which babies are primarily with their mothers or are also interacting with other adults and older children. Among the Efe

TABLE 6.1 Episodes in the Strange Situation

Episode	Event Initiating Episode	Persons Present During Episode
1	Parent and infant enter room	Parent and infant
2	Stranger joins parent and infant	Parent, infant, and stranger
3	Parent leaves room	Infant and stranger
4	Parent returns to room; stranger leaves	Parent and infant
5	Parent leaves	Infant alone
6	Stranger returns	Infant and stranger
7	Parent returns; stranger leaves	Parent and infant

people, who live by hunting and foraging in the forests of Zaire, infants spend about half the time in social contact with people other than their mothers. This figure rises to 70 percent by the time children are 3 (Tronick, Morelli, & Ivey, 1992). Box 6.2 presents an account of daily life among the Efe.

Measuring Attachment

The most popular procedure for assessing security of attachment was devised by Mary Ainsworth and her colleagues (1978); it is called the **Strange Situation**. This procedure consists of a series of seven 3-minute episodes during which infants are observed with a parent, with a stranger, with a parent and a stranger, and alone, as shown in Table 6.1.

The two key episodes in the Strange Situation are 4 and 7, those in which the parent returns after being out of the room. The type of behavior shown when the parent returns is used as the principal index of the infant's attachment to him or her.

Three major patterns of attachment were described by Ainsworth, and a fourth has been added more recently. First, children who seek or greet the parent when he or she returns—and who are easily comforted by the parent (if distressed)—are described as **securely attached**. They typically show mild protest following the parent's departure, although protest can also be absent or even fairly marked. Three other patterns of behavior have been described, all of which are varieties of **insecure attachment**. Children who ignore and actively avoid the parent upon his or her return are usually classified as **avoidant**. When the parent leaves the room, these children often do not protest and simply continue to play. Children who, after the parent returns, alternately cling to the parent and push him or her away are described as **resistant**. These children are often extremely distressed when the parent leaves. In samples of American 1-year-olds, about 65 percent are usually classified as securely attached, about 21 percent as avoidant, and about 14 percent as resistant (van IJzendoorn & Kroonenberg, 1988).

Recently, a fourth pattern of response in the Strange Situation has been described (Main & Solomon, 1986, 1990). Some children observed in the Strange Situation did not seem to fit any of the available categories, because they showed elements of both avoidant and resistant insecurity. In addition, they sometimes showed odd behaviors that seemed to suggest fear or confusion. This pattern has been called **disorganized**. It seems to occur with high frequency in children who have been maltreated (Carlson, Cicchetti, Barnett, & Braunwold, 1989), in children of depressed mothers (Radke-Yarrow, Cummings, Kuczynski, & Chapman, 1985)

BOX 6.2
DAILY LIFE AMONG THE EFE

Human cultures have developed a very wide variety of lifestyles. The patterns with which we are familiar in Western industrialized countries are not found everywhere and, in fact, are not likely to have characterized life for most of the history of our species. The following passage gives some idea of daily life among the Efe people of Zaire.

The Efe subsist mainly by cooperative bow hunting with metal-tipped arrows and by gathering forest resources such as nuts, fruits, and honey. A considerable portion of their diet is also composed of cultivated foods obtained through the exchange of forest products or labor with neighboring Lese horticulturalists. . . . To meet the unpredictability and seasonality of food resources, the economic activities of both Efe men and women are diverse. There is also overlap in the subsistence activities of individual camp members. Men most often bow hunt cooperatively in small groups with other men who live in the same camp or with men from neighboring camps. The work load of Efe women is very high. Women often engage in multiple activities and spend a considerable amount of time gathering food and fuel and preparing the food that they have acquired. . . . This work is typically conducted in the company of other women and children. Parties of women travel together with their children in the forest to collect seasonal fruits, nuts, and mushrooms, cooperatively fish in small streams, and work side by side in the gardens of their Lese horticultural neighbors. Men may accompany their wives foraging, especially if the resource is particularly risky to acquire, such as palm fruit, which requires scaling trees to a significant height. On the other hand, women rarely accompany men on hunts; when they do, they do not kill game but serve primarily as beaters to flush the animals out toward the bowmen.

Day-to-day activities do not appear to be highly coordinated among individual camp members. During the mid-morning and early afternoon hours when most out-of-camp activities take place, one or several individuals are likely to be found in the camp resting, taking care of children, preparing food, or socializing. The nearly continuous presence of people in the camp may provide mothers with an opportunity to leave their children in camp while they engage in such out-of-camp activities as foraging for forest foods or working in gardens.

Daytime camp activities are highly varied; nighttime activities tend to be less varied. Typically, nighttime activities center around consumption of the day's last meal at about dusk, followed by storytelling and singing or dancing for a few hours into the night. During this time, infants often nurse themselves to sleep, draped across their mothers' laps; toddlers and older children may hover close to their family's campfire, or they may play, but this is difficult unless the moon is full and high enough to cast light into the clearing. Children may fall asleep, but more often they wait until the family beds down. At night, camp members often wake several times to stir the coals and add fuel to the smoldering fires, to converse with each other, to play instruments, or to sing. The infants may be passed to a familiar caregiver, such as a sister or an aunt, to play or sleep for some period. Toddlers may also freely change their sleeping arrangements during the night to be with others.

Efe infants and children have diverse opportunities to be socially and physically involved in ongoing daily camp activities with a variety of community members. This is true whether the child is in the camp (. . . infants and toddlers spend most of their time in the camp) or foraging with other people (usually caregivers and children). For the infant the distinction between daytime and nighttime events is not sharp, and social activities continue throughout the night.

Source: From "The Efe Forager Infant and Toddler's Pattern of Social Relationships: Multiple and Simultaneous," by E. Z. Tronick, G. A. Morelli, and P. K. Ivey, 1992, *Developmental Psychology, 28,* p. 570. Copyright © 1992 by American Psychological Association. Reprinted by permission.

and in children whose mothers are affected by an unresolved loss of one of their own attachment figures (Main & Hesse, 1990).

Although the Strange Situation may seem artificial, classifications based on it do predict other qualities that theoretically should be related to the security of children's attachment. Children who were classified as securely or insecurely attached in the Strange Situation when they were 12 to 18 months old were observed at later ages ranging from 21 months to 5 years. Securely attached children were generally more socially outgoing with adults and with other children, more cooperative and compliant with their mothers and with strange adults, better able to cope with stress, and more curious than children who were classified as insecurely attached (Arend, Gove, & Sroufe, 1979; Londerville & Main, 1981; Pastor, 1981; Waters, Wippman, & Sroufe, 1979). When securely attached children were observed in their own homes, they sought physical contact with their mothers less often than did children who were classified as insecurely attached (Clarke-Stewart & Hevey, 1981). These longitudinal relations are not always seen, however, and it may be that predictability will prove to be more marked in some circumstances than others (Howes, Matheson, & Hamilton, 1994).

Limitations of the Strange Situation. Although these findings indicate that the Strange Situation may be a sensitive index of quality of attachment, several things should be kept in mind in interpreting responses in the situation as an indication of security or insecurity. First, classifications are not immutable. In fact, many children change their attachment classifications during the period between 12 and 19 months, and more change thereafter. The changes are sometimes associated with changes in family circumstances, such as changes in residence or economic status. Children are just as likely to shift from insecure to secure attachment as the other way around (R. A. Thompson, Lamb, & Estes, 1982).

Second, the child's temperament and the cultural values of his environment may have an impact on Strange Situation classifications. The primary basis for classifying a child as securely or insecurely attached is the child's reaction when the parent returns to the room. However, that reaction is determined partly by how upset the child became when the parent left the infant alone or with the stranger. Children who do not cry when the parent leaves because they are not especially anxious about the departure are also unlikely to approach the parent for comfort when he or she comes back. Such children are likely to be classified as avoidant and insecurely attached. Similarly, children who cannot be soothed easily (called resistant and insecurely attached) are likely to be those who become extremely upset by the maternal departure.

Some infants who are temperamentally vulnerable to becoming anxious and frightened by unexpected parental departure may also be more difficult to soothe in the Strange Situation. Many 1-year-old children who are classified as resistant— compared with securely attached children—are very irritable and difficult to care for from the first days of life through the first birthday (Belsky & Rovine, 1987; Calkins & Fox, 1992).

One-year-olds who are classified as resistant and insecurely attached may have been born with a nervous system that causes them to be unusually reactive to changes in stimulation. One indication of sensitivity is the infant's reaction to a change in the taste of liquids. Newborn infants were allowed to suck on a nipple that first delivered plain water. After 2 minutes the solution was changed to a mildly sweet liquid, and after 2 more minutes it was changed to an even sweeter liquid.

Some newborns did not increase their rate of sucking very much despite the change from plain water to sweet liquid. However, other infants were very reactive to the change in taste and showed a large increase in sucking rate. When these children were seen at 18 months of age, those who had reacted to the sweet taste with an increase in sucking were more likely to be classified as showing resistant attachments (LaGasse, Gruber, & Lipsitt, 1989).

Another factor that may influence the child's behavior in the Strange Situation is the degree to which parents encourage their infants to control signs of fear during the first year. A child with an attentive and loving parent who encourages self-reliance and control of fear is less likely to cry when the parent leaves and, therefore, is less likely to approach the parent when he or she returns. Such a child may be classified as avoidant. Patterns of attachment differ in different cultures, suggesting that cultural values and child-rearing practices influence children's behavior in the Strange Situation. In Germany, about 35 percent of infants are classified as avoidant. The authors of one study wrote that their 1-year-old subjects may have received "a strong push in the direction of affective reserve" from their parents and other adults in the German culture (Grossmann, Grossmann, Huber, & Wartner, 1981, p. 179). In Japan and Israel, where parents are considerably more protective, higher percentages of children are classified as resistant. There are also large differences between samples from the same country, perhaps because of different parental practices and life experiences for children in those samples (van IJzendoorn & Kroonenberg, 1988).

Caregiving and Attachment

Although the human infant appears to have an innate tendency to form attachments, the targets selected and the strength and quality of those attachments depend partly on the parents' behavior in relation to the child. Recent efforts to determine what parental qualities are important for attachment have shown that attachment does not result only from parental actions that satisfy the child's need for food, water, warmth, and relief from pain. Moreover, the sheer amount of time the child spends with the parent seems not to determine the quality of the child's attachment. For example, a group of Swedish children whose fathers had been their primary caregivers for some part of infancy showed no different patterns of attachment to their fathers than children whose fathers had been away working full time (Lamb, Hwang, Frodi, & Frodi, 1982).

What qualities of social interactions between parent and child are most important for the development of attachment? A major dimension of importance has been variously described as sensitivity, synchrony, and reciprocity. Parents of strongly attached children generally respond quickly and positively to their children's social overtures and act in response to the infant's signals, whether they are cries, glances, smiles, or vocalizations. They initiate playful, pleasant exchanges in ways that fit the baby's mood and cognitive abilities. A key dimension of sensitive interaction is the ability to act in harmony with the child's signals and behaviors (Ainsworth et al., 1978). Consider the following examples of two parents who show equal amounts of affection and interaction with their children but differ in their sensitivity:

Darcy, an 18-month-old, is playing with some toys on the floor. Her mother finishes some work at her desk and turns to watch her. She comments, "Those are

Sensitive and mutually enjoyable interaction is the key to an attachment bond.

nice blocks, Darcy. You are making a fine tower with them." Darcy smiles. Mother picks up a book and begins to read. In a few minutes, after finishing her tower, Darcy walks to Mother with a children's book in her hand, saying, "Book," and trying to crawl into Mother's lap. Mother takes Darcy in her lap, puts down her own book, and says, "Do you want to read this book?" Darcy says yes, and Mother reads.

Stacy, another 18-month-old, is playing on her living room floor when her mother finishes some desk work. Mother says, "Come here, Stacy. I'll read your book to you." Stacy looks up but continues building a block tower in which she is apparently engrossed. Mother goes to Stacy and says, "Let's read now," picking her up and giving her a hug. Stacy squirms and whimpers. Mother puts her down, and Stacy returns to her tower. Later, having finished her tower, Stacy picks up the book and tries to crawl into Mother's lap, saying, "Book." Mother says, "No, you didn't want to read when I was ready. I'm busy now."

These two mothers provide their children with equal amounts of attention, but the first is more sensitive and responsive to the child than the second. The second shows characteristics of both intrusiveness (interfering with her child's ongoing activity) and rejection or withdrawal (refusing to read when her child requests it). Overall, the pattern is one of inconsistency. Behavior of this sort has been identified as predicting insecure attachment. Specifically, maternal-infant interaction leading to avoidant attachment seems to be characterized by intrusiveness and overstimula-

tion, while interaction preceding resistant attachment seems to be poorly coordinated, with mothers being underinvolved and inconsistent (Isabella & Belsky, 1991).

Most infants develop clear attachments to fathers as well as to mothers, and
some social critics have suggested that infants could benefit from receiving frequent
care from their fathers as well as their mothers. Two questions about the role of
fathers have been addressed in recent research: (1) Do fathers have the capacity to
provide appropriate and sensitive care to infants? (2) What kind of interactions do
fathers typically have with their infants? Observations of fathers in standardized situations reveal that they show as much sensitivity, affection, and skill as their wives
when feeding and holding their newborn infants (Parke & Tinsley, 1981). However,
in American middle-class families fathers and mothers play with babies in different
ways. The fathers are more likely to provide tactile and physical stimulation, while
the mothers are more verbal with their infants. This difference may be unique to
American families; similar differences were not observed in Israeli or Swedish families (Lamb et al., 1982; Sagi, Lamb, & Gardner, 1986).

The observation that parent-infant interaction differs between secure and insecure infants leaves open the question of how these interaction patterns arise. Belsky
and Isabella (1988) have presented evidence that three classes of variables are
related to attachment security: (1) the mother's personality before giving birth; (2)
characteristics of the marriage; (3) infant temperament. Mothers who seemed more
mentally healthy initially, who had stronger marriages, and who had less difficult
infants were the most likely to have secure infants. Further, if only one of these factors was negative, secure infants were still the likely outcome. Only when two or
more areas showed problems did insecurity become likely. One account of a couple
in whom maternal personality and marital struggle posed problems can be seen in
Box 6.3.

An intriguing way of thinking about maternal personality comes from the
recent work of Mary Main, who has argued that men's and women's representations of their own attachment relationships affect their caregiving patterns and the
security of their infants (Main, Kaplan, & Cassidy, 1985). The parent's state of
mind with regard to childhood attachment experiences has been assessed using an
Adult Attachment Interview (AAI) developed by George, Kaplan, and Main
(1985). In the interview, people are asked to describe their childhood relationships
with their mother and father, both generally and in terms of specific memories.
Coding is based not so much on the actual recollections but on the ways in which
the experiences are described. Three patterns of discourse have been distinguished.
One pattern is the **autonomous** or secure pattern (also termed "free to recall").
These individuals describe their attachment history, whether negative or positive, in
a coherent way, recognizing the importance of these experiences. A second pattern
is called **dismissing**. These individuals deny the importance of attachment. They
often idealize their parents but without being able to remember concrete supporting evidence. A third pattern is called **preoccupied**. These individuals seem overin-
volved with their attachment experiences and have difficulty describing them
coherently and reflectively. Recent research has supported the reliability and validity of the AAI (Bakermans-Kranenburg & van IJzendoorn, 1993). However, controversy continues to surround whether and in what way the AAI is dependent on
childhood experience, or whether it is simply a measure of healthy psychological
functioning in adulthood (Fox, 1995).

The AAI was developed so that the patterns would correspond with the

BOX 6.3
PARENTAL PERSONALITY AND MARITAL DISCORD: BABY AS "HOT POTATO"

In ideal circumstances, when "baby makes three" the adults in the situation are able to adapt to the dramatic changes in their lifestyle, with humor and patience at least, if with some sense of loss. However, in some cases, the addition of a baby exposes or exacerbates difficulties parents have in dealing with their own emotional lives and with their relationship with their spouse. A report on a family intervention project conducted at Pennsylvania State University gives one some sense of what can happen. Here, disagreements between partners on who takes care of the increased responsibilities are discussed.

> In one case in which the mother openly acknowledged problems with her husband over child-care responsibilities, the intensity of this conflict appeared so strong that the needs of the child were often sacrificed. The mother described a morning routine that involved both parents heatedly arguing over whose turn it was to get up with the baby and change its diaper. The argument typically lasted from 15 to 30 minutes with the baby's cries in the back-

ground. It was very important to this mother that she not appear to give in, so she made a point of not picking up the baby—despite its cries—until the argument was concluded by her husband getting out of bed and stomping off to the bathroom. On the occasions when this mother felt she had won the argument, the verbal exchange was the same but the mother got to the bathroom first, leaving the husband to cope with the crying baby. In this marriage in which the baby appeared to frequently play the role of "hot potato," the child's signals were not simply ignored but the stimulus for active avoidance and emotional conflict. Clearly, these dynamics could create a negative understanding of self, others, and the world. And, in particular, they might well teach a child to restrain or hide any overt signs of her/his needs or feelings in order to prevent parental fighting and unavailability.

Source: From *Clinical Implications on Attachment* (p. 368), by T. Nezworski, W. J. Tolan, and J. Belsky, 1988, Hillsdale, NJ: LEA.

attachment classifications of infants from the Strange Situation. That is, scoring was planned so as to reflect the characteristics of parents of secure and insecure children. Thus, free-to-recall adults generally have secure babies, while dismissing parents tend to have avoidant babies and preoccupied parents tend to have resistant babies (van IJzendoorn, 1995). Parents with different adult representations of attachment also differ in the sensitivity with which they take care of infants and children (van IJzendoorn, 1995). However, variations in caretaking do not fully explain the relation between adult attachment and infant attachment; biologically transmitted temperamental characteristics may play a role in the relation as well (Fox, 1995).

Research on clinical populations shows that mothers with a history of mental health problems were more likely to have babies with insecure attachments than mothers without such a history (van IJzendoorn, Goldberg, Kroonenberg, & Frenkel, 1992). Such an outcome is not surprising, given the demands sensitive child-rearing makes upon the psychological and social resources of parents. Interestingly, however, insecure attachments did not seem to be elevated in cases where the child had problems such as physical disabilities.

CONSEQUENCES OF VARIATIONS IN CAREGIVING ARRANGEMENTS

Psychologists assume that the feelings of security produced by attachment to adults will vary with the regularity of that relationship and the degree to which it is satisfying. Thus, infants who experience irregular, unpredictable, or unsatisfying interactions with adults should show signs of anxiety and, perhaps, symptoms such as fears or antisocial behaviors when they are adolescents or adults. Historically, such predictions were first studied in groups of children being reared in institutions such as orphanages, in which it is often virtually impossible to have stable relationships between children and adults. More recently, the focus has shifted to examine situations in which substantial amounts of care are provided by an individual (or by several people) other than the mother.

Institutional Care. Residential institutional care for young children (e.g., in orphanages or homes for children whose parents are unable to take care of them) is sometimes necessary in the United States and is common in poorer countries. Under these circumstances, the number of adults available to care for the child and the amount of intellectual stimulation provided are critical factors. Some children who have grown up in such institutions are more dependent, seek more attention from adults, and are more disruptive in school than children who have been reared at home (Rutter, 1979).

Orphanages care for the physical needs of children, but it is difficult to develop emotional bonds in such a setting.

I don't agree

However, it is not clear whether there will always be undesirable long-term consequences if a young child does not have a consistent attachment figure. In one study, institutionally reared English girls were studied as adults. If they had married faithful, loving husbands, they did not show obvious signs of anxiety. However, many of the women had difficulty finding a satisfactory husband, and many had chosen a deviant man as a spouse. These women were anxious, but an important cause of their anxiety was an unsatisfactory marriage (Rutter, Quinton, & Hill, 1990).

Partial Nonmaternal Care. In the United States increasing numbers of women with young children are employed outside the home. In 1993, 57 percent of children under 6 had either two working parents or a single working parent, and 50 percent of working women returned to work within one year of having a baby. Similar trends are evident in most western European nations, and maternal employment is the norm in eastern European countries, the former Soviet Union, and China (as well as among foraging groups such as the Efe; see Box 6.2). Maternal employment has created a need for new child-care arrangements. These are quite varied: 51 percent of families in the United States use relative care (30 percent grandparents), 26 percent use center-based care, 19 percent use family day-care (group care in the home of a nonrelative), and 4 percent have in-home care by a nonrelative (Scarr & Eisenberg, 1993).

There has been considerable controversy about the effects of nonmaternal care on infants' development. The controversy revolves around two issues, which need to be sharply distinguished from each other. First, is the presence of one primary caregiver during infancy critical to children's emotional, social, and/or cognitive development? Theories stressing the importance of attachment lead some psychologists to predict that attachment to the primary caregiver may be disrupted if infants spend many hours a day in the care of someone other than their biological mother. We might call this the "one mother" hypothesis. Second, is nonmaternal care sometimes lower-quality care, care that is insensitive or unstimulating, and does this pose a risk to infant development?

The "one mother" hypothesis is decisively refuted by several demonstrations that secure attachment and positive child outcomes can be observed in situations where there are multiple caregivers. Thus, 80 percent of infants growing up on rural collectives (called kibbutzim) in Israel—in which they are cared for much of the day by a nonrelative caretaker—have secure attachments to their mothers (Aviezer, Van IJzendoorn, Sagi, & Schuengel, 1994). This proportion is comparable to, or even higher than, the rate typically seen in home-reared American infants. Similarly, B. E. Anderson (1989) reported that early entrance into day care in Sweden was associated with *more* favorable child outcomes (in both the cognitive and socioemotional realms) at age 8 years than was later entrance or home care. In the United States, Field (1991) has also reported better cognitive and socioemotional outcomes for school-aged children who attended early day care. But note that all these studies involved situations in which child care was of generally high quality.

The second issue surrounding nonmaternal care concerns the quality of the available care at home or away from home. Not all day care creates conditions for healthy development. Important factors are warm and frequent interactions between adults and children, verbal stimulation, opportunities for exploration and stimulation, space, and materials that are varied and age appropriate. Some signs that parents can use to evaluate quality of child care are a small adult–child ratio (e.g., 1:3), small group size, caregivers with training in child development or early-childhood education, and space designed for children (Phillips, 1987).

Much infant day care in the United States is not high in quality. The interactions of caregivers with children are less sensitive than parents' typical interactions with their own children. Most infants are in care settings that vary greatly in quality, and these settings are difficult to monitor. Perhaps even more important, changes in caregivers and settings are the rule rather than the exception for infants in day care. Personnel turnover is high because the pay is often set at the minimum wage. Family day-care providers change, get "burned out," or go out of business. Also, many infants are cared for in two or three different settings; they may stay with a neighbor in the morning, then go to a relative's house in the afternoon. Frequent changes in people and places might be stressful for some children.

In sum, many infants in regular day care show healthy development. Quality of care, whether at home or elsewhere, is important for social and cognitive development, but high-quality care away from home is scarce and expensive. Unlike many other countries, the United States has not developed a system of quality child care at low cost to parents.

An additional problem especially marked in the United States is that it is often difficult to remain at home with a young infant without losing one's job. In many European nations, employed parents have an alternative to placing their infants in child care shortly after birth: they receive parental leaves of six to nine months at partial or nearly full pay. In the United States paid maternity leaves are unusual. Even unpaid leaves have typically lasted only four to six weeks (Kamerman, Kahn, & Kingston, 1983). The Family and Medical Leave Act, which went into effect in 1993 after much opposition, only requires 12 weeks of unpaid leave and does not cover all employed people.

☼ CULTURAL IDEALS AND CHILD REARING

All theories about infants' social development and the child-rearing practices associated with healthy development must be considered within a cultural context. Different cultures have different conceptions of the ideal child, and these beliefs determine how parents rear their children. Puritan parents in colonial New England believed that infants were willful and had to be tamed. They punished young children severely, and the children were generally conforming. Contemporary parents in Calcutta believe that children are uncontrollable. Accordingly, they are more tolerant of tantrums in 2-year-olds, and their children are less obedient than Puritan children were.

The differences in behavior between Japanese and American mothers provide another contrast. American mothers conceive of their mission as molding their children into active, independent beings by stimulating them and teaching them self-reliance and social skills. Japanese mothers see their task as building a close loyalty to and dependence on the mother and other members of the family. In line with these values, American mothers put their children in rooms of their own, and they play with their infants to make them vocalize, smile, and laugh. By contrast, Japanese mothers remain very close to their young children; they respond quickly to crying by soothing and quieting more often than stimulating their babies. It is not surprising that American infants are more active, vocal, and spontaneous than Japanese infants.

Japanese and American ideals of interaction with infants are different. Parents in each society seek to develop an adult adapted to the culture.

Even within our own society there have been major differences in how mothers have handled their infants in the past 70 years. Government pamphlets published in 1914 containing advice to American mothers told them that because babies have extremely sensitive nervous systems, mothers should avoid excessive stimulation of their infants. By the 1960s, such pamphlets instructed mothers to let their infants experience as much stimulation as they wished, because that is the way they learn about the world. In 1914, mothers were told not to feed or play with their babies every time they cried because those actions would spoil them. A half century later, mothers were told that they should not be afraid of spoiling their babies and that children will feel trusting and secure if their mothers always come to nurture them when they cry.

Contemporary Americans believe that it is essential to minimize anxiety in their 1-year-olds and to maximize their babies' comfort and security. These changes in advice reflect variations in philosophy and in the cultural concept of the ideal child. In spite of these variations, most children in each generation grow up to function well in their culture. Thus it is clear that there are many paths to adaptive social development.

☼ SUMMARY

In everyday conversation the word *emotion* is used to refer to conscious awareness of a specific change in internal feeling tone, often accompanied by thoughts about the quality of the feeling and the events that produced it. Because it is impossible for infants to report on their perceptions and thoughts, however, developmentalists have studied emotion in infants by examining changes in the brain and body that follow encounters with pain, deprivation, novelty, danger, and other events.

Infants display many reactions that suggest emotional states. Between 7 and 12 months of age, for example, a moderately unfamiliar event can produce a state of uncertainty. If the infant has no behavior it can use to divert its attention, the event may give rise to states that we call fear or anxiety. One of the most common emotions exhibited late in the first year is stranger anxiety. Infants also show fear of temporary separation from a familiar caregiver. These fears appear to be associated with the improvement in the infant's recall memory that occurs at about 8 months. They can be alleviated by the presence of a familiar person or a familiar setting.

Avoidance of the visual cliff also occurs at about 8 months, at the same time that infants begin to crawl or creep. It is believed that the infant's self-produced locomotion acts to crystallize cognitive abilities by causing the infant to pay increased attention to its environment.

Infants display a range of facial expressions that seem to indicate emotional states. However, because different observers may interpret an expression in different ways, psychologists are not certain that it is possible to know the emotional state of an infant simply by looking at its face.

Initially the infant's smile is a reflex, but by 2 months it occurs in response to human faces and voices. It may occur when the infant recognizes that an event resembles a previously acquired schema. Later, laughing occurs in response to social interaction, visual surprises, and tickling. Psychologists distinguish between the smiling or laughing that occurs in response to tickling and that which accompanies assimilation of a schema or mastery of a motor skill.

It appears that some babies are born with a bias toward certain moods and reaction styles, termed temperament. Scientists have studied a small set of temperamental dimensions, including activity, fussiness, fearfulness, sensitivity to stimuli, and attentiveness. Their research has shown that over time, parents come to react to children with difficult temperaments in special ways that can affect the children's behavior and adjustment later in life.

Studies of infants' activity levels have found a moderate genetic influence at 8 months but not at later ages. On the other hand, differences among infants in irritability may be modestly preserved for the first two years. Two of the most stable temperamental qualities are shyness and sociability; they have been found to persist throughout childhood and adolescence. Child-rearing conditions can influence the degree to which these tendencies are actualized, however.

The reciprocal influence of parental behavior and infant temperament forms the basis for the principle of bidirectionality. This principle states that children's development is a product of the interaction between their own characteristics and those of the people who socialize them.

Most theorists assume that the pattern of social interaction between the infant and its caregivers influences the infant's psychological growth in important ways. Sigmund Freud proposed a theory of development in which the infant passes through a series of psychosexual stages; in each stage a particular source of gratification (e.g., feeding) becomes central, and too much or too little gratification can slow the child's progress into the next stage. Erik Erikson's developmental theory emphasized psychosocial as opposed to psychosexual stages. A parallel theoretical approach, social learning theory, was based on the idea that social development occurs as a result of the reinforcement of certain responses through the reduction of biological drives.

Ethologists, in contrast, have studied the fixed action patterns exhibited by newborn animals and have attempted to find comparable patterns in humans.

The predominant theoretical framework for analyzing parent-child relationships is now attachment theory, proposed by the English psychiatrist John Bowlby. In this theory, a major result of parent-child interactions is the development in the infant of an emotional attachment to the caregiver, who is best able to soothe the baby and whom the baby approaches most often for play and consolation when aroused by novelty, danger, or distress. All normal infants form attachments, and many theorists propose that a strong or secure attachment provides a basis for healthy emotional and social development during later childhood.

Three major patterns of attachment have been described: Children who seek the parent when he or she returns after a brief separation in a laboratory setting are described as securely attached. Those who ignore the parent upon his or her return are classified as avoidant and insecurely attached. And children who alternately cling to the parent and push him or her away are described as resistant and insecurely attached. A fourth pattern, called disorganized, has been delineated more recently. Securely attached infants have been found to be more socially outgoing and cooperative than insecurely attached infants at age 5.

The targets of a child's attachments and the strength and quality of those attachments depend partly on the parents' behavior in relation to the child. Sensitive and responsive interaction is especially important, and this is more common in the presence of well-adjusted parents, a harmonious marriage or other social support, and an adaptable infant.

Some children who have grown up in institutions are more dependent and disruptive than children who have been reared at home. Controversies about partial nonmaternal care need to be separated into questions. First, one hypothesis states that "one mother" is necessary for healthy development; this does not seem to be correct. Second, a different hypothesis focuses on the fact that nonmaternal care is not always sensitive and of high quality. Quality of care does seem to have an effect on healthy development.

It should also be remembered that each child is reared within a particular cultural context and that most children in each generation grow up to function well in their culture.

REVIEW QUESTIONS

1. Distinguish between the meaning of *emotion* in everyday conversation and the meaning of the term as it is used by developmental psychologists.

2. What conditions give rise to fear or anxiety in an 8-month-old infant? How is the emergence of these emotions explained by contemporary psychologists?

3. Describe the visual cliff. How has this device contributed to the understanding of infants' cognitive development?

4. What events cause the infant to smile or laugh at birth, 2 months, 4 months, and 1 year?

5. What is meant by a temperamental quality?

6. What temperamental qualities of infants have been found to be most stable?

7. Briefly discuss four theoretical perspectives on social and emotional development in infancy.

8. What is meant by attachment? What role does it play in social and emotional development?

9. How is attachment measured? Briefly describe the four major patterns of attachment that have been identified.

10. How do variations in the quality of children's attachment in infancy affect their later development?

CRITICAL THINKING ABOUT THE CHAPTER

1. Imagine being the parent of an inhibited child. What issues would arise in child rearing? How would you attempt to deal with them? What about an uninhibited child? What issues might arise in this case?

2. American society has seen intense debate recently concerning how best to raise young children. One popular magazine has even coined the term the "Mommy Wars" to refer to the day care debate. Why is this discussion so emotional? How does it relate to other themes in contemporary society? Do you see a resolution at hand?

KEY TERMS

anal stage
attachment
autonomous
avoidant attachment
bidirectionality
dismissing
disorganized attachment
emotion
ethology
fixed action patterns
inhibited/uninhibited
insecure attachment

libido
oral stage
preoccupied
primary reinforcer
releasers
resistant attachment
secondary reinforcer
secure attachment
social referencing
Strange Situation
temperament
visual cliff

SUGGESTED READINGS

Ainsworth, M. D. S., Blehar, M. C., Waters, E., & Wall, S. (1978). *Patterns of attachment.* Hillsdale, NJ: Erlbaum. Summarizes the information that led to the use of the Strange Situation to classify children as securely or insecurely attached.

Averill, J. R. (1982). *Anger and aggression.* New York: Springer-Verlag. This insightful book examines the available knowledge on the emotion of anger and associated aggressive behavior.

Bowlby, J. (1969). *Attachment* (Vol. 1). New York: Basic Books. In this classic work Bowlby summarizes his theoretical ideas about the origins of attachment and its consequences.

Kagan, J. (1984). *The nature of the child.* New York: Basic Books. A collection of essays that includes chapters on the meaning of emotion, the consequences of temperament, and the significance of the concept of attachment.

Karen, R. (1994). *Becoming attached.* New York: Warner Books. A very readable account of the origins and development of attachment theory. Written by a clinical psychologist enthusiastic about the approach, although there is also coverage of critics.

Thomas, A., & Chess, S. (1977). *Temperament and development.* New York: Brunner Mazel. Summarizes the pioneering research of two psychiatrists who reintroduced the concept of temperament into discussions of development.

PART IV

THE TRANSITION TO CHILDHOOD

CHAPTER

7

THE SECOND AND THIRD YEARS

SYMBOLIC ABILITY

Symbolic Play
Imitation
Drawing
Seeing Models as Representations

THE ONSET OF SELF-AWARENESS

Self-Recognition
Describing One's Own Behavior
A Sense of Possession

EMPATHY AND A MORAL SENSE

Empathy
Standards
Violations of Rules

FAMILY INTERACTIONS IN THE SECOND AND THIRD YEARS

One hot day in August, LaDoris Washington was getting ready for her daughter's first birthday. She put flowers on the table and set places for the guests: herself and her husband, Harold; her father and mother and Harold's father; her sister; and their next-door neighbors. When everyone had gathered, they sang "Happy Birthday" to Michelle, who was wearing a new ruffled dress that her aunt had made for the occasion. LaDoris blew out the candle on the cake (encouraging Michelle to make a few blowing sounds along with her), and everyone had a slice of the applesauce-and-raisin cake that was LaDoris's specialty. Michelle didn't seem to like it, so LaDoris gave her a chocolate pudding instead. Soon, smears of pudding adorned the new dress. LaDoris sighed, thinking of what she would have to go through to wash out all that chocolate. But Michelle was smiling so broadly, LaDoris couldn't bring herself to take the pudding away.

Two years later, Michelle was bouncing around the house, excited as could be about her upcoming third birthday party. She had picked a cake with chocolate icing and multicolor flowers at the bakery, and decided to wear her favorite purple overalls. Her friends were coming: Jill, Angela, Walter, Ismail, and her best friend, Maria. They would play some games and then watch a tape of a magic show. As she helped her mother by setting out paper plates and plastic spoons, she came on a spoon with a crack. "No good," she said to her mother, holding up the spoon. "Do we have another one?"

The two years that follow the first birthday see an amazing transformation in children. Michelle was a baby at her first birthday party, a baby who enjoyed being with people and seeing them excited, who tried to imitate her mother blowing out the candles, but who was still a baby for whom her family made almost all decisions. By age three, she had become a child (who didn't like being called a baby!) with likes and dislikes she could clearly express in language. She had definite ideas regarding such matters as what to wear, what to eat, and who to have at her party. She increasingly claimed her place in social interactions, establishing herself as a family member and a member of a peer group. And she had clear standards for what things should be like, as shown by her rejection of the broken spoon.

In the preceding chapters we have emphasized the many things infants can do and think about. In the next two chapters of the book, we explore some of the things they can't do or can't do very well, together with the changes that occur in the years between age 1 and age 3, the period in which the child moves from infancy to childhood. In this chapter, we consider three broad classes of behavior that change a great deal in this period. One important change involves the strengthening and flowering of the representational capacities of the infant into the powerful symbolic capacities seen in older children. Changes in these capacities—an aspect of development emphasized by Piaget—underlie changes in play and imitation that occur in the toddler period. A second class of behavior emerging in toddlerhood is self-awareness. A third is empathy and a moral sense. The final topic in this chapter concerns the challenges that the emerging capabilities of the 1- and 2-year-old can pose for adults interacting with them. The emergence of language—a very important part of the transition from infancy to childhood—is examined in the next chapter.

Between the ages of 1 and 3 years, children change in important ways, but this sister and brother can also find mutual interests.

⚙ SYMBOLIC ABILITY

Letting one thing stand for another is one of the distinctive aspects of human thought. While species other than our own may be able to symbolize their experience to some degree, the **symbolic ability** of humans includes many different capacities to create and accept arbitrary relationships between objects and ideas. We develop a large variety of creative and powerful systems of representation. Notably, we can communicate using language, letting distinctive acoustic strings stand for things we know. But symbolism goes beyond language and is a pervasive aspect of human thought. For example, people can construct models and diagrams, can pretend that one thing is another, and can imagine states of affairs that they have never encountered. In this section, we discuss the emergence between the ages of 1 and 3 of some of these aspects of symbolic ability.

Symbolic Play

All normal children play. The notion of play is a familiar one, and it may seem quite obvious that, for instance, a child playing a toy xylophone is playing. But play is actually fairly difficult to define. For instance, is a grand master actually "playing" when playing chess? The long hours of study and preparation and the seriousness of the battle involved in a chess match at this level suggest that "play" is more a convenient term than an accurate description of the activity.

Catherine Garvey (1977) has helped formalize our understanding of play by listing the criteria that most observers use in defining **play**:

1. Play is pleasurable and enjoyable.
2. Play has no extrinsic goals. The child's motivations are subjective and serve no practical purpose.
3. Play is spontaneous and voluntary, freely chosen by the player.
4. Play involves some active engagement on the part of the player.

Infants play by banging objects, swinging them, and putting them in their mouths. However, around the first birthday, their play changes. Children transform experience and impose their own ideas on objects, rather than simply adjusting their actions to an object's physical properties. In the hands of a 10-month-old, a rubber ball is an object to squeeze and throw and a cup is something to hold and put to the mouth. However, by the second birthday children invent new and often original uses for these and other objects. They may treat a ball as a piece of food, a cup as a hat, a plate as a blanket, or a ball of yarn as a balloon. In other words, children are now capable of symbolism; they can both create and accept an arbitrary relationship between an object and an idea. It is likely that this is a uniquely human quality (P. K. Smith, 1982). No one has ever observed any animal engaging in pretend play without prior training.

Symbolic ability develops in phases, with a sequence that is highly predictable from infant to infant (Belsky & Most, 1981). The earliest kind of play with objects is putting objects into the mouth (an action that poses a very significant danger of choking if an object is small or has detachable parts) and simple manipulation (that is, handling—such as indiscriminate waving or banging—that is in no way specific to the object or its function). Such play is very common at 7.5 months, but, as seen in Figure 7.1, it declines steadily to 16.5 months and then levels out (while not

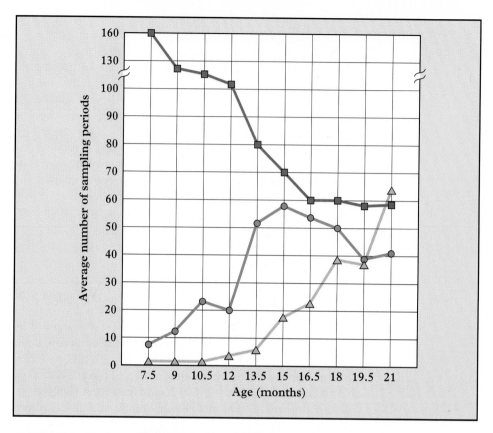

FIGURE 7.1 Changes with age in infant play. Squares show amount of simple exploration, circles show relational play, and triangles show pretend play. After "From Exploration to Play: A Cross-Sectional Study of Infant Free Play Behavior, " by J. Belsky and R. K. Most, 1981, *Developmental Psychology, 17*, p. 636. Adapted with permsission of the American Psychological Association.

completely dropping out of the child's repertoire). Around 12 months children begin to treat objects more relationally, bringing one into contact with another, sometimes appropriately (for example, putting a cup on a saucer). They also begin to treat a toy cup as if it were real—for instance, by raising it to the lips. Although the degree of distortion imposed on these objects is minimal, no 7-month-old would behave in this way. By the middle of the second year, children go one step further and impose new functions on objects. They might turn a doll upside down and treat it as a salt shaker or play with a wooden block as if it were a chair.

Many 2-year-olds seem capable of simple metaphor. For example, they will treat two wooden balls that differ only in size as if they were a parent and child. Two-year-olds are also capable of following sequences of pretend actions in which some of the components are purely imaginary (Harris & Kavanaugh, 1993; Harris, Kavanaugh, & Meredith, 1994). For example, if a teddy bear is made to take a teapot and pretend to pour its contents over a doll, 2-year-olds will say that the bear poured "tea" over the doll and made her "wet."

An interesting change occurs late in the second year. At this time children begin to replace themselves with a toy as the active agent in play. For example, a child may put a toy bottle to a doll's mouth rather than to her own, or place a toy telephone beside an animal's head rather than her own. The role of these toys has changed. Instead of being mere participants in the child's sensorimotor schemes, they have become symbolic agents in play that the child is both inventing and directing (Kagan, 1981).

Changes in symbolic play with objects across age occur at about the same time across very different cultures: in American children, in children living on islands in the Fiji chain, and in children living in Vietnamese families that have recently immigrated to the United States (Kagan, 1981). Similar sequences of development in symbolic play have also been observed in deaf children, whose play is less directed by language if they grow up with hearing parents who cannot sign (Blum, Fields, Scharfman, & Silber, 1994), and in Down syndrome children, whose development occurs at a slower rate and ultimately stops at lower levels than that of normal children (Cicchetti, Beeghly, & Weiss-Perry, 1994).

Some theorists emphasize the role of play in attempting to cope with anxiety and conflict. For example, a child acting out an interaction between a mother and a doll might scold and punish the doll because he is trying to work through pressures currently exerted on him. However, while acting out psychic conflicts can be one reason for play, most play is not motivated by inner unrest (K. H. Rubin, Fein, & Vandenberg, 1983).

Other investigators stress the role of play in the development of intellectual skills (Bruner, Jolly, & Sylva, 1976). In play, children can experiment without interference, and in so doing they may develop complex abilities. Playing with crayons and paper facilitates drawing skills; manipulating blocks teaches the child something about mechanics; playing with objects promotes the ability to generate new ways of using these objects. For example, children who had played with a set of sticks and colored chalk solved a "problem" that required them to clamp two sticks together to get the chalk out of a box. They were as quick and efficient as children who had watched someone else solve the problem (Sylva, Bruner, & Genova, 1976).

A current conception of play emphasizes both its cognitive and social aspects, seeing these two sides as deeply interwoven (Slade & Wolf, 1994). Play can be solitary, but it is more commonly interactional. It can be facilitated and supported by responsive adults, as discussed by attachment theory (see Chapter 6). The amount and developmental level of symbolic play seems, in fact, to be a sensitive indicator of the nature of the relationship between an adult and a young child (Greenspan & Lieberman, 1994).

As children play with objects in a more symbolic manner, their reactions to other children also change. Before the first birthday a meaningful interaction between two children is rare. Ten-month-olds treat other children as if they were animate toys; they pull at their hair, poke at their eyes, and babble to them. But between 13 and 24 months, children become capable of engaging in complementary social interaction (Howes, 1987). That is, children run and chase, hide and seek, offer and receive. Their behaviors with familiar peers are at a higher level than those seen with unacquainted children, indicating that they have developed knowledge of the other child's preferences and established routines that are fun and interesting for both partners. In fact, a fascinating finding in recent work on social development is that 1-year-olds can, in fact, form stable friendships. (See Box 7.1.)

Between 25 and 36 months, children take another step in their peer play, beginning to engage in cooperative social pretend play, such as bus driver and passenger or store owner and customer (Howes, 1987). This kind of play is the social analogue of the pretend skills children are also building up in their solitary play.

⬙ **BOX 7.1**

FRIENDS FROM BABYHOOD

Howes (1987) has described the onset of stable friendship patterns in children as young as 1 year and has shown evidence that these relationships facilitate the social and emotional development of the participants. An illustration of this phenomenon comes from the response of a 9-year-old girl to an invitation to write about a person who had influenced her life.

One person that influenced my life is Stephanie Rogers. I met Stephanie when I was four months old! We met because we went to the same school back then. The school was Temple Day Care. Stephanie lives in Merchantville, New Jersey, and goes to Morristown Friends. While I live in Merion, Pennsylvania and go to Cynwyd School.

Stephanie has had a big influence in my life because for one thing she discovered the summer camp I go to currently. She has helped me in other ways, too. I have helped her, too.

Stephanie has been with me most of my life and is a special friend. (Talia Lerner)

Being with familiar peers and friends enhances children's ability to pretend, because specific roles and routines can be established. It is not until children are 3 and 4 that they can easily direct other children about their roles in a pretend scenario ("You be the teacher and I'll be the little girl"). At that point, social relationships become more flexible. Two-year-olds will work together at a doll house, talk to each other on the telephone, and imitate each other in jumping off a couch. But they do not play games with rules, and their play episodes last only a few minutes. Nevertheless, interactive experiences with other children facilitate cooperative play later on (Kagan, 1981; Mueller & Brenner, 1977).

Imitation

Symbolic play is one kind of evidence of increasingly powerful symbolic abilities in children. As we have seen, children show growing capacities to let one thing stand for another—even when there is no obvious relation between the symbol and what is symbolized—and become able to interweave multiple symbols in complex sequences of pretend or make-believe. Another capacity developing from 1 to 3— that has been linked to symbolic ability, especially by Piaget—is children's selective **imitation**, or ability to duplicate particular observed actions of others.

While there is controversy about the existence of imitation in newborns or very young infants (Jacobson, 1979; Meltzoff & Moore, 1977), there is no doubt—as we saw in Chapter 5—that imitation, even delayed imitation of actions seen some time ago, becomes possible before the first birthday (Meltzoff, 1988). Infants of 11 months can even remember two-step sequences of novel events, such as making a rattle by putting a button in a box with a slot in it and then shaking it. They show imitation of such sequences even after a delay of three months (Mandler & McDonough, 1995). However, imitation becomes both more frequent and more complex during the next several years. By 30 months, children are able to retain substantial portions of complicated sequences containing eight events (Bauer & Fivush, 1992).

Children are much more likely to imitate their parents than to imitate their brothers and sisters or even characters seen regularly on television. In one study, 71 percent of the imitative acts of 2-year-old children, as recorded by their mothers, were imitations of maternal acts (Kuczynski, Zahn-Waxler, & Radke-Yarrow, 1987). Most of these imitations occurred hours, days, or weeks after they had been seen, especially if the acts were punishments (see Figure 7.2).

Imitation is an efficient way to learn and perfect new actions. Thus, the capacity to imitate another person is a major foundation for the advanced intellectual and technological development of the human species. Imitation is quite rare even among chimpanzees, and it seems to represent one of the adaptations that allow human beings to survive and reproduce with great success (Tomasello, Kruger, & Ratner, 1993). Imitation seems to be an almost universal maturational phenomenon, "a capacity that is built into the human species" (Yando, Seitz, & Zigler, 1978, p. 4). Interestingly, however, there is at least one exception to this rule. Children with autism, a severe developmental problem whose origin is currently unclear (see Chapter 16), have great difficulty with imitation (I. M. Smith & Bryson, 1994). The fact that autistic children also sometimes show advanced representational abilities (see Box 7.2) poses an intriguing problem for understanding the bases of the development of representation.

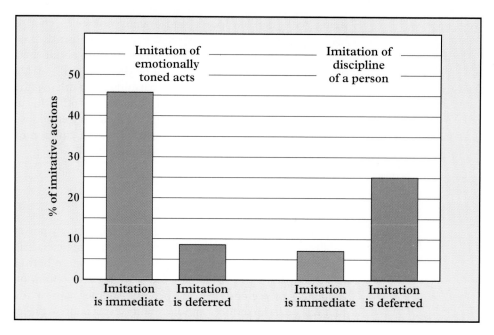

FIGURE 7.2 Two-year-olds are likely to imitate emotionally toned acts immediately but are more likely to imitate disciplinary acts after a delay. After "Development and Content of Imitation in the Second and Third Year of Life," by L. Kuczynski, C. Zahn-Waxler, and M. Radke-Yarrow, 1987, *Developmental Psychology, 23*, pp. 276–282. Copyright by the American Psychological Association. Adapted with permission of the American Psychological Association.

What are the determinants of imitation? Children observe many more behaviors of other people than they ever duplicate in their own actions. Why do they imitate only a small number of the many acts they have observed? Four hypotheses about the determinants of imitation are listed and evaluated in the following paragraphs.

1. *Imitation to promote social interactions.* When an infant imitates a parent, the parent often smiles, tells the baby how wonderful and intelligent it is, and imitates the baby in return. The responsiveness of the parent may reinforce the baby's imitative behavior. Such social reinforcements increase the baby's general tendency to imitate, and they influence which behaviors the baby chooses to imitate. Children are more likely to imitate an action that has received approval, such as eating with a spoon, than a response that is ignored, such as banging two forks together.

2. *Imitation to enhance similarity to another.* Another basis for imitation emerges as the child enters the third year and begins to imitate specific individuals rather than particular acts. By the second birthday most children are aware that they have qualities that make them more similar to some people than to others. For example, the boy recognizes that he and the father share the properties of short hair, trousers, and similar genital anatomy. The recognition of similarities to the father and other males leads the boy to assume that he belongs to the same category as other males. Correspondingly, girls assume that they belong to the same category as other females. This insight provokes each child to make an active effort to search for additional similarities to other people in order to firmly establish the category to which they belong. They do this by imitating the actions of those people.

BOX 7.2
EXCEPTIONAL DRAWING ABILITY IN AN AUTISTIC CHILD

Left: typical drawing of a rooster drawn by a 6- or 7-year-old. Right: Nadia's drawing of a rooster. From *Nadia: A Case of Extraordinary Drawing Ability in an Autistic Child* (Figures 11 and 33), by L. Selfe, 1977, New York: Academic Press. Reprinted with permission.

In normal children, drawing develops through the primitive stages described in the text, in highly predictable sequences. Even at age 6 or so, most normal children will draw recognizable figures or objects, but without use of perspective, shading, or other artistic devices. For instance, above, at the left, is a typical picture of a rooster as drawn by a 6- to 7-year-old. A fascinating exception to this rule is seen in the drawings produced by an autistic girl called Nadia (Selfe, 1977). Beginning about age 3, and despite an inability to speak at this time or to relate normally to other people, Nadia produced some highly sophisticated drawings (see her drawing of a rooster, at the right, also produced at 6 years). The nature of the neurological and psychological organization that allowed Nadia to draw in this way is not known, but her story provides an intriguing glimpse of the extent to which human abilities can develop in isolation from each other.

3. *Emotional arousal as a basis for imitating.* Children more often imitate their parents than other adults. One reason may be that parents are a more continuous source of emotional arousal—both pleasant and unpleasant—than are most other people. Individuals who have the power to arouse the child emotionally—whether to joy, uncertainty, anger, or fear—recruit the child's attention, and as a result the

Imitation is the basis for much of human learning.

child more thoroughly watches their actions than those of people who command less attention. A similar process occurs among children playing together. When pairs of unacquainted 2-year-olds play together, it is often the passive, quieter child who imitates the more dominant, active, loquacious one. The inhibited youngster appears to be apprehensive about losing a toy to the other and watches the dominant child closely. When the dominant one performs an action that the passive child might be able to master (e.g., jumping off a table), the latter is likely to imitate that act within the next few minutes.

4. *Imitation to gain goals.* Imitation can be a self-conscious attempt to gain pleasure, power, property, or any number of other desired goals. For example, a child who is trying to build a house with blocks may watch carefully as another child or an adult builds a similar structure, and may then imitate those actions. Or a 3-year-old may imitate the bullying behavior of another child because that behavior succeeds in getting desired toys away from other children. This basis for imitation typically emerges after the second birthday. At this point it is appropriate to say that children are motivated to imitate others, because they have an idea of a goal to be gained through the imitative act.

In summary, imitation may occur because of response uncertainty, social reinforcement, a desire to be more like another person, or a desire to attain particular goals. The behaviors imitated during the first 3 years of life depend partly on the child's level of cognitive development, which determines what behaviors the child perceives as challenging but not impossible. The motivation to be similar to another and the degree of emotional arousal induced by another person determine whom the child will imitate, and the motivation for certain goals determines what will be imitated.

Drawing

Children begin to engage in ever more sophisticated and complex pretend play in the period between 1 and 3 years, and their capacity to remember and imitate action becomes surer. They also begin to acquire the ability to understand and produce notations of experience, that is, to master systems of symbolization in which one thing stands for another. One important kind of notation humans use is artistic. While visual art may seem to represent the world in an obvious way, because drawings share properties with the objects they represent, reducing a complex three-dimensional world to paper is actually not an obvious process. Humans have solved the problems involved in varying ways; compare the representations of the ancient Egyptians found in pyramids with the perspective drawings of Leonardo da Vinci. Children need to learn how to accomplish the task of representing the world in drawing.

Children's drawings become more symbolic during the second and third years. Sometime in the second year children begin to scribble, but they rarely try to draw familiar objects. Although their drawings do not portray specific objects, if they are asked to label a set of scribbles they may call it a dog, a cat, or a person. But by 3 years of age children create symbolic forms that look like animals or people (see Figure 7.3).

FIGURE 7.3 Drawings of a person by a 2-year-old (left) and a 3-year-old (right). From *The Second Year* by J. Kagan, 1981, Cambridge, MA: Harvard University Press.

FIGURE 7.4 A picture of a face drawn by an adult examiner and shown to young children. From *The Second Year* by J. Kagan, 1981, Cambridge, MA: Harvard University Press.

In one study, an examiner drew a schematic face on a piece of white paper, as illustrated in Figure 7.4. She then gave the child a piece of paper and told the child to make that drawing. The developmental sequence was very similar for children from different cultures. The first attempt to copy the face, around 16 months, usually resulted in a scribbling of parallel lines. During the next phase, which began to appear at about 20 months, children created an approximation of a crude circle but included no internal elements to represent the eyes, nose, or mouth. By the second birthday, most middle-class American children were able to draw a circle, and at 30 months most children attempted to place a few dots or lines inside the circle to represent parts of the face (Kagan, 1981) (see Figure 7.5).

Seeing Models as Representations

Drawing is one medium humans can use to represent the world. Another symbolic possibility is to construct models, that is, smaller (and usually simpler) versions of something to be represented. For instance, architects commonly construct models of buildings they are designing. As with drawing, it might seem that the relation between the model and the real world is so obvious that it would be present from very early in life. This is not the case, however. DeLoache (1989) has described a very abrupt change, generally occurring between 2.5 and 3 years, in children's ability to see a model as standing for the real world.

In DeLoache's studies, the experimenter played a game with children in which a toy was hidden in an ordinary-size room. The child was then asked to find a miniature version of the hidden object in a miniature room that was a scale model of the big one. For instance, if a Snoopy dog had been hidden under a chair in the real room, a small Snoopy could be found under a miniature chair in the scale model. At 2.5 years, very few children could find the toy when they had to go from room to model (or vice versa). However, they had no trouble finding the toy in the space in which they originally saw it hidden, showing that their problem was not a problem with memory. In dramatic contrast, almost all 3-year-olds could solve these tasks.

DeLoache argues that younger children have difficulty with this task because they are not able to see something as both what it is (a little room) and as a repre-

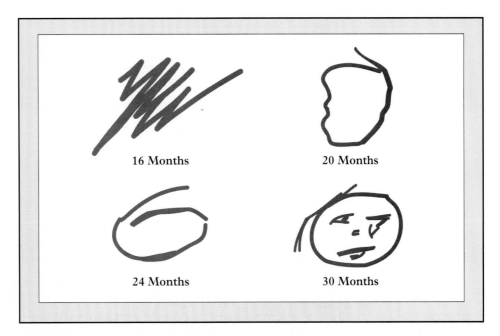

FIGURE 7.5 Drawings made by children of four ages when asked to make a picture like the one done by the examiner shown in Figure 7.4. From *The Second Year* by J. Kagan, 1981, Cambridge, MA: Harvard University Press.

sentation (of the larger room). They see the model room as an object-in-itself, not necessarily related to the big room. One support for this argument is that children have much less difficulty using a photograph as a tool to help in finding the toy, presumably because a photograph is more obviously a representation and less obviously something of interest in its own right. DeLoache's work shows that the development of the ability to let one thing stand for another (or to represent) can have a protracted history and involve many subcomponents of skill. Each advance in representational power is an important addition to the armamentarium of powerful and flexible problem solving at which the human species excels.

THE ONSET OF SELF-AWARENESS

Each of us is familiar with the experience of reflecting upon our feelings and thoughts, knowing whether we are able to solve a particular problem, and initiating or inhibiting a goal-directed sequence of behaviors. In other words, we are conscious of our qualities and potentials for action. The last half of the second year is a time when children begin to have **self-awareness**, a capacity to perceive their own qualities, states, and abilities. Observations of children in our own and other cultures reveal the appearance of a set of behaviors that can be called self-awareness.

Self-Recognition

One of the most basic indicators of the emergence of self-awareness during the second year comes from studies of children's recognition of themselves in a mirror (Lewis & Brooks-Gunn, 1979). Children from 9 to 24 months of age were first

This 18-month-old is showing signs of recognizing himself in a mirror.

allowed to look at themselves in a mirror. Then their mothers surreptitiously marked their noses with rouge, and the children were allowed to look at themselves in the mirror again. Children younger than about 18 to 21 months did not touch their nose or face when they saw the rouge in their reflected image, but by 24 months two-thirds of the children put their finger to their nose. Soon after children began to point to their rouge-colored nose, they also began to use the pronouns I, me, and you, suggesting that they were now distinguishing clearly between the self and other people.

There may be a contribution of maturation to the emergence of a sense of self. One argument for this conclusion comes from a longitudinal study of a deaf child (born of deaf parents) who was learning to communicate with American Sign Language. In the middle of her second year, the same time that hearing children begin to describe their actions as they are performing them, the deaf child began to use signs that made reference to herself (Petitto, 1983). Thus, the emergence of self-reference appears to occur at about the same time in children acquiring very different kinds of systems of self-reference.

Describing One's Own Behavior

Children show self-awareness not only by referring to themselves but also by being aware of their own actions. When children begin to speak in three- and four-word sentences that contain verbs, they often describe their own actions as they are performing them. The 2-year-old says, "Go up" as he climbs up on a chair, "I fix" as he tries to rebuild a fallen tower of blocks, or "Want cookie" as he goes to the kitchen.

Children are more likely to describe their own activities than the behaviors of others (Huttenlocher, Smiley, & Charney, 1983). There are several possible reasons for this. One is that children are most interested in their own activities. As a consequence, children describe their behaviors (but not those of others). Another possibility, however, for why children initially describe their own actions rather than those of others is that children do not initially realize that other people are agents of actions in the same way that they themselves are. Their access to inner knowledge about the reasons for what they do may lead to a more vivid sense of agency for the self, one which is only subsequently extended to other human beings (Huttenlocher et al., 1983). Support for this argument is provided by the observation that when children begin to talk about the actions of other people, they talk about actions involving characteristic movements (e.g., running, throwing) before they talk about actions involving unobservables, such as having goals and being a cause (e.g., opening).

A Sense of Possession

Social interactions between children provide additional signs of self-awareness. Consider the following example. Two 3-year-old boys, total strangers, were playing on opposite sides of an unfamiliar room with their mothers present. During the first 20 minutes of play, Jack took toys from Bill on four separate occasions. On each occasion Bill did nothing. He did not protest, cry, whine, retaliate, or retreat to his mother for help. But after the fourth seizure Bill left his toys, walked across the room, took a toy that Jack had been playing with earlier, and brought it back to his own play area. Several minutes later, while Bill was playing with a wagon, Jack tried to take it. This time Bill held on and successfully resisted Jack's attempts at appropriation.

Why did Bill resist Jack on the fifth occasion, though he had not done so on the first four? One reason may be that the continued experience of losing toys finally evoked in Bill an idea of personal possession, even though he was playing with these toys for the first time. When objects are lost or seized, the child may try to reaffirm his sense of possession by resisting or by taking the other child's toys. These arguments are based on the assumption that the child has the concept of a "self" that can possess objects, even temporarily, and maintain control over them.

Two-year-old children who attain a sense of self-awareness a little earlier than other children are usually more possessive. In one study, 2-year-old boys were first tested for degree of self-awareness using the mirror test described previously. They were also evaluated in terms of their understanding of the pronouns *my, you,* and *I* and their ability to adopt the perspective of another person. The boys were then observed in pairs in a free play session. The boys who had a firmer understanding of self were much more possessive of the toys, more often yelling and screaming, "My ball" when the other child came toward them (Levine, 1983).

These findings suggest that as children mature and become consciously aware of themselves, they also become more possessive and more likely to become involved in quarrels. Perhaps this is the price humans pay for the gift of self-consciousness. However, the values of the society in which the child is raised can either amplify or mute this natural possessiveness. If adults discourage such behavior, as they do on Israeli kibbutzim or on communes in China, children will be less possessive with objects than they are in most American homes, where private property is highly valued.

✧ EMPATHY AND A MORAL SENSE

The emergence of self-awareness is accompanied by other important emerging abilities. One is the occurrence of **empathy**: the ability to appreciate the perceptions and feelings of others. Traditionally, many theorists, including Piaget, have argued that young children are lacking in the ability to understand how the world appears to anyone but themselves. However, recent research has shown clear evidence that sometime toward the second birthday, children do begin to show signs of empathy, with increasing frequency and clarity in the year between the second and third birthdays (Zahn-Waxler & Radke-Yarrow, 1990). Another emerging ability, likely linked to the ability to show empathy, is the development of standards and a moral sense.

Empathy

The ability to infer the emotional state of another person is often most clearly revealed in the behavior of children when they see a person who is hurt or in distress. In one study, mothers were asked to keep diaries about their children's everyday behavior. The diary data showed a major change in the children's actions during the last half of the second year. During this period children show an increased tendency to hug or kiss a person who has been hurt, or to give a victim a toy or food. These prosocial or helpful behaviors are relatively rare during the first part of the second year (Radke-Yarrow, Zahn-Waxler, & Chapman, 1983).

Anecdotes can convey the existence of early empathy very clearly. One especially precocious incident is recounted by Dunn and Kendrick (1982). A 15-month-old boy, Len, was in the garden with his brother. Len was a stocky boy who often played a game with his parents that made them laugh. He would come toward the parents, walking in an odd way and pulling up his T-shirt and showing his stomach. On the day in question, Len's brother had fallen and was crying vigorously. Len first watched solemnly and then approached his brother, pulled up his T-shirt, showed his tummy, and spoke to his brother as if he were trying to make him laugh and thus dilute his distress. An even more complex sequence of behavior is shown in Figure 7.6, in which a 21-month-old is responding to his mother's acting the emotion of sadness. He looks at her, then asks her what's wrong, then tries to distract her with a hand puppet, then asks for help from the experimenter, and finally gives his mother a hug while making consoling sounds. The fact that most 2-year-olds are capable of inferring a psychological and emotional state in another person implies that children can recall their own earlier emotional experiences and act on that information.

Standards

During the last 6 months of the second year, children begin to create idealized representations of objects, events, and behaviors. Shirts should have all their buttons; clothes should have no rips. And, as we saw with Michelle in the vignette that opened the chapter, spoons should have no cracks. These representations are termed **standards**. At the same time, children acquire standards about correct and incorrect behavior in specific situations, often dealing with cleanliness, control of

FIGURE 7.6 This 21-month-old's mother was asked to pretend to be sad. This sequence of pictures shows his empathic response. From "The Origin of Empathetic Concern" by C. Zahn-Waxler and M. Radke-Yarrow, 1990, *Motivation and Emotion, 14,* pp. 116–117.

aggression, and obedience to parents. These standards are the beginning of the child's understanding of right and wrong, good and bad; they are the first step in the development of a sense of morality.

If events match children's standards, they may smile, but events that violate a standard may produce signs of anxiety or distress. For example, children will point to broken objects, torn clothing, missing buttons, and the like, and show concern in their voice and face. They will point to a crack in a plastic toy and say, "Oh-oh," "Broke," or "Yukky." When they witness a mishap, they will also sometimes attempt to correct or repair it (P. M. Cole, Barrett, & Zahn-Waxler, 1992).

In one study (Kagan, 1981), 14- and 19-month-olds were brought to a laboratory playroom containing a large number of toys, some of which were purposely flawed (a doll's face was marked with black crayon; the clothes on another doll were torn; the head of an animal was removed). None of the 14-month-old infants paid any special attention to the damaged toys, but over half the 19-month-olds were obviously preoccupied with them. They brought them to their mother, pointed to the damaged part, stuck their finger in the place where an animal's head had been removed, or, if they could talk, indicated that something was wrong by saying "fix" or "broke."

Parents often report that during the few months before the second birthday, children suddenly show concern over dirty hands, torn clothes, and broken cups. Parents do not suddenly begin to punish destruction of property or dirty hands at 18 months; so why do the signs of concern appear at this age? It seems that children are developing the ability to infer that events have causes (even when they do not observe the cause). For example, a 21-month-old child sees a baby crying and immediately assumes that the baby is hungry or hurt. When children react emotionally to a broken toy or a shirt without a button, they are assuming that the flaw is not an inherent property of the object but has been caused by something or someone. For example, American 2- and 3-year-olds, as well as Mayan children living in villages in the Yucatan peninsula, looked longer at a picture of a human face with distorted features than at a normal face. The children's verbalizations—"What happened to his nose?" or "Who hit him in the nose?"—implied concern about the forces that might have damaged the face and inferences as to the events that might

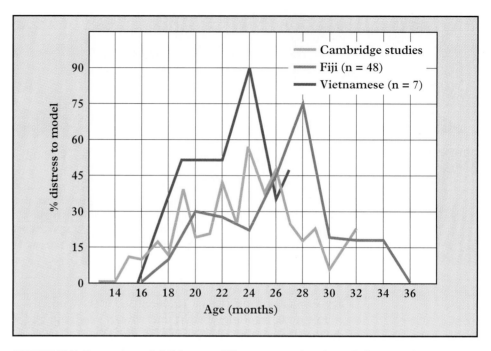

FIGURE 7.7 Percentage of children at different ages who showed distress when a model demonstrated a behavior that was moderately difficult for them to imitate. In three cultures, children around the age of 2 years showed considerable distress, suggesting concern over attaining standards. After *The Second Year* by J. Kagan, 1981, Cambridge, MA: Harvard University Press..

have produced the distortion. These observations suggest that by the second birthday, children are ready to show concern about events that violate their standards and to assume that these events were produced by some external force (Kagan, 1981).

Also around the second birthday, children display distress if they are unable to meet standards of behavior imposed by others. If 1- to 2-year-olds are only a little uncertain of their ability to perform a witnessed act, they will imitate. If they are too uncertain, they may show signs of distress. In one series of observations, many 2-year-olds stopped playing, protested, clung to their mother, and even cried after having watched a researcher display actions that were a little too difficult to assimilate or to remember well (Kagan, 1981). The distress reactions did not occur when the actions displayed were either easy to imitate or far beyond the child's ability (see Figure 7.7). This means that 2-year-olds have some awareness of their ability to imitate an act, and become anxious if they are uncertain. If an act is very hard, they do not cry, because they are not uncertain and will not try to imitate it.

Another phenomenon implying that children possess standards of correct and incorrect performance is the appearance of a smile when they meet a self-imposed standard that requires the investment of effort. Children who take 5 minutes to complete a six-piece puzzle often smile when they finish the task. They do not look at the mother while smiling; rather, the smile is a private response reflecting the recognition that they have met the standard they set for themselves. Children will also smile if they are about to do or are in the middle of a forbidden act that violates a standard, such as putting a hand in the toilet or threatening to spill some milk on the floor (Dunn, 1988).

Violations of Rules

As children grow from infancy into childhood, they become more likely to be interested in exploring violations of adult rules and events that will provoke disgust or disapproval in others. It is common to see 2-year-olds explore all the possible variations on acceptable behavior in the presence of siblings and parents. Two-year-olds enjoy jokes that involve violations of standards about love relationships (e.g., "I don't love you, Mummy!") or about sex-appropriate behavior, disobedience, honesty, the mistakes of other people, and incongruities in family routines (e.g., eating in a bathrobe if that is not common in a particular family) (Dunn, 1988).

The age at which this appreciation of right and wrong behaviors appears is remarkably similar in children from many different cultures and families. One investigator visited the homes of four children every two weeks when the children were 13 to 23 months of age, and recorded the children's behaviors on each occasion (Lamb, 1988). Between 15 and 17 months, every one of the children began to show a sudden increase in concern about objects that were broken or dirty and about violations in adult standards, as well as spontaneous smiles upon mastering a task. The age at which these reactions appeared was similar despite the fact that the children were growing up in different homes (see Figure 7.8).

Mothers from many different cultures begin to hold their children responsible for their actions by the second or third birthday. For example, mothers living in the Fiji Islands comment that their children naturally become more responsible after the second birthday. At that time the children acquire a sense of right and wrong, which the Fijians call *vakayalo*.

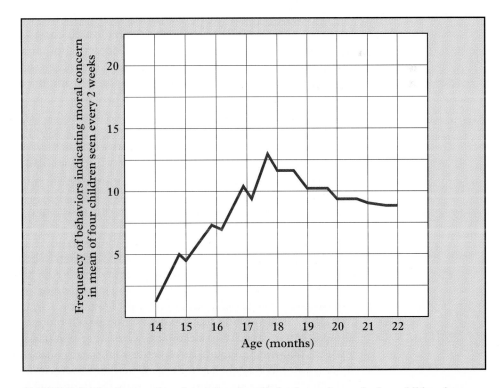

FIGURE 7.8 The frequencies of morally related behaviors at home for four children between 14 and 22 months of age. After *The Emergence of Moral Concern in the Second Year of Life* by S. Lamb, unpublished doctoral dissertation, Harvard University.

In sum, at 2 years children begin to evaluate actions and events as good or bad, and they often show distress when events do not meet their standards. These capacities are common to children from many cultures, probably because they result from cognitive developmental changes that occur around the second birthday. Children's use of standards to evaluate events and behavior is the beginning of their moral sense of right and wrong. (We discuss this issue further in Chapter 11.)

⚙ FAMILY INTERACTIONS IN THE SECOND AND THIRD YEARS

The growth of symbolic ability, of self-awareness, and of a sense of standards in the second and third years might seem to be clearly valuable developments. Children are growing and maturing and acquiring new skills; what could be better? However, for many parents and others who deal with toddlers, the changes of these years don't *feel* like good ones. In fact, this period of life is often referred to colloquially as the "terrible twos."

There are challenges to taking care of infants (e.g., inconsolable crying, lack of regular sleep patterns), but, as our opening vignettes illustrate, infants rarely have highly specific ideas about how they want things to happen, and they lack the physical and cognitive skills to stubbornly pursue their ends. All this changes in the second year of life. As infants grow into children with definite ideas and values of their own, these desires increasingly conflict with those of the adults around them and can lead to problems in caretaking.

One area of potential conflict at this age can be toilet training, which generally occurs at some point between 1 and 3 years (with considerable cross-cultural and cross-ethnic variation in when it is considered appropriate). Toilet training was emphasized, in fact, by Freud and Erikson in their discussions of the developmental issues of toddlers. However, the wishes of children and the desires of adults can also clash on many other issues, including aggression, standards of cleanliness, times to leave the park or to go to bed, and other aspects of daily living. In fact, Minton, Kagan, and Levine (1971) found that mothers' interaction with normal 27-month-olds in their homes contained very frequent instances of "violation sequences," in which a child did something in which the mother had to intervene. Violation sequences occurred nine times per hour on the average and took up half the time of total mother-child interaction. If you think about what these figures mean for the feelings of the adults involved, you can see why this period is known as the "terrible twos"!

The capacity to listen to adult prohibitions and to cooperate on tasks does improve over the years from 1 to 3. Vaughn, Kopp, and Krakow (1984) showed that children grew steadily more able to tolerate delays (e.g., "Don't open your present yet") as they neared the age of 3 years, and steadily more compliant in response to mothers' requests for help on tasks (e.g., "It's time to clean up now"). At each age, Vaughn et al. also found that children who seemed more cognitively advanced also showed better capacity to delay and were more compliant. This finding supports the idea that the development of better representational and thinking capacities is at least partially responsible for age-related improvement in self-control.

Parents, however, cannot simply wait for their children to mature. Each day, they must care for their toddlers in such a way as to best safeguard their children

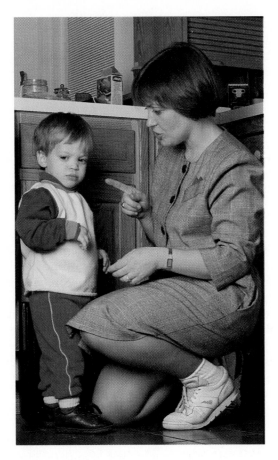

Violations of rules are a frequent feature
of daily life with a toddler.

from physical harm and foster in them a sense of responsibility and morality, while
at the same time not squelching their developing autonomy. We discuss research
and theory on parenting practices very shortly, but a few points need to be made
before plunging into such a discourse.

First, many discussions of child rearing seem to be based on the premise that
parents act on totally malleable young organisms and therefore bear most of the
responsibility for their children's behavior and personality. However, the child's
own temperament and personality have an effect on the interaction as well. In fact,
some parents see themselves as holding the reins of a high-spirited animal charging
through a forest. They try to monitor the speed and direction a little, but they
believe that some of the child's growth is beyond their control. The latter view is
consistent with current assumptions that children play an active role in their own
development (see Chapter 1) and that parent-child influences are bidirectional (see
Chapter 6).

Second, the child-rearing techniques that parents choose depend in part on
their beliefs about development and on the qualities they regard as most important
for children to acquire. These beliefs vary across cultures and historical periods. In
modern America, parents value traits such as independence and autonomy. But
these traits may be less valued in other cultures, and hence parents may be more
power assertive with their children in order to achieve the outcome valued by that
society (Maccoby & Martin, 1983; Whiting & Whiting, 1975).

TABLE 7.1 Parenting Patterns: A Two-Dimensional Classification

	Accepting, Responsive, Child-Centered	Rejecting, Unresponsive, Parent-Centered
Demanding, Controlling	Authoritative	Authoritarian
Undemanding, Low in Control Attempts	Permissive	Rejecting-Neglecting

Source: After "Socialization in the Context of the Family: Parent-Child Interaction," by E. E. Maccoby and J. A. Martin, in *Handbook of Child Psychology, Vol. 4, Socialization, Personality, and Social Behavior* (4th ed., pp. 1–102), edited by P. H. Mussen amd E. M. Hetherington, 1983. Adapted with permission.

This being said, let us look at some of the variations in styles of parenting that have been studied by psychologists. One way to conceptualize such variation is to define parenting styles in terms of their position on two dimensions (Maccoby & Martin, 1983). These dimensions are shown in Table 7.1. This conceptualization of parenting styles has proved very useful to work on effective parenting at several developmental periods, and it is used again in later discussions in this book.

The first dimension on which parents vary can be labeled warmth. It appears on Table 7.1 as "accepting, responsive, child-centered" versus "rejecting, unresponsive, parent-centered." The dimension of warmth has much in common with the sensitive and loving interaction that attachment theorists see as central to a secure attachment relationship (see Chapter 6). Secure attachment has been found to be associated with the development of children who are cooperative and responsive to adult requests (Matas, Arend, & Sroufe, 1978); the literature on parental warmth also supports the relation of warmth and responsiveness to desirable child outcomes. Thus, there is a convergence of findings across investigators guided by differing theoretical ideas and using different methodologies.

Parental warmth and its opposite, parental anger and punitiveness, themselves have developmental histories. For instance, Crockenberg (1987) found that adolescent mothers were more likely to act in an angry and punitive way to their toddlers during a clean-up task when they themselves had been rejected as children *and* when they did not currently have supportive social relationships. Importantly, however, mothers who did have supportive relationships interacted effectively with their toddlers, even when they had histories of childhood rejection. Similar findings by Quinton and Rutter (1985) support the hopeful conclusion that early experience does not doom parents to perpetuate a cycle of rejection; rather, this cycle can be broken if the individual manages to establish better adult life circumstances.

The second dimension on Table 7.1 is also important for optimal parenting. The dimension is labeled "demanding, controlling" versus "undemanding, low in control attempts." The work of Diana Baumrind (e.g., 1967, 1973, 1988) has been important in defining and showing the influence of this dimension. Parents who are high in firm control but also high in warmth are called **authoritative** parents by Baumrind. Such parents demand mature behavior (of an age-appropriate kind) with clarity and consistency. Their maturity demands are not harshly enforced and physical punishment is rare. Rather, authoritative parents generally explain reasons for their actions to their children verbally; questions and discussion are not dismissed. However, parents remain in charge. Parents who are demanding but low in warmth are called **authoritarian**, parents who are undemanding but high in warmth are termed **permissive**, and parents who are low on both dimensions are termed **rejecting-neglecting**.

The typology in Table 7.1 is helpful in conceptualizing effective parenting, but other processes should be considered as well. As discussed earlier, children begin to imitate others in the second year of life. Hence, observation becomes one means of socialization. Children are more likely to imitate models who behave warmly, so observational learning is a more effective means of parenting when adults are high in the first dimension of Table 7.1.

Observation is most effective when people display the desirable behavior consistently. If a parent sometimes uses harsh physical punishment, the child is unlikely to accept control of aggression as the proper way to behave, because the child sees how effective aggression is in controlling others. But if a child never sees physical aggression at home, nonaggressive ways of handling frustration will be learned as the appropriate standard.

However, children are exposed to many more models for imitation than just parents alone. For instance, even when parents do not use physical punishment, the child is likely to observe physical aggression elsewhere, among playmates or perhaps on television. In societies like ours, where there is so much behavioral diversity, observation of the parents alone is not always sufficient to override the influence of other agents of socialization.

In sum, the most effective and beneficial methods of socializing the toddler include acting as a consistent model of desired behavior, establishing a warm, affectionate relationship with the child during the first two years, and exerting firm control. As children begin to exhibit behavior that parents want to change, parents need to think carefully about what behaviors they want to socialize. Then they can use verbal disapproval and provide reasons for restrictions. Physical punishment may be less effective than consistent reprimands and gentle interventions such as pulling the child's hand away from a hot stove. The effects of any of these child-rearing practices depend, however, on their fit with the social context in which they occur.

⚙ SUMMARY

Around the first birthday, children become able to treat an object as if it were something other than it is; they are now capable of symbolism. Once they have gained this competence, their representations of experience become expanded.

Important evidence for the development of symbolism is seen in play with objects. During the second year, children manipulate objects in ways that reproduce acts that they have seen adults perform. Children begin to replace themselves with a toy as the active agent in play, and they may pretend to be another person. Children's drawings also become symbolic during the second and third years, and they become able to see models as representations of the real world.

As children play with objects in a symbolic manner, their reactions to other children also change. At about 18 months they become inhibited in the presence of another child, but by age 2 this reaction begins to disappear; 3-year-old children engage in reciprocal play and use other children as models.

Imitation is selective duplication of the behavior of a model. It begins at 7 or 8 months and becomes increasingly frequent and complex thereafter. Delayed imitation appears before the first birthday and is common during the second year. Children often imitate behavior that has an instrumental goal, but they are less likely to imitate emotional expressions. They are much more likely to imitate their parents than to imitate anyone else.

Imitation is a universal maturational phenomenon. However, children imitate some models and behaviors more than others. There are several hypotheses about the determinants of imitation. One reason children might engage in imitation is to promote social interactions and to enhance similarity to another person; they are most likely to imitate people who arouse them emotionally. In addition, imitation can be a self-conscious attempt to gain pleasure, power, property, or other desired goals.

During the last half of the second year, children begin to be aware of their own qualities, states, and abilities. Children indicate this self-awareness by describing their own behavior as they perform it, recognizing themselves in a mirror, and affirming personal possession of objects. The emergence of self-awareness is accompanied by an improvement in the ability to appreciate the perceptions and feelings of others.

During the last 6 months of the second year, children begin to create standards—idealized representations of objects, events, and behaviors. Events that violate a standard may produce signs of anxiety or distress. This reaction may be due to the development of the ability to infer that events have causes, even when the causes are not observed. Children's concern about violations of standards suggests that they have developed ideal representations of the "right" or "correct" way things should be.

Around the second birthday, children display distress if they are unable to meet standards of behavior imposed by others, but they show pleasure when they meet standards they have set for themselves. In addition, they are amused by violations of adult rules and by events that will provoke disgust or disapproval in others. The age at which this appreciation of right and wrong behavior appears is similar in children from different cultures and families.

The development of symbolism, imitation, standards, and self-awareness depends on experiences with other people. The most important experiences occur within the family and are directly related to the parents' beliefs about the qualities children should acquire. The process by which children learn the standards, values, and expected behaviors of their culture is termed socialization. Parents socialize their children by serving as models of behavior, expressing acceptance and warmth, providing restrictions on freedom, and punishing unacceptable behavior.

REVIEW QUESTIONS

1. What is symbolic representation?

2. In what ways does play reflect the growth of symbolic representation?

3. Describe the ways in which children react to and interact with other children in the first two years.

4. What are the defining characteristics of imitation?

5. Why do children imitate some models and behaviors more often than others?

6. What are standards? How do children indicate that they have begun to use standards to evaluate events and behavior?

7. In what ways do children indicate that they have become aware of their own qualities, states, and abilities?

8. How is self-awareness related to the appearance of empathy?

9. What challenges exist to effective caretaking of the 1- and 2-year-old? How can these challenges best be met?

CRITICAL THINKING ABOUT THE CHAPTER

1. Observe the play of a 1-year-old and a 3-year-old. (If you don't know any young children, go to a park and observe discreetly, guessing the ages of the children.) What kind and amount of symbolic play do you see in the 1-year-olds? In the 3-year-olds? What changes do you see in their social interaction with other children and with caretakers?

2. Why don't all parents act authoritatively with their children? List some of the impediments to authoritative parenting. Then consider which might be changeable and how one might go about changing them.

KEY TERMS

authoritative   permissive
authoritarian   rejecting-neglecting
empathy   symbolic ability
imitation   self-awareness
play

SUGGESTED READINGS

Dunn, J. (1988). *The beginnings of social understanding.* Cambridge, MA: Harvard University Press. Presents information based on observations in the home during the second year that reveal the effects of social interaction on empathy with others.

Kagan, J. (1981). *The second year.* Cambridge, MA: Harvard University Press. Summarizes a longitudinal study of children in the second year that focused on the emergence of a moral sense and the first signs of self-awareness.

Kagan, J., & Lamb, S. (Eds.). (1988). *The emergence of morality in young children.* Chicago: University of Chicago Press. Contains essays by leading scholars on the development of standards and discusses the role of cultural setting, biology, and family experience on the emergence of morality.

Shatz, M. (1994). *A toddler's life: Becoming a child.* New York: Oxford University Press. Discusses how toddlers develop abilities to reflect on their behavior and engage others. Illustrates and explores these changes in a case study, tracing the development of Shatz's grandson, Ricky.

CHAPTER 8

LANGUAGE AND COMMUNICATION

THE FUNCTIONS OF LANGUAGE

THE PUZZLE OF LANGUAGE ACQUISITION

A DESCRIPTION OF LANGUAGE ACQUISITION

EXPLANATIONS OF LANGUAGE ACQUISITION

In the short span of 2 years or so, roughly from ages 1 to 3 years, children perform an astonishing feat: they progress from uttering their first word to speaking grammatically correct sentences. Consider the case of Eve, a little girl whose speech was carefully recorded and studied (R. Brown, 1973). When she was 18 months old, Eve produced many two-word sentences, for example:

"Right down."

"Mommy read."

"Look dollie."

Just nine months later, at the age of 27 months, she communicated with much more complete and complex sentences, for example:

"I go get a pencil 'n' write."

"We're going to make a blue house."

"How 'bout another eggnog instead of cheese sandwich?"

The contrast between Eve's utterances at 18 months and the sentences she spoke at 27 months highlights the speed with which language skills are acquired and improved. In this chapter, we consider what we know about the ways children perform the task of learning language rapidly, universally (across a wide variety of environments and kinds of languages), and without explicit training. The fact that all normal children learn such a complex task so naturally has made language acquisition a central issue for research in child development.

⚙ THE FUNCTIONS OF LANGUAGE

Every animal species possesses a small number of special abilities that give it unique advantages in the struggle for reproduction (and hence, survival of the species). Among birds, for instance, the ability to sing and to fly are two unique talents. Among humans, significant competences include upright posture, tool use, and language—the ability to communicate with others using words and sentences. Language is a powerful component of the human biological heritage.

The most obvious function of language is to communicate. Children use language to communicate their needs. By the first year some children will say simple words like "milk" or "cookie" when they are hungry. While many animals, especially primates, can use facial expressions and gestures as well as shrieks and calls to influence the behavior of others, language is more precise. By simply saying "Hand hurts," for instance, a child can induce a parent to do something to make the hurt go away. Language is also used, even by young children, to communicate ideas and to comment on situations. Early in language acquisition, children will point out that certain objects belong to certain people ("Daddy shoe"), or that certain events are happening ("Doggie run").

The ability to communicate ideas has many additional effects on human functioning. For instance, language is an integral part of the establishment of human society and culture. Before there were schools, books, or newspapers, listening to adults and peers gave children knowledge about their culture and their world. A young baboon has to learn the hard way to avoid fights with larger animals or to remember where food is located. For humans, much of this information is packaged in words.

A second use of language is to help children establish and maintain relationships with others. In other species, social bonds are initiated and maintained by actions such as mating dances or mutual grooming. Among humans, conversations at the dinner table, between friends and associates, and of course, between lovers and spouses, fill analogous purposes.

A third function of language is to help to demarcate categories. As indicated in Chapter 5, animals and human infants represent the world around them in the form of perceptual and conceptual categories. Language, however, makes possible more symbolic and abstract ways of representing the world. Language permits one to classify objects into symbolic, linguistic categories, which are efficient modes of representation. The word *tree* does not just mean a particular object in the backyard; it refers to a variety of botanical forms that share certain important attributes. Thus language enables a person to categorize diverse events that share some common features.

The use of language to classify experience into symbolic categories is related to a fourth use of language: as an aid in inference and deduction, which comprise the essence of human reasoning. For instance, if one knows that something is a dog, one can infer that it moves, barks, has a heart, fetches sticks, eats meat, and so forth.

THE PUZZLE OF LANGUAGE ACQUISITION

Given even minimal linguistic input, normal children acquire language quickly and easily. This achievement poses a theoretical puzzle for psychologists and linguists. What accounts for the rapid improvement in children's comprehension and use of complicated grammatical structures and rules? What role, if any, do innate mechanisms play? Is the child active in the process of language acquisition, searching for rules and regularities, formulating and testing hypotheses about grammar and meaning? Are reinforcement and modeling important? To what extent is progress in language dependent on the growth of cognitive capacities? Do parents and other people interacting with the child influence the course of linguistic development?

The answers to these critical questions are still controversial. But in the past few decades we have made substantial progress in understanding how to answer them. We have also learned a great deal about how language development proceeds. For example, we know what competencies emerge at what ages and the sequences in which abilities develop with a good degree of precision. In this chapter, we first discuss what has been discovered on a descriptive level about language acquisition: what occurs in what order and at what age. We then return to the question of *how* the process occurs.

A DESCRIPTION OF LANGUAGE ACQUISITION

Sentences are the basic unit for the communication of an idea. However, children cannot begin the task of learning language with sentences. To acquire language, children must master several subsystems of language. These include the *phonemic system* (or the sound system) of their language, the *semantic system* (or the meaning system, beginning with the meanings of individual words), the *syntax* (or grammar) of their language, and the *pragmatics* of language use (or the social rules governing what to say, how and when and to whom). We consider each of these four systems in turn in describing the course of language acquisition.

Phonemes and Babbling

Phonemes are the basic sounds that are combined to make words. Languages vary in the number of phonemes they use, from a low of 11 phonemes to a high of 141 phonemes. English uses 40 phonemes, slightly above the average for the world's languages (Halle, 1990). In English, the phonemes correspond roughly to the sounds of the spoken letters of the alphabet. For example, one phoneme in English is the sound *t* as it is pronounced in words like *tap, bat,* or *later.* Even though the sounds of *t* in these three words are slightly different, *t* is regarded as a single phoneme by speakers of English. Similarly, the *a* sound in the word *baby* differs in subtle ways each time we say it, but we can recognize that sound not only across these minor variations but also despite differences in the pronunciation of *baby* by people from Maine, Mississippi, or Australia.

English contains some phonemes that are rare in other languages; one example is the *th* sound in *this*. On the other hand, some African languages contain unique phonemes in the form of click sounds. In some languages, such as Chinese, a rising or falling vocal tone applied to a word is a phoneme. Every language specifies how phonemes may and may not be combined to make words. These specifications permit some combinations and prohibit others. For example, in English there are no words that begin with the phonemes that correspond to *ng, zb,* or *tn,* although these can begin words in some other languages.

Perceiving Phonemes and Linguistic Structure. If you have ever listened to people speaking a foreign language, especially one that is completely unfamiliar to you, you know that at first it sounds like gibberish. It is difficult to know where one word ends and another begins, or even where one sentence ends and the next begins. The sounds seem odd and difficult to discriminate. Imagine, then, the task confronting the language-learning child! Even beginning to "crack the code" would seem an almost hopeless task.

Fortunately, infants begin language acquisition with a few legs up on the process. One important advantage they have is that they are able, apparently from birth, to discriminate between similar phonemes. For example, they can discriminate *ba* from *bu* or from *da* (Bertoncini, Bijelac-Babic, Jusczyk, Kennedy, & Mehler, 1988; Eimas, 1975). This ability has been demonstrated using the habituation method described in Chapter 4. A nipple is placed in an infant's mouth; when she sucks on the nipple at a particular rate, a loudspeaker emits a particular syllable, such as *ba*. When the infant's rate of sucking begins to slow because she is becoming habituated to (bored by) the sound *ba*, the syllable emitted by the loudspeaker is changed. Half the infants hear a new syllable, such as *bu* or *da*. The other half continue to hear *ba*. As Figure 8.1 shows, if infants continue to hear the same syllable, they do not show an increase in sucking rate. But if they hear a new syllable, they show an increase in sucking rate, indicating that they perceive a difference between the original syllable and the new syllables.

This ability to tell sounds apart helps infants to group language sounds in what will be a linguistically meaningful way. Human infants can in fact make many more phonemic discriminations than are required by their language; they are prepared to make discriminations that would be useful in languages other than the one to which they are exposed. After all, a newborn does not know her future linguistic community; babies have to be equally prepared to learn English, Chinese, Swahili, or any of the thousands of other human languages. However, if a particular phonemic discrimination is not part of their language, they will eventually lose the power to make that discrimination (Werker & Tees, 1984). For example, although infants can discriminate between the phonemes *ra* and *la,* this distinction does not occur in Japanese, and Japanese adults do not make this discrimination easily.

Infants have another leg up on language acquisition, in addition to their abilities at phonemic discrimination. This is the ability to perceive the overall rhythmic and tonal structure of utterances, the prosody or "sound envelope" that groups the speech stream into sentences, clauses, and phrases. By at least 4.5 months of age, infants prefer to listen to speech with normal spacing of pauses between clauses than to listen to speech with pauses arbitrarily cut into the speech stream. Interestingly, this is true for infants from an English-speaking environment when listening both to English and to Polish. However, as with phonemic discriminations, by a later age (6 months) infants

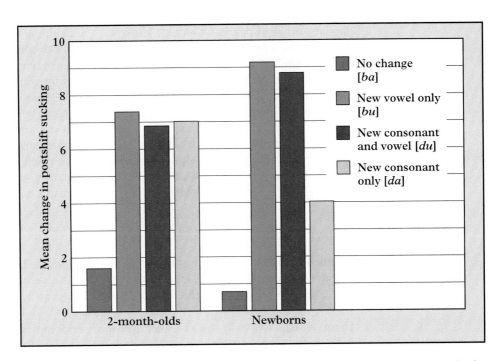

FIGURE 8.1 Data showing that infants can discriminate among phonemes. Changes in the phoneme lead to increases in sucking rates. After "An Investigation of Young Infants' Perceptual Representations of Speech Sounds," by J. Bertoncini, B. Bijelac-Babic, P. W. Jusczyk, L. J. Kennedy, and J. Mehler, 1988, *Journal of Experimental Psychology: General, 115*, pp. 21–33. Adapted with permission.

lose their ability to make discriminations in a foreign language, while retaining their preference for the more familiarly divided English (Hirsh-Pasek & Golinkoff, 1993).

Babbling. Although 1-month-old infants can discriminate among phonemes, they are unable to produce them. Newborns cry, burp, cough, and sneeze, but the speech areas of the brain and their connections to the vocal cords are not yet mature enough to produce the phonemes of their language. It is not until the third month that infants begin to coo and make vowel sounds while playing alone or with others. These sounds represent the infant's first phonemes. At 5 or 6 months of age, all infants spontaneously begin to babble by combining vowel and consonant sounds in strings of syllables that sound like *ba-ba-ba* or *da-da-da*. These babbling sounds often sound like real speech because of their rising and falling intonations. The fact that babbling appears in all infants around 6 months of age suggests that maturation of the brain as well as growth of the vocal system has made it possible for the infant to babble when it is excited. Although babbling has no symbolic meaning, it increases in frequency until infants are about 1 year old and speak their first meaningful words. From then on, babbling decreases.

The frequency of babbling before the first birthday does not predict how early or late normal children will begin to speak words or the size of their vocabulary when they enter school. Babbling reflects the child's degree of excitability and tendency to express excitement in vocal sounds. Support for this conclusion is provided by the fact that deaf children, who cannot hear their own voice or the voices of others, also begin to babble at about 6 months of age, and their babbling is very similar to that of hearing children. However, the babbling of deaf children quickly declines after a month or two, suggesting that in order to continue vocalizing, infants need to hear themselves babble as well as receive feedback from other people.

Deaf children have provided further evidence of the importance of the babbling stage, through a kind of "manual babbling" that develops when they are exposed to sign language (Petitto & Marentette, 1991). Deaf infants perform signlike hand gestures, different from natural expressive gestures but not yet meaningful signs. This observation indicates that the babbling period is critical and natural preparation for meaningful language. It also shows that what matures when babbling begins—rather than being a specifically sound-based or articulatory mechanism—is a much broader linguistic capability that includes manual signing as well as oral speech.

Semantics: Learning the Meanings of Words

Semantics refers to the meaning system of a language. Learning how particular strings of sounds (or particular hand shapes and movements) correspond to what is in the world is a basic (and challenging) task in language acquisition.

First Words. Around the first birthday most children begin to speak their first meaningful sounds, usually in the form of single words. The first words are generally names for toys, familiar objects in the home, articles of clothing, animals, and body parts, as well as words that tell their parents what they want—such as *up, down, open, more,* and *no.* It is interesting that the first words spoken are usually names for people with whom the baby interacts and for objects that change or that the child plays with often. However, simple exposure to people and objects does not lead to early naming. For instance, names for animals and vehicles, both of which move, are more common early words than names of rooms and plants, which do not move. Words for food, toys, and articles of clothing that children can remove easily (*juice, cookie, ball, sock*) are common in children's early vocabulary; words for immovable objects and those that are not easily acted upon (*wall, table, window*) occur less frequently. Box 8.1 provides a list of one child's early active vocabulary.

Figure 8.2 shows data on the number of words produced by children from 8 to 16 months, as reported by parent observers in a large national study (E. Bates, Dale, & Thal, 1994). One point to note about this graph is that there are very marked differences among children in word learning. The middle curve shows the development of an average child, and 80 percent of children will develop in a manner in between the top and the bottom curves. But 10 percent of children develop as slowly as the bottom curve (or slower), and 10 percent develop as fast as the top curve (or faster). These variations in rate of language learning are completely normal, although parents often worry about the slower developers. Only when development falls well outside the curves shown on this graph is it necessary to consider consulting a pediatrician or speech pathologist.

Variations in speed of vocabulary development are related, in part, to how much parents and other adults speak to their children (Huttenlocher, Haight, Bryk, Seltzer, & Lyons, 1991). Also, girls begin to speak earlier than boys, on the average, although this difference basically disappears after the age of 2 years (Huttenlocher et al., 1991).

Another interesting point can be seen by comparing Figures 8.2 and 8.3. Figure 8.3 shows development of word *comprehension* for the same sample of children

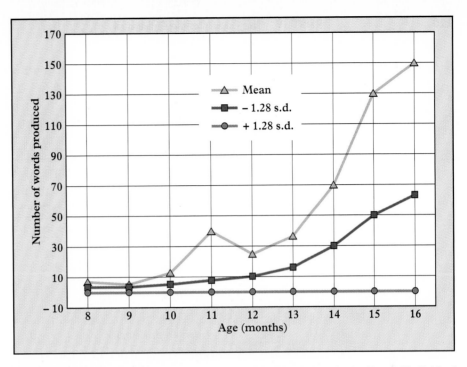

FIGURE 8.2 Word production on the MacArthur CDI Infant Scale. From "Individual Differences and Their Implications for Theories of Language Development," by E. Bates, P. S. Dale, and D. Thal, in *Handbook of Child Language*, edited by P. Fletcher and B. MacWhinney, 1993, Oxford: Basil Blackwell. Reprinted with permission.

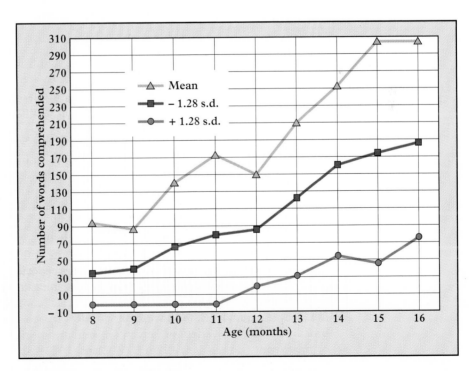

FIGURE 8.3 Word comprehension on the MacArthur CDI Infant Scale. From "Individual Differences and Their Implications for Theories of Language Development," by E. Bates, P. S. Dale, and D. Thal, in *Handbook of Child Language*, edited by P. Fletcher and B. MacWhinney, 1993, Oxford: Basil Blackwell. Reprinted with permission.

BOX 8.1

FIRST WORDS

When children first begin to learn words, they learn them fairly slowly and it is possible to keep a diary of what words they say. Below is a list of the words learned by one child, Andrew, by the age of 14 months. What characteristics of early words mentioned in the text are illustrated in this list?

mama	steps	bus
book	boom	hotdog
ball	look	apple
flower	touch	hot
bike	move	lawnmower
shoe	back (= put back)	door
turtle	upside (= upside down)	up
Ernie	dada	out
throw	hi	off
yes	night-night	more
no	truck	dog

(E. Bates et al., 1994). Comparing Figures 8.2 and 8.3 shows that children understand many more words than they actually speak—technically that their comprehension exceeds their production. Infants who are not yet saying words will often respond to questions or instructions like "Where is your bottle?" or "Pat the doggy" with appropriate actions.

Comprehension in children who don't speak can be shown in controlled experimental conditions, as well as in parental reports. In one study, a group of 1-year-olds, many of whom were not saying words, were brought to a laboratory. The infants sat on their mothers' laps facing a screen on which slides were projected. A pair of pictures appeared on the screen—say, a dog and a frog—and the mother asked, "Where is the dog?" The infants often looked at the picture of the dog, indicating that they knew the word *dog* (Reznick, 1990).

The meanings children attribute to words may not always be exactly the same as adult meanings for those words. Some errors reported in the literature are what is called **overextensions**, or applications of meanings that are too wide. For example, a child may say "doggie" to refer also to cats, cows, horses, rabbits, and other four-legged animals. Some investigators have argued that overextensions can be broadly based on a variety of perceptual similarities in shape, size, sound, texture, or movement (Bowerman, 1976; E. V. Clark, 1973), as well as similarities in function (Nelson, 1975), as when *moon* or *ball* is used for many objects that are round, including cakes, oranges, and the letter *o.* Other errors in early word meaning are said to be **underextensions**, or words that are defined too narrowly. For example, one 9-month-old used the word *car* to refer to cars moving on the street below but not to cars standing still or to pictures of cars (L. Bloom, 1973).

However, over- and underextensions may not be that important or common a phenomenon in early speech. First, it is important to remember that overextensions often occur in the production of speech but not in comprehension. A child who overgeneralizes *apple,* applying that word to tomatoes as well, has no difficulty pointing to the apple in a set of pictures of round objects including tomatoes (Gruendel, 1977; J. R. Thompson & Chapman, 1977). Second, overextended definitions usually last only a short time, fading out as new words enter the child's vocabulary. When the child learns the word *cow* and understands that this animal has features such as moo sounds and horns, the meaning of *cow* is differentiated from the meaning of *dog* (E. V. Clark, 1973). Taken together, these observations suggest that over- and underextension errors in production may reflect the child's desire to communicate—with a limited repertoire of words—rather than indicating true errors of conceptual grouping. That is, a child who wishes to draw attention to the moon may say "cookie" not because she thinks the moon *is* a cookie but simply because it's the only word she knows that captures *any* aspect of the object that she wishes to communicate about. In fact, in a careful look at children's word production, Huttenlocher and Smiley (1987) found that very few, if any, overextensions in early child speech appear to completely violate adult conceptual categories, as when *moon* is used to label a cake (Huttenlocher & Smiley, 1987). Most such errors seemed due to the simple desire to communicate.

The Process of Word Learning. By the time children are 6 years of age, they will have learned about 10,000 to 13,000 different words (Anglin, 1993; Benedict, 1979; Kagan, 1981). This is a vast learning task, and psychologists have been very interested in how it occurs. The challenge of the task is not simply that so many words are learned (although that's part of the issue) but also that it's not easily apparent how children decide what any of the words they hear could mean.

For instance, many new words seem to be acquired through "naming rituals" that parents indulge in from the time their babies first utter something that sounds like a word (Ninio & Bruner, 1976). Parents point to objects, name them, and correct the child's attempts to repeat the names. Often young children establish effective routines for eliciting the names of objects from their parents. For instance, they repeatedly say, "What's that?" But how do children arrive at meanings even from a simple situation such as pointing and naming? Imagine a parent pointing to a picture of a rabbit and saying "bunny." From the point of view of the language-learning child, "bunny" could equally well be the name of that particular rabbit (analogous to "Flopsy" or "Cottontail") or could mean some part of the rabbit ("tail") or "picture" or "animal," or it could mean "Look at that," and so on. The amazing thing, on this analysis, is that children learn any words at all, at least without great labor at ruling out all the rival meanings. This lack of determinacy has inspired a great deal of research and thought in the past decades.

One help to children learning words comes from adult naming practices. As first pointed out by Roger Brown in an essay on "the original word game" (1966), adults can label objects at several different levels of generality. A pet is called Prince and is also a dalmatian, a dog, a mammal, or an animal. When speaking to children,

This father has asked his daughter, "Where's my nose?" and his daughter is answering. Some psychologists think such games are important in language learning; others disagree.

however, adults overwhelmingly choose to use terms at an intermediate level of generality (sometimes called the "basic" level). Thus, children between 1 and 3 years old are likely to hear a beagle called a "dog" rather than a "beagle" (more specific) or an "animal" (more general) (Anglin, 1977).

A second help to language-learning children appears to be their own biases (or hypotheses) about what a word could mean. One of these biases is that, if an adult uses an unfamiliar word and there is an object in the environment for which the child does not currently know a label, the child's first guess will be that the new word refers to the object with no current name. Golinkoff, Hirsh-Pasek, Bailey, and Wenger (1992) call this the *novel name–nameless category* (or N3C) principle.

In one experiment showing this kind of phenomenon (Heibeck & Markman, 1987; also Carey & Bartlett, 1978), children 2 to 4 years old were asked to help the experimenter. They were asked to retrieve one of two objects from a chair in a corner of the room. One of the objects was a familiar one for which the child had a word; the other object was unfamiliar, and the child did not know the correct name for it. For example, when the experimenter wanted the child to learn a new color word, she might say to the child, "There is something that you could do to help me. Do you see those two books on the chair? Could you bring me the chartreuse one? Not the red one, the chartreuse one." Generally, given this instruction, the child ignored the red object and brought the chartreuse object. About ten minutes later the children were tested to see whether, on the basis of a single experience with the new word, they would spontaneously name the new color. Children readily learned new words for colors. However, even though the children learned new words for colors, they did not use those words often in their spontaneous speech (Heibeck & Markman, 1987).

A second principle that may help children learn new words is called the **whole-object assumption**. Children seem to first assume that a word refers to a whole object (e.g., a rabbit) rather than to a part of the object (the tail), an attribute of the object (furry), or an aspect of the context (carrot-eating). A third principle, very closely related to the whole-object principle, is the **taxonomic assumption** (Markman & Hutchinson, 1984). That is, a child whose parent points to a rabbit and says "rabbit" will not only assume that the word labels the rabbit, rather than attributes such as soft or associated objects such as carrots; he will also assume that the word will extend to other rabbits. This bias is shown when words are part of the situation, but not in other task situations, indicating that the taxonomic principle is specifically linked to language. For instance, if shown a picture of a cow and told that it is a "dax," children will pick a taxonomically related item (e.g., a pig) rather than a thematically related item (e.g., milk) when asked to "find another dax." They are much less likely to make the taxonomic choice if asked simply to "find another one." Apparently the use of a specific label focuses children's attention on taxonomy (Markman & Hutchinson, 1984; Waxman & Gelman, 1986).

Syntax: Combining Words into Sentences

Learning words is an important part of language acquisition. Yet the infinite productivity and flexibility of human language rest on much more than just words: they derive from people's ability to combine words in an incredibly large number of ways, according to rules understood by all users of that language, in order to express novel ideas and fine gradations of meaning. These rules are called **syntax**, or grammar. Children begin the task of acquiring syntax by expressing single relations such as possession ("Mommy's hat"). They progress to acquire more and more complex grammatical constructions (one child who was nearly 3 said, "I'm sorry I can't do that because it fell over when I pushed it").

First Word Combinations. As children reach the middle of the second year, when their speaking vocabulary is about 50 words, they begin to express simple relations between words or concepts. In English and some other languages, relations are generally communicated by word order. That is, in English, "Mary hit Sue" means something quite different from "Sue hit Mary." Thus children acquiring English—and other languages emphasizing word order—begin to express relations by putting words together, generally in the correct order. For example, in producing a combination meant to communicate "I would like to eat a cookie," children will say "Eat cookie," not "Cookie eat." Almost all of children's two-word sentences place words in the appropriate order.

In languages with freer word order, relations are often expressed by means of suffixes or prefixes to base words. For instance, in classical Latin, *vir* (man) would have to be the subject of a sentence, no matter in what position it appeared in the sentence, while *virum* would have to be the object, again regardless of order. The suffix *-um* tells the listener that the word is being used as an object. Given definite markings of grammatical relations, words can appear in a sentence in almost any order. When the *Aeneid* begins with the line "Arma virumque cano" (I sing of arms and the man), the meaning is clear, even though the objects of the sentence come before the verb ("cano"). Children acquiring these inflected languages may enter the "two-word" stage by beginning to produce such modifications to their base words.

Figure 8.4 shows development with age in the percentage of English-speaking children combining words. The top curve shows children who combine words "at least sometimes," and the bottom curve shows children who combine words "frequently" (E. Bates et al., 1994). As you can see from the bottom curve, around the second birthday there is a major increase in the frequency of combinations. A similar story is told by a case study of one boy, who spoke his first two-word sentence at 19 months and used 14 different two-word combinations during that month. During the next six months the number of different two-word combinations spoken by that boy increased dramatically; the totals for those months were 24, 54, 89, 250, 1,400, and over 2,500, respectively (Braine, 1963).

Typical of these two-word sentences are "See doggy," "Where daddy?" "All gone," "Throw ball," and "More car." Understanding these sentences sometimes requires adults to take context into account. For example, the last sentence, "More car," might mean "Drive around the block some more" if the child has been going for a ride, or it might communicate the fact that the child has seen a long line of cars, if the child is looking out the window.

Table 8.1 lists some important classes of sentences that are produced in two-word utterances. The relations listed in the table occur in all languages, which suggests that they are based on concepts that are acquired by children as a result of cognitive maturation.

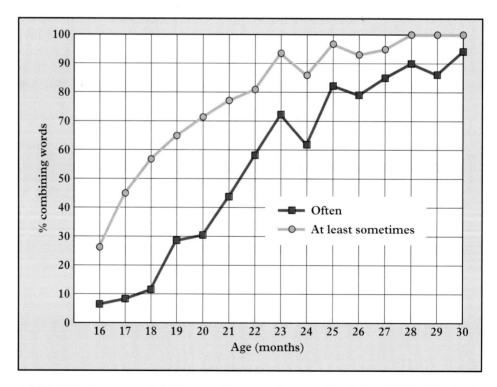

FIGURE 8.4 Percentage of children combining words on the MacArthur CDI Toddler Scale. From "Individual Differences and Their Implications for Theories of Language Development," by E. Bates, P. S. Dale, and D. Thal, in *Handbook of Child Language*, edited by P. Fletcher and B. MacWhinney, 1994, Oxford: Basil Blackwell. Reprinted with permission.

TABLE 8.1 Meanings Expressed in Telegraphic Speech

Meaning	Example
Locate, name	See doggie, book there
Demand, desire	More milk, want candy
Nonexistence	Allgone milk
Negation	Not kitty
Possession	My candy
Attribution	Big car
Agent-action	Mama walk
Action-object	Hit you
Agent-object	Mama book
Action-location	Sit chair
Action-recipient	Give papa
Action-instrument	Cut knife
Question	Where ball?

Source: From *Psycholinguistics*, by D. I. Slobin, 1971, Glenview: IL: Scott, Foresman. Reprinted with permission.

Learning Syntactic Rules. The child's first two-word sentences, and the three- and four-word sentences that follow, have been likened to telegrams or abbreviated versions of adult sentences. Like a telegram, these sentences contain only essential words. They lack prepositions (*in, on, by*), conjunctions (*and, but, or*), articles (*a, the*), and many grammatical niceties, such as verb tense. The language-learning child must acquire all of these finer points in order to sound like a mature speaker.

In order to discuss language development from telegraphic speech to adult speech, we need to introduce the concept of grammatical **morphemes**, or the smallest units of meaning in a language; a morpheme cannot be broken into any smaller parts that have meaning. However, linguists make a distinction between two kinds of morphemes. An **unbound morpheme** is a word that can stand alone. The words *cat, milk,* and *danger* each consist of one unbound morpheme. Although *danger* has two syllables, neither has meaning by itself, and thus *danger* is a single morpheme. Other morphemes, called **bound morphemes**, cannot stand alone and are always parts of words. Prefixes, suffixes, plurals, and possessives are all bound morphemes that are connected to other morphemes. Thus, the bound morpheme *-ness,* when added to the unbound morpheme *happy,* produces the word *happiness;* the bound morpheme *-s* following the unbound morpheme *dog* becomes the word *dogs.* Bound morphemes also indicate the tense of a verb and the possessive case.

Children master the grammatical morphemes of their language in a particular order. Roger Brown of Harvard University discovered this order for English by studying three children who were called Adam, Eve, and Sarah. The order in which 14 English grammatical morphemes were mastered by these children is shown in Table 8.2. Most children first learn the present progressive ending *-ing* (as in *walking*), followed by correct use of the prepositions *in* and *on,* the plural, the irregular past tense (*he went, she ate*), the possessive (*Mary's*), the correct use of *are* and *is,* articles like *the* and *a,* and the regular past tense (*he walked, she stopped*). These victories are followed by mastery of the third person present tense (*she walks*), the third person present tense irregular (*she does*), auxiliary verbs that are not contracted (*I am walking*), the contractible form of the verb to be (*that's*), and finally, the contractible form of auxiliary verbs (*I'm walking*).

TABLE 8.2 Average Order of Acquisition of 14 Grammatical Morphemes by Three Children Studied by R. Brown (1973)

1.	Present progressive
2,3.	Prepositions (*in/on*)
4.	Plural
5.	Irregular past tense
6.	Possessive
7.	Copula, uncontractible
8.	Articles
9.	Regular past tense
10.	Third person present tense, regular
11.	Third person present tense, irregular
12.	Auxiliary, uncontractible
13.	Copula, contractible
14.	Auxiliary, contractible

The first few morphemes that are mastered—for example, adding *-ing*—are produced early because these sounds are perceptually distinctive. The order of mastery is different in other languages. For example, in languages in which the plural is not perceptually distinctive, it appears at a later age.

You may have noticed that acquisition of the irregular past tense occurs before the regular past tense in the list. This fact (and some other phenomena like it) have been argued to be very important in understanding language acquisition. The order of acquisition suggests that children initially *memorize* words like *went* as the past tense of *go*. However, later, they learn general rules for forming the past tense (in English, by adding *-ed* to the verb). That a *rule* is in fact learned—rather than simply a long list of memorized words—is suggested by a phenomenon called **over-regularization**. A child who once used the word *went* correctly may begin to say "I goed" when she intends to use the past tense because she has learned the rule that one should add *-ed* to indicate an event that happened in the past. Such mistakes are not that common, occurring about 2.5 percent of the time in child speech (G. F. Marcus, Pinker, Ullman, Hollander, Rosen, & Xu, 1992). But the fact that they occur at all suggests that a rule is acquired, rather than language being a product of simple memorization. The same conclusion is suggested by the fact that when children (or adults) are shown an unfamiliar action and given a verb for it ("This is a man who knows how to rick"), they can immediately, on request, use it in the past tense ("Yesterday he ricked"). There is no need for even one exposure to the word *ricked* (Berko, 1958).

As children grow older and acquire these grammatical morphemes, their speech sounds less telegraphic and their utterances become longer. In fact, the length of utterances is a good indicator of the level of a child's syntactic development, at least during the period from 1½ to 4 years of age. Psychologists compute the average length of a sample of utterances from a particular child and call that index the **mean length of utterance**, or MLU. The MLU is based on the average number of morphemes in a set of utterances, not on the number of words.

There are ways of scoring children's syntactic competence other than MLU, but until recently, all have been based on laborious processes of coding lengthy samples of children's spontaneous speech. However, a technique has now been devised to estimate syntactic competence from parent responses on a test of the kinds of things

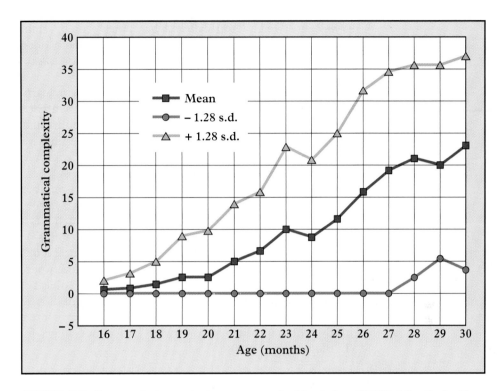

FIGURE 8.5 Grammatical complexity scores on the MacArthur CDI Toddler Scale. From "Individual Differences and Their Implications for Theories of Language Development," by E. Bates, P. S. Dale, and D. Thal, in *Handbook of Child Language*, edited by P. Fletcher and B. MacWhinney, 1994, Oxford: Basil Blackwell. Reprinted with permission.

their child is most likely to say. Parents are given two sentences a child might say— one using a bound morpheme to express the possessive ("Daddy's car"), for instance, and the other not ("Daddy car")—and asked which sentence sounds more like what their child might currently say. This technique makes it possible to gather much larger sets of data on grammatical development. Grammatical development based on such studies is shown as a function of age in Figure 8.5 (E. Bates et al., 1994).

As is clear from Figure 8.5, there are dramatic differences among children in mean length of utterance. A study of children followed from 10 to 28 months old found that the 28-month-olds with the greatest MLU scores were those who had uttered a large number of nouns when they were 1 year old and a large number of verbs when they were 2 years old. These facts suggest that the differences in language ability of preschool children can be predicted and that the use of nouns by 1-year-olds to name objects in the environment—rather than the use of words like *bye-bye* or of commands to others—is a particularly sensitive sign of later language precocity (E. Bates, Bretherton, & Snyder, 1988).

Development of Complex Syntax. In addition to learning the grammatical morphemes studied by Brown, children learn a variety of grammatical complexities in the years from 2 to 4. We examine a few of them here.

Combining Sentences. Speakers sometimes want to express the relation between sentences. This can be done by joining sentences using a conjunction such as *and* or *or* (e.g., "You call and he comes") or by embedding one sentence in another (e.g., "I hope that I don't hurt it"). Some embedded sentences are called *wh* clauses (those that begin with *what, who, where,* or *when*). Examples are "I know where it is" and "When I get big, I can lift you up."

To construct complex sentences, children have to learn the rules for combining larger groups of words (phrases, clauses, and even sentences) and using connective words (e.g., *and, but, because*). *And* is generally the first and most frequently occurring connective in a child's vocabulary during the third year. *Because, what, when,* and *so* are also used frequently; *then, but, if,* and *that* appear less frequently (L. Bloom, Lahey, Hood, Lifter, & Fiess, 1980).

Children's early complex sentences express a number of different meanings. The order of appearance of semantic relationships is fairly constant, although some children begin the sequence earlier and move through it faster than others. Additive relationships ("You can carry that and I can carry this") are expressed first, followed by temporal and causal statements ("You better look for it when you get back home," "She put a Band-Aid on her shoe and it maked it feel better"). Contrast or opposition ("I was tired but now I'm not tired"), object specification ("The man who fixes the door"), and notice ("Watch what I am doing") appear still later. During the third year, progress in the use of complex sentences is usually slow and steady, with no sudden leaps forward or abrupt changes from one form to another (L. Bloom et al., 1980).

Questions.   Advances in linguistic development are also reflected in a gradual but regular improvement in the production and comprehension of questions. Two-year-olds understand yes-no questions ("Are you hungry?") as well as questions beginning with *where, who,* and *what,* and they generally answer appropriately. These questions pertain to people, objects, and locations—precisely the things that children are interested in and talk about in their first sentences. At this age, children generally do not understand questions beginning with *when, how,* or *why,* and they may answer them as if asked *what* or *where* (Q: "Why are you eating that?" A: "It's an apple"). However, at about age 3 children begin to respond to *why* questions appropriately (Ervin-Tripp, 1977).

In terms of production, children learn first to invert the auxiliary verb and noun in yes-no questions ("Are you going to help me?"). However, they still fail to make this inversion in *wh* questions ("Why kitty can't stand up?"). *Wh* questions are more complex grammatically than yes-no questions because they require two operations: inserting the question word and inverting the subject and verb. At this stage the child can perform each of these operations separately but cannot yet combine them in the same sentence.

Deictic Words.   Deictic words are pairs of words like *here* and *there, this* and *that,* or *mine* and *yours,* whose correct use requires considering the differing relations of objects to the speaker and the listener. What is "mine" when I'm talking is "yours" when you're talking to me; what's "here" for me is "there" for you. Children's comprehension of these words is quite good by 3 years.

In one study of this topic, a child between 2 and 5 years of age sat at a table opposite the experimenter. Facing a low wall across the center of the table, the child and the experimenter played a game together. Each player had an overturned cup. While the child's eyes were closed, the experimenter hid a piece of candy under one of the cups. The experimenter then gave the child clues such as "The candy is on *this* side of the wall" (or "under the cup" or "here" or "in front of the wall"). To obtain the candy the child had to translate the experimenter's viewpoint into his or her own—"*this* (the experimenter's) side of the wall" was, from the child's perspective, *that* side. All the children readily distinguished between *mine* and *yours,* but 2-year-olds had difficulty when a shift of perspective was required. Three-year-olds are adept at taking the speaker's perspective, since they correctly interpret *this* and *that, here* and *there,* and *in front of* and *behind* (de Villiers & de Villiers, 1974).

Passive Sentences. The passive voice ("The window was broken by the dog") is rarely used by children under 4 years of age, but after that time children begin to master this syntactic form. By age 5 children will act out, with toys, a passive sentence such as "The boy was kissed by the girl" or "The truck was hit by the car." Although 4-year-olds do not ordinarily use passive sentences when they talk, they can understand them if the context is unusual. For example, an animal attacking a person is an unusual and salient event. Therefore, upon seeing that event, school-children will spontaneously utter a passive sentence like "He is being bitten by the dog" (Lempert, 1984).

Negatives. There is also a regular sequence in children's acquisition of the ability to speak grammatically correct negative sentences. At first, many children put the word *no* at the beginning of the sentence—"No sit down," "No go bed." A little later, the child moves the word *no* inside the sentence—"I no like it," "I no want bed." Finally, the child masters the correct form (Pea, 1980).

Pragmatics: Language in Context

One of the most important functions of language is communication. Effective communication requires not only knowledge of the rules of grammar (syntax) and the meanings of words (semantics) but also the "ability to say the appropriate thing at the appropriate time and place to the appropriate listeners and in relation to the appropriate topics" (Dore, 1979, p. 337). To communicate effectively, children must learn to relate language to the physical and social context in which it is used. This aspect of language is called **pragmatics**.

Babies communicate before they speak, using actions and gestures to express emotional states and to get help in gratifying their needs. Babies will reach toward an object they want, hand a mechanical toy to an adult so that the adult will start it, and shake their heads or make pushing gestures to indicate refusal (Pea, 1980). The child's earliest intentional vocal communication may accompany these gestures. Other early communicative sounds draw attention to objects or events or serve as part of a ritual game such as waving goodbye or playing peek-a-boo. These actions and vocalizations may be the precursors of communication through language (Bruner, 1975).

Young children speaking one-word utterances also have pragmatic aims. They can use single words to ask for something they want, to label something, or to describe an event that has happened. The mother who has just heard her child say "milk" has to use the context as well as the tone of voice and facial expression to decide whether the child wants some milk, saw a quart of milk and named it, or has just spilled some milk. The same utterance can have at least three different meanings.

Conversation requires a variety of pragmatic skills.

With words and sentences, children can communicate much more efficiently and converse more effectively. Competence in conversation draws upon many social, speaking, and listening skills: taking turns; recognizing one's own turn to speak; taking account of the listener's competence, knowledge, interests, and needs; refraining from dominating the interaction or interrupting one's conversational partners; recognizing when a message is not understood and clarifying ambiguous statements; signaling attention and willingness to continue the interaction by non-verbal means such as eye contact (Dore, 1979).

Do young children possess the cognitive capacities needed to develop these communication skills? Piaget's observations led him to conclude that they do not; he stated that early speech is essentially noncommunicative or egocentric (Piaget, 1926). Children of this age, Piaget said, are not aware that a listener's point of view may be different from their own. They talk as if they were thinking aloud, often describing their own actions, and they engage in "collective monologues" in which two children each follow a line of conversation with little evidence that they are responding to the other's comments. (Sara: "Here goes my train." Sally: "The horse is hurt." Sara: "It's going faster.") Piaget thought that only at the age of 6 or 7 is egocentric speech replaced by "socialized" speech, which takes into account the viewpoint of the listener and thus makes real dialogue possible (Piaget, 1926).

It is now generally agreed that Piaget greatly underestimated young children's competence in communicating. Two-year-olds speak directly to each other and to adults, usually in staccato utterances referring to familiar objects in the immediate environment. Most such messages bring adequate responses; if they do not, the communicator is likely to repeat the message. Short utterances are typical, but longer, more elaborate communications occur in some play situations, for example, when children try to cooperate in moving a piece of furniture from one place to another.

In conversations initiated by adults, 2-year-olds often simply repeat what the adult says. Three-year-olds take turns with an adult conversational partner, and about half of their responses add new and relevant information to what the adult has said. The conversation is short, however, seldom continuing for more than two turns (L. Bloom, Rocissano, & Hood, 1976). In talking with other 3-year-olds, children sometimes sustain much longer turn-taking sequences. One pair of 3-year-olds took 21 turns, asking and replying to questions about a camping trip (Garvey, 1975, 1977).

By the age of 4, children know how to make major adjustments in their conversational strategies when their audience requires it. The 4-year-olds in one study were observed talking to 2-year-olds, to peers, and to adults during spontaneous play and while explaining how a toy works. When talking to 2-year-olds they used simpler, shorter sentences and more attention-getting words like *hey* and *look* than they did when talking to adults or other 4-year-olds. Sentences addressed to adults and peers were longer and more complex, containing more coordinate and subordinate clauses (Shatz & Gelman, 1973).

Beginning at about age 3, children's spontaneous conversations include contingent queries, that is, questions about what another child has said or done. These questions are frequently requests for elaboration, clarification, or explanation, the most common being "What?" or its synonym "Huh?" For example, let us examine the following conversation:

Lenny: Lookit, we found a parrot in our house.

Phil: A what?

Lenny: A parrot. A bird.

Phil: Wow!

In this conversation—a representative interaction between 3-year-olds—the query "A what?" (spoken with rising intonation) was clearly a request for repetition. After making his inquiry, the listener gave the speaker his turn to respond, and the speaker gave the expected response plus an expansion. The listener then responded, acknowledging that the speaker's initial statement had been clarified (Garvey, 1975).

Pragmatic skills also involve knowledge about the social context. The use of polite forms is part of pragmatics. A child who is a dinner guest at another child's house may say, "Please pass the potatoes" or "May I have some potatoes?" When eating in the school cafeteria, it may be more socially appropriate to say, "Give me the potatoes." Children who want a favor from their parents will often adopt a special tone of voice and a particular rate of speech if they are uncertain about the parents' response.

Between the ages of 2 and 3 years, children use some of the "polite" forms for requests, such as using a question rather than a command. But there is little evidence that they understand that it is polite; it is merely an alternative way of issuing a command. They will, for example, repeat the "question" insistently, or switch back and forth between questions and commands (Newcombe & Zaslow, 1981). Within a few years, however, children use different tones and words when speaking to their peers, to their younger siblings, or to their parents, indicating that they recognize that there are social and cultural rules for the content and tone of speech that vary with the social context.

⚙ EXPLANATIONS OF LANGUAGE ACQUISITION

Now that we have described the course of children's acquisition of language, we are in a position to discuss theories that try to account for language development. Early attempts to account for language acquisition using learning theory are generally agreed to have failed, and we briefly describe the reasons for this conclusion. Current theories all place stress on the innate capacities humans bring to the task of learning language. But there are very sharp differences, within this broad agreement, between theorists who believe that the innate equipment must be *language specific,* that is, involve rules and mechanisms that pertain only to language, and those who think the innate equipment can be better characterized as similar to human capacities for other forms of learning and problem solving.

Learning Theory

During the first half of this century, learning theory dominated American psychological thinking and research. Learning theorists viewed positive and negative reinforcement, punishment, and imitation of models as the principal mechanisms governing the acquisition and modification of most behavior, including language. Learning theory stressed nurture rather than nature as the most powerful influence on development, holding that children speak in ways that increasingly conform with adult speech because this is the behavior that environmental reinforcers model and that they shape and maintain.

Certainly children do need models to learn language: they cannot acquire a vocabulary or the grammatical structure of their language without exposure. Children in the United States learn English; children in China learn Chinese. They gather information about their own language by hearing others speak it. However, developmental psycholinguists have pointed out that learning theory does not describe or explain the underlying capacities that enable a child to acquire linguistic knowledge and skills. Reinforcement alone cannot account for the astonishing rate of language development in young children; we can hardly imagine what an enormous number of utterances would have to be rewarded if progress depended on that alone. Nor can reinforcement fully explain the acquisition and use of the rules or principles of grammatically correct speech. When an utterance is not reinforced, the child has no way of knowing what was wrong or how to correct the error. When it is reinforced, the child has no information about what was correct. The real problem, the psycholinguists argue, is to determine how children come to understand the principles for ordering words and parts of words so that they make sense (Slobin, 1971).

Developmental psycholinguists also argue that observation and imitation do not fully explain language acquisition. For one thing, some of a child's first two-word utterances are unique and creative combinations of words that adults are unlikely to use (e.g., "allgone bye-bye"). Similarly, when children overregularize ("The mouses runned"), they use language forms that they are unlikely to have heard from adults, and that show they are learning general rules, rather than particular routines. When children are observed at home, some children imitate the utterances of other people a great deal and some do not, but amount of imitation is *not* correlated with rate of language acquisition (L. Bloom, Hood, & Lightbown, 1974).

An even stronger argument comes from observation of blind children learning language. They acquire consistent meanings for words such as *look* and *see,* which they not only can't observe but for which they have very different experiences than those around them (see Figure 8.6). Clearly, imitation and observation of others play a role in language production, but simple imitation of the speech of others cannot be the principal means of acquiring language.

Nativist Theory

The nativist view of language acquisition stresses innate biological determinants of language—the influence of nature rather than nurture. The evidence for an innate aspect of language acquisition includes the universality and regularity of trends in children's production of sounds, which we discussed earlier. Regardless of the language they are learning, children progress through the same sequence: babbling, saying their first word at 1 year, using two-word combinations in the second half of the second year, and mastering most grammatical rules of their language by the age of 4 or 5. First words and sentences in all languages express the same basic set of semantic relationships.

FIGURE 8.6 A blind child lifts her hands in response to the request "Look up." A sighted child wearing a blindfold lifts her head. From *Language and Experience* (pp. 57–58), by B. Landau and L. R. Gleitman, 1985, Cambridge, MA: Harvard University Press. Reprinted with permission.

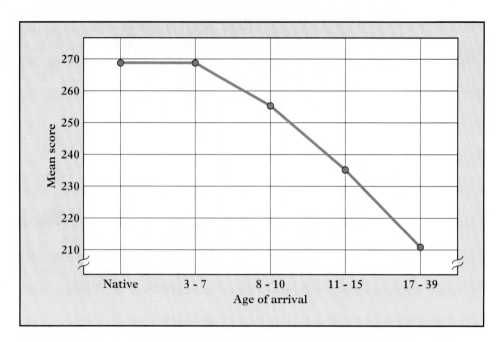

FIGURE 8.7 People arriving in the United States and beginning to learn English learned very well if they arrived at age 7 or younger. After that, their total correct score on a test of English grammar declined progressively. From "Critical Period Effects in Second Language Learning: The Influence of Maturational State on the Acquisition of English as a Second Language," by J. S. Johnson and E. L. Newport, 1989, *Cognitive Psychology, 21,* pp. 60–99. Reprinted with permission.

Critical Period. An additional argument for a nativist approach to language acquisition comes from evidence that the brain is especially "ready" for language acquisition in childhood; that is, that there is a critical period for language acquisition. "Within this period language acquisition is expected to proceed normally but outside it language acquisition is difficult if not impossible" (A. J. Elliot, 1981, p. 23).

One way to test the critical-period hypothesis is to determine whether a person who had not learned any language as a child could do so later on. But where could one find such a person? A girl of 13 who had been isolated by her parents and knew very little language was discovered in Los Angeles in 1970. Box 8.2 presents an account of "Genie's" early history. After her rescue she went to live in a foster home, where she heard normal language, although she had no special speech training at first. Within a short time she began to imitate words and learn names, at first speaking in a monotone or a whisper but gradually raising her voice and using more varied tones. Her language development was in many ways similar to that of a young child, although in some respects she progressed at a faster rate. She began to produce single words spontaneously about 5 months after she went to live in the foster home, and began to use two-word utterances about 3 months after that. Her earliest two-word combinations expressed the same relationships that young children express first, for example, agent-action, action-object, possession, and location. Gradually she produced longer sentences.

Nevertheless, Genie's language development was deficient in some respects. Five years after she began to acquire language and extensive speech training, her speech was essentially telegraphic. She was still unable to use negative auxiliaries (such as *haven't, isn't, hadn't*) correctly, had difficulty forming past tenses (using *-ed* endings), asked no spontaneous questions (although she asked questions that she was specifically trained to ask), could not combine several ideas in a sentence, and confused opposite words such as *over* and *under.* In addition, she performed poorly on tests of comprehension (Curtiss, 1977).

Clearly, Genie was able to acquire some basic language after puberty, that is, after the end of the so-called "critical period" for language acquisition. Genie's case provides partial support for the critical-period hypothesis, however, because she did not acquire language with the completeness that a preschool child would. Some of her problems might be due to the socioemotional effects of her isolation, however.

There is other evidence for the critical-period view that is more compelling. First, consider the observation that adult immigrants generally find learning a new language difficult and almost always retain a foreign accent, while their preadolescent children learn the new language quickly, make few errors, and speak without an accent (Labov, 1970). This observation has been substantiated by research by J. S. Johnson and Newport (1989). Their data show that the ability to make subtle syntactic distinctions in English is closely related to when people first began to learn English (see Figure 8.7). There is similar evidence regarding acquisition of sign language; those who learn it as adults do not acquire complete control of the grammar, but children become completely fluent (Pinker, 1994).

A second argument in favor of the critical-period hypothesis is that children are linguistically inventive in a way that adults are not. When people from different cultures come together, they often evolve a crude common language that has bits of each of their languages thrown into it, called a *pidgin.* Over time, this pidgin can evolve into a true language with its own consistent rules; such a blended language is called a *creole.* Bickerton (1981) has presented evidence that this process of creating a creole language in the Hawaiian Islands was driven by the inventiveness of children. Similar evidence has recently come from the language development of iso-

Children exposed to sign language acquire a fluency extremely difficult for adult learners.

BOX 8.2
GENIE: LANGUAGE ACQUISITION AFTER PUBERTY

When Genie was brought to the attention of the authorities, she was 13.5 years old and past puberty, but she was so malnourished that she weighed only 60 pounds and looked like a young child. She was mute, incontinent, and unable to stand erect. The story of her life was incredible. Her tyrannical father believed she was retarded because she was slow in learning to walk (actually this was due to a hip deformity). When she was 20 months old he locked her into a small, closed room. She remained imprisoned there until she was discovered almost 12 years later, when her mother, who was almost blind, came to the authorities for help. Here is an account of her early years.

In the house Genie was confined to a small bedroom, harnessed to an infant's potty seat. Genie's father sewed the harness himself; unclad except for the harness, Genie was left to sit on that chair. Unable to move anything except her fingers and hands, feet and toes, Genie was left to sit, tied-up, hour after hour, often into the night, day after day, month after month, year after year. At night, when Genie was not forgotten, she was removed from her harness only to be placed into another restraining garment—a sleeping bag which her father had fashioned to hold Genie's arms stationary (allegedly to prevent her from taking it off). In effect, it was a straightjacket. Therein constrained, Genie was put into an infant's crib with wire mesh sides and a wire mesh cover overhead. Caged by night, harnessed by day, Genie was left to somehow endure the hours and years of her life.

Source: From *Genie: A Psycholinguistic Study of a Modern-Day "Wild-Child"* (p. 5) by S. Curtiss, 1977, New York: Academic Press.

lated deaf people in Nicaragua when first offered the opportunity to sign. Children evolved a true sign language, but adults didn't (Pinker, 1994).

Two Kinds of Nativist Theory. As we pointed out, there is widespread agreement that language acquisition depends on innate abilities that are specific to humans (although at least some may be shared with some species of nonhuman primates). However, there is disagreement between those who have insisted that the innate equipment children bring to language acquisition must include information that is specifically linguistic and those who think that more general cognitive abilities are sufficient to account for language learning. Hirsh-Pasek and Golinkoff (in press) have termed these theories the "inside out" theories and the "outside in" theories, respectively.

The "inside out" theories suggest that children already know quite a bit about the possible structure of a language and that they listen to the language they are acquiring primarily to decide which linguistic devices, of a small possible set of options, are in fact in use in that language. For instance, children must find out whether their language expresses relations among words by word order or by inflections. In this view, the input language has primarily a triggering function. Noam Chomsky, a leading proponent of this point of view, maintains that humans possess an inborn brain mechanism that is specialized for the job of acquiring language. Chomsky has called this mechanism a language acquisition device (LAD) (Chomsky, 1957, 1959). Such theorists interpret the critical-period phenomenon as indicating that the LAD will only operate effectively early in development.

Other theorists do not subscribe to the idea of an inborn mechanism specialized for language acquisition. For them, language development is dependent on cognitive, information-processing, and motivational predispositions that are inborn but not specific to language. In this kind of theory, a phenomenon such as the critical period can be explained in terms of general changes that occur in development, such as the gradual increase in short-term memory, which we discuss in the next chapter (Newport, 1991).

One instance of a theory emphasizing general mechanisms in language development was proposed by Dan Slobin. He has suggested that children in all societies are equipped with certain information-processing abilities or strategies that they use in learning language. His cross-cultural studies of language acquisition convinced him that children formulate and follow a set of "operating principles." One operating principle is "Pay attention to the ends of words." Children find ends of words more salient than beginnings and middles, perhaps for reasons of attention and memory. For instance, languages that indicate place or position with morphemes that come after the noun (i.e., suffixes) are easier for children to learn (in this regard) than languages that use markers placed before the noun. In Turkish, for example, a suffix marks the place of an object (the equivalent of saying "pot stove-on"), whereas in English the preposition comes before its object ("pot on stove"). Turkish-speaking children learn these suffixed place markers before English-speaking children learn prepositions (Johnston & Slobin, 1979).

Another operating principle is "Pay attention to the order of words." Word order in children's early speech reflects word order in the adult speech the child hears. Children also seem to have strong preferences for consistent and regular systems; a third operating principle, thus, is "Avoid exceptions." As a result, overregularization is common in children's early speech (e.g., "bringed").

The "outside in" theories put more stress on the input language than do the "inside out" theories. They suggest that children are able to learn language in part because the language they hear is simplified and adjusted to their cognitive and linguistic level, and that they make inferences about grammatical rules based on what they hear. "Outside in" theories often take a very close look at the nature of the evidence children get about language, both from what they hear addressed to them and from how adults respond to what they say.

Theoretical Controversies

A good part of the disagreement between the two preceding approaches has centered on two empirical issues. First, what *is* the nature of the feedback children receive about their utterances? Second, it is known that adults speak in a distinctive way to children, slowing and simplifying their speech. Is this simplified speech important for language acquisition or simply something adults do as a matter of style?

Negative Feedback. An early study by R. Brown and Hanlon (1970) suggested that adults rarely correct children's grammatical errors. That is, children do not often get what is called **negative feedback**, or information that some grammatical hypothesis they have about language is incorrect. Rather, adults seem to correct children's language primarily based on the truth of what they are asserting. Brown and Hanlon cited a famous pair of examples to make this point. In one exchange, Adam said, perfectly grammatically, that the Walt Disney show came on a certain day, and an adult corrected him, because the show actually occurred on another day.

Adam: And Walt Disney comes on Tuesday.

Mother: No, he does not.

But in another exchange, Adam said something ungrammatical, and was not corrected at all, because the essential idea was true.

Adam: Mama isn't boy, he a girl.

Mother: That's right.

The issue of negative feedback is theoretically important because it has been shown that, without negative feedback, no general-purpose learning mechanism could *ever* arrive at a correct grammar (Pinker, 1979). Thus, the language-specific innate knowledge approach would seem to be the only one possible to hold, if in fact children do not get negative evidence.

However, there is some evidence to challenge Brown and Hanlon's conclusion. For instance, Hirsh-Pasek, Treiman, and Schneiderman (1984) have shown that parents are more likely to repeat or question early ungrammatical utterances, perhaps because they don't understand them. This is not explicit negative evidence, but it may well serve the same function. Children want to be understood. If they see that they are not getting their point across, they might be led to revise their hypotheses about language structure.

The extent and possible use of negative evidence are still, however, quite controversial. J. L. Morgan and Travis (1989) reported that adults reacted inconsistently to overregularization errors and errors in making *wh* questions in early child speech. No contingent relation between child errors and adult reaction was found at all for later child speech. This report undermines the argument that negative feedback plays a role in language learning. If children cannot tell what is being corrected, or are corrected only part of the time, then the negative feedback they get won't be very beneficial.

Child-Directed Language. Proponents of "outside in" views emphasize the fact that the way parents speak to children is extremely important. Adults talking to children emphasize the important content words in a sentence, slow the rate of their speech, repeat themselves if the child does not seem to understand, and add critical nonverbal information like pointing or frowning in order to help the child understand what it is they are saying. They may use a special vocabulary (including words like *tummy* and *choo-choo*). The pitch of the voice tends to be higher, and intonation is exaggerated. Sentences are short, simple, and grammatically correct; they contain fewer verbs and modifiers, function words, subordinate clauses, and embeddings. There are more questions, imperatives, and repetitions, and speech is more fluent and intelligible (Newport, Gleitman, & Gleitman, 1977; Snow, 1974; Vorster, 1974).

When talking to children, adults use a special style of speech. One aspect of such child-directed language is that there is very often a joint focus of attention, as seen here.

Although the nature of child-directed language varies somewhat across cultures, adults in all cultures implement some of these changes to some degree when speaking with young children. Given this universal dramatic shift in the nature of speech to language learners, it has been argued that **child-directed language** supplies a scaffold for the child to build upon in learning language.

A number of studies indicate that child-directed language may facilitate early language development. In one study, the speech of mother-child pairs in their homes was recorded twice, first when the babies were 18 months old (at the one-word stage) and again 9 months later, after the children had begun talking in sentences. If a mother used relatively simplified language when speaking to her 18-month-old (e.g., many yes-no questions and a high proportion of nouns, such as *boy*, relative to pronouns, such as *he*), her child was likely to show a high level of linguistic competence at 27 months (longer sentences and more verbs, noun phrases, and auxiliary verbs). The children of mothers who used longer and more complex sentences during the first observation progressed more slowly. The investigators concluded that child-directed language may be an effective teaching language for very young children (Furrow, Nelson, & Benedict, 1979).

Another investigator, working with somewhat older children, compared the speech of mothers whose children showed accelerated speech development with that of mothers whose children were making normal progress in language. Although the sentences that the two groups of mothers used in talking to their children did not differ in simplicity or length, mothers of accelerated children spoke more clearly, made fewer ambiguous or unintelligible statements, let their children lead in conversation, and responded to the children's utterances with related contributions. In effect, they tailored what they said to what the child said, often repeating or expanding the child's statement. For example, if Sally drops a ball and says, "Ball fall," her mother replies with the correct expanded sentence: "The ball fell down." And if Sally says correctly, "The ball fell down," her mother says, "Yes, the ball fell down because you dropped it" (Penner, 1987). Such "fine tuning" effects have also been shown in analyses by Sokolov (1993).

These naturalistic studies have been supplemented by experimentally controlled "training" studies, showing how tailored input can accelerate children's acquisition of complex grammatical forms. For instance, before one experiment began, the 28-month-olds in the study did not spontaneously use either tag questions (e.g., "I found it, didn't I?") or negative questions (e.g., "Doesn't it hurt?"). They also did not use future or conditional verbs (e.g., "He will eat it," "He could find it"). One group of children was given five training sessions demonstrating the use of questions, while another group had five sessions emphasizing verb forms. The training consisted of recasting or rewording the child's sentences in the form to be acquired. For instance, when a child in a question training session said, "You can't have it," the experimenter would reply, "Oh I can't have it, can I!" In a verb training session, the experimenter would answer a question like "Where it go?" with "It will go there."

The training proved to be effective. All the children who were exposed to tag and negative questions acquired the ability to frame and produce such questions, but they made no progress in the use of future or conditional verbs. Similarly, all the children in the verb training group produced new verb constructions, but they did not add tag or negative questions to their language repertoires. The two groups of children showed the same degree of progress on other measures of language development, such as length of utterances and number of words used. Training by means of rephrasing or recasting sentences apparently had very specific, selective effects (Nelson, 1975).

The findings of these studies may be interpreted as supporting the "outside in" view that environmental input is important in language development. At the same time, it should be noted that these studies are taking increasingly finer looks at the language acquisition process and are still not totally clear. "Inside out" theorists strongly contend that the magnitude of the information provided by fine tuning and by negative evidence is insufficient to account for the rapidity and ease of language acquisition.

☼ SUMMARY

Language has five basic functions. It makes it possible to communicate ideas, allows the user to understand his or her society and culture, helps in establishing and maintaining social relationships, permits the user to classify events in linguistic categories, and aids in reasoning.

Language is also a multifaceted system, with four different components. *Phonemes* are the basic sounds that are combined to make words. Every language has rules governing the combination of two or more phonemes to make words. Infants only a few days old can discriminate between similar phonemes and in fact can make many more phonemic discriminations than are required by their language. However, they cannot produce phonemes themselves. At 5 or 6 months of age, all infants spontaneously begin to babble by combining vowel and consonant sounds in strings of syllables. This babbling has no symbolic meaning.

Semantics or meaning can be seen around the first birthday, when most children begin to speak their first meaningful sounds, usually single words. Most of the words used by children in the second year stand for things or people. Children understand many more words than they actually speak. Many of their new words are acquired through "naming rituals" that parents engage in with their children from the time the infant first utters something that sounds like a word.

The meanings children attribute to words are often quite different from adult meanings for those words. Some are overextensions, in which a word is used to refer to objects that are similar to the one the word actually designates. Others are underextensions, in which the meaning of the word is defined too narrowly.

Syntax is apparent about the middle of the second year, when children begin to put two words together and speak their first sentences. The variety of children's two- and three-word combinations increases greatly as they approach their second birthday. Typically, children's speech preserves correct word order for their language.

As children grow older, their sentences become longer. Mean length of utterance (MLU) increases dramatically between the ages of 2 and 4. At the same time, children master the grammatical morphemes of their language—the present progressive ending (*-ing*), correct use of *in* and *on,* the plural, and so forth. They also begin to utter complex sentences consisting of two or more simple sentences joined by *and* or of one thought embedded in another. To construct such sentences, children have to learn the rules for combining larger groups of words and using connective words. They thus become able to produce questions; use deictic words like *here, there, this,* and *that;* construct passive sentences; and use negatives.

Pragmatics, or the ability to communicate effectively, goes beyond meanings and grammatical rules. Children must learn to relate language to the physical and social context in which it is used. Even young children speaking one-word utterances have different pragmatic aims. Pragmatic skills increase throughout childhood with increased awareness of the social context of speech.

There are a number of theories about how language is acquired. According to learning theory, the principal mechanisms governing the acquisition of language are reinforcement (reward) and imitation of models. Certainly children imitate what they hear others say; they cannot acquire a vocabulary or the grammatical structure of their language without exposure to models. However, observation and imitation do not fully explain language acquisition.

The nativist view of language acquisition stresses innate biological determinants. There is controversy, however, between theorists who stress innate knowledge that is language-specific and those who stress more general cognitive abilities that are guided by the nature of language input.

REVIEW QUESTIONS

1. What are the basic functions of language?
2. What are phonemes? Briefly discuss the infant's ability to perceive and produce phonemes.

3. What is meant by bound morphemes and unbound morphemes?

4. How do children learn the meanings of new words?

5. Briefly describe the process through which children learn to combine words into simple and complex sentences.

6. What is meant by the ability to employ pragmatics in speech?

7. Briefly discuss the main theories of language acquisition.

CRITICAL THINKING ABOUT THE CHAPTER

1. Suppose someone said to you that children obviously learn language through imitation. How would you persuade them they were wrong?

2. Now that sign language is recognized as a true language, many deaf individuals argue that they have their own culture and would not want to hear even if this became possible. Think about and try to describe how you might feel about this issue if you were deaf.

KEY TERMS

bound morpheme
child-directed language
mean length of utterance
morpheme
negative feedback
overextension
over-regularization
phonemes

pragmatics
semantics
syntax
taxonomic assumption
unbound morpheme
underextensions
whole-object assumption

SUGGESTED READINGS

Berko-Gleason, J. B., & Bernstein Ratner, N. (Eds.). (1993). *Psycholinguistics*. New York: Holt Rinehart. Articles give overviews of important topics in the psychology of language and language development.

Pinker, S. (1994). *The language instinct: How the mind creates language*. New York: William Morrow. An engaging account written for the general reader by one of the foremost proponents of a nativist approach to language instinct.

Rymer, Russ (1993). *Genie: An abused child's flight from silence*. New York: HarperCollins. An account of Genie's discovery and of efforts to teach her language. An interesting look inside science, describing tensions and rivalries among the investigators working with Genie. Also discusses current views of language acquisition in a very readable fashion.

Winner, E. (1988). *The point of words*. Cambridge, MA: Harvard University Press. This excellent essay describes in depth the young child's understanding of figurative aspects of language, including metaphor and irony.

P A R T

V

THE CHILDHOOD YEARS

CHAPTER

9

COGNITIVE DEVELOPMENT IN CHILDHOOD

Five-year-old Josh was sitting in the bathtub with the water running, while in the bedroom beyond his mother Carol busied herself with changing the baby's diaper and getting him into his sleeper. "Mom!" Josh called. "The water's getting too cold!" With the baby half in a sleeper and half out, Carol decided not to rush in. Instead, she called, "Why don't you fix it? If you turn up the hot or turn down the cold, it'll get better." (Carol felt OK about doing this because long ago she had turned down the temperature on the hot water heater so that even if a person ran pure hot water, scalding was impossible.) But soon she heard, "Now it's even worse!"

Finishing zipping the baby, Carol put him in his crib. On entering the bathroom, she saw Josh shivering. She adjusted the water and tried to explain how he could set the temperature himself. But it was very hard for him to understand the idea that the crucial thing was the ratio of the hot to the cold water. She said, "If you turn on the hot a lot, you should turn on the cold the same amount. If you turn the hot only a little, do the same with the cold. Then, whatever you've done, if it's too cold, either add hot or cut down on the cold. . . ." Josh looked baffled, and Carol gave up. For now, she'd just take care of it herself.

Why is it hard for Josh to understand something that seems simple and obvious to an adult? Researchers in cognitive development seek the answers to questions such as this. A wide variety of answers have been offered. Jean Piaget, the Swiss theorist of cognitive development whose general views we introduced in Chapter 5, would say that Josh is not yet in the "stage of concrete operations." Because his thinking is still "preoperational," he has difficulty with problems that require him to think about ordered quantities or continua, such as temperature or amount of water.

Other theorists would offer different explanations. For instance, perhaps Josh has trouble because the problem is too complex. There are two taps that each produce water at a certain rate but with different temperatures (hot and cold). The process of combining all this information may simply be too much for a young child. This kind of answer would be offered by an "information processing" psychologist.

Yet another answer might be that perhaps Josh simply hasn't had enough experience with temperature and needs to acquire more knowledge about it through greater exposure and interaction. This would be the answer of a psychologist who emphasized the role of the "knowledge base" in children's thinking. A similar answer with a slightly different emphasis would be offered by someone who suggested that children's "theories" of heat and temperature are too simple and need to undergo conceptual change through interaction and experimentation.

In this chapter we begin by discussing Piaget's view, as well as questions raised about his theory. We then introduce three other theoretical perspectives on cognitive development: information-processing approaches, domain-specific learning, and work inspired by a Russian developmental theorist, Lev Vygotsky. In a final section, we offer an integration of these views.

✦ PIAGET'S DESCRIPTION

Preoperational Thought

As we saw in Chapter 7, between about 18 months and 2 years, children show increasingly robust evidence of mental representation in the phenomena of delayed imitation and symbolic play. Piaget interpreted these new behaviors as showing that children acquire the ability to think about objects and events that are not present in the immediate environment—to represent them in mental pictures, sounds, images, words, or other forms. He believed that this transition marked the end of the sensorimotor period of cognitive development and the beginning of a period he termed *preoperational*.

Despite the achievement of symbolic thought, preoperational children lack some important forms of logical understanding, according to Piaget. First, as we discussed in Chapter 8, Piaget believed that their thought and speech are often *egocentric*. That is, children do not understand that other people have a different perspective or point of view than they do. Such egocentrism may be shown in speech that is not adjusted to the needs of the listener, as we mentioned in the last chapter.

Piaget demonstrated another form of egocentrism (spatial egocentrism) using the "three mountains task." A three-dimensional scale model of three mountains of different shapes was shown to the child. The child was then asked what the model would look like to people sitting in other places around the table. Young children (before age 6) said that the other person would see the same view of the mountains that they did. They apparently did not understand that the scene would look different to a person sitting in a different place. (For another account of childhood thinking that Piaget would call egocentric, see Box 9.1.)

In addition to seeing preoperational children as egocentric, Piaget suggested that their thought showed three other characteristics: a lack of reversibility or flexibility, domination by perceptual appearances, and focus or centration on only one aspect of a situation at a time. To define each of these attributes, we consider them together with their concrete-operational opposites.

Box 9.1
Does the moon follow me or you?

Young children often interpret natural phenomena in the light of their own current understanding. The result is often what, to an adult, seem humorous theories and amusing misunderstandings. The following account of one child's early beliefs about the moon is an illustration.

For a long time I gloated over the happy secret that when I played outdoors in the moonlight the moon followed me, whichever way I ran. The moon was so happy when I came out to play, that it ran shining and shouting after me like a pretty puppy dog. The other children didn't count.

But, I was rudely shaken out of this when I confided my happy secret to Carrie Roberts, my chum. It was cruel. She not only scorned my claim, she said that the moon was paying me no mind at all. The moon, my own happy, private-playing moon, was out in its play yard to race and play with her.

We disputed the matter with hot jealousy, and nothing would do but we must run a race to prove which one the moon was loving. First, we both ran a race side by side, but that proved nothing because we both contended that the moon was going that way on account of us. I just knew that the moon was there to be with me, but Carrie kept on saying that it was herself that the moon preferred. So then it came to me that we ought to run in opposite directions so that Carrie could come to her senses and realize that the moon was mine. So we both stood with our backs to our gate, counted three and tore out in opposite directions.

"Look! Look, Carrie!" I cried exultantly. "You see the moon is following me!"

"Aw, youse a tale-teller. You know it's chasing me."

So Carrie and I parted company, mad as we could be with each other. When the other children found out what the quarrel was about, they laughed it off. They told me that the moon always followed them.

Source: From *Dust Tracks on a Road: An Autobiography* (pp. 26–27), by Zora Neale Hurston, 1991, New York: HarperCollins Publishers.

The Stage of Concrete Operations

Piaget hypothesized that children enter a new stage of thought, the stage of concrete operations, some time between about 6 and 8 years of age. Piaget defined the **operation** as a basic cognitive structure that is used to transform information, or "operate" on it. One achievement that is characteristic of this stage is the ability to engage in mental operations that have **reversibility**. For example, children understand that subtracting a few pennies from a jar of pennies can be reversed by adding the same number of pennies to the jar.

Second, concrete operational thinkers are capable of **decentration**; that is, they can focus their attention on several attributes of an object or event simultaneously and understand the relations among dimensions or attributes. They understand that objects have more than one dimension—for example, weight and size—and that these dimensions are separable. A pebble is both small and light; a bowling ball is both small and heavy; a balloon may be both large and light; a car is both large and heavy.

Third, children shift from relying on perceptual information to using logical principles. One important logical principle is the *identity principle,* which states that basic attributes of an object do not change. If a box of Lincoln logs contains 32 pieces, a house built using all of those logs will also contain 32 pieces. The *equivalence principle* is closely related to the identity principle. It states that if A is equal to B in some attribute (e.g., length) and B is equal to C, then A must be equal to C. For example, if Mary wears the same size shoe as Denise and Denise wears the same size shoe as Valerie, can Mary wear Valerie's shoes? Concrete operational thinking enables the child to answer "Yes."

Many of Piaget's best-known experiments focus on phenomena surrounding the transition to concrete operational thought. Indeed, the best way to understand what he meant by the stage is to examine the phenomena that convinced him that the reasoning of children of preschool age is qualitatively different from that of older children.

Conservation. Piaget's famous conservation experiments demonstrate all three features of concrete operational thinking previously mentioned: reversibility of mental operations, decentration, and change from perceptual to logical judgments. In one type of experiment, shown in Figure 9.1, the child is shown two identical glasses, both of which contain the same quantity of colored liquid. After the child agrees that both glasses contain the same amount of liquid, the interviewer pours the liquid from one of the glasses into a taller, thinner glass and asks, "Does this glass (the taller one) have the same amount, more, or less liquid than this one (the shorter one)?" Preoperational children often say that the taller glass contains more. Concrete operational children understand that the amount of liquid has not changed despite the change in its appearance.

A critical part of the experiment is questioning the child about *why* the amount is the same or different. A child in the concrete operational stage may say, "If you poured it back into the original glass, it would look (be) the same again" (reversibility), or, "The second one is taller, but it is also thinner" (decentration, relations between dimensions), or, "You didn't take any away, so it must be the same" (logical identity rule). A preoperational child, even if he hit on the answer "same," would be unable to explain why that answer was correct and might be easily persuaded by the experimenter to change his mind.

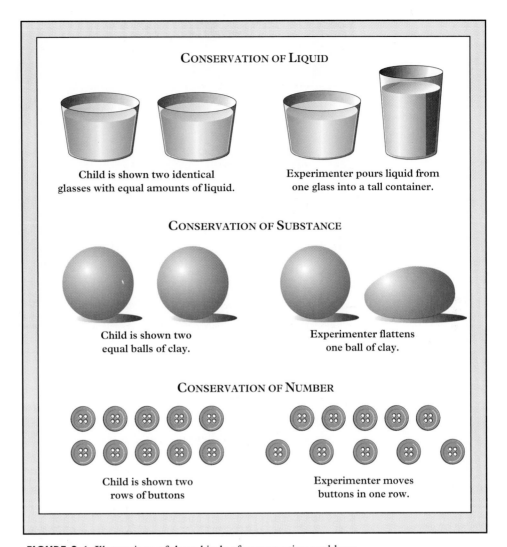

FIGURE 9.1 Illustrations of three kinds of conservation problems.

The experiments with liquid and clay shown in Figure 9.1 demonstrate **conservation of substance** (understanding that the amount of a substance does not change just because its shape or configuration changes). The experiment with buttons demonstrates **conservation of number** (understanding that the number of objects present does not change when the objects are rearranged). In a typical number-conservation experiment, the child is shown two identical rows of buttons. After the child agrees that the number of buttons in the two rows is the same, the buttons in one row are spread out. Preoperational children are likely to say that the longer row has more buttons because they focus on one dimension (length) and use perceptual cues rather than logical principles. Concrete operational thinkers can mentally reverse the operation (move the buttons back to their original positions), decenter (consider both length and density), and use the identity principle to conclude that rearrangement does not change the number of buttons in a row.

Many card games depend on an understanding of the serial order of the cards.

Seriation and Transitive Reasoning. Another characteristic of the concrete operational stage is the ability to arrange objects according to some quantified dimension such as weight or size. This ability is called **seriation**. An 8-year-old can arrange eight sticks of different lengths in order from shortest to longest. Understanding of serial order can also be demonstrated in the card game known as War, a favorite of children in the early years of the concrete operational stage. The players each play one card, and the card with the higher value wins the trick. Children must understand the sequence of the numbers 2 through 10, and they must learn that kings are worth more than queens and jacks. Seriation is critical to understanding the relationships of numbers to one another, and therefore it is essential in learning arithmetic.

Seriation underlies the child's grasp of another important logical principle, **transitivity**, which states that there are certain fixed relationships among the qualities of objects. For example, if A is longer than B and B is longer than C, then it must be true that A is longer than C. Children in the stage of concrete operations recognize the validity of this rule even if they have never seen objects A, B, and C.

One reason concrete operational children can engage in transitive reasoning is that they appreciate the fact that many terms, such as *taller, shorter,* and *darker,* refer to relations rather than to absolute qualities. Younger children tend to think in absolute terms and thus interpret *darker* as meaning "very dark" rather than "darker than another object." If they are shown two light objects—one of which is slightly darker than the other—and asked to pick the darker one, they may not answer or may say that neither object is darker.

Class Inclusion. Children's understanding of **class inclusion** illustrates the logical principle that there are hierarchical relations among categories. If 8-year-olds are shown eight yellow candies and four brown candies and asked, "Are there more yellow candies or more candies?" they will usually say that there are more candies. However, when given the same problem, 5-year-olds are likely to say that there are more yellow candies, even though they are capable of counting the candies and understand what yellow candies and all candies are. Their difficulty, Piaget believed, reflects their lack of understanding of hierarchical relations as well as the inability to reason about a part and the whole simultaneously.

Concrete operational children appreciate the fact that some sets of categories nest or fit into each other. For example, all oranges belong to the category of fruits, and all fruits belong to the larger category of foods. Moreover, the child can perform an operation and mentally take apart every category of objects and put them back together. The class of foods, therefore, consists of all foods that are fruits and all foods that are not fruits.

Second, the concrete operational child realizes that objects can belong to more than one category or more than one relationship at any one time, a principle called the *multiplication of classes or relations*. For classes of objects, "multiplication" means that children appreciate the fact that bananas can belong simultaneously to the category of natural foods and the category of sweet foods; bread can belong to the category of manufactured foods and the category of starchy foods; a person can be both a computer programmer and a mother. Similarly, for relations among objects, "multiplication" means that a snowball can be both light in weight and light in color; a rock can be both heavy and dark.

Although concrete operational children have advanced beyond children at the preoperational stage in reasoning, problem solving, and logic, they are not yet, according to Piaget, at an adult level. Much of their thinking continues to be

Successful arrangement of a rock collection depends on a child's understanding of what Piaget called multiplication of classes and relations.

restricted to the here and now of concrete objects and relations. At this stage children conserve quantity and number and can order and classify real objects and things, but they cannot reason as well about abstractions, hypothetical propositions, or imaginary events. Such reasoning only occurs with the transition to Piaget's final stage, the stage of formal operations, which he believed occurs during adolescence. We defer consideration of this stage to Chapter 14.

✿ QUESTIONS ABOUT PIAGET'S THEORY

Every great scholar generates revisions, extensions, and outright dispute. Piaget was no exception. In fact, he himself revised and extended his views until his death in 1980, and his associates in Geneva continued the process (Bullinger & Chatillon, 1983). By the end of the 1970s, many researchers had raised serious questions about important aspects of Piaget's theory. But even as parts of the theory have been rejected, it has served an important role in stimulating studies that have yielded new knowledge about children's cognitive development. In this section, we look at the research that has led to significant modification in contemporary views of Piagetian theory.

Can Cognitive Development Be Accelerated?

One question that people often raise about children's difficulties with tasks like conservation is whether teaching can explain the underlying principles and allow children to answer correctly. However, according to Piaget, training in basic cognitive skills like conservation is not likely to be effective for genuinely preoperational children, because true acquisition requires interaction between a "ready" organism and an appropriate environment. He predicted that training would be helpful only for children who were already engaged in the transition to concrete operations, because they would be developmentally ready for such training.

Neither of these predictions has been clearly supported by research findings. By now, many studies have shown that preoperational children can benefit from training in conservation and other types of concrete operational thinking. Moreover, children who are deemed "ready" on the basis of their current level of functioning do not learn more easily than those who do not appear to be ready (Brainerd, 1983). Preoperational children may become transitional following training, and transitional children may acquire concrete operations, but both types of children improve.

Can Preschoolers Show Concrete Operational Abilities?

If preschool children can in fact benefit from training in concrete operational skills, many researchers have reasoned that perhaps, even without training, they understand much more about conservation, the relations of classes, and so on, than Piaget believed. By now, a large number of studies have been done indicating that this is the case. In this section, we examine a few such demonstrations.

Conservation of Number. Very young children demonstrate conservation of number when given a simplified task. In the "magic game," children were shown two plates, each of which contained a row of toy mice. On one plate were two mice;

on the other were three, arranged in rows of the same length. Children then played a game in which the plates were covered and they had to guess which plate was the winner on a series of trials. Three mice always won. Then the experimenter began to change one of the plates surreptitiously, either by adding or subtracting mice or by lengthening or shortening rows. Even children 2.5 or 3 years old responded correctly to the changes in number and ignored changes in row length (Gelman & Baillargeon, 1983). Not only do these findings contradict Piaget's notion that preoperational children do not conserve number, but they suggest that very young children have numerical concepts.

Class Inclusion. In one of Piaget's tests, children are given sets of objects such as four red flowers and two white ones and asked, "Are there more red flowers or more flowers?" Preoperational children often say that there are more red flowers, a response that Piaget attributed to their inability to decenter, or think simultaneously of a subclass and a class. Other experiments with 4-year-olds, however, demonstrate that they can use class inclusion to draw inferences. For example, the children were asked questions like the following: "A yam is a kind of food, but not meat. Is a yam a hamburger?" "A pawpaw is a kind of fruit, but not a banana. Is a pawpaw food?" In one study, children answered such questions correctly 91 percent of the time. Clearly they had some understanding of classes and subclasses (Gelman & Baillargeon, 1983).

Spatial Egocentrism. Contrary to Piaget's theory, preschool children can take other people's perspectives. In one study, for example, children between 1 and 3 years old were given open wooden cubes with photographs pasted on the inside back surface. They were told to show the picture to the adult sitting across from them. Almost all children age 2 or older turned the cube toward the adult and away from themselves (Lempers, Flavell, & Flavell, 1978). They understood that the adult's perspective was different and that an adjustment of the cube's position was needed so that the adult could see the pictures.

Slightly older preschool children can discern other people's perspectives in more complicated situations, including indicating the precise spatial relations between the other people and objects. Newcombe and Huttenlocher (1992) showed that children's mistakes in the "three mountains" perspective-taking situation occurred only when children were asked to pick which of several pictures showed the other person's view. Picking a picture is actually a very confusing task because, since the child remains in his original position, the picture showing the other person's point of view is not correctly aligned with the landmarks in the room (see Figure 9.2). However, when children are simply asked what would be close to, far from, or on the left or right of the observer, children as young as 3 years show above-chance success. These young children are capable of taking another person's perspective.

Why the New Findings? Why do psychologists investigating similar topics reach opposite conclusions? Is it simply a case of experts who do not agree, or the courtroom phenomenon in which one can find an expert to take any position? We do not think so. Both Piaget's original theory and the newer research contradicting some of its conclusions have made important contributions to our understanding of children's thought. In fact, careful examination of the differences between Piaget's earlier studies and the newer ones shed light on developmental differences between preschool-age children and those in middle childhood.

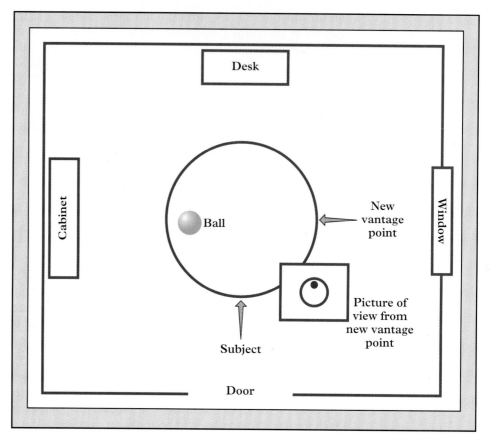

FIGURE 9.2 A perspective-taking task. The subject is looking at a ball in a certain position on a table. In order to select a picture showing where the ball would be from a new vantage point, the subject has to ignore the fact that the picture shows the ball in the wrong relations to the landmarks in the room, such as the window and the desk. From "Children's Early Ability to Solve Perspective-Taking Problems," by N. Newcombe and J. Huttenlocher, 1992, *Developmental Psychology, 28,* p. 636. Copyright © 1992 by American Psychological Association. Reprinted by permission.

First, Piaget's studies relied on children's understanding of abstract language, for example, the words *more, less,* and *same.* Preschool children are often confused by these words, but they can understand a game in which they are to pick a winner or carry out a simple instruction. Children in middle childhood not only understand the basic principle but can apply it in the context of instructions using abstract words.

Second, Piaget's tasks were often more complex than those that were later used successfully with preschool children, even though they required the child to use the same basic principle. For instance, picking a picture in the "three mountains" task is a far more difficult task, even for adults, than responding to a question about which item is in a particular location with respect to an observer.

Finally, studies of preschoolers have included clever ways to test children's implicit knowledge. When a person can use a principle but cannot explain it, we say that his or her knowledge is implicit. For example, preschool children can use the rule to form the past tense, but they cannot explain that the rule is to add -*ed* to the verb (see Chapter 8). In the research just discussed, ingenious ways were found to get children to demonstrate their implicit knowledge of number, class inclusion, and other principles that Piaget believed required concrete operations. What is added in middle childhood is the ability to explain the principles, that is, explicit knowledge about number, class, relations, and logic.

Is Cognitive Development Domain General or Domain Specific?

In Piaget's theory developmental stages cover broad domains of thought; Piaget believed that children use the same cognitive structures across a wide range of tasks. Once children understand the use of hierarchical classification for foods, for example, they should be able to use hierarchies of classes for animals, people, motor vehicles, and so on. In addition, Piaget thought that classification abilities should be related to the other concrete operational abilities, such as conservation and seriation. This hypothesis led him to postulate a "stage" of concrete operational thought.

However, decades of research indicate that development is rarely stagelike in this sense. Children may succeed at seriation but fail at conservation, or they may perceive conservation of number years before they perceive conservation of mass. Piaget was aware of this phenomenon and even invented a name for it. He called it **horizontal décalage** and attributed it, somewhat vaguely, to the different properties of the different tasks and to the interest and experience of children with the materials. But for many theorists of cognitive development, the issue is more serious, because it challenges the whole notion of cognitive development as stagelike. They have proposed that, instead, development occurs in a domain-specific fashion. That is, children acquire knowledge about specific areas of knowledge, such as number, space, or temperature, separately. Learning about one domain does not usually result in much learning about another domain. Each domain needs to be mastered individually and poses its own specific obstacles to understanding.

Evaluation of Piaget's Theory

There are important problems with some aspects of Piaget's theory, but this should not distract us from its merits. Many of its basic assumptions are now so widely accepted that we take them for granted. Most psychologists agree that human organisms function according to general principles of organization and adaptation. They agree that children actively construct their world rather than being passive registers for external stimuli, and that cognitive development is a product of continual interactions between the child and the environment.

On the other hand, many psychologists now reject Piaget's notions of discontinuous broad stages of development in favor of more narrowly defined advances in cognitive skills. Also, although qualitative changes in thought can be identified, many skills appear to develop more gradually and continuously than Piaget's theory suggests.

INFORMATION-PROCESSING RESEARCH ON COGNITIVE DEVELOPMENT

The General Approach

The major goals of psychologists in the information-processing tradition are similar to those of Piaget. First, they want to describe the nature of thought—to analyze how the human mind represents and manipulates information. Second, these psychologists try to specify how cognitive processes change with age and experience.

There are also differences in goals, assumptions, and techniques between information-processing theorists and Piaget. One major difference is that information-processing approaches assume that thinking *is* information processing (Siegler, 1991). That is, thinking is considered to be analyzable into components. In this way of thinking, children have certain knowledge and encode certain aspects of situations. This knowledge can be manipulated and experimented on, and the outcome of these thought manipulations may alter the contents of the knowledge store. Memory limits may affect children's ability to store information and to manipulate knowledge. All of this needs to be carefully analyzed, in these psychologists' view, in order to provide a "process" account of knowledge and its development. A second difference is that advocates of information-processing theories generally propose that developmental changes are gradual and continuous rather than discontinuous and qualitative, as Piaget thought. Third, psychologists in this tradition generally reject notions of cross-task generalities or stages. In fact, one of the major thrusts of some information-processing research is to determine the effects of task variations on children's processing.

The information-processing tradition is not a unitary school of thought. Some investigators have concentrated on particular tasks, sometimes tasks Piaget used, trying to analyze them from the perspective of what children encode and represent about the problem, what rules or concepts they apply to encoded information, and how these rules can change as a result of feedback from the environment. We discuss research on the balance beam problem to exemplify this variety of information-processing research. Other investigators have looked at the problem in a more domain-general way, analyzing mental processes that cut across particular tasks and subject matter. We discuss research on the development of attention and memory to exemplify this variety of information-processing research.

Information-Processing Analysis of Particular Tasks

Robert Siegler (1983) has analyzed in detail the age changes in the rules children use to make judgments about certain problems. Particularly interesting problems for the study of cognitive development are those in which two dimensions must be considered together. One example is a task known as the balance beam, illustrated in Figure 9.3. The examiner places individual weights on one peg on each side of the fulcrum and asks the child to predict whether the beam will tip to the right, tip to the left, or remain balanced when its ends are released. Before reading on, stop for a moment to see whether you know the rule that applies to this "teeter-totter" task.

Siegler (1983) identified a developmental sequence consisting of four types of rules. Rule 1 is to use only one dimension, usually weight. Children predict that the side with more weights will tip down; if the number of weights is equal, they predict that the beam will balance. Rule 2 is to use a second dimension, distance, but only when the number of weights is equal. If the number of weights is the same, the children predict that the side with weights that are more distant from the fulcrum will tip down. If the weights are unequal, they predict that the side with more weights

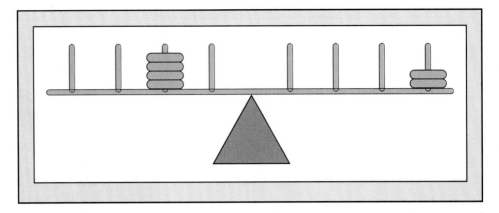

FIGURE 9.3 A diagram of the balance beam used in Siegler's research. The correct solution involves considering both the number of weights on the pegs and the distance of the weights from the center, in order to decide if the beam will balance, tip to the right, or tip to the left.

will tip down regardless of distance. Rule 3 is a transition in which children recognize that the earlier simple rules do not work on some problems, but they do not know the correct rule, so they guess. The final level, rule 4, involves knowing that one multiplies the number of weights by the distance on each side to predict which way the beam will tip.

Siegler found, first, that 90 percent of children's performance can be successfully categorized as following one or another of these rules. Second, children's rule use follows an orderly progression, with 5-year-olds mostly using rule 1, 9-year-olds using rules 2 or 3, and 13- and 17-year-olds using rule 3. Interestingly, almost no one used rule 4, even though the high school students had had explicit instruction in solving problems of this kind in their high school physics classes.

This research has much in common with Piagetian research, and, indeed, Piaget also examined children's thinking about balance beam problems. However, in contrast to Piaget, Siegler focused on the knowledge children encoded about the situation (weights, distances) and the processes or rules they used to combine the encoded information. Change from one rule to another was seen as more incremental than stagelike, and as specific to understanding of balance problems rather than as indicating broad characteristics of thought.

Development of Selective Attention

A second variety of information-processing investigation focuses more on vital cognitive processes that are needed in a wide variety of tasks. One such component process whose development has been examined is attention. We frequently hear instructions like "Turn your attention to the picture on the south wall" or "Jeremy, pay attention to what I'm telling you." Attention acts as a filter or gatekeeper—we selectively orient our perceptual activity toward certain inputs and ignore other inputs. However, attention involves more than simply pointing one's eyes at a particular object; it is a central cognitive process through which information is admitted or focused upon for further processing.

Robert Siegler's research has delineated an orderly sequence of rules governing children's understanding of balance problems.

Imagine a 5-year-old attending a three-ring circus for the first time. The multitude of colorful costumes, circus acts, music, clowns, and popcorn sellers is overwhelming. The child's attention is likely to shift quickly from one thing to another in an unsystematic way. She looks at a clown in front of her until she is attracted by a loud fanfare introducing the lion act in the center ring; then she notices people on the high trapezes and looks at them. If the circus comes to town every year, by the time our child is 10 she'll be much more familiar with the circus and will guide her attention more directly. She will watch for the high-wire act because she especially likes it; she'll ignore the dogs riding bareback but attend quickly when the dancing bears appear.

This example illustrates several developmental changes. First, children become better able to control the deployment of attention—to "decide" what they will and will not attend to. Second, children's attentional patterns become more adaptive to the situation; for instance, they can scan several areas broadly if that is called for, or they can focus narrowly if that is appropriate. Third, children become more able to plan ahead. Rather than simply selecting from what is available, they anticipate what they want to see or hear and search accordingly. Fourth, children become increasingly able to extend their attention, sometimes dividing it among different activities over time. For example, they might attend sporadically to a baseball game on television while playing a game of Monopoly.

The circus example illustrates another important point: when we use the term developmental change, we do not mean just maturational changes that occur with age. We also refer to changes that occur over time as a result of experience. Part of the reason the 10-year-old can control her attention adaptively at the circus is because she has seen it before. Another 10-year-old attending her first circus would probably show more attentional control than the 5-year-old but less than the experienced 10-year-old.

Memory Development

Memory is in some ways the core of cognition. Without memory, cognition would have little meaning because none of its products would be lasting. Psychologists distinguish among three types of memory: sensory, short-term, and long-term. **Sensory memory** (or the sensory register) is very brief. If a picture or sound is not stored or in some way related to existing knowledge within about 1 second, it vanishes. Thus, as you drive down a highway, the trees along the road are registered in your sensory memory but are not retained unless you think about them or process them in some way. **Short-term memory** holds information for a maximum of about 30 seconds. If you look up a phone number, for example, you will remember it for about 30 seconds unless you repeat it to yourself or otherwise make an effort to retain it. **Long-term memory** refers to knowledge that is potentially available for a long time, perhaps forever. Information is stored in long-term memory by being integrated with already existing knowledge—for instance, with existing schemata, images, or concepts. Several important developmental changes occur in these memory systems.

Short-Term Memory. With age there is an improvement in the speed and capacity of short-term memory. As children grow older, they can search their memory for information more quickly. For example, in one experiment people from 8 to 21 years of age were shown series of digits (e.g., 4, 7, 3, 1, 8) on a computer screen for 2 seconds; then they were shown one digit (e.g., 5) and told to decide whether it was part of the set they had just seen. This task requires people to search their memories of the set they just saw. Although subjects of all ages could perform the task, there was a regular increase with age in the speed of performance. In fact, similar changes in speed occur for many cognitive tasks (Kail, 1988).

Long-Term Memory Retrieval. Long-term memory improves strikingly in some cases but less so in others. This may seem self-contradictory until we analyze the task requirements of different means of asking about the contents of long-term memory. Recognition ("Which of these did you see before?") is better than recall ("Tell me what you saw") at all ages, but the difference is greatest for young children. Another way of stating the same thing is to say that recall improves with age more than recognition does. A 10-year-old who has seen 12 pictures can usually recall about 8 of them and recognize all 12. A 4-year-old also recognizes all 12 pictures but recalls only 2 or 3.

The ability to retrieve information from long-term memory in a recall task improves with age for many reasons. One is that the knowledge base used to encode and retrieve information improves. Children acquire more schemata and general knowledge, and they have more complex and organized concepts. However, in some cases, children may have more knowledge of a paricular area than an adult. In this case, one might expect that the child would show better memory for that mate-

Memory skills develop with age, but by age 7, children play Concentration very well.

rial than the adult would. This seems to be the case. Children who were recruited from a chess tournament were found to recall the positions of chess pieces on a board better than adults who knew little about chess (Chi, 1978).

A second reason for developmental change in memory retrieval is development of memory strategies. Suppose a preschool teacher says to her class of 4-year-olds, "I'm going to read you a story. I want you to listen very carefully because I'm going to ask you questions about it." In all likelihood those children will not remember any more than a group of children who hear the story without instructions to remember. By the age of 8 or 10, however, performance improves considerably if children are told to try to remember. One reason seems to be that the older children have learned strategies for remembering, including increasingly efficient strategies for encoding, rehearsal, and retrieval.

Let's take a closer look at one of these strategies. One useful memory strategy is to allocate encoding and study time predominantly to vital information. In fact, with age, children become more skilled at selecting important items to remember, that is, at distinguishing central from incidental information. For example, in one study of this question, children were shown a board with two rows of six doors on it (see Figure 9.4). Half of the doors had cages on them and each of these doors covered a drawing of an animal; the other half had houses on them and each covered a picture of a household object. The children were given one of two different tasks: (1) to decide whether the pictures in the top row were the same as or different from those in the bottom row or (2) to remember all the animals (or all the household objects). Before each trial they were told to open the doors one at a time and study the pictures. The most efficient strategy for the same-different judgment is to open a door in the top row and then a door below it, comparing pairs of pictures. For the recall task, it is more efficient to open only the doors for the category you need to remember. Eight- and 10-year-old children used these different strategies more consistently than 6-year-olds did. The younger children tended to open all the doors or to open the doors in an unsystematic order even when told only to remember one category (P. H. Miller, Haynes, DeMarie-Dreblow, & Woody-Ramsey, 1986).

Within a given age group, there are also individual differences in use of strategies. For example, when given an extra period to study, a majority of children in grades 5, 6, and 7 merely reread their books. However, some children underlined some passages or took notes. Not only did this minority select important information for encoding, but they actively restructured and grouped the information in their own ways. Not surprisingly, those children performed better on a subsequent test (A. L. Brown, Bransford, Ferrara, & Campione, 1983).

An important applied question about children's memory retrieval concerns whether they can serve as acceptable witnesses in court. This issue has currently been of intense public concern, especially in highly publicized cases involving allegations of childhood sexual abuse. A recent review of literature on this issue (Ceci & Bruck, 1993) suggests that preschool children, while they can remember much more than is sometimes believed, may be more subject to suggestibility effects than older children and adults. (See Box 9.2 for a story involving early childhood memory and doubts about its accuracy.)

Metamemory Processes. As well as remembering and doing things in order to remember, adults also have some knowledge of how their memory systems work and how to make them work better. For instance, an adult not only rehearses a phone number while crossing the room to dial, he understands that this procedure is vital to retaining the number. Such knowledge about memory is called **metamemory**.

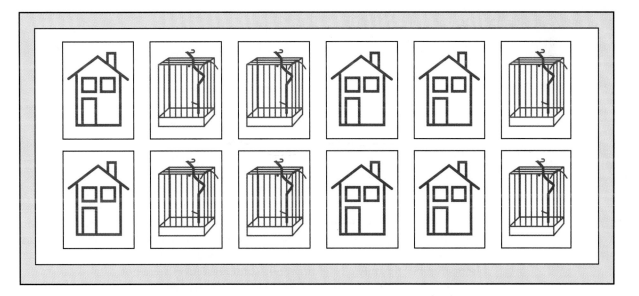

FIGURE 9.4 A test of children's memory strategies. Children could open doors to see animals (cages) or household objects (houses). They used different strategies when asked if the rows were identical and when asked to memorize all the household items. After "Children's Strategies for Gathering Information in Three Tasks," by P. H. Miller, V. F. Haynes, D. DeMarie-Dreblow, and J. Woody-Ramsey, 1986, *Child Development, 57,* pp. 1429–1439. Adapted with permission.

BOX 9.2

HOW ACCURATELY DO ADULTS REMEMBER CHILDHOOD?

Controversy about childhood memory involves more than the issue of child witnesses discussed in the text. There are also cases of adults claiming to remember events from their childhood that they had forgotten, including being witness to a murder or being sexually abused by a relative. How valid are these stories? Unfortunately, the answer must be, "There's no way to tell." We have good evidence both that such retrievals *can* happen, and also that the opposite can occur: something can be "remembered" that never occurred (Loftus, 1993). The following is a passage in which a fictional character wonders about such a childhood memory.

> I had my mother's death on my mind. One of my few plain childhood memories was of that day. I was not quite three, Hallie was newborn, and I'm told I couldn't possibly remember it because I wasn't there. The picture I have in my mind is nonetheless clear: two men in white pants handling the stretcher like a fragile, important package. The helicopter blade beating, sending out currents of air across the alfalfa field behind the hospital. This was up above the canyon, in the days when they grew crops up there. The flattened-down alfalfa plants showed their silvery undersides in patterns that looked like waves. The field became the ocean I'd seen in storybooks, here in the middle of the desert, like some miracle.
>
> Then the rotor slowed and stopped, setting the people in the crowd to murmuring: What? Why? And then the door opened and the long white bundle of my mother came out again, carried differently now, no longer an urgent matter.
>
> According to generally agreed-upon history, Hallie and I were home with a babysitter. This is my problem—I clearly remember things I haven't seen, sometimes things that never happened. And draw a blank on the things I've lived through.

Source: From *Animal Dreams* (p. 48), by Barbara Kingsolver, 1991, New York: HarperCollins Publishers.

Flavell and his associates (Kreutzer, Leonard, & Flavell, 1975) demonstrated children's development of knowledge about memory (metamemory). For example, children were asked who would learn the names of all the birds in their city faster— a boy who had learned them last year and then forgotten them, or a boy who had never learned them. By the third grade, the children knew that relearning was likely to be faster than new learning. In another study, children were asked, "If you wanted to phone your friend and someone told you the phone number, would it make any difference if you called right away after you heard the number or if you got a drink of water first?" Fifth-graders were aware that they would remember the phone number for only a brief time, but kindergarteners were not.

One can also have metamemory knowledge about people, tasks, and strategies (Flavell, 1985). Knowledge about people includes accurate assessment of one's own cognitive abilities in relation to particular tasks. As children grow older they gain a more accurate picture of their own abilities, and they become more accurate in predicting individual differences among other people. They also know that some tasks are more difficult than others (e.g., that recognition is easier than recall). By late childhood children can articulate strategies for remembering. When asked how they would go about remembering a name or a phone number, they may suggest rehearsal, writing it on your sleeve, associating it with something familiar, and other such strategies.

While metamemory skills change with age, it is less clear how they relate to improvement in memory per se. There are only moderate correlations between children's knowledge about memory and their performance on memory tasks (A. L. Brown et al., 1983). However, teaching experiments have found that children are more likely to increase their use of relevant memory strategies when the reasons for using these strategies are carefully explained to them (Paris, Newman, & McVey, 1982). This finding suggests that metamemory can actually motivate the development of memory skills.

Evaluation of the Information-Processing Approach

Psychologists working within the general framework of information processing have generated a great deal of knowledge about how children's cognitive structures and processes work. Because they are not guided by one clear-cut theory, their explanations are not subject to disproof in the same sense that learning theory and Piagetian theory are. A few reservations are in order, however. While much has been learned about the specifics of what rules children use at what ages on certain tasks or what memory strategies develop when, the overall picture of children's development is sometimes fragmented. To some extent, this is the inevitable consequence of the assumption that change is task-specific, but investigators in this tradition have not always tried as hard as they might to look for common themes.

Linked to these issues, these models have been criticized for being static, that is, for failing to describe how changes in cognitive units and processes occur. Explaining as well as describing change has actually been a goal of this approach (Siegler, 1991), but relatively little research has seemed to move us much closer to understanding the change process.

⚙ DOMAIN-SPECIFIC RESEARCH ON COGNITIVE DEVELOPMENT

Rejection of Piaget's broad stages of development does not mean that developmental sequences or regular patterns of change are no longer of interest. Recent theorists have set themselves a more modest goal than Piaget's: to delineate developmental sequences in particular cognitive domains.

One reason cognitive skills are domain specific is that knowledge of information within a content domain is important. Children and adults perform at "higher" cognitive levels when they know a lot about a topic. In fact, some people have argued that most changes that occur with age are primarily a result of the fact that individuals accumulate knowledge about many diverse topics as they grow older. We have already seen that knowledge allows children to demonstrate memory that is, in some cases, better than the memory of adults for the same material (Chi, 1978).

A second reason for domain specificity may be that different kinds of representations and processes are required for the different areas. For instance, the kinds of understanding and cognitive manipulation that are required to understand number and numerical operations may have nothing, or very little, in common with the kinds of understanding and thought that are required to understand other people and their motivations and actions. In some cases, there may even be different parts of the brain engaged in these different kinds of thought, so that one would naturally not expect much overlap in the developmental course of learning in the different domains.

Theory of Mind

As adults, we assume that other human beings have minds similar to ours. Our reasons for acting are likely to be similar to theirs, and our abilities to know or to perceive aspects of the world are probably similar to theirs. At the same time, we recognize that we may know certain things others don't (as when we are told a secret) or that we may have different beliefs than others based on our varying experiences.

Children take some time to develop this full understanding of other minds and their workings. From as young as 1 year of age (see Chapter 7) they show some capacity for empathy, or understanding of others' emotions, when they are signaled by sounds or facial expressions. By the age of 2 years, children understand that others will act in accord with their own wishes, even if those differ from those of the child. For example, they may understand that Mom may choose a pickle instead of a cupcake for a snack, even though they would never make this choice. They have more difficulty, however, with the beliefs of others, and may not understand, for example, that one person could think or know something different from what they think or know. For instance, a 2-year-old boy being read a book in which someone is baking a birthday cake as a surprise for another character may not understand that the cake will be a surprise. He may insist that if the Mom and the kids know about the cake, the Dad does too.

By the age of 3 years, children clearly understand that other people may act on their own beliefs, even when those differ from those of other people (Wellman, 1990). In addition, they understand that thoughts (as well as dreams and memories) are not physical entities. However, while 3-year-olds have some sophisticated understanding of mental events, they are still lacking in some important respects. In particular, they think that other people will know what *they* know, even when the other people have not had an opportunity to acquire this knowledge. For instance, a child who is shown a picture of an elephant and then shown the same picture covered by a sheet of paper, with only a small square cut away to show a patch of gray, may predict that a new observer will be able to identify the patch of color as an elephant (M. Taylor, 1988). By the age of 4, children are much less likely to make this mistake.

Three-year-olds also differ markedly from 4- and 5-year-olds in their understanding of the distinction between appearance and reality (Flavell, 1986). During the second year of life, as we discussed in Chapter 7, children begin to use objects as though they were something different (object substitution) and to use themselves or toys as pretend people (self-other substitution). Young children understand the difference between pretending and reality—even a 2-year-old knows that his teddy bear is not really eating when he holds a spoon to its face. Yet 3- and 4-year-olds do not completely understand a more fundamental difference: the distinction between appearance and reality.

Consider the following dilemmas, which were presented to a series of children. First the children were shown a very realistic looking fake rock made of sponge rubber. They were allowed to handle and squeeze it. Then they were asked, "Is this really

Understanding of what others know and don't know is the basis for surprise. This ability develops over the preschool age range.

and truly a sponge, or is it really and truly a rock?" "When you look at this with your eyes right now, does it look like a rock or does it look like a sponge?" Other children were shown a white piece of paper, which was then placed behind a blue filter; they were asked about its real color and its apparent color. These tasks are among those used by John Flavell (1986) and his associates to test children's understanding of the difference between appearance and reality. Three- and even 4-year-old children have difficulty with these questions, but by age 5 most children get them right.

Why should young children have so much difficulty with these tasks? They understand that the sponge "rock" is a "pretend rock." What seems to be difficult for them to understand is that something can have two identities simultaneously; one identity is its appearance and another is its reality. When an object is "pretend," it is just that—a pretend rock or spoon or astronaut. But if children think an object is a real sponge, they tend to say it looks like a sponge. If it looks blue, it is blue.

Understanding of Number

Understanding number and numerical quantity is an obviously essential aspect of daily life in our culture. Even in considerably less complex societies, numerical transactions are an important part of human interaction. Thus, tracing children's development of number has been an important focus of recent research in cognitive development.

There have been reports that infants understand number, in some sense. Infants as young as 4 months distinguish one object from two and two objects from three, as shown by their looking times in habituation experiments, although they cannot discriminate four objects from five or six (Starkey & Cooper, 1980; Strauss & Curtis, 1981). In addition, infants have recently been shown to have some understanding of the operation of addition. Wynn (1990) found that infants showed longer looking times when they viewed an object hidden behind a screen, saw another object added to it, and then saw the screen removed to reveal three objects, and shorter looking times when two objects were revealed, as might be expected. Findings of this sort have led to speculation that number has an innate basis.

However, it is important to clarify the nature of infant competence. Huttenlocher, Levine, and Jordan (1994) have recently shown that it is not until almost 3 years of age that children can solve addition and subtraction problems presented nonverbally, when they need to represent the outcome for themselves. That is, in a fashion similar to Wynn's study, children would see a certain number of objects hidden behind a screen, with some then either added or subtracted. However, rather than being shown the outcome of the transformation, as in Wynn's study, they were then asked to set up a display using their own objects, in order to show how many objects were behind the screen. Two-year-olds could not do this task. The contrast between results suggests that infant number representation may be an inexact estimation mechanism rather than a precise mental representation of the sort that allows for a child to set up a replica of the display (Gallistel & Gelman, 1992; Huttenlocher et al., 1995).

An important aspect of early number ability is counting. Preschool children have been found to use counting principles, even when they don't count exactly correctly by adult standards. Ask a 3-year-old to count eight blocks. You may hear, "1, 2, 3, 4, 6, 10, 13, 20." You rarely hear a sequence like "10, 6, 20, 13." When you ask the child how many there are, the answer will probably be 20. If you then ask her to count eight sandwiches, she will go through a similar sequence. What does this child know about the principles of counting? First, she knows one-to-one correspondence—a number label goes with each object. Second, she uses the number labels in a stable order—larger ones always come after smaller ones; this is the ordinal principle. Third, she knows that the final label in a sequence represents the total number of objects; this is the cardinal principle. Fourth, she knows that number labels can be applied to any object—the abstraction principle. Fifth, she knows that the order of the objects does not matter—she can count any one of the blocks first or second, and so on (Gelman & Gallistel, 1978). Thus, even though she does not count many objects accurately, this 3-year-old has a considerable amount of basic number knowledge.

Despite the fact that children have a good understanding of number by the time they enter school, they still need to work to acquire facility with operations such as addition and subtraction and to memorize their "number facts" so that they can be accessed easily and automatically, thus allowing for their use in more complicated problems. Siegler (1986) observed that, when children encountered problems they had encountered frequently (e.g., 2 + 2), they answered quickly from rote memory. When problems were unfamiliar, children had to work out the answer, by counting on their fingers or counting aloud. As these problems were encountered more, these overt strategies were less used and answers came more quickly.

Even preschoolers understand counting principles. By age 6, children such as the girl pictured usually count quite competently, using adult number words.

Spatial Representation

No mobile organism could survive in the world without a concept of space. The ability to find food and shelter and avoid predators depends on it. Human beings are in some ways less spatially skilled than other species; we have no magnetic sense, as do migrating birds, nor can we easily remember the location of hundreds of seeds, as can birds that cache their food. But we can orient in ways that animals cannot, using symbolic means such as verbal directions and maps to supplement our mental representations of where things are and how they are related to each other.

As with number and theory of mind, we have recently learned that the roots of mature competence in dealing with space can be found in the infant period. By the age of 16 months, children can locate hidden objects in a sandbox with great accuracy. They do this even when they move after seeing the hiding, so the coding of the location does not depend on noting the relation of the hiding place to the self (Huttenlocher, Newcombe, & Sandberg, 1994).

Children also show developmental change in their spatial understanding. They develop the ability to construct and understand maps across the elementary school years (Liben & Downs, 1989). They also develop the ability to deal with situations in which there is conflict between different methods of coding location, as occurs in the "three mountains" task as originally presented by Piaget and as in the preceding discussion (Newcombe & Huttenlocher, 1992). They hone their accuracy in judging direction and distance, not reaching adult levels until early adolescence (Cousins, Siegel, & Maxwell, 1983).

✺ THE VYGOTSKYAN APPROACH TO COGNITIVE DEVELOPMENT

All of the ways of looking at cognitive development examined so far have a tendency to focus on the individual child. Children are considered to gain in their understanding of problems, to improve their memory abilities, and so on as they struggle to find more and more effective ways of coping with the demands of everyday life and of comprehending the phenomena they observe in the world. Some developmental psychologists have argued recently that this way of looking at cognitive development does not assign enough importance to the social environment and the role of culture. Following the lead of a Russian psychologist, Lev Vygotsky, they have emphasized the role of adults in arranging the contexts within which children learn and guiding children in exploring these contexts (Laboratory of Comparative Human Cognition, 1983; Rogoff, 1990).

One way in which culture is crucial to cognitive development is through "setting the menu" of the array of activities to which children are exposed. For instance, in many cultures weaving or fishing are important skills that children can observe and be taught about; in our own culture, these activities are not part of children's usual experience. In industrialized countries, children are more likely to observe reading, writing, and negotiating as important skills of adult life.

Cultures also vary in how activities are presented and related to each other. In Western industrialized countries, skills are often taught as part of a school curriculum, and, hence, these skills are *decontextualized*, or taught in the abstract. Children work with clay as part of an art curriculum, not in order to make a pot, for instance. In other cultures, activities that children experience are more closely linked to the demands of everyday life.

A third way in which the social world is crucial to cognitive development is by introducing tasks to children in ways that fit their current cognitive level, and gradually increasing their level of involvement as their skills are seen to grow. Vygotsky described this adult structuring of the child's interaction with the world as fostering growth in the **zone of proximal development**. Other terms have been used by other writers. For instance, Rogoff (1990) talks about adults as providing *guided participation* to children with whom they interact.

Examples of adult-child (or, more generally, expert-novice) interaction in the zone of proximal development help to illustrate the Vygotskyan approach. In research in the United States, using a decontextualized task typical of the culture, namely, putting together a puzzle, Wertsch, McNamee, McLane, and Budwig (1980) studied how mothers and their preschool children worked together to do a puzzle that was challenging but possible for the children and well within the mothers' competence. Mothers began with simple directives, such as "Put the red one here." As their children developed facility with the puzzle, mothers acted less directively. They might ask, for example, more open-endedly "Where does the red one go?" This utterance still directs a child's attention to a certain piece but leaves some of the activity unspecified, for a child to think about individually.

Similar sequences of interaction have been found in research on weaving skills in Mexico (Childs & Greenfield, 1982). Adults spend 93 percent of the time with the children who are working on their first weaving project, directly pointing out what the children are to do and not do. Adult participation declines as weaving experience increases, and comments are increasingly more subtle and indirect.

In all cultures, adults guide children's participation in valued skills, adjusting their level of support as the children's understanding increases.

⊙ AN EMERGING NEW VIEW

Despite their different theoretical assumptions and methods, research on cognitive development from various approaches and theories has converged in the past several years. All researchers see cognitive development as an active and constructive process proceeding from some innate givens. There is disagreement about the strength of those innate givens, however, as well as about whether subsequent change can be qualitative and fundamental or is merely quantitative and incremental. Research on these issues is increasingly conducted in a domain-specific fashion, using a wide variety of techniques. The cultural context in which the domain is learned and the guidance provided by adults in learning about it is taken into account. One can be optimistic that ongoing research will help to resolve areas of controversy, isolating and defining both the starting points of different lines of development and the nature of the changes occurring along the way.

Despite continued theoretical controversy, there is also some consensus about some of the cognitive processes that change in important ways with development. The following list is a partial summary of those changes, taken from a variety of sources. As you read it, keep in mind that changes may result from maturation, experience, or (in most cases) the interaction of innate equipment with the evidence about the world obtained by children's active exploration of it.

We illustrate the list by discussing why 14-year-old Leslie might be able to design and build a backyard playhouse, while 6-year-old Chris probably could not do so.

♦ **Knowledge Base.** Leslie has learned about building materials and principles from her parents and from a course, World of Construction, that she took in the seventh grade.

♦ **Accessibility of Skills.** Leslie has more advanced math skills than Chris does. She is also probably better at applying them to a new situation such as figuring out the dimensions needed to build the playhouse.

♦ **Use of Task-Appropriate Strategies.** Leslie will probably make drawings of the house before beginning to build it; Chris might just begin to nail boards together.

♦ **Flexibility in Approaching Tasks.** If the wood that Leslie planned to use will make the house too heavy, she will try to obtain some other material that is lighter.

♦ **Speed of Information Processing.** Leslie can plan, measure, and figure more quickly than Chris can.

♦ **Capacity to Deal with Large Amounts of Information.** Leslie will be able to deal with the designs for several parts of the house, keeping in mind how they will fit together.

♦ **Ability to Consider More Than One Dimension or Factor in Making a Judgment.** Leslie will be able to consider height (tall enough to stand up in), weight (light enough to move), and floor area simultaneously in deciding on the final product.

♦ **Metacognitive Knowledge.** Leslie can describe how she should go about figuring out dimensions and remembering to follow the steps in the right order.

♦ **Ability to Plan.** Leslie thinks ahead to the final product, then decides what intervening steps are needed.

♦ **Ability to Resist Distraction.** When Leslie is working on her playhouse, she ignores the television, her brothers and sisters, and her mother's demand that she take out the trash.

♦ **Ability to be Exhaustive and Systematic in Solving Problems.** Before Leslie begins construction, she double-checks her plans to make sure she has considered all the parts of the house and that she has all the materials she needs. (Based on A. L. Brown et al., 1983; Kagan, 1984; Sternberg, 1985.)

All of these changes are part of the cognitive development that takes place during the school years. The changes occur partly in individual interaction with the physical world and partly in social interaction with others who are expert in the component processes. Some of the changes occur fairly abruptly, while others mature gradually over the years. Different approaches to cognitive development often simply emphasize different aspects of the complex picture that constitutes cognitive development.

✺ SUMMARY

Piaget offered one prominent description of the course of cognitive development in childhood. He hypothesized that the preschooler is typically in a preoperational stage of thought, which begins when he acquires the ability to use and manipulate symbols at about 18 months. Despite these achievements, the child's thought and speech are often egocentric, inflexible, centered on only one aspect of a situation at a time, and lacking in logical principles.

Sometime between 6 and 8 years of age, in Piaget's view, children enter the stage of concrete operations. They become able to engage in mental operations that are flexible and fully reversible, and they can decenter; that is, they can focus on several attributes of an object or event simultaneously. In addition, they shift from relying on perceptual information to using logical principles such as the identity principle and the equivalence principle.

Tasks that demonstrate these characteristics of the concrete operational stage include: conservation, the ability to identify when quantities are unchanged despite changes in their appearance; seriation, the ability to arrange objects according to a quantified dimension; and class inclusion, the ability to appreciate the fact that some sets of categories fit into each other, as well as the realization that objects can belong to more than one category or relationship at a time.

Recent studies have raised questions about aspects of Piaget's theory. Preoperational children can benefit from training in conservation and other types of concrete operational training, demonstrate conservation of number when given a simplified task, and use class inclusion to draw inferences. In addition, studies have shown that preschool children can take other people's spatial perspectives. Also, development does not seem to proceed in as general a fashion as Piaget's stage concept would seem to imply.

Although many psychologists no longer accept the notion that children move from one form of thought to a completely different form at various points in development, they do accept the notion that some qualitative changes in thinking occur between the preschool and school years. In addition, they believe that developmental changes are gradual rather than sudden, and that they tend to be specific to particular content domains.

Many psychologists have moved toward an information-processing approach. This perspective, like Piaget's, views children as active in selecting, constructing, and interpreting the information they receive. However, it focuses on more task-specific analyses than did Piaget, analyzing children's approaches to tasks in terms of their encoding and manipulation of specific information. Other researchers in this tradition have examined domain-general cognitive processes such as attention and memory.

Attention acts as a filter or gatekeeper to orient perceptual activity selectively toward certain inputs. As they grow older, children become better able to control the deployment of attention. In addition, their attentional patterns become more adaptive to the situation and they become more able to plan ahead and more able to extend their attention over time.

Psychologists distinguish among three types of memory. Sensory memory lasts less than a second. Short-term memory holds information for a maximum of about 30 seconds. Long-term memory refers to knowledge that is potentially available for a long time. Information is stored in long-term memory by being integrated with already existing knowledge. Information is transferred from working memory to long-term memory through the process of encoding, while the process of retrieval recovers information from memory.

With age, there is an improvement in the speed and capacity of working memory. Recognition is better than recall at all ages, but recall improves with age more than recognition does. Age-related improvement in retrieval from long-term memory is due to several factors. Children become increasingly skilled at selecting important items to remember. Older children have learned strategies for remembering.

The term *metamemory* refers to knowledge about one's own memory processes. One can have metamemory knowledge about people, tasks, and strategies. In general, children gain competence in remembering earlier than they gain metamemory knowledge about how those processes work, although explaining the workings of memory may facilitate their acquisition of memory strategies.

Researchers have increasingly examined the development of children's understanding of specific cognitive domains, such as understanding of number, space, and other people's minds. In each of these areas, there are competences that are evident early in life, as well as specific and important changes that occur as development progresses.

REVIEW QUESTIONS

1. What is an operation?

2. What is meant by conservation of number? Of substance?

3. What is seriation? What is transitive reasoning?

4. In what ways has recent research challenged aspects of Piaget's theory?

5. Psychologists today believe cognitive skills are more domain specific than Piaget thought. Why is this the case?

6. What is attention? How does it change with age?

7. Distinguish among the three types of memory. How does memory change with age?

8. What is metacognition?

9. Summarize what is known about cognitive development in a particular domain, such as theory of mind or understanding of number.

CRITICAL THINKING ABOUT THE CHAPTER

1. Students reading about Piaget's experiments on conservation often have trouble believing that young children make the kind of mistakes Piaget described. One common question raised is that children would avoid mistakes if they were properly motivated, for instance, if a valued food were used in the experiment. If you can arrange to interact with a child of about 4 years, ask the conservation of number questions using candies. Try the questions out on an older child as well.

2. What implications does the research in this chapter have for effective elementary education? What further questions would you like to see answered to provide a basis for improved elementary education?

KEY TERMS

class inclusion   reversibility
conservation of number   sensory memory
conservation of substance   seriation
decentration   short-term memory
horizontal décalage   transitivity
long-term memory   zone of proximal development
metamemory
operation

SUGGESTED READINGS

There are several excellent textbooks that cover the area of cognitive development. They vary in their emphasis, and some also cover the periods of infancy (Chapter 5) and adolescence (Chapter 14) as well as individual differences (Chapter 10). Some possibilities are:

Flavell, J. H. (1985). *Cognitive development* (2nd ed). Englewood Cliffs, NJ: Prentice-Hall. An excellent text by one of the major translators of Piaget's theory. Covers many aspects of cognitive development, with particular emphasis on memory.

Siegler, R.S. (1991). *Children's thinking* (2nd ed). Englewood Cliffs, NJ: Prentice-Hall. Another excellent text, this time by one of the leading investigators of the information-processing school.

Small, M.Y. (1990). *Cognitive development.* San Diego: Harcourt Brace Jovanovich. This book has a special strength in covering recent research while blending theoretical perspectives.

You may also want to read books on specific topics in cognitive development.

Ceci, S. J., Toglia, M. P., & Ross, D. F. (Eds.). (1987). *Children's eyewitness memory.* New York: Springer-Verlag. Contains a variety of interesting essays on how children's memory processes operate in important situations, particularly those in which strong emotions may occur.

Gelman, R, & Gallistel, C. R. (1978). *The child's understanding of number.* Cambridge, MA: Harvard University Press. A ground-breaking set of investigations showing that very young children understand many of the basic principles of number. This work was important for demonstrating that young children can use some of the principles of concrete-operational thinking.

CHAPTER

10

INTELLIGENCE AND ACHIEVEMENT

Matthew Smith, fourth grader, chewed on his pencil as he stared at the multiple-choice test on his desk. This was the third day his class had had to spend most of their day on these tests, and he was sick of them. He knew that his parents cared a lot about how he did, and that his teachers would use the test results to put kids in smart groups or dumb groups or maybe even send him to a special class for dummies. (Grown-ups called it a "resource room," but kids knew better.) But he just couldn't tell if he was doing well or not, and besides, the tests were boring. He was nervous and tired and wished he could just be at home, relaxing, playing ball, throwing sticks to the dog, or . . . really ANYTHING rather than filling in one more box with a no. 2 pencil!

In the last chapter we described developmental patterns in children's cognitive processes with a focus on the universals, or common features, of children's thinking and learning. In this chapter we take a different perspective and examine individual differences in intellectual functioning. For many years psychologists and educators have searched for ways to predict which children will learn more quickly and which ones will learn more slowly in standard educational programs. The intelligence test and the notion of IQ were invented in the early 1900s to help meet this need.

IQ tests are widely used today, and you have all probably lived through days like the one Matthew is going through. But there is a great deal of controversy about the proper use and interpretation of IQ tests. Why do individuals differ in IQ? To what extent is intelligence genetically determined? How do family, school, and culture affect IQ? Why do we see differences in IQ among different groups in society?

One reason for measuring intelligence is to predict school performance. School is, after all, the major arena in which our society expects children to use their cognitive abilities. School performance depends partly on intelligence, but it also depends on motivation, expectancies regarding success, socialization experiences, and the social context of the classroom. In this chapter we examine how intelligence and school achievement are affected by these factors. First, however, we must have a thorough understanding of how intelligence is defined and measured.

❂ DEFINING AND CONCEPTUALIZING INTELLIGENCE

Among the many definitions of **intelligence**, the following seems most sensible to us: Intelligence is the capacity to learn and use the skills that are required for successful adaptation to the demands of one's culture and environment. Different cultures may require skills in social interaction, language, mathematics, memory, fine motor coordination, sports, or many other domains. Because widely diverse abilities are required for adaptation in different cultures, it follows that people who are regarded as intelligent in one culture will have different talents than people who are regarded as intelligent in another culture. Thus, modern Americans emphasize speech, reading, and mathematics. Children and adults who excel in these skills are described as intelligent. By contrast, the !Kung San of the Kalahari Desert in southern Africa prize superior hunting skills; South Pacific islanders value outstanding navigational ability. The specific talents that are valued depend on the society's requirements for survival and on the beliefs of its population.

One Ability or Many?

Initially, intelligence was defined as a general competence—an ability that could be displayed across a wide variety of tasks. Before long, however, this view was challenged by those who argued that different intellectual skills do not necessarily occur together. This issue—whether intellectual ability is a general quality that applies to many task situations or a set of specific cognitive abilities—has been debated for years.

Although the issue is not entirely settled, most psychologists agree that patterns of abilities differ from one individual to another. Some children are especially good

Cultures value skills important to success in the setting in which they are located.

at learning verbal skills; others are good at visualizing spatial relations; still others are talented at mathematics. Similar variation in abilities is found in other cultures. Among Quechua-speaking children in Peru and Mayan Indian children from Guatemala, there is little relation between the ability to remember a pattern of pictures and the ability to remember words or sentences; children who do well on one of these tasks are not necessarily proficient on the others (Kagan, Klein, Finley, Rogoff, & Nolan, 1979; Stevenson, Parker, Wilkinson, Bonnaveaux, & Gonzalez, 1978). Thus, averaging a child's performance across a variety of tasks may make it impossible to detect the child's particular strengths and weaknesses.

Intellectual skills are also specific to the particular environmental contexts in which they are learned and practiced. For example, Kpelle rice farmers in Nigeria perform better than American adults when asked to estimate the amounts of rice in bowls of different sizes, but less well when asked to estimate the lengths of objects. This can be explained in part by the fact that the Kpelle have a standardized system for measuring volume that is used in buying and selling rice; there is no standard system for measuring length (Laboratory of Comparative Human Cognition, 1983).

What Are the Dimensions of Intelligence?

Although many experts agree that intelligence is multidimensional and includes several abilities, they do not always agree on the nature of these abilities. Some divide abilities according to the content of the task—for example, verbal comprehension, number comprehension, spatial relations, social skills, and musical ability (Anastasi, 1987). Others emphasize cognitive processes such as memory, inference, and problem solving. Guilford (1979) proposed a model in which there were 120 different subtypes of intelligence! In this section, we examine several proposals currently being used to conceptualize intellectual abilities.

Crystallized and Fluid Abilities. One important theory distinguishes between crystallized and fluid abilities (Horn, 1968). **Crystallized abilities** refer to the knowledge a person has accumulated. Vocabulary tests measure crystallized ability because they measure how much knowledge about word meanings one has acquired. **Fluid abilities** refer to the processes we use in solving problems and dealing with new information. They require some knowledge, but they also entail reasoning, memory, logical thinking, seeing connections, and inference. Analogies like "Doctor is to patient as lawyer is to _____" measure fluid abilities. As people grow older, their fluid abilities decline faster than their crystallized abilities.

Gardner's Multiple Intelligences. Howard Gardner (1983) has also proposed that there is more than one kind of intelligence. His proposal regarding what types of intelligence there are has been especially influenced by data indicating that particular forms of intelligence can develop in striking autonomy from other forms. For instance, children with very deficient abilities in some domains, such as language, sometimes show quite startling abilities in other domains, as we saw in Chapter 7 in the case of the drawing ability of an autistic child. In addition, normal children can sometimes show extraordinary talent in a particular area, as when children master a musical instrument well enough to play professionally. A vignette on one such child with talent in a specific area is presented in Box 10.1.

On the basis of this kind of evidence, Gardner suggests six candidates for his multiple intelligences: linguistic intelligence, musical intelligence, logical-mathematical intelligence, spatial intelligence, bodily-kinesthetic intelligence, and the personal intelligences. The last entry is plural, because Gardner distinguishes intelligence regarding one's own emotions and inner workings from a social intelligence regarding the needs and feelings of others. Gardner emphasizes that his list is tentative and that additions or subtractions could probably be made. Nevertheless, he sees the general approach as productive in its emphasis on a variety of reasonably autonomous abilities.

Intelligence as Adaptation: A Triarchic Theory. Sternberg (1985; Sternberg & Suben, 1986) has proposed an expanded theory of intelligence that incorporates cognitive skills but also includes the individual's wider life experience and adaptive skills. His triarchic theory has three major components.

The first component consists of *cognitive processes and knowledge*. There are several subcomponents to this category. First, this component includes problem-solving skills. For instance, during the test you compare the potential answers for critical differences, and you look for giveaways to wrong answers, such as the use of "always" or "never." A second subcomponent consists of metacognitive processes (see Chapter 9)—planning, monitoring, and evaluating one's task performance. For example, in a multiple-choice test one decides whether to read for detail or general ideas, plans how much time to devote to each question, and develops strategies for optimal performance. The third subcomponent includes knowledge acquisition, or adding to one's store of knowledge. In the test example, you study for the test by deciding what information in the reading and lectures is relevant; then you relate it to what you already know.

The second major component in the triarchic model is how easily and quickly individuals deal with new experiences, that is, *how rapidly they learn*. Behavior is intelligent if a person applies cognitive processes to new situations and if such

BOX 10.1

A CHESS PRODIGY

Some areas seem to produce prodigies more easily than others. One striking kind of child prodigy is the child who plays chess at internationally competitive levels. Feldman (1986) studied such children. His book *Nature's Gambit* contains case studies of several child prodigies. Mastery of chess, however, does not fit neatly into any of Gardner's (1983) multiple intelligences. Chess proficiency may depend on extraordinary attainments in one or both of two of Gardner's abilities: spatial intelligence and logico-mathematical intelligence.

Franklin was a small, dark, intense eight-year-old when I met him at the Marshall Chess Club in New York. He was a no-nonsense chess player at an age when most boys were busy with sports and superheroes. One of my clearest memories of Franklin is watching him play an eight-hour tournament without moving from his seat while his adult opponents tired, snacked, looked over other tables, and even took time out to go to the bathroom. In spite of his father's ministrations, Franklin staunchly pushed aside sodas, sandwiches, and even candy as unwanted distractions.

According to Frank and Jane Montana this intensity is characteristic of their son—once he

takes on a project he does it with a vengeance. . . . In the case of chess, Franklin's parents reported that he seemed to catch on fire almost instantly. He first saw the game played by Fischer and Spassky in the World Championship matches in 1972. His father had a passing interest in chess, and like many others that spring he occasionally tuned in to the much-publicized and dramatic event. Four-year-old Franklin began watching the matches out of curiosity (and probably as a way to get to spend a little extra time with his hard-working dad). His interest piqued, he asked Frank to teach him to play. Father and son dug up the Montanas' chessboard, and Frank showed Franklin how to set it up and make rudimentary moves. Franklin began to spend many hours with the chessboard. Jane recalls that Frank left on an extended business trip shortly after he and Franklin had begun to play together, stranding her—a nonplayer—with a child who besieged her all day long to play with him. . . .

Source: From *Nature's Gambit* (pp. 27–28), by David Henry Feldman, 1986, New York: Basic Books.

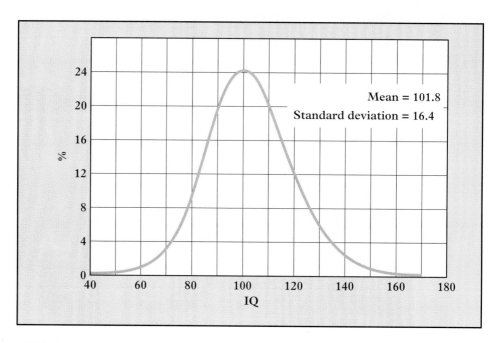

FIGURE 10.1 Distribution of IQs on the Stanford-Binet in the 1937 standardization group. After *Stanford-Binet Intelligence Scale: Manual for the Third Revision of Form L-M* (p. 18), by L. M. Terman and M. A. Merrill, 1973, Boston: Houghton Mifflin. Copyright © 1973 by Houghton Mifflin Company. Adapted with permission of the publisher, the Riverside Publishing Company.

applications become automatic fairly quickly. For example, when a child sees a sign in a store saying that the price of tennis racquets is 25 percent off, she will figure out what mathematical operations are required to calculate the price, then do the calculation. After a few similar shopping experiences, she will know automatically to multiply the price by 0.75.

The third component refers to the *ability to adapt to one's social and cultural environment*. Adaptation does not consist merely of changing yourself or your ways of thinking. It also involves shaping your environment to fit your needs or selecting a new environment. For example, a child who learns how to ask the teacher good questions will get answers that help him learn—he is shaping his environment. When he reaches junior and senior high school, he can select teachers and courses to a limited extent; that is, he can select his own learning environments. Intelligence in the broad sense can be manifested by all of these ways of adapting to and influencing the environmental context in which one performs everyday skills.

One might expect that tests of intelligence would be created to fit these various theories. Historically, however, efforts to measure intelligence preceded the development of theories about intelligence.

Early Efforts to Measure Intelligence

The first intelligence tests were created in the early 1900s by a Frenchman, Alfred Binet. He had a practical purpose: to predict which children would succeed or fail in school. The research strategy was empirical. The researchers administered a variety of questions to children who were doing well in school and to children who were not doing well. The questions finally selected for the intelligence test were those on which the high achievers performed better than the poor achievers. The quality the researchers were trying to measure was not an abstract, theoretical entity; it was the children's potential for performance in the specific situation of school.

This test was later modified for use in the United States by Lewis Terman and Maude Merrill at Stanford University. Now known as the Stanford-Binet, the test contains a large number of items designed to measure everyday information, verbal ability, memory, perception, and logical reasoning. To standardize the test, items were administered to a representative sample of children of different ages. Then the items were assigned to age levels. For example, the items assigned to the 3-year level were those that were passed by about half of the 3-year-olds; the items placed at the 6-year level were those that were passed by about half of the 6-year-olds; and so on. The IQ (intelligence quotient) was calculated by comparing the child's score with averages for other children of the same age.

Figure 10.1 shows the distribution of IQ scores for the population used in standardizing the Stanford-Binet. The test was constructed so that the distribution of scores would closely resemble the normal bell-shaped curve, with the center or mean of the curve at IQ 100, and higher and lower IQs about equally common. Table 10.1 shows the percentage of individuals in different IQ ranges and the interpretive label for each range.

Multidimensional Intelligence Tests

The early Stanford-Binet provided only a summary IQ score; the authors assumed that intelligence is a generalized quality. Other scales, which are widely used today, include subtests for many dimensions of intelligence. One of these scales is the

TABLE 10.1 Percent of Children at Different Levels of IQ in the 1937 Standardization Group of the Stanford-Binet

IQ	Percent	Classification
160–169	0.03	
150–159	0.2	Very superior
140–149	1.1	
130–139	3.1	Superior
120–129	8.2	
110–119	18.1	High average
100–109	23.5	Normal or average
90–99	23.0	
80–89	14.5	Low average
70–79	5.6	Borderline defective
60–69	2.0	
50–59	0.4	Mentally defective
40–49	0.2	
30–39	0.03	

Source: From *Stanford-Binet Intelligence Scale: Manual for the Third Revision of Form L-M* (p. 18), by L. M. Terman and M. A. Merrill, 1973, Boston: Houghton Mifflin. Copyright © 1973 by Houghton Mifflin Company. Reproduced by permission of The Riverside Publishing Company.

Wechsler Intelligence Scales, devised by the psychologist David Wechsler. The items were selected in much the same way as those included in the early Stanford-Binet, but they are arranged in subtests measuring particular skills such as vocabulary, discerning similarities and differences, memory for numbers, and constructing designs with colored blocks. The subtests can be scored separately, but they are also grouped into two scales: the Verbal IQ, which is based on items using language (e.g., vocabulary) and numbers, and the Performance IQ, which is based on subtests that do not require language (e.g., assembling parts of a puzzle). The Full Scale IQ is an average of the Verbal and Performance IQs.

Some other tests of intelligence are even more clearly based on the multidimensional view. For instance, the Primary Mental Abilities Test, designed for elementary schoolchildren, and the Differential Aptitude Test, designed for older children and adolescents, both contain separate tests for skills such as verbal reasoning, number facility, spatial relations, and perceptual speed. The child obtains scores on each subtest but is not given an average or overall score. Although many of these tests correlate with the Stanford-Binet and the Wechsler, multidimensional tests are especially useful when one has questions about specific abilities, such as ability to visualize spatial relations (Anastasi, 1987).

Tests Based on Cognitive Processes

The intelligence-testing movement and the development of theories about cognitive development occurred separately. The testing movement had a practical goal that was approached through a trial-and-error process. Psychologists studying cognitive development, on the other hand, were concerned with generating theory and knowledge about children. They usually had little interest in applying their work to the measurement of individual differences. Recently these two groups have begun to work together. Theories of intelligence have incorporated what we know about cognitive processing, and intelligence tests are increasingly based on those theories.

The fourth major revision of the Stanford-Binet (Thorndike, Hagen, & Sattler, 1986) and the Kaufman A-B-C tests are both recent examples of a theory-based approach (Anastasi, 1987). The authors of the Stanford-Binet still assume that some aspects of intelligence are generalized. However, items are grouped to represent three components of intelligence: crystallized abilities (e.g., vocabulary and mathematical calculations), fluid-analytic abilities (e.g., constructing block designs and identifying missing parts in a picture), and short-term memory (e.g., remembering a string of digits). A person receives scores for each component as well as an overall score. As on virtually all intelligence tests, scores are calculated by comparing the individual's performance to that of others of the same age from the same country on a scale with a mean of 100 and a standard deviation of 16 (see Figure 10.1). However, the score is called a Standard Age Score (SAS), not an IQ. In the next section, we consider why the test authors made this change.

Limitations on Measures of IQ

The public and many professionals have imbued the IQ with almost mystical qualities. Many people seem to believe that the tester can peer into the mind and discover a number that is predetermined by heredity, fixed for life, and determined by one's innate potential. It is this belief framework that is making Matthew, in our opening vignette, so desperately nervous. Yet none of these assumptions is exactly correct.

IQ is not a "pure" index of innate potential by any means. An IQ score measures how much you know about certain topics and how well developed certain skills are at the time that the test is given. Your score is influenced by your past experiences and familiarity with the skills and information contained in the test as well as by your genetic and biological makeup. Just as your performance on a reading test depends partly on your previous experience with reading, your performance on an intelligence test is affected by your opportunities to learn and use vocabulary, information, arithmetic, memory, and spatial skills. Your genetic endowment plays a role in how quickly you learn from experience, but that is true for any kind of cognitive achievement, not just IQ.

Further, contrary to popular belief, IQ is not fixed for life. Intelligence test scores are among the most stable human qualities that psychologists measure, but a person's score does not remain the same throughout life. Even over a few weeks, test scores can vary by as much as 10 points because of changes in motivation, variations in attention, or fatigue. Over longer periods, while there is some stability in intelligence test scores after about age 2 (that is, a score at one age predicts scores at later ages), there is also considerable change for many individuals. In other words, IQ tests at one age predict IQ at a later age much better than chance, but not in a "hand of fate" fashion.

Evidence for this statement comes from two longitudinal studies in which the same children were tested from ages 2 to 18 (Honzik, Macfarlane, & Allen, 1948; Sontag, Baker, & Nelson, 1958). Two generalizations describe the results of these studies: (1) As children advance in age, their test scores become increasingly better predictors of later performance. For instance, the correlation between IQs at ages 3 and 5 is lower than the correlation between scores at ages 8 and 10. (2) The shorter the interval between tests, the higher the correlations between them; that is, the more similar the scores.

Nevertheless, some children show marked changes in IQ as they grow older. In a longitudinal study that followed children between the ages of 2.5 and 17, the difference between the average child's highest and lowest scores was 28.5 points (McCall, Appelbaum, & Hogarty, 1973). Even after age 6, when IQ scores are relatively stable, the scores of some children show large changes, increasing as well as decreasing. The average changes between the ages of 6 and 18 for children in two groups studied at the University of California are shown in Table 10.2. The scores of the majority of the children shifted 15 points or more, and in over one-third of the cases they shifted 20 points or more.

TABLE 10.2 Changes in IQ Between Ages 6 and 18

Change in IQ	Guidance N = 114(%)	Control N = 108(%)	Total N = 222(%)
50 or more IQ points	1	—	.5
30 or more IQ points	9	10	9
20 or more IQ points	32	42	35
15 or more IQ points	58	60	58
10 or more IQ points	87	83	85
9 or fewer IQ points	18	17	15

Source: After "The Stability of Mental Test Performance Between Two and Eighteen Years," by M. P. Honzik, J. W. Macfarlane, and L. Allen," 1948, *Journal of Experimental Education, 17*. A publication of the Helen Dwight Reid Educational Foundation. Adapted with permission.

Larger changes in IQ are less common. It would be rare (though not impossible) for a child's score to shift from 70 to 130 or from 130 to 70. For practical purposes, we can predict that a child with a high score is unlikely to change to a very low score and vice versa, but we cannot predict with any precision what score a child will have a few years from now.

Does IQ measure aptitude or achievement? **Aptitude** refers to the ability to learn a new skill or to do well in some future learning situation. For example, the Scholastic Aptitude Test, which is given to high school students throughout the United States, is designed to predict their academic performance in college. **Achievement**, on the other hand, describes how much a person has learned in a particular course or school subject. The standardized achievement tests given in most public school systems are used primarily to measure how well students have learned reading, math, and other academic subjects. Aptitude tests often cover a wide range of content, whereas achievement tests measure a specific set of information or skills (Anastasi, 1987). In fact, however, there is no clear separation between aptitude and achievement. Performance on intelligence tests depends on what one knows, and conversely, achievement tests can be used to predict future academic success. Therefore, intelligence tests measure both aptitude and achievement.

Does performance reflect competence? People who interpret test scores must constantly remind themselves of the difference between competence and performance. If children perform well on a test, one can be reasonably confident that they have the competences measured by the test. However, if a child does not answer the questions correctly, one cannot be sure that those competences are lacking—only that they were not demonstrated. When children do not perform correctly, we must be cautious about saying that they cannot do so.

How Should the IQ Test Be Used?

All of these cautions about the meaning of the IQ score raise questions about its use. Two of the points made earlier in the chapter are pertinent to this issue. First, because intelligence is multidimensional, it is probably more useful to examine tests of specific skills than to rely solely on a single IQ score. Rather than saying that a child is intelligent, we might say that she is good at language, math, spatial reasoning, creative writing, or artistic composition.

Second, because intelligence tests are basically tests of achievement across a wide range of cognitive domains, the label "IQ" could be replaced by a term like "school ability," "academic aptitude," or "Standard Age Score" (Reschly, 1981; Thorndike et al., 1986). These labels might avoid the implications that test scores are an index of innate potential or a fixed entity that the person carries throughout life. They might better convey the notion that tests of cognitive performance can be useful for educational diagnosis while reducing the possibility that children will be stigmatized with a label that says they are unable to learn.

Even with these restrictions, we must recognize that IQ is not the only determinant of success in school, work, or other life situations. Intelligence accounts for only part of individual variations in school performance (Anastasi, 1987). Existing tests do not measure all aspects of intelligent behavior. For instance, most tests do not measure all the components defined in Sternberg's triarchic theory. They rarely measure children's ability to learn from experience or to adapt to new environ-

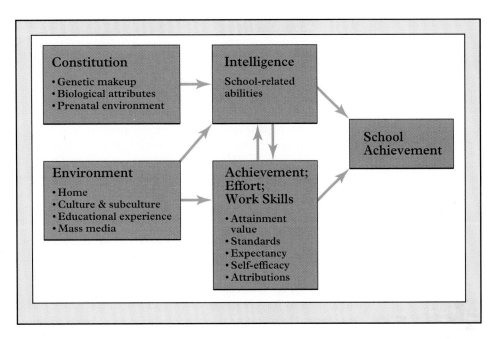

FIGURE 10.2 The major influences on intellectual functioning and school achievement.

ments. Moreover, qualities other than intelligence are important for achievement. In short, we need to look beyond IQ and consider such factors as motivation and expectancies.

These points seem especially vivid when we look at accounts of the life stories of individuals who were identified in childhood as having IQ scores in the genius range. Some achieved at expected levels, but the lives of others were disappointing. See Box 10.2 for one such story.

MOTIVATION AND SCHOOL ACHIEVEMENT

Achievement in school and in adult life depends not only on people's abilities but also on their motivation, attitudes, work skills, and emotional reactions to school and other achievement situations. The diagram in Figure 10.2 illustrates the contributions of ability and motivational variables to achievement.

Achievement Motivation

Achievement motivation is "an overall tendency to evaluate one's performance against standards of excellence, to strive for successful performance, and to experience pleasure contingent on successful performance" (Feld, Rutland, & Gold, 1979, p. 45). It is the desire to do well in a particular domain (e.g., football or music), together with a tendency to evaluate one's own performance spontaneously. We often infer achievement motivation from achievement behaviors such as persisting at a difficult task, working intensely or striving for mastery, and selecting challenging but not impossibly difficult tasks, that is, setting a moderate level of aspiration.

BOX 10.2
ONE OF "TERMAN'S KIDS"

Lewis Terman was the Stanford psychologist who was responsible for adapting Binet's original intelligence test into the Stanford-Binet. In the 1920s, he began a study of intellectually gifted children, which has been carried on for decades, continued by psychologists such as Robert and Pauline Sears. Some of the life stories of the participants (or Termites, as they were nicknamed) are presented in a book by Joel Shurkin (1992).

The children did not always lead lives matching their early potential. This is illustrated in the story of "Beatrice," who had graduated from Stanford at the age of 17 and seemed gifted at sculpture. However, she never found an adult occupation in which she could be productive. In this extract, we take up Beatrice's life story after she has finished college.

A strange transformation came over Beatrice. Perhaps tired of being a prodigy (certainly no longer qualified to be a child prodigy), perhaps weary of trying to fulfill her mother's aspirations, she seemed to unplug her mind from the complexities of higher intellect. . . . In April 1943 she married a private in the army, Leon Johnson. . . . Shortly after the war Beatrice had a daughter, Ingrid. Terman, who kept in touch with her, noticed an increasing distance about Beatrice. She left it to her husband to teach Ingrid how to read. Her conversation became an unending chain of cliches with no sign of the bright, burning intellect of the young "genius.". . . Warfare with her mother continued. . . . In 1955 Beatrice visited Terman at Stanford. [Terman wrote that] "Beatrice is better dressed than on past visits and obviously came up alone in order to impress me with her development. Fewer cliches than usual but too much pose and mysterious hints about her accomplishments that I could not very well clear up."

During the next ten years Beatrice and her husband dabbled in real estate. Then in 1965 Beatrice and Leon divorced. She lived with Ingrid, who became a lawyer like her grandfather. Beatrice stopped sculpting. She died of breast cancer in 1985. Her death certificate listed her profession as "landlady."

Source: From *Terman's Kids* (pp. 186–187), by Joel N. Shurkin, 1992, Boston: Little, Brown and Company.

It is easy to see that these achievement behaviors could contribute to school success. Consider two children whose IQs are both 100 in the first few grades of school. Sara begins learning to read with enthusiasm. She concentrates on the books and worksheets that the teacher provides, and she persists in attempting to solve problems that are difficult for her. When she goes to a learning center where there is a choice of activities, she selects a book that has some difficult words as well as some words that she knows. Linda begins with the same level of skill but is inclined to be distracted from assignments when a teacher is not working with her. When she encounters difficult words, she gives up easily. At the learning center she chooses a very easy book. Over time, Sara will probably learn more reading skills than Linda will, and her teachers will like her more.

Like intellectual abilities, achievement motivation and behavior vary across tasks and situations. Even if we restrict the discussion to school achievement, children's levels of motivation may vary from one subject area to another or from one time period to the next. One child may be very persistent and involved when working on art projects but make little effort in math. Another may read avidly, selecting

Children who value certain kinds of achievement will work long and hard on projects related to their goals.

challenging books, but seek the easiest position in a team sport. Of course, the greatest social concern arises when children show less than optimal motivation in hard-core school subjects, especially reading and math.

What determines a child's level of motivation or effort in a particular task area? Some of the factors involved are attainment value (the value the child attaches to success); standards of performance; expectancies and beliefs about one's abilities; attributions about the reasons for success or failure; and the child's "theories" of intelligence, in particular, whether she sees intelligence as fixed or as something that can be developed.

Attainment Value. Questions like "How important is it to you to do well in music?" "How important do you think math will be in your future work?" and "How much would you like to be good at leadership?" are used to assess attainment value, that is, how much value a person attaches to attainment in a particular area. Attainment value influences children's selection of achievement activities.

Jacquelynne Eccles and her colleagues at the University of Michigan investigated achievement in mathematics among a group of 668 students in grades 5 through 12 using a large battery of questions about motivations and attitudes. All of the students were assessed again a year after the original test, so that comparisons over time could be made. The investigators were interested in two outcomes: math grades and selection of advanced math courses as electives. Course choices were particularly important because students who stop taking mathematics in junior or senior high school are effectively disqualified from later courses of study and college majors that require advanced math. One reason that males perform better than females on math tests during high school and college is that more males take advanced math courses (Fennema & Peterson, 1985).

The attainment value attached to math was the best predictor of students' intention to take advanced math. Students who considered math important and thought it would be useful to them in the future were most likely to say that they intended to take elective math courses. Girls considered math less useful and important for their future lives than boys did. Boys' higher attainment value for math was a major reason that boys took more elective math courses than girls did (Eccles, Adler, & Meece, 1984).

Standards of Performance. Evaluating performance means comparing it with a standard of excellence. You may evaluate how well you do something on the basis of your own past performance (e.g., "I ran a mile in less time than I have run it before"), on the basis of a goal that you have selected for yourself (e.g., "I set a goal of reading 20 books this summer, and I did it"), or on the basis of comparisons with others (e.g., "I was fifth highest in my class on that test"). When the standards you adopt are personal or are based on comparisons with your own past performance, they are **autonomous standards**. When they are based on comparisons with other people's performance, they are described as **social-comparison standards** (Veroff, 1969). Children begin to use social-comparison processes to evaluate their performance around age 5 or 6, in part because the advent of concrete-operational thought enables them to compare their performance with that of others and to consider a standard that orders performances on a continuum. In American society the emphasis on competition and individual achievement contributes to increasingly heavy reliance on social comparison as a basis for evaluating performance during the school years.

Expectancies and Beliefs About One's Abilities. As children progress through school, they form beliefs about their abilities in different subject areas, such as reading, math, and music. When they encounter a specific task, such as a math test, they have expectancies about how well they will perform that are based partly on their self-concepts of ability in math and partly on their own past performance in that particular course (e.g., algebra). Expectancies of success not only result from previous success; they also contribute to effective performance. Children who believe they have good math ability are likely to select advanced math courses as electives (Eccles, 1983).

One's self-concept of ability is an example of **perceived self-efficacy**, a characteristic described by Albert Bandura (1981, 1982). "Perceived self-efficacy is concerned with judgments of how well one can execute courses of action required to deal with prospective situations" (Bandura, 1982, p. 122). A sense of efficacy influences achievement behavior—what kinds of activities you choose to try and how much effort and persistence you exhibit (Bandura, 1981).

Some people have concluded that school achievement can be improved by raising children's self-esteem or sense of efficacy. However, training programs designed to raise children's self-esteem have generally failed to change their school performance (Scheirer & Kraut, 1979). One reason is the failure of such programs to realize that self-concepts are specific to particular domains. In a group of fifth-graders, for instance, achievement in reading and math were associated with high academic self-concepts but were not related to self-concepts in nonacademic domains (Marsh, Smith, & Barnes, 1985). In other words, making children feel good about their athletic skills or their general worth as people does not usually have much effect on their reading skills. Interventions that focus on self-concepts about particular domains of achievement are more likely to be effective.

Attributions About Success and Failure. Expectancies of success and concepts of one's abilities are not simply a result of past successes. Children with the same levels of performance often have different perceptions of their abilities, different expectations about future success (Vollmer, 1986). For example, across a wide range of achievement areas boys often have higher expectancies than girls, even when their average past performance is similar or lower (Crandall, 1969; Eccles, 1983; Stein & Bailey, 1973).

Children's expectancies may differ because they interpret their successes and failures differently. That is, they make different attributions about the reasons for their successes and failures. **Attributions** are inferences about the causes of one's own or someone else's behavior. Whether or not we are aware of it, we are constantly making attributions: Mary must be grouchy today because she didn't get enough sleep. Joe is usually a poor student; if he got an A, it must be an easy course.

Attributions about the reasons for successes and failures affect achievement behavior and expectancies about future performance (Bar-Tal, 1978; Dweck & Elliot, 1983). Four major causes of success or failure have been defined: (1) ability (or lack of it), (2) effort (or lack of it), (3) task difficulty (or ease), and (4) luck (good or bad). Examples of each are shown in Table 10.3.

As you can see, the four attributions are classified along two dimensions. One dimension is internal/external. Ability and effort are internal causes because they originate within the individual and are, to some degree, within that person's control. Task difficulty and luck are external causes because they arise outside the individual and are often beyond his or her control. This internal/external dimension is sometimes called locus of control.

The second dimension is stable/unstable. Ability and task difficulty are stable characteristics that are not easily changed, while effort and luck are unstable and can change readily. Attributing success or failure to stable causes is more likely to affect future expectancies than attributing them to unstable causes. For example, a person who believes that a good tennis score reflects ability will probably expect to do well in the next game. One who thinks that the score was due to extraordinary effort or to luck will not expect to do as well.

Consider the case of Jennifer, a 12-year-old who is trying to become a good swimmer. Every day she counts the number of laps she swims and times how long it takes her. Like most of us, she does well on some days and less well on others. If she

TABLE 10.3 Examples of Attributions About Success and Failure

		Internal	**External**	**Effect on Expectancy**
		Ability	*Task Difficulty*	
Stable	*Success*	"I'm good at math."	"It was an easy test."	Expect future success.
	Failure	"I'm lousy at math."	"It was a hard test."	Expect future failure.
		Effort	*Luck*	
Unstable	*Success*	"I studied hard."	"I guessed right."	Don't know.
	Failure	"I didn't study enough."	"I guessed wrong."	Future could be different.

considers her good days an index of her ability and interprets her bad days as times when she is not trying as hard as she might, she will probably feel good about her swimming ability. She will also redouble her efforts after a setback or a string of poor performances. On the other hand, if she thinks that her good days are flukes or a result of superhuman effort, but that her bad days show that she really does not have the ability to become a high-powered swimmer, she will probably become discouraged.

A pattern of maladaptive attributions—believing that your successes do not reflect ability and that your failures cannot be reversed by effort—has been labeled **learned helplessness** (Dweck & Elliot, 1983). Some children believe that the causes of failure are lack of ability, task difficulty, or bad luck—reasons that are outside their control or cannot be changed. As a result, they feel helpless and give up easily when they fail (Diener & Dweck, 1978, 1980). Such children do not necessarily experience any more failures or successes than other children do, but they interpret them differently.

Children's "Theories of Intelligence." Dweck and Leggett (1988) have considered what the origins of learned helplessness and its opposite, mastery-oriented behavior, might be. They suggest that learned helplessness is associated with an "entity view" of intelligence. That is, children who think that intelligence is fixed and immutable (just the beliefs we've been criticizing in this chapter) set as their performance goal to attract positive evaluation and avoid negative evaluation. If they see themselves as having high ability, this can work out, but if they see themselves as having low ability, they will show helpless behavior in which they avoid challenge. By contrast, children who have an "incremental view" of intelligence and see intelligence as changeable, will seek to increase their competence, showing mastery behavior and seeking challenge even if they see themselves as initially low in ability.

Changing Attributions and Achievement Behavior

People who are easily discouraged by failure can sometimes be helped by being taught new attributions and coping strategies. In some experimental programs, children and adults were taught to attribute their failure on a task to lack of effort. For example, when children failed on a set of math problems, an adult told them that they should have tried harder. Children who received this form of "attribution retraining" after failure performed better on math tests than children who had been given easy problems on which they succeeded 100 percent of the time (Dweck, 1975). In general, attribution retraining leads not only to changes in attribution but also to improved expectancies of success, perceptions of self-efficacy, task persistence, and task performance in the task domain on which training is focused (Forsterling, 1985). However, a few cautions are in order.

Teaching children that their failures are due to lack of effort may be harmful if they lack the appropriate skills for the task (Covington & Omelich, 1979). In these instances it is more useful to teach strategies for approaching problems. For example, children's self-efficacy, achievement effort, and performance improved most when they were taught strategies for solving math problems as well as "adaptive" attributions. The most effective strategy was modeling and practice—the children watched an adult talking about how to solve problems as he did them, and they practiced verbalizing to themselves as they did problems (Schunk & Cox, 1986).

A second caution is that there may be cases where children really do lack the basis for success in a certain area. Not everyone has artistic, musical, or linguistic talent. In this case, it is important to help children to set realistic objectives for what they do need and want to achieve in that area, and to help them to see that there may be other arenas in which they can achieve more success.

Developmental Patterns

Perceptions of self-efficacy, attributions, and attainment values develop gradually throughout childhood. As they grow older, children develop more refined abilities to think about and adopt standards of performance and to use information about the performance of others in their self-evaluations (Ruble, Boggiano, Feldman, & Loebl, 1980). Preschool children show achievement behavior: they persist at tasks and make efforts to master new skills, and there is some correspondence between their expectancies of success and their efforts to achieve (Crandall, 1978). Compared to elementary schoolchildren, however, they more often choose easy rather than challenging tasks (Stein & Bailey, 1973).

During the first few years of school, several changes occur: (1) Children's stated expectancies become more realistic, that is, more closely related to their actual performance (Nicholls, 1978; Ruble, Parsons, & Ross, 1976). (2) Children increasingly use social comparison in evaluating their own performance (Feld et al., 1979; Ruble, Boggiano, et al., 1980). (3) Children set higher levels of aspiration for themselves; that is, they choose more difficult tasks (Feld et al., 1979).(4) Children express more anxiety about failure when responding to questionnaires designed to measure test anxiety (Rholes, Blackwell, Jordan, & Walters, 1980; Sarason, Hill, & Zimbardo, 1964).

With age, children differentiate the causes of success and failure along the lines described in Table 10.3. Younger children sometimes do not distinguish clearly among effort, ability, and luck. In one study, 5- and 6-year-old children did not see the difference between tasks requiring luck and skill. In the "luck" task, they were asked to match pictures that they could not see because the cards were turned face down; in the "skill" task, they could see the pictures to be matched. Clear differentiation between the two tasks occurred only for children in the 9-to-14 age range (Nicholls & Miller, 1985).

The distinction between ability and effort is even more subtle and is not well understood by young children. For instance, kindergarten and first-grade children assume that people who try harder are smarter—even if they fail. It is not until the ages of 10 to 13 that most children clearly distinguish effort from ability (Shantz, 1983).

Whether these age-related changes are due to cognitive development, school experience, or both, we do not know. Cognitive growth is probably important in enabling children to compare themselves with a standard and to understand different types of attributions. At the same time, for most American children, elementary school serves as their initiation into the world of grades, evaluations, failures, competition, and clear comparisons with peers. Beginning in the first grade, children in many schools are placed in reading and arithmetic groups according to "ability" (i.e., current level of skill). They are evaluated on report cards, their papers are graded, and they are tested. These school experiences may teach children to evaluate themselves, to compare themselves with peers, to make attributions about their successes and failures, and to be anxious about failure.

Test Anxiety

American schools increasingly rely on tests—standardized achievement tests, minimum-competency tests, and entrance examinations—to make decisions about educational placement and judgments about students' achievement. During the first few years of school, many children (like Matthew in our opening vignette) may develop a pattern of anxiety over testing that interferes with their performance. In one longitudinal study, 713 elementary schoolchildren were followed for four years. Children with high test anxiety performed more poorly than those with low test anxiety. The differences between high- and low-anxiety children became more pronounced as the children grew older (K. T. Hill & Sarason, 1966).

One reason to believe that anxiety affects performance adversely is that the performance of highly anxious children changes when testing conditions are altered. K. T. Hill (1980) gave children math problems under four testing conditions: standard instructions stating that the test measured the children's ability; "diagnostic" instructions stating that the test would tell where they needed help; "expectancy reassurance" instructions, in which they were told that no one gets all the answers right; and "normative" instructions, in which they were told that individual scores were not important. The performance of children with high, medium, and low test anxiety is shown in Figure 10.3. The highly anxious children performed much better when the instructions provided reassurance or removed the threat of individual evaluation.

Hill (1980) also reported on ways of reducing the negative effects of text anxiety on children in their everyday school experiences. Children can be taught about

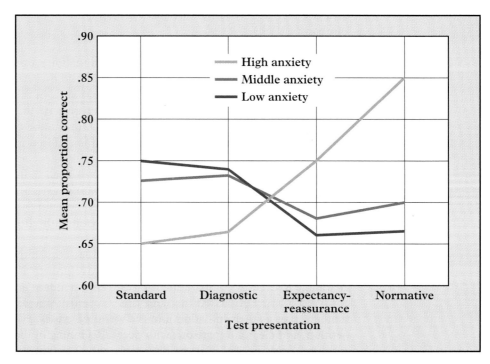

FIGURE 10.3 Test performance of children with high, medium, or low anxiety under four types of test instructions. After "Motivation, Evaluation, and Educational Testing Policy," by K. T. Hill, in *Achievement Motivation: Recent Trends in Theory and Research* (p. 65), edited by L. J. Fryans, 1980, New York: Plenum. Adapted with permission.

test formats, how to deal with timed tests, and the purposes of testing. Report cards can contain specific feedback about strengths and weaknesses instead of letter grades. Children's own accomplishments can be emphasized and comparison with others minimized. Evaluations suggest that this approach is particularly helpful to children with high test anxiety.

In summary, children's achievement in school depends not only on their intellectual abilities but also on their motivations and their interpretations of achievement situations. Achievement behaviors such as task persistence and setting moderate levels of aspiration can facilitate learning. Attainment value, realistic standards of performance, expectancy of success, positive self-concepts about one's abilities, and appropriate attributions about the reasons for success and failure are all factors that affect children's selection of achievement activities and the amount of effort they expend when they are involved in such activities. Anxiety about failure can interfere with performance, but its effects can be alleviated through training and by reducing situational cues for anxiety.

One theme that emerges from this research will be familiar by now: Skills, motivations, and beliefs about achievement are specific to particular task situations. It is not usually useful to talk about generalized achievement motivation or a general self-concept, to mention only two examples. Instead, one must examine a child's self-concept and motives for reading, math, football, or basket weaving in order to predict behavior within any one of those domains.

✿ GROUP DIFFERENCES IN INTELLIGENCE AND ACHIEVEMENT

As we discussed in Chapter 2, there is substantial evidence that a reasonably large part of the differences among people in IQ have a genetic basis. As we have been emphasizing in this chapter, however, to go from this conclusion to the argument that IQ is innate and fixed is unwarranted. A still less defensible argument is to say that differences in school achievement are related to innate and fixed causes, because school achievement and IQ, while related, are far from identical, and as we saw in Chapter 2, genetic influence on school achievement is much less marked than genetic influence on IQ. With these ideas in mind, in this section we take a look at group differences in intelligence: between males and females, between countries, and between racial and ethnic groups within the United States and other industrialized countries.

Sex Differences

Among American children there are few consistent sex differences in intellectual performance and school achievement. When the Stanford-Binet and other intelligence tests were constructed, items were discarded if the average performance of boys and girls differed. That is, the tests were constructed so as to avoid particular types of content or skills on which males and females differed. Nevertheless, girls have slightly higher IQs in the early years than boys do (Broman, Nichols, & Kennedy, 1975). In addition, girls also earn higher grades than boys do throughout the school years, but the difference decreases in high school and college.

Males and females, on the average, have often been said to show different patterns of performance in different intellectual domains. In particular, Maccoby and Jacklin (1974) concluded that girls excelled in verbal abilities, while boys were better in mathematical and spatial ability, at least beginning in adolescence. All of these conclusions, however, have been altered in the next two decades of research.

As we mentioned in Chapter 8, girls do learn their first words at a faster rate than boys, but this difference fades after the age of 2 years. In childhood and adulthood, no significant differences in a large number of verbal abilities could be detected in a statistical analysis integrating the results of various studies (Hyde & Linn, 1988).

During elementary school, males and females perform about equally well in mathematics, but males begin to do better in high school and clearly excel in college. At least some of this difference may have to do with cultural perceptions of mathematics as a field more useful to men. American children learn early that mechanical, athletic, and mathematical skills are socially defined as masculine (Stein & Bailey, 1973). Males and females also learn different attribution patterns. Males are more likely to show adaptive attributions; that is, they attribute their successes to ability and their failures to luck. Females more often attribute their failures to lack of ability, a maladaptive pattern (Hansen & O'Leary, 1986). These attribution patterns may be especially important for mathematics achievement, because mathematics is a field in which eventual understanding and success is frequently preceded by unambiguous failures to "get the right answer." In addition, the social dynamics of the average math class may not favor girls, and some schools have even tried single-sex classes as an antidote (see Box 10.3).

The idea that males perform better, on the average, on tasks that require visual-spatial reasoning—such as imagining how a cube constructed of black and white blocks would look from another side—has been supported, although the difference may be confined to particular subtypes of spatial ability (M. C. Linn & Petersen, 1985), and seems evident much earlier in childhood than adolescence (E. S. Johnson & Meade, 1987; Newcombe, 1982).

Of course, average scores do not represent any individual; there are many girls who do very well at spatial reasoning. Nevertheless, the reasons for the average differences have been hotly debated by scientists. There is some evidence that prenatal exposure to male hormones may play a role in the difference. S. M. Resnick, Berenbaum, Gottesman, and Bouchard (1986) found that girls with a syndrome called chronic adrenal hyperplasia, in which the prenatally developing adrenal glands oversecrete masculine hormones, scored higher on tests of spatial ability than relatives who did not have this syndrome. On the other hand, there is also evidence that girls who are intellectually assertive and seek clear answers to problems develop better spatial skills (Newcombe & Dubas, 1992; Ozer, 1987).

Social Class and Ethnic Group Differences

Cross-National Comparisons. Do children in Asian countries accomplish more in school, especially in mathematics, than American children? If so, are they more intelligent? These questions guided a carefully designed comparison of achievement levels and cognitive development among first- and fifth-grade children in Japan, Taiwan, and the United States, conducted by Harold Stevenson of the University of Michigan and his collaborators. By the fifth grade, Chinese and Japanese children had higher levels of performance in math and some areas of reading than American children. The three groups did not differ on various tests of gen-

BOX 10.3
SINGLE-SEX MATH CLASSES?

Sex differences in math achievement are highly related to sex differences in taking math courses. Girls often avoid taking math classes when they become electives in high school. One reason is that they do not perceive that math is relevant to their future careers (a grave error in a technological society). Another issue has been proposed to be the social interactions that occur in mixed-sex math classes, and single-sex classes have been proposed as a remedy. This extract describes the all-girl math class. After reading it, reflect on whether you think this format is one you would advocate.

In Laura Gamb's high school mathematics and science classes last year, the boys would make fun of her if she said million when she meant billion, and she learned to deflect their ridicule by saying, "Just kidding," or "Never mind." In Amber West's middle school math class, she was so afraid of sounding stupid when she didn't understand something that she swallowed her questions, whispering them to a teacher between periods, or waited until she got home and asked her mother. And in Cara Raysinger's high school math class, she often couldn't concentrate or get the teacher's attention because

there were so many rowdy boys jumping out of their seats and throwing pencils across the room and making noises like airplanes.

But Laura, Amber and Cara don't feel embarrassed, intimidated, distracted or ignored any more because now they are learning math and science in all-girl classrooms in three California schools. The schools have adopted segregation as a way of solving the widely acknowledged problem of girls lagging behind boys in math and science from middle school onward. . . .

Many of the girls . . . said it was a relief to be able to learn at their own pace and help each other rather than be rushed along by the boys. "The boys want to hurry up and get it done so they can say, 'I beat you,'" said Missy West, a seventh-grader. . . . The girls added that they were more comfortable taking leadership roles in single-sex classes and acknowledging that they were smart. . . .

Source: From "All-Girl Classes to Help Girls Keep Up with the Boys," by Jane Gross, *The New York Times,* November 24, 1993, pp. A1 and B8. Copyright 1993 by The New York Times. Reprinted by permission.

eral intellectual ability, however, suggesting that the difference is not due to genetic or constitutional differences among nationalities.

Instead, the differences appear to result from differences in educational systems and in parents' socialization practices. Children in Japan and Taiwan spend more time in school than children in the United States; they have longer school days and their school year is longer. When they are in school they spend more time in math instruction, and they are less likely to spend that time in irrelevant "off-task" activity. Teachers in those societies spend more time in group instruction than American teachers do. In addition, they are more enthusiastic and better trained in math. Within the three countries, these features of the classroom are correlated with children's math achievement (Stigler, Lee, & Stevenson, 1987). Another important contributor to the superior performance of Chinese and Japanese children may be the emphasis placed on achievement by parents and other people in the culture and the fact that they attribute success in mathematics to effort and hard work, whereas American parents tend to believe mathematics performance is determined by innate ability (Stevenson et al., 1985).

Within-Country Comparisons. Many of the environmental factors that exert the greatest impact on the child's IQ and achievement are associated with the social class and ethnic group of the family. Social class typically correlates with IQ and school grades (the average correlation is about .50). For example, in a study that followed 26,760 children from before birth to age 4, the best predictor of IQ at age 4 was the mother's education and social status. Neither the child's prenatal and birth history nor the child's performance on an infant intelligence scale predicted IQ as accurately (Broman et al., 1975). Children from economically disadvantaged minority groups in both the United States and Europe, many of whom are non-white, obtain lower IQ scores and perform less well in school than the average child from the majority group in the same country (Scarr, Caparulo, Ferdman, Tower, & Caplan, 1983).

There is also a difference in average IQ scores between black children and white children, a difference that is confounded with social class (Broman et al., 1975; Hall & Kaye, 1980). Periodically during the twentieth century, certain scholars (e.g., Jensen, 1969) have claimed that the differences in IQ between blacks and whites are a result of genetic factors. Like many other psychologists, we disagree. The available evidence does not support the conclusion that one race is genetically inferior to another; rather, it suggests that black children have lower IQ scores because of experiences in their families, neighborhoods, and schools, as well as the events associated with economic disadvantage and racial discrimination (Scarr, 1981).

The importance of family environment is demonstrated by studies of black children who have been adopted by middle-class white or black families. The IQs of adopted black children are above average and are similar to those of adopted white children. Children who were adopted as infants have higher averages than those who were adopted when they were 1 year old or older (Scarr & Weinberg, 1976).

Genetic explanations have also been suggested for social-class differences in average IQ, and similar arguments against such explanations can be offered. Children who were born to lower-class families in France and were adopted by upper-middle-class families had average IQ scores of 110, 18 points higher than those of siblings who had remained in their lower-class homes. The proportion of school failure was 12 percent for the adopted children and 70 percent for the brothers and sisters who remained with their original families (Schiff et al., 1978). In a second French sample, the proportion of school failures for adopted children was similar to that for other children in the social class of their adoptive families, not to that for children in the social class of their biological parents (see Figure 10.4) (Duyme, 1988). Thus, social class and ethnic group differences in school achievement and test performance are not due primarily to genetic factors.

Difference vs. Deficit

Although we have argued that social experience makes a major contribution to ethnic and class differences in IQ, we must avoid the trap of assuming that minority and lower-class children have deficient intelligence when intelligence is defined according to the broad definitions offered at the beginning of the chapter. That approach is sometimes called the deficit model.

It is more accurate to say that nonwhite and lower-class children often learn different skills; what they sometimes lack are the school-related skills that are valued in white middle-class society (Boykin, 1983). They learn what is adaptive in their subcultures. Consider the children in Trackton, a lower-class black commu-

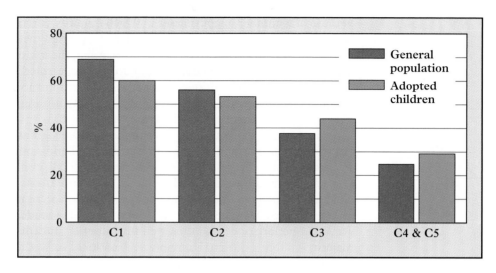

FIGURE 10.4 Percentages of school success by social class. (C1 = professionals, higher management; C2 = middle management; C3 = craftsmen, tradesmen, or lower management; C4 and C5 = unskilled workers.) After "School Success and Social Class: An Adoption Study," by M. Duyme, 1988, *Developmental Psychology*, 24, pp. 203–209. Adapted with permission.

nity in the Carolina hills. When Trackton children go to school, they do not understand indirect requests from the teacher, such as "It's time for everyone to put away your crayons," because such requests are not part of their home experience. They sometimes fail even to answer the question "What is your name?" because they are used to nicknames like Frog and Red Girl, which teachers sometimes refuse to use (Sternberg & Suben, 1986).

Middle-class parents often ask children questions to which the adult knows the answer. "What is this picture, Jennifer?" In some subcultures children are not accustomed to such questions. For example, during a study of the speech of Oakland black youngsters a psychologist asked one child, "Where do you live? How do you get there from here?" The child's answer was vague. A little later the psychologist's husband asked the same question. The answer he got was, "You go down the stairs, turn left, walk three blocks . . ." What was the difference? Her husband had never been to the child's house, but she had picked the child up there (Ervin-Tripp, 1972, p. 145).

When assessments are properly designed, children from different racial and social-class groups show cognitive skills acquired from common experiences. Preschool and kindergarten boys from middle- and lower-class black and white families were tested on their understanding of mathematical concepts that can be acquired from experience with everyday objects. Tasks were designed to measure the children's understanding of "more," addition and subtraction, basic counting, and conservation of number. There were few differences in performance among children of different races or social classes (Ginsburg & Russell, 1981).

Test Bias. One implication of the "difference" model is that tests of intelligence are biased against lower-class and minority children. That is, the tests sample skills and information that are part of middle-class culture, not the skills and information that minority children learn. This problem has been recognized for many years, but there was a resurgence of concern about it during the 1970s and 1980s, partly because of a number of court cases in which minority parents challenged the use of IQ tests to place their children in classes for the mentally retarded. In the 1979–1980 school year, two court cases regarding the use of intelligence tests were decided—in opposite directions. A California judge ruled that standardized tests could not be used to identify or place black children in special classes for the mentally retarded. Meanwhile an Illinois judge ruled that using tests for placement did not discriminate against black children (Bersoff, 1981).

Should IQ tests be used to make educational decisions for any child, particularly a member of a minority group? On the one hand, some people argue that an IQ test measures the skills needed to achieve in school, even though such tests may also have a middle-class bias. That is, a test may indicate how much a minority child has learned about the requirements for achievement in the middle-class society represented by schools. In fact, among college students, test scores predict academic performance about as well for minority students as for those from the majority culture (Cleary, Humphreys, Kendrick, & Wesman, 1975; N. S. Cole, 1981). Moreover, an "objective" test may provide an opportunity for academically talented minority students to be identified even when biased teachers fail to recognize their ability.

On the other hand, there is considerable danger that teachers and parents will label a child who scores low on an IQ test as stupid and incapable of learning, particularly if that child is black or Hispanic. It is difficult to escape from the widely held misconceptions about IQ, the notion that a person's IQ is innate or that it is immutable. Teachers might convey low expectancies for success and fail to put forth their best efforts to teach a child with a low IQ. Once children are placed in a special class for retarded children, they may be further labeled and have little chance of making normal progress in school.

The content of most IQ tests is probably more familiar to middle-class white children than to many minority children. For example, a middle-class white child might be more familiar with the word *lecture* than a lower-class black child would be. Although some content bias of this kind undoubtedly occurs, it is not as simple as it appears. When Anglo, Hispanic, and African-American college students rated items on an IQ test for bias, there was very little agreement among members of each group about which items were biased. Still more disconcerting was the fact that the items the adults thought were biased were not those on which minority children performed poorly (Sandoval & Millie, 1980). This may only indicate, however, that it is difficult to assess the life experiences of others.

More general differences in life experience probably do make IQ tests difficult for minority children. For many ethnic minorities in the United States, standard English is a second language that is less familiar than the language spoken at home or in their neighborhoods. In addition, minority children may have less opportunity to learn test-taking skills or to become familiar with the process of testing. Finally, fear of failure (test anxiety) and low concepts of their own abilities appear to be especially severe among lower-class and minority children.

✺ INDIVIDUAL DIFFERENCES IN INTELLIGENCE AND ACHIEVEMENT

We are now ready to ask what accounts for individual differences in intelligence and achievement behavior. The diagram in Figure 10.2 provides an overview of different types of influences. Intelligence is partly a function of genetic and constitutional influences, as discussed in Chapters 2 and 3. In this section, we focus on the environment.

The Home Environment

What elements of the environment are important for promoting intelligence and achievement? One way to answer this question is to study the environments of children who achieve at different levels and try to identify factors that correlate with performance. This method has one major flaw, which was discussed in Chapter 1: Correlations do not imply causation. If we find that parents of brighter children behave differently from parents of children who do not perform well, we do not know whether the parents' behavior stimulated the child or the parents responded to certain characteristics of their children. For example, in the United States the amount of time parents spend helping their children with homework is negatively correlated with the children's school achievement. That is, the poorer students get more help. Does parental help interfere with school achievement? Probably not. It is more likely that poor achievers need or ask for help more often. With these cautions in mind, let us examine the evidence.

The Physical and Social Aspects of the Home Environment. A systematic evaluation of both the physical and social qualities of children's homes is provided by the Home Observation for Measurement of the Environment (HOME). It includes six features of the home environment: (1) how emotionally and verbally responsive the mother is to the child; (2) the mother's acceptance of the child; (3) the mother's involvement or interest in the child; (4) the degree of organization in the household—whether there are regular times for meals, going to bed, and the like; (5) whether appropriate play materials are available, and (6) the variety of daily stimulation—changes in activities, opportunities to go places, and the like.

The HOME was used in several investigations of low-income families, many of which were black. The qualities of the home environment when children were quite young (age 2) predicted performance on the Stanford-Binet at age 3 and school achievement several years later (Bradley & Caldwell 1984; Bradley, Caldwell, & Elardo, 1977; Van Doorninck, Caldwell, Wright, & Frankenburg, 1981). Children with high IQs and achievement levels had mothers who were involved with them, were affectionate and verbally responsive, and avoided restriction and punishment. There were predictable routines, such as regular times for naps and meals, but there was also some variety in daily activities. Of particular importance was the availability of appropriate play materials.

One feature of the physical environment that can interfere with intellectual functioning is excessive noise and disorganization. For example, in a group of 39 children who were studied between the ages of 12 and 24 months, the presence of noise from television, other children, traffic, or appliances was consistently associated with relatively poor performance on tests of intellectual functioning (Wachs, 1979).

Affection and Involvement with the Child. In general, high-achieving children have parents who are at least moderately affectionate and involved with them. In one investigation the researchers defined "affective quality" by observing mothers' responsiveness to the child's activities, flexibility (e.g., allowing the child to change activities), concern for the child's feelings (e.g., asking why the child does

Parents play an important role in developing children's academic skills.

not want to do something), and acceptance (e.g., "I let her do things at her own pace"). Affective quality at age 4 predicted children's school readiness at ages 5–6, IQ at age 6, and school achievement at age 12 (Estrada, Arsenio, Hess, & Holloway, 1987).

A positive parent-child relationship can affect achievement because it forms a basis for the child to accept the parent's expectations and demands. If the parent does not expect achievement but encourages dependency, affection does not lead to high levels of achievement effort (Stein & Bailey, 1973). Parental affection may also increase the child's social competence and willingness to explore and take risks. Rejection, on the other hand, leads to a variety of antisocial, aggressive, or maladaptive behaviors that conflict with achievement (Huesmann & Eron, 1986).

Parents' Beliefs, Expectations, and Values. Children's achievement efforts are affected by their attainment values, expectancies of success, concepts about their abilities, and attributions. They get those beliefs and values partly from their parents. In the University of Michigan study of math achievement, the value that parents attached to different areas of achievement influenced their children's values. For example, parents considered math more important for their sons' future than for that of their daughters. The children's attainment values reflected those priorities.

Parents' perceptions of their children's abilities appear to have a direct influence on the children's sense of efficacy and their expectancies of success. An investigation of third-graders who were doing well in school but had low academic self-concepts (an "illusion of incompetence") suggests that these self-concepts resulted from their parents' low evaluation of their abilities (Phillips, 1987). In the University of Michigan study, students' expectancies of success were more closely related to their parents' expectancies than to their own past performance (Parsons, Adler, & Kaczala, 1982).

Parenting Styles and Discipline. One way in which parents communicate confidence in their children's abilities is to set high standards and demand mature behavior. When they do, they convey the message, "I think you are capable of doing this." In fact, achievement and task persistence are associated with the authoritative parenting style we first discussed as regards toddlers in Chapter 7 (Baumrind, 1973). As you recall, authoritative parents are affectionate, but they have clear standards and expect children to behave maturely. They enforce rules firmly, perhaps sometimes using punishment, but they explain the reasons for rules and involve their children in decision making about rules.

Both cross-sectional and longitudinal studies show that high achievement in school is associated with authoritative parenting. In one large sample, high school students with the highest grades had parents who were authoritative. The lowest grades occurred among students with authoritarian parents (Dornbusch, Ritter, Leiderman, Roberts, & Fraleigh, 1987).

Another investigation observed mothers' behavior with their preschool children and followed up the children in kindergarten and sixth grade. High achievers had mothers who had high expectations for mature behavior and achievement, communicated effectively with their children, and were affectionate (Hess, Holloway, Dickson, & Price, 1984). Mothers of high achievers controlled their children's behavior with explanations of reasons and consequences. For example, when the child refused to eat, the mother said, "If you don't eat, you won't be healthy and get bigger" (Hess & McDevitt, 1984, p. 2020). Mothers of low achievers more often used authoritarian methods such as threatening to spank the child if she did not eat.

Parents' Teaching Behavior. When parents play with young children, they can teach at the same time. Direct observation of parents working with their children on problem-solving tasks helps us understand what parents do and how different teaching methods affect children's skills and motivation.

Mothers of high achievers praise the child's efforts (e.g., "That's an interesting idea") rather than criticizing (e.g., "You know that doesn't look right") (E. G. J. Moore, 1986). They ask the child to think of different possible answers. They give suggestions that provide guidance about strategies for solving problems (e.g., "Why don't you try turning the pieces around to see if some of them fit that way") rather than giving the child the answer (e.g., "Try this piece here") (Hess & McDevitt, 1984). The parent's strategy suggestions provide guidance without solving the problem for the child. In earlier studies of Dutch and American families, parents were especially likely to tell girls the answers while encouraging boys to solve problems independently (J. H. Block, 1984; Hermans, Ter Laak, & Maes, 1972).

Alternative Interpretations. Having reviewed some factors in the home environment that are related to higher IQ and/or higher achievement, let us return to the caution with which we opened the section: Correlation does not imply causality. Alternative interpretations of the correlations are possible. In particular, behavior geneticists such as Sandra Scarr and Robert Plomin (see Chapter 2) have drawn our attention to the possibility that the correlations have a genetic basis. Genetic effects could operate in several ways. Brighter parents could produce brighter children, while incidentally behaving differently and buying different kinds of toys. Brighter children could also elicit from their parents more stimulating games, more effective teaching styles, and so on. Evidence for such possibilities has been provided by adoption studies (Braungart, Fulker, & Plomin, 1992). However, an important limitation of adoption studies is that adoption agencies screen prospective adoptive parents very carefully. Thus, adoptive parents differ less from each other than biological parents do. One is unlikely to find extremes of deprivation or neglect, or even of maladaptive parenting or homes low in stimulation, in studying adoptive families. This is currently a lively and controversial area of research.

Early Intervention

Given the evidence that environment can have an important impact on the development of intellectual skills, it seems natural to attempt to improve the environments of children whose normal lives seem to place them at risk of not developing as fully as they might be able to. In this section, we review some intervention efforts.

Head Start. Perhaps the best known of early intervention projects is Project Head Start. The first Head Start programs were established during the summer of 1965 for 500,000 children. One goal of Head Start was to provide economically deprived children with the skills they would need when they entered public school. Although the program was also intended to contribute to children's physical, social, emotional, and cognitive development, most of the evaluations of Head Start's success have focused on school-related skills, particularly IQ (Zigler & Valentine, 1979).

Extensive evaluations were conducted in the early years of Head Start. The results were scrutinized by educators and legislators to determine whether the benefits of the program were sufficient to merit continued support by the federal government. These evaluations consistently showed that children in Head Start programs made significant gains in IQ, vocabulary, and school readiness skills such as understanding letters, numbers, and concepts. The gains were especially large for children with initially low IQs (Horowitz & Paden, 1973; Zigler & Valentine, 1979).

A few years after Head Start began, evaluations of the program began to be less optimistic—they suggested that short-term gains tended to fade out during the early school years. In many cases, however, these evaluations were faulty because all Head Start programs were grouped together without attention to the quality of the program, the skills of the teachers, and the like. More important, there usually were no appropriate control groups with which Head Start children could be compared. Often they were compared to other children in their neighborhoods or in their schools. We now know that the children selected for Head Start were significantly more deprived than others in their neighborhoods. That is, they began with fewer skills and lower test scores. Their parents were less well educated; they were more often black; their homes were more crowded; they had larger families but fewer had fathers at home; and their mothers read to them less in comparison to children who attended other kinds of preschools or did not go to preschool (Lee, Brooks-Gunn, & Schnur, 1988). Follow-ups using appropriate control groups have shown that Head Start children perform better in school and have fewer academic problems than comparable children without Head Start experience, even several years after entering school (Zigler & Valentine, 1979).

Well-controlled studies of preschool intervention programs show clear long-

Head Start provides children with experiences they may not get in their homes. Here, children explore plants using a magnifying glass.

term effects. In 1976, eleven investigators in different parts of the country who had directed experimental early-education programs in the 1960s formed a consortium to follow up their graduates, who were then 10 to 17 years old. Many of the programs had been the models on which Project Head Start was based. The programs were selected because they all were initially evaluated with control groups of children selected to be comparable to the children participating in the educational program. (Most other Head Start evaluations were difficult to interpret because they lacked such control groups.) All of the children were from low-income families, and over 90 percent were black. Each investigator collected information on grade levels, special class placements, achievement test scores, and IQ.

In 1976 the experimental groups (those who had participated in the preschool programs) more often fulfilled the achievement requirements of their schools than did children in the matched control groups. They less often repeated a grade or were assigned to special classes for slow learners. They also performed better on reading and mathematics achievement tests during much of elementary school and on intelligence tests for three or four years after they left preschool.

In a few programs students were followed through the high school years. Those who had participated in preschool programs more often completed high school and were more likely to be employed after high school. Female students from the experimental groups were as likely as females in the control groups to become pregnant before completing high school, but they more often returned to school after having their babies. Of the experimental group, 25 percent were enrolled in some form of post–high school education, compared with 3 percent of the control group (Lazar & Darlington, 1982). These findings contradict earlier reports that Head Start programs produce no long-term effects on children's intellectual development. They suggest that carefully designed early-education programs can produce lasting benefits for economically disadvantaged children.

The long-term effects of intervention may reflect lasting changes in home environments as well as changes in the children themselves. Parents whose children participate in such programs appear to learn new ways to convey skills and encouragement to their children. For instance, in the follow-up study by Lazar and Darlington (1982), mothers of children who had participated in an early-intervention program had higher aspirations for their children and were more positive about their children's school performance than mothers in a control group. Programs teaching mothers how to provide cognitive stimulation for their children have effects also on the children's younger sisters and brothers, presumably because the mothers use the skills they learn in the programs (Klaus & Gray, 1968; Seitz & Apfel, 1994).

After a period of criticism and of neglect, Head Start programs are being revived in the 1990s through increased federal funding. However, more money will not solve the problem by itself. Continued efforts are needed to improve and monitor quality and to evaluate the most cost-effective components of Head Start (Zigler & Styfco, 1993).

Intervention in Infancy. Although poor children who have experienced preschool intervention have improved chances to achieve, their intellectual performance still tends to be below average. More intensive intervention, beginning in infancy, can lead to IQs in the average range for high-risk children. The Carolina Abecedarian Project, for example, provides educational day care for children beginning at 3 months and continuing throughout the preschool years. During infancy the major emphasis is on verbal stimulation. Teachers talk to infants and play games with them. After age 3 the curriculum includes math, music, science, and prereading skills.

Children receiving this intensive educational day care were compared to comparable children in a control group. All the children in both groups received nutritional supplements and health care. The results of intelligence tests administered during the first 4 years of life are illustrated in Figure 10.5. Although both groups performed in the average range during infancy, the scores of the control group declined. Apparently, early intervention can reverse the decline in intellectual functioning that characterizes children from intellectually and materially impoverished environments (Ramey et al., 1984).

Intervention with Television. The late 1960s also witnessed a major effort to use television in teaching disadvantaged children. A group of educators, psychologists, television writers, and producers combined their talents to create *Sesame Street* and *The Electric Company*. Production techniques from advertising and cartoons were used to package information about reading, cognitive skills, self-esteem, and prosocial behavior. Since that time other educational programs designed to teach science (*3-2-1 Contact*) and math (*Square One*) have been created. These programs reach a large number of children in a wide range of social groups. Evaluations have demonstrated that children learn letters, numbers, and other cognitive skills from these programs.

Sesame Street was evaluated in several parts of the country during its first two years. In the first of these evaluations, children who watched the program frequently were compared with children who did not. In the second, the researchers used a field experimental design in which children were randomly assigned to view or not to view the program at home. The experimental group was given cable connections or UHF sets (needed in order to receive the program), and their mothers

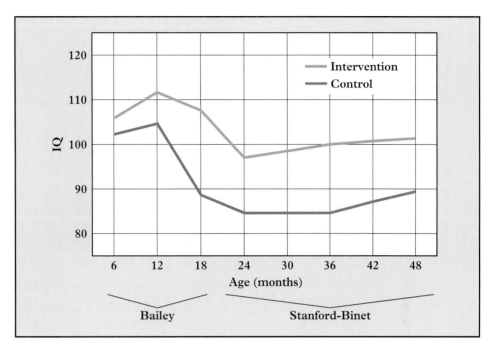

FIGURE 10.5 Performance on intelligence tests for children who received intervention from early infancy through age 4 as compared to a control group. The drop for both groups at 24 months is probably due to a change in the tests used. After "The Plasticity of Intellectual Development: Insights from Preventive Intervention," by C. T. Ramey, K. O. Yeates, and E. J. Short, 1984, *Child Development, 55*, pp. 1913–1925. Adapted with permission.

were asked to encourage the children to watch the program. The control group did not receive extra TV reception aids or encouragement to watch the program. Both groups of children took a test of cognitive skills before and about six months after the viewing season. The results of the first evaluation are shown in Figure 10.6, and these were supported by the results of the second evaluation. As you can see, the children who watched most often gained significantly more than those who watched infrequently. Children do learn from *Sesame Street* (Bogatz & Ball, 1971; Cook et al., 1975; Rice, Huston, Wright, & Truglio, 1988).

Interaction Between Constitution and Environment

In Figure 10.2 the child's constitution (genetic and biological attributes) and the environment are shown as the two major influences on intellectual development. Most psychologists agree that both are important. Each contributes to a child's intellectual skills and academic accomplishments.

We sometimes say rather glibly that there is an interaction between constitution and environment. By this we mean more than "both contribute." We mean that the effects of the child's constitution depend on the environment and the effects of the environment depend on the child's constitution. Consider the following example: In the Carolina Abecedarian Project discussed earlier, children were classified as high or low risk at birth on the basis of their Apgar scores. As you will recall from Chapter 3, the Apgar score is an index of the child's basic responsiveness at birth; a

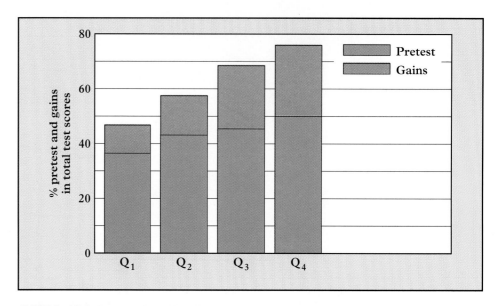

FIGURE 10.6 Pretest and gain scores on skills taught by *Sesame Street.* Children were divided by how much they watched the show (Q1 = once a week or less; Q2 = two or three times per week; Q3 = three or four times per week; Q4 = five or more times per week). After *The First Year of 'Sesame Street': An Evaluation*, by S. Ball and G. A. Bogatz, 1970, Princeton, NJ: Educational Testing Service. Adapted with permission.

low Apgar score suggests some constitutional vulnerability. The children were randomly assigned to educational day care or to a control group; that is, they experienced two types of environment.

The intelligence test scores of the children with two types of constitution in two environments are shown in Figure 10.7. Children who received educational day care performed well regardless of their Apgar scores. That is, in a stimulating environment constitutional vulnerability made little difference. In the control group, however, the high-Apgar-score children performed better than the low-Apgar-score children. In the control environment constitutional vulnerability did make a difference. One can also read Figure 10.7 to say that children with optimal constitutional attributes were less affected by poor environments than children with signs of constitutional vulnerability.

A model for understanding one type of interaction between organism and environment is shown in Figure 10.8 (Horowitz, 1987). In this model, organisms are placed on a continuum from constitutionally invulnerable to vulnerable and environments are classified on a continuum from facilitative to nonfacilitative. Children with relatively invulnerable constitutions are expected to develop normally even in environments that are not highly stimulating or facilitating. Children in facilitative environments are expected to develop normally even when they have vulnerable constitutional attributes. The model is not intended to suggest that any child is completely invulnerable; a sufficiently bad environment can affect even a constitutionally strong child. Instead, it is intended to show that the greatest risk occurs for children who are biologically vulnerable and experience nonfacilitative environments.

This general model can be applied to understanding particular aspects of children's intellectual development. For instance, children with low birth weight or neurological problems in infancy are vulnerable to developing poor cognitive and

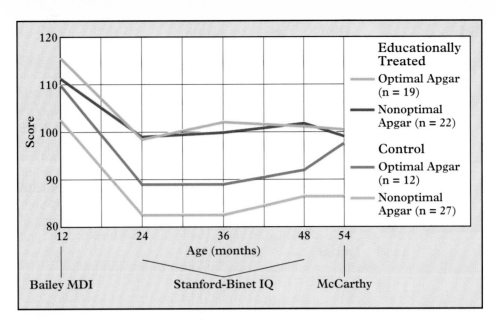

FIGURE 10.7 Mental test performance of high-risk children during the first 4.5 years as a function of educational history (environment) and Apgar status (biological status at birth). After "Biological Nonoptimality and Quality of Postnatal Environment as Codeterminants of Intellectual Development," by B. J. Breitmayer and C. T. Ramey, 1986, *Child Development, 57*, pp. 1151–1165. Adapted with permission.

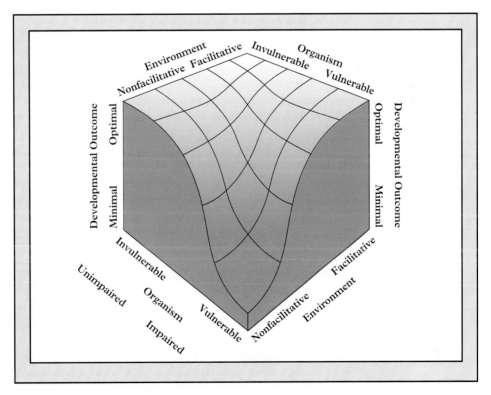

FIGURE 10.8 A model of developmental outcome illustrating the interaction of biology and environment. After *Exploring Development Theories: Toward a Structural/Behavioral Model of Development*, by F. D. Horowitz, 1987, Hillsdale, NJ: LEA. Adapted with permission.

academic skills (see Chapter 3). However, when these constitutionally vulnerable children grow up in supportive, stimulating environments, they do not usually develop achievement problems in school. One group of psychologists followed all the children born in one year on the Hawaiian island of Kauai from before birth to adulthood. In stable, supportive middle-class families, by age 10 the school performance of children with neurological problems in infancy was indistinguishable from that of children with no signs of vulnerability in infancy. By contrast, early biological problems were exacerbated for children who lived in poverty in unstable homes with poorly educated parents (E. E. Werner & Smith, 1982). In the United States, children living in poverty are at higher risk than children in affluent families for both biological vulnerability (e.g., low birth weight) and nonfacilitative environments.

⚙ SUMMARY

Intelligence is the capacity to learn and use the skills that are required for successful adaptation to the demands of one's culture and environment. Initially, it was defined as a general competence, but today most psychologists agree that patterns of abilities differ from one individual to another. Intellectual skills are also specific to the particular environmental contexts in which they are learned and practiced.

Although many experts agree that intelligence includes many abilities, they do not always agree on the nature of those abilities. One theory distinguishes between crystallized abilities, or the knowledge a person has accumulated, and fluid abilities, or the processes we use in solving problems and dealing with new information. Another approach, the structure of intellect model, classifies intellectual abilities along three dimensions: task content, operations, and the product or outcome of intellectual activity. Yet another approach is a triarchic theory with three major components: cognitive processes and knowledge, ability to deal with new experiences, and the adaptation to the environment.

The first intelligence tests were created in the early 1900s to predict which children would succeed or fail in school; they provided only a summary IQ score. The Wechsler Intelligence Scales, which are widely used today, include subtests for several dimensions of intelligence; the subtests can be scored separately but are also grouped into verbal and performance scales. Some other tests of intelligence contain separate tests for various abilities and do not yield an average or overall score. Recent tests are increasingly based on theories about cognitive processes.

Popular assumptions about the nature of IQ and the value of IQ tests are incorrect. IQ is not a pure index of innate potential and is not fixed for life. Intelligence tests measure both aptitude and achievement, but performance on an IQ test does not necessarily reflect competence. Many experts believe it is more useful to examine tests of specific skills than to rely solely on a single IQ score.

Achievement motivation is an overall tendency to evaluate one's performance against standards of excellence, to strive for successful performance, and to experience pleasure contingent on successful performance. It can be inferred from achievement behaviors such as persisting at a difficult task or setting a moderate level of aspiration. The factors that determine a child's level of motivation include attainment value (the value the child attaches to success), standards of performance, expectancies about one's abilities (an aspect of perceived self-efficacy), and attributions about the reasons for success or failure.

Perceptions of self-efficacy, attributions, and attainment values develop gradually throughout childhood. During the first few years of school, children's expectancies become more realistic; they increasingly use social comparison in evaluating their own performance; they set higher levels of aspiration for themselves; and they express more anxiety about failure. Many children develop a pattern of anxiety over testing that interferes with their performance.

Among American children there are consistent sex differences in intellectual performance and school achievement. On the average, males and females have different patterns of performance in different intellectual domains. These patterns are consistent with cultural stereotypes about appropriate behaviors for men and women. Intellectual achievement also differs among different cultural groups, social classes, and ethnic groups. The claim that differences in IQ between blacks and whites are a result of genetic factors is not supported by the available evidence.

Although social experience makes a major contribution to ethnic and class differences in IQ, this does not mean that minority and lower-class children have deficient intelligence. It is more accurate to say that nonwhite and lower-class children often learn different skills than white middle-class children. One implication of this "difference" model is that intelligence tests are biased against lower-class and minority children. It is probably true that general differences in life experience make IQ tests difficult for minority children: among other factors, such children are less familiar with standard English, they have less opportunity to learn test-taking skills, and they are especially prone to fear of failure and low concepts of their own ability.

Various aspects of the home environment contribute to individual differences in intelligence and achievement. Among these are features of the physical and social environment, such as whether parents are affectionate and verbally responsive and the level of noise and disorganization in the home. A positive relationship between parent and child can affect achievement because it forms a basis for the child to accept the parent's expectations and demands. Parents' beliefs, expectations, and values affect the achievement efforts of their children, as do parenting styles, discipline, and parents' teaching behavior. These differences in home environment and parental behavior are probably responsible for some of the differences in IQ among ethnic and social-class groups.

Intervention programs designed to enhance the intellectual achievement of preschool and elementary schoolchildren were established in the 1960s and are collectively known as Head Start. Well-controlled studies of such programs show that they have positive long-term effects, probably reflecting changes in the child's environment as well as in children themselves. More extensive intervention, beginning in infancy, can lead to IQs in the average range for high-risk children.

The 1960s also witnessed a major effort to use television in teaching disadvantaged children through such programs as *Sesame Street* and *The Electric Company*. Such programs have been shown to have a positive effect on children's academic skills.

Psychologists often say that there is an interaction between constitution and environment. By this they mean that the effects of the child's constitution depend on the environment and vice versa. In a stimulating environment, constitutional vulnerability makes a relatively small difference; conversely, children with optimal constitutional attributes are less affected by poor environments than are more vulnerable children. This general model can be applied to understanding particular aspects of children's intellectual development.

REVIEW QUESTIONS

1. What is intelligence?

2. Briefly describe three theories about the dimensions of intelligence.

3. When were the first intelligence tests created? How have intelligence tests evolved since that time?

4. What are some limitations on measures of IQ?

5. What is meant by achievement motivation? What factors determine a child's level of motivation in a particular task area?

6. Briefly describe developmental patterns in achievement motivation.

7. How do the patterns of intellectual performance differ for males and females?

8. Contrast the "deficit" and "difference" models of ethnic and class differences in IQ.

9. What elements of the home environment may be important for promoting intelligence and achievement?

10. Discuss the effects of intervention programs designed to enhance the intellectual achievement of preschool and elementary schoolchildren.

CRITICAL THINKING ABOUT THE CHAPTER

1. What good and what bad effects has intelligence testing had on society? On balance, do you think testing has a place in society? If you think it does, explain just how you think it should be used.

2. Imagine you have been asked to consult with an elementary school about how to increase their students' achievement. What aspects of their teaching and school environment would you want to find out about? What would you want to tell them about current understanding of young children's achievement motivation?

KEY TERMS

achievement
achievement motivation
aptitude
attributions
autonomous standards
crystallized abilities

fluid abilities
intelligence
learned helplessness
perceived self-efficacy
social-comparison standards

SUGGESTED READINGS

Gould, S. J. (1981). *The mismeasure of man.* New York: Norton. A critical analysis that views the mental testing movement in a broad societal context.

Howe, M. J. A. (Ed.). (1983). *Learning from television: Psychological and educational research.* New York: Academic Press. Contains chapters by several authors describing how children and adults learn from television programs designed for education.

Scarr, S. (1981). *Race, social class, and individual differences in IQ.* Hillsdale, NJ: Erlbaum. A collection of essays by one of the most prominent investigators of genetic and environmental contributions to intelligence.

Spence, J. T. (Ed.). (1983). *Achievement and achievement motives: Psychological and sociological approaches.* San Francisco: W. H. Freeman. Contains chapters by several authors who have investigated achievement motivation. Most of the important views on this topic are represented.

Werner, E. E., & Smith, R. S. (1982). *Vulnerable, but invincible: A longitudinal study of resilient children and youth.* New York: McGraw-Hill. A report on a longitudinal study of children on the Hawaiian island of Kauai. All of the children were followed from birth to adulthood.

DEVELOPMENT OF SOCIAL BEHAVIOR IN CHILDHOOD

Josefina (who is 4 years old) and Rosa (who is 8) are playing family. Josefina, wearing an old pair of high heels and lipstick, is the mother and Rosa is the father. Their 2-year-old brother, Ramon, is playing too. They said he could, if he dressed up as a girl and was the daughter. He agreed. Anything to be included with the big kids! He's actually quite proud of how he looks in a party dress and a hairbow.

After 20 minutes of happy play, however, Rosa and Josefina start arguing. Rosa wants to trade places and be the mother. Josefina refuses, saying, "I'm a girl, so I CAN'T be the Daddy!" Rosa argues that SHE is a girl, and she was the father for a good long time. She says, "It doesn't matter if you play a man. You're still who you are when the game's over." But Josefina won't listen and gets angrier by the second. "I'm a girl and that's what I am!" she shouts. Finally, she kicks off her high heels so hard they hit the wall, and stomps off to her room in a flood of tears.

One of the central tasks of growing up is developing a sense of self, a sense of both who one is and how one fits into society. Development of a sense of self, as an individual and as a member of salient social categories, is the basis for children's becoming increasingly responsible members of their culture. In the next three chapters, we examine social development, describing changes as they occur at the individual level (Chapter 11) and relating these changes to family processes (Chapter 12) and to the wider social context of development (Chapter 13).

This chapter presents current understanding of how social behavior develops between toddlerhood and adolescence. Two broad topics are addressed. First, we examine sense of self. In the years between toddlerhood and adolescence, children build a progressively more complete sense of who they are. They define their self-concept, establish levels of self-esteem, and achieve certain levels and patterns of self-control. In addition, because gender and ethnicity are central social categories in most cultures, children must learn to understand these categories and incorporate them into self-definition. Second, we examine important aspects of social interaction. A child's developing sense of self is closely linked to the development of abilities to interact with others and to be a responsible member of social groups. Being able to act in prosocial ways (for instance, to help others who need help) and to control aggression are two aspects of taking one's place in society that we examine in this chapter.

❂ DEVELOPING A SENSE OF SELF

William James, one of the earliest psychologists to write on the self, divided the self into two components, the "me" and the "I." The "me" is "the sum total of all a person can call his" (James, 1892/1961, p. 44), including abilities, social and personality characteristics, and material possessions. The "I" is the "self as knower." This aspect of the self "continually organizes and interprets experience, people, objects, and events in a purely subjective manner" (Damon & Hart, 1982, p. 844). In other words, the "I" is reflective, aware of its own nature. Research in self-concept encompasses both the "I" and the "me" aspects of the self.

Not all cultures give as much primacy to the sense of self as Western cultures do. To us, people are autonomous individuals whose identity and privacy are important. We give children their own rooms and accord them some rights to private thoughts and activities. Our self-descriptions emphasize such traits as kindness, assertiveness, or athletic talent. In many cultures, however, people are defined in relation to their social and group contexts—as part of a larger whole. People in those cultures emphasize their social roles (e.g., mother, community builder) and social contexts (e.g., member of the Miranda family) (Shweder & Bourne, 1984).

Self-Concept

As explained in Chapter 7, the beginnings of self-awareness appear during the second year of life. At around 18 months of age children recognize their own face and point to pictures of themselves when someone says their name (Damon & Hart, 1982). During the childhood years, however, this rudimentary sense of self

TABLE 11.1 Self-Concept at Different Ages

Responses to the question "What would you have to change about yourself for you to become your best friend?"
Numbers are percent of children who gave each category of response.

	Grade Level		
Type of characteristic described	*First*	*Third*	*Sixth*
External (physical attributes, name, possessions, age)	85	36	8
Behavioral (regular behavior or traits)	5	56	76
Internal (thoughts, feelings, knowledge)	10	8	16

Source: After "Development of Attributes of Personal Identity," by D. M. Mohr, 1978, *Developmental Psychology, 14*, pp. 427–428. Copyright The American Psychological Association. Adapted with permission.

grows into an elaborated and relatively stable network of self-perceptions and feelings.

Self-concepts have often been measured by asking people to describe themselves or to tell how they are different from others. For example, a child might be asked to tell how he would describe himself in a diary that no one else would see, or how he would be different if he were his best friend. Such measures of self-concept are intended to identify the kind of attributes that the person considers most important.

Using these techniques, we see regular developmental changes in the categories children use when asked to describe themselves. Until about age 7 children tend to define themselves in physical terms. They name concrete, observable features of themselves, such as hair color, height, or favorite activities ("I like to play ball"). They are less likely to name comparative qualities such as reading ability or bravery, or to discuss inner psychological experiences (Selman, 1980). During middle childhood, descriptions of self shift gradually to more abstract statements of facts ("I don't get into fights") and psychological traits (Damon & Hart, 1982; Harter, 1983; Selman, 1980). Children begin to feel distinct from others because of unique thoughts and feelings (see Table 11.1).

These changes can be seen in our opening story. At 4, Josefina had difficulty with playing a role that contradicted the obvious fact that she was a girl, while at 8, Rosa had less difficulty with this idea, perhaps because she had a dawning idea of "who she was" that was based on more abstract psychological characteristics.

The information gained in studies of children's verbal reports does not, however, do complete justice to the capabilities of young children. Recent evidence suggests that preschool children have begun to develop aspects of a self-concept, although they have difficulty expressing it in spontaneous speech. Eder (1990) showed that children as young as 3 years could give meaningful descriptions of themselves when given a simple choice between statements and asked to pick the option that best described them. For instance, when children were asked to choose between the statements "It's not fun to scare people" and "It's fun to scare people," they did so in consistent ways that seemed to capture what they were like. These findings suggest that what develops with age is the availability of psychological categories and their use in self-description, rather than the existence of the categories themselves.

Self-Esteem

As children form self-concepts, they implicitly assign positive or negative values to their own attributes. Collectively, these self-evaluations constitute their **self-esteem**. Self-esteem differs from self-concept because it involves evaluation. The self-concept can be a set of ideas about oneself that is descriptive but not judgmental. The fact that one has dark hair and a soft voice can be part of one's self-concept, but those qualities are not judged as good or bad; they are neutral. Self-esteem, on the other hand, refers to one's evaluations of one's own qualities. Consider an 8-year-old boy who views himself as someone who fights a lot. If he values his ability to fight and stand up for himself, that quality may add to his self-esteem. If he is unhappy about his tendency to get into fights, this behavior might detract from his self-esteem.

Measuring self-esteem is difficult. When children under 7 are asked questions about how much they like themselves or how they evaluate their abilities, they almost always say they are satisfied and happy with themselves, accompanying their comments with a slightly mystified look. By age 9 or 10, children more often report low self-evaluations, and they probably have a more clearly formulated sense of their worth and competence in different areas (Harter, 1983). Even older children, however, may not want to admit that they have undesirable qualities or may be unaware that certain qualities are considered undesirable by others.

One measure designed to reduce response bias is the Self Perception Profile for Children. For each question, descriptions of two types of children are presented and the child is asked which group he or she belongs to. Typical descriptions are "Some kids feel there are a lot of things about themselves that they would change if they could" versus "Other kids would like to stay pretty much the same" (Harter, 1985). This scale succeeds in measuring children's self-perceptions more accurately than earlier measures, partly because it includes questions about different types of behavior. Although individuals seem to have a general sense of self-worth, self-esteem varies for different domains of behavior (Marsh, 1985).

The fact that self-evaluations vary for different content domains is an important point for parents and teachers to remember. Adults may be able to help children by emphasizing areas in which the children are competent and building self-esteem in those areas. On the other hand, they should not expect positive self-evaluations in one domain to carry over directly into another.

Self-Control

One of the prerequisites for establishing and maintaining satisfactory social relationships is the ability to regulate and control one's own behavior in ways that take other people's needs and feelings into account and, at the same time, conform to the standards of one's society or culture. As children grow older, they become more able to do this; they gradually become more skilled in role taking and adopt their culture's rules and restrictions.

Many hypotheses about self-control originated in psychoanalytic theory. Freud suggested that the personality has three components: the id, which represents unconscious drives and impulses; the superego, which incorporates conscience or sense of right and wrong; and the ego, which is responsible for balancing or modulating the conflicting demands of one's own needs and impulses, one's

Children's self-evaluations are different in different domains. For instance, feeling good (or bad) about one's skill in basketball may not relate to self-esteem in the classroom or satisfaction with one's appearance.

conscience, and reality. Ego processes are the rational components of the personality that help people devise means of satisfying some of their basic needs (or obtaining pleasure) without incurring punishment—including social disapproval—or violating their own moral standards. This often entails suppressing certain impulses, delaying gratification, or finding socially acceptable ways of expressing impulses.

There are other approaches to self-control as well. Social-learning theorists see self-control, resistance to distraction, and delay of gratification as outcomes of reinforcements and observational learning (modeling and imitation). If a child is rewarded (given reinforcements) for delaying gratification or controlling impulses, these responses are strengthened and therefore are more likely to occur on future occasions. In addition, if children are exposed to models who display these responses, they are likely to emulate the models' behavior.

Developing Self-Control. One way to measure self-control is in terms of the child's ability or willingness to postpone immediate gratification of a desire in order to obtain something more valuable later on. In many developmental studies of self-control, children are given a choice between two alternatives, one of which is immediately available but less desirable while the other is more attractive but available only after a delay. For example, in one laboratory study children were left alone for 15 minutes in a room with a relatively unattractive pretzel and a highly attractive marshmallow. They were told that they could eat only one of them; they could eat the pretzel at any time or, if they were willing to wait 15 minutes, they could have the marshmallow. Presented with this choice, older children were more likely than younger ones to delay gratification, that is, to choose the more valuable alternative, for which they would have to wait, over the less valuable, but immediately available, alternative (Mischel & Metzner, 1962). Children who are more able to delay gratification have been found to be more responsible and mature than other children. They are also higher in achievement motivation, more intelligent, better students, and more likely to follow rules, even when they are working alone without supervision (Mischel, 1966).

Many factors influence the ability to delay gratification. Some involve the situation. When the delay is very long or the delayed reward is not much more valuable than the alternative, children are more likely to choose the immediately available reward (Mischel, 1966, 1974; Schwarz, Schrager, & Lyons, 1983). Also, if rewards are visible rather than covered, children are less likely to delay gratification (Mischel & Ebbesen, 1970).

Training techniques may enhance children's cognitive controls and, hence, their ability to delay gratification. We will review five such techniques. First, children can be taught to distract their attention from the desirable qualities of the delayed incentive—essentially, learn not to think about those qualities. In one study, one group of children were instructed to think about the taste and feeling of the relatively undesirable pretzel and the desirable marshmallow in front of them, whereas another group were told to imagine that the marshmallows were fluffy white clouds and the pretzels were logs for a cabin. The children in the second group, distracted from thinking about the positive qualities of the delayed reward, waited almost twice as long as those who were thinking about the taste of the candy (Mischel & Patterson, 1978).

A second technique to regulate self-control is self-instruction, which can be used even by very young children. Patterson (1982) offered preschool children an attractive reward for completing a long, repetitive task (copying letters of the alphabet) but warned them that a talking "clown box" might try to distract them while they worked. Some of the children were instructed to repeat to themselves short sentences or "plans," such as "I'm not going to look at Mr. Clown," when this occurred. These children were less distracted and did more work than children in control groups who were not given these instructions.

A third technique, usable by older children, is to learn to monitor themselves so as to resist distraction (Pressley, 1979). For example, sixth-graders in an individualized math curriculum were trained to record instances of "off-task behavior" (e.g., talking to others, fooling around) and to use them as signals to return to work. These children spent more time concentrating on their work and performed better on mathematics tests than children in control groups who did not receive this training (Sagotsky, Patterson, & Lepper, 1978).

Positive labeling is a fourth strategy that may increase the ability to delay gratification. Before playing a "candy game," girls in the first and second grades chatted briefly with the experimenter. During the chat, the experimenter told half of the participants, "I hear you are very patient because you can wait for nice things when you can't get them right away" (positive label); the other half were told, "I hear that you have some very nice friends here at school" (irrelevant label). In the game, a machine dispensed one M&M every 60 seconds, and all the accumulated candies belonged to the child. However, as soon as she took any of them the machine stopped and the game was over. The results showed that the experimenter had created a self-fulfilling prophesy: The children who had been labeled "patient" showed significantly greater ability to delay gratification, waiting about twice as long as the others (Toner, Moore, & Emmons, 1980).

Self-control, patience, and the ability to delay gratification are important in children's acquisition of many culturally valued skills.

Finally, observation of a model who defers gratification can also alter a child's level of self-control (Bandura & Mischel, 1965). Thus, parents and other agents of socialization may successfully promote a tendency to delay immediate gratification in order to achieve more desirable long-range objectives by training children in techniques of cognitive control such as self-monitoring, or by serving as models of self-control.

Over- and Undercontrol. Although self-control is a key component of social adjustment, extremes of control may be maladaptive. J. H. Block and Block (1980) studied what they called **ego control** and found that 3-year-old children classified as *overcontrollers* showed strong tendencies toward conformity, inhibition, undue delay of gratification, and reluctance to explore new situations, as well as positive characteristics such as planfulness and perseverance. Overcontrolled children also showed minimal emotional expression, had narrow, unchanging interests, and manifested their needs indirectly rather than directly. In sharp contrast, the *undercontrollers* were emotionally expressive and spontaneous, nonconforming, and exploratory, but also distractible and unable to delay gratification of desires. Clearly, neither extreme was desirable.

A second dimension important in thinking about self-control involves the fact that it is often adaptive to shift from greater to less control (or vice versa) as circumstances change. For instance, expected behavior at school and on the playground varies widely. For this reason, J. H. Block and Block (1980) also assessed what they called **ego resilience**, an index of flexibility or adaptability. Highly resilient children can exercise strong control when it is called for; they can also "let go," acting spontaneously and expressively in other situations. High ego resilience seems to be helpful to children's functioning. Early ego resilience was associated with empathy, social responsiveness, and caring.

Ego control and ego resilience remain relatively stable through early childhood. At age 7, four years after the initial classification in the Block and Block study, undercontrollers were more energetic, curious, restless, and expressive of impulses than more controlled children were. In their relationships with peers they exhibited more teasing, manipulativeness, and aggression.

Children who were overcontrollers at age 3 were shy and inhibited at age 7. Other effects of high ego control were different, depending on the children's level of ego resilience. The combination of high ego control and high ego resilience at age 3 was predictive of excellent adjustment at age 7—specifically, a high degree of socialization and a relative absence of anxiety. The combination of high ego control and low ego resilience at age 3 predicted poor adjustment at age 7; these children suffered from anxiety and feelings of inadequacy, and they viewed the world as threatening and unpredictable (J. H. Block & Block, 1980).

The Gendered Self

A child's sense of self is intimately tied to the social categories or groups to which the child is assigned by his or her culture. One of the most basic social categories in almost every society is gender. Often the first question asked about a baby is "Is it a boy or a girl?" Our culture and most others define a host of interests, personality attributes, and behaviors as "feminine" or "masculine." Some of these definitions may have their roots in biological differences, while many others are likely the products of particular cultural histories.

Babies are often dressed and adorned so that there is no question about their sex, showing how fundamental a social category sex is.

TABLE 11.2 A Taxonomy of Sex Typing

Content Area	Construct			
	Identity (how you perceive yourself)	*Concepts* (knowledge about gender and social stereotypes)	*Preference* (what you would like)	*Adoption* (what you do; how other people see you)
Biological gender	Gender identity Sex role identity	Gender constancy	Wish to be male or female	Clothing, hair, surgical sex change
Activities and interests	Perception of your own interests	Concepts about sex typing of toys, activities, interests	Preferred toys, games, interests	Spending time with toys, games, interests
Personality attributes, social behavior	Perception of your own personality	Concepts about sex typing of aggression, kindness, and the like	What attributes you value, would like to have	Observed aggression, kindness, and the like
Gender-based social relationships	Perception of your patterns of friendship, sexual orientation	Concepts about norms for same-sex friends, opposite-sex lovers, and the like	Preference for male or female friends, lovers, models to emulate	Selecting others for social or sexual contact on the basis of gender (e.g., same-sex peer choices)

Psychologists have used the term **sex typing** to describe the ways in which biological gender and its cultural associations are incorporated into the child's self-perceptions and behavior. Sex typing is not, however, a single process. Table 11.2 illustrates one way of describing its components. Across the top of the table are four features of sex typing. The first feature is identity or self-perception. **Gender identity** is acceptance of one's basic biological nature as female or male—the fundamental sense of being a girl or a boy. **Sex role identity** is a sense of being feminine or masculine—that is, a feeling that one's interests, personality, and behavior conform to one's own definitions of femininity or masculinity. The second feature is concepts or knowledge about what society defines as masculine or feminine. We all know many of the social stereotypes and expectations for males and females, whether or not we agree with them or adopt them for ourselves. The third feature is sex role preferences, what a person values or would like to be. The fourth feature, sex role adoption, involves acting in ways that are culturally defined as feminine or masculine. Each of these features is somewhat independent. For example, sex role identity describes children's personal and private definition of self; sex role adoption refers to their overt behavior.

The vertical divisions in Table 11.2 show different content areas that are part of sex typing. Femininity or masculinity is defined not only by biological gender but also by activities and interests (e.g., playing with dolls or guns), personality characteristics (e.g., being sensitive or independent), and gender-based social relationships (e.g., playing mostly with girls or with boys).

Masculine and feminine qualities are not mutually exclusive. A woman may enjoy cooking and may also be interested in repairing cars; she may have a firm sense of her identity as a female even though she has interests that are culturally defined as both feminine and masculine. A man may be both independent and kind; he may regard both of these qualities as consistent with his masculine identity even though others define kindness as a feminine trait. A man may enjoy cooking and knitting while also preferring heterosexual relationships. In each case the person's basic gender identity as female or male remains solid. It is a rare person who conforms to all of his or her society's sex role expectations.

A person who combines feminine psychological qualities with masculine attributes is sometimes described as psychologically **androgynous** (Bem, 1974; Spence & Helmreich, 1978). Since the concept of androgyny was introduced in the 1970s, many people have argued that it represents a healthier pattern than traditional sex typing because a person with the capacity to be kind, gentle, and nurturant as well as assertive and independent could adapt to many situations. Thus, a girl in a science class may find verbal assertiveness more adaptive than traditional feminine kindness and gentleness. A boy who can be gentle and kind may be better able to establish a close relationship than one who is dominant and unemotional.

Development of Sex Typing. Children develop at least a rudimentary gender identity sometime between 18 months and 3 years of age. They learn to label themselves and others correctly as females or males. Nevertheless, during the preschool years understanding of gender is limited. One 3-year-old boy upset his parents by announcing that he was going to be a mommy when he grew up. Another child became alarmed when she saw her mother dressed in a man's business suit for a Halloween party. Ramon, in our opening vignette, was perfectly willing to wear a dress and hairbow to win the approval of his big sisters. Children of this age have an imperfect understanding of biological gender; they lack what cognitive theorists call **gender constancy** (see Table 11.2).

Gender constancy refers to a child's understanding that gender does not change. Gender constancy is acquired in three steps. First, children acquire gender identity. Next, they learn (around age 4) that gender does not change over time. By age 5 or 6, most children also understand that gender remains the same regardless of changes in appearance, clothing, or activities. Before that age, children may say that a boy who wears a dress or plays with a doll is a girl.

Bem (1989) has argued that confusion on gender identity and constancy questions reflects children's difficulties in knowing what the valid cues are for gender classifications when adults are reluctant to talk about them. That is, adults may not discuss genital or biological sex with children and may actually use cues such as dress or hairstyle to define sex for their children, leading to ambiguity. This reasoning predicts that difficulty with gender constancy would be most common for children who do not know that genitals are the critical basis for deciding whether a person is male or female. In fact, Bem found that children who are aware of genital differences are more likely to understand that gender does not change with new clothing or haircuts.

By the time American children reach their third birthday, they not only classify people correctly as female or male but also have a remarkable amount of information about social expectations for the two sexes (Weinraub, Clemens, et al., 1984). They know that girls are supposed to play with dolls and dress up like women, while boys are supposed to play with trucks and pretend to be firemen. By the age of 4 or 5 they know most of the stereotypes for adult occupations. They expect women to be teachers and nurses and men to have a variety of occupations such as pilot and police officer. A young child may adamantly assert that "women can't be doctors" or "men don't change diapers."

Preschool children often assume that sex stereotypes are absolute prescriptions for correct behavior, and they sometimes enforce them more rigidly than older people do. By around age 5, children begin to learn stereotypes about personality and social behavior. Boys are believed to be big, loud, aggressive, independent, and competent; girls are thought to be small, quiet, nurturant, obedient, and emotional. Stereotypes for personality traits are probably learned later than those for play activities and interests because personality attributes are abstractions. In addition, sex differences in related behaviors are less pronounced and therefore are less likely to be observed by children than differences in dress, play activities, and jobs.

In middle childhood, children continue to refine their understanding of social expectations for females and males. At the same time, their thinking sometimes (but not always) becomes less rigid (Katz & Ksansnak, 1994; Powlishta, Serbin, Doyle, & White, 1994; Serbin, Powlishta, & Gulko, 1993). They seem more ready than younger children to recognize that people can combine behaviors that are stereotyped as masculine and feminine, and they are better able to accept departures from sex role prescriptions. Some of this developmental change seems to be linked to cognitive advances, in particular, to using more than one basis for classifying people and objects (Bigler & Liben, 1992).

Like their thinking and judgments, children's behavior is sex typed very early. By age 2, children in preschool select toys and activities that fit sex stereotypes (O'Brien & Huston, 1985); see Figure 11.1. The same pattern is seen when 2-year-old children are observed at home. Girls more often play with soft toys and dolls, ask for help, and dress up in adult clothes. Boys more often play with blocks and manipulate objects or toys (Fagot, 1974).

Children also begin to select same-sex playmates during the preschool years. If you observe a typical preschool, you are likely to see groups of girls, often playing in the housekeeping area, and groups of boys, often playing with blocks or trucks. In elementary school, sex segregation becomes extreme. In a one-room day camp attended by 8- to 10-year-old children, boys interacted with other boys almost three times as much as they socialized with girls; girls interacted primarily with other girls (A. C. Huston, Carpenter, Atwater, & Johnson, 1986).

Although there are early and clear sex differences in games, activities, and peer selection, sex typing in personality and social behavior is less pronounced, even in middle childhood. Boys are, on the average, more aggressive than girls, as we discuss shortly, but there are no reliable differences between the sexes in dependency, altruism, independence, or most other personal qualities (A. C. Huston, 1983; Maccoby & Jacklin, 1974; Shibley-Hyde & Linn, 1986).

How Does Sex Typing Come About? Several explanations of sex typing have been suggested. Two older theories, based on theories of cognitive development and of social learning, are often seen as opposed to each other. More recently, theorists have emphasized a different cognitive approach to understanding of gender as a social category, which can be more easily integrated with concepts from social learning theory. We examine each of these three approaches in turn.

Lawrence Kohlberg (1966) proposed a cognitive-developmental theory of sex typing, suggesting that sex typing results from cognitive-developmental changes. This view departed radically from the accepted wisdom of the time. Kohlberg suggested that children achieve gender identity (i.e., classify themselves as girls or boys) as part of the general tendency to think in categories. Once gender identity is established, children actively look for information about the activities, values, and behaviors that distinguish boys from girls. They do not need to be given direct

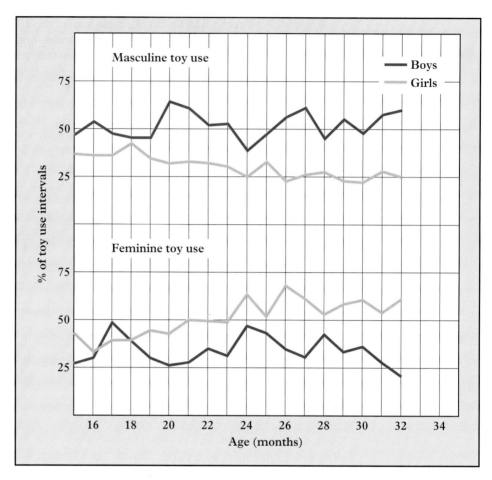

FIGURE 11.1 Percentage of playtime that toddler boys and girls spent with stereotypically masculine and feminine toys. After "Development of Sex-Typed Play Behavior in Toddlers," by M. O'Brien and A. C. Huston, 1985, *Developmental Psychology, 21*, pp. 866–871. Copyright 1985 by the American Psychological Association. Adapted with permission.

instruction or encouragement by adults; they acquire information about sex typing spontaneously, by constructing knowledge about the roles assigned to each gender in their surroundings. It is then a natural step for children to value the patterns associated with their own gender. In effect, a boy says, "I am a boy. Therefore, I want to do 'boy' things." Kohlberg proposed that this process is completed when children achieve gender constancy—an accomplishment that accompanies concrete-operational thought.

Some parts of this theory are well supported by evidence, but others are not. The idea that children are active in seeking information about salient categories in their social world fits well with current theoretical views of development (see Chapter 1). However, evidence does not support the prediction that gender constancy is important for sex typing; children who acquire gender constancy early are no more likely to be sex typed than those who acquire it later. Moreover, not all children value the role prescribed for their gender, even though they understand it.

Mischel (1970) argued for a social learning theory approach to sex typing in which sex-typed behavior is learned through the same processes that operate for other forms of behavior: instrumental conditioning and observation. In this view, boys and girls are reinforced and punished for different behaviors from early childhood on, and children learn to expect certain roles for females and males by observing others.

Careful observational studies in homes and preschools support the assertion that parents, teachers, and peers reinforce different kinds of behavior in girls and boys. For instance, parents of children between 20 and 24 months of age more often reacted favorably when the children engaged in activities that were "sex appropriate" than when they performed behaviors that were deemed appropriate for the other sex. They responded positively when girls played with dolls, asked for help, followed an adult around, and helped with an adult task. They reacted positively when boys played with blocks, manipulated objects, and were physically active (see Table 11.3). When interviewed, many of these parents said that they treated children of both sexes similarly. There was little correlation between their observed behavior and the attitudes they expressed in the interviews.

Children also have many opportunities to observe sex-typed behavior in their daily lives. Parents are not the only models, but they are extremely important because of children's strong attachments to them. Children are especially likely to imitate par-

TABLE 11.3 Parents' Reactions to Behavior of Toddler Boys and Girls

The proportions in this table represent the percentage of occasions on which parents responded positively (by praising, guiding, comforting, explaining, or joining the child's activity) or negatively (by criticizing, restricting, punishing, or stopping play) when their children engaged in each of the behaviors listed. The information was obtained by observing parents and their 20- to 24-month-old children at home. The asterisks indicate that the difference between treatment of boys and girls was statistically significant.

| | **Parent Reaction** | | | |
| | Positive | | Negative | |
Child Behavior	*To boys*	*To girls*	*To boys*	*To girls*
Masculine Behavior				
Block play	.36	.00*	.00	.00
Manipulates objects	.46	.46	.02	.26*
Transportation-toy play	.61	.57	.00	.02
Rough-and-tumble play	.91	.84	.03	.02
Aggression: hit, push	.23	.18	.50	.53
Running and jumping	.39	.32	.00	.07
Climbing	.39	.43	.12	.24*
Riding trikes	.60	.90	.04	.06
Feminine Behavior				
Play with dolls	.39	.63*	.14	.04*
Dance	.00	.50	.00	.00
Ask for help	.72	.87*	.13	.06*
Play dress up	.50	.71	.50	.00
Help adult with task	.74	.94*	.17	.06*
Follow parent around	.39	.79*	.07	.07

Source: From "The Influence of Sex of Child on Parental Reactions to Toddler Children," by B. I. Fagot, 1978, *Child Development,* 49, pp. 459–465. Copyright © 1978 by The Society for Child Development. Reprinted by permission.

ents who are warm and powerful (i.e., are dominant and decisive and exercise control over the child's life). Parental example does influence children's sex typing. For instance, children of employed mothers have less traditional sex role concepts than children whose mothers work at home full-time; daughters of employed mothers also have higher educational and career aspirations than daughters of nonemployed mothers (A. C. Huston, 1983). However, parents' attitudes about their roles are also important. For instance, having a father who participated in household work did not change children's sex stereotypes unless their mothers adopted nontraditional attitudes about the male role. If the mother thinks it is consistent with masculinity for the father to cook and change diapers, the child's sex role schemata incorporate the father's nontraditional behavior (Baruch & Barnett, 1986).

Children also learn the social expectations of their culture by observing other adults, peers, teachers, and the mass media. Television may be an especially potent source because children spend many hours each week watching TV and because the portrayal of women and men on television is often highly stereotyped. Television women cook, clean, care for children, and try to look beautiful (often while managing a demanding job); television men are aggressive, adventurous, and successful (Calvert & Huston, 1987).

Recent theorists have proposed a *schema theory* approach to sex typing, in which children's cognitions about gender—their gender schemata—explain sex typing (Liben & Signorella, 1987; C. L. Martin & Halverson, 1981). According to this theory, once children have acquired gender role schemata, they interpret events in their world according to those schemata. When events violate sex stereotypes, the child may fail to notice or remember. For example, children saw a large number of pictures showing men and women in sex-stereotyped roles (e.g., a female nurse, a male judge) and counter-stereotyped roles (e.g., a female dentist, a male typist). A few minutes later they were asked to select the pictures they had seen from a larger set containing similar pictures. The children recognized more pictures that were consistent with sex stereotypes than pictures that were inconsistent (Cann & Newbern, 1984).

Memory can be distorted by sex stereotypes. In one study, groups of 6-year-olds saw one of four short films about a doctor and a nurse. The only difference between the films was the gender of the two actors (two males; two females; male doctor, female nurse; female doctor, male nurse). Children who saw the traditional version (male doctor, female nurse) remembered the actors and their roles correctly. Those who saw female doctors or male nurses often remembered incorrectly. Some thought the male nurse was a doctor (Cordua, McGraw, & Drabman, 1979).

Schema theory explains individual differences in sex typing by proposing that gender may be more salient or important to some children than to others (Bem, 1981). Although all members of a society are well aware of the social expectations for males and females, gender may be a particularly salient category for some people. They interpret the world through gender-based glasses. Others may judge people and situations according to different categories. Consider Sue, who goes to a picnic in a park where a lot of people are playing Frisbee. She is trying to decide whether to join the game. If gender schemata are salient to her, she might consider whether it is feminine to play Frisbee. She will probably notice whether other girls are playing, or think about whether she will be attractive to boys if she plays. Tammy, for whom gender schemata are not very salient, might consider whether she has enjoyed playing Frisbee in the past, whether she is so uncoordinated that she will look foolish if she plays, or whether she sees another activity that she prefers. She is basing her decision on criteria unrelated to gender. Both girls might make the same decision, but for different reasons.

Children for whom gender is especially salient show strong sex-typed preferences and behavior. They choose games and activities that are socially prescribed for their gender, and they are especially likely to play with same-sex peers (Serbin & Sprafkin, 1986). They are also more likely to remember events that fit sex stereotypes and forget those that do not (Signorella & Liben, 1984).

Using the theory of gender salience, Sandra Bem (1983) has presented a series of proposals for socializing children in a nonsexist manner, stemming from the premise that gender as a category has assumed too much significance in our culture. It is used even when it is irrelevant. For example, in an elementary school classroom the monitors are one boy and one girl each day; boys and girls are put on opposing teams or are selected alternately for teams. Teachers do not use race, eye color, or other categories to sort children. As a result of the attention gender receives from adults, it becomes highly salient in children's thinking and takes on more importance than it otherwise might. Empirical support for this idea comes from work by Bigler (1994), who found greater gender stereotyping when teachers divided classrooms according to sex than when they used arbitrary classifications such as the "red" and "green" groups.

Bem suggests that one way to counteract this pattern is to teach children early that gender is a biological fact defined by reproductive capacities and anatomy. Parents can stress that genitals, not clothes or behavior, define a person as a girl or a boy. Many parents, even those who teach their children labels for everything around them, avoid labeling genitals or talking directly about biological sex. Yet such labels and discussion enable the child to understand what is critical to being a girl or a boy and what is not.

These three approaches to sex typing are complementary. Children may learn some social expectations for the sexes through direct reinforcement and other norms by observing others. They process that information actively, integrating it with other knowledge that they have acquired to construct concepts of gender appropriateness. Knowledge of social stereotypes alone, however, does not lead individuals to acquire sex-typed identities and preferences. If gender becomes a salient basis for thinking about everyday life, children are likely to act in accordance with social expectations for their gender. Their preferences and behavior also depend on the social value and reinforcement they receive from important people in their surroundings.

The Ethnic Self

Children's self-concepts include the racial, ethnic, and religious groups to which they belong. Many of the principles that govern acquisition of sex-typing probably also apply to other social categories. This is especially true in the case of ethnic categories, which are salient ones in many cultures.

Virtually all of the research on ethnicity and self-concept has been carried out with black children. As early as age 3, both black and white children classify people according to skin color, just as they classify people by gender or by age. They may recognize different racial groups before that, but children younger than age 3 have not been studied (P. A. Katz, 1976; Powell, 1985).

The group differences recognized by very young children (through about age 6) are based on obvious physical characteristics such as skin color and facial features. During middle childhood, black children develop a complex concept of race that includes social cues that differentiate blacks from whites, such as style of dress, speech patterns, culinary tastes, musical preferences, history, and ancestry (Alejandro-Wright, 1985). Young children are also more likely to understand ethnic

BOX 11.1
A CHILD LEARNS WHAT IT MEANS TO BE BLACK IN AMERICA

Richard Wright's autobiography, *Black Boy* (1945), contains many perceptive recollections of a child's efforts to understand racial distinctions. Some especially telling passages from Wright's book are presented here.

I soon made a nuisance of myself by asking far too many questions. . . . It was in this manner that I first stumbled upon the relations between whites and blacks, and what I learned frightened me. Though I had long known that there were people called "white" people, it had never meant anything to me emotionally. I had seen white men and women upon the streets a thousand times, but they had never looked particularly "white." . . . It might have been that my tardiness in learning to sense white people as "white" people came from the fact that many of my relatives were "white"-looking people. . . . And when the word circulated among the black people of the neighborhood that a "black" boy had been severely beaten by a "white" man, I felt that the "white" man had had a right to beat the "black" boy, for I naively assumed that the "white" man must have been the "black" boy's

father. . . . A paternal right was the only right, to my understanding, that a man had to beat a child. But when my mother told me that the "white" man was not the father of the "black" boy, was no kin to him at all, I was puzzled.

"Then why did the 'white' man whip the 'black' boy?" I asked my mother.

"The 'white' man did not whip the 'black' boy," my mother told me. "He beat the 'black' boy."

"But why?"

"You're too young to understand." (pp. 30–31)

At last we were at the railroad station . . . and for the first time I noticed that there were two lines of people at the ticket window, a "white" line and a "black" line. During my visit at Granny's a sense of the two races had been born in me with a sharp concreteness that would never die until I died. When I boarded the train I was aware that we Negroes were in one part of the train and that the whites were in another. Naively I wanted to go and see how the whites looked while sitting in their part of the train.

distinctions that are emphasized in their culture than ones that are not considered important. In the United States, white children are relatively unaware of differences between light- and dark-skinned African-Americans, even though their physical appearance is quite different, but they classify light-skinned African-Americans as different from Caucasians, despite the physical similarity between the two groups.

Minority children are aware of ethnic differences earlier than nonminority children. (See Box 11.1 for a personal account of the dawning of such awareness.) Ethnic differences have more profound social consequences for minorities, and in the formation of self-concept there is a general tendency for distinctive qualities to be salient. (For example, very short people mention height when they define themselves more often than people of average stature [McGuire, McGuire, Child, & Fujioka, 1978].) Even in adulthood, being black is probably a more salient aspect of one's identity than being white, at least in a predominantly white culture like ours. This is illustrated by one survey of black adolescents. In response to the question "Who are you?" 95 percent mentioned being black or Negro. It would be most surprising to find white teenagers mentioning being white in response to the same question (Powell, 1973).

"Can I go and peep at the white folks?" I asked my mother.

"You keep quiet," she said. . . .

I had begun to notice that my mother became irritated when I questioned her about whites and blacks, and I could not quite understand it. I wanted to understand these two sets of people who lived side by side and never touched, it seemed, except in violence. Now, there was my grandmother. . . . Was she white? Just how white was she? What did the whites think of her whiteness?

"Mama, is Granny white?" I asked as the train rolled through the darkness.

"If you've got eyes, you can see what color she is," my mother said.

"I mean, do the white folks think she's white?"

"Why don't you ask the white folks that?" she countered.

"But you know," I insisted. . . . "Granny looks white," I said, hoping to establish one fact, at least. "Then why is she living with us colored folks?" . . .

"Don't you want Granny to live with us?" she asked, blunting my question. . . .

"Did Granny become colored when she married Grandpa?"

"Granny didn't become colored," my mother said angrily. "She was born the color she is now."

Again I was being shut out of the secret, the thing, the reality I felt somewhere beneath all the words and silences. . . .

"What has Papa got in him?" I asked.

"Some white and some red and some black," she said.

"Indian, white, and Negro?"

"Yes."

"Then what am I?"

"They'll call you a colored man when you grow up," she said. She turned to me and smiled mockingly and asked: "Do you mind, Mr. Wright?"

I was angry and I did not answer. I did not object to being called colored, but I knew that there was something my mother was holding back. She was not concealing facts, but feelings, attitudes, convictions which she did not want me to know; and she became angry when I prodded her. All right, I would find out someday. Just wait. All right, I was colored. It was fine. I did not know enough to be afraid or to anticipate in a concrete manner. True, I had heard that colored people were killed and beaten, but so far it all had seemed remote. There was, of course, a vague uneasiness about it all, but I would be able to handle that when I came to it. (pp. 55–56)

Source: From *Black Boy* by Richard Wright, 1945, New York: Harper & Row.

In the 1940s and 1950s many researchers concluded that black children had negative self-images because they preferred white people to black people in a variety of tests. It appeared that black children had accepted the devaluation of their group by the majority culture. More recent studies have been contradictory—black children sometimes express positive and sometimes negative attitudes toward their own group. At the same time, black children report high self-esteem on questionnaires like those described earlier, perhaps because the measures are based on self-reports (Harter, 1983; P. A. Katz, 1976; Rosenberg, 1985).

The contradiction between self-esteem and group attitudes may reflect the difference between group identity and personal identity. Group identity includes both ethnic-group awareness (e.g., "I am Cuban" or "I am African-American") and attitudes (e.g., "Black people help each other"). Personal identity includes both self-concept (e.g., "I am tall," "I am shy") and self-esteem (e.g., "I am a good athlete"). Group identity might contribute to personal identity, but many factors other than one's ethnic-group identity could influence self-concept and self-esteem. A black child might have a strong positive academic self-concept and think of himself as smart even

Research on ethnic identity has mostly concerned African-American children in the United States. Other ethnicities and the development of children from mixed ethnic backgrounds is now beginning to be explored.

if he believes that many black children are poor students. Conversely, he might consider himself a poor athlete even though he thinks blacks are generally superior athletes. In fact, when measures of both group identity and personal identity are given to children and adolescents, there is little relationship between the two (Cross, 1985).

The social changes that have taken place in the past 40 years may also have produced changes in group attitudes among black people. Studies conducted before 1960 consistently showed that black children had negative attitudes about their racial group. The 1953 school desegregation decision, followed by the civil rights movement and the Black Power movement in the 1960s, produced a new group image for black people. Studies conducted between 1968 and 1977 suggest that children's attitudes reflected that change; the majority of those studies found that black children had positive attitudes toward blacks. Although in the 1980s black children faced reduced opportunities, more poverty, and less social support than had been available in the previous two decades, positive changes appear to have been maintained, particularly when parents have taught pro-black attitudes (Cross, 1985).

Almost no information exists about ethnic identity for other minorities, such as Asian-Americans, American Indians, or Hispanics. We might expect that children's awareness of these groups would depend on visible physical cues and on the social importance of group distinctions, just as it does for black Americans. We need more information, however, particularly as increasing numbers of children in these groups become part of the American population. In addition, there are beginning to be studies of children growing up in bi-ethnic or multiethnic households. L. D. Phillips (1991) has presented data showing that adolescents who come from mixed racial backgrounds (black and white in the United States) seem to be better adjusted when they identify themselves as black. The determinants of this correlation need to be better understood.

⊛ THE DEVELOPING SELF AND OTHERS

So far in this chapter, we have learned about children's development as individuals. Their self-concepts develop in a social world in which children receive information about themselves and about the salient categories in their society. However, children's social development also centrally concerns interpersonal behavior: how children fit into society and interact with others. In order to accomplish this task successfully, children must acquire certain skills and dispositions. In the second section of the chapter, we examine two important domains of interpersonal development: prosocial behavior and control of aggression.

Prosocial Behavior

The term prosocial behavior refers to positive social actions, including altruism, helping, sharing, caring, and sympathizing. Prosocial behavior can be seen in infants and toddlers (Hay, 1979; Leung & Rheingold, 1981), but the incidence of sharing, helping, sympathy, and empathy increases dramatically during the elementary school years (Emler & Rushton, 1974; Rushton & Weiner, 1975; Ugurel-Semin, 1952).

Is there a general prosocial trait; that is, are cooperative children also more generous and helpful to others? The findings of a number of observational studies conducted in naturalistic settings suggest that the answer is yes. For example, among preschool children observed during free play there were substantial associations among different types of prosocial interactions, including sharing, helping, and cooperating; some children were consistently more generous and also more helpful than others (Strayer, Waring, & Rushton, 1979). Other studies have yielded more modest, although generally positive, relationships among different types of prosocial behavior (e.g., Krebs & Sturrup, 1982; Payne, 1980). Closely related types of behavior, such as sharing and donating, are most highly correlated (B. S. Moore & Eisenberg, 1984).

Longitudinal studies demonstrate that prosocial tendencies are fairly stable over time (Bar-Tal & Raviv, 1979; J. Block & Block, 1973). In one study, the correlations between measures of prosocial behavior taken during nursery school and again five or six years later were substantial (.60 for boys and .37 for girls) (Baumrind, 1971). In the last two decades many investigators have attempted to discover the determinants of these individual differences. Among the most significant determinants are cultural background and empathy.

Variations in prosocial behavior are related to the culture in which children are growing up. A child who is reared in a culture whose economy and way of life are based on cooperation among members of the family and the community will be trained for cooperation, whereas a child who is brought up in a competitive society will be socialized in different ways. When playing a game like the one illustrated in Figure 11.2, in which they must work together to win prizes, children from traditional subcultures and small agricultural communal settlements in Mexico and Israel are much more cooperative—and far less competitive—than their conterparts in middle-class urban areas (Madsen, 1967; Madsen & Shapira, 1970; Shapira & Madsen, 1974). The differences in the children's behaviors are undoubtedly related to the values and economic systems of the communities in which they were raised. Competitiveness is punished in societies where it threatens to undermine the culture but is encouraged in societies in which it is advantageous in the struggle for survival.

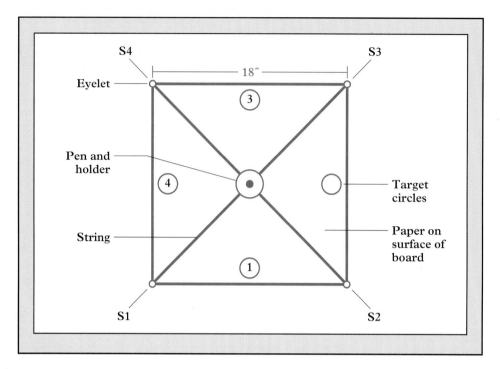

FIGURE 11.2 A cooperation game that can be played by four children. A pen is suspended at the center. Strings attached to the pen pass through eyelets at the four corners of the board. The object is to pull the pen through the circles on the board. Because each child controls one string, all must cooperate to move the pen to any of the circles. After "Cooperation and Competitive Behavior of Urban Afro-American, Anglo-American, Mexican-American, and Mexican Village Children," by A. Shapira and M. C. Madsen, 1970, *Developmental Psychology, 3*, pp. 16–20. Adapted with permission.

Children may also differ in prosocial behavior as a function of differences in empathy (M. L. Hoffman, 1981). Individual differences in level and pattern of empathic responses are apparent from very early childhood, and these differences tend to be quite stable. Some toddlers react to the distress of peers with loud crying or agitation, whereas others respond in calmer, more cognitive ways (e.g., exploring and asking questions); some behave aggressively (e.g., hitting a child who hit another child) or in an anxious or avoidant manner (e.g., turning and looking away). In one longitudinal study, two-thirds of the children made responses at age 7 that were similar to those they had made at age 2 (Radke-Yarrow & Zahn-Waxler, 1984).

The relation between empathy and prosocial behavior increases with age. Among preschool children, the association is weak but positive; empathy with another child's sadness and worry is correlated with prosocial behavior, but empathy with happiness or anger is not (Feshbach, 1978; Lennon, Eisenberg, & Carroll, 1986). However, among older children, adolescents, and adults there are stronger associations between indices of empathy and prosocial responses such as helping others in distress (Eisenberg & Miller, 1987). For example, 5- and 6-year-old children who showed great empathy (judged from facial expressions) with a child who had lost a marble collection subsequently worked harder to replace the other child's loss than did children who showed no empathic reaction (Leiman, 1978).

Experiences in role taking may raise the level of empathy with others and, consequently, the level of altruism. Six-year-olds who practiced taking roles—often switching roles—in a series of skits and who answered questions about the motives and feelings of characters they were portraying were more likely to share candies with needy children than were children who had no role-playing experience (Iannotti, 1985).

Another factor promoting the development of high levels of empathic response may be secure attachment. Compared with infants who lack secure attachments, those who are judged to have secure attachments to their mothers at 1 year show greater concern with distressed adult playmates nine months later, and at 3 years of age they are more sympathetic with peers in distress (Main, Weston, & Wakeling, 1979; Waters et al., 1979).

The caregiver's child-rearing practices and disciplinary techniques—especially reactions to the toddler's hurting or frustrating another child—also contribute to the development of empathy. According to the results of one study, the reactions that are most likely to lead to high levels of empathy are clear cognitive messages stressing the consequences of the child's behavior, accompanied by displays of emotion and statements of principles (e.g., "Look what you did! Don't you see you hurt Amy? Don't ever pull hair!") (Zahn-Waxler, Radke-Yarrow, & King, 1979).

Facilitating Prosocial Behavior. In their efforts to promote their children's prosocial behavior, parents use a variety of techniques, including modeling, reasoning, direct instruction, and assigning responsibility to the child. We examine each of these four factors, each of which seems to have a role to play in raising prosocial children.

First, modeling helps to develop altruism, as we have already found it to influence many other behaviors. In an ingenious experimental study, one group of children observed a model exhibiting "symbolic" altruism. Using toy animals and people and three-dimensional plastic settings, the model portrayed scenes in which someone needed help, for example, a monkey trying to get a banana that was outside its cage and beyond its reach. The model helped the toy person or animal, at the same time expressing awareness of the distress and sympathy, using the word *help* to highlight what she had done. The child, using a duplicate set of toys, then emulated the model's altruism, and the model pointed out how helpful the child had been (Yarrow, Scott, & Waxler, 1973). Another group of children observed this symbolic modeling and, in addition, witnessed the model in an act of real altruism: a second woman came into the room, tried to retrieve something under a table, and "accidentally" banged her head and acted as if she were in pain. The model responded warmly, putting her hand on the woman's shoulder and saying, "I hope you aren't hurt. Do you want to sit down a minute?" The victim responded appreciatively. With half the children in each modeling condition, the model was nurturant, helpful, and supportive; with the other half of the children, she was nonnurturant, aloof, and only minimally helpful.

The differential effects of the two kinds of modeling were apparent two weeks later in tests involving other imaginary or symbolic situations as well as actual opportunities to help in real-life situations. Symbolic modeling alone—in effect, giving "lessons"—resulted in increased helping, verbalizations, and actions only in symbolic or imaginary situations. However, observing a nurturant adult modeling real altruism produced an increase in real-life altruism (e.g., helping a mother by picking up a basket of spools that had spilled or retrieving toys that a baby had dropped out of its crib). Drawing upon these findings, the investigators concluded that if parents want to socialize their children to high levels of altruism, they should not only try to inculcate the principles of altruism in the children but also exhibit altruism in their everyday interactions (Yarrow et al., 1973).

Empathy is basic to prosocial actions such as comforting a friend.

The personal histories of unusually altruistic adults provide impressive evidence of the contribution of parental modeling and identification to prosocial behavior. Non-Jews who risked their lives trying to rescue Jews from the Nazis during World War II tended to be strongly identified with parents who held strong moral convictions and acted in accordance with them (London, 1970). (See Box 11.2 for further insight into such "rescuers.") In another study, fully committed workers in the civil rights movement of the 1960s—those who made extensive sacrifices to work for equal opportunities for people of all races—described their parents as vigorous workers in the cause of justice and human welfare, and as warm, loving, and willing to express their feelings about moral issues. In contrast, workers who were only partially committed to the movement—those who did some work, but without making great sacrifices—did not regard their parents as good models of altruistic behavior. Their parents, they reported, gave lip service to humane causes but did not actually work for those causes and they were cool, aloof, and avoidant in their relationships with their children—behavior that was hardly likely to promote strong identification with them (Rosenhan, 1969).

The prosocial participants in another recent study were volunteers at a crisis counseling center who underwent rigorous training and worked very hard, making major investments of time and effort. Among the volunteers, those who had had warm, positive relationships with altruistic parents during childhood completed their six-month commitment to this prosocial work even if they found the training difficult and unrewarding. However, those who had had poor relationships with nonaltruistic parents sustained their crisis work only if they found the training situation personally rewarding (Clary & Miller, 1986).

Modeling is not the only factor caretakers can use to develop prosocial behavior. A second technique is discipline through **induction**, a term that refers to reasoning with children and pointing out the painful consequences of misbehavior.

BOX 11.2
THE CHILDHOODS OF RESCUERS

What sort of person risks his or her life to save the life of others? In interviews conducted with people who acted to save the lives of Jewish people during the Holocaust, Drucker and Block (1992) found a great diversity of backgrounds and motivations. Rescuers acted in many different countries. They were Catholic and Protestant, male and female, educated and uneducated. Some were nuns, some were aristocrats, some were peasants. Some acted out of political conviction, while others just thought they were doing the decent and normal thing. Many, but not all, remembered childhoods which had shaped and modeled their altruism and courage, albeit in different ways. For instance:

My parents used to say to me, "I can't go after you to watch what you do all day, but someone watches you and don't forget it. Ask yourself, 'Can I take responsibility for what I'm doing?' " (Semmy Riekirk)

My father had died in the First World War, and it was very difficult to grow up without a man in the house. My mother was very gener-

ous. Everyone in town knew to come to her house. We weren't rich, but she always gave wheat and flour to people who needed something to eat. If there was someone who was alone and not being cared for, she would go. . . . When children see people in the house helping others, it makes them want to help. The things you learn in your own house are the things you grow up to do. (Emilie Guth)

I think it was my parents' unusual way of child-rearing that provided the motivation for me to behave the way I did during the war. I was never punished and always encouraged to express my feelings, both the negative and the positive ones, in words. And when I asked questions I got answers. I was never told I was too young or anything like that. I was treated with respect and consideration from the time I was born. (Marion Pritchard)

Source: From *Rescuers: Portraits in Moral Courage in the Holocaust* (pp. 33, 72, and 118), by M. Drucker and G. Block, 1992, New York: Holmes & Meier. Reprinted with permission.

Children whose parents use induction are more likely to make prosocial responses to the distress of others and to be helpful and considerate (M. L. Hoffman, 1970; M. L. Hoffman & Saltzstein, 1967; Zahn-Waxler et al., 1979). More assertive, power-based techniques—control by means of power or material resources (including physical punishment, withdrawal of privileges, and threats)—led to socially negative outcomes, lack of consideration for others, stinginess in donations, and self-centered values (Dlugokinski & Firestone, 1974). The disciplinary pattern that is most likely to enhance prosocial behavior consists of frequent use of induction and infrequent use of power.

Induction is viewed as an effective technique for eliciting the child's natural tendency toward empathy (M. L. Hoffman, 1970), which may then lead to attempts to help. Parents who make extensive use of techniques based on power, on the other hand, may communicate to children that following rules established by authorities yields better results than considering the possible effects of their actions.

Parents often lecture their children about the virtues of prosocial behavior. According to some research evidence, such direct instruction may have some generalized positive effects. For example, when children were told that they ought to donate some of their winnings in a game to poor children, they exhibited greater generosity than children in a control group who were not told what they ought to do; these effects were discerned both immediately and eight weeks later (Rushton, 1975). The effects of such instructions about expected behavior may produce as much immediate and enduring generosity as is produced by modeling (Grusec, Saas-Kortsaak, & Simutis, 1978; Rice & Grusec, 1975).

A final factor parents can use to develop prosocial behavior is to give children responsibility. Children who are given responsibility for household chores, taking care of siblings, or contributing to the economic well-being of the family are more likely than others to develop high levels of prosocial responsiveness. Children reared in cultures in which they are routinely assigned such responsibilities are more prosocial than children reared in cultures in which this is not done (Whiting & Whiting, 1973, 1975). Within our own culture, parental demands for mature behavior—pressure to assume responsibility and to achieve in accordance with one's abilities—also promote the development of high levels of altruism and nurturance toward others (Baumrind, 1971).

In summary, the development of high levels of altruism and other prosocial behavior depends on all the major processes of socialization in the family—modeling and imitation, explaining, assigning responsibility, and direct instruction. Each of these processes probably reinforces the effects of the others. (The contributions of school and the media to the development of prosocial behavior are discussed in Chapter 13.)

Aggression

Anger is a basic emotion, felt from infancy. Anger is a component of many conflicts, both between children (as with Rosa and Josefina in our opening story) and among adults. However, anger only sometimes results in aggression. How and when aggression occurs, against whom and in what form, are matters that human society typically regulates and socializes. All societies must find ways of preventing their members from injuring, killing, and doing serious harm to one another, but they vary enormously in the extent to which they regulate aggression. For example, among American Indian tribes, the Comanche and the Apache raised their children to be warriors, whereas the Hopi and the Zuni teach peaceful, nonviolent behavior. In some American subcultures aggression and toughness are highly valued, whereas among the Hutterites and Amish pacifism is a way of life and children are trained to be nonaggressive.

Patterns of Agressive Behavior. As children develop, their patterns of aggressive behavior change. Two- and 3-year-olds frequently fight and quarrel, usually over possession of toys or other desirable objects (i.e., instrumental aggression). The total amount of aggression displayed peaks at about 4 years of age. As children reach elementary school age, aggressive acts become less frequent and instrumental, and more often hostile. Verbal aggression, such as teasing or name calling, increases during the preschool and early elementary school years. Because older children are better able to understand other people's intentions, more of their aggression, both physical and verbal, is retaliatory, consisting of responses to frustration or attacks by others (Hartup, 1974).

Although the form aggression takes changes with age, aggressiveness is stable over time. Highly aggressive nursery schoolchildren are likely to become highly aggressive kindergarteners. The amount of physical and verbal aggression expressed at ages 6 to 10 is correlated with aggression toward peers at ages 10 to 14

Rearing children to participate in the work of the household seems to help develop prosocial behavior.

(Emmerich, 1966; Kagan & Moss, 1962; Olweus, 1979). The most impressive evidence of the stability of aggression comes from a 22-year longitudinal study that began with a large number of 8-year-olds in the third grade. At that time the children were asked to name classmates who behaved in certain ways, including aggression (e.g., "Who pushes or shoves children?") (Huesmann, Eron, Lefkowitz, & Walder, 1984). Aggression was measured several times in the ensuing years. Children who were rated as aggressive by their peers when they were 8 years old tended to be rated as aggressive by their peers ten years later. Moreover, those who were rated as aggressive by their peers tended to rate themselves as aggressive, to rate others as aggressive, and to see the world as an aggressive place (Eron, 1987; Huesmann et al., 1984; Lefkowitz, Eron, Walder, & Huesmann, 1977). In addition, those who were rated as highly aggressive at age 8 were three times more likely to have police records by the time they were 19 than those who were not so rated, and at age 30 signifcantly more of them had been convicted of criminal behavior, were aggressive toward their spouses, and tended to punish their own children severely.

By contrast, children who were regarded by their classmates as highly prosocial at age 8 (i.e., those who were frequently named as "never fighting when picked on" and "being polite to others") showed very little antisocial behavior in subsequent years. Figure 11.3 illustrates these findings, showing that both males and females who were high in aggression at age 8 had a relatively high number of criminal convictions by age 30, while those who were high in prosocial behavior had very few. These data sug-

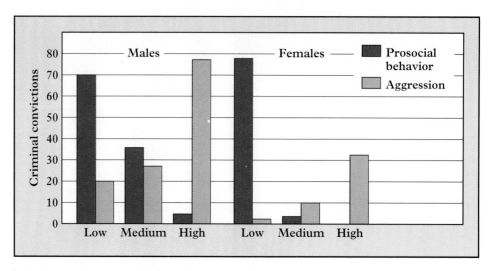

FIGURE 11.3 Mean number of criminal convictions by age 30 as a function of levels of aggression and prosocial behavior at age 8. After "The Stability of Aggression over Time and Generations," by L. R. Huesmann, L. D. Eron, M. M. Lefkowitz, and L. O. Walden, 1984, *Developmental Psychology*, 20, pp. 1120–1134. Copyright 1984 by the American Psychological Association. Adapted with permission.

gest that aggression and prosocial behavior represent opposite kinds of interpersonal problem-solving strategies that are learned early in life (Eron, 1987; Eron, Walder, & Lefkowitz, 1971; A. Goldstein, 1981; Patterson, G. R., 1982)

The aggressive child's cognitions, interpretations of the behavior of others, and ways of processing information help explain why aggressiveness is stable over time. Highly aggressive boys are more ready than their nonaggressive peers to perceive hostility in the actions of others. Thus, when questioned about some hypothetical ambiguous events (e.g., being hit in the back with a ball or having one's toys knocked to the ground by a peer), aggressive boys are likely to assume hostile intent. When they view the peer as acting in a hostile way toward them, they are inclined to retaliate with what they feel is justified aggression. In this way an ambiguous, possibly accidental act by a peer may lead to an intentional aggressive act by the aggressive child (Dodge, 1980, 1985, 1986).

This view of the world as hostile is based at least in part on actual experience, for aggressive boys are in fact likely to be the targets of aggression by their peers. In this way a spiral of aggression and counteraggression is created and perpetuated. When unacquainted 7-year-old boys were brought together to play freely for several sessions, those who were highly aggressive in their early interactions frequently became the targets of aggression in later sessions, and those who were initially the targets of aggression became more aggressive in later sessions. These findings support the notion that aggressiveness develops from reciprocal influences (Dodge, 1986).

Sex Differences. Sex differences in aggression are evident from the age of 2 or 3 on. In nursery school, boys instigate aggression—both verbal and physical—more often than girls do and are more likely to retaliate after being attacked. Boys are also more frequently the targets of aggression (Darville & Cheyne, 1981; Maccoby & Jacklin, 1980). Sex differences in aggressive behavior are found in all social classes and all cultures (Parke & Slaby, 1983) and at almost all ages, although the differences are most marked during puberty and early adulthood (Cairns, 1983). (See Figure 11.4.)

What accounts for these consistent sex differences? Both biology and learning are involved. Some argue that the prevalence of sex differences across human cultures, and in almost all species, is strong evidence for biological determinants. In addition, however, the social experiences of boys and girls with respect to aggression are very different. Aggressive behavior is part of the masculine stereotype in our culture; it is expected and often implicitly encouraged in boys. For instance, in one study preschool boys received more attention for their aggressive actions than girls did both from adults and from peers (Fagot & Hagan, 1982). The attention was sometimes positive (e.g., smiling or joining the child's play) and sometimes mildly negative (e.g., moving the child to another activity); either form of attention can encourage aggression more than simply ignoring it will.

Determinants of Aggression. What are the roots of individual differences in aggressiveness? Biological factors, as we mentioned earlier, play some role. For example, the testosterone levels of adolescent boys are significantly correlated with self-reports of physical and verbal aggression, tolerance for frustration, and irritability. Temperament may also have a lasting impact: children who had been irritable and hard to soothe as infants were anxious, hyperactive, and hostile when they were 3 years old (J. E. Bates, 1982). Moreover, infants who are very active, irregular, dis-

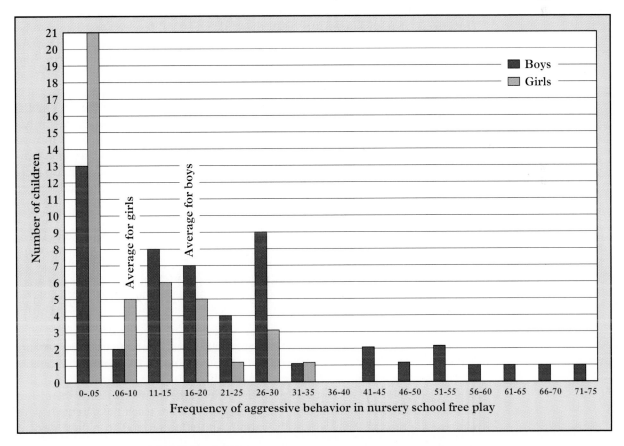

FIGURE 11.4 Frequency of interpersonal aggressive behavior for 4-year-old boys and girls in a preschool classroom. After data reported in "Aggressive and Prosocial Television Programs and the Natural Behavior of Preschool Children," by L. K. Friedrich and A. H. Stein, 1973, *Monographs of the Society for Research in Child Development, 38* [4, Serial No. 1511]. Adapted with permsssion.

tractible, and low in adaptability ("hot-headed") are more likely than others to develop aggressive behavior in subsequent years (Olweus, 1980; A. Thomas, Chess, & Birch, 1968).

Clearly, these biological influences interact with social experiences. Conditions in the child's environment may serve both to facilitate and to restrain the expression of biological tendencies (Parke & Slaby, 1983). Among those conditions, the most significant is the influence of the family.

Both parental rejection and permissiveness are conducive to high levels of aggression in children. In rejecting their child, parents probably often ignore the young child's expressions of discomfort and bids for nurturance and support. Such parents are also not likely to give positive reinforcements or rewards, which makes the parent less effective as a teacher for the control of aggression (B. Martin, 1975). Also, if parents are overly permissive and accepting in the early years and fail to set clear limits on the child's aggressiveness, the child's aggressive responses become strong and persistent (Olweus, 1980). Children of both sexes who do not identify closely with their parents tend to express more aggression than those with a strong identification with their parents (Eron, 1987).

Physical punishment, especially if it is used frequently, erratically, and inconsistently, may result in enduring high levels of aggression and hostility (Eron & Huesmann, 1984; Eron, Walder, et al., 1971; Lefkowitz et al., 1977; Patterson, 1982). The effects of punishment vary with the child's general level of aggression; relatively nonaggressive children are likely to suppress their hostile responses if they are punished, but highly aggressive children who are punished will persist in, or even increase, their aggressive behavior (Eron et al., 1971).

Family interactions frequently take the form of an escalating pattern of coercion that serves to maintain and increase aggression in the family. When a child is hostile, other family members are likely to do something that increases the probability of further aggression. For example, a brother yells at his sister; she in turn yells back, calling him names; he then hits her; she hits him back; and so on. A similar pattern of escalation may develop between parent and child—the child reacts defiantly and the parent makes stronger threats and punishes the child more severely. Aggressive children usually are unresponsive to social disapproval and unlikely to react to mild verbal discipline.

To study the socialization of aggression in the family, Gerald Patterson (1976, 1980) and his associates observed children with aggressive behavior problems both at home and at school. The parents of these children were generally hostile and lax in their enforcement of rules and standards. The mothers sometimes reacted positively to both deviant and prosocial behaviors; on other occasions they ignored or punished similar kinds of behavior.

Patterson and his colleagues developed a comprehensive program of behavior modification for retraining parents of highly aggressive children. First the parents study techniques of child management, such as how to notice and reinforce desirable behavior and how to enforce rules consistently. Next they are taught to observe and record their children's deviant and prosocial actions, the events that elicit them, and their consequences. Modeling and role playing are used to teach the parents how to reinforce appropriate behaviors with warmth and affection and to reduce deviant behavior by not giving in to the child's aggression and not allowing their own coercion to escalate. Techniques of control using rewards for desirable responses and calm forms of punishment such as "time out" (removing the child from an activity until she stops using coercive tactics) are substituted for more severe forms of punishment.

Detailed observations demonstrate that this program is very successful in reducing aggressive behavior, and observations a year later show that the beneficial effects of the treatment generally persist. Clearly, parents can learn more effective, nonpunitive ways of interacting with their aggressive children, and this can be accomplished in a relatively short period (Patterson, 1976, 1980).

Of course, the child's level of aggressiveness is also affected by many other factors. For example, frequent exposure to television violence may lead to increases in aggression, whereas some school experiences may reduce the expression of hostility. These influences are discussed in Chapter 13.

⚙ SUMMARY

An important task of growing up is developing a sense of self. The beginnings of self-awareness appear during the second year of life. Until about age 7 children tend to define themselves in physical terms. During middle childhood, descriptions of self shift to behavior patterns and psychological traits. People evaluate themselves more subjectively than they evaluate others.

The positive or negative values one assigns to one's own attributes constitute one's self-esteem. Self-esteem is difficult to measure in children under 7. Even older children may give biased responses. Self-esteem varies for different domains of behavior.

Children's self-control increases as they grow older. According to psychoanalytic theory, ego processes (the rational components of the personality) balance the conflicting demands of the individual's needs and desires, conscience, and reality. In contrast, social-learning theorists see self-control and delay of gratification as outcomes of reinforcements and observational learning.

Children who are generally self-controlled and able to delay gratification are more responsible and mature than other children. Training techniques can be used to enhance children's cognitive controls and, hence, their ability to delay gratification. Positive labeling and observation of a model can also increase children's ability to delay gratification.

The process of sex typing describes the ways in which biological gender and its cultural associations are incorporated into the child's self-perceptions and behavior. It has four facets: gender and sex role identity, concepts or knowledge about what society defines as masculine and feminine, sex role preferences, and sex role adoption. A person who combines feminine and masculine attributes is sometimes described as psychologically androgynous.

Children develop at least a rudimentary gender identity by age 3. Later they acquire gender constancy, the understanding that gender does not change. Preschool children often assume that sex stereotypes are absolute prescriptions for correct behavior. In middle childhood, children's understanding of social expectations for females and males is refined and their thinking becomes less rigid.

Children's behavior is sex-typed very early: by age 2 they select toys and activities that fit sex stereotypes, and they begin to select same-sex playmates during the preschool years. According to Kohlberg, sex typing is based on cognitive-developmental changes; for example, gender identity is related to the ability to think in categories. Social-learning theorists believe that sex-typed behavior is learned through the same processes that operate for other forms of behavior. Information-processing theorists explain sex typing in terms of schemata—once children have acquired gender role schemata, they interpret events according to those schemata. Schema theory explains individual differences in sex typing by proposing that gender may be more salient to some children than to others.

Children's identities include the racial, ethnic, and religious groups to which they belong. The group differences recognized by very young children are based on obvious physical characteristics. During middle childhood children develop a complex concept of ethnic group that includes social as well as physical cues. Minority children are aware of ethnic differences earlier than nonminority children.

Although empathy and helping are seen in infancy and toddlerhood, the incidence of sharing, helping, sympathy, and empathy increases dramatically during the elementary school years. Longitudinal studies demonstrate that prosocial tendencies are fairly stable over time. Individual differences in prosocial tendency are influenced by cultural background and empathy. Infants with more secure attachment to their caregivers appear to develop higher levels of empathic response.

A variety of techniques have been used in efforts to socialize children to engage in prosocial behaviors. They include modeling and observation, induction (reasoning with the child), direct instruction, and early assignment of responsibility.

As children develop, their patterns of aggressive behavior change. The total amount of aggression displayed peaks at about 4 years of age. In elementary school, aggressive acts are more likely to be hostile than instrumental; also, verbal aggression increases during the preschool and early elementary school years. Sex differences in aggression are evident from the age of 2 or 3 on. For both males and females, aggressiveness is stable over time.

Among the determinants of aggression are biological factors such as testosterone level and family influences such as parental rejection and permissiveness. Parents of highly aggressive children can be retrained to break the escalating pattern of coercion that serves to maintain and increase aggression in the family.

REVIEW QUESTIONS

1. What regular developmental changes occur in the development of self-concept?

2. Distinguish between self-concept and self-esteem.

3. How is children's self-control measured? How can their ability to delay gratification be increased?

4. What are the four facets of sex typing?

5. What is gender constancy? What are Kohlberg's and Bem's views of its development?

6. Describe the various explanations of sex typing that have been proposed by theorists. What is a contemporary integration?

7. How do children's conceptions of ethnic groups and ethnic identity develop?

8. What is meant by prosocial behavior and what are its most significant determinants?

9. What techniques are used in attempting to socialize children to engage in prosocial behaviors?

10. How do patterns of aggressive behavior change as children develop?

CRITICAL THINKING ABOUT THE CHAPTER

1. It is sometimes suggested that teachers should make an effort to bolster the self-esteem of children in their classes through special self-esteem programs. Critics argue that self-esteem should flow from achievement and that efforts to make children "feel good" may backfire if they feel no need to earn pride through achievement. What is your opinion? Justify your point of view using evidence from the text.

2. This chapter contains discussion of how to reduce sex typing. Do you agree that this is a desirable social goal? Why or why not?

3. Write a brief "parenting column" in which you tell your readers how to work with their children to increase prosocial behavior and reduce aggression.

KEY TERMS

androgynous   induction
ego control   self-concept
ego resilience   self-esteem
gender constancy   sex role identity
gender identity   sex typing

SUGGESTED READINGS

Eisenberg, N. (1992). *The caring child.* Cambridge, MA: Harvard University Press. An overview of prosocial behavior and altruism and how it can be fostered within and outside the home.

Lewis, M., & Saarni, C. (Eds.). (1985). *The socialization of emotion.* New York: Plenum. Chapters in this book cover many aspects of emotional development in childhood, including cross-cultural comparisons. The authors take a perspective that emphasizes learned aspects of emotion, particularly the influence of language on emotional experience and expression.

Liben, L. S., & Signorella, M. L. (Eds.). (1987). *New directions in child development: Vol. 38. Children's gender schemata.* San Francisco: Jossey-Bass. Six chapters address the formation and effects of gender schemata. Basic developmental patterns are described, and individual differences are examined. Effects of family, school, and television on children's gender schemata are discussed. One chapter reviews interventions designed to change children's gender schemata.

Olweus, D., Block, J., & Radke-Yarrow, M. (1986). *Development of antisocial and prosocial behavior.* Orlando, FL: Academic Press. This thought-provoking volume consists of seventeen essays, each by an expert in the field, focused on research, theory, and issues in the domains of aggression, delinquency, cooperation, and altruism. The principal themes are biosocial approaches, early developmental patterns, impulse control, socialization in the family and peer groups, and continuities in social development.

Spencer, M. B., Brookins, E., Geraldine K., & Allen, W. R. (Eds.). (1985). *Beginnings: The social and affective development of black children.* Hillsdale, NJ: Erlbaum. An edited collection of recent psychological studies of black children. Contains several articles about self-esteem and identity, socialization, and academic development. The authors present a well-rounded, perceptive, and sympathetic picture of black children.

CHAPTER

12

SOCIALIZATION IN THE FAMILY SETTING

DETERMINANTS OF CHILD-REARING PRACTICES

Parental Characteristics and Beliefs
Children's Personality and Behavior
Social Contexts
Marital Relationship
Parental Support Systems

CHILD-REARING PRACTICES AND THEIR CONSEQUENCES

Reinforcement
Punishment
Inductive Techniques
Imitation and Identification
Patterns and Styles of Parental Behavior
Toward a Theory of Disciplinary Techniques

VARIATIONS IN FAMILY STRUCTURE

Siblings
What Adults Are in the Home?
Divorced Parents
Stepparents
Unmarried Parents

FAMILY PROBLEMS: THE CASE OF CHILD ABUSE

A SYSTEMS APPROACH TO FAMILY SOCIALIZATION

Consider two healthy, attractive 6-year-old girls, Nancy and Tracy, both of whom are above average in intellectual ability (IQs around 115). They attend the same first-grade class in a medium-sized American community. Nancy is energetic, eager, outgoing, and cheerful, and she is doing well in school. Her teacher regards her as one of the brightest children in the class (although she isn't). When a question is asked, Nancy frequently raises her hand or calls out, "I know, I know," even when she may only be guessing at the answer. When faced with a difficult problem, Nancy is persistent, trying one solution after another; if she cannot solve the problem herself, she is comfortable asking the teacher for help. She is popular with her classmates, a leader in group activities, considerate of her peers, and generally helpful.

Tracy is a much different kind of child—slow-moving, quiet, and shy. She is doing poorly in school and is considered unintelligent by her teacher (although she isn't). She never volunteers answers to the teacher's questions, and she gives up quickly when faced with a difficult problem—"I just can't do it." Tracy has few friends, shows little interest in group games or activities, and seldom shares things with others or helps peers in any way.

What accounts for the vast differences between the two girls in personality and social behavior? Obviously, the determinants are many and varied. The contributions of factors such as heredity, temperament, and variations in early attachments were reviewed in earlier chapters. However, in any discussion of social and personality development, the concept of socialization also looms large.

Socialization is the process through which children acquire the behavior, skills, motives, values, beliefs, and standards that are characteristic, appropriate, and desirable in their culture. The agents of socialization are the individuals and institutions that participate in the process—such as parents, siblings, peers, teachers, members of the clergy, and television and other media. Although all of these agents may influence the child in important ways (see Chapter 13), ordinarily the family is the most salient part of the child's environment. For this reason, it is generally regarded as the primary or most powerful agent of socialization, playing the key role in shaping personality, characteristics, and motives; guiding social behavior; and transmitting the values, beliefs, and norms of the culture.

The goals of socialization—that is, the attributes and social responses to be acquired by the child—vary from one culture to another, as do the techniques used to socialize the child. For example, in American culture, independence, self-reliance, intellectual ability, considerateness, popularity, self-confidence, assertiveness, and standing up for one's rights are generally valued (Kagan, Reznick, Davies, et al., 1986). By contrast, Japanese culture values a sense of dependence on one's group and community, emotional control, obedience, willingness to work hard to achieve long-range goals, courteous behavior, and self-effacement (Caudill & Frost, 1973; Goodnow, 1985; E. E. Werner, 1979). In keeping with this emphasis on the importance of the social group, Japanese parents frequently use shame as a technique to control nonconforming behavior; for example, they may ask the child questions like "What will other people think?" (Harrison, Serafica, & McAdoo, 1984).

What kinds of family environments and experiences enhance children's learning, emotional and social development, competence, and happiness? What family experiences are detrimental to personality and well-being? How have the radical changes in the structure of the family that have occurred during the last few decades—for example, the enormous increases in divorce rates and single parenthood—affected children's behavior and development? What roles do brothers and sisters play in shaping the child's behavior and personality? This chapter deals with these and related questions.

✿ DETERMINANTS OF CHILD-REARING PRACTICES

Every parent's style and techniques of child rearing are a function of many interacting factors. As noted earlier, cultural background is one of these—Japanese parents are much more likely than Americans to use shame as a disciplinary technique. Within American culture, parents in some subcultures and social-class groups are prone to punish children physically for misbehaving, whereas parents in other groups seldom resort to physical punishment. Another factor that affects disciplinary techniques is the child's developmental level. In general, parents' use of physical punishment declines as children grow older, and physical displays of affection such as caressing tend to be replaced by other ways of expressing affection and approval. As the child's language skills improve, parents can make greater use of

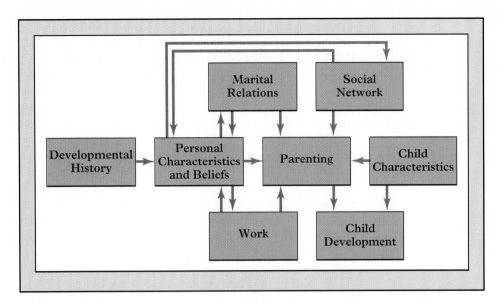

FIGURE 12.1 A process model of the determinants of parenting. After "The Determinants of Parenting: A Process Model," by J. Belsky, 1984, *Child Development, 55,* pp. 83–96. Adapted with permission.

verbal guidance, explanations, and reasoning. "The more the child can speak intelligibly, the more efficient the parent becomes in responding to the child's bids for attention and help" (Maccoby, 1984, p. 322).

According to Belsky (1984), factors that influence parents' child-rearing practices fall into three major categories: (1) forces emanating from within the parent (personality; expectations; beliefs about the goals of socialization, the nature of children, and effective socialization techniques); (2) attributes of the child (personality characteristics and cognitive abilities); and (3) the broader social context in which the parent-child relationship is embedded, including the parents' marital relations, their social networks, and their occupational experiences. Figure 12.1 presents a model illustrating the impacts of these factors on parenting. We consider each of these three kinds of influence in this section.

Parental Characteristics and Beliefs

Styles of parenting and disciplinary techniques inevitably reflect the caregiver's personality characteristics and belief systems. Emotionally mature, well-adjusted parents are more likely to react with sensitivity and nurturance to their children's signals and needs than less psychologically healthy parents are; sensitive parenting promotes emotional security, independence, social competence, and intellectual achievement (Belsky, Lerner, & Spanier, 1984). Parents who are self-confident, have trusting attitudes toward others, and believe that they can control what happens to them show greater warmth, acceptance, and helpfulness in their relationships with their children (Mondell & Tyler, 1981).

The impact of parental characteristics on parenting can be seen especially clearly in looking at how parents suffering from depression interact with their children. Depressed mothers seem to set up disruptive, hostile, and rejecting home environments that have adverse effects on their children's development (Colletta,

1983; Hammen, Burge & Stansbury, 1990). While some adverse outcomes in children of depressed mothers would be expected based on genetic transmission (see Chapter 2), the fact that the children also show elevated rates of nondepressive disorders—including aggression, attention problems, and social incompetence—argues for a role of the environment created by the depressed parent in leading to problems (Dodge, 1990). There are many aspects of the home environment in which a parent is depressed that may be relevant to elevation in children's risks for developing problem behaviors. One recent study focused on children's feelings of responsibility, finding that children with depressed mothers were *more* likely than normal children to express feelings of responsibility for other's feelings at the age of 5 or 6, whereas, by 7 to 9 years, they were *less* likely to have such feelings (Zahn-Waxler, Kochanska, Krupnick, & McKnew, 1990). This striking pattern, shown in Figure 12.2, suggests that a normal pattern of development of responsibility is disrupted when mothers are depressed. It may be that depressed mothers thrust emotional responsibility on their children at ages too young for them to deal effectively with the emotions.

In addition to their personality characteristics, parents' cognitions and beliefs about children's motivations and abilities are significant in shaping disciplinary practices (Dix & Grusec, 1985). As they attempt to socialize their children to

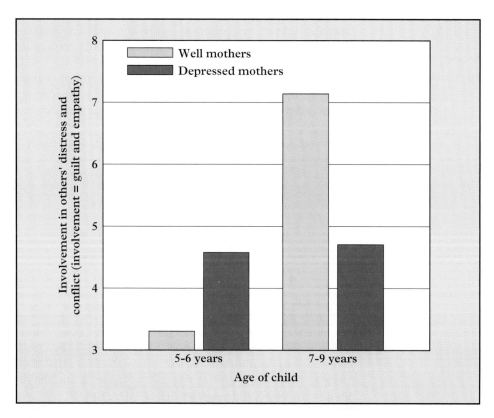

FIGURE 12.2 The average number of themes of responsibility in stories told by younger and older children of depressed and well mothers. After "Patterns of Guilt in Children with Depressed and Well Mothers," by C. Zahn-Waxler, G. Kochansky, J. Krupnick, and D. McKnew, 1990, *Developmental Psychology, 26*, pp. 51–59. Adapted with permission.

Parents who see children as active learners are likely to explain social interactions to their children.

become accepted, well-functioning, happy members of society, parents generally evaluate their children's actions as good or bad, mature or immature, to be encouraged or to be eliminated (Bacon & Ashmore, 1986). Thus, a mother who believes that her 3-year-old daughter pushed another child accidentally is not likely to be upset or to reprimand her. But if she believes the act was intentional, she may punish the child or try to modify her behavior in other ways. Similarly, a mother is not likely to react punitively to her 3-year-old son's temper tantrums if she considers him too young to control his behavior or if the tantrum was a reaction to some temporary frustration; under these circumstances she will probably be sympathetic and comforting. However, if she thinks the child's tantrum was a reflection of a self-centered, impatient disposition, she is likely to try to eliminate this response (Dix & Grusec, 1985).

Some parents believe that children are constructive, self-regulating learners who acquire knowledge through experimentation. They discuss issues with their children and ask them many questions, thereby stimulating them to think and reason. Furthermore, those who perceive children as naturally capable, rapid learners believe that they should not be rigidly directive. In contrast, parents who think children are primarily passive learners use directives and commands that are less likely to promote cognitive development (Goodnow, 1985; Sigel, 1986; Sigel, McGillicuddy-DeLisi, & Goodnow, 1992).

Parents' social orientations—their general conceptions of others—also affect their interactions with their children. Parents who stress psychological characteristics, motives, and feelings—in contrast to those who think primarily in terms of concrete features such as physical appearance, occupation, or position in society—tend to use person-centered disciplinary techniques. They call their children's attention to the feelings and motives of others and encourage them to reflect on their own behavior and emotions. This approach contributes to the development of the child's understanding, sense of personal responsibility, and autonomy (Applegate, Burke, Burleson, Delia, & Klein, 1983).

In sum, parents' cognitions—their inferences about children's behavior and motivations; their beliefs, opinions, and social orientations—are significant determinants of their child-rearing practices and disciplinary techniques. However, ideas about childhood and parenting are not fixed and immutable. Beliefs about child rearing may change in fundamental ways as a result of the experience of raising a child, noticing the differences between siblings, getting advice from more experienced parents about how to handle new situations (e.g., preparing the child to enter school), and consulting with experts, especially when children have health or psychological problems (Goodnow, 1985).

Children's Personality and Behavior

The principle of bidirectionality is clearly illustrated in parent-child interactions: The child's temperament and attributes influence the quality and quantity of the care he or she receives, just as the parents' child-rearing practices influence the child's characteristics. An irritable and sleepless infant is likely to be very frustrating to its caregivers, eliciting hostile reactions that, in turn, serve to increase the infant's irritability (A. Thomas & Chess, 1977). Mothers who consider their infants "difficult" interact with them less and respond less sensitively to their cries than other mothers do (S. Campbell, 1979). Mothers' reactions seem to have a basis in fact: negative cycles of mother-infant interaction can also be discerned when indices of negative infant emotionality are obtained from objective observers looking at babies just after birth (van den Boom & Hoeksma, 1994). By 4 to 8 years of age, children who are relatively lacking in self-control—and who ask more questions and comply less readily with instructions than do normal children—have mothers who are more controlling and give more instructions and criticisms (Mash & Johnston, 1982).

One way of thinking about the mutual influence of parents and children is to suppose that parents have upper and lower limits for acceptable behavior. When the child's behavior is above or below those limits, the parents respond with efforts to change the behavior. For example, if a very aggressive child exceeds the parent's upper limit of tolerance for aggression, the parent may punish her and attempt to restrain her aggressive impulses. The same parent might respond to a timid child by encouraging him to act more assertively.

Social Contexts

Marital Relationship. Satisfactory, supportive marital relationships facilitate adaptation to parental roles (Grossman, Eichler, Winickoff, et al., 1980), and secure, satisfying husband-wife relationships are associated with sensitive parenting, which, in turn, is related to secure attachments between parent and child (Goldberg & Easterbrooks, 1984). This is not due simply to more emotionally mature people having both better marriages and making better parents; better marital relationships are associated with more sensitive parenting even when the effects of parents' individual psychological health are controlled (Cox, Owen, Lewis, & Henderson, 1989).

Support from a spouse appears to affect parenting in several ways (Belsky & Vondra, 1989; Simons, Lorenz, Wu, & Conger, 1993). One effect is an indirect one: supportive interaction with a spouse reduces the kind of emotional distress that inevitably appears from time to time in life; this personal reinforcement makes a parent feel happier and hence able to interact more positively with the children. Spouses also seem to have a direct effect on each other's parenting, perhaps by modeling effective interventions, by taking over when a spouse is tired or the children are being difficult, or by discussing the children and coming to mutual decisions about them.

Parental Support Systems. As well as the social support obtained from a marital relationship, social support from relatives and friends is important to parenting. Parents with supportive social networks feel less stress in parenting, have more positive attitudes toward themselves and their children, are more responsive and less rejecting, and provide better care; parents with less support tend to be more restrictive and punitive in their relationships with their children (Colletta, 1981, 1983; Crockenberg, 1981). Social support networks seem to play a particularly significant role under conditions of stress; stress is more debilitating and support more beneficial for single mothers than for married ones (Weinraub & Gringlas, 1995).

Social support may act more indirectly, however, than marital support. Social support appears to have its primary effect on parenting by influencing parents' emotionality (Simons et al., 1993). Relatives and friends are less likely to take over child care or intervene directly with children than a spouse is. In addition, social support from relatives and friends is probably inherently less powerful than marital support, because marital relationships are generally much more intense parts of adults' social lives than other social ties (Belsky & Vondra, 1989).

⚙ CHILD-REARING PRACTICES AND THEIR CONSEQUENCES

Almost all parents have implicit or explicit ideals regarding what their children should be like, that is, what knowledge, moral values, and patterns of behavior their children should acquire as they develop. In their efforts to achieve these ideals, parents ordinarily try a variety of strategies, since different techniques are useful for different purposes. In using these disciplinary techniques, parents are attempting to promote compliance with their own and/or society's values and standards of acceptable behavior, not only at home or under the surveillance of adults but also when the child is alone. In fact, the goal of successful socialization can be regarded as facilitating the development of self-regulation (Lepper, 1983). That is, the ultimate aim of disciplinary techniques is the achievement of intrinsic motivation in which the child has a personal desire to behave in socially acceptable ways. In this section, we examine four frequently-used techniques: reinforcement, punishment, induction (or reasoning), and imitation (or identification). We then examine Diana Baumrind's work on characterizing styles of parental interaction, already mentioned in Chapters 7 and 10. Finally, we present a recent integrative overview of how disciplinary techniques work (Grusec & Goodnow, 1994).

Reinforcement

Reinforcers or rewards can be social (praise, affection) or nonsocial (material goods, special privileges). For young children, reinforcements are most effective when they are given immediately after the desired behavior has occurred, so that the connection between the action and the reward is obvious (Millar & Watson, 1979). Immediate rewards probably are less important for older children, who are more capable of delaying gratification and of understanding the relationship between their behaviors and rewards that come later (Maccoby & Martin, 1983).

Extrinsic rewards must be administered cautiously, especially for spontaneous, intrinsically motivated behavior, because under certain circumstances such rewards may actually diminish the child's interest in the rewarded behavior. This was demonstrated in an experiment in which children were rewarded with prizes for drawing with felt pens, an activity they were highly motivated to engage in and that they found very interesting; they subsequently manifested much less interest in this activity. The most appropriate rewards are those that fit the **minimum-sufficiency principle** (Lepper, 1983), which states that the most effective means of changing a child's behavior over the long term are rewards that are just sufficient to engage the child in the new behavior. In other words, rewards should help to "hook" the child on a new means of doing something but should not be such a prominent feature of the situation that the child focuses primarily on the rewards themselves. With such minimally sufficient rewards, standards are likely to be internalized (Damon, 1983).

Reinforcement is sometimes given unintentionally, as when children get attention for misbehaving. Consider the following example: Sally is playing with her friend in one room of the house while her mother works in another room. Sally and her friend decide to play a chase game, running through the room where Sally's mother is working. Mother looks up from her work and tells them not to run through the room. They run through the room again, and Mother tells them a little more firmly to stop it. They repeat the action, and Mother gets up from her work, takes them back to the room where they were playing, and suggests that they play with some puzzles. Just as Mother settles back to her work, they run through again.

What has happened here? It appears that the mother's attention is serving as a positive reinforcer for interrupting her. What could this mother do differently? One technique that sometimes works is **extinction**. If attention is reinforcing, then ignoring the behavior may stop it. The mother might pay no attention to the running children. After a few tries, they might stop running because that behavior is not being reinforced. In this way the undesirable behavior is extinguished.

Punishment

Most parents believe that they have to resort to punishment in some situations, especially when they are trying to teach their children to avoid danger (Trickett & Kuczynski, 1986; Zahn-Waxler & Chapman, 1982). Punishment may have some negative consequences, but it can be applied effectively to reduce or inhibit undesirable responses and to promote the development of self-control and appropriate social behavior. To accomplish these goals, punishment must be administered in accordance with some well-established principles.

First, timing is of the utmost importance; the shorter the delay between the undesirable behavior and the punishment, the more effective the punishment will be.

THE DANGERS OF INFLATION—By BERNARD M. BARUCH

Norman Rockwell's cover for a 1933 *Saturday Evening Post* was not controversial at the time, but research now suggests that physical punishment is not an effective method of discipline and has many unintended negative effects.

The ideal time to stop an unacceptable act is just before it occurs or as it is beginning (Aronfreed, 1968; Parke, 1977). For example, if a young child repeatedly runs into the street, the best time to administer punishment is when he is just about to step off the curb. Second, punishment from a nurturant, affectionate parent is more likely to produce the desired result than punishment from a cold or hostile parent. Third, if the goal is to inhibit or extinguish unacceptable actions, consistency in punishment is essential. Inconsistent or erratic punishment—punishing a particular behavior on some occasions and ignoring it on others—is likely to cause the behavior to persist. The parents of juvenile delinquents and highly aggressive boys are more inconsistent in their use of rewards and punishment than are parents of nondelinquents (Parke, 1977). Fourth, in accordance with the minimum-sufficiency principle, the punishment for a prohibited action should be just severe enough to induce compliance (Lepper, 1981). Severe punishments may bring future compliance with rules but may also generate resentment and fear, which, in turn, may lead the child to resist accepting and internalizing those rules. Prohibitions and punishments are most likely to have their intended effects if they are accompanied by explanations of the underlying reasons (LaVoi, 1973; Parke, 1977).

These principles are applied in many homes and schools in a disciplinary strategy known as "time out," in which a prohibited activity is prevented by having the

BOX 12.1
SOME THOUGHTS ON HOW TO PUNISH A CHILD

The question of what to do when a child misbehaves is an old one. Physical punishment was more acceptable in earlier historical periods than it is today. But how can one make sure that children will stop doing things that are dangerous and disagreeable? The text gives answers from psychological research. Here we look at the musings of the aunt and guardian of one of the best-known misbehaving children in American literature, Tom Sawyer, following a trick he has played on her.

Hang the boy, can't I never learn anything? Ain't he played me tricks enough like that for me to be looking out for him by this time? But old fools is the biggest fools there is. Can't learn any dog new tricks, as the saying is. But, my goodness, he never plays them alike two days, and how is a body to know what's coming? He 'pears to know just how long he can torment me before I get my dander up, and he knows if he can make out to put me off for a minute or make me laugh, it's all down again, and I can't hit him a lick. I ain't doing my duty by that boy, and that's the Lord's truth, goodness knows. Spare the rod and spile the child, as the good book says. I'm a-laying up sin and suffering for us both, I know. He's full of the old scratch, but laws-a-me! he's my own dead sister's boy, poor thing, and I ain't got the heart to lash him, somehow. . . . I'll just be obliged to make him work tomorrow, to punish him. It's mighty hard to make him work Saturdays, when all the boys is having a holiday, but he hates work more than he hates anything else, and I've got to do some of my duty by him, or I'll be the ruination of the child.

Source: From *The Adventures of Tom Sawyer* by Mark Twain.

child sit on the sidelines for a short time without any attention from adults or other children. This form of discipline can be administered quickly and calmly; the reasons underlying it can be explained clearly; and it is not physically or emotionally harmful to the child (Hawkins, 1977; Parke, 1977). There are many other forms of punishment as well; for some thoughts on the issue, see Box 12.1.

Punishment must be used cautiously, however, because it can have undesirable side effects. Severe punishment may generate such anxiety in children that they do not learn the lesson the punishment was designed to teach. Moreover, as a reaction to punishment that they regard as unfair, children may avoid punitive parents, who therefore will have fewer opportunities to teach and guide the child. In addition, parents who use physical punishment provide aggressive models. A child who is regularly slapped, spanked, shaken, or shouted at may learn to use these forms of aggression in interactions with peers.

Inductive Techniques

As noted in our discussion of the development of prosocial behavior in the last chapter, **inductive techniques** or reasoning about misdeeds is often a very effective means of bringing about lasting improvements in children's behavior (Damon, 1983; M. L. Hoffman, 1988). Examples of other-oriented inductive statements are "Don't yell at me; that hurts my feelings" and "Don't push him or he'll fall and cry." These strategies "lead children to focus on the actual standards that their parents are trying to communicate rather than on the disciplinary means by which the parents enforce

Children learn a great deal through imitation. This girl is not only learning how to sew boots but is also learning values of patience, attention to detail, and hard work.

these standards" (Damon, 1983, p. 180). Successful application of inductive techniques depends on good communication between parent and child, as well as on the child's understanding of and ability to internalize the reasons for rules and directives.

A series of studies by Martin Hoffman and his colleagues (1967, 1970, 1975, 1981, 1983) have demonstrated that parents whose principal disciplinary techniques are inductive enhance their children's moral maturity, moral reasoning and behavior, and ability to feel guilt and shame. In contrast, power assertive techniques (e.g., threats, withholding of privileges, or physical punishment) do not promote the internalization of moral values and may actually inhibit moral development. Inductive discipline that orients the child toward the feelings of others is also effective in motivating compliance with rules and regulations, such as not playing with a certain toy at a certain time (Kuczinski, 1983).

Imitation and Identification

Direct training techniques such as rewards, punishments, and reasoning are intentionally employed by parents in their attempts to enforce rules and to regulate or modify their children's responses. But these are not the only means by which children are socialized. Parental example obviously is also extremely important.

Children acquire many of their parents' behavior patterns, idiosyncrasies, motives, attitudes, and values through the processes of **imitation** and **identification**. These processes operate without the parents deliberately teaching or attempting to influence the child and without the child intentionally trying to learn. In fact, children often imitate behavior that parents would rather not teach them. A 4-year-old who swears when he hits his finger with a hammer is demonstrating the power of imitative learning.

Imitation may be defined simply as copying someone else's specific behaviors. Identification is a similar but not identical concept, derived from psychoanalysis, referring to a more subtle process in which a person incorporates the characteristics and global behavior patterns of another person. Freud maintained that by identifying with parents, particularly the parent of the same sex, a child acquires his or her superego or conscience, moral values, and standards as well as the responses and attitudes appropriate to his or her sex. Thus, through identification a young girl may adopt her mother's behavior patterns, attitudes, values, interests, mannerisms, and standards.

Research findings support the theoretical prediction that children identify most strongly with warm, nurturant, dominant, and powerful parents. For example, children with warm parents were rated as more similar to their parents and showed a greater tendency to imitate them than did children with relatively cold parents. In marriages in which power was unbalanced—one partner made decisions and led the other most of the time—children were more likely to imitate the dominant parent (Hetherington, 1967; Lavine, 1982).

Patterns and Styles of Parental Behavior

Parental disciplinary techniques and the strength of the child's identification may be seen as rooted in broad patterns of parent-child interaction or child-rearing styles. Diana Baumrind has focused on the connections between such patterns of parental behavior and children's behavior, using the two dimensions of responsiveness (or warmth) and control (or demandingness) to define types of parents termed authoritative, authoritarian, permissive and rejecting (or neglectful).

Baumrind began her longitudinal work with preschoolers. In reassessing the parents and children when the children were 9 years old, Baumrind (1988, 1991) found continued evidence that authoritative child rearing—the pattern combining high demandingness with high levels of warmth and responsiveness—had the most positive consequences for children. The children who experienced an authoritative upbringing were the most socially competent, responsive, and intellectually able, as well as more achievement oriented and planful than children in any of the other categories.

The daughters of authoritarian parents who were highly demanding but not responsive were socially assertive, whereas both permissive and rejecting-neglecting parents produced daughters who were lacking in social competence. The sons of rejecting parents tended to be domineering but deficient in leadership skills and lacking in social competence.

These findings suggest that children's behavior depends on the entire pattern of parental practices rather than on a single dimension or disciplinary practice. The authoritative pattern stands out as the one that is most likely to have enduring benefits for the child's personality and social behavior. Baumrind concludes that

> there are only a few ways to be an optimally competent parent whereas departures from competence may take many forms. Permissive parents give too much room, asking too little and leaving too many decisions up to the child. Authoritarian parents give too little room, asking too much and leaving

too few decision up to the child.... Authoritative ... parents are more ideal and rejecting-neglecting parents are less ideal than most parents in most areas. (Baumrind, 1988, p. 223)

However, in considering this research, the principle of bidirectionality must again be considered. Perhaps temperamentally "easy" children, who are more obedient, socially outgoing, and independent from the start, are most readily disciplined in authoritative ways, whereas such methods are impractical or ineffective in dealing with temperamentally "difficult" children. Although the value of authoritative child-rearing practices seems well established, it may not be possible to apply such practices successfully to all children.

Toward a Theory of Disciplinary Techniques

Everyday discussions of discipline often have an absolutist quality. People want to know what kind of discipline is most effective, and they often have strong opinions about certain forms of discipline. One way to deal with the complexity of the issues is the typological approach suggested by Baumrind, in which certain correlated practices are used to define types of parenting.

A second way to deal with the issue is to focus on the child's processing of disciplinary messages. Kinds of discipline are more and less appropriate, depending on the nature of the misdeed; the personality, past history, and age of the child; the personality of the parent and the nature of the parents' relationship with the child; and the interaction of forms of discipline with each other and with the other variables (e.g., many forms of discipline work better in the context of an overall warm or secure relationship). These considerations have recently been integrated into a theory of parental discipline by Grusec and Goodnow (1994).

The Grusec and Goodnow model focuses on two steps in children's processing of parental disciplinary messages. First, children must *understand* the messages clearly, or the messages cannot be effective. Understanding is enhanced by sending clear and consistent messages that are age-appropriate. Discipline through reasoning is helpful, in this view, because it often makes clear the general principle that the parent is trying to convey. For instance, if a child calls his sister a "jerk," saying "Stop that!" is less informative than saying "Brothers and sisters should be nice to one another." However, other disciplinary techniques also enter into achieving understanding. For instance, a time-out procedure might be necessary to calm a child before an explanation could be understood.

The second step Grusec and Goodnow posit in successful discipline is that children must not only understand but also *accept* a disciplinary message. Acceptance is affected by many variables in the situation. One important factor is whether the type of discipline used is perceived by the child as appropriate to the misdeed. Children, like adults, have strong intuitions about what interventions fit what behaviors and when parental intervention is appropriate at all (Grusec & Pedersen, 1989; Smetana, 1988). For instance, children, like adults, accept that punishment may be required when a child is in physical danger, but, on the other hand, they think that some subjects, such as choice of clothes or how a bedroom is kept, are personal and not their parents' business. A second important factor is whether the child is motivated to accept the message; the nature of the relationship with the adult is very important to such motivation, which may be why warmth and responsiveness and secure attachment are vital to effective socialization. Motivation to accept a disciplinary message may also be higher when adults do not threaten a child's autonomy too much. For example, parents may use humor or indirect requests ("What's the magic word?") to correct their children, rather than direct commands.

✺ VARIATIONS IN FAMILY STRUCTURE

In the discussion of the family thus far, we have focused on parents, without considering other family members who may be in the home, such as siblings, and without considering that, increasingly, many families do not consist of children living with two biological parents, neither of whom has been married before. While the traditional family in the United States is the nuclear family—which consists of a mother and father living in one household with their children—over the last three or four decades increasing numbers of American children have grown up in family settings that are quite different from the traditional family. In this section of the chapter, we begin by examining the role of siblings in socialization, and then go on to discuss parenting by divorced parents, by stepparents, and by never-married parents.

Siblings

More than 80 percent of American children have one or more sisters or brothers. These siblings may be highly significant agents of socialization. One-year-olds spend as much time in interaction with their siblings as they do with their mothers

This Orthodox Jewish family has a traditional nuclear structure consisting of parents and their children.

(and far more than they do with their fathers); 4- to 6-year-olds spend over twice as much time in the company of brothers and sisters as they do with their parents (Bank & Kahn, 1975). While rivalry or aggression appear in sibling relationships, young siblings at home also spend a great deal of time playing together: cooperating in games; showing concern, understanding, and physical affection; imitating each other, especially younger ones imitating older ones; and attempting to help and comfort each other (Dunn, 1983; Dunn & Kendrick, 1982; Pepler, Abramovitch, & Corter, 1981). Thus, siblings can be expected to have important effects on each other's development.

In relationships between preschool-age siblings, the older one tends to be dominant, initiates more interactions (both helpful and cooperative and interfering and aggressive), and gives more orders and suggestions (Berndt & Bulleit, 1985). Firstborn males tend to use more techniques based on physical power with their younger siblings, whereas firstborn females are more likely to explain, ask, and take turns with their younger brothers and sisters (Sutton-Smith & Rosenberg, 1970). Younger siblings are not completely submissive, however. As they grow older, they become equal partners in interactions with their older siblings; they initiate more positive actions and also become less compliant and more aggressive (Dunn, 1983; Pepler et al., 1981). Apparently, interactions with older siblings are intellectually and socially stimulating, for compared with other preschoolers, younger siblings talk more about their fantasies, ask and answer more questions, and engage in more cooperative play (Berndt & Bulleit, 1985). As early as preschool, older siblings can serve as effective teachers for younger ones, instructing and guiding them, monitoring their behavior, and modifying their own directives to help the younger child (Stewart, 1983). The majority of secondborn children feel strong attachment to their older siblings (Bryant & Crockenberg, 1980).

Siblings' responses to each other are regulated partially by their relationships with their mother. For example, mothers who talk frankly about the new baby's needs and feelings and invite participation in discussions and decisions about the infant's care (e.g., asking questions such as "What do you think he wants?") stimulate close, friendly relations between the siblings. Mothers who do not discuss the baby in this way produce siblings who are less likely to make positive approaches to each other. Firstborn girls who have particularly intense and playful relationships with their mothers are likely to become hostile toward a new baby, who, in turn, is likely to develop negative attitudes toward the older sibling (Dunn & Kendrick, 1981).

Longitudinal data indicate that siblings' interactions are quite stable over time. Children who were friendly to their new baby sibling were still friendly toward that sibling three or four years later; those who initially withdrew from a newborn sibling were more aggressive toward that sibling at later ages (Dunn & Kendrick, 1982; Stilwell, 1983). Stability is especially marked once children are 5 years old; after that, correlations across periods as long as 7 to 8 years indicate stability in the sibling relationship (Dunn, Slomkowski, & Beardsall, 1994).

The quality of early sibling interactions may have consequences for the child's later behavior. Close, affectionate sibling relationships augment the development of desirable characteristics and responses, including role-taking and communication skills, social sensitivity, cooperation, and understanding of social rules and roles (Dunn & Kendrick, 1982). One mechanism for advance in role-taking skills may be sibling arguments. Such arguments are different in many ways from arguments children have with parents, and they may be specifically associated with advances in the ability to take the perspective of others (Slomkowski & Dunn, 1992). Sibling interaction may also help to advance children's understanding of related abilities, such as

Sibling interaction has a distinctive quality.

knowing what facts another person is aware of and not aware of (Dunn, Brown, Slomkowski, Tesla, & Youngblade, 1991; Perner, Ruffman, & Leekam, 1994). On the negative side, hostile sibling relationships in 3- and 4-year-olds are associated with antisocial behavior five years later (Richman, Graham, & Stevenson, 1982).

Another positive effect of having siblings may be to provide comfort in times of adversity. Dunn, Slomkowski, and Beardsall (1994) found that siblings gave each other support in cases of problems such as maternal illness, school difficulties, and so on. When parents divorce, the pattern is not as clear. Increased conflict between siblings is sometimes reported after divorce, but the pattern may depend on the pre-divorce sibling relationship. If it was close, the siblings may support each other through the divorce (Hetherington, 1988; Jenkins, 1992).

Given the many positive influences of siblings we have discussed, it may seem that being an only child would cause problems. In fact, the only child is frequently described in negative terms, for example, as "maladjusted, self-centered and self-willed, attention-seeking and dependent on others, temperamental and anxious, generally unhappy and unlikable, and yet somewhat more autonomous than a child with siblings" (V. D. Thompson, 1974, pp. 95–96). However, a systematic analysis of over 100 relevant studies suggests that only children do *not* generally suffer any of these problems.

Only children surpass those with many siblings in intelligence and achievement motivation. They resemble firstborns and children from two-child families in these respects and also in measures of sociability, character, and adjustment. Compared with children in large families, only children, firstborns, and children in two-child families probably receive more parental attention, which helps the child acquire more sophisticated intellectual skills, such as vocabulary, as well as more mature behavior patterns (Falbo & Polit, 1986). Many people have a strong intuition that only children are different in some respects from children with siblings, but if so, the differences must be on variables not studied so far.

What Adults Are in the Home?

The percentage of children in the United States living with only one parent has increased from about 9 percent in 1960 to about 25 percent in 1990 (U.S. Bureau of the Census, 1992). The increase has occurred across racial and ethnic groups, but living with a single parent is especially prevalent for African-Americans (55 percent). The increase in this statistic has prompted intensive examination of child rearing by unpartnered parents (Weinraub & Gringlas, 1995).

Early research on single parents conceptualized the important variable as "father absence." The reasons for the father's absence (divorce, death, never married) were often not considered, and the fact that single mothers ordinarily experience more stress than mothers in nuclear families was not taken into account. Single mothers have more financial problems, a greater workload, and stronger feelings of isolation and loneliness than partnered parents, and any or all of these facts—as well as the absence of a father—could produce effects on their children.

The "father absence" literature showed a variety of negative correlates in children. For instance, 2-year-old Israeli boys whose fathers had been killed before they were born and who were living with widowed mothers showed more dependency, more anxiety about separation, more aggression, and less autonomy than compara-

Being a single mother can be stressful, especially when there is poverty and lack of social support.

ble boys who were living with both parents (Levy-Shiff, 1982). Children reared in mother-only households performed less well in school and on tests of intelligence and achievement than children reared in two-parent families, and they were more likely to be inattentive and disruptive in class (Guidubaldi, Perry, & Cleminshaw, 1983; Hetherington, Camara, & Featherman, 1983). However, to understand how and why these correlates come about, it is important to differentiate various kinds of single parents.

Divorced Parents. The most common cause of living in a single-parent household is divorce or separation. In 1990, 62 percent of the children living in single-parent households in the United States did so following divorce or separation (Weinraub & Gringlas, 1995). Divorce is preceded and followed, in most cases, by at least some degree of conflict and discord. Such disagreements may be key elements in the adverse effects of divorce.

An extensive longitudinal study in which divorcing parents and their 4-year-old children were followed for six years after the divorce and compared with a matched group of children in intact families who were studied for the same period (Hetherington, Cox, & Cox, 1982; Hetherington, 1989) showed that the first year after the divorce was the most stressful for the parents. They encountered many new and difficult problems in managing their households, finances, and working arrangements. After a divorce the income of mother-only families (the most common situation) usually drops appreciably. When a divorce occurs, families often sell their home and move to a new neighborhood; in many cases the move leads to further disruption and problems of adjustment in addition to those directly related to the divorce itself. Under these circumstances, it is not surprising that parents' self-concepts deteriorate and that feelings of anxiety, depression, anger, rejection, and incompetence and inadequacy in establishing meaningful relationships are common at this time.

As might be expected, the stress and insecurity of the divorced parents are reflected in their relationships with the children. Compared with other parents, those who had divorced recently were less affectionate and more restrictive, made fewer demands for mature behavior, communicated more poorly, were inconsistent in their discipline, and lacked control over their children. Mother-son relationships were particularly poor at this time. In the first two months after the divorce, fathers, eager to maintain contact with their children, typically initiated many interactions. However, this changed rapidly; after the first few months, most divorced fathers have little contact with their children.

Two years after the divorce parents coped with their problems more adequately; their self-concepts were better; and there were marked improvements in parent-child relationships. Mothers became more nurturant and consistent in their disciplinary practices, better able to control their children, and more demanding of mature behavior; they communicated better and used more explanation and reasoning in dealing with their children. Divorced fathers also became more demanding of mature behavior, communicated better, and were more consistent in their disciplinary techniques. With time, however, they became less nurturant and affectionate and more detached from their children.

As would be predicted from these parental reactions, the major adverse impact of divorce on children was evident during the first year, and the effects appeared to be more severe and enduring for boys than for girls. After their parents divorced, the boys showed more problems in cognitive, emotional, and social areas; they were more likely than girls to become unruly, aggressive, and impulsive, yet at the same time to be dependent, anxious, and lacking in task orientation. (However, not all studies have replicated the greater effect on boys. Allison and Furstenberg [1989] found no sex differences, or, occasionally, worse effects on girls, in following a large, nationally representative sample.)

Whether children are more vulnerable to effects of divorce at a certain age is not clear. Allison and Furstenberg (1989) found larger effects of divorce among children who were younger when the divorce occurred, but Hetherington (1991) drew the opposite conclusion from comparing her study with young children, which we have described in detail, to a subsequent study she undertook with adolescents. It may be that there are different vulnerabilities at different ages. Preschoolers' level of cognitive development may lead them to misinterpret what is happening and to blame themselves for the separation. As children grow older, they may understand the causes of the adult conflict better and blame themselves less. But they may be less adaptable, having clearer memories of a time when their parents lived together in relative harmony.

As the parents' psychological well-being and adjustment improves during the second year after the divorce, so does the children's. In the Hetherington et al. study, the adverse consequences had dissipated substantially and, in the case of girls, practically disappeared two years after the divorce. These findings suggest that in the long run it is not a good idea for parents to remain in a conflicted marriage for the sake of the children if the alternative is a stable, one-parent household. In fact, marital conflict has been found to predict significant adjustment problems in children, and some of the research on "effects of divorce" may actually be picking up, at least in part, the effects of pre-divorce conflict. J. H. Block, Block, and Gjerde (1986) found that children whose parents later divorced showed behavioral problems *prior* to the divorce. Marital conflict may be associated with behavioral problems in children because conflict often leads to poor parenting behavior, such as lax control and rejection (Fauber, Forehand, Thomas, & Wierson, 1990).

In line with this emphasis on how parents' psychological states influence their parenting behavior, the detrimental effects of divorce on children may be reduced if household routines are well organized and discipline is authoritative and consistent (Hetherington et al., 1982). Living with a happy, well-adjusted parent with whom they have a warm relationship and good communication enables children to cope better with divorce. Also, a boy who lives with his mother after divorce benefits from a good relationship with his father. Boys who maintain such relationships exercise greater self-control and get better school grades, especially in math, and higher scores on achievement tests (Guidubaldi et al., 1983).

The interactions between the divorced parents also play a significant role in children's adaptation. High parental conflict and hostility and low parental cooperation often make children feel "caught" between their warring parents. This feeling often leads to problems in adjustment (Buchanan, Maccoby, & Dornbusch, 1991). Children are especially likely to feel caught in situations where they go back and forth between their parents, if the parents have not managed to create a working relationship. Thus, dual residence may not be a good idea in these cases, although it can work very well if the ex-spouses are not in conflict (Buchanan et al., 1991).

Almost all studies of divorce have involved white middle-class parents and children originally living in nuclear family groups (i.e., father, mother, and children). Generalizations from these studies must be made very cautiously. For example, the organization and economic status of black families may be quite different from that of most middle-class white families (Wilson & Saft, 1993). A much higher proportion of black than of white families are extended families (including grandparents and other relatives), and many more black than white families have incomes below the official poverty line. In addition, black family structure is more likely to fluctuate as a result of frequent changes in family composition and membership, as well as frequent changes in living quarters and arrangements. Any or all of these factors can be expected to influence parents' and children's reactions to divorce when it occurs.

Stepparents. Approximately 75 percent of parents who divorce remarry. This means that 35 percent of the children born in the United States in the early 1980s will spend part of their lives living with a stepparent (Glick, 1984). Because in 90 percent of divorce cases custody of the child is given to the mother, many more children live with stepfathers than with stepmothers.

After a period of adjustment to living with only one parent (often an unsettling experience), many children must cope with another major change: living in a new nuclear family with a stepparent. Young children and adolescents appear to adjust to this situation better than children between the ages of 9 and 13. Problems may be aggravated if both parents bring children to the new marriage (Hetherington et al., 1982).

In fiction, stepparents are often depicted as cruel and evil and as making life miserable for their stepchildren, but research shows that the opposite is often true: Boys often benefit from having a stepparent, particularly a stepfather. Thus, 6- to 11-year-old boys with stepfathers tended to be more mature, better adjusted, and more socially competent than boys living with single mothers (Santrock & Warshak, 1979). These positive outcomes are probably due to the fact that many young boys are excited about having a new stepfather and rapidly become attached to him (Wallerstein & Kelly, 1980); moreover, stepfathers are often attentive, competent parents. In addition, remarried mothers are generally happier and more secure than those who are single, and because their workloads, financial worries, and loneliness are reduced, they can devote more time and energy to their children. Thus, remarried mothers exercise firmer control over their children than single mothers do, and they are more intellectually stimulating and expressive, particularly with their sons (Santrock, Warshak, Lindbergh, & Meadows, 1982).

Girls with stepfathers fared less well, however; they expressed more anxiety than girls in intact families. There is likely to be more friction between a girl and her remarried mother than between a boy and his remarried mother (Santrock et al., 1982; Vuchinich, Hetherington, Vuchinich, & Clingempeel, 1991). On the other hand, an accepting and nurturant stepmother may enhance a young girl's adjustment. Stepmother-stepdaughter relationships generally improve over time, and girls develop more positive perceptions of their families, less aggressive behavior, and fewer inhibitions (Furstenberg, Nord, Petersen, & Zill, 1983). Frequent contact with their biological mothers may have some adverse effects for these girls, leading to a poorer self-concept and a less positive relationship with the stepmother (Clingempeel & Segal, 1986; Furstenberg et al., 1983).

Successful stepparenting—that is, stepparenting that benefits the child—is not simply a function of the stepparent's gender or residence in the home but, rather, of his or her personality characteristics, interest in the child, attitudes, and child-rearing practices, as well as the quality of the new marriage. In addition, remarriage may improve the natural parent's emotional adjustment and self-concept, and these factors, in turn, may lead to better interactions between parent and child, with beneficial effects on the child's personal and social adjustment. However, a danger in step-fathering is a tendency to distance oneself from parenting, particularly of adolescents (Hetherington, 1991).

Unmarried Parents. The birth of children to mothers who have never married is increasing among women of all educational levels and ethnic backgrounds (see Figure 12.3). Many of these births are to adolescent mothers, but the group showing the fastest increases in births outside marriage is Caucasian, employed, college-educated women. Birth outside marriage is now the second most common cause (at 31 percent), after divorce, of children living in a single-parent household.

Weinraub and Gringlas (1995) argue that one must distinguish between adolescent unmarried mothers and other unmarried mothers. About one-third of births to unmarried mothers are to adolescent mothers, who seem to suffer some unique disadvantages in rearing their children. Their problems include poverty, lack of education, and low levels of aspiration for the future (B. C. Miller & Moore,

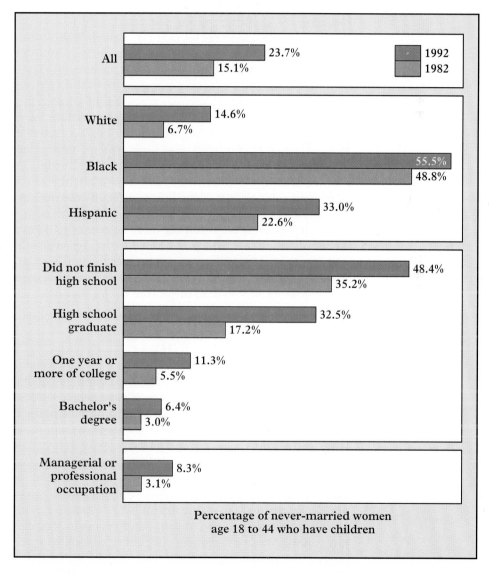

FIGURE 12.3 The percentages of never-married women who had children, in 1982 and in 1992. From "Never Married, With Children," *The New York Times*, July 14, 1993, p. 14. Reprinted with permission.

1990; Scott-Jones, 1991). Many of these problems predate the pregnancy. The facts that adolescent mothers have high rates of unemployment or employment at minimum wage may be as attributable to their educational background and world view as to their having a child (Brooks-Gunn & Chase-Lansdale, 1995).

Due to their age and poverty, many adolescent mothers live with their own mothers, depending on them for advice and help with child care. Negotiating some autonomy from their own mother and developing an identity are likely to be difficult in this case (Brooks-Gunn & Chase-Lansdale, 1995). Adolescent mothers are more likely to be depressed than older mothers (Carter, Osofsky, & Hann, 1991).

The picture is not entirely bleak, however. Longitudinal follow-up of adolescent mothers has shown that, 17 years after the birth of their first child, many women had obtained more schooling and that almost three-quarters were employed (Furstenberg et al., 1987a, 1987b). Understanding how young mothers negotiate the challenges facing them and what factors encourage successful outcomes is a major challenge for current research in this area. Efforts aimed at education and employment seem more promising than interventions aimed directly at parenting skills (Brooks-Gunn & Chase-Lansdale, 1995).

Older and better-educated single mothers also face challenges, but their situation is probably somewhat easier than that of adolescent mothers, although they have been less well-studied. Longitudinal observations begun by Weinraub and Wolf (1983) and overviewed by Weinraub and Gringlas (1995) show that, even with college education and professional employment, unmarried mothers work longer hours, report more financial problems and daily hassles, and experience less social support than do women with husbands. When the children were preschoolers, unmarried mothers of sons had more difficulty controlling their behavior than did married mothers. By preadolescence, children of both sexes being reared by unmarried mothers were showing more behavior problems and lower social competence and school performance. Many of these behaviors, however, were correlated with the mothers' social support. This fact suggests that an important determinant of single parenting is whether or not friends or relatives are available to reduce the mother's sense of isolation, to provide advice and help, and to bolster her spirits.

✿ FAMILY PROBLEMS: THE CASE OF CHILD ABUSE

Raising children is one of the most difficult and demanding responsibilities a person can take on, and it is one for which most people have little preparation or training. Some adults have emotional problems or life stresses that make it difficult for them to be good parents, and as a result some of them subject their children to violence, sexual abuse, or extreme neglect.

Although precise data are virtually impossible to obtain, it is estimated that over a million children are abused each year—maimed, injured, severely beaten, sexually molested, starved, stabbed, whipped, kept in isolation, or subjected to other extreme forms of maltreatment. Child abuse is reported more often in lower-class than in middle-class families, but it occurs in all social classes, races, and ethnic groups. Abusive treatment, like other disciplinary practices, is a function of interactions among the parents' personal and cognitive attributes, the child's behavior and attitudes, and the social context (Belsky, 1993).

Many abusive parents experienced abuse and rejection themselves as youngsters and seem to be perpetuating this pattern, especially when they are under stress and lack social supports (R. Conger, Burgess, & Barrett, 1979; Egeland, Jacobvitz,

& Papatola, 1987). At the same time, it is important to remember that a history of abuse does not make abuse inevitable, and that many parents do succeed in breaking the cycle of abuse (J. Kaufman & Zigler, 1989). Only 10 percent of child abusers have serious mental illnesses, but many more manifest personality and behavioral characteristics associated with poor parenting and inability to handle stress adequately (Kempe & Kempe, 1978). Compared with mothers who take excellent care of their children, abusive mothers are less intelligent and more aggressive, defensive, anxious, irritable, and immature. They have relatively low expectations about their relationships with their children, and their attempts at discipline are erratic and unpredictable; they may make equally positive (or negative) responses to desirable and undesirable behavior (Belsky, 1993; Egeland, Breitenbucher, & Rosenberg, 1980; Mash, Johnston, & Kovitz, 1983).

Children who are victims of abuse may inadvertently contribute to their own maltreatment because they are difficult to deal with and place strain on family relations. Irritable, unresponsive, highly demanding infants—as well as physically unattractive, hyperactive, disobedient children—are more likely to be targets of abuse than children who are responsive, attractive, quiet, undemanding, and compliant (B. Johnson & Moore, 1968; Parke & Collmer, 1975). In addition, younger children and those in poor health are more likely to suffer abuse, perhaps because caring for them is more demanding (Belsky, 1993).

Child abuse is frequently part of a pattern of family violence, and it has been hypothesized that anger at a spouse is often displaced onto the relatively defenseless child. Threats, physical punishment, criticism, sarcasm, disapproval, and anger are characteristic of the reactions of abusive and severely neglecting parents; smiles, praises, and expressions of affection occur much less frequently in abusive families than in nonabusive families (Burgess & Conger, 1978) (see Figure 12.4). In addi-

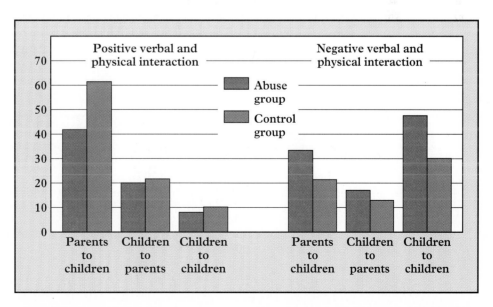

FIGURE 12.4 Rates of positive and negative verbal and physical interactions in families with and without a history of abuse. After "Family Interaction in Abusive, Neglectful, and Normal Families," by R. L. Burgess and R. D. Conger, 1978, *Child Development, 49,* p. 1170. Adapted with permission.

tion, siblings in abusive families are more hostile toward each other than are siblings in nonabusive families (Parke & Slaby, 1983).

Social and economic stress increases parents' potential for abusing children. The incidence of abuse is highest among adolescent, poor, uneducated, and socially isolated parents, particularly those with large families. When unemployment rates in a community rise, the incidence of child abuse also increases in the next few months, suggesting that the stresses of unemployment build up over time (Steinberg, Catalano, & Dooley, 1981). However, some poor neighborhoods are "high risk" for child abuse whereas others that are equally poor are "low risk." Families in the "high risk" neighborhoods tend to regard themselves as under stress, socially isolated, and in need of support; they hardly ever use available community services such as child-care and recreational centers. In contrast, families in "low risk" areas have greater pride in their neighborhood, engage in more neighborly exchanges, and make more use of available community resources (Garbarino & Sherman, 1980).

The consequences of child abuse may become apparent very early. In interactions with their mothers, abused infants show much more avoidant, resistant, and noncompliant behavior than nonabused children do (Egeland & Sroufe, 1981). In day care centers, toddlers who have been abused tend to be more aggressive toward their peers and more wary and ambivalent toward their caregivers, whom they seem to distrust and sometimes threaten or attack. Abused toddlers who were observed in a day care center sometimes reacted to others' distress with fear, aggression, or anger, and no abused toddler ever showed concern or an empathic response, although more than half of the nonabused children showed sadness or empathy under these circumstances (Main & George, 1979). Clearly, many abused children learn to distrust adults and to react aggressively to others, a pattern that they may maintain and use when they become parents. Nevertheless, many abused children develop into well-functioning, empathic, kindly individuals who become excellent parents (R. Conger et al., 1979).

Several treatment programs have been effective in teaching abusive parents new, less violent methods of discipline through role playing, modeling, and home visits (Zigler, 1980). The incidence of child abuse can be reduced if the community provides adequate resources and support systems for families that are under stress, including employment and educational opportunities for mothers and children, support groups for parents, child-care facilities, homemaker services, public service programs on television, and hotlines (Belsky, 1993; Parke & Slaby, 1983).

Child abuse is often differentiated from neglectful care, in which children are simply not given enough to eat or are poorly clothed or laxly supervised, without being physically hurt. However, the distinction between abuse and neglect is often difficult to make and the two problems often co-occur. The correlates of abuse and neglect are very similar (Belsky, 1993). In fact, apparently unintentional childhood accidents appear to be related to the abuse-neglect syndrome as well, presumably because lax supervision and neglect are likely to increase the probability of accidents (Peterson & Brown, 1994).

⬡ A SYSTEMS APPROACH TO FAMILY SOCIALIZATION

Much research on the family has centered on one significant dyadic (two-person) relationship, usually that between a mother and her child. However, if you think about your own family and other families you have known, you will recognize that each family constitutes a complex system that is made up of many subsystems (e.g., mother-father, mother-child, brother-sister, mother-father-brother, grandmother-grandchild, etc.) that interact with and influence one another. Thus, as noted earlier, the quality of the relationship between the mother and father (the mother-father system) may affect the mother-child and father-child systems: a stable, happy marital relationship is likely to be associated with warm, nurturant parenting, whereas unsatisfactory husband-wife relationships may generate parental tensions and anxieties that are reflected in poor parenting. On the other hand, some parents, most often mothers, may become more involved and supportive in their parenting in order to compensate for unhappy marital situations. Or a young boy who is treated harshly by his parents may avoid social and emotional maladjustment because he finds warmth and nurturance in his relationships with an older sister or an understanding grandparent.

In a systems approach, each family member is seen as an active participant in a number of interacting subsystems. To understand an individual child's development and personality, the whole family system and its subsystems must be considered and investigated. This approach is advocated by family therapists; they work with entire family units, observing many interactions within the family network, in order to help resolve a child's problems and reduce conflicts. Patricia Minuchin, a developmental psychologist who is also a family therapist, has given a lucid, succinct account of the systems point of view and has spelled out the implications of this view for research (P. Minuchin, 1985).

From the systems perspective, a particular dyadic relationship like the father-child relationship is never independent and can be understood only in the context of the family and its various subsystems. The family is an "open" system, which means that it undergoes periods of stability and periods of change. Many features of the family system and patterns of interaction among its members that have become well established keep the family functioning in stable, adaptive, and reasonably smooth ways. But sometimes situations change radically—perhaps the family inherits a great deal of money, the father loses his job, the mother becomes critically ill or is seriously injured, a grandparent moves into the home, or an adolescent daughter becomes pregnant. Under such conditions the established patterns are disrupted, precipitating changes in emotional reactions and restructuring of relationships. New and different individual, as well as family, goals may be generated. Alternatives to the established family system must be explored and tried, and the family system, as well as its various subsystems, is likely to become reorganized and considerably changed. (For a view of how family systems theory views families going through divorce, see Box 12.2.)

Systems theory and the experiences of family therapists challenge traditional ways of thinking about child development and research in socialization. If children are regarded as interdependent, contributing participants in systems and subsystems that control their behavior, they must be studied in the context of the organization and functioning of their natural families; they cannot be studied meaningfully in isolation from the family and its subsystems.

This argument implies that dyads such as mother-child are not the only salient units for research; rather, a variety of naturally occurring systems—mother-father-child and mother-father-grandparents-child, for example—must be viewed as units and be the targets of systematic developmental studies. This kind of research is needed to determine how patterns of relationship are established and changed and how each subsystem relates to the child's personality and social behavior.

BOX 12.2
THE FAMILY SYSTEM AFTER DIVORCE

In this chapter, we have examined the literature on the effects of divorce on the family and have also introduced the ideas of a systems approach to the family. In the following passage and excerpt from an interview, Salvador Minuchin, one of the founders of family systems theory, presents a case of a family going through the divorce process.

The period after the separation is always stressful for family members. They must negotiate new patterns of functioning while the blueprints that governed the old family still control their habitual responses. Family therapists who see families in the period of transition may misdiagnose the search for new patterns and the ensuing pain. We may label as deviant what is actually the creative attempt of a family organism to develop a new shape—the shedding and becoming that precede a butterfly.

We need to explore separation and divorce so as to develop ways of helping family members move from one pattern to another. As a step in such exploration, I interviewed the Jansons. At the first interview, the spouses had been separated for over a year and were in the process of divorcing. The two daughters, Natalie, thirteen, and Vicky, ten, had remained with their mother, but visited their father most weekends. . . .

Minuchin: So, you understand the purpose of the meeting. I want to explore the ways in which your family has changed since Mr. Janson left the house. Is it okay if I start with the children? (Mother nods.) Your name is Vicky, is that right? How has life changed now that you're three people instead of four?

Vicky: Well, I guess—it seems that my sister and I get into fights more than we used to. We can't get as many things because my father's not living with us. So we can't buy as much, and stuff like that.

Minuchin: How has life changed for you in particular?

Vicky: Well, I've changed schools. And we might have to move.

Minuchin: Why is that?

Vicky: Because my dad doesn't live with us. The house is big, and . . .

Minuchin: And that will be a problem for you?

Vicky: Yes. All my friends live here.

Source: From *Family Kaleidoscope* (pp. 20–21) by S. Minuchin, 1984, Cambridge, MA: Harvard University Press. Copyright © 1984 by S. Minuchin. Reprinted by permission of Harvard University Press.

Unfortunately, psychologists do not yet have adequate methods for investigating and evaluating either the complex interacting subsystems—such as child-parent-sibling subsystems—or the family as an integrated unit. When such methods are devised, research in socialization will yield richer and more meaningful findings that can be applied not only in the practice of therapy but also in making wise decisions about public policy.

❂ SUMMARY

Parental child-rearing techniques are a function of many interacting factors. These include cultural and social-class background, the child's developmental level, personal attributes of both parent and child, and the social context in which the parent-child relationship is embedded, especially the relationship between the parents.

Among the parental characteristics that affect parenting styles and disciplinary techniques are maturity and emotional adjustment. Parents' cognitions and beliefs about children's motivations and abilities are also significant in shaping disciplinary practices. Parents are more likely to react punitively to misbehavior if they believe it was intentional and that the child is old enough to control his or her behavior. Parents who believe children are constructive, self-regulating learners have different parenting styles than those who believe children are primarily passive learners.

The techniques that are most commonly used in child rearing are rewards, punishments, and reasoning or induction. Rewards (reinforcers) can be social (e.g., praise) or nonsocial (e.g., special privileges). The effectiveness of social reinforcements depends partly on the child's relationship with the adult. Reinforcement is sometimes given unintentionally, as when children get attention for misbehaving. Under such conditions the parent may attempt to extinguish the undesirable behavior by ignoring it.

If reinforcement strategies fail, parents may feel that they must use punishment. For punishment to be applied effectively, however, it must be administered as soon as possible after the undesirable behavior. Punishment is more effective if it comes from a nurturant, affectionate parent, and consistency is essential if it is to inhibit unacceptable actions. In accordance with the minimum-sufficiency principle, the punishment for a prohibited action should be just severe enough to induce compliance. Prohibitions and punishments are most likely to have their intended effects if they are accompanied by explanations of the reasons underlying them. If punishment is severe or unfair, it can have negative side effects.

Nonpunitive disciplinary strategies—which are referred to as inductive techniques—include reasoning, pointing out the consequences of undesirable actions, or appealing to the child's pride or desire for mastery. Successful application of these techniques depends on good communication between parent and child, as well as on the child's understanding of the reasons for rules and directives.

Children are socialized not only by direct training techniques but also by parental example, that is, through the processes of imitation and identification. Imitation is copying someone else's specific responses. Identification is a more subtle process in which a person incorporates the characteristics and global behavior patterns of another person. Identification depends on the presence of a strong emotional tie to the person whose behavior is adopted and on the child's perception of himself or herself as similar to the model.

Child-rearing styles vary from one culture to another and from one historical era to another; they also differ from one family to another. Researchers have identified four general patterns of parental control: authoritative, authoritarian, permissive-indulgent, and rejecting-neglecting. The authoritative pattern, which combines high demandingness with high levels of warmth and responsiveness, appears to have the most positive consequences for the child.

Siblings are an important aspect of family life. Sibling interactions may be antagonistic or may be stimulating and warm. Relationships with the mother may affect which pattern develops. Sibling relationships show a good deal of continuity over time. Only children, contrary to some popular opinion, do not seem to develop negative attributes.

For children of divorced parents, the first year after the divorce is the most stressful one. The stress and insecurity felt by the parents are reflected in their relationships with the children. Preschool-age children seem to be most vulnerable to the negative effects of divorce. School-age children may be better able to cope with divorce because they have a better understanding of their parents' problems and the reasons for the divorce. The interactions between the divorced parents play a significant role in children's adaptation to divorce.

Child rearing is often stressful for single parents, especially those who are still adolescent. Poverty, lack of prospects, and the need to negotiate one's own autonomy and identity while also mothering are significant issues for adolescent mothers. Nevertheless, outcomes for these mothers are sometimes more positive than one might expect, and educational and employment assistance appears to help them.

Child abuse occurs in all social classes, races, and ethnic groups. It is a function of interactions among the parents' personal and cognitive attributes, the child's behavior and attitudes, and the social context. Many abusive parents experienced abuse and rejection themselves as youngsters and seem to be perpetuating this pattern. Child abuse is frequently part of a pattern of family violence, and it increases in situations of social and economic stress.

A family can be viewed as a complex system made up of many subsystems that interact with and influence one another. In a systems approach to family socialization, each family member is seen as an active participant in a number of interacting subsystems. To understand an individual child's development and personality, therefore, the whole family system and its subsystems must be considered and investigated.

REVIEW QUESTIONS

1. What factors interact to shape each parent's style or techniques of child rearing?
2. What is a reinforcer? Under what conditions are reinforcements most effective?
3. What general principles govern the effectiveness of punishment?
4. Give some examples of inductive or nonpunitive strategies for modifying children's behavior.
5. Distinguish between imitation and identification.
6. Researchers have identified four general patterns or styles of parental behavior. Name them and describe each briefly.
7. What effects do siblings have on a child's development?
8. Describe the impacts of divorce and remarriage on preschool and school-age children.
9. What is a systems approach to family interaction?

CRITICAL THINKING ABOUT THE CHAPTER

1. Think about the techniques of child rearing that were used by your parents. What do you think was helpful or not helpful about them? Why do you think your parents had the style they had?
2. Design an intervention designed to reduce child abuse. Think about how you would identify a target audience and what you would say to them. Also, discuss what ethical issues you might face in your work.

KEY TERMS

extinction   minimum-sufficiency principle
identification   reinforcer
imitation   socialization
inductive techniques

SUGGESTED READINGS

Bornstein, M. H. (Ed.) (1995). *Handbook of parenting.* Hillsdale, NJ: Lawrence Erlbaum. A four-volume handbook containing recent treatments of 59 different topics in parenting.

Cicchetti, D., & Carlson, V. (Eds.). (1989). *Child maltreatment: Theory and research on the causes and consequences of child abuse and neglect.* New York: Cambridge University Press. An edited collection containing chapters by the leading experts in the field.

Dunn, J. (1985). *Sisters and brothers.* Cambridge, MA: Harvard University Press. A broad survey of sibling relationships and their impact on development, illustrated with many realistic examples.

Furstenberg, F. F., & Cherlin, A. J. (1991). *Divided families: What happens to children when parents part.* Cambridge, MA: Harvard University Press. An account of what is known about the effects of divorce on children, written by two sociologists who have done a great deal of the relevant research.

Maccoby, E. E., & Mnookin, R. H. (1992). *Dividing the child: Social and legal dilemmas of custody.* Cambridge, MA: Harvard University Press. Written by a developmental psychologist and a lawyer.

CHAPTER

13

SOCIALIZATION BEYOND THE FAMILY

RELATIONSHIPS WITH PEERS

Developmental Changes in Peer Interaction
Peer Relations and Group Structure
Friendship

DAY CARE AND SCHOOL AS CONTEXTS FOR DEVELOPMENT

Day Care and Preschool
Elementary School

TELEVISION AS A SOCIALIZING INFLUENCE

Description of Children's Television Viewing
Parents' Influence on Children's Viewing
Television vs. No Television
How Children Understand Television
What Is Learned from Television?

GOVERNMENT AND ECONOMIC INFLUENCES

Social Trends and Social Policy
Relations Between the Family and Other Social Systems

Letifa is a 10-year-old girl whose parents immigrated to the United States from Saudi Arabia. She is the youngest of six children. Her mother wears traditional Saudi dresses, keeps her head covered in public, and generally retreats quietly to the kitchen when a stranger enters the house. She rarely speaks to adults whom she does not know, perhaps because her English is not very proficient. Letifa's father wears Western clothes but speaks English with a heavy accent. The family are practicing Muslims, and they speak Arabic at home in an attempt to maintain their culture.

Letifa and her older sisters dress in the standard garb of American children and adolescents—blue jeans and sweatshirts. They speak English fluently with no trace of an Arabic accent. The older girls drive cars, go to college, and readily greet visitors to their home. The Americanization evident in their dress and manner also goes deeper: it pervades their values, beliefs, and expectations about human relationships.

In Chapter 12, we discussed how families socialize their children. But an example such as that of Letifa reminds us how many important factors there are in socialization, and that many influences do not come from the family. Why are Letifa and her siblings so different from their parents? Some answers come readily to mind. First, because Letifa's family is the only Saudi family in her community, her friends are all middle-class white Americans. Second, Letifa attends an American school, where the content of the instruction, the teachers' attitudes and personalities, and the social organization of the work are all distinctively Western. Third, the family owns a television and a videocassette recorder. Although the VCR permits the family to watch Arabic language tapes that may help them preserve their original culture, much of their time is spent viewing American television.

Developmental psychologists have increasingly recognized the importance of studying socialization in a wider social context than simply the parent-child relationship (Bronfenbrenner, 1979; Lerner, 1991). As we discussed in Chapter 12, children interact with their parents in a context that encompasses the whole family system, including the husband-wife relationship, siblings and other relatives, and parents' social support networks. In this chapter, we broaden the discussion yet further, to discuss how children are influenced by their classmates and friends, by the schools they attend, and by the mass media. We also study the issue of the effects of economic conditions and government policies on children. Social policy and economics profoundly influence the work lives and economic opportunities of children's parents, as well as the nature of educational and vocational opportunities children are offered.

✦ RELATIONSHIPS WITH PEERS

Children who spend time together at school and in their neighborhoods—or in settings such as Little League teams, church groups or children's theater groups—constitute a miniature society. Peers (that is, age-mates) contribute in unique and major ways to the shaping of a child's personality, social behavior, values, and attitudes. The peer group instructs or trains children in critical social skills that cannot be learned in the same way from adults: how to interact with age-mates, how to relate to a leader, how to deal with hostility and dominance. In later childhood, peers can help one another deal with personal problems and anxieties.

Developmental Changes in Peer Interaction

Children's peer relationships are a central part of their lives. Most preschool children seek out and enjoy their peers, and if they find themselves alone they are likely to try to join ongoing activities with others (Corsaro, 1981). During the preschool years, children have sharp increases in the strength of their attachment to peers generally (Almy, Monighan, Scales, & Van Hoorn, 1983), and their social relationships—primarily between playmates of the same sex—become closer, more frequent, and more sustained. Communication improves as children accommodate their language to that of their peers. Also, as they become older, children are more willing to participate in joint efforts, coordinate their activities more effectively, and often collaborate successfully in solving problems (C. R. Cooper, 1977).

Compared with younger children, school-age children engage in more task-

Children's peer groups provide children with critical social skills not easily learned from adults.

related interactions, which tend to be increasingly better organized (P. K. Smith, 1977). Cooperation and other kinds of prosocial behavior, such as sharing and altruism, increase throughout the school years, while aggression and quarreling decrease. With greater understanding of other people's motivations and intentions and improved use of feedback from others, communication among peers becomes more effective and more highly valued (Hartup, Brady, & Newcomb, 1981). By adolescence, time spent with peers exceeds time spent with adults, including parents (Hartup, 1970; Medrich, Rosen, Rubin, & Buckley, 1982).

The primary vehicle for the development of relationships with peers is play with other children. We already examined the early development of play in Chapter 7. While solitary and parallel play are common in preschoolers, by 5 years the predominant mode of play has shifted to group play (Monighan-Nourot, Scales, Van Hoorn, & Almy, 1987). The proportion of pretend or dramatic group play rises steadily between the ages of 3 and 6 or 7; over time this form of play gradually becomes more elaborate. At school age, we also see the beginning of games with rules, which require the cognitive ability to understand and accept rules, as well as the ability to deal with competitiveness. Participation in simple group games and board games generally begins between the ages of 4 and 7, but participation in games with more abstract rules is more likely during the period from age 7 to age 12 (Eifermann, 1970; K. H. Rubin et al., 1983).

Age-related changes in social interaction and play are to some extent a function of increasing skill in role taking, that is, the ability to put oneself mentally in someone else's position. It has been hypothesized that underlying role-taking ability is empathy—or the recognition, understanding, and vicarious feeling of another person's emotions (Feshbach, 1978). As noted in Chapter 7, 2- and 3-year-olds already show a basic awareness of other people's feelings and desires, recognizing such states as happiness, sadness, and anger. However, after seeing another child fall and hurt herself, a toddler may not know how to help the distressed child effectively, although she may give attention and affection, express sympathy, or offer him a toy (Dunn & Kendrick, 1979; Rheingold, Hay, & West, 1976). Skills in perspective or role taking are manifested much more clearly in the early elementary school years (LeMare & Rubin, 1987).

To trace the development of role-taking skills from the preschool period through adolescence, Robert Selman presented children of various ages with story dilemmas designed to elicit reasoning about social or moral situations. Here is an example:

> Holly is an 8-year-old girl who likes to climb trees. She is the best tree climber in the neighborhood. One day while climbing down from a tall tree, she falls off the bottom branch but does not hurt herself. Her father sees her fall. He is upset and asks her to promise not to climb trees any more. Holly promises.
>
> Later that day, Holly and her friends meet Shawn. Shawn's kitten is caught up in a tree and can't get down. Something has to be done right away, or the kitten may fall. Holly is the only one who climbs trees well enough to reach the kitten and get it down, but she remembers her promise to her father (Selman, 1980, p. 36).

After reading children a story, Selman asked questions such as: "Does Holly know how Shawn feels about the kitten? Why?" "How will Holly's father feel if he finds out she climbed the tree?" "What does Holly think her father will think of her if he finds out?" The responses were coded for the child's explanation of the thoughts and feelings of each individual in the story and the relationships among their various perspectives. The data indicated that role-taking skills develop through a series of qualitatively distinct stages, described in Table 13.1.

Role-taking ability is correlated with general intelligence (Shantz, 1983) and with moral behavior, including altruism, helping, sharing, and consideration for others. Deficiencies in role-taking skills are characteristic of juvenile delinquents, and training in perspective taking may sometimes help reduce their problem behaviors (Chandler, 1973).

With more extensive social experience and advances in cognitive abilities—particularly role-taking skills and the ability to conceptualize thoughts and feelings—children's conceptions of others become more abstract, more complex, and more focused on psychological (rather than external) characteristics. In fact, developmental trends in conceptions of others are strikingly parallel to the changes in self-concept and self-description reviewed in Chapter 11. When asked, "Tell me about Bill" or "What sort of person is Edna?" children younger than age 7 usually refer to external, concrete attributes such as physical characteristics, appearance, possessions, and overt behavior. Although they frequently use global evaluative adjectives like *good*, *bad*, *mean*, and *nice*, they do not usually refer to psychological attributes. In middle childhood, beginning around age 8, there are major changes in person perceptions. We see increased use of abstract adjectives referring to traits, motives, beliefs, values, and attitudes (Livesley & Bromley, 1973; Peevers & Secord, 1973).

TABLE 13.1 Stages in the Development of Role-Taking Skills

Stage	*Age*	*Skills*
0: Egocentric viewpoint	Below 5	Young children fail to distinguish between their own interpretation of an event and someone else's. Children at this stage do not realize that others can see a social situation differently than they do. For example, in response to the question "How will Holly's father feel when he finds out?" the child says, "Happy; he likes kittens."
1: Social informational role taking	5–8	Children are aware that other people have different perspectives, thoughts, and feelings about things because they are in different situations or have different information. A child might say, "Holly's father will be mad because he doesn't want her to climb trees."
2: Self-reflection	8–10	Children recognize that each individual is aware of other people's thoughts and feelings and knows that the other person is also aware of the child's perspective. Moreover, the child is conscious of the fact that this mutual awareness influences each person's view of the other. For example, a child who was asked, "Will Holly's father punish her?" replied, "She knows her father will understand why she climbed the tree, so he won't punish her."
3: Mutual role taking	10–12	Children can consider an interaction simultaneously from their own point of view and from that of another person, and recognize that the other person can do the same. The child can take the perspective of a disinterested third person—an onlooker, parent, or mutual friend—and anticipate how each participant (including herself) will react to the viewpoint of the partner. A question about her father might be answered in this way: "Holly and her father trust each other, so they can talk about why she climbed the tree."
4: Social and conventional system role taking	12–15+ to adult	Children realize that there are integrated networks of perspectives that are shared by the members of a group, such as an "American" or "Catholic" point of view. "The subject realizes that each self considers the shared point of view of the social system in order to facilitate accurate communication with and understanding of others."

Source: After "Social Cognitive Understanding: A Guide to Educational and Clinical Practice," by R. L. Selman, in *Moral Development and Behavior: Theory, Research, and Social Issues,"* (pp. 302–307), edited by T. Likona, 1976, New York: Holt, Rinehart and Winston. Adapted with permission.

The descriptions given by children age 12 to 14 are generally better organized and show greater sensitivity to the complexity (and sometimes contradictory nature) of personality characteristics and behavior. Qualifying terms such as *sometimes* and *quite* are used frequently, and explanations of behavior are common. At this age children seem to understand that an individual's behavior depends not only on personality traits but also on situations and cognitive factors (Shantz, 1983). The following is a 15-year-old's description of a friend:

Andy is very modest. He is even shyer than I am when near strangers and yet is very talkative with people he knows and likes. He always seems good tempered and I have never seen him in a bad temper. He tends to degrade other people's achievements, and yet never praises his own. He does not seem to voice his opinions to anyone. He easily gets nervous (Livesley & Bromley, 1973, p. 221).

Peer Relations and Group Structure

Within any classroom or social group, some children are popular with their peers and some are not. Social status may be evaluated by means of observation, particularly in nursery school. More commonly, researchers have used what are called **sociometric techniques**. Children respond to questions such as "Who in the class is your best friend?" and "Who are the ones that aren't liked by others?" by listing the names of classmates. Another technique is to ask children to cast a "class play" by giving names of classmates who would be most appropriate for specific kinds of roles (Masten, Morison, & Pellegrini, 1985). On the basis of such peer nominations, children can be classified as popular (receiving many positive and few negative mentions); rejected (receiving many negative and few positive nominations); controversial (receiving both high negative and high positive nominations); and neglected or ignored (receiving neither positive nor negative nominations). In addition, some children are average, not fitting any of the four extreme groups. During the school years the statuses of "popular" and "ignored" are fairly stable, and the status of "rejected" is highly stable (Coie & Dodge, 1983; Hymel, Rubin, Rowden, & LeMare, 1990).

What determines whether children are popular or unpopular, accepted or rejected by their peers? Studies on this topic have been reviewed recently by Newcomb, Bukowski, and Pattee (1993). Popular children, as one might expect, prove to have a wide array of cognitive and social competencies. They have well-developed role-taking skills (Kurdek & Krile, 1982) and friendly, outgoing, sympathetic orientations toward others (Renshaw & Asher, 1983). They understand effective ways of interacting; for instance, when asked how they would react in several hypothetical social situations (e.g., observing a child being teased), popular first-, second-, and third-graders are more likely than less popular children to suggest solutions that are active, assertive, and likely to maintain and advance positive relationships (Asher & Renshaw, 1981; Putallaz, 1987). Popular children are also likely to have personal characteristics that are highly valued by the culture in which a child is raised, such as physical attractiveness (Cavior & Dokecki, 1973; Lerner & Lerner, 1977).

Rejected children are more frequently the initiators or targets of teasing, fighting, and arguing, and they act in immature, antisocial, disruptive, inappropriate, or deviant ways (Asher & Hymel, 1981; Gottman, 1977). Overall, they are high in aggression and withdrawal and low in sociability and incognitive skills (Newcomb et al., 1993). However, it may be possible to distinguish distinct subgroups of rejected children. Bierman, Smoot, and Aumiller (1993) found that aggressive-rejected boys were a distinct group from nonaggressive rejected boys; the nonaggressive rejected boys were high in social awkwardness and insensitivity. Interestingly, not all aggressive boys were rejected. Those aggressive boys who were rejected had more severe conduct problems, however, and were less adaptable.

Nonaggressive rejected boys may actually be very submissive and may be the victims of chronic bullying. D. Schwartz, Dodge, and Coie (1993) found that 6- and 8-year-old boys who came to be victimized by their peers as they got acquainted showed initially high levels of submissiveness and nonassertiveness,

Aggression often (but not invariably) leads to social rejection.

which seemed to lead to cyclically increasing patterns of aggression against them and to peer dislike.

Neglected children seem to be low in both aggression and sociability (Newcomb et al., 1993). There may be a variety of kinds of social withdrawal (K. H. Rubin & Asendorpf, 1993). Being nonsocial when in a social situation may consist in being reticent (hovering on the edge of the action), in engaging oneself in quiet and constructive solitary activity, or in active solitary play (such as self-dramatizing). These three behaviors are quite distinct in preschoolers. Reticence is associated with shyness and anxiety, while active solitary play is associated with impulsivity (Coplan, Rubin, Fox, Calkins, & Stewart, 1994). Quiet solitary play may be adaptive in preschoolers, but it appears to become associated with reticence and related to anxiety and low social competence by 7 to 9 years of age (Asendorpf, 1991; K. H. Rubin & Mills, 1988).

Controversial children are an interesting but relatively little-studied group of children. They appear to be individuals who are high in undesirable qualities such as aggression but who are also high in cognitive and social skills (Newcomb et al., 1993). Their mix of attractive and unattractive qualities is likely the basis for the fact that others may both like and dislike them.

Styles of interacting with peers may be acquired in—and generalized from—children's relationships within their families. When interacting with their first-graders, mothers of unpopular children were more negative and controlling than mothers of high-status children. Mothers of high-status children were more likely to interact in positive, agreeable ways and showed more concern with their own and their children's feelings (Putallaz, 1987). In another study, fathers' and mothers' emotional expressiveness was found to be linked to their children's acceptance by peers (Cassidy, Parke, Butkovsky, & Braungart, 1992). It may be that families who express their emotions clearly may help children develop skills for effective interaction with peers.

Children's relationships with peers seem to be sensitive indicators of later outcome. Rejected children, especially those who are aggressive, are at risk for later problems such as theft and truancy, dropping out of school, and criminal behavior (Achenbach & Edelbrock, 1981; Coie & Cillessen, 1993; Hymel et al., 1990; Morison & Masten, 1991; Parker & Asher, 1987; Roff, Sells, & Golden, 1972). It has been less clear whether social sensitivity and isolation have long-term predictive value, but recent studies indicate some relationships. Hymel et al. found that social isolation in second grade predicted problems with fearfulness and anxiety in fifth grade. In another study, children observed in elementary school were followed up seven years later, as adolescents. Earlier sensitivity and isolation were associated with less peer acceptance in adolescence. For boys, sensitivity also predicted less involvement in sports and in organizations and lower self-esteem. The greater significance of social sensitivity for boys than for girls is consistent with findings of Caspi, Elder, and Bem (1988) that, while childhood shyness did not predict psychopathology for either men or women, men who were shy as children took longer to achieve stable careers and marriages.

Fortunately, both isolated and rejected children can sometimes be coached in the kinds of skills that are effective in establishing better social relationships. Socially isolated third- and fourth-grade children have been found to gain greater acceptance from peers after they had participated in five sessions of instruction and practice in social skills such as cooperation (e.g., taking turns and sharing things) and communication (conversing with another child). A year later these children showed further gains in popularity (Oden & Asher, 1977; Shantz, 1983).

For preschool children, Myrna Shure and George Spivak (Spivak & Shure, 1976; Shure & DiGeronimo, 1994) believe that the difficulties experienced by children in their social relationships are due at least in part to lack of understanding of others and lack of skill in social problem solving. They therefore developed extensive training programs to teach preschool children three types of skills.

One skill was finding alternatives—generating as many different solutions to a problem situation as possible. For example, children were shown some pictures and were told, "Johnny wants a chance to play with this shovel, but Jimmy keeps on playing with it. What can Johnny do so he can have a chance to play with the shovel?" The children were encouraged to think of as many different possibilities as they could. A second skill was anticipating the consequences of actions. For instance, a child character was described as having taken an object, such as a flashlight, from an adult without asking. The children were asked to anticipate how the adult might react. The third skill was understanding cause and effect. In one story, the children were told, "Debbie is crying. She is talking to her mother." They were encouraged to speculate about why the events in the story were happening, that is, to suggest that someone may have hit Debbie or that she might have fallen.

Teachers rated the behavioral adjustment of children before and after the training. Among the children who were initially poorly adjusted, those who received the training were rated as better adjusted afterward, whereas those who did not receive the training had not improved. These findings support the notion that specific cognitive skills can help children function more successfully in their social relationships.

Friendship

Outside the family circle, the child's most significant social relationships are with friends. There seems to be an important distinction between being accepted by a peer group and having a mutual relationship with an age-mate (Bukowski & Hoza, 1989). A classic discussion of children's friendships by Sullivan (1953) suggested that true friendships emerge in the preadolescent period, when interpersonal needs fulfilled earlier in the context of the peer group develop into a need for intimacy and personal disclosure. In Sullivan's view, having a friend—or what Sullivan called a "chum"—at the age of 9 or 10 years constituted a key developmental step in interpersonal development. Lacking such a relationship could inhibit the development of the ability to engage in truly intimate relationships as an adult. Sullivan also suggested that it was at this age that children first became able to experience the emotion of loneliness, based on missing an intimate. Children not with their parents experience anxiety and children without playmates experience boredom; only when true friendship began was loneliness possible.

Empirical research on friendship has been inspired by Sullivan's theorizing, although much of the work has been generally descriptive in nature and has not actually tested the theory (Newcomb & Bagwell, 1995). In this section, we examine what is known about three topics: children's concepts of friendship; how children form friendships; and how children maintain relationships at different ages and maintain them differently with friends than with acquaintances.

Concepts of Friendship. As would be expected, children's ideas of friendship change as they mature. To investigate children's conceptions of friendship,

Ten-year-old girls playing Monopoly. Sullivan suggested that true intimacy in friendship first arose at about this age.

researchers use interview techniques ("Who is your best friend?" "Why is Nancy your best friend?") (Damon, 1977; Selman, 1980; Youniss, 1980) or present children with hypothetical dilemmas and ask questions about them (Selman, 1976b). For example, in one dilemma two girls, Kathy and Debbie, have been friends since they were 5. A new girl, Jeanette, moves into their neighborhood. Jeanette invites Kathy to go to the circus with her on a day that Kathy has promised to play with Debbie. Questions follow about what Kathy will do and about friendship and social relationships.

According to some theorists, there are stages in the development of conceptions of friendship that parallel the stages in the development of role-taking skills (Selman, 1981). Thus, although many preschool children form friendships with each other, they are not concerned with lasting relationships and characteristically view friends as "momentary physical playmates"; to them, a friend is whomever one is playing with at the time (Z. Rubin, 1980). Older children, however, think of friendships as relationships that continue beyond single, brief interactions. Between the age of 5 and adolescence, children's conceptions of friendship evolve through three major levels (Damon, 1977). At the first level, which is typical of 5- to 7-year-olds, friends are the playmates whom the child sees most frequently, usually neighbors or schoolmates. They share things such as food and toys, "act nice," and are "fun to be with." Friendships have no permanent status and are easily established and terminated; there is no sense of liking or disliking the stable personal traits of another child. One 5-year-old reported that "when I don't play with them they don't like me" (Damon, 1977, p. 156).

Between the ages of 8 and 11, children regard friends as people with whom they cooperate, exchange good deeds, and share. Mutual trust, shared interests, reciprocity, response to each other's needs, and possession of desirable attributes such as kindness and considerateness are also critical features of friendships. Thus, Betty, age 10, likes Karen "because she's nice; she gives me jewelry and candy, and I give her things, too" (Damon, 1977, p. 158).

Beginning at about 12 years of age, friendships are judged in terms of mutual understanding and sharing of thoughts, feelings, and other secrets, and they are usually stable over long periods. Friends help each other handle psychological problems such as loneliness and fear, and they avoid upsetting each other. According to one 13-year-old boy, "You need someone you can tell anything to, all kinds of things that you don't want spread around. That's why you are someone's friend" (Damon, 1977, p. 163).

Forming Friendships. If you ask children how to make friends, their answers will reflect their conceptions of friendship. Thus, for young children the way to form a friendship is simply to play with another child. Older children view the process as more complicated and gradual; friendships become deeper as people gain greater insight into one another's traits, interests, and values. A 13-year-old said, "You don't really pick your friends, it just grows on you. You find out that you can talk to someone, you can tell them your problems, when you understand each other" (Z. Rubin, 1980, p. 35).

The social processes involved in becoming friends were investigated in two complementary studies in which the conversations of pairs of children between the ages of 3 and 9 were tape-recorded while they were playing together. In the first study, the interactions of children playing with their best friends were compared with those of children playing with strangers their own age. Six social processes related to friendship formation were examined: (1) connectedness and communication clarity, (2) information exchange, (3) establishing common ground, (4) resolution of conflict, (5) positive reciprocity, and (6) self-disclosure. These are defined in Table 13.2. Children playing with friends surpassed those playing with strangers in the manifestation of all six of these social processes.

In the second study, the investigator attempted to trace children's progress toward friendship by pairing previously unacquainted children for three sessions and recording their conversations. Among these children, those who hit it off and were likely to become friends scored higher on each of the six social dimensions than children who did not become friendly with each other. The researcher concluded that when two unacquainted children meet, they need to begin with simple interaction—exchanging information, establishing shared activities, and managing any conflicts that arise. As the relationship proceeds, they need to communicate clearly and exchange information, exploring similarities and differences and engaging in self-disclosure (Gottman, 1983). (See Box 13.1 for a literary account of the formation of a new friendship.)

A parent's style of interacting with his or her child may serve as a model for the child's approach to strangers who are potential friends. Children in the first grade were observed as they played a game with their mothers and as they played with age-mates whom they had not met before. Children of disagreeable, demanding, and highly controlling mothers were characteristically preoccupied with themselves

TABLE 13.2 Social Processes in Friendship Formation

Process	Definition	Example
1. Communication clarity and connectedness	Request for clarification of a message followed by appropriate clarification.	"Which truck do you want?" "The dumpster."
2. Information exchange	A question-answer sequence; one child asks a question and the other answers.	"Hey, you know what?" "No, what?" "Sometime you can come to my house."
3. Establishing common ground	Finding something to do together or exploring similarities and differences.	"Let's play house." "We're both 4."
4. Conflict resolution	Successfully resolving arguments and disagreements.	"Give me the green crayon." "No, I'm using it; here, try the blue one." "OK. That's just as good."
5. Positive reciprocity	One child responds to the other's positive behavior and extends a positive interchange, as in chains of gossip, joking, or fantasy.	"Katie's too bossy." "Yeah, and she's mean, too."
6. Self-disclosure	One child asks about the other's feelings, and the other expresses her feelings.	"Are you scared of taking swimming lessons?" "Yeah, I'm scared of the water. You scared?" "Not anymore."

Source: After "How Children Become Friends," by J. M. Gottman, 1983, *Monographs of the Society for Research in Child Development, 48* (Serial No. 201). Adapted with permission.

Box 13.1
A FAMOUS FRIENDSHIP

Children need friends as well as loving adults in order to be happy and to grow up in a healthy way. In the following passage taken from a well-known book, Anne Shirley, who has recently acquired parental figures when adopted by Matthew and Marilla Cuthbert, makes a friend.

When Marilla and Anne went home Diana went with them as far as the log bridge. The two little girls walked with their arms about each other. At the brook they parted with many promises to spend the next afternoon together.

"Well, did you find Diana a kindred spirit?" asked Marilla as they went up through the garden of Green Gables.

"Oh, yes," sighed Anne, blissfully unconscious of any sarcasm on Marilla's part. "Oh, Marilla, I'm the happiest girl on Prince Edward Island this very moment. I assure you I'll say my prayers with a right good-will tonight. Diana and I are going to build a playhouse in Mr. William Bell's birch grove tomorrow. Can I have those pieces of broken china that are out in the woodshed? Diana's birthday is in February and mine is in March. Don't you think that is a very strange coincidence? Diana is going to lend me a book to read. She says it's perfectly splendid and tremenjusly exciting. She's going to show me a place back in the woods where rice liles grow. Don't you think Diana has got very soulful eyes? I wish I had soulful eyes. Diana is going to teach me to sing a song called 'Nelly in the Hazel Dell.' She's going to give me a picture to put up in my room; it's a perfectly beautiful picture, she says—a lovely lady in a pale blue silk dress. A sewing-machine agent gave it to her. I wish I had something to give Diana. I'm an inch taller than Diana, but she is ever so much fatter; she says she'd like to be thin because it's so much more graceful, but I'm afraid she only said it to soothe my feelings. We're going to the shore some day to gather shells. We have agreed to call the spring down by the log bridge the Dryad's Bubble. Isn't that a perfectly elegant name? I read a story once about a spring called that. A dryad is a sort of grown-up fairy, I think."

"Well, all I hope is you won't talk Diana to death," said Marilla.

Source: From *Anne of Green Gables,* by L. M. Montgomery.

---

and with getting their own way when interacting with other children—behavior that hardly made them attractive as friends. The results of this study are consistent with what one might expect when behaviors are modeled by an adult (Putallaz, 1987).

Maintaining Friendships. As we have seen, early friendships are often fragile; they are quickly formed and easily terminated. Yet even in the preschool years some children maintain strong bonds of friendship. Such friendships are generally formed with children who live nearby, share interests and favorite activities, and have interesting playthings; however, there is no single basis for these friendships (D. S. Hayes, 1978). The friendships of preschool children have many functions. According to one researcher, "Friends are security givers, standards against whom one can measure oneself, partners in activities that cannot be engaged in alone, guides to unfamiliar places, and apprentices who confirm one's own developing sense of competence and expertise" (Z. Rubin, 1980, p. 69).

Schoolchildren tend to select friends of their own age, sex, and race (Asher,

Singleton, & Taylor, 1982; Kandel, 1978; Singleton & Asher, 1979). In middle childhood, friends tend to share interests, attitudes, social orientations (e.g., the tendency to seek or avoid social participation), and values, but they do not generally resemble each other closely in intelligence or personality characteristics (Byrne & Griffitt, 1966; Challman, 1932; Davitz, 1955). In adolescence, college-bound children are likely to have college-bound friends, while those who are not planning to go to college choose friends whose educational goals are similar to their own (O. D. Duncan, Featherman, & Duncan, 1972).

As children grow older, their friendships become more stable and enduring. The fourth- and eighth-graders in one study answered questionnaires about their friendships at both the beginning and the end of the school year. Over two-thirds of those who were close friends at the beginning of the year were still close friends at the end. Enduring friendships were characterized by frequent interactions and a high degree of liking for each other, whereas unstable friendships were relatively lacking in intimacy at both times measured. Not surprisingly, the children who were involved in weaker friendships reported less intimacy and less similarity to their friends—and more disloyalty or unfaithfulness—in the spring than they had in the fall. In evaluating their friendships, eighth-graders emphasized intimacy and stimulation more than fourth-graders did, and girls stressed intimacy, loyalty, and faithfulness more than boys did (Berndt, Hawkins, & Hoyle, 1986).

A recent review of the literature on children's friendships (Newcomb & Bagwell, 1995) reveals that friends do not differ from acquaintances in the frequency with which they are in conflict. Friendships are not uniformly harmonious. But friends do differ from acquaintances in how much they are concerned with conflict resolution. When they fight, friends want to make up. This fact suggests support for an idea that can be traced back to Sullivan: that friendships are vital to children's developing skills in maintaining close interpersonal ties with equals, skills that are central to life as an adult.

Friends may also foster each other's cognitive and emotional growth in other ways. Azmitia and Montgomery (1993) point out that friends are more likely than acquaintances to exchange ideas in a candid way, testing them and engaging in collaborative resolutions. This may help to build identity and understanding of the world. On the other hand, Berndt (1993) has reminded us that friendships also involve teasing, rivalry, and conflict. These painful features of some friendships may lead to negative effects on development and need investigation.

✺ DAY CARE AND SCHOOL AS CONTEXTS FOR DEVELOPMENT

In the first part of the chapter, we examined the importance of peers and friends for children's social development. In industrialized societies, much of this interaction with age-mates takes place in the context of organized group settings. Children generally begin formal schooling sometime between the ages of 5 and 7, but for increasing numbers of children, socialization in a school context begins much earlier, as they attend preschools, Head Start programs, or day care centers. All these kinds of schools constitute small social systems, in which children learn rules of morality, social conventions, attitudes, and modes of relating to others, as well as academic skills.

Day Care and Preschool

For years many middle-class children in the United States and other industrialized countries have attended preschools designed to provide them with social and intellectual stimulation for a few hours a week. Early-education programs like Head Start have been available to a few children from low-income American families since the 1960s, but the vast majority have not had access to such services (Children's Defense Fund, 1987). Expansion of Head Start is, however, planned for the 1990s (Kassebaum, 1994; Takanishi & DeLeon, 1994). In addition, in recent decades mothers of young children have entered the labor market in increasing numbers, and many of their children have been placed in day care arrangements of various kinds. In this section, we discuss two topics about the existence and structuring of early-childhood group experiences that are currently under debate.

Effects of Early Group Care. While early education for a few hours a day before the age of 5 is uncontroversial, there has been much discussion recently about the effects of more extended periods in group settings for young children. We have already discussed the controversy over infant day care in Chapter 6, concluding that separation from an attachment figure does not appear to lead to negative outcomes when there is high-quality care. Here, we revisit the issue of day care, concentrating on studies of preschoolers and looking at what determines the quality of a program for preschool children.

Studies of the correlates of being in day care have produced mixed results. In some studies children who have participated in day care are more socially skilled, cooperative, and task oriented than children who have spent their preschool years at home (D. Phillips, McCartney, & Scarr, 1987). Moreover, it has been found that the longer children are in day care, the more time they spend in social participation and constructive play rather than being unoccupied or watching others play (Schindler, Moely, & Frank, 1987). On the other hand, children with day care experience have also been found to be more poorly adjusted, less compliant, and more aggressive than children with less such experience (Baydar & Brooks-Gunn, 1991; Haskins, 1985; Vandell & Corasiniti, 1990). One study found a mixture of positive and negative results, with day care experience related to less positive and more negative adjustment in kindergarten, but also to lower amounts of internalizing problems such as fearfulness and anxiety (J. E. Bates, Marvinney, et al., 1994).

What is going on here? Actually, it should be no surprise that the effects of day care are not uniform; the care provided varies greatly in both form and quality. The quality of day care has been shown to have important effects on the short- and long-term effects on children's social and academic development. For instance, Howes and Stewart (1987) studied a group of children from 11 to 30 months old who were in family day care, that is, group care in someone's home. They evaluated both the quality of the child care and characteristics of the children's homes. The children's peer interactions were rated for competence, defined by the extent of complementary and interactive interchanges with peers. Play with objects was rated for complexity and originality. Both the quality of child care and the attributes of the home contributed to the children's peer interactions and competent play. Children in high-quality child care played more competently than those in low-quality care. These differences existed even when family characteristics were equated. Families that were nurturant and had strong support systems had children who played

High-quality preschool environments are associated with good outcomes for children.

more competently than children from families that were restrictive and were experiencing high levels of stress.

Howes (1988b) also conducted a longitudinal investigation of children who had entered high- and low-quality care during their infant and preschool years. Children who had experienced low-quality care were less compliant and less likely to show self-regulation as toddlers; they were less competent with peers as preschoolers; and they were more hostile and less task oriented in kindergarten. These effects were more pronounced for children who entered low-quality care before their first birthday, but they were also observed for children who entered child care between ages 1 and 4.

An increasing number of studies support the commonsense idea that day care of high quality supports healthy development while day care of low quality impedes it. For instance, Vandell, Henderson, and Wilson (1988) found that children in better-quality day care were more socially competent and happier at age 8 than children in lower-quality care. Howes, Phillips, and Whitebook (1992) observed that high-quality day care was associated with secure attachment to teachers and to peer competence. Secure attachment to teachers is associated in turn with lower aggression and more complex play (Howes, Hamilton, & Matheson, 1994).

Not all researchers accept the idea that any effects of day care on children are basically the result of high- versus low-quality care (e.g., J. E. Bates et al., 1994). Other possible mediators of effects of day care, such as variation in family stress levels, may be important. However, no observers argue that quality of care is unimportant for children. Thus, it is important to define what constitutes high-quality care for preschool children.

One important component of quality care is adult-child interaction, particularly verbal interaction. Children in centers with frequent adult-child interaction learn language earlier, gain better communication skills, and acquire more social skills than children in centers with low rates of interaction (McCartney, Scarr, Phillips, & Grajek, 1985). The smaller the group of children and the higher the ratio of adults to children, the more adults talk to children. Caregiver training is also important; caregivers with specialized training in working with young children often provide a richer experience than that provided by untrained caregivers (Whitebook, Howes, & Phillips, 1990).

The physical setting, group size, and play materials are also important determinants of quality. Most states have regulations about minimum amount of space per child and other aspects of the physical environment, but these are often less than optimal. Experimental study has documented the effects of such physical variables on children. When children in different play groups were randomly assigned to classes with different environmental characteristics, and their behavior was observed over the course of an entire school year, the results showed that children in large groups spent more time doing "table activities," did more chasing and rough-and-tumble play, and spent more time in same-sex interactions than did children in small groups. When groups were small, children engaged in more fantasy and imaginative play. Density, or space per child, did not have many effects on behavior except when spaces were very crowded (15 square feet per child). In such cases there was a decrease in cooperative play and some increase in aggression. Amount of equipment was more important than amount of space. When classes had several of each type of plaything, children were less aggressive and less likely to cry than they were when there were only one or two of each item. But in settings with scarce equipment, children shared equipment and played together more (P. K. Smith & Connolly, 1980).

These findings suggest that a preschool classroom that is crowded or inadequately equipped may produce aggression and other kinds of stress for children. On the other hand, small spaces can be carefully organized, and children can learn to share when equipment is limited. In addition, the effects of space and equipment may depend on the child's culture and other experiences. For instance, in Holland, where living quarters are typically small, children displayed positive social interactions and little solitary play in preschools with only 12.5 square feet of space per child (Fagot, 1977).

Toys and activities also affect the nature of play and social interaction among children. Blocks often elicit aggression and, not surprisingly, constructive play. Art and fine motor activities (e.g., playing with Lego blocks) tend to reduce social interaction; children often participate in these activities by themselves. Housekeeping and dramatic play centers stimulate cooperation and role taking (Pellegrini, 1985; Stoneman, Cantrell, & Hoover-Dempsey, 1983).

The attributes of quality day care are not unique to day care settings. The nature of parent-child interaction, the availability of appropriate toys and materials, and freedom to explore in a context of organized routines are important aspects of children's home environments. There exist clear standards for quality day care, known as the Federal Interagency Day Care Requirements (FIDCR). However, although these criteria were developed in the early 1980s and have been shown to relate to child outcome (Howes, Phillips, & Whitebook, 1992), they have never been fully implemented.

Adult Structuring. Whether preschool group experience is extensive or limited to a few hours in the morning, some disagreement exists about what kind of experience is most beneficial for children. In one way of looking at this issue, teachers' methods can be classified along a continuum from teacher-directed to learner-directed. High levels of adult structuring or teacher direction occur when the teacher tells children which activity or task they should carry out, gives them directions about how to do the task, provides written instructions, or offers specific praise or criticism for their performance. Low levels of structure occur when children choose their own activities and tasks and decide how they should be carried out without adult direction. Of course, there are many points on this continuum, and some people argue that intermediate levels of structure provide opportunities that do not occur at either extreme. Variations in structure can also exist within a classroom. Some activities may be closely supervised while others are relatively unsupervised.

Observations and experimental studies in preschool classrooms show that children in highly structured classes or activities attend well during learning tasks, comply with teachers' directions, and turn to the teacher for approval and recognition. They also follow classroom rules and procedures, such as putting away materials after using them, with relatively few reminders from teachers. They spend a lot of time interacting with the teacher and relatively little time in peer interactions.

Low structure, by contrast, encourages positive interactions with peers—helping, cooperation, empathy—as well as aggression, assertiveness, and leadership. Children in less structured classes and activities also spend more time in fantasy and imaginative play (A. C. Huston & Carpenter, 1985; Huston-Stein, Friedrich-Cofer, & Susman, 1977; P. K. Smith & Connolly, 1980; N. G. Thomas & Berk, 1981). One author concludes that low levels of structure encourage children to create their own structure in play activities, while high levels of structure encourage them to adopt or fit into structures offered by others (Carpenter, 1983).

Structure is not always imposed on children; both in classrooms and at home children can often choose among different activities. From the early preschool years on, girls are more likely to select activities structured by adults, while boys more often select less-structured activities. This sex difference was evident in observations of preschool children in a number of classrooms over the course of several months. Although different activities were structured by adults in different classrooms, girls chose structured activities more often than boys did (Carpenter, 1983). This difference was even more striking in observations of 8- to 10-year-olds in a day camp where identical activities were available with and without adult structuring. Girls participated in the adult-structured activities 60 percent of the time, whereas boys did so 35 percent of the time (A. C. Huston et al., 1986). Children's responses to structure illustrate an important principle: Although environments influence behavior, children also choose their environments. Scarr and McCartney (1983) refer to this process as "niche building," as discussed in Chapter 2.

Elementary School

The social structure of elementary schools is a very different topic from the structure of preschools, in large part because education from the age of 5 or 6 years is

Box 13.2

SCHOOL AS A CONTEXT FOR DEVELOPMENT IN NINETEENTH-CENTURY ENGLAND

Schools in the United States and elsewhere have typically been the target of a great deal of criticism; school reform has probably been a topic of conversation since shortly after schooling began. However, in thinking about the current failures of our schools and inventing ways in which they could be improved, it is important to have historical perspective. When Charles Dickens wrote *Nicholas Nickleby* in 1838, his caricature of Yorkshire boarding schools was sufficiently based on fact that lawsuits were threatened, reputations were ruined, and several schools closed. In this famous passage, Mr. Squeers, headmaster of Dotheboys Hall, introduces Nicholas to the school and its methods.

"This is the first class in English spelling and philosophy, Nickleby," said Squeers, beckoning Nicholas to stand beside him. "We'll get up a Latin one, and hand that over to you. Now, then, where's the first boy?"

"Please, sir, he's cleaning the back parlour window," said the temporary head of the philosophical class.

"So he is, to be sure," rejoined Squeers. "We go on the practical mode of teaching, Nickleby; the regular education system. C-l-e-a-n, clean, verb active, to make bright, to scour. W-i-n, win, d-e-r, der, winder, a casement. When the boy knows this out of book, he goes and does it. It's just the same principle as the use of the globes. Where's the second boy!"

"Please, sir, he's weeding the garden," replied a small voice.

"To be sure," said Squeers, by no means disconcerted. "So he is. B-o-t, bot, t-i-n, tin, botin, n-e-y, ney, bottinney, noun substantive, a knowledge of plants. When he has learned that bottinney means a knowledge of plants, he goes and knows 'em. That's our system, Nickleby; what do you think of it?"

"It's a very useful one, at any rate," answered Nicholas.

Source: From *Nicholas Nickleby,* by Charles Dickens.

legally mandated and universal in most countries. However, it is interesting to remember that, in the nineteenth century, there was much more variation in the requirements and the ubiquity of schooling for children from 6 to 12 years, and scandalously low-quality schools existed in some cases (see Box 13.2).

In discussing current elementary schooling, we focus on four issues: the effect of teachers' expectancies on children, the effect of cooperative learning groups, racial and ethnic integration, and mainstreaming of physically and cognitively disabled children into regular classrooms.

Teachers' Expectancies. In the late 1960s both educators and the public were startled by the publication of a book called *Pygmalion in the Classroom,* which proposed that teachers' beliefs about a child's IQ could affect that child's performance. The authors argued that children would learn more when teachers expected high performance than when they did not (R. Rosenthal & Jacobson, 1968). Since then a large body of research has accumulated showing that teachers' expectancies can, under some circumstances, affect learning independently of the child's abilities (P. P. Minuchin & Shapiro, 1983; R. Rosenthal, 1976). For example, a teacher may decide that a child who is a little dirty and poorly dressed probably is not very smart; the teacher may then demand less from the child or ignore him. As a result, that child may show lowered performance and have low expectations of success, low motivation, and low self-esteem.

How are teacher expectancies communicated to children? For one thing, teachers are friendlier, smile more often, and show more positive feelings toward the students they consider bright than toward those they think are less able. Children shown video clips of teachers talking to students who are strong or weak academically have been found to be able to guess which student the teacher is addressing, solely on the basis of nonverbal cues (Babad, Bernieri, & Rosenthal, 1991). Also, when a student for whom a teacher has high expectancy fails to answer a question, the teacher often asks the question again, perhaps giving clues and pressing the student to try again. When a low-expectancy student fails to answer the question, the teacher asks someone else, possibly to avoid embarrassing the student. Through these actions teachers unintentionally teach attributions: The high-expectancy student's failure is due to insufficient effort, but the low-expectancy student's failure is due to lack of ability (H. M. Cooper, 1979).

Cooperative Learning vs. Competition. In the traditional American classroom, individual learning is stressed. Children are forbidden to look at another person's paper or talk to other children; they take tests individually; and they receive an evaluation (a grade) that tells them not only how well they did but how their performance compares with that of their classmates. The goal is to promote learning by encouraging individual effort and competition.

Encouraging cooperation among students can also promote learning and better interpersonal relationships among pupils (Slavin, 1987). Cooperative learning programs are based on two critical elements: group interaction or discussion and a group reward structure. For example, in one method children are placed on study teams of about five people; the teams are matched on the basis of previous achievement. Group members study together, discuss the material, and quiz one another. Sometimes each child is given different parts of the material that all members of the group must learn. Then each member of the team is tested to see how well they know the information, and the team whose members do best wins an award. Each student is individually accountable for the material, so the weaker students cannot goof off while the better students do all the work. At the same time, each team member benefits from the successes of the others, so there is a strong incentive to work together (Aronson, Blaney, Stephan, Sikes, & Snapp, 1978; Slavin, 1987).

Cooperative learning structures not only improve learning in some instances but also contribute to positive attitudes toward other students and concern for the welfare of others. In one investigation, children in cooperative learning classrooms showed improved self-esteem, and they liked their classmates better than those in comparison classrooms (Aronson et al., 1978).

Desegregation and Integration. School desegregation was originally ordered by the Supreme Court to provide all children in the nation with an equal opportunity for a good education. However, the effects of desegregation on students' self-perceptions, aspirations, and intergroup relations may be at least as important as its potential effects on academic achievement. Nevertheless, official desegregation does not necessarily lead to social or academic integration. Minority students are often resegregated into different classrooms within a school or different groups within a classroom on the basis of ability and in other ways. Social segregation in

Cooperative learning groups can improve both learning outcomes and social interaction.

lunchrooms and on playgrounds is also common. However, much of this segregation may stem from the fact that ethnicity and socioeconomic status are generally confounded. In a university-based school where students were selected for ethnic and socioeconomic diversity, Howes and Wu (1990) found that cross-ethnic interaction and friendship increased between kindergarten and third grade. For third graders, from 34 percent of friendships (for European-Americans) to 50 percent of friendships (for Asian-Americans) were cross-ethnic, with Hispanic children and African-American children falling in between.

Friendly relations among members of different ethnic groups are more likely when the school organization promotes cooperation rather than competition and when individual achievement is deemphasized. Children in classes using cooperative learning structures have better intergroup relations than children in comparable classes organized more conventionally (Aronson et al., 1978; Hallinan & Teixeira, 1987; P. P. Minuchin & Shapiro, 1983; Slavin, 1987).

Meaningful contact among members of different ethnic groups may be more likely in elementary school, where children spend most of their time in a single classroom, than in junior and senior high school, where they move from class to class. In a longitudinal study of children who entered integrated schools in kindergarten, both black and white children had generally positive attitudes toward members of each group. Children were asked how much they would like to play with and work with each of their classmates. In the third, seventh, and tenth grades, the children's cross-race and own-race ratings were fairly similar. When they were asked who their best friends were, however, their choices were overwhelmingly members of their own race. In the seventh and tenth grades, the students also knew more members of their own group than of the other racial group (Asher, Singleton, & Taylor, 1982).

In sum, school integration alone does not automatically improve self-esteem or intergroup relations, but cooperative, equal-status interactions among children do lead to increased self-esteem and positive intergroup attitudes. Although intergroup relations are often positive in integrated schools, friendships tend to form along ethnic lines. When not extreme, this tendency may be positive, because it helps to facilitate a sense of one's own ethnic identity (Spencer, 1983). Positive intergroup relations are most likely in classrooms where students are similar in level of achievement and social status. Where the backgrounds of children are quite different, mutual respect can be fostered by placing them in cooperative structures in which each person has a valued role to play.

Mainstreaming. The integration of children with physical and mental handicaps into regular classrooms is called **mainstreaming**. Proponents of mainstreaming argue that it provides handicapped children with the best possible opportunities for educational advancement and normal social relations with other children. Like school integration, however, mainstreaming does not always achieve these goals. Some handicapped children who are mainstreamed find that they are stigmatized in the classroom and have relatively fewer social interactions with classmates than handicapped children in special classes do. A number of studies have shown that nonhandicapped children in both preschool and elementary school classes interact more with other nonhandicapped peers than with handicapped children (Ipsa,

Mainstreaming of disabled children needs to be done very carefully to be effective.

1981). Even mildly retarded children were rejected by peers, were anxious and dissatisfied in their peer relationships, and displayed disturbed behavior. Some were shy and withdrawn; others were aggressive and disruptive (A. R. Taylor, Asher, & Williams, 1987). Experiences of rejection may lead to diminished self-esteem and a sense of inadequacy, which may also adversely affect the child's ability to learn (Caparulo & Zigler, 1983).

⚙ TELEVISION AS A SOCIALIZING INFLUENCE

From the beginning of most children's lives, television is an important socializing influence. Television is an "early window" on the outside world, conveying information and values from the broader society in which children live long before they are exposed to formal schooling or to peers (Liebert & Sprafkin, 1988).

Description of Children's Television Viewing

American children spend more time watching television than engaging in any other single activity except sleeping. Popular media often report that children watch an average of 25 to 35 hours of television a week, but most systematic investigations lead to estimates of 12 to 20 hours a week—2 or 3 hours a day. Individual differences are large, with children in one study watching from 0 to almost 76 hours a week (A. C. Huston, Wright, Rice, Kerkman, & St. Peters, 1990). Viewing increases with age until the child enters school; then it drops slightly. It rises again until age 10 to 13; then it declines, probably because adolescents are more mobile and spend more time away from home. Children in families of lower socioeconomic status watch more than children in middle-class families do; within social classes, black children watch more than white children do.

For research purposes, "viewing television" is sometimes defined as being in the same room with an operating television set. Because sets are usually in central living spaces, children may often be present but uninvolved in what others are watching. A group of investigators at the University of Massachusetts videotaped more than 100 families during all of their viewing for ten days. They calculated the percentage of time that each person in the room looked at the set. They found that attention rose rapidly during the preschool years, reaching a peak in middle childhood (D. R. Anderson & Field, 1983) (see Figure 13.1). Clearly, young children become attuned to the television set well before they reach school age.

Television viewing is sometimes discussed as though all TV programs were alike, but they are not. Two distinctions are particularly important: (1) the intended audience—whether the program is designed for children or for adults—and (2) informative content—whether the program is designed to educate and inform about the world or merely to entertain. In a longitudinal study conducted at the University of Kansas, parents of children between the ages of 3 and 7 kept diaries of the family's viewing for one week every six months for two years. The amount of time the children spent viewing different types of programs is shown in Figure 13.2. Two points are especially noteworthy. First, young children spend a large amount of time watching programs that are not designed for children and that they probably do not understand fully. Second, viewing of informative children's pro-

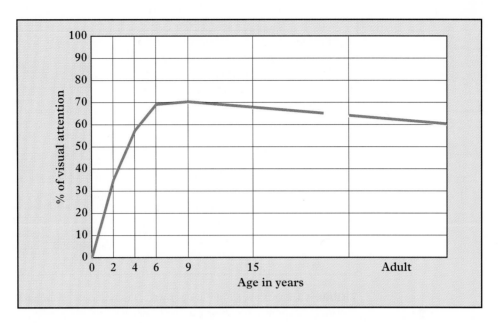

FIGURE 13.1 Percentage of time that children of different ages looked at the television set when it was turned on in their homes. After "Children's Attention to Television: Implications for Production," by D. R. Anderson and D. E. Field, in *Children and the Formal Features of Television*, edited by M. Meyer, 1983, Munich: Saur. Adapted with permission.

gramming drops with age while viewing of cartoons increases, at least until age 5 (A. C. Huston, Wright, Rice, et al., 1990).

Parents' Influence on Children's Viewing

It is often suggested that poor viewing habits arise from lack of parental supervision. Critics envision "latchkey" children as glued to the television set when no adult is at home. Contrary to this view, research suggests that children develop their viewing habits as a result of being with their parents (St. Peters, Fitch, Huston, Wright, & Eakins, 1991). In the University of Kansas study, a parent was present during most (67 percent) of the adult programs watched by 3- to 7-year-olds (see Figure 13.2). Preschool children who stay at home with their mothers watch more television than those whose mothers are employed (Pinon, Huston, & Wright, 1989). Once children reach school age, they watch similar amounts of television whether their mothers are employed or not (Messaris & Hornik, 1983). Thus, it may be true that unsupervised children watch a lot of television, but supervised children do, too. Most parents impose few if any restrictions on their children's viewing.

When parents and children watch television together, the parents can make the experience more profitable for the children, though they do not always take advantage of this opportunity. For example, children learn more from educational television when an adult watches with them than they do by themselves (Salomon, 1977). With very young children, programs like *Sesame Street* can be treated as "talking picture books" that parents and children discuss (Lemish & Rice, 1986). Parents of older children can use television as an occasion to discuss values, morality, and factual information with their children. Increases in the availability of multiple channels on cable and the spread of videotape players give parents a greater

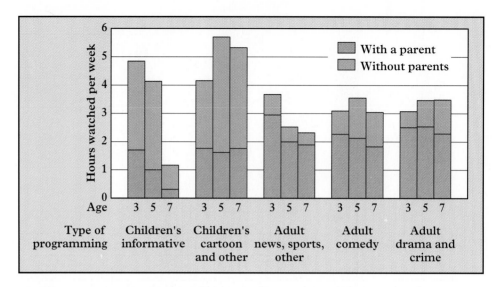

FIGURE 13.2 Number of hours per week that children from ages 3 to 7 watched different categories of television programs with and without their parents. After "Development of Television Viewing Patterns in Early Childhood: A Longitudinal Investigation," by A. C. Huston, J. C. Wright, M. L. Rice, D. Kerkman, and M. St. Peters, 1990, *Developmental Psychology, 26* (pp. 409–420). Adapted with permission.

range of choices in selecting programs to suit their children's needs and level of understanding.

Television vs. No Television

Some critics and theorists suggest that television as a medium, regardless of its content, can affect thought, social activity, and other aspects of life (e.g., Valkenburg & van der Voort, 1994; Winn, 1987). They argue that television replaces family interaction, play, and other activities; that it has negative effects on health and physical fitness and on school achievement; and that it induces passive approaches to learning, reducing creativity and imagination.

These claims are difficult to evaluate with carefully collected evidence because virtually everyone is exposed to television. The small groups of nonviewers cannot be studied for comparison to viewers because they probably differ from television users in many characteristics other than exposure to television. In British Columbia and Australia, however, two different groups of investigators were able to conduct "natural experiments." Each group located a town that did not have television reception as well as towns that were similar in other respects and did receive television (Murray & Kippax, 1978; T. M. Williams, 1986). In this section we discuss their results, along with correlational studies, in relation to the criticisms just noted.

Displacement of Other Activities. Television affects the structure of leisure time, displacing some activities much more than others. When television is introduced, children reduce their use of radio, records, movies, and similar media, but the effect on the time they spend reading is small. Television does lead to reduced participation in some community activities, particularly sports, clubs, dances, and

Parents who watch TV with their children can use the opportunity to discuss important issues.

parties (T. M. Williams, 1986). For adults, there is a corresponding increase in time spent on home hobbies like needlepoint and carpentry, which may be combined with television viewing (Murray & Kippax, 1978). Television does not reduce the time families spend together, but it may reduce their level of interaction (Dorr, 1986).

Health and Physical Fitness. The British Columbia study showed that television viewing leads to reduced participation in sports, which might well affect physical fitness. Large-scale studies in the United States also show a correlation between amount of time spent watching television and obesity. Longitudinal analyses show that childhood viewing predicts adolescent obesity, even when childhood obesity is taken into account (Dietz & Gortmaker, 1985). Children who spend a lot of time watching television are inactive and snack often; both may contribute to obesity.

School Achievement and Cognitive Processes. Large-scale correlational studies consistently show a small relationship between heavy television viewing and low levels of achievement in school. In a review of 23 studies including thousands of children, the pattern shown in Figure 13.3 emerged. For children who watched more than about 10 hours a week, more television viewing was generally associated with lower achievement. However, achievement actually improved with increased television viewing up to about 10 hours a week (P. A. Williams, Haertel, Walberg, & Haertel, 1982).

Several researchers have tried to determine whether the relation between television viewing and low achievement may be due to the fact that both are associated

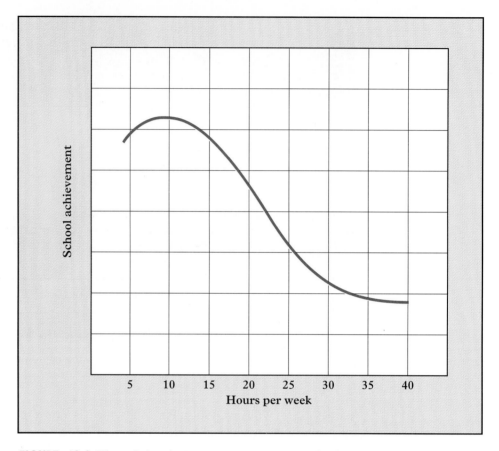

FIGURE 13.3 The relation between average amount of television viewing and school achievement, from data in 23 large-scale studies. After "The Impact of Leisure-Time Television on School Learning: A Research Synthesis," by P. A. Williams, E. H. Haertel, H. J. Walberg, & G. D. Haertel, 1982, *American Educational Research Journal, 19*, pp. 19–50. Adapted by permission.

with other factors, such as social class and intelligence. Although children from lower-class homes watch more television and perform less well in school than those from middle-class homes, the association between viewing and achievement holds true even within social classes. However, when children are of equivalent intelligence there is little association between the total amount of television viewed and most types of school achievement or cognitive functioning (D. R. Anderson & Collins, 1988).

Reading is the one subject that may be negatively influenced by television, but the effects are small. In the British Columbia study, for example, young children in the town without television reception performed better on reading tests than comparable children in the towns that received television. Two years later, after television was introduced in the "no TV" town, children in the early elementary school grades had poorer reading skills (T. M. Williams, 1986). Among children in the United States who have grown up with television, heavy viewing of entertainment television is slightly associated with poor reading skills. However, reading skill is much more directly affected by practice and by attitudes toward print. Children who watch television and also become familiar with books are likely to become good readers (M. Morgan & Gross, 1982; Ritchie, Price, & Roberts, 1987).

Different types of television programs have different effects on achievement and cognitive functioning. As we have already pointed out, children learn vocabulary, letters, and number skills from programs like *Sesame Street*. Documentaries and instructional television can be used effectively to teach a wide range of information (Liebert & Sprafkin, 1988).

Television can also teach cognitive skills through example. A camera can demonstrate visual analysis (i.e., finding parts of a complex stimulus) by zooming in on sections of the stimulus and zooming out to show the whole thing. In one series of studies children who watched several demonstrations of such zooms performed better than a control group on a test of visual analysis (Salomon, 1979).

Intellectual Passivity. Because children usually watch television for entertainment rather than for educational reasons, they often treat it as an occasion to relax and put forth minimal mental effort (Salomon, 1983). On the other hand, children are not passive receivers of stimuli from the TV tube. From a very early age they make choices about what, when, and how attentively to watch. Their attention is attracted by vivid, rapidly moving productions that contain many audiovisual gimmicks and special effects, but such production features alone are not enough to maintain their interest (A. C. Huston & Wright, 1983). They attend to content that they can understand (D. R. Anderson & Lorch, 1983) and to content that is funny or interesting (Zillmann, Williams, Bryant, Boynton, & Wolf, 1980). They think actively about what they are viewing, perhaps more than adults do.

How Children Understand Television

Attention to TV. Certain features of television programs hold children's attention. These include humor, character movement, sound effects and auditory changes, children's and women's voices, and animation. Children tend to lose interest when programs contain men's voices, complex speech, live-animal photography, and long zooms (D. R. Anderson, Lorch, Field, & Sanders, 1981; A. C. Huston & Wright, 1983). For the most part, violence and aggression do not increase attention to a program that has other attractive features (Potts, Huston, & Wright, 1986). Violence is not necessary to hold children's interest; they like nonviolent programs with humor, animation, and other attention-getting features.

Cognitive Development. The extent to which children understand what they see on television depends partly on their level of cognitive understanding. Although children watch many programs that are specifically designed for children, much of what they view is intended for adult audiences (St. Peters et al., 1991). The plots, characters, and situations they encounter in adult programs are often unfamiliar to them. Until age 9 or 10 they have difficulty understanding adult programs because they lack some of the relevant cognitive skills. As a result, they may obtain different messages from those programs than most adults do.

Young children have at least three problems understanding some TV shows. First, they sometimes have difficulty discriminating central, important content from content that is tangential to the main point. An incidental sight gag (Fat Albert falling flat on his face, for instance) may seem at least as important as the central theme (he and his gang are trying to help a girl who is unhappy about her parents' divorce). Second, children may fail to integrate different elements of a story that occur at different times. For example, a child may not connect the scene of a masked man holding up a bank with a scene occurring half an hour later in which a man is arrested and taken to jail. With age, children watch programs increasingly demanding of temporal integration (A. C. Huston et al., 1990). Third, children sometimes have difficulty making inferences about events that are not explicitly shown and about the feelings and intentions of characters (Collins, 1982; D. S. Hayes & Casey, 1992). For instance, children in the Hayes and Casey (1992) study had great difficulty recalling and describing the emotions of characters in segments of *Sesame Street*. Thus, even when watching programs carefully designed for them, children may understand and remember less of what is going on than adults assume.

What Is Learned from Television?

Concern about television viewing often focuses on the content of television, as well as the time spent watching. Worry has centered on three domains, which we review in this section: learning stereotypes, learning aggression, and being inordinately influenced by advertising. There may be positive effects of television as well; most such commentary has centered on learning prosocial behavior.

Stereotypes. Children learn social stereotypes of women, men, minorities, elderly people, and many other groups, including children themselves, from television. When there are historical changes in American society, television images typically lag far behind. For instance, as women entered the labor force during the years from 1950 to 1980 the percentage of employed women in television fiction increased, but it remained considerably lower than the percentage of employed women in the United States population (Calvert & Huston, 1987).

Children learn from these portrayals, particularly when they have little contact with the group being portrayed. For example, white children who knew few black people derived many of their ideas about blacks from television (Berry & Mitchell-Kernan, 1982; Greenberg, 1972, 1986; U.S. Commission on Civil Rights, 1977). Perhaps more important, portrayals that run counter to prevalent stereotypes can make a significant change in children's views about a group of people. One television series, called *Freestyle*, was specifically designed to counteract gender and ethnic stereotypes that might influence children's career interests. Thirteen half-hour programs were made to be shown on public television and in school classrooms. Most of the programs were dramatic stories about children. For instance, "Grease Monkey" was about a girl who loved working on cars. Her experiences getting and keeping a job in a service station made a good story.

Children's responses to the programs were evaluated in classrooms where additional materials for reading and discussion were supplied and in classrooms without the additional materials. The children generally liked the series, and many of them chose to watch it at home. The program was successful in reducing children's stereotypes about what girls and boys (or women and men) should do. They became more accepting of nontraditional activities, occupations, and family roles. However, when they were asked what they planned to do themselves, there was less change. Girls said that they intended to do more mechanical and athletic activities, but boys' intentions were not influenced by the program. The most pronounced changes occurred when supplemental materials and discussion were used in the classroom (J. Johnston & Ettema, 1982).

Violence. Violent scenes abound on American television, and violent crime is widespread in American society. The rates of both homicide and television violence are considerably higher in the United States than in many other countries. The effects of television violence on viewers have been studied more extensively than any other aspect of television. The evidence accumulated from a wide variety of sources indicates that television violence can cause aggressive behavior (Liebert & Sprafkin, 1988).

Laboratory experiments, field experiments, and longitudinal correlational studies have been used to study television violence (see Chapter 1 for a discussion of these research methods). One group of investigators conducted parallel longitudinal studies in five countries: Poland, Israel, Australia, Finland, and the United States. Children's aggressive behavior in school and the amount of television violence they watched were measured on three occasions over a two-year span. The findings varied slightly from one nation to another, but in general the children who watched a lot of television violence became more aggressive over time than those who did not. It was also true that those who were initially aggressive developed an increasing taste for TV violence, indicating a self-perpetuating circle (Huesmann & Eron, 1986).

Although many people may not be inspired to physical violence by television, their attitudes and reactions to other people's violent actions may be influenced. People who watch a lot of violence on television are more likely to approve of aggressive behavior. They also become desensitized—they are less likely to respond to real-world violence with horror or to make an effort to help a victim (Liebert & Sprafkin, 1988).

Advertising. Commercials for foods, toys, and other products are an integral part of American children's television-viewing experiences. Young children are particularly susceptible to persuasion by advertising because they lack the cognitive skills to understand its purposes. Until about age 5, children have considerable difficulty telling programs and ads apart. Even at age 6, they use concrete perceptual cues. For example, they often say that you can tell a commercial from a program because it is short.

Children's ability to understand the purposes of advertising may be related to their cognitive-developmental level and perspective-taking skills. Such skills may enable children to comprehend that advertisements are made by someone who has a purpose (i.e., to sell), who may not be truthful, and who intends the message for a particular audience. Children's improving skills in role taking between the ages of 6 and 11 may lessen their credulity about advertising (Liebert & Sprafkin, 1988). By the age of 10 or 11 most children are skeptical of advertising messages, but they are still vulnerable to subtle forms of deception (Wartella & Hunter, 1983).

Prosocial Behavior. Prosocial interactions such as altruism and sympathy are also shown often on television. Children can learn prosocial approaches to problem solving (e.g., negotiation) when they see them on television. Programs, such as *Mr.*

Rogers' Neighborhood, that are deliberately designed to teach positive social behavior—cooperation, helping, understanding others—influence children's behavior in their everyday interactions (Stein & Friedrich, 1975). In fact, in a review of a large number of studies, Hearold (1986) concluded that prosocial portrayals have a greater effect on behavior than antisocial portrayals do.

⚙ GOVERNMENT AND ECONOMIC INFLUENCES

So far, our discussion of socializing influences on children has dealt primarily with the direct effects of children's interactions with people (family and peers) and institutions (schools and media). But social influences can be more indirect. For example, the nature of parents' jobs affects the amount of time they can spend with their children, their levels of psychological stress, and the city and neighborhood in which they choose to live. These factors in turn influence parent-child interactions and the types of peers and schools to which the child is exposed, to give just a few examples.

Bronfenbrenner (1979) emphasized the importance of wider cultural and social systems in his ecological theory of human development. He conceptualized development as the "progressive, mutual accommodation between an active, growing human being and the changing properties of the immediate settings in which the developing person lives, as this process is affected by relations between these settings, and by the larger contexts in which the settings are embedded" (Bronfenbrenner, 1979, p. 21).

The "larger contexts" referred to by Bronfenbrenner are created by social policies and programs and by the economic policies of the workplace. Government policies affect family income (e.g., tax exemptions for dependents or tax credits for child care); the types of services available to families (e.g., free immunizations, Head Start), and many aspects of family life. Economic policies affect parental employment, wage rates, working hours, health benefits, and the like. In this section we consider a few of the many ways in which economic events and government policies influence families and children.

Social Trends and Social Policy

Poverty and Children. Poverty for children decreased in the United States during the 1960s, but it has been increasing since. The number of poor children under the age of 3 rose by 26 percent between 1980 and 1990 (Dixon, 1994). Approximately 21 percent of all children in the United States live in families with incomes below the poverty line (Kassebaum, 1994). This rate is at least double that of other industrialized nations (A. Huston, McLoyd, & Coll, 1994). Poverty rates in the United States are especially high for African-American and Latino children (A. Huston et al., 1994).

Three interrelated factors account for the increasing number of children living in poverty (A. Huston et al., 1994). The first is the nature of the economy, including both the types and the number of jobs available. Many of the new jobs created during the past decade pay low wages and have few if any benefits like health insurance. Young workers in particular often cannot earn enough to rise out of poverty or support a family (Children's Defense Fund, 1987). The second factor has been a decline in government-sponsored income support for poor families. Major support programs, such as Aid to Families with Dependent Children (AFDC) and child-care funding, were reduced at the same time that the need for them increased. The third factor is increases in the divorce rate and in the number of single-parent families, most of which are headed by women. Such families are especially vulnerable to poverty because in the majority of cases there is only one wage earner. That wage earner is usually a woman, and women's average wages are about two-thirds of the average earned by men.

Recent investigations have helped to clarify the nature of the impact of poverty on children. While poor children are more likely than better-off children to live in mother-headed households or with parents with lower levels of education, being poor has an effect on the children's cognitive and social development even when the effects of these other variables are controlled (G. J. Duncan, Brooks-Gunn, & Klebanov, 1994). Furthermore, the longer the period of poverty during childhood, the worse the effects on developmental outcome (G. J. Duncan et al., 1994). Much of the detrimental effect of poverty on development is mediated by the effects poverty has on the parent and the home environment. Improvements in family income have strong effects on improving home environments, especially for the poorest children (Garrett, Ng'andu, & Ferron, 1994).

In considering research on poverty in the United States and other industrialized countries, we should not forget that poverty is even more profound and widespread in developing countries. The effects of malnutrition on prenatal and postnatal development (discussed in Chapter 3) are, for instance, especially manifest in these countries. A recent study of the development of Brazilian children living on the street showed striking physical and psychological risks for these extremely deprived children (R. Campos et al., 1994). Worldwide, approximately 100 million children and adolescents are growing up in these circumstances (UNICEF, 1989).

Effects of Income Loss on Families. Many families are not chronically poor, but they may experience periods of poverty or major fluctuations in income. A University of Michigan study found, for instance, that over a span of ten years 25 percent of an adult sample had incomes below the poverty line for at least one year, but fewer than 3 percent were chronically poor (i.e., poor for eight years or more). The major cause of income loss for men was losing a job; the major cause for women was dissolution of a marriage through divorce or death (G. J. Duncan, 1984).

When a parent loses a job, severe stresses occur within the family. The effects of income loss on families have been studied for two periods of high unemployment: the Great Depression of the 1930s and the recession of the early 1980s. Longitudinal data on families with children collected during the 1930s permitted comparisons of families that experienced major income loss (reductions of more than 35 percent) with families that did not. When a family's income dropped, there were increases in the children's behavior problems—specifically, temper tantrums and uncontrolled outbursts. The cause appeared to be the father's behavior: fathers who were experiencing economic stress became more punitive, and the children reacted with tantrums and angry outbursts (Elder & Caspi, 1988).

Men who were unemployed in the 1980s spent more time with their children

Children growing up on the street face difficult physical and psychological risks.

than employed men did, partly so that their wives could work at jobs outside the home, but they were less nurturing toward their children than employed fathers were. Once they returned to work, their involvement with the children returned to the same level as that of continuously employed men (R. Goldsmith & Radin, 1987).

A systems analysis of the effects of income loss on families is shown in Figure 13.4. Children in families that have experienced serious income loss manifest socioemotional problems, somatic symptoms (e.g., stomachaches), and reduced aspirations and expectations for higher education and job success. The father's response to income loss and his behavior toward the child are among the primary causes of these effects. Depression and demoralization in mothers as a result of economic instability seem to predict additional amounts of variation in child outcomes (R. D. Conger et al., 1992). In families in which fathers maintain a nurturant relationship with the child and in which the mother can provide support, income loss may have relatively small effects on children (McLoyd, 1989).

Mothers' unemployment or work loss may have similar effects to that of fathers. McLoyd, Jayaratne, Ceballo, and Borquez (1994) studied single African-American mothers, a group particularly economically vulnerable. They found, consistent with earlier studies of fathers, that adverse effects of economic loss on children were mediated by effects on adults. Under stress, the mothers were at risk for depression and for becoming less effective parents, for instance, more punitive. These personality and behavioral changes were, in turn, associated with negative effects in the children.

Policies Affecting Mother-Headed Households. Many of the long-term consequences of divorce and single parenting for children's development are partly due to income loss and poverty (I. Garfinkel & McLanahan, 1986). The incomes of

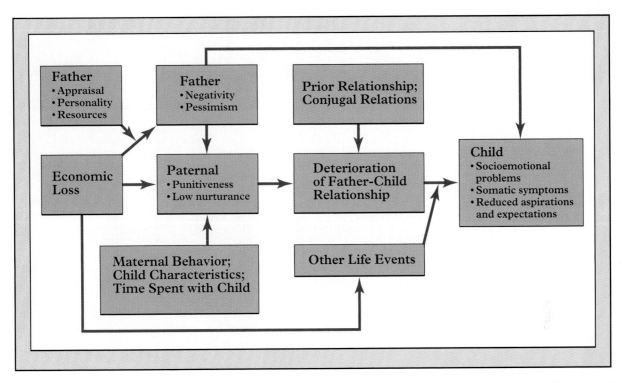

FIGURE 13.4 A model of how parental income loss affects children. After "Socialization and Development in a Changing Economy: The Effects of Paternal Job and Income Loss on Children," by V. C. McLoyd, 1989, *American Psychologist, 44,* p. 294. Adapted by permission.

families headed by women typically are about half of the family's income before a divorce. Government policies determine the types of services and financial aid that are available to single-parent families that are experiencing economic strains. Programs that provide medical care and nutritional supplements for infants and pregnant women are generally approved and have well-documented benefits for children (Schorr, 1988). However, programs that provide income to single mothers carry the social stigma of "welfare." Despite the intense public interest in these programs, psychologists know little about their effects on family processes or on children's development.

Government policies also define the legal obligations of a nonresident parent, whether or not the parents were originally married. Lax enforcement of child support obligations, which was typical in the United States until recently, leaves many single-parent families entirely dependent on maternal earnings or welfare. In the 1980s, enforcement of support obligations was improved and awards were increased in many areas (I. Garfinkel & McLanahan, 1986). Psychologists are now beginning to examine how these policies affect relationships among family members. For example, do parents who are forced to pay child support give their children more attention, or do they express hostility and resentment toward them?

Homelessness. An American tragedy of increasing proportions, and one that will inevitably affect children's social, emotional, and cognitive development, is homelessness. It is virtually impossible to obtain an accurate census of homeless people, but it is estimated that there are more than 2 million in the United States; the vast

Homeless families are a challenge to government social policy.

majority of these are families with children. The average homeless family includes one parent and two or three children. Many live in temporary shelters or long-term hotels provided by civic, federal, or private agencies. Family life as it is generally known is virtually destroyed; fathers are frequently separated from their families, and in large cities the families are shifted from one shelter or hotel to another. In the words of an official New York City report, "the seemingly endless shuttling between hotels and shelters can come to resemble a game of 'human pinball.'" Two-thirds of the "pinballs" are dependent children.

Living conditions in these hotels and shelters are deplorable—cramped, filthy, noisy, and unsanitary. The children are inadequately nourished and often hungry; their parents are desperate and depressed; drugs and violence abound in their surroundings; and the children attend school sporadically, if at all. One school principal in New York estimates that one-quarter of the children in hotels and shelters for the homeless are two or three years behind their peers in academic skills, which makes them even more reluctant to attend.

A keen observer of homeless families highlighted the devastating effects of homelessness on children:

> All but a few of the children [in hotels for the homeless] will fail to thrive in any meaningful respect. Early death or stunted cognitive development are not the only risks these children face. Emotional damage may be expected, too. . . . A psychiatrist . . . speaks of interviewing children who are more depressed than those she would expect to find in psychiatric clinics. She describes a 19-month-old baby who had started having nightmares and stopped eating, and

a 10-year-old who, ridden with anxiety, has begun to mutilate himself: he has pulled out his permanent teeth.

Anger that does not turn in upon the child frequently turns out to vent itself on society. Children at [these] hotels . . . live with a number of good reasons for intense hostility and with very few for acquiescence in those norms by which societies must live. Such children, if they do not cause disruption in the streets and the hotels, may do so in school (Kozol, 1988a, p. 80; see also Kozol, 1988b).

Relations Between the Family and Other Social Systems

Relations between families and other social systems occur within a context of cultural values and beliefs about children and families. In the United States the underlying ideology is highly individualistic: Children are considered to be the sole responsibility of their parents. We view government actions as intrusions into the privacy of the family, justified only when the parents fail to fulfill their obligations, for example, in cases of child abuse and neglect (Grubb & Lazerson, 1988). The one clear exception is education; government is expected to provide schools and educational opportunities for all.

In societies with a more communal ideology, there is a somewhat different division of responsibility between parents and other social institutions. For instance, in some Israeli kibbutzim (agricultural communities based on a communal ideology), children are raised in a children's house by a specially trained caregiver. They see their parents each day, but their parents are not solely responsible for their upbringing.

Even in societies with a less clear communal ideology than the kibbutzim, the responsibility for socializing children is shared by individuals, communities, and institutions outside the family. For instance, an American psychologist living in Paris was struck by observing that adults other than parents felt free to correct children playing in a public park. It seemed to be taken for granted that any adult had the right, and perhaps the responsibility, to intervene in children's behavior. In the United States, an adult who corrected another person's child would be considered a busybody or worse.

Perhaps because of our individualistic ideology, government policies affecting children in the United States are quite different from those in most other industrialized countries. The United States could probably benefit from the experience of other nations in finding ways to provide for the welfare of children, even though particular solutions must be adapted to different cultural contexts.

✿ SUMMARY

The primary vehicle for the development of relationships with peers is play, beginning around age 2. Between the ages of 2 and 5, children's interactions become more frequent, more sustained, more social, and more complex. Group dramatic play and games will become part of the child's play repertoire.

Age-related changes in social interaction and play are to some extent a function of increasing skill in role taking. Role-taking ability appears to develop through a series of qualitatively distinct stages and is correlated with general intelligence and moral behavior.

With more extensive social experience and advances in cognitive abilities, children's conceptions of others become more abstract, more complex, and more focused on psychological characteristics. Beginning around age 8, children make increased use of abstract adjectives referring to traits, beliefs, values, and attitudes. The descriptions given by children age 12 to 14 are generally better organized and show greater sensitivity to the complexity of personality characteristics and behavior.

Many factors influence the social status of children. Among the cognitive attributes associated with popularity are well-developed role-taking skills and friendly, outgoing, sympathetic orientations toward others. Children with high social status also have greater social knowledge and understanding of effective ways of interacting. Moderately high self-esteem is more likely to lead to acceptance by peers than either very high or very low self-esteem.

Children's ideas about friendship change as they mature. Whereas preschool children are not concerned with lasting relationships, older children think of friendships as relationships that continue beyond single, brief interactions. Between the age of 5 and adolescence, children's conceptions of friendship evolve from a stage in which friends are the playmates whom the child sees most frequently, through one in which friends are the people with whom they cooperate and share, to one in which friendships are judged in terms of mutual understanding.

Many children attend preschools and early-education programs, and many more are in day care. The quality of child care has important effects on development. Components of quality include the amount of adult-child interaction and group size. The physical setting (available materials and space) is also important. An inadequately equipped classroom may produce increased aggression and other kinds of stress, but children also learn to share when equipment is limited. Toys and activities can affect behavior by encouraging aggression, prosocial behavior, high levels of activity, and the like.

Another variable is adult structuring of children's activities. Children in highly structured classes attend well, comply with directions, and turn to the teacher for approval. They interact almost exclusively with the teacher and relatively little with peers. Low structure, in contrast, encourages positive interactions with peers as well as aggression, assertiveness, and leadership. Girls are more likely to participate in adult-structured activities than boys are.

Recent research has shown that teachers' expectancies can, under some circumstances, affect learning independently of the child's abilities. Expectancies are communicated to children through behaviors such as smiling and showing positive feelings toward students who are considered to be bright. Cooperative learning programs are based on group interaction and a group reward structure. They improve learning in some instances and also contribute to positive attitudes toward other students and concern for the welfare of others. Racial integration is more successful when the school organization promotes cooperation rather than competition and when individual achievement is deemphasized. Mainstreaming, or integrating children with physical and mental handicaps into regular classrooms, is less successful than its advocates originally hoped, but programs stressing peer interaction and cooperation can make mainstreaming more effective.

An important socializing influence within the home is television; on the average, children watch two or three hours of television a day. Young children often watch programs that are not designed for children. Television viewing is sometimes thought to replace family interaction, play, and other activities; to have negative effects on health and physical fitness and school achievement; and to induce passive approaches to learning. Researchers have found that television does affect the structure of leisure time and that it leads to reduced participation in sports, which may affect physical fitness. Television viewing is associated with lower achievement in school for children who watch more than about 10 hours a week. It does not appear to make children intellectually passive. In fact, children think actively while viewing, and if the program content is informative, they learn a great deal from television.

The extent to which children understand what they see on television depends partly on their level of cognitive understanding. Young children sometimes have difficulty discriminating central, important content from content that is tangential to the main point. They may also fail to integrate different elements of a story that occur at different times, and may have difficulty making inferences about events that are not explicitly shown.

Children acquire much of their knowledge about social relationships and behavior from television. They also learn social stereotypes. In addition, television violence can cause aggressive behavior. Children can also learn prosocial approaches to problem solving when they see them on television.

Children are affected by governmental policies and programs and by the economic policies of the workplace, in part because their parents are affected. Government policies affect family income, the types of services available to families, and many aspects of family life. Such workplace policies as parental leave for childbirth, wage rates, working hours, health benefits, and the like affect parental employment and the quality of family life. Major social trends such as high rates of poverty and homelessness have long-term consequences for the development of the current generation of children.

REVIEW QUESTIONS

1. How does children's play contribute to the development of peer relationships?
2. What is meant by role taking? How is skill in role taking related to empathy?
3. In what ways do children's perceptions of others change as they grow older?
4. What factors determine the social status of children among their peers?
5. What social processes are involved in the formation of friendships? What factors play a role in the maintenance of friendships?
6. How do preschool and day care environments affect social, emotional, and cognitive development?
7. What effects do the physical and academic organization of schools have on children's development?
8. How do teachers influence children?
9. Briefly discuss cooperative learning, desegregation and integration, and mainstreaming in terms of their effects on children.
10. How much time do children spend watching television and what kinds of programs do they watch?
11. What are the effects of television viewing on family interaction, physical fitness, school achievement, and learning?
12. What kinds of knowledge do children acquire from television?
13. In what ways do social and economic policies influence the lives of children?

CRITICAL THINKING ABOUT THE CHAPTER

1. Think back to the friends you had in preschool, elementary school, and middle school or junior high. How did your friendships differ at these different ages? What effect did these friendships have in creating the person you now are?

2. There is currently a great deal of debate about educational reform. Pick an issue of importance in your area (such as adoption of outcome-based education, or the formula for funding schools and reducing inequities among school districts) and follow it by reading newspapers and even attending community meetings. Then write a paper on your position on the issue.

3. Find out what a single mother of two preschool children could obtain in government support in your community. Then construct a budget for her to live on. To do this, you will need to research the cost of housing, a market basket of food, diapers and baby supplies, and so on. Write a paper on what you found out and what the experience makes you think about government policy.

KEY TERMS

mainstreaming
sociometric techniques

SUGGESTED READINGS

Elder, G. H., Jr. (1977). *Children of the Great Depression: Social change in life experience.* Chicago: University of Chicago Press. An analysis of families that experienced severe income loss during the depression of the 1930s. Longitudinal data are examined to compare children whose families lost income with those whose families did not.

Leavitt, L., & Fox, N. (Eds.) (1993). *Psychological effects of war and violence on children.* Hillsdale, NJ: Erlbaum. A recent look at an issue just beginning to occupy psychologists, and of importance to children around the world.

Liebert, R. N., & Sprafkin, J. N. (1988). *The early window: Effects of television on children* (3rd ed.). New York: Pergamon. A readable review of the literature on the effects of television. Provides a historical examination of the research in relation to changes in the industry and government policy over the 40 years since television was introduced in the United States.

Scarr, S. (1984). *Mother care/Other care.* New York: Basic Books. Presents a summary of the research on day care, taking the position that day care is not harmful to children and in many cases can be beneficial.

Schorr, L. B. (1988). *Within our reach: Breaking the cycle of disadvantage.* New York: Anchor Press. The author argues that we know a great deal about how to help disadvantaged children and families break out of persistent poverty. She reviews interventions that have been successful in producing long-term change in such domains as child health, education, and adolescent pregnancy, and draws clear implications for national policy.

Shure, M. B., & DiGeronimo, T. F. (1994). *Raising a thinking child.* New York: Henry Holt. Describes the I Can Problem Solve program devised by Myrna Shure in easy-to-learn steps.

P A R T

VI

ADOLESCENCE

▼

CHAPTER

14

PHYSICAL AND COGNITIVE DEVELOPMENT IN ADOLESCENCE

PHYSICAL GROWTH IN ADOLESCENCE

Hormonal Factors in Development
The Adolescent Growth Spurt
Sexual Maturation
   Sexual Development in Males
   Sexual Development in Females
   Normal Variations in Development

PSYCHOLOGICAL ASPECTS OF MATURATION

Onset of Puberty
   Females
   Males
Timing of Puberty
   Early and Late Maturation in Males
   Early and Late Maturation in Females

ADOLESCENT SEXUALITY

Premarital Sexual Intercourse
Sexually Transmitted Diseases, Pregnancy, and Contraception
Homosexual Behavior and Orientation

COGNITIVE DEVELOPMENT IN ADOLESCENCE

Formal Operations

Shirley looked over at her 12-year-old daughter Ilana in the pediatrician's office. They were waiting for Ilana's well-child physical, and Shirley had mixed emotions. It seemed only yesterday that she had been bringing her firstborn child to this same office in diapers, for shots and for what had seemed like an endless series of checkups to monitor the chronic ear infections Ilana had had as a child. Now Ilana was a healthy seventh-grader (with newly pierced ears) who needed to go to frequent checkups at the orthodontist's. She was also showing definite signs of puberty, with a newly rounded figure and a growth spurt in full swing. Shirley suspected that, sometime in the next year, Ilana would start having periods. While she believed Ilana was ready for this in one sense, with a good understanding of the physical changes of adolescence, Shirley wondered what psychological changes puberty would bring. And she was scared stiff about how Ilana would handle sexual issues, fearing that mistakes could carry a heavy price, in an era when sexually transmitted diseases were a real threat.

Shirley is not alone in her fears for her daughter. Adolescence has traditionally been considered a more difficult developmental period than middle childhood, both for children and for their parents. It is a time of physical, cognitive, and emotional changes that move children into adulthood. These changes are often positive and pleasurable, but there are awkward moments and difficult passages as well. As long ago as 300 B.C., Aristotle complained that adolescents were "passionate, irascible, and apt to be carried away by their impulses" (Kiell, 1967, pp. 18–19). Plato advised that boys not be allowed to drink before the age of 18 because of their excitability: "Fire must not be poured on fire" (Plato, 1953, p. 14). And in a funeral sermon, a seventeenth-century clergyman compared youth to "a new ship launching out into the main ocean without a helm or ballast or pilot to steer her" (S. R. Smith, 1975, p. 497).

Psychologists have sometimes concurred with this view of adolescence. For instance, G. Stanley Hall, founder of the American Psychological Association and originator of the scientific study of adolescence, viewed adolescence as a period of "storm and stress." Sigmund Freud and his daughter, Anna Freud, spoke of adolescence as a period during which the conflicts of the oral, anal, and phallic stages of development are revisited, following the relative peace of middle childhood, which they called the latency stage.

Empirical investigations of typical adolescents suggest, however, that the extent of adolescent turmoil during this period has been greatly exaggerated (Steinberg, 1990). A better conception of adolescence may be as a challenging and sometimes difficult stage of life, during which several major life transitions occur. Adolescence is, above all, a period of change. The child turning into an adolescent undergoes dramatic physical, sexual, cognitive, and emotional transformations. In addition, there are changes in the social demands made by parents, peers, teachers, and society itself. In this chapter we examine the physical changes of adolescence and their effects on psychological development. We also explore the basic cognitive changes that occur at this time. In the next chapter, we deal with social development and changes in interpersonal relationships.

✺ PHYSICAL GROWTH IN ADOLESCENCE

The term **adolescence** comes from the Latin verb *adolescere*, which means "to grow into adulthood." It begins with the onset of puberty and ends with the assumption of adult responsibilities. As one philosopher remarked, adolescence begins in biology and ends in culture. Because societies vary in when individuals are considered sufficiently skilled and mature to take on adult responsibilities, the period we call adolescence varies in length. It may be brief, as it is in some simpler societies, or relatively prolonged, as it is in our own relatively complex society. Despite such variations, one aspect of adolescence is universal and separates it from earlier stages of development: the physical and physiological changes of puberty that mark its beginning.

The term **puberty** refers to the first phase of adolescence, in which sexual maturation becomes evident. Strictly speaking, puberty begins with hormonal increases and their manifestations, such as gradual enlargement of the ovaries in females and testicular cell growth in males. But because these changes are not outwardly observable, the onset of puberty is often measured by such events as the emergence of pubic hair, the beginning of elevation of the breasts in girls, and an increase in the size of the penis and testes in boys. Sexual maturation is accompanied by a "growth spurt" in height and weight that usually lasts about four years.

Hormonal Factors in Development

Of critical importance in the regulation of pubertal growth is the pituitary gland. This gland is located at the base of the brain, to which it is connected by nerve fibers. When the cells of the hypothalamus "mature" (an event that occurs at different times in different individuals), signals are sent to the pituitary gland to begin releasing previously inhibited hormones (Grumbach, 1978). The hormones released by the pituitary have a stimulating effect on most other endocrine glands, including the thyroid and adrenal glands and the testes and ovaries, which in turn begin releasing hormones that affect growth and sexual development. These include androgens (masculinizing hormones), estrogens (feminizing hormones), and progestins (pregnancy hormones). They interact with other hormones in complex ways to stimulate an orderly progression of physical and physiological development.

In the early days of sex-hormone research, when sex differences were viewed as dichotomous and absolute, it was assumed that females produce only female sex hormones and males only male sex hormones. We now know that there is some overlap; the hormones of both sexes are present in both men and women (Gupta, Attanasio, & Raaf, 1975; Marshall, 1978). The hormonal difference between the sexes is a difference in the *proportions* of masculinizing and feminizing hormones present in males and females. Looking at Figure 14.1, we see that as puberty pro-

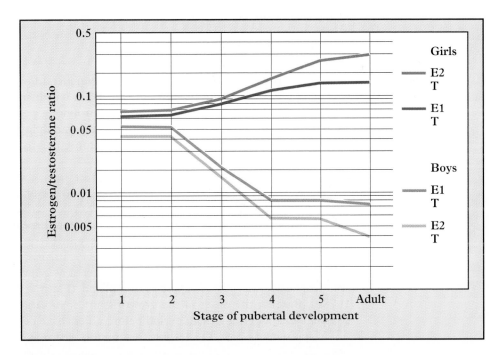

FIGURE 14.1 Mean trends in estrogen-to-testosterone ratios during pubertal development for girls and boys. Two measures of estrogen level are used, resulting in two ratios for each sex. After "Plasma Estrogen and Androgen Concentrations in Children During Adolescence," by D. Gupta, A. Attanasio, and S. Raaf, 1975, *Journal of Clinical Endocrinology and Metabolism, 40,* pp. 636–643. Adapted with permission.

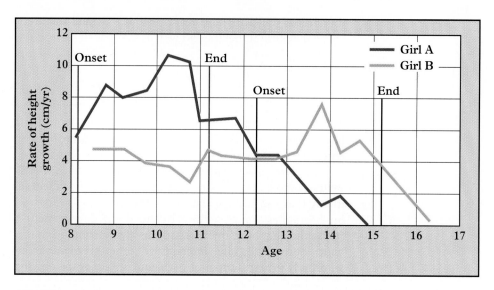

FIGURE 14.2 Differences in timing of the pubertal growth spurt. The early developing girl (A) reached the end of the pubertal spurt before the late-developing girl (B) reached the onset. After "Somatic Development of Adolescent Girls," by M. S. Faust, 1977, *Monographs of the Society for Research in Child Development, 42* (1, Serial No. 169). Copyright © The Society for Research in Child Development. Adapted with permission.

ceeds, the ratio of estrogen levels to testosterone levels increases in females and decreases in males.

The Adolescent Growth Spurt

The term **growth spurt** refers to the accelerated rate of increase in height and weight that occurs at puberty. This increase varies widely in intensity, duration, and age of onset from one child to another, even among perfectly normal children. Unfortunately, the degree of normal individual variability is often poorly understood by adolescents and their parents and consequently is a source of needless concern.

In both sexes, the adolescent growth spurt lasts about 4.5 years (Boxer & Petersen, 1986; Faust, 1984; Marshall, 1978). For the average male, the growth rate peaks at age 13; in females this occurs about two years earlier, at age 11. In the average boy, the growth spurt begins a few months before his eleventh birthday, though it may begin as early as age 9; similarly, the growth spurt is usually completed shortly after age 15 but may continue until age 17. In girls, the growth spurt usually begins and ends about two years earlier. Further slow growth may continue for several years after the growth spurt is completed (Faust, 1983; Falkner & Tanner, 1978b). Because the onset of the growth spurt is so variable, some young people complete the pubertal growth period before others have begun it (see Figure 14.2).

Many parents have the feeling that rapidly growing adolescents, particularly boys, are "eating us out of house and home." Indeed, the nutritional needs of young people increase considerably during the years of rapid growth, although there are wide individual variations, depending on such factors as body size and activity level. On the average, boys need more calories at every age than girls. However, a large, very active girl obviously will have greater nutritional needs than a small,

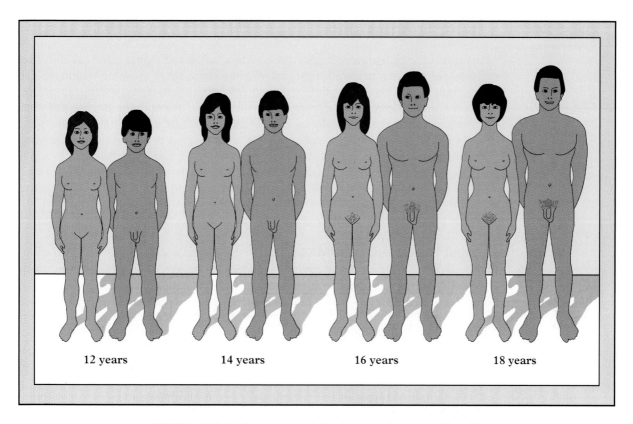

FIGURE 14.3 Body growth and development from ages 12 to 18 years.

inactive boy. Similarly, late maturers need fewer calories than early maturers of the same age.

Changes in height and weight are accompanied by changes in body proportions in both boys and girls. The head, hands, and feet reach adult size first. The arms and legs grow faster than the trunk, which stops growing last. As the English pediatrician James Tanner has written, "A boy stops growing out of his trousers (at least in length) a year before he stops growing out of his jackets" (1971, p. 94). These differences in the rate of growth in different parts of the body largely account for the feelings of awkwardness that some adolescents have, especially those who are growing fastest. For brief periods, some young people may feel that their hands and feet are too big or that they are "all legs." Of course, thoughtless comments by adults may intensify the adolescent's feelings of awkwardness.

Sex differences in body shape also are magnified during early adolescence. Although even in childhood girls have wider hips than boys do, the difference becomes more pronounced at puberty. Conversely, males develop thicker as well as larger bones, more muscle tissue, and broader shoulders (see Figure 14.3). Partly as a result, males become and remain stronger than females (particularly in the upper body) as adolescence proceeds. Other reasons for males' greater physical strength relative to their size are that they develop larger hearts and lungs, higher systolic blood pressure, a greater capacity for carrying oxygen in the blood, and a lower heart rate while resting. They are also more resistant chemically to fatigue from exercise (Forbes, 1978; Tanner, 1970, 1971).

Sexual Maturation

As in the case of the growth spurt, there are marked individual differences in the age at which sexual maturation begins. While there is some variation within developmental sequences—for example, breast development in girls may appear before or after the development of pubic hair—physical development during puberty and adolescence generally follows a rather orderly progression (Boxer & Petersen, 1986; Faust, 1984). Thus, a male who has an early growth spurt is more likely to develop pubic hair and other attributes of sexual maturation early; a female who shows early breast development is likely to have early menarche (onset of menstruation). Preadolescents with advanced skeletal development will probably have an early growth spurt and early sexual maturation (Roche, 1978; Tanner, 1970, 1971).

Sexual Development in Males. Although testicular cell growth and secretion of male sex hormone begin earlier—typically about age 11.5—the first outward sign of impending sexual maturity in males is usually an increase in the growth of the testes and scrotum (the baglike structure enclosing the testes) beginning at about age 12.5. There may also be some growth of pubic hair. Approximately a year later, an acceleration in growth of the penis accompanies the beginning of the growth spurt in height. Axillary (armpit) and facial hair usually make their first appearance about two years after the beginning of pubic-hair growth, although in a few children axillary hair appears first (Marshall & Tanner, 1970).

A definite lowering of the voice usually occurs fairly late in puberty. In some young men this change is abrupt and dramatic, while in others it is so gradual that it is hardly perceptible. During this process the larynx (Adam's apple) enlarges significantly and the vocal cords (which it contains) approximately double in length, with a consequent drop in pitch of about an octave.

During adolescence the male breast also undergoes changes. The diameter of the areola (the area surrounding the nipple) increases considerably (although not as much as in girls) and is accompanied by elevation of the nipple. In some males (perhaps 20 to 30 percent) there may be a distinct enlargement of the breast about midway through adolescence. Usually this disappears within a year or so (R. Bell, 1980). Prepubescent boys may also show a tendency toward adiposity (fatness) of the lower torso, which, again, may suggest feminine body contours to the apprehensive adolescent or adult. Although these bodily configurations typically disappear with time, they may represent a source of needless anxiety for both adolescents and parents. There is no evidence that (in the absence of specific pathology) either of these conditions is related to any deficiency in sexual functioning.

Sexual Development in Females. The appearance of unpigmented, downy pubic hair is usually the first outward sign of sexual maturity in girls, although the so-called bud stage of breast development may sometimes precede it (Faust, 1984). Budding of the breasts is accompanied by the emergence of downy, unpigmented axillary hair and increases in the secretion of estrogen (female sex hormone). In the following year the uterus and vagina show accelerated growth; the labia and clitoris also enlarge. **Menarche**, the onset of menstruation, occurs relatively late in the developmental sequence (about age 12.75), almost always after the growth spurt has begun to slow down (Faust, 1977, 1984; Tanner, 1970).

There is frequently a period of a year or more following the beginning of men-

TABLE 14.1 Maturation in Boys and in Girls

Although there may be some individual—and perfectly normal—variations in the sequence of events leading to physical and sexual maturity in boys, the following sequence is typical:

1. Testes and scrotum begin to increase in size.
2. Pubic hair begins to appear.
3. Adolescent growth spurt starts; the penis begins to enlarge.
4. Voice deepens as the larynx grows.
5. Hair begins to appear under the arms and on the upper lip.
6. Sperm production increases, and nocturnal emission (ejaculation of semen during sleep) may occur.
7. Growth spurt reaches peak rate; pubic hair becomes pigmented.
8. Prostate gland enlarges.
9. Sperm production becomes sufficient for fertility; growth rate decreases.
10. Physical strength reaches a peak.

Although, as in the case of boys, there may be normal variations in the sequence of physical and sexual maturation in girls, a typical sequence of events is as follows:

1. Adolescent growth spurt begins.
2. Downy, nonpigmented pubic hair makes its initial appearance.
3. Elevation of the breast (the so-called bud stage of development) and rounding of the hips begin, accompanied by the beginning of downy axillary (armpit) hair.
4. The uterus and vagina, as well as labia and clitoris, increase in size.
5. Pubic hair grows rapidly and becomes slightly pigmented.
6. Breasts develop further; nipple pigmentation begins; areola increases in size; axillary hair becomes slightly pigmented.
7. Growth spurt reaches peak rate and then declines.
8. Menarche (onset of menstruation) occurs.
9. Pubic hair development is completed, followed by mature breast development and completion of axillary hair development.
10. Period of "adolescent sterility" ends, and girl becomes capable of conception (up to a year or so after menarche).

struation during which the adolescent female is not yet able to conceive. Similarly, males are able to have intercourse long before they produce live spermatozoa. Obviously, however, because of significant individual differences, younger adolescents should not assume that they are "safe" because of their age. Some young women are able to conceive within the first year after menarche (Boxer & Petersen, 1986; Zabin, Kantner, & Zelnik, 1979). The typical sequences of sexual maturation for boys and girls are summarized in Table 14.1.

Normal Variations in Development. Differences from group norms in rate of development and physical appearance are agonizing for many adolescents and can impair their self-esteem (Simmons, Blyth, & McKinney, 1983; Simmons & Rosenberg, 1975; Tobin-Richards, Boxer, & Petersen, 1984). It should be emphasized that the average developmental sequences discussed here are just that—average. Among perfectly normal adolescents there are wide variations in the age of onset of the developmental sequence (and sometimes in the order of the events in the sequence). For example, while maturation of the penis may be complete by age 13.5 in some boys, in others it may not be complete until age 17 or even later. The bud stage of breast development may occur as early as age 8 in some girls, as late as age 13 in others. Age at menarche may vary from about 9 to 16.5. The marked differences that occur among normal adolescents in their rates of development are illustrated in Figure 14.4, which shows the differing degrees of pubertal maturity among three normal males, all aged 14.75 years, and three normal females, all aged 12.75 years.

Normal variations in pubertal timing are largely linked to genetic and nutritional factors (Garn, 1980). However, there is intriguing new evidence that, for girls, a psychological factor may be relevant as well. Girls who experience family conflict and father absence may reach menarche somewhat earlier than girls who do not (Moffitt, Caspi, Belsky, & Silva, 1992; Steinberg, 1988; Surbey, 1990). However, the association of family conflict and earlier menarche could be a basically genetic relation. The mothers of earlier maturers may have been themselves early maturers, who are known to marry earlier and be more likely to divorce than average or later maturers (Udry & Cliquet, 1982).

✳ PSYCHOLOGICAL ASPECTS OF MATURATION

The momentous physical changes of puberty have psychological consequences. As children change physically to look increasingly like adults, they evoke different reactions from others (parents, teachers, and peers) and expect different things of themselves. Furthermore, the underlying hormonal changes that create and orchestrate physical change may have direct effects on adolescents' emotions and behaviors, although research on the exact nature of these relations does not yet give a completely clear picture of the links (Buchanan, Eccles, & Becker, 1992). Research on the psychological consequences of going through puberty has looked at two aspects of adolescent physical changes. First, what effects do the physical changes have on adolescent personality and on the relationships of adolescents, especially with parents? Second, because there is wide individual variation in the age when the physical changes occur, we may ask whether being early, average, or late in reaching puberty with respect to one's peers have any psychological effects. Each of these questions needs to be examined separately for girls and for boys.

Onset of Puberty

Females. While sexual development in girls begins, as we have seen, with breast development and the growth of axillary and pubic hair, probably the central event of puberty is the beginning of menstruation. Menstruation is much more to the adolescent girl than a physiological readjustment. It is a symbol of sexual maturity—of the girl's future status as a woman (Brooks-Gunn & Ruble, 1983; Greif & Ulman, 1982; Ruble & Brooks-Gunn, 1982). In the words of one older adolescent, "It seemed that all my friends had gotten their period already, or were just having it. I felt left out. I began to think of it as a symbol. When I got my period, I would be a woman."

However, there are also negative aspects to how adolescents see menstruation. In several studies (Boxer & Petersen, 1986; Brooks-Gunn & Ruble, 1982, 1984; Greif & Ulman, 1982), many preadolescent and adolescent American girls saw menstruation as having negative aspects; most felt that menstruation "is something

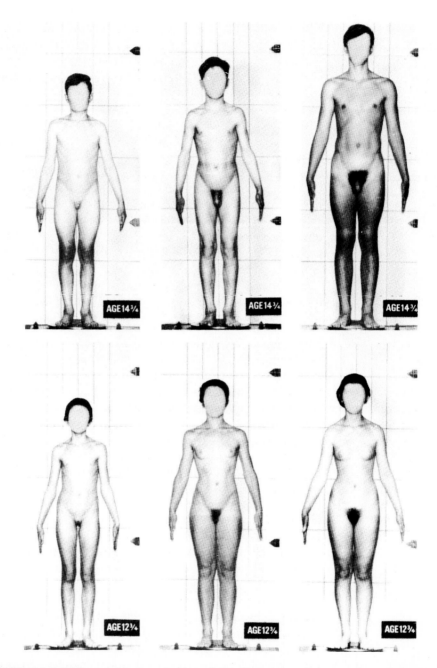

FIGURE 14.4 Different degrees of pubertal development at the same chronological ages. The upper row shows three boys, all aged 14.75 years. The bottom row shows three girls, all aged 12.75 years. From "Growth and Endocrinology of the Adolescent," by J. M. Tanner, in *Endocrine and Genetic Diseases of Childhood*, edited by J. L. Gardner, 1969, Philadelphia: W. B. Saunders. Reprinted with permission.

Children who are 11 to 13 years old may show a very wide range of physical growth patterns. Some still look like children; others much more closely resemble adults.

women just have to put up with." Its most positive aspect was as a sign of maturity; its most negative aspect was "the hassle" of needing to be prepared for its occurrence (Ruble & Brooks-Gunn, 1982). Overall, very few adolescents saw menarche as either wholly positive or wholly negative.

Why do so many adolescent girls react at least somewhat negatively to the onset of menstruation? One reason is the negative attitudes of others. If a girl's parents and friends act as though she requires sympathy for her "plight"—an attitude indicated by such labels as "the curse"—she is likely to react in a similar fashion. Negative reactions may also be self-fulfilling prophecies. Brooks-Gunn and Ruble (1982) found that what premenarcheal girls *expected* of menstruation was correlated with what they reported experiencing after menarche, although postmenarcheal reports were, overall, less negative than the premenarcheal expectations. Negative reactions to menstruation may also stem from physical discomfort, including headaches, backaches, cramps, and abdominal pain. A majority of American adolescent females (aged 12 to 17 years) report experiencing at least mild pain before or during menses. However, only 14 percent of those reporting cramps or other pain describe it as severe (Klein & Litt, 1984). Regular exercise, proper diet (including avoidance of excessive amounts of salt, sugar, and caffeine), sufficient rest, and proper use of pain medication help to reduce discomfort.

Menarche is related to several psychological changes. Girls increase in body awareness and in self-consciousness after menarche (Brooks-Gunn & Ruble, 1982; Koff, Rierdan, & Jacobson, 1981), and they also show increases in social maturity,

Conflict with parents following the onset of puberty is common and may serve a function in individual and family development.

peer reputation, and self-esteem (Garwood & Allen, 1979). There may be negative effects on relationships with parents, however. Mother-daughter conflict increases immediately following menarche (J. P. Hill, 1988; Holmbeck & Hill, 1991). This initial conflict subsides but seems to be replaced with increased interpersonal distance (Holmbeck & Hill, 1991).

While uncomfortable for the participants, conflict and disengagement following menarche may not be maladaptive. Many developmental theories suggest that increasing emotional autonomy is central to adolescence, and conflict may be a part of the development of autonomy. In addition, from an evolutionary perspective, conflict following adolescence may be a part of the process that leads adolescents to leave home and to seek mates outside the family circle (Steinberg, 1990).

Males. Just as the onset of menstruation may cause concern to adolescent girls, adolescent boys may be surprised and worried by spontaneous erection and the first occurrences of ejaculation. Although genital stimulation, like other forms of bodily stimulation, is pleasurable for children, erection and genital stimulation usually carry a greater sense of sexual urgency after puberty. During this period the penis begins to tumesce very readily, either spontaneously or in response to a variety of stimuli. Although males may be proud of their capacity for erection as a symbol of emerging virility, they may also be worried or embarrassed by their apparent inability to control this response. They may become apprehensive about dancing or even having to stand up in a classroom to give a report. They may wonder if other males experience a similar apparent lack of control (R. Bell, 1980).

The adolescent male's first ejaculation is likely to occur within a year after the onset of the growth spurt (around age 14, although it may occur as early as 11 or as late as 16). First ejaculation may occur as a result of masturbation or nocturnal emission (ejaculation of seminal fluid during sleep, often accompanied by erotic dreams). A boy who has previously masturbated, with accompanying pleasant sensations but without ejaculation, may wonder if the ejaculation of seminal fluid is harmful or an indication that something is physically wrong with him. Others have no such concern. As one 15-year-old put it, "I think a first wet dream is a powerful moment. It marks becoming a man. I was really excited about it" (R. Bell, 1980, p. 15).

As with girls, the occurrence of puberty in boys is correlated with psychological changes. Independent of the age when puberty occurs, pubertal maturation is associated with increased conflict and distance in boys' relationships with their parents (Steinberg, 1977, 1981, 1988). This conflict is most marked in the middle of pubertal change and may concentrate initially in sons' relationships with mothers, with conflicts with fathers occurring later.

Timing of Puberty

As we have already seen, young people vary widely in the age at which they reach puberty. At age 15 one boy may be small, with no pubertal development of reproductive organs or pubic hair. At the same age another boy may appear to be virtually a grown man, with broad shoulders, strong muscles, adult genitalia, and a bass voice (Tanner, 1970, 1971). Similarly, at age 13, one girl may appear childlike, with a flat chest and no pubic hair, while another may look like a woman. Even though such variations are perfectly normal, they can affect the way adolescents view themselves—and the way they are viewed by others.

Early and Late Maturation in Males. Adults and other adolescents tend to think of the 14- or 15-year-old who looks 17 or 18 as older than he actually is. They are likely to expect more mature behavior from him than they would from a physically less developed male of the same age (Steinberg & Hill, 1978). Because there is less discrepancy in height between an early-maturing boy and most girls his own age (who typically experience an earlier growth spurt), the boy may become involved in boy-girl relationships sooner and with more self-confidence. Moreover, a physically more developed male has an advantage in many activities, especially athletics. Although a boy who matures much faster than most of his peers may feel somewhat different, he is not likely to feel insecure about the difference. After all, with his more rugged physique, increased strength, and greater sexual maturity, he can assure himself that he is simply changing in the direction society expects and approves (Blyth et al., 1981; Petersen, 1988; Simmons, Blyth, Van Cleave, & Bush, 1979; Simmons et al., 1983).

In contrast, the late-maturing male is more likely to be "treated like a child." He is likely to have a harder time excelling in athletics and other activities and establishing relationships with females. He may wonder when, if ever, he will reach full physical and sexual maturity.

Not surprisingly, all of this results, on the average, in personality differences between early and late maturers. Extensive long-term research at the University of California found that males who matured late tended to be less poised, more tense and talkative, and more self-conscious and affected than males who matured early. They were also likely to be "overeager" and more restless, impulsive, bossy, and "attention seeking." Though obviously there are exceptions to these patterns, late maturers tended to be less popular with peers, and fewer of them were leaders. Early maturers, on the other hand, appeared more reserved, self-assured, and matter-of-

Pubertal changes in males are generally seen as clearly positive; the same is not true for females.

fact, and were more likely to engage easily in socially appropriate behavior. They were also more likely to be able to laugh at themselves. Later studies have obtained similar results (Clausen, 1975; M. C. Jones, 1957; Mussen & Jones, 1957; Simmons et al., 1979, 1983).

While early-maturing boys generally have an advantage over those who mature late, the picture is not entirely one-sided. When early- and late-maturing groups were compared at or after (but not before) puberty, late-maturing boys emerged as more intellectually curious and higher in exploratory behavior and social initiative (Livson & Peskin, 1980; Peskin, 1967). In contrast, early maturers tended to avoid problem solving or new situations unless urged. "The early maturers appeared to approach cognitive tasks cautiously and timidly, with a preference for rules, routines, and imitative action" (Livson & Peskin, 1980, p. 73).

A far-ranging follow-up study of the participants in the University of California studies, conducted when the subjects were 38 years old, demonstrated that differences between early and late maturers—both positive and negative—can persist into adulthood (Clausen, 1975; M. C. Jones, 1957; Livson & Peskin, 1980). As adults, the early-maturing males were more responsible, cooperative, sociable, and self-contained but also more conventional, conforming, moralistic, humorless, and concerned with making a good impression. On the other hand, the late maturers remained less controlled, less responsible, and more impulsive and assertive but also "more insightful, perceptive, creatively playful, and able to cope with the ambiguity of new situations" (Livson & Peskin, 1980, p. 71).

Much can be done by parents, teachers, and others to minimize the anxiety and other negative psychological effects of late maturation. Adults can make a conscious effort to avoid treating a late maturer as younger than he actually is. They can help him realize that his slower maturation is normal—that he will indeed "grow up" and be just as physically and sexually masculine as his peers. And they can help him achieve success in activities in which his smaller size and strength are not a handicap. For example, while immaturity and smaller size can be a handicap for a football player, they may be assets for a diver or a tumbler.

Conversely, parents and others can assist early maturers by not forming unrealistic expectations of maturity based on physical appearance. They can also encourage early-maturing boys to take time to catch up psychologically and socially instead of rushing headlong into adult activities.

Early and Late Maturation in Females. Early or at least average maturation is generally easier for adolescent boys to deal with than late maturation, although, as we have seen, differences between early- and late-maturing males in adulthood show a more mixed picture. Early research on the effects of timing of puberty in girls seemed to show fewer differences related to timing of puberty in girls than boys and a greater mixture of positive and negative effects (Crockett & Petersen, 1987; Faust, 1960, 1977, 1984; Livson & Peskin, 1980; Simmons et al., 1979, 1983). However, more recently, a growing body of evidence suggests predominantly negative effects of early maturing for girls, a very different pattern than that seen with boys.

Early-maturing girls tend to be less satisfied with their body image than average or late maturers. While the early-maturing boy is steadily developing in the direction of favored adult norms, this is not typically the case for early-maturing girls, who tend to be bigger, heavier, and fatter than their more petite late-maturing peers (Simmons et al., 1983; Tobin-Richards, Boxer, & Petersen, 1984). The exaggerated emphasis our society places on being tall and slim may help explain the finding that the heavier a girl is—or thinks she is—the more dissatisfied she is with both her weight and her body shape.

In addition to being dissatisfied with their bodies, early-maturing girls seem to be more easily disorganized under stress; more restless, listless, moody, and complaining; and less popular with same-sex peers than late-maturing girls (Blyth et al., 1981; Faust, 1960, 1977; Peskin, 1973; Petersen, 1988). They are more likely to perform poorly in school, score lower on achievement tests, exhibit problem behaviors in school, and have lower academic aspirations (Simmons et al., 1979, 1983). While findings that they are more independent, more popular with opposite-sex peers, and more interested in dating may appear positive, studies suggest that involvement with boys, often older boys, at a young age may have negative consequences. Early-maturing girls show more behavioral problems, precocious sexual behavior and early marriage than later maturers (Caspi & Moffitt, 1991; Stattin & Magnusson, 1990; Udry & Cliquet, 1982). Many behavioral problems are produced specifically by the girls' involvement with older boys (Caspi, Lynam, Moffitt, & Silva, 1993).

Influences from opposite-sex peers are not the only contributor to early-maturing girls' greater risk of behavioral problems. Another important factor is prepubertal personality and temperament. Behavioral problems are especially likely in adolescence if early-maturing girls already had problems at age 9 (Caspi & Moffitt, 1991). The prior existence of problems and early maturing seem to work together as risk factors, amplifying the effects of either factor taken alone. That is, the girl with earlier behavior problems who matures on time or late, and the girl who matures early but has no history of problems, are at much less risk.

Why is early maturation a more favorable event for boys and a negative one for girls? First, early-maturing girls are in a minority among their peers; early-maturing boys are changing when girls in their classes have already matured (Simmons et al., 1983). Second, society favors early maturity in males more clearly and less ambiguously than in females. In boys, early maturation means greater strength and physical prowess. Among girls, early maturation may mean being heavier than one's female peers and taller than everyone one's own age. Third, in our society it may also mean being subjected to more conflicting sexual messages than is the case for males. In the case of an early-maturing female, parents and other adults should be careful to support her in avoiding opposite-sex relationships beyond her psychological maturity level. They can help her develop her own interests and maintain her friendships with peers her own age.

⚙ ADOLESCENT SEXUALITY

Among the many developmental events that characterize puberty and the onset of adolescence, none is more dramatic than the physical and psychological changes associated with sexual development. These changes require many new adjustments on the part of the young person and contribute significantly to a changing self-image. As one 16-year-old expressed it, "When I was 14, my body started to go crazy" (R. Bell, 1980, p. 73).

Although sexuality in the broadest sense is a lifelong part of being human (even babies love to be held and may fondle their genitals), the hormonal changes accompanying puberty lead to stronger sexual feelings. These feelings are manifested differently in different individuals; even in the same person they may be expressed differently at different times. Some adolescents find themselves thinking a great deal about sex; others are less aware of sexual feelings and more excited by other interests. At the same age, one adolescent may be in love and going steady, another may be involved in sexual experimentation, and a third may feel that it is much too early for such activities (R. Bell, 1980).

Premarital Sexual Intercourse

Intense interest has been focused on the question of adolescents' engaging in sexual intercourse, because this sexual behavior is associated with risks for adolescents of unintended adolescent pregnancy and of sexually transmitted diseases (STDs), including AIDS. American adults tend to overestimate, however, the precocity of the age at which adolescents typically initiate intercourse. The majority of people over the age of 18 estimate that first intercourse generally occurs before the age of 16 (Centers for Disease Control and Prevention, 1991). However, the actual proportions of adolescent females who have had intercourse, as estimated from survey responses, tell a somewhat different story. Proportions increase regularly with age, as shown in Figure 14.5, from very low percentages at age 12. The proportions reach a level where over half the group have had intercourse at age 18 (rather than prior to 16, as adults had estimated).

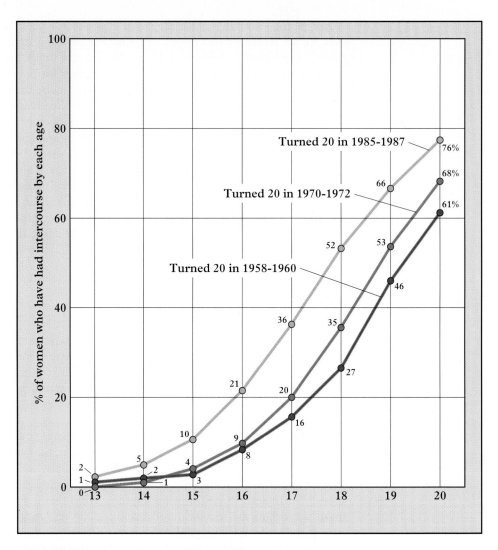

FIGURE 14.5 Proportions of females who have had sexual intercourse, at ages 13 to 20, for three different birth cohorts in the United States. From Figure 12, "Percent of Women Who Have Had Intercourse by Each Age," in *Sex and America's Teenagers* (p. 23). Reprinted with permission of the Alan Guttmacher Institute.

There has been clear historical change in occurrence of sexual intercourse in American adolescents during the twentieth century. Figure 14.5 shows for three birth cohorts the proportion of adolescent females at each age who have had intercourse. At each age, figures are higher for more recent historical periods (Alan Guttmacher Institute, 1994).

Data for males are similar in many respects to those for females. Figure 14.6 shows that proportions of males having had intercourse increase regularly with age for males, with over half the group having experienced intercourse at least once by the age of 17. As with girls, at each age except the youngest, larger proportions of adolescent boys report having had intercourse in more recent historical periods.

Comparing Figures 14.5 and 14.6 shows that boys are more likely than girls at each age to have experienced intercourse. This is an especially striking fact when we remember that boys experience puberty later than girls do. One reason for the fact that adolescent males are more likely to have sexual intercourse is that they experi-

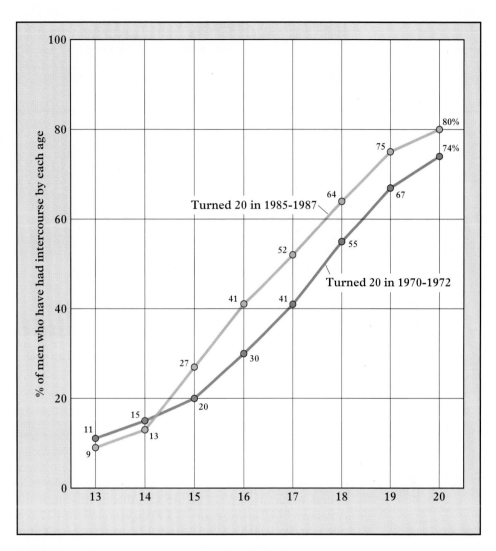

FIGURE 14.6 Proportions of males who have had sexual intercourse, at ages 13 to 20, for two different birth cohorts in the United States. From Figure 11, "Percent of Men Who Have Had Intercourse by Each Age," in *Sex and America's Teenagers* (p. 22). Reprinted with permission of the Alan Guttmacher Institute.

ence marked increases in testosterone levels at puberty. It has been demonstrated that this hormone increases sexual behavior in members of both sexes under experimental conditions (Hamburg & Trudeau, 1981; Katchadourian, 1985; Petersen, 1988). Another reason is certainly that norms and expectations about sex differ for males and females, with sex still considered more acceptable for males. However, this difference in norms for the two sexes may lead not only to real differences in behavior but also to differences in reporting (Smith, 1988). Girls may underreport sexual experience out of a feeling that it is unacceptable, and boys may overreport sexual experience because they feel it is expected. It is important to remember that the data in Figures 14.5 and 14.6 are based on what people said in interviews.

There are differences in sexual intercourse as a function of socioeconomic class and ethnic background. Males and females from families that are poor or low-income initiate sex earlier. The point at which over half the respondents report sexual intercourse occurs six months earlier for males from such families compared to

Sexual activity in adolescents (and adults) poses risks and challenges for responsible behavior.

those from better-off families, and four months earlier for females from such families (Alan Guttmacher Institute, 1994). Black adolescents are more sexually active than whites or Hispanics, although the size of the difference has been decreasing over past decades. The point at which half the respondents report sexual intercourse occurs two years earlier for African-American males than for European-American or Hispanic males (15 years versus almost 17 years), and the difference is one year for females (16.5 versus 17.5 years) (Alan Guttmacher Institute, 1994).

Focusing solely on whether adolescents have or have not experienced sexual intercourse does not, however, give a complete picture of adolescents' sexual lives. First, it is important to remember that adolescents typically have sex quite sporadically. This fact is partly linked to the fact that they are usually not married or cohabiting, but unmarried adolescents also have sex less frequently than unmarried people in their twenties (Alan Guttmacher Institute, 1994). The sporadic nature of adolescent sex is important to consider in offering contraceptive education to adolescents, a topic we discuss shortly.

Second, not all of the adolescent women who report experience with sexual intercourse have had voluntary sex (K. A. Moore, Nord, & Peterson, 1989). This phenomenon is especially marked among the younger girls who report sexual experience, with 60 percent of girls who had sex before the age of 15 reporting that they had sex involuntarily (Alan Guttmacher Institute, 1994). Involuntary sex is a situation in which it is generally impossible for an adolescent girl to protect herself from pregnancy or sexually transmitted diseases. Even more alarmingly, having such experience seems to create difficulty in practicing protective behavior in future sexual encounters (Cassese, 1993; Kidman, 1993). Sexual abuse is a risk factor for the development of various psychological problems, including depression (Kendall-

Tackett, Williams, & Finkelhor, 1993), and these problems may lead in turn to difficulty practicing protective behavior.

Sexually Transmitted Diseases, Pregnancy, and Contraception

Adolescents who are sexually active face the challenge of protecting themselves from the possibility of unintended pregnancy and from sexually transmitted diseases, including those for which there is currently no cure, such as genital herpes and acquired immune deficiency syndrome (AIDS). A sexually active adolescent woman not using contraception has a 90 percent chance of being pregnant within a year (Harlap, Kost, & Forrest, 1991). The rate will be lower, however, to the extent that intercourse is sporadic, a fact that may give adolescents a false sense of security. A single act of unprotected intercourse with an infected partner poses a risk of transmission, for women, ranging from 1 percent for HIV to 30 percent for genital herpes and 50 percent for gonorrhea. Chances for transmission to men are somewhat lower for some diseases, but are still 0.9 percent for HIV, 30 percent for genital herpes, and 25 percent for gonorrhea (Harlap, Kost, & Forrest, 1991).

Preventing unintended pregnancy is possible with a wide range of methods, including birth-control pills, intrauterine devices (IUDs), diaphragms, and condoms. There has been significant progress in adolescents' use of some form of contraception. About two-thirds of American adolescents now report using contraception the first time they have intercourse. However, the likelihood of doing so increases with age. When intercourse occurred before age 15, 52 percent of women report having used contraception, whereas the rate is 68 percent for those who were 15 to 17 at first intercourse, and 77 percent for those who were 18 or 19 (Alan Guttmacher Institute, 1994; Sonenstein, Pleck, & Ku, 1989).

Adolescents now do about as well as adult women at using contraceptive methods as they are designed to be used and in preventing unintended pregnancy (E. F. Jones & Forrest, 1992). However, it is important to realize that usage patterns are far from perfect at all ages. Examining effective use of condoms is particularly illuminating, given that this contraceptive method is the only method that additionally offers any protection against sexually transmitted diseases. To use condoms correctly requires, first, that a condom be put on the penis before penetration rather than after; second, that withdrawal occur while the penis is still erect after orgasm; third, that the condom be held in place during withdrawal; and, fourth, that a condom be used for every act of intercourse. In a sample of women relying on condoms for contraception, from 73 to 80 percent of women across the age range from 15 to over 30 followed the first rule, but compliance rates for the second were 40 to 56 percent, for the third were 28 to 40 percent, and for the fourth were 31 to 56 percent (Alan Guttmacher Institute, 1994). Clearly, while it is encouraging to find that condoms are being used at higher rates than was true formerly, their usage needs improvement.

While contraceptive use is increasing, the fact that larger numbers of adolescents are having sex than in prior historical periods, combined with the fact that contraceptive use is far from perfect, leads to high rates of unintended adolescent pregnancy. In the United States about 11 percent of girls aged 15 to 19 become pregnant each year (Azar, 1994). More than two-thirds of teenagers giving birth each year are unmarried. One way to look at these statistics is this: out of every 20 girls now aged 14, 8 will get pregnant as teenagers. Of these, 4 will give birth (Azar,

1994). Rates of teenage pregnancy are higher in the United States than in most other countries. American rates are more than double those found in Great Britain, Canada, and New Zealand, and more than triple that seen in Finland, Denmark, and the Netherlands (Alan Guttmacher Institute, 1994).

In addition to the risks of pregnancy—which are greater for teenagers than for women in their twenties—adolescent mothers, as we saw in Chapter 12, face significant problems in other areas. They are twice as likely as their peers to drop out of school, less likely to gain employment, and more likely to end up on welfare (Burt, 1986; Edelman, 1987; Furstenberg, 1976; Furstenberg, Brooks-Gunn, & Morgan, 1987a, 1987b). Many still need mothering themselves and are ill prepared to take on the psychological, social, and economic responsibilities of motherhood; their knowledge of an infant's needs and capabilities is often unrealistic, leading to expectations and demands that their infants cannot meet (J. J. Conger, 1988). Moreover, single adolescent mothers have less chance of getting married than their peers, and a much greater chance of divorce if they do marry (Furstenberg & Brooks-Gunn, 1986). Even adolescents who are already married when they become pregnant, or who marry prior to the birth of their child, are far more likely to divorce than those who become mothers after age 20. Nevertheless, with adequate social support, substantial numbers of adolescent mothers do go on to complete high school, become effective parents, escape public assistance, and find fixed regular employment (Furstenberg, Brooks-Gunn, & Morgan, 1987b).

Psychological studies comparing sexually active adolescent girls who do and do not use contraceptives (or use them rarely) have found that those who do not use contraceptives are more likely to have fatalistic attitudes: to feel powerless to control their own lives, to have a low sense of personal competence, and to have a passive, dependent approach to male-female relationships. They are also more inclined to take risks and to cope with anxiety by attempting to deny dangers rather than face up to them. In contrast, consistent contraceptive use is more likely among female adolescents who are older, are in love and involved in an ongoing relationship, have high levels of self-esteem and self-confidence, are making normal progress in school, have positive attitudes toward their parents, and received sex education early and at home, rather than from an acquaintance (Chilman, 1983).

Some adolescents avoid using contraceptives because they fear that it would spoil the spontaneity of the relationship or because they think it would indicate that they expect to have intercourse. One sign that the double standard persists in some circles is that frank pursuit of sexual relations is still considered more acceptable for boys than for girls (Goodchilds & Zellman, 1984; Santrock, 1987). For a significant number of adolescents, it is more acceptable for a girl to be swept away by the passion of the moment than to take contraceptive precautions (Morrison, 1985). Interestingly, girls who frankly accept their sexuality and girls who are able to discuss sexual matters easily with their parents are more likely to use contraceptives than those who deny it to themselves or others (Chilman, 1983; J. J. Conger, 1987; Hornick, Doran, & Crawford, 1979).

Among male adolescents, those who are most likely to employ contraceptive measures are older, more experienced in dating, and more organized and responsible in their general approach to life. They also tend to have parents who approve of their sexual involvement. Males who are least likely to employ contraception tend either to be sexually naive or to be permissively reared and "exploitive," believing that contraception is the female's responsibility (Goldfarb et al., 1977; Kelley, 1979).

Contrary to frequently expressed opinions on the subject, only one in fifteen pregnant adolescents in a national sample stated that she did not use contraceptives because she was trying to have a baby, and only one in eleven indicated that she "didn't mind" getting pregnant. However, among adolescents who either seek or do not object to pregnancy, a common theme is emotional deprivation. In the words of one pregnant 15-year-old, "I guess for once in my life, I wanted to have something I could call my own, that I could love and that would love me." Other, related motivations may include being accepted as an adult, getting back at one's parents, "holding" a boyfriend, gaining attention from peers, escaping from school, or just looking for some change in an unrewarding existence (Chilman, 1983).

A key ingredient in helping adolescents to engage in reponsible sexual behavior is education and communication with adults. While it is sometimes feared that discussing sex with adolescents sends the message that having sex is condoned or actually encouraged, this does not appear to be the case. Adolescents who report that they are able to discuss sex freely and openly with their parents are less, rather than more, likely to engage in premarital intercourse (J. J. Conger, 1988; Sorensen, 1973); of this group, those who are sexually active are less likely to become pregnant. Sex education programs are associated with better communication with parents about pregnancy and conception (Dawson, 1986; "Sex education," 1986). There is no consistent evidence that sex education, including information about contraception, increases the likelihood of becoming sexually active. On the other hand, there is considerable evidence that sexually active adolescents who have had sex education are more likely to use effective contraceptive methods. In addition, teenagers who have had sex education courses are, if anything, less likely to become pregnant (Dawson, 1986; Marsiglio & Mott, 1986; "Sex education," 1986).

Kirby et al. (1994) have summarized the characteristics of effective school-based pregnancy- and STD-prevention programs. These characteristics include: (1) being based in an understanding of social learning and social influence, (2) focusing fairly narrowly on reducing specific risky behaviors, (3) including experiential and personalized activities to ensure comprehension of information on risks and how to avoid them, (4) instructing participants on social pressure, (5) reinforcing norms against unprotected sex, and (6) having activities to practice relevant skills and confidence in those skills. (See Box 14.1 for an account of sex education in one fictional high school class.)

Homosexual Behavior and Orientation

Although a large majority of young people develop an exclusively heterosexual orientation by the end of adolescence, a significant minority develop an exclusively or predominantly homosexual orientation. Contrary to some popular conceptions, the incidence of homosexuality in our society does not appear to have increased in the last 40 years, although openness about homosexuality has increased dramatically (A. P. Bell, Weinberg, & Hammersmith, 1981; Chilman, 1983; M. Hunt, 1974; Kinsey, Pomeroy, & Martin, 1948; Kinsey, Pomeroy, Martin, & Gebhard, 1953). Uncertainty about how many adults are homosexual is linked to definitions of what homosexuality is and also to how samples are obtained for surveys on sexual behavior. A national survey of Americans from 18 to 59 years found that 2.8 percent of men and 1.4 percent of women identified themselves as homosexual or bisexual (Dunlap, 1994).

Why some young people become homosexual while most become heterosexual

BOX 14.1
SEX EDUCATION

The following is a fictional account of a teacher in a very small town in the Southwestern United States, who decides, somewhat impulsively, that it is essential for her high school biology class to know more about contraception than they do.

On the last Monday of October Rita Cardenal made three announcements to the class: she was quitting school, this was her last day, and if anybody wanted her fetal pig they could have it, it was as good as new.... Rita wore about half a dozen earrings in one ear and had a tough-cookie attitude, and I liked her. She'd been a good student. She seemed sorry to go but also resigned to her fate, in that uniquely teenage way of looking at life, as if the whole production were a thing inflicted on young people by some humorless committee of grownups with bad fashion sense. I was disappointed but unsurprised to lose Rita. I'd been watching her jeans get tight. The pregnancy dropout rate in Grace was way ahead of motor-vehicle accidents, as a teenage hazard. Rita was a statistic. On Tuesday I made my own announcement: we were doing an unscheduled unit on birth control.

The reaction in the ranks was equal parts embarrassment and amazement. You'd think I suggested orgies in study hall. There was some hysteria when I got to the visual aids. "Look, there's nothing funny about a condom," I said, pretending to be puzzled by their laughter. "It's a piece of equipment with a practical purpose, like a. . . " Only the most unfortunate analogies came to mind. Shower cap. Tea cozy. "Like a glove," I said, settling for the cliche. I turned from the blackboard and narrowed my eyes. "If you think this thing is funny, you should see the ridiculous-looking piece of equipment it fits over." The guys widened their eyes but shut up. I was getting the hang of this.

"Miss," said Raymo. They'd never learned to call me Codi.

"What is it?"

"You're gonna get busted for this."

Source: From *Animal Dreams* (pp. 145–146) by Barbara Kingsolver, 1990, New York: HarperPerennial.

is still unclear. Some theorists have stressed the potential importance of social and psychological influences (e.g., disturbances in parent-child relationships); others emphasize genetic, hormonal, or other biological factors (Beach, 1977; A. P. Bell & Weinberg, 1978; Green, 1980, 1987). It may well be that a complex interaction of biological, psychological, and social factors beginning early in life is involved and that the nature of the interaction may vary from one individual to another (Bell, Weinberg, & Hammersmith, 1981). It is clear, as Alan Bell and his colleagues at the Kinsey Institute have observed, that "neither homosexuals nor heterosexuals are what they are by design. Homosexuals, in particular, cannot be dismissed as persons who simply refuse to conform. There is no reason to think it would be any easier for homosexual men or women to reverse their sexual orientation than it would be for heterosexual [individuals] to become predominantly or exclusively homosexual" (A. P. Bell & Weinberg, 1978, p. 222).

Adolescents dealing with a dawning awareness of homosexuality often go through stages of identity reorganization. Troiden (1989) described a progression consisting of four stages. First, prior to puberty, children are often sensitive to differences between themselves and other children, without being aware of their

BOX 14.2
FORMING A HOMOSEXUAL IDENTITY

Exactly why some people are homosexual and others are heterosexual is still not well understood. However, for whatever reason a sexual orientation is formed, once people become aware of it they need to integrate their sexual selves with their overall concept of themselves. This process may be particularly difficult for homosexuals due to social stigma.

Recollecting my years as a high school lesbian, the images that stick in my mind are those of feeling alone, sneaking around, feeling hunted, and fighting with my parents. I felt that neither my parents nor my friends would understand my sexual choice, so I kept my secret well. I think if it had not been for the other lesbians I knew, my life would have been unbearable. By the same token, if it had not been for them, my home life would have run much smoother.

I came out to myself as a fourteen-year-old high school sophomore. My field hockey teammates had been spreading rumors that our coach was a lesbian. I felt angered that they should let such a thing influence their opinion of her. Having never knowingly met any gays, I knew nothing about homosexuality. Yet from my uneducated standpoint, I decided that the accusations were unjust.

The constant talk about gays made me curious and I went to the library to read up on the subject so I could better understand my coach if indeed she was gay. One day, a short time after starting to read about lesbians, I was sitting in English class and like a bolt of lightning, I realized that I was gay. The "bolt of lightning" line may sound rather dramatic. What happened was that suddenly all the feelings of attraction I had been having for women, and the isolated feelings about myself due to my lack of "femininity" came together and pointed to the label, *Lesbian*..

Source: From *One Teenager in Ten: Writings by Gay and Lesbian Youth* "(Joanne," pp. 9–10), edited by A. Heron, 1983, Boston: Alyson Publications.

meaning or attaching significance to them. Second, as they realize the significance of the differences during adolescence, they may be confused about their sexual identity. But if they are successful in dealing with this confusion, they may proceed to stage 3, identity assumption, and stage 4, commitment to a new identity. (See Box 14.2 for a personal description of this process of "coming out.")

COGNITIVE DEVELOPMENT IN ADOLESCENCE

The physical changes of adolescence are dramatic indeed. But there are also important cognitive changes occurring at this time that play a vital role in transforming children into adults. In fact, the comment that adolescence begins in biology, which we mentioned at the beginning of the chapter, may be incomplete. Adolescence also appears to begin with a series of changes in cognitive ability, which lead to children's becoming much more able to think and reason like adults. Such a change clearly is central to the gradual assumption of adult roles and responsibilities that characterizes adolescence. Cognitive changes play a critical role in helping adolescents deal with complex educational and vocational demands.

Formal Operations

The most comprehensive description of cognitive changes in adolescence comes from Jean Piaget. His general view of cognitive development has already been presented in Chapters 5 and 9. Here, we examine his view that there is a qualititative change in cognition at adolescence. Piaget used the term *formal operations* to decribe the mature level of thought that he saw as beginning in adolescence. In the formal operations stage, which begins at about age 12 and extends through adulthood, the limitations of the previous stage (the concrete operational stage of thought) are overcome. The person begins to use a wider variety of cognitive operations and strategies in solving problems, is highly versatile and flexible in thought and reasoning, and can see things from a number of perspectives or points of view (Ginsburg & Opper, 1979).

One of the most striking features of the stage of formal operations is the development of the ability to reason about *hypothetical* problems—about what might be— as well as about real ones, and to think about *possibilities* as well as actualities. The concrete operational child mentally manipulates objects and events; in the stage of formal operations, the child can manipulate ideas about hypothetical situations. For example, an older child can reach a logical conclusion when asked, "If all Martians have yellow feet and this creature is a Martian, does this creature have yellow feet ?" A 7-year-old has difficulty reasoning about improbable or impossible events and is likely to say, "I never saw a Martian" or "Things don't have yellow feet."

Another hallmark of problem solving in the stage of formal operations is *systematic searching for solutions.* Faced with a novel problem, an adolescent attempts to consider all possible means of solving it and checks the logic and effectiveness of each one. When planning to drive to the seashore, for example, adolescents can mentally review all the possible routes, systematically assessing which one is safest, shortest, and fastest (though they may not employ this competence in a specific instance). Systematic evaluation of alternatives is central to scientific experimentation and also to effective everyday problem solving, about problems such as what could cause a car to malfunction.

In formal operational thought, mental operations are organized into higher-order operations. Higher-order operations are ways of using abstract rules to solve a whole class of problems. For example, in solving the problem "What number is 30 less than 2 times itself ?" concrete operational children are likely to try first one number and then another, using addition and multiplication until they finally arrive at the correct answer. An adolescent combines the separate operations of addition and multiplication into a single, more complex operation that can be expressed as an algebraic equation, and quickly finds the answer: 30.

In Piaget's investigations of formal operations, which he conducted in collaboration with his longtime colleague Barbel Inhelder, children were asked to solve a variety of logical and scientific problems. The problems called for conclusions about the behavior of floating objects, oscillating pendulums, balance beams, and chemical mixtures. For example, in one experiment children were given five bottles containing colorless liquids and instructed to find a way of combining them that would produce a yellow liquid. In attempting to solve this problem, children in the stage of concrete operations use a trial-and-error approach, trying out a number of solutions, generally in an inefficient way. They often test each chemical individually with one or two others but fail to consider all the possible combinations. In contrast, adolescents act more like adult scientists or logicians, considering all the possible solutions in an

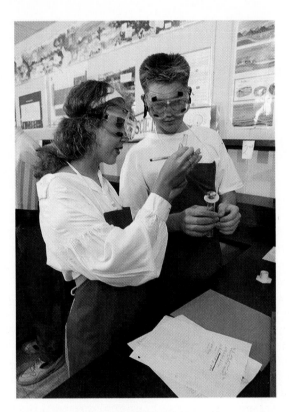

Adolescents become able to systematically evaluate solutions and possibilities, an essential ability for understanding science.

exhaustive way, formulating hypotheses about outcomes, and systematically designing tests of the hypotheses. They try out all the possible combinations of chemicals and draw accurate conclusions through deductive, logical reasoning.

As occurred with Piaget's hypotheses about younger children, researchers have found some problems with Piaget's formulation of a stage of formal operations. Not only is the age of onset of formal operational thinking more variable than Piaget envisaged, but this change occurs less suddenly and is less universal and more specific to particular areas in which the individual is especially competent, such as physics or politics (Keating, 1980). Thus, investigators have found some aspects of formal thinking in highly intelligent younger children (Keating, 1975, 1980). Conversely, some adolescents and adults never acquire true formal operational thought because of limited ability or cultural limitations, both in our own and in other countries (Keating, 1980; Neimark, 1975a; R. J. Ross, 1973). Even very bright adolescents and adults do not always employ their capacity for formal operational thinking—for example, when a problem seems too far removed from reality or when they are bored, tired, frustrated, or overly involved emotionally (Neimark, 1975a, 1975b).

From an information-processing perspective, there are additional cognitive changes to those described by Piaget. Adolescents are generally able to process more, and more complex, information than younger children, and to do so more quickly and efficiently. They appear to be able to accomplish this in part because of their increased ability to pay careful attention and to remember, and partly because they have developed a variety of information-processing strategies (e.g., increasingly powerful rules for solving problems) and are able to employ them selectively

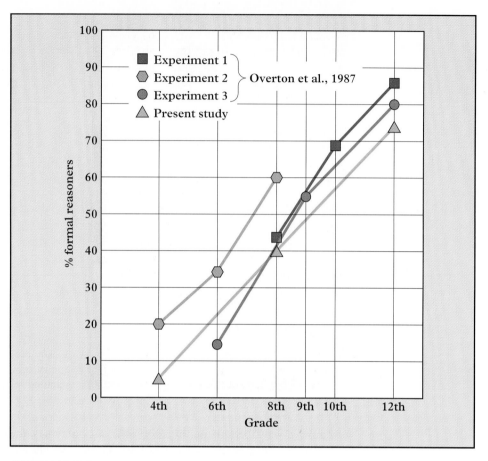

FIGURE 14.7 Percentages of subjects at grades 4 through 12 who achieve a criterion for formal reasoning. After "Semantic Familiarity, Relevance, and the Development of Deductive Reasoning," by S. L. Ward and W. F. Overton, 1990, *Developmental Psychology, 26*, p. 491. Adapted with permission.

in accordance with the demands of a particular task (A. L. Brown, 1975; A. L. Brown et al., 1983; Flavell, 1985; Sternberg, 1984).

The Piagetian and information-processing points of view are not diametrically opposed, however, because Piaget was less interested in the precise age or rate of acquisition of cognitive abilities than with the fact of their logical sequence. Research focused on children's and adolescents' ability to reason logically about verbal problems has found highly regular and reproducible linear increases with age in the proportion of subjects who reach criterion performance (Overton, Ward, Noveck, Black, & O'Brien, 1987; Ward & Overton, 1990). As can be seen in Figure 14.7, small proportions of children reach criterion even at Grade 4, when they are 9 or 10 years old; high school seniors, on the other hand, do not all reach criterion. The fact that individual differences exist in age of attainment does not pose a serious problem for Piaget, especially since the differences may be coherent and explainable. For instance, age at acquisition of formal reasoning ability is related to training experiences and to differences in cognitive style (Overton, Byrnes, & O'Brien, 1985). Differences in age at acquisition are also related to social class (Demetriou, Efklides, Papadaki, Papantoniou & Economou, 1993), perhaps because cognitive and social experiences vary with social class.

Once the ability to reason with formal logic is acquired, whether or not it is deployed may depend on one's familiarity with the content area of a problem and one's motivation to solve it. For instance, Ward and Overton (1990) gave logical reasoning problems to students in Grades 6, 9, and 12 that were either of high meaning and relevance or more artificial and contrived. For the sixth graders, few of whom would be expected to be able to reason logically at all, this manipulation made little difference. However, the two older groups showed much clearer evidence of logical reasoning with high-relevance problems than with contrived problems. Reasoning logically apparently requires both competence and motivation.

There are some important implications of the changes observed in adolescent thinking. For example, many adolescents show a newfound (and sometimes wearing) talent for discovering a previously idealized parent's feet of clay—questioning the parent's values, comparing them with other parents, or accusing them of hypocritical inconsistencies between professed values and behavior.

In addition, on entering the stage of formal operations, adolescents may begin to think about their own thoughts, evaluating them and searching for inconsistencies and fallacies. A 14-year-old may brood about the following two propositions:

1. God loves humanity.

2. There are many suffering human beings.

These two beliefs seem incompatible, causing the adolescent to look for ways of resolving the tension created by the inconsistency.

Another characteristic of adolescent thought is a preoccupation with thought itself, particularly with one's own thoughts about oneself. An adolescent girl or boy is likely to become more introspective and analytical. In addition, thought and behavior may appear to be egocentric (Elkind, 1968; Enright, Lapsley, & Shukla, 1979). Because adolescents think about themselves a lot, they are likely to conclude that other people, too, are subjecting their thoughts and feelings, personality characteristics, behavior, and appearance to critical scrutiny. This idea may well increase the adolescent's already strong feelings of self-consciousness.

⚙ SUMMARY

Adolescence is a period of rapid physical, sexual, psychological, cognitive, and social change. It begins with puberty, the developmental phase in which sexual maturation becomes evident. At this time the pituitary gland begins releasing previously inhibited hormones, which in turn stimulate other glands to begin releasing hormones that affect growth and sexual development. The hormonal difference between the sexes is a difference in the proportions of masculinizing and feminizing hormones present in males and females.

A growth spurt—an accelerated rate of increase in height and weight—occurs at puberty. In both sexes the growth spurt lasts about 4.5 years, but it peaks about two years earlier in girls than in boys. Changes in height and weight are accompanied by changes in body proportions. Sex differences in body shape also are magnified during early adolescence.

In males, sexual maturation begins with an increase in the growth of the testes and scrotum, followed by an acceleration in growth of the penis, the appearance of axillary hair, and a lowering of the voice. In females, the first sign of sexual maturity is the appearance of pubic hair and "budding" of the breasts. These changes are followed by accelerated growth of the reproductive organs and finally by menarche (onset of menstruation).

For adolescent girls, the onset of menstruation is a symbol of "becoming a woman." However, a majority of American adolescent girls react negatively to menarche, partly because of the negative attitudes of others and partly because of the associated physical discomfort. For adolescent boys, uncontrolled erection and initial ejaculation may be a source of worry and embarrassment.

Early-maturing males face higher expectations of mature behavior and have an advantage in many activities, especially athletics. Late-maturing males are more likely to be "treated like children" and are likely to have more difficulty excelling in athletics and other activities. These differences result in personality differences that tend to favor early-maturing boys, who are likely to be more self-assured and able to engage easily in socially appropriate behavior.

Early-maturing girls tend to be less satisfied with their body image, more restless and moody, and less popular with same-sex peers than late-maturing girls. Their popularity with boys, especially older boys, may be an element in the higher risk of early maturing girls for behavior problems. However, this risk seems particularly high in the early maturing girl who also has a prior history of behavior problems before puberty.

Perhaps the most dramatic changes associated with adolescence have to do with sexuality. Rates of premarital intercourse have increased among teenagers, especially girls, over recent historical periods in the United States. Among the problems associated with adolescent sexuality are the possibility of pregnancy and sexually transmitted diseases. Contraceptive use is now as good among adolescents as among adults; however, inadequacies in contraceptive behaviors at all ages are troubling. Adolescents who decide to keep their babies are twice as likely as their peers to drop out of school, less likely to gain employment, and more likely to end up on welfare.

Teenagers who do not use contraceptives either believe (usually mistakenly) that they cannot become pregnant or are unable to obtain contraceptives when they need them. Compared with those who use contraceptives, they are more likely to have fatalistic attitudes and are more inclined to take risks.

Continuing cognitive development, including the advent of the stage of formal operations, allows adolescents to think more abstractly, to formulate and test hypotheses, and to consider what might be, not merely what is. These abilities often lead adolescents to criticize parental and social values. Adolescent thought and behavior may also appear egocentric; young people may conclude that others are as preoccupied with their behavior and appearance as they themselves are. Adolescent cognitive development also plays an important role in personality development and in the formation of a clear sense of identity.

REVIEW QUESTIONS

1. Briefly describe the role of hormonal factors in adolescent physical development.

2. How does sexual development progress in adolescent males and females?

3. What effects does maturation, particularly early versus late maturation, have on the psychological well-being of adolescent boys and girls?

4. Briefly describe recent social changes in sexual behavior by males and females. How do these vary among different sectors of the population?

5. Why do sexually active adolescents often fail to use contraceptive measures?

6. Name four cognitive capabilities that are likely to develop during adolescence. What are some implications of these cognitive changes?

CRITICAL THINKING ABOUT THE CHAPTER

1. There is continuing debate about the kind of sex education children and adolescents should receive. What material do you think should be taught, at what age, by whom and how? Whatever program you advocate, use the material presented in this chapter to provide a factual context for your response.

2. Consider the psychological challenges posed by sexual maturation. Do you think these challenges make adolescence a time of storm and stress, as some observers of adolescence have claimed, or do you disagree? Why might observers' answers to this question vary across different cultural groups or at different historical periods?

KEY TERMS

adolescence
growth spurt

menarche
puberty

SUGGESTED READINGS

Bell, R. (1987). *Changing bodies, changing lives: A book for teens on sex and relationships.* New York: Random House (paperback). A valuable source of information on physical and sexual development in adolescence and the effects of these changes on feelings and relationships.

Feldman, S. S., & Elliott, G. R. (Eds.). (1990). *At the threshold.* Cambridge, MA: Harvard University Press. Chapters on a wide variety of topics in adolescence, written by leading experts.

Flavell, J. (1985). *Cognitive development* (2nd ed.). Englewood Cliffs, NJ: Prentice-Hall (paperback). A sophisticated but readable discussion of cognitive development, including excellent chapters on middle childhood and adolescence.

Hayes, C. D. (Ed.). (1987). *Risking the future: Vol. 1. Adolescent sexuality, pregnancy, and childbearing.* Washington, DC: National Academy Press (paperback). A comprehensive summary of current knowledge about causes, incidence, and consequences of adolescent sexuality, pregnancy, and childbearing.

Steinberg, L., & Levine, A. (1990). *You and your adolescent: A parent's guide for ages 10–20.* New York: Harper & Row. A self-help book written by a leading researcher on adolescent development. Interesting for those who work with adolescents, as well as for parents.

Youniss, J., & Smollar, J. (1985). *Adolescent relations with mothers, fathers, and friends.* Chicago: University of Chicago Press. An informative study of the role of parents and friends in helping adolescents become autonomous adults. Does an excellent job of integrating theory and empirical data.

CHAPTER

15

AUTONOMY, INTIMACY, IDENTITY, AND VALUES IN ADOLESCENCE

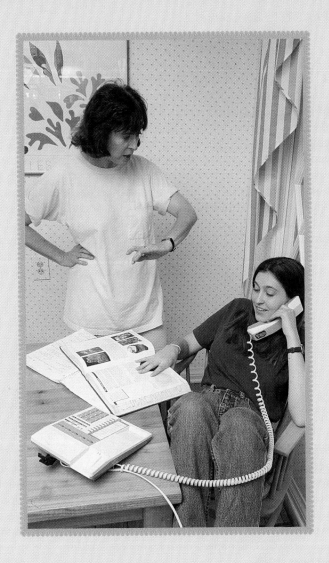

It's 6 p.m. at the Polk house. Three people are home, all in the kitchen together, but they're doing different things and thinking very different thoughts. Mindy Polk, 43, is chopping carrots as fast as she can while keeping an eye on several simmering pots and on her two adolescent children. Sam, 16, is doing his homework at the kitchen table while wearing headphones, a habit Mindy deeply disapproves of. But she's too tired and too busy to fight with him about it right now. He needs to get his homework done so that he can go to his part-time job delivering pizza. Sasha, 13, is talking on the telephone to one of her girlfriends. Mindy signals to her to hang up and get started on her homework, but Sasha turns her back. Mindy figures that's another problem she'll tackle when dinner is over.

Sighing, Mindy throws the carrots in a pot and looks up as Bruce Polk, 45, arrives back from dropping off one of their cars for much-needed repair. "The shop will need to keep the car two days," he says in a disgusted voice. "So I better call Bob and see if I can get a ride to work tomorrow and Wednesday. Sasha, will you please get off the phone?"

Adolescence, as you have seen already in Chapter 14, is a time of transitions. In addition to undergoing biological and cognitive transformations, adolescents undergo psychological and social changes on the way to adulthood. Four main lines of change can be delineated. First, adolescents renegotiate their relationships with their parents, establishing a greater autonomy than was possible or desirable in childhood. Sometimes minor friction results, as in the Polk family, when adolescents' sense of what is appropriate clashes with that of their parents. Second, adolescents begin to spend increasing amounts of time with friends, as Sasha was in holding her lengthy phone conversation. They establish more intimate relationships with peers than they had in childhood, including relationships with the opposite sex. Third, adolescents define an identity more firmly, making decisions about education and possible work life. Fourth, adolescents become increasingly able to reason in adult terms about moral issues and to define religious, political, and moral values. In this chapter, we examine changes in adolescence in all four of these important areas.

PARENTAL RELATIONSHIPS AND THE DEVELOPMENT OF AUTONOMY

A central task of adolescence is for parents and their children to establish new kinds of relationships with one another. Adolescents need increased, age-appropriate independence and sufficient freedom from parental control to express themselves as individuals with needs and feelings of their own, to make decisions about their own lives, and to take responsibility for the consequences of those decisions (Steinberg & Hill, 1978; Youniss & Smollar, 1985). At the same time, the development of age-appropriate autonomy does not require that the adolescent abandon family ties. Indeed, under favorable circumstances the development of age-appropriate autonomy is a dual process, providing both for separateness, individuality, and self-exploration and for continuing family connectedness, encouragement, and mutual support (C.R. Cooper, Grotevant, & Condon, 1983; Youniss, 1983; Youniss & Smollar, 1985).

Changing Interaction Patterns in the Family

Adolescents' relationships with their parents change in at least three ways as they mature. First, as adolescents gain in cognitive ability, their *perceptions* of their parents undergo a corresponding shift (Youniss, 1980). Younger children are likely to perceive their parents as "figures who have knowledge and power to get things done, especially those things children need or want" (Youniss & Smollar, 1985, p. 75). In contrast, adolescents are better able to differentiate parents as persons (with unique needs and feelings) from the roles parents play in carrying out their responsibilities as mothers and fathers. As one older adolescent girl said about her current relationship with her mother, "I'm more independent of her. Also, I am more free with my opinions even when I disagree. I realize she's not only my mother but an individual herself and I take her more on that level now. We still turn to each other when we have problems. We're still close" (Youniss & Smollar, 1985, p. 80). Similarly, a 15-year-old girl said of her mother: "She respects me more and lets me be on my own more. Treats me like a person, consults my opinion. I am a voice that is heard. Five years ago she was just a mother, now she's a person" (Youniss & Smollar, 1985, p. 80).

Second, as children grow into adolescence, they spend *less and less time* with their parents and families. One study of time use in adolescence addressed the question of changes in time use in adolescence in a very direct way, asking participants from 9 to 15 years to carry electronic pagers for a week. Subjects were signaled at random times—except school hours—and they reported where they were, who they were with, and how they were feeling (R. Larson & Richards, 1991). As you can see in Figure 15.1, both boys and girls reported less time with family as they grew older. For boys, time with family was replaced largely with time alone, while for girls time with family was replaced both by time alone and by time with friends. Larson and Richards (1991) also found that, when adolescents were with their families, both boys and girls reported feeling less positive about those experiences in seventh grade than they did in fifth grade. By ninth grade, boys felt more positive again about family experience, but feelings had not rebounded for girls.

As well as changing perceptions of their parents and decreasing time spent with family, adolescents are more prone to *conflict* with their parents than they were when they were children (Paikoff & Brooks-Gunn, 1991). We have already looked at research on this topic in Chapter 14; much of the increase in conflict appears to be linked to the biological changes of early adolescence. However, there are other determinants as well (Laursen & Collins, 1994; Paikoff & Brooks-Gunn, 1991). Many other life events occur in early adolescence, including transitions to junior high or middle school and the beginning of dating. The cumulative impact of these changes may affect adolescents' feelings about themselves (Simmons, Burgeson, Carlton-Ford, & Blyth, 1987), which may in turn affect their family relationships. In addition, the timing of adolescence with respect to changes in the parents may affect conflict. Paikoff, Brooks-Gunn, and Carlton-Ford (1991) found that mother-daughter relationships were affected by the timing of the daughter's puberty with

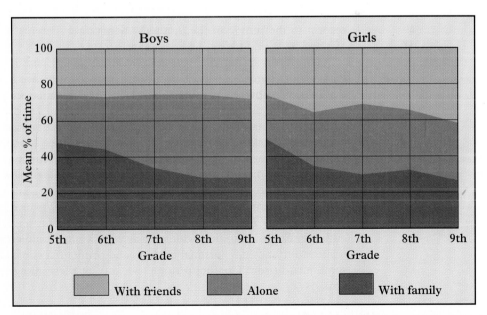

FIGURE 15.1 Amount of waking time not spent in class that adolescents of various ages are with friends, alone, or with family. After "Daily Championship in Late Childhood and Early Adolescence: Changing Developmental Contexts," by R. Larson and M. H. Richards, 1991, *Child Development, 62,* p. 289. Adapted with permission.

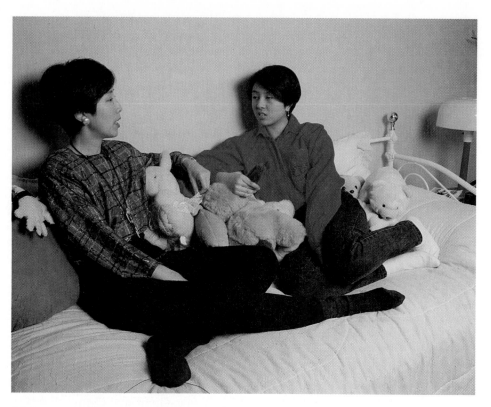

Adolescents and parents are sometimes in conflict, but these disputes are likely to focus on predictable areas rather than central values.

respect to the timing of the mother's menopause. Parents' self-definitions may be affected by their children's adolescence.

The topics of conflict between adolescents and parents are fairly predictable and focus on areas in which adolescents and parents are likely to disagree about whose responsibility it is to make decisions. For instance, in one study of this question, Smetana and Asquith (1994) asked adolescents and their parents to judge whether parents had authority over—or adolescents had personal autonomy regarding—decisions in several spheres of daily life. These domains were moral issues (e.g., stealing); conventional behavior (e.g., cursing); friendship behavior (e.g., seeing a friend parents don't like); personal behavior (e.g., choosing own clothes); and prudential items, or matters of life and health (e.g., smoking). Adolescents and parents agreed that parents had authority over moral and conventional issues, but they disagreed on the other domains. Parents tended to feel that parental authority extended to these domains as well, whereas adolescents felt that behavior related to friendship, personal choices, and prudential choices was within their personal jurisdiction. Conflict resulted because of these disagreements over jurisdiction.

Variations in Parental Behavior

Changing long-established patterns of parent-child interaction in order to adapt to the changes brought on by puberty and adolescence is seldom easy, either for par-

DIFFICULTY IN ESTABLISHING AUTONOMY

The following first-person account is taken from a collection of essays written by college students as part of their course work.

I guess the reason I thought my father was perfect for such a long time is that whenever we do anything together, he always gives advice and I always follow it, so it took me a long time to discover that there is more than one correct way to do everything. When I don't follow his advice, it leaves me feeling anxious, like I've done something wrong in opposing him. I always notice an interesting occurrence when we have disagreements: I stop thinking. As soon as he says, "Why did you. . . ?" or "Why don't you. . . ?" my mind simply shuts down. It either refuses entirely to come up with an adequate defense or else views the reasons with a sudden involuntary attitude of belittlement.

A case in point: when my parents drove me to school at the beginning of freshman year, they came with me to the bank to open a checking account. I brought them with me because I'd never had a checking account

before and I felt unsure about the procedure. The clerk left me with a form to sign, and I put down my full three names. My father immediately asked me, "Why did you sign it that way?" (with a little laugh). "That means you have to sign all your checks that way. It's much easier just to put down your first and last name."

"I, ah, I don't know. I just thought, well . . . " I couldn't think of a reason. As I think back now, I had signed that way simply because I had never had a checking account before and I thought maybe the bank required a full signature for identification. It didn't occur to me at the time that that was sufficient justification of my action. I would have liked to have looked him in the eye and said (with a faint smile curling my lips), "What the hell difference does it make?" But that didn't occur to me either.

Source: From *Experiencing Youth: First Person Accounts* (2nd ed.) (pp. 127–128) by G. W. Goethals and D. S. Klos, 1976, Boston: Little, Brown. Copyright © 1976 by G. W. Goethals and D. S. Klos. Reprinted by permission of Little, Brown and Company.

ents or for their children. But transitional difficulties and conflicts can be greatly reduced by effective communication and openness within the family (H. Barnes & Olson, 1985; Grotevant & Cooper, 1983; Youniss, 1983). In one large study of normal families, it was found that families with better communication between parents and adolescents were also higher in family cohesion, adaptability, and satisfaction (H. Barnes & Olson, 1985). Indeed, effective communication plays a vital role in helping family members strike a balance between separateness from and connectedness to one another (H. Barnes & Olson, 1985; Grotevant & Cooper, 1983). Effective family communication also fosters adolescent identity formation and mature role-taking ability (C. R. Cooper, Grotevant, & Condon, 1983). In contrast, studies of parent-child interaction in troubled families—or in families with a mentally ill parent or child—have often found distortions in the capacity of parents and child to communicate effectively with one another (Goldstein, Baker, & Jamison, 1980; Rutter, 1980; Wynne, Singer, Bartko, & Toohey, 1976). (See Box 15.1 for a personal account of difficulties in communication and in establishing emotional autonomy from parents.)

Effective communication may be one element of the larger constellation of effective parenting practices that have been called authoritative parenting. As already discussed in Chapters 7, 10, and 12, authoritative parents are those who value both autonomous will and disciplined behavior in their children (Baumrind, 1968, 1975; Elder, 1980). They encourage verbal give-and-take, and when they exercise parental authority in the form of demands or prohibitions, they explain their reasons for doing so (Cohler & Boxer, 1984; Lesser & Kandel, 1969). Authoritative parents differ from authoritarian ones, who discipline but do not explain and are seen as low in warmth; from permissive parents, who love but don't monitor and discipline; and from neglectful parents, who neither discipline nor show love.

In adolescence, authoritative parenting may be thought of as consisting of three components instead of two: warmth, behavioral supervision and monitoring, and granting of psychological autonomy (Steinberg, 1990; Steinberg, Mounts, Lamborn, & Dornbusch, 1991). The importance of granting autonomy, which can also be discussed as conducting family decision-making democratically, becomes a salient issue after childhood, as families negotiate the increased autonomy necessary for adulthood. The following description of authoritative parents, written by a 16-year-old girl, captures this family style:

> I guess the thing I think is great about my parents, compared to those of a lot of kids, is that they really listen. And they realize that eventually I'm going to have to live my own life—what I'm going to do with it. A lot of the time when I explain what I want to do, they'll go along with it. Sometimes, they'll warn me of the consequences I'll have to face if I'm wrong, or just give me advice. And sometimes, they just plain tell me no. But when they do, they explain why, and that makes it easier to take. (Conger, 1979, p. 49)

Authoritative parenting of adolescents has been found to be associated with a wide variety of positive adolescent characteristics, including academic achievement and greater involvement in school activities. The link between parental authoritativeness and school success appears to be causal in nature rather than correlational; it is evident in both early and late adolescence; and it occurs across a variety of socioeconomic and ethnic groups (Dornbusch et al., 1987; Lamborn, Mounts, Steinberg, & Dornbusch, 1991; Steinberg, Elman, et al., 1989; Steinberg, Lamborn, et al., 1992; Steinberg, Mounts, et al., 1991). However, the effect may be somewhat weaker in African-American adolescents, for whom the attitudes of peers may be relatively more important (Steinberg, Dornbusch, & Brown, 1992).

☼ ADOLESCENTS AND THEIR PEERS

As we saw in Figure 15.1, adolescents spend less time with their families than they did as children. A correlated trend is that peers play an increasingly important role in the psychological and social development of adolescents. For instance, one study of African-American, Anglo-American, and Hispanic children and adolescents asked subjects to name the individuals who gave them psychological support and help. The results, shown in Figure 15.2, indicate that close family relations persist across age but that peers emerge as support providers in adolescence (Levitt, Guacci-Franco, & Levitt, 1993). The same phenomenon of the emergent importance of peers is shown by work in which more than two out of three adolescents said that a close friend understood them better than their parents did; that they felt more "themselves" with their friend; and that at this time

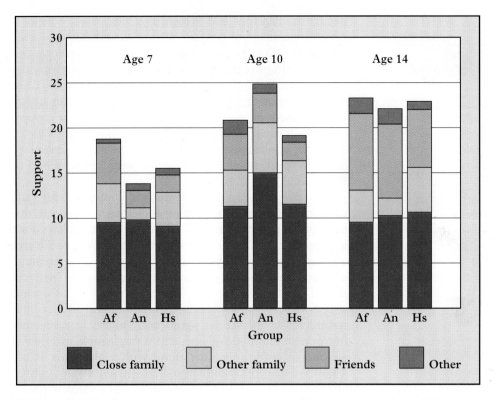

FIGURE 15.2 Feelings of psychological support reported by African-Americans (Af), Anglo-Americans (An), and Hispanics (Hs) at ages 7, 10, and 14 years from close family, extended family, friends, and other sources. After "Convoys of Social Support in Childhood and Early Adolescence: Structure and Function," by M. J. Levitt, N. Guacci-Franco, and J. L. Levitt, 1993, *Developmental Psychology, 29*, p. 815. Adapted with permission.

in their life they could learn more from their friend than from their parents (Youniss & Smollar, 1985).

The importance of peers is probably especially evident in age-segregated technologically based societies, in which entry into the adult world of work and family responsibility is delayed well past biological maturity. Adolescents are more dependent on peer relationships than younger children are, both because their ties to parents become progressively looser as they gain greater independence and because conflicts with parents, especially in early adolescence, may impede emotional disclosure.

Peer Groups

Peer groups are sometimes seen as threats to adult culture and as the enforcers of conformity, often to antisocial norms. However, this image is largely unjustified, in particular because it ignores the fact that peer groups are generally differentiated into distinct types or crowds, with very different reputations and norms (B. B. Brown, 1990). In most American high schools, students can easily identify a number of social groups. Common ones include popular adolescents—who are socially competent and who achieve academically—who also engage in some moderate delinquent behavior and drug use; "jocks," who are less academic and whose drug use focuses more on alcohol; "brains," who do very well academically and avoid delinquent behavior and drug and alcohol use; "normal" adolescents, who avoid deviant activities but who are otherwise undistinctive; and outcast groups, including "druggies" and "nerds" (Brown, Mounts, Lamborn, & Steinberg, 1993).

Peer groups of these very different kinds clearly vary dramatically in whether or not they arouse concern in adult observers. Further, it is important to recognize that the choice of peer groups an adolescent makes depends in large part on the characteristics of the adolescent. That is, while peer groups do exert some pressure on the individuals within them to engage in certain behaviors, there is a strong tendency for adolescents to seek out groups in the first place because they have (or aspire to have) characteristics that fit them for that group (B. B. Brown, 1990; B. B. Brown et al., 1993).

It is also true that the motivation to conform to the values, customs, and fads of the peer culture increases during adolescence. However, this phenomenon seems to be a special phenomenon of early adolescence, waning during middle and late adolescence (Berndt, 1979; Hartup, 1983; Steinberg & Silverberg, 1986). The need to conform to peers may vary with socioeconomic background, relationships with parents and other adults, school environment, and personality factors (Clasen & Brown, 1985; C. R. Cooper & Ayers-Lopez, 1985; Costanzo & Shaw, 1966; Steinberg & Silverberg). For example, children and adolescents with a strong tendency toward self-blame scored significantly higher in conformity than those who were low or medium in self-blame, and young people with low status among their peers are more conforming than those with high status (Coleman, 1980; Costanzo, 1970). Adolescents with high self-esteem and strong feelings of competence are less conforming than their peers (C. R. Cooper & Ayers-Lopez, 1985; Hartup, 1983). In addition, the need for conformity varies enormously from one adolescent to another (Berndt, 1979; J. J. Conger, 1979; L. E. Larson, 1972a, 1972b; Steinberg & Silverberg, 1986). More self-confident, authoritatively reared adolescents may be able to profit from the views and learning experiences provided by both parents and peers without being strongly dependent on either or unduly troubled by differences between them (C. R. Cooper & Ayers-Lopez, 1985; Hartup, 1983).

Many people believe that parental and adolescent peer group values are mutually exclusive and that heightened peer group dependence and conformity lead to a sharp decline in parental influence. This is not the case, however, at least for most adolescents. First, parent and peer values are not usually fundamentally different; there is typically a considerable overlap between the values of parents and those of peers. One reason for such overlap is that there are often similarities in the cultural backgrounds of families in the same neighborhood (B. B. Brown, 1990; Lerner & Knapp, 1975). An additional reason for overlap in values is that parenting seems to influence the nature of adolescents' peer group choices. Parents' monitoring, encouragement of academic achievement, and use of democratic decision-making affect their adolescents' behaviors, which in turn influence choice of peer groups (B. B. Brown et al., 1993).

Second, parental and peer norms clash less than is often imagined because neither parental nor peer influence is monolithic, extending to all areas of adolescent decision-making and behavior (Clasen & Brown, 1985; L. E. Larson, 1972a, 1972b; Wilks, 1986). The weight given to a parent's or peer's opinion depends to a large extent on the adolescent's appraisal of its relative value in a specific situation. For example, peer influence (especially that of same-sex peers) is more likely to dominate in such matters as tastes in music and entertainment, fashions in clothing and language, patterns of same- and opposite-sex peer interaction, and the like. Parental influence is more likely to dominate in such areas as underlying moral and social values and understanding of the adult world (Brittain, 1966, 1969; Sebald & White, 1980; Wilks, 1986).

Friendships

Friendships hold a special place among adolescents' peer relationships. Compared to other peer interactions, friendships typically are more intimate, involve more intense feelings, are more honest and open, and are less concerned with self-conscious attempts at role playing in order to gain popularity and social acceptance (Berndt, 1982; Douvan & Adelson, 1966; Youniss & Smollar, 1985). In one intensive study, middle-class adolescents of both sexes selected "close friend" as the person with whom they were most likely to "talk openly" and share "true feelings." The relationship was viewed as reciprocal; close friends "are not afraid to talk about . . . doubts and fears"; they "depend on each other for advice"; and even when they disagree, they listen to each others' reasons for thinking as they do (Youniss & Smollar, 1985, p. 103).

In view of the sensitivity of adolescents to the potential dangers involved in revealing their inner feelings, it is not surprising that they place particular emphasis on the need for security when they discuss the requirements of friendship: they want the friend to be loyal, trustworthy, and a reliable source of support in any emotional crisis (Berndt, 1982; C. R. Cooper & Ayers-Lopez, 1985). Indeed,

Peer group relationships and friendships are increasingly important to adolescents.

untrustworthy behavior is cited by adolescents as the primary cause of serious conflict between close friends (Hartup, 1983; Youniss & Smollar, 1985). In the words of a 14-year-old girl from an urban ghetto, "A friend don't talk behind your back. If they are a true friend they help you get out of trouble and they will always be right behind you and they help you get through stuff. And they never snitch on you. That's what a friend is" (Konopka, 1976, p. 85).

Owing to the freedom of close friends to criticize each other, an adolescent can learn to modify behavior, tastes, or ideas without the painful experience of rejection. At their best, friendships help young people learn to deal both with their own complex feelings and with those of others. They can serve as a kind of therapy by allowing free expression of suppressed feelings of anger or anxiety and by providing evidence that others share many of the same doubts, hopes, fears, and seemingly dangerous feelings. As one 16-year-old girl expressed it, "My best friend means a lot to me. We can talk about a lot of things I could never talk about with my parents or other kids—like hassles we're getting or problems we're worried about, and like ideals and things. It really helps to know you're not the only one that has things that bother them" (J. J. Conger, 1979, p. 70).

Close friendships may play a crucial role in helping young people develop a sense of their own identity. By sharing their experiences, their plans, their hopes and fears—in brief, by explaining themselves to each other—adolescent friends are also learning to understand themselves. There is an implicit awareness that self-definition and a coherent view of external reality cannot be achieved solely through reflection, that without the corrective functions of an external voice, one "risks self-delusion or egoism" (Youniss & Smollar, 1985, p. 167). In the words of one adolescent, "You can't always decide what you want to do yourself. You need a second opinion" (Youniss & Smollar, 1985, pp. 164–165). There is also awareness that mutual understanding is a reciprocal process: "You have to give a friend advice when he has a problem because a lot of times when a person is involved in a problem, he can't see it too well" (Youniss & Smollar, 1985, p. 164). In addition, when a friend who "really understands" you still likes you and values you, your own confidence and self-esteem are bolstered (R. Bell, 1980; Erikson, 1968). In short, under favorable circumstances friendships may help the adolescent define his or her identity and gain greater confidence and pride in it. (However, friendships may pose problems and challenges in some circumstances. See Box 15.2 for an account of how members of minority groups may feel when their friends belong the majority.)

Romantic Relationships

As children grow into adolescents, their interest in the opposite sex increases. This is especially true for girls (Savin-Williams & Berndt, 1990). Although same-sex individuals generally constitute the majority of an adolescent's friends, especially in early adolescence, the determinants of popularity with the same and with the opposite sex appear to be quite similar, at least in early adolescence (Bukowski, Gauze, Hoza, & Newcomb, 1993). With increasing age, emotional intimacy and disclosure in opposite-sex relationships increase (Savin-Williams & Berndt, 1990).

Remarkably little is known about romantic relationships in adolescence. Theorists have made opposing suggestions about the nature of these relationships. Erik Erikson believed that the central task of adolescence was forging an identity, a topic we discuss shortly, and argued that true emotional intimacy was impossible in the

---

BOX 15.2

FORMING A BLACK IDENTITY IN A WHITE CULTURE

Friends play an important role in identity formation in adolescence. However, when friends do not understand important components of one's identity, as may be true when minority adolescents interact with nonminority adolescents, this process can be more difficult. The following passage is taken from the memoir of a black woman who attended a largely white, very exclusive prep school on a scholarship.

I did not, however, tell the girls what I was thinking. We did not talk about how differently we saw the world. Indeed my black and their white heritage was not a starting point for our relationship, but rather was the outer boundary. I could not cross it, because there sprang up a hard wall of denial impervious to my inexperienced and insecure assault. "Well, as far as I'm concerned," one girl after another would say,

"it doesn't matter to me if somebody's white or black or green or purple. I mean people are just people."

The motion, having been made, would invariably be seconded.

"Really. I mean, it's the person that counts."

Having castigated whites' widespread inability to see individuals for the skin in which they were wrapped, I could hardly argue with "it's the person that counts." I didn't know why they always chose green and purple to dramatize their indifference, but my ethnicity seemed diminished when the talk turned to Muppets. It was like they were taking something from me.

"I'm not purple." What else could you say?

Source: From *Black Ice* (pp. 83–84) by Lorene Cary, 1992, New York: Alfred A. Knopf.

---

absence of an identity. Erikson assigned the achievement of an open and intimate relationship to the next stage of life, after adolescence, for this reason. By contrast, Harry Stack Sullivan argued that the same-sex "chumships" of late childhood allow the development of interpersonal abilities that are basic for romantic relationships in adolescence. Sullivan saw emotional intimacy in adolescence as closely interwoven with the establishment of identity, arguing that romantic relationships provided an arena in which adolescents could experiment with identity and see the consequences of tentative identity choices reflected in the reactions of their partner. (Goethals & Klos, 1976).

One of the few descriptions of adolescent transitions from the world of same-sex interaction to a world that includes opposite-sex relationships comes from a classic observational study conducted some time ago in Australia (Dunphy, 1963). Dunphy saw small same-sex friendship groups in early adolescence begin to engage in tentative cross-sex interaction, often led by individuals who were popular and central in their same-sex friendship groups. Eventually, cliques formed that included both sexes. As adolescence went on, Dunphy saw the increasing predominance of dating couples as the unit of social interaction, with a disintegration of same-sex cliques. However, although his work is intriguing and often cited, it has never been replicated or extended to other social groups or historical periods (B. B. Brown, 1990).

✿ IDENTITY

As we have seen, Erik Erikson is the developmental theorist most responsible for stressing a characterization of adolescence as a period for self-definition and for the formation of an identity. Adolescents and adults with a strong sense of their own identity see themselves as separate, distinctive individuals, with a need for self-consistency, a feeling of wholeness. When Erikson spoke of the integrity of the self, he had in mind both separateness from others and unity of the self—a workable integration of the person's needs, motives, and patterns of responding. In Erikson's words, the adolescent "in order to experience wholeness, must feel a progressive continuity between that which he has come to be during the long years of child-hood and that which he promises to become in the anticipated future" (1956, p. 91). In writing of identity, Erikson also had in mind a sense of identity in which identity is not purely individual and internal. An important component of a true identity, Erikson thought, is consistency between how the adolescent conceives her-self to be and how she perceives others to see her. An identity is both personal and social.

Developing a Sense of Identity

The development of a sense of identity does not begin or end in adolescence. An individual's identity is already being shaped during earlier periods of life, begin-ning, in Erikson's view, with the establishment of basic trust or mistrust of the peo-ple and the world around the infant. Further, many adults become more genuinely individual as they grow older. However, even though identity development may be a lifelong process, the search for a sense of identity is especially relevant during ado-lescence. As we have already noted, during adolescence the young person is con-fronted with a host of psychological, physiological, sexual, and cognitive changes, as well as by new and varied intellectual, social, and cognitive demands.

Achieving a clear sense of identity depends partly on cognitive skills. The young person must be able to conceptualize herself or himself in abstract terms. The capacities for abstract and hypothetical thinking discussed in Chapter 14 aid the adolescent in the search for an individual identity. At the same time, they make the search more difficult because they open up a wider range of possibilities to choose among.

An adolescent's freedom to explore a variety of possibilities in pursuit of an individual identity is significantly influenced by relationships within the family (C. R. Cooper, Grotevant, & Condon, 1983; Marcia, 1980; Youniss & Smollar, 1985). In one study of family interactions, adolescents who scored high on a mea-sure of identity exploration were more likely to come from families in which self-assertion and freedom to disagree ("separateness") were encouraged along with "connectedness" to the family, including openness or responsiveness to the views of others ("plurality") and sensitivity to and respect for the ideas of others ("mutual-ity"). In the words of one high-scoring participant in the study, "I have a say but not a deciding vote in family decisions" (C. R. Cooper et al., 1983, p. 54). In contrast, adolescents who scored lower in identity exploration were more likely to come from families in which individuality was not encouraged and mutual support and agree-ment were emphasized. One low-scoring young woman commented with respect to career choice, "I'm having a hard time deciding what to do. It would be easier if

Adolescent boys have a special need for mutual understanding with parents, especially fathers.

they would tell me what to do, but of course I don't want that" (Grotevant & Cooper, 1983, p. 55).

Other studies have shown that opportunities for separateness in family interactions appear to be especially important for girls' development, while connectedness in family relations, particularly with the father, appears to be especially important for boys (C. R. Cooper & Grotevant, 1987; Grotevant & Cooper, 1985). Perhaps the greater importance of separateness for females reflects the effort needed to overcome the greater restrictiveness they experience relative to males. Boys, on the other hand, are more likely to be pressured by society to be autonomous and assertive in identity exploration. Consequently, their greatest need in family interaction may be for mutual understanding, respect, and support, particularly from their fathers, who serve as gender-role models (C. R. Cooper & Grotevant, 1987; Hauser et al., 1987; T. Huston & Ashmore, 1986; Youniss & Ketterlinus, 1987).

Varieties of Identity Status

Erikson (1968) described an ideal process of identity formation in which an adolescent proceeded through a period of questioning and exploration, sometimes called a **moratorium** period, to a phase of identity achievement. He also pointed to two important ways in which the search for identity can go wrong: it may be prematurely foreclosed (i.e., crystallized too early), or it may be indefinitely extended.

Identity Foreclosure. **Identity foreclosure** is an interruption in the process of identity formation. Adolescents who foreclose do not engage in the period of questioning and exploration that Erikson saw as important for identity. The reasons for this fact, and its implications, are somewhat controversial.

One view of foreclosure follows Erikson in emphasizing its negative aspects. Adolescents in foreclosure are seen as likely to be highly approval oriented, basing their sense of self-esteem largely on recognition by others, and to be more conforming and less autonomous than other youth. They are also less thoughtful and reflective and more stereotyped and superficial, as well as less close and intimate in both same-sex and opposite-sex relationships. Although they do not differ from their peers in overall intelligence, young people whose identity has become fixed have difficulty being flexible and responding appropriately when confronted with stressful cognitive tasks; they seem to welcome structure and order in their lives.

A somewhat different view points to positive features of foreclosure. Foreclosed adolescents are less anxious than other adolescents and have a high degree of respect for authority. They tend to have close relationships with their parents (especially in the case of sons and their fathers). Their parents, in turn, generally appear to be accepting and encouraging while at the same time exerting considerable pressure for conformity to family values (Bourne, 1978a, 1978b; Donovan, 1975; Marcia, 1980; St. Clair & Day, 1979; Weinmann & Newcombe, 1990). This picture of a foreclosed adolescent suggests that such an individual, while rather traditional, may not be less well adjusted than adolescents going through a period of active questioning of identity.

The adaptive value of identity foreclosure probably varies with social circumstances. For instance, some early findings showed that self-esteem was highest for women in the foreclosure status and lowest for women who showed identity achievement (Marcia & Friedman, 1970; Toder & Marcia, 1973). However, as women have become more prevalent in the work world, this situation may well be changing (Harter, 1990). Similarly, Hauser and Kasendorf (1983) find that African-American adolescents are more likely to be in identity foreclosure than whites. They attribute this finding to the lack of occupational opportunities for African-American adolescents, the pressing economic pressures that make a moratorium period a luxury, and the lack of African-American role models.

Identity Diffusion. In contrast to adolescents in foreclosure, some adolescents go through a prolonged period of **identity diffusion**. Some never develop a strong, clear sense of identity; these are adolescents who cannot "find themselves," who keep themselves loose and unattached (Douvan & Adelson, 1966). Such a person may exhibit a pathologically prolonged identity crisis, never achieving any consistent loyalties or commitments.

Young people who experience identity diffusion often have low self-esteem and immature moral reasoning. They are impulsive; their thinking is disorganized; and they have difficulty taking responsibility for their own lives. They tend to be focused on themselves, and their relationships are often superficial and sporadic. Although generally dissatisfied with their parents' way of life, they have difficulty fashioning one of their own (G. R. Adams, Abraham, & Markstrom, 1987; Donovan, 1975; Marcia, 1980; Orlofsky, 1978; Waterman & Waterman, 1974).

Identity Achievement. The aim of identity exploration is **identity achievement**. Individuals who have achieved a strong sense of identity after a period of active searching are likely to be more autonomous, creative, and complex in their thinking than other adolescents. They also show a greater capacity for intimacy, a more confident sexual identity, a more positive self-concept, and more mature moral reasoning. While their relationships with their parents are generally positive,

Adolescent girls' search for identity more closely resembles that of boys when there are a variety of roles to which they may aspire. This girl has taken a steer to a livestock auction in Texas.

they have typically achieved considerable independence from their families (Hodgson & Fischer, 1978; Orlofsky, 1978; Orlofsky, Marcia, & Lesser, 1973; St. Clair & Day, 1979).

Research comparisons show that young people who have achieved a clear sense of identity weighed a variety of occupational and ideological options and arrived at conclusions to which they are committed. They also yielded less to pressure for conformity and were less uncomfortable in resisting such pressure (Toder & Marcia, 1973). They chose relatively difficult college majors, and they manifested fewer negative feelings, such as anxiety, hostility, or depression, than those who lacked a firm identity (Marcia, 1980).

Entering the World of Work

It has been argued that one of the most stressful aspects of adolescence in industrialized society is the fact that there is such a long time period between biological markers of adulthood and the ability to support oneself and establish an independent life. Some observers of this dilemma suggest that a partial solution is for adolescents to enter the work world on a part-time basis, thus giving adolescents the possibility to demonstrate responsibility and independence, to gain relevant work

Most adolescents who work have jobs at minimum wage; their duties are likely to be repetitive and unchallenging.

experience and establish work habits, and to become economically more self-sufficient (National Commission on Youth, 1980). At any time in the school year, about two-thirds of high school juniors and seniors in the United States are employed, and about half of the seniors work for more than 20 hours per week (Bachman & Schulenberg, 1993).

Empirical evidence on the issue of part-time employment for adolescents paints a rather different picture, however, of this proposed remedy for the length of adolescence. Employment turns out to be correlated with a variety of negative consequences for adolescents, including problem behaviors, such as drug and alcohol use and delinquency, and lower school performance (e.g., Greenberger & Steinberg, 1986; Steinberg & Dornbusch, 1991). The greater the number of hours worked, the worse the consequences seemed to be. While it is possible that correlations of part-time employment with lower academic performance and with problem behavior are due to the fact that adolescents who dislike school and do poorly are more likely to work, research following adolescents over time shows that, over and above such selection effects, part-time employment has negative effects (Bachman & Schulenberg, 1993; Steinberg, Fegley, & Dornbusch, 1993).

Some of the negative effects of part-time employment for adolescents are likely to be linked to the kind of jobs adolescents usually hold. They are usually minimum-wage jobs, repetitive and unchallenging, which may do little to develop a sense of responsibility and engagement in the work world. Instead, the more adolescents work, the less time they have for school, and the less time they also have even for habits basic to a healthy lifestyle, such as getting sufficient sleep or eating breakfast (Bachman & Schulenberg, 1993).

✿ MORAL DEVELOPMENT AND VALUES

The increased cognitive capacities of adolescents foster greater awareness of moral issues and values and more sophistication in dealing with them. At the same time, the problem of developing a strong sense of identity cannot be separated from the problem of values. Thus, there are at least two reasons why adolescents would be expected to show change and growth in their thinking about complex social and political issues: their increased cognitive abilities and their work on forming an identity. In this section, we examine work on the development of moral reasoning.

Piaget's Approach

The first work on moral reasoning was done by Piaget. Based on observation of children of different ages at play—and on interviews with children about the rules of games, the nature of justice, and the morality of characters in stories—Piaget suggested there were two stages of moral development. During the stage of **moral realism**, the child believes that rules are handed down by authorities (e.g., parents and teachers) and therefore are fixed, absolute, and sacred. Ideas about right and wrong are also inflexible, and justice is subordinate to adult authority. The young children whom Piaget interviewed did not think it was ever right to tell a lie, and when asked about a story in which the commands of a parent conflicted with justice or equality, they usually chose obedience to adults as the correct course of action. At this stage, actions are judged more by their consequences than by the intentions of the actor. Piaget asked children who was naughtier, a boy who was trying to help his mother and accidentally upset a tray and broke 15 glasses, or another boy who, while trying to sneak a cookie out of a cupboard, broke one glass. Most moral realists said that the first boy was naughtier because he broke more glasses (Piaget, 1932/1965).

Piaget proposed that the second stage, **moral relativism**, began at the age of 10 or 11. During this stage, ideas of reciprocity in human interactions and the belief that everyone has an equal right to justice and consideration predominate in moral thinking. During the stage of moral relativism, children realize that many social rules, including the rules of games, are simply statements of convention and can be changed by agreement or consensus. Blind obedience to authority is rejected, and moral rules are regarded as the products of cooperation, reciprocity, and interaction among peers. Consequently, children at this stage are more flexible in their moral judgments, taking into consideration the circumstances of an individual's actions as well as the actor's point of view, emotions, and feelings. Disobedience, lying, or violation of rules are sometimes justified, and not all wrongdoing will inevitably be punished. Children now believe in equal justice for all, and their judgments about transgressions take into account the intentions of the actor and the nature and extent of the harm done.

Piaget maintained that progress from moral realism to moral relativism is a joint function of the child's greater cognitive abilities and more extensive social experiences. The most significant cognitive changes, he believed, are a decline in egocentrism and an increase in the ability to take roles and assume another person's perspective. Also, as a result of more numerous and more enduring contacts with peers, children learn to work cooperatively—and often make compromises—with others of equal status. Unilateral respect for adult authority is thereby reduced, and respect for peers and their points of view increases. Piaget suggested

Piaget thought that only older children and adolescents could understand games as socially invented interactions with rules that could be changed if a group agreed to do so.

that parents can help their children achieve higher levels of moral thinking by being less authoritarian and maintaining egalitarian relationships with them (Piaget, 1932/1965).

Subsequent research has shown that youngsters' understanding of intentions is more advanced than Piaget thought. The difference between deliberate and accidental wrongdoing is clear even to preschoolers (Karniol, 1978), and they take intentions into account when judging another's actions (Costanzo, Coie, Grumet, & Farnill, 1973). "I did it on accident, Mom," said one preschooler when she had done something wrong. In fact, when evaluating an individual's actions, young children consider many factors, including whether the results are positive or negative and whether the object of an action is an inanimate object, an animal, or a person (Rest, 1983).

In summary, as with much of Piaget's thinking about development, contemporary research has revealed a view of the young child as more sophisticated than Piaget believed. However, being able to think abstractly about rules and conventions, about morality and social justice, are clearly achievements of adolescence. One approach to the development, based on Piaget's thinking—which focuses attention on these changes in later childhood, adolescence—and even adulthood—is that of Lawrence Kohlberg.

Kohlberg's Approach

About 30 years after Piaget published his studies of moral development, Kohlberg began to extend and amplify Piaget's work. Kohlberg and his associates presented children and adolescents with a series of moral dilemmas and asked them to resolve them, stating their reasoning. An example is the situation of Heinz, a man whose wife is dying. He does not have enough money to buy a drug that will save her life. The druggist refuses to lower the price or delay the payment, so Heinz breaks into the drugstore and steals the drug. Should Heinz have done that? Why or why not? The individual's level of moral judgment is assessed on the basis of the structure or kind of reasoning used, not the content of the judgment. In other words, a person could receive a high score for saying that Heinz was right or for saying that he was wrong; the score depends on the reasons for the judgment (Kohlberg, 1963, 1964).

Analyses of the responses to these dilemmas led Kohlberg to propose three levels of moral judgment, each of which is further subdivided into two stages. At the preconventional level, children judge right and wrong primarily by the consequences of actions. In the earliest stage (stage 1), right and wrong are judged in terms of obeying rules in order to avoid punishment. In stage 2, a simple doctrine of reciprocity develops. People should act to meet their own needs and let others do the same; doing what is "fair" constitutes an equal exchange. The saying "You scratch my back and I'll scratch yours" fits this stage. The child's moral orientation is still primarily individualistic, egocentric, and concrete, although the rights of others are seen as coexisting with the child's rights (Colby, Kohlberg, Gibbs, & Lieberman, 1983; Kohlberg, 1976).

At the second level, conventional morality, the focus is on interpersonal relationships and social values; these take precedence over individual interests. Initially, at stage 3, a child may put strong emphasis on being "a good person in your own eyes and those of others" (Kohlberg, 1976, p. 34), which means having worthy motives and showing concern about others. Typically, conformity to stereotyped images of natural behavior (i.e., the behavior of the majority) is emphasized. The intention behind an action acquires major importance; one seeks approval by "being good." At stage 4, a social or member-of-society perspective takes precedence. The child shows concern not only with conformity to the social order but also with maintaining, supporting, and justifying this order. "Right behavior consists of doing one's duty, showing respect for authority, and maintaining the given social order for its own sake" (Kohlberg & Gilligan, 1972, p. 160).

At the postconventional and principled levels (stages 5 and 6), moral judgments are based on broad abstract principles, principles that are accepted because they are believed to be inherently right rather than because society considers them right. At stage 5, the individual willingly participates in the social order and, in effect, enters into a social contract with others in which equal distribution of power and protection of each person's liberties and rights are ensured. The emphasis at this stage is on democratic processes, impartiality in applying the laws of society, and opposition to laws if they violate the principles of equality, liberty, and justice. Stage 6, the highest (and most ideal) stage of moral development, is characterized by a rational moral perspective and involves the application of universal, absolute principles of justice, equality, and respect for human life and human rights. When Martin Luther King said that disobeying segregation laws was morally right because he was obeying a higher law, he was making a principled moral argument. This level is characterized by a "major thrust toward abstract moral principles which are universally applicable, and not tied to any particular social group" (Kohlberg & Gilligan, 1972, p. 159). (A detailed explanation of each stage appears in Table 15.1.)

Like Piaget, Kohlberg believed that moral development depends on advances in general cognitive abilities and that, like those advances, moral stages emerge in

TABLE 15.1 Six Stages of Moral Judgment

Lawrence Kohlberg (1976) proposed six stages of moral judgment. This table lists those stages and gives some examples and definitions for each.

	Content of Stage	
Level and stage	*What is right*	*Reasons for doing right*
Level I—Preconventional		
Stage 1: Heteronomous morality	Not breaking rules backed by punishment; obedience for its own sake; avoiding physical damage to persons and property.	Avoidance of punishment; the superior power of authorities.
Stage 2: Individualism, instrumental purpose, and exchange	Following rules only when it is to someone's immediate interest; acting to meet one's own interests and needs and letting others do the same. Right is also what's fair, an equal exchange, a deal, an agreement.	To serve one's own needs or interests in a world where one must recognize that other people have interests, too.
Level II—Conventional		
Stage 3: Mutual interpersonal expectations, relationships, and interpersonal conformity	Living up to what is expected by people close to you or what people generally expect of people in your role. "Being good" is important and means having good motives and showing concern about others. It also means maintaining mutual relationships, such as trust, loyalty, respect, and gratitude.	The need to be a good person in one's own eyes and those of others. Caring for others. Belief in the Golden Rule. Desire to maintain rules and authority that support stereotypical good behavior.
Stage 4: Social system and conscience	Fulfilling the actual duties to which one has agreed. Laws are to be upheld except in extreme cases in which they conflict with other fixed social duties. Right is also contributing to society, the group, or an institution.	To keep the institution going as a whole, to avoid the breakdown in the system that would occur "if everyone did it." (Easily confused with stage 3 belief in rules and authority.)
Level III—Postconventional or Principled		
Stage 5: Social contract or utility and individual rights	Being aware that people hold a variety of values and opinions, that most values and rules are relative to one's own group. These relative rules should usually be upheld, however, in the interest of impartiality and because they are the social contract. Some nonrelative values and rights like *life* and *liberty*, however, must be upheld in any society and regardless of majority opinion.	A sense of obligation to law because of one's social contract to make and abide by laws for the welfare of all and for the protection of all people's rights. A feeling of contractual commitment, freely entered upon, to family, friendship, trust, and work obligations. Concern that laws and duties be based on rational calculation of overall utility, "the greatest good for the greatest number."
Stage 6: Universal ethical principles	Following self-chosen ethical principles. Particular laws or social agreements are usually valid because they rest on such principles. When laws violate these principles, one acts in accordance with the principle. Principles are universal principles of justice.	Belief as a rational person in the validity of universal moral principles, and a sense of personal commitment to them.

Source: After "Morality," by J. Rest, in *Handbook of Child Psychology: Vol. 3. Cognitive Development* (4th ed.), edited by P. H. Mussen, J. Flavell, and E. Markman, 1983, New York: Wiley. Adapted with permission.

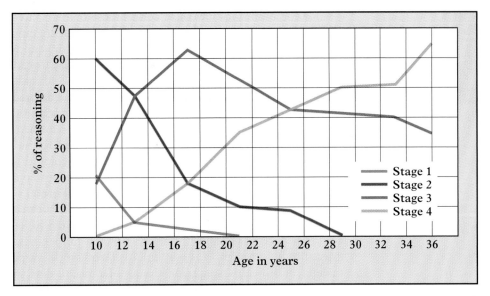

FIGURE 15.3 Percentage of moral reasoning at each of Kohlberg's first four stages for each of age group. After "A Longitudinal Study of Moral Judgment," by A. Colby, L. Kohlberg, J. Gibbs, and M. Lieberman, 1983, *Monographs of the Society for Research in Child Development, 48* (Serial No. 200). Adapted with permission.

an invariant sequence, each stage evolving from, and replacing, the preceding one. Piaget believed that egalitarian relationships with peers stimulate progress from moral realism to moral relativism. Similarly, Kohlberg asserted that participation in a democratic institution leads to greater moral maturity.

Most adults are at stage 3 or 4 of Kohlberg's sequence. Although stage 5 responses appear with increasing frequency in late adolescence and during the college years, only a small percentage of the population reaches this stage. Indeed, stage 6 reasoning is found so rarely that it has been dropped from the scoring system (Kohlberg, 1978).

Research on Kohlberg's Theory. Kohlberg's theory has had considerable influence and has stimulated a great deal of research as well as controversy. Evidence supports the hypothesis that the moral stages represent an orderly, universal, and invariant progression in moral development. As predicted from this hypothesis, preconventional reasoning declines sharply with age, accounting for 80 percent of 10-year-olds' moral judgments, 18 percent of 16- to 18-year-olds', and only 3 percent of 24-year-olds'. The proportion of conventional moral judgments increases from 22 percent at age 10 to almost 90 percent at age 22. Similar trends have been found in cultures as divergent as those of Taiwan, Turkey, Central America, India, and Nigeria (Edwards, 1981; Kohlberg, 1969; Magsud, 1979; Turiel, Edwards, & Kohlberg, 1978).

A 20-year longitudinal study of a group of American men who were tested at four-year intervals between preadolescence and their mid-30s provides further evidence that successive moral stages are attained in the predicted order (see Figure 15.3). None of the subjects skipped any stage. Their judgments at any period tended to be remarkably consistent; that is, the vast majority of an individual's responses in a testing session were at the same level of moral reasoning (Colby et al., 1983). Longitudinal studies in other cultures have yielded similar results (Nisan & Kohlberg, 1982; White, Bushnell, & Regnemer, 1978).

Research findings have also confirmed Kohlberg's hypothesis that advances in moral judgments are related to changes in general cognitive abilities. For example, conventional reasoning (levels 3 and 4) is said to depend on the individual's ability to assume the perspectives of others. In one study, 11-year-old girls who were good at role taking were at the conventional level of moral reasoning, whereas poor role takers were generally at stage 2 (Moir, 1974). Also as predicted, formal operations and abstract thinking are prerequisites for postconventional moral reasoning (level 5): preadolescent girls and college women who reasoned at the postconventional level in response to the Kohlberg dilemmas used formal operational thinking in cognitive tests. However, not all those who had achieved the level of formal operations on the general cognitive tests were at the postconventional level in moral judgment (Tomlinson-Keasey & Keasey, 1974). Formal operations apparently are necessary, but not sufficient, for the development of postconventional morality.

Maturity of moral judgment is positively related to level and quality of formal education, extent of exposure to the arts and humanities, breadth of cultural and intercultural experiences, assumption of real-world responsibilities and decision making, and such personal qualities as tolerance of diversity and open and trusting relationships with others (Rest, 1986; Schomberg, 1978; Spickelmier, 1983).

Both as high school students and later as young adults, students who score high in moral development are more likely than those who score low to display "growing awareness of the social world and one's place in it" (Rest, 1986, p. 57). They emerge as people who enjoy intellectual stimulation, seek challenges, make plans and set goals, and take responsibility for themselves and their environs (Spickelmier, 1983). Not surprisingly, they are more likely to "come from stimulating and challenging environments, and from social milieus that support their work, interest them, and reward their accomplishments" (Rest, 1986, p. 57).

Criticisms of Kohlberg's Theory. Kohlberg's work has been criticized on grounds of both theory and method. Some critics argue that all morality is culturally relative and that it is ethnocentric to view one kind of moral thought as "higher" than another. Principled judgments that oppose the laws of a society might not be considered the most advanced form of moral thinking in another culture or at another time (Baumrind, 1978). Kohlberg's conclusion that young children's moral judgments are based exclusively on rewards, avoidance of punishment, and deference to authority has also been challenged. According to some investigators, children have more profound knowledge and understanding of morality than they are able to articulate; they have "an intuitive moral competence that displays itself in the way they answer questions about moral rules and in the way they excuse their transgressions and react to the transgressions of others" (Schweder, Turiel, & Much, 1981, p. 288).

Young children are capable of recognizing moral issues (general principles relating to justice, fairness, and the welfare of others), and of distinguishing these from social conventions (arbitrary rules of conduct sanctioned by custom and tradition). In one study, children between 5 and 11 years of age were asked about school policies that permit children to hit each other or to take off their clothes in school. The majority of children of all ages said that a school should not permit hitting but could allow children to undress (Weston & Turiel, 1980). Thus, it is clear that social-conventional thinking and morality are distinct conceptual systems in children's thinking (Turiel, 1983). In addition, children will argue that it is wrong to hit or steal (moral issues) even in the absence of rules or laws against such acts, and they often react spontaneously to their peers' violations of moral rules by citing reasons for obeying those rules (Nucci & Nucci, 1982; Nucci & Turiel, 1978; Smetana, 1981).

Another criticism of Kohlberg's work has been that his scoring system is biased in favor of males because high scores in moral maturity depend on an orientation toward justice. Carol Gilligan (1977, 1982) has argued that a justice orientation is stressed in the socialization of males, whereas females are socialized to be nurturant, empathic, and caring. She has suggested that women's moral reasoning is more likely to be based on this ethic of care. She presented interviews with women who were thinking about how to deal with an unwanted pregnancy to support this argument. Young women who reached a higher level of moral reasoning when they made a decision about abortion showed better subsequent adjustment than those who regressed (Gilligan & Belenky, 1982).

Gilligan did not study men's reasoning about personally relevant moral dilemmas. Thus, we do not know whether men and women differ in moral reasoning from her work. Recent reviews of studies using hypothetical problems conclude that in fact males do not score higher on Kohlberg's dilemmas than females do (L. J. Walker, 1984; Rest, 1986). Whether there are sex differences in everyday life remains unsettled.

Moral Judgment and Behavior. Because the Kohlberg sequence of stages is based on responses to hypothetical situations rather than responses to issues and dilemmas that people actually confront, some critics are doubtful about its meaningfulness and the extent to which it can be generalized (Baumrind, 1978). Can children's moral behavior be predicted on the basis of their reasoning about moral issues? The answer to this question may vary with age.

Young children's moral judgments are not related to resistance to cheating or violation of social norms (Blasi, 1980, 1983; Santrock, 1975), and their actions may be inconsistent with their stated beliefs about fairness and justice. Thus, in one study children worked in groups of four, making bracelets. The situation was arranged so that some children made more and prettier bracelets than others; for example, one child was younger and less skilled, so she worked more slowly than the others. In individual interviews about the fairest way to divide the reward among the participants, many children said that all should share equally because they had all worked hard and contributed to the best of their ability. However, when they were actually distributing the rewards, children often acted in ways that were dictated by their self-interest. Children at all ages studied tended to favor themselves somewhat more than others (Damon, 1983; Gerson & Damon, 1978). Thus, the children's reasoning did not completely determine their actual social conduct (Damon, 1983).

The moral behavior of older children, adolescents, and adults is more likely to be consistent with their moral judgments. Given opportunities to cheat, only 15 percent of college students at the postconventional level of moral development actually did so, in contrast to 55 percent of those at the conventional level and 70 percent of those at the preconventional level. Similarly, during the 1965 Berkeley Free Speech movement, some students acted consistently with their strong moral position and "sat in" at the administration building to protest the university's rules prohibiting political activity on the campus. They did this at great personal risk, for many were forcibly evicted or arrested. Yet 73 percent of the students who were at stage 5 on the Kohlberg scale became active protesters, in contrast to only 40 percent of those at stage 4 and 10 percent of those at stage 3 (Haan, Smith, & Block, 1968).

Judging from available evidence, we can make only tentative predictions from moral judgments to social behavior because the relationship between the two is at best a moderate one and is closer among older individuals than among younger ones. Perhaps this is what we should expect, because beliefs about what is right, fair, or just are only one of many factors that determine how an individual will act in any particular situation.

✸ SUMMARY

Four central tasks in the psychosocial development of the adolescent are to develop autonomy from parents and family, to establish satisfying peer relationships and friendships, to develop an identity, and to develop skills at moral reasoning.

Developing autonomy is, in favorable circumstances, a process in which separateness is developed and yet connections are maintained. Adolescents typically develop different perceptions of their parents as people, spend less time with their families, and experience some conflict with their parents, especially as they reach puberty, focusing on areas where parents and adolescents tend to differ as to who has jurisdiction. Variations in parental behavior affect the ease with which adolescents make the transition from dependent child to independent adult. Authoritative parents, who value both autonomous will and disciplined behavior, are most likely to foster the development of confidence, responsibility, and autonomy.

Peers play a crucial role in the psychological and social development of most adolescents. Relations with peers serve as prototypes for adult relationships. Motivation to conform to the peer culture increases during early adolescence; however, conformity to peer group values does not usually cause a sharp decline in parental influence.

Friendships are especially important in adolescence. They provide emotional support and allow the adolescent to modify behavior, tastes, or ideas without experiencing rejection; they may play a crucial role in helping adolescents develop a sense of their own identity. Relations with opposite-sex peers are especially significant in adolescence.

A third task of adolescence is developing a sense of one's own identity, that is, a sense of oneself as a separate, distinctive individual. A sense of identity requires a perception of oneself as separate from others, a feeling of self-consistency or wholeness, and a sense of continuity of the self over time. It also requires consistency between one's own and other people's perceptions of one's identity.

Although identity development is a lifelong process, the search for identity is especially relevant during adolescence. Achieving a clear sense of identity takes time and depends partly on cognitive skills. The search for identity is significantly influenced by relationships within the family; adolescents who feel free to explore a variety of possibilities come from families in which individuality is encouraged.

The search for identity can go wrong in either of two ways: It can be prematurely foreclosed or indefinitely extended. Identity foreclosure is a premature fixing of one's self-image that interferes with the development of other potentials and possibilities for self-definition. For example, it may result in lack of flexibility and inability to respond appropriately to stressful cognitive tasks. Identity diffusion, on the other hand, results from a long, inconclusive search for identity; individuals who are unable to transcend identity diffusion are likely to be immature and to have low self-esteem.

The increased cognitive capacities of adolescents foster greater awareness of moral issues and values and more sophistication in dealing with them. The groundwork for research on moral development was laid by Jean Piaget, who proposed that young children are at a stage of moral realism, in which they believe that rules are handed down by authorities and therefore are fixed and absolute, but that, beginning around age 10, children attain the state of moral relativism, in which ideas of reciprocity and the belief that everyone has an equal right to justice predominate. Piaget's work was extended by Lawrence Kohlberg, who proposed three levels of moral judgment that are achieved in an orderly progression. At the preconventional level, children judge right and wrong primarily by the consequences of actions. At the conventional level, interpersonal relationships and social values take precedence over individual interests. At the postconventional level, moral judgments are based on broad abstract principles.

Adolescent thinking about moral issues has usually advanced at least to the level of conventional morality. Adolescents begin to question the social and political beliefs of adults. Their personal values and opinions become less absolute, and their political thought becomes less authoritarian. They do not, however, always act in accordance with their moral values.

REVIEW QUESTIONS

1. How do children's relationships with their parents change during adolescence?
2. What effects do variations in parental behavior (e.g., authoritative vs. authoritarian) have on adolescents' ability to develop an appropriate degree of autonomy?
3. Why do peer relations play a crucial role in the psychological and social development of adolescents?
4. What do we know about the relative influence of parents and peers on the adolescent?
5. Describe the three main characteristics of a fully developed identity.
6. What role does the family play in the development of identity?
7. What is meant by identity foreclosure and identity diffusion?
8. Outline Kohlberg's description of the development of moral reasoning.

CRITICAL THINKING ABOUT THE CHAPTER

1. Write about the social structure of your high school. What peer groups existed and what were they called? What influenced who belonged to what group? How important were the groups to social and psychological development?
2. Do you think Kohlberg's approach to moral reasoning is overly culturally specific? Give reasons for your answer.

KEY TERMS

identity achievement
identity diffusion
identity foreclosure

moratorium
moral realism
moral relativism

SUGGESTED READINGS

Erikson, E. H. (1968). *Identity: Youth and crisis.* New York: Norton (paperback). A classic series of essays on identity development.

Greenberger, E., & Steinberg, L. (1988). *When teenagers work: The psychological and social costs of adolescent employment.* New York: Basic Books. This well-researched book argues convincingly that much current teenage employment is of questionable value and, in some instances at least, may actually interfere with optimal educational, psychological, and even social development.

Grotevant, H. D., & Cooper, C. R. (Eds.). (1983). *Adolescent development in the family.* San Francisco: Jossey-Bass. The various studies described in this book indicate that adolescent development involves not an abandonment but, rather, a transformation of parent-child relationships. Continued "connectedness" to the family is needed even as the young person pursues the goals of autonomy and individuality.

PSYCHOPATHOLOGY

CHAPTER

16

DEVELOPMENTAL PSYCHOPATHOLOGY

Darcy Malloy and Scott Nakamura were having a quick conference in the teachers' lounge. Darcy was a fifth-grade teacher and Scott the counseling psychologist who visited the school twice a week. Darcy was worried about several kids in her class, and she wanted to ask Scott's advice.

The chief problem was Michael, a boy who was constantly in trouble. He neglected his schoolwork, teased other kids, mouthed off to Darcy and seemed impossible to reach. His parents didn't respond to requests to come in for conferences. Worst of all, Darcy was pretty sure that Michael was behind the mysterious disappearances of children's possessions that had been plaguing the class, although she couldn't prove it.

Michael was the thorn in Darcy's side, but she was worried about other kids as well, especially Jana. Jana never bothered anyone; that was part of her problem. She was very quiet and withdrawn, seemed to have no friends, and frequently looked very sad. At lunchtime she only nibbled at her food. She didn't run or play at recess or read or draw, either. She just sat leaning on the building, almost appearing to be asleep.

Wlat is wrong with Michael and with Jana? Is Michael headed for delinquency? Is Jana depressed? What leads to such problems and what can be done about them? In this chapter we shift from "normal" emotional and behavioral development to some of the emotional problems and behavior disorders of childhood and adolescence.

◉ STUDYING PROBLEMS IN DEVELOPMENT

Taking a Developmental Perspective

Disturbed or pathological behavior is not, in most instances, qualitatively different from "normal" behavior. Typically, it represents an extreme of behaviors that have been discussed throughout this book. Taking a developmental perspective on the causes of disturbed behavior, we study problem behavior by knowing the causes of normal behavior. For instance, we can understand depression by examining what leads to sadness and anxiety among children in general. Or we can understand social withdrawal by knowing how children gain social skills and confidence in general. Furthermore, when problems become severe, we understand these problems by looking both at long-term background factors (such as learning problems or family dysfunction) and at short-run factors (such as stressful events or meeting deviant peers) that may have tipped the balance toward the negative. This approach to understanding disturbances in development has been called **developmental psychopathology**.

Taking a developmental perspective on emotional problems in childhood and adolescence also means that any seemingly abnormal behavior must be evaluated with knowledge of what is normal for a given age. If a parent regards a 2-year-old who has difficulty sharing or who doesn't comply easily with requests to clean up as having a problem, an observer who knows something about 2-year-olds in general will be able to see the situation as a problem of overly high parental expectations rather than one of a child who is abnormal.

Using a developmental perspective to study children's emotional problems may seem natural and obvious, but it has not always been the stance adopted. Until recently, there were not many efforts to trace the developmental history of a problem (Achenbach, 1990). If investigators did look at developmental history, it was retrospectively. That is, given a child who had a problem, what factors in the past could explain it? The preferred method in developmental psychopathology, however, is the **prospective study**, in which a group of normal children—or, perhaps, children at high risk for developing a problem but not yet showing it—are studied longitudinally (Lewis, 1990). This method gives one a more complete and more objective look at what factors may lead to disorder. In addition, and very importantly, the method allows one to look as well at what factors lead to *not* developing the disorder, that is, what experiences can buffer and protect children at risk. Unfortunately, we do not yet have a great deal of such prospective information on the development of many childhood disorders.

Types of Emotional Disturbance

Studying disordered behavior requires researchers to come to some agreement on how to group and categorize the many possible symptoms that troubled individuals can exhibit. The effort to construct diagnostic categories for children (as well as for adults) has turned out to require an enormous amount of work. Over the years, labels have been changed and criteria for using them revised. As a positive consequence of these revisions, the field has made substantial progress in arriving at a diagnostic system that can be used with a high degree of agreement by observers and that seems to group together individuals who have a common set of problems (Costello, 1990). Furthermore, there is increased recognition that children may show more than one kind of problem (a situation called **comorbidity**) and that, in such cases, all the problem types should be diagnosed rather than simply to assign the child to one category. A third improvement has been to recognize that various informants—including children themselves as well as parents, teachers, and other professionals—should be consulted in order to achieve an accurate picture of children's functioning. Talking to children themselves (although this is difficult when children are under 10 years) is important because adults often turn out to be unaware of children's inner lives. For instance, children report higher levels of phobias, depression, and suicidal thoughts than their parents report about them (Costello, 1990).

The many specific problems of children are now often understood as falling into three broad categories: **externalizing problems** (or problems of undercontrol), **internalizing problems** (or problems of overcontrol), and **major developmental deviations** (sometimes called psychoses). *Externalizing* syndromes include various kinds of "acting out" behavior. One such behavior is aggression; some of the family patterns that contribute to excessive aggression, and some of the treatments for such behavior patterns, have already been discussed in Chapter 11. In this chapter, we discuss attention deficit hyperactivity disorder, conduct disorders and delinquency, and substance abuse. *Internalizing* syndromes include anxiety, depression, self-deprecation, and eating disorders. We discuss such problems in this chapter and also examine suicide, which is often linked to anxiety and depression. Finally, we take a look at the two major developmental deviations: **infantile autism**, a profound disorder in early development, and **schizophrenia**, an "adult" problem that may begin to strike in adolescence.

Prevalence of Emotional Disturbance

How many children show serious emotional disturbance at some time during childhood? In answering this question, it is important to remember that disturbance is defined as deviance from behavior that is normal or usual for the child's age. For instance, it is not unusual for a 2-year-old to cling to her mother in a strange place, but it is unusual for a 12-year-old to do so. As we have seen, we must always define psychopathology in the context of what we know about normal development.

Trying to determine how many children are seriously disturbed also turns out to be expensive. Clearly, we cannot simply examine how many of them seek some kind of psychological help, because many children (and adults) who could benefit from such help do not obtain it. Even worse in regard to understanding disturbances in children, there are important biases in who is referred for help. For instance, black males have been found to be only one-third as likely as black females or white children of either sex to be treated for anxiety disorders (Costello & Janiszewski, 1990). Thus, to determine the prevalence of emotional problems in children, we need to define a sample of children that represents the population we wish to know about, and to obtain information about their psychological functioning.

TABLE 16.1 Items from the Behavior Problems Checklist

These items differentiate children referred for professional help with emotional problems from children who are not referred.

Acts too young	Poor peer relations	Stomachaches, cramps
Argues a lot	Lacks guilt	Attacks people
Can't concentrate	Easily jealous	Poor schoolwork
Obsessions	Feels unloved	Refuses to talk
Hyperactive	Feels persecuted	Screams a lot
Too dependent	Feels worthless	Secretive
Lonely	Fighting	Stubborn, sullen, or irritable
Confused	Is teased	Moody
Cries a lot	Hangs around with children who get into trouble	Sulks a lot
Cruel to others		Swearing
Daydreams	Impulsive	Temper tantrums
Demands attention	Lying or cheating	Threatens people
Destroys own things	Nervous	Unhappy, sad, or depressed
Destroys others' things	Not liked	Withdrawn, worrying
Disobedient at home	Too fearful or anxious	
Disobedient at school	Feels too guilty	

How can we obtain the needed information? One way to assess children is to conduct structured interviews with them and also with their parents and teachers. An important early study of this kind was conducted in the 1960s by Michael Rutter and his associates on the Isle of Wight, a small island off the south coast of England, and this data base has continued to be of current interest and use (Rutter, 1989). More recently, there have been several large-scale studies using interview techniques conducted in a variety of settings, including New Zealand (J. C. Anderson, Williams, McGee, & Silva, 1987); Puerto Rico (Bird et al., 1988); the United States (Costello et al., 1988; Velez, Johnson, & Cohen, 1989); and Canada (Offord et al., 1987). These studies converge very closely on the conclusion that about 1 in 5 children, at any point in time, can be diagnosed as suffering from some kind of disturbance. Estimates in the various studies ranged only from 17.6 percent to 22 percent (Costello, 1990), a very close agreement considering the variety of settings and methods used. The number of children with persistent problems is probably somewhat lower. In the New Zealand study, slightly over 10 percent of the children were considered a problem by every teacher who rated them over a three-year period (J.C. Anderson et al., 1987).

Another approach to obtaining information about children's problem behavior involves asking children, parents, and teachers to complete checklists of possible problems, indicating which apply. One well-validated technique of this kind is called the Child Behavior Checklist (CBCL). The behavior problems on the CBCL that differentiate children who are referred for emotional problems from those who are not are shown in Table 16.1 (Achenbach & Edelbrock, 1981).

Using symptom checklists is clearly a great deal easier and cheaper than using diagnostic interviews. However, symptom checklists do not precisely identify children with problems that would trigger a psychiatric diagnosis. More than half of the children with high scores on behavior checklists do not receive a diagnosis when interviewed (Costello, 1990). These tools are useful for screening populations and identifying high-risk samples for further study; they are also useful for research on the continuum of behavior from normal to deviant.

Symptom checklists such as the CBCL have been used to track problem behaviors in children over time. Disturbingly, a recent study indicates that behavioral and emotional problems in children may be worsening in the United States. Achenbach and Howell (1993) compared child behavior as reported by parents on the Child Behavior Checklist in 1976, and then again, by a comparable sample of parents, in 1989. They found that problem behaviors were more common and competent behaviors less common in 1989 than in 1976. The changes were seen across both sexes and a variety of ethnic and socioeconomic backgrounds. Furthermore, the changes were not concentrated in one area, such as aggression. Rather, increases were seen across the board, particularly in withdrawal, attention problems, delinquency, and depression. The study was not designed to shed light on the reasons for the changes seen, but the fact that they exist is worrisome and suggests the need for more intense study of the determinants of child problems.

The CBCL has also been used to examine cross-cultural and cross-ethnic differences in whether children's emotional problems are of the externalizing or internalizing kinds. One such study was conducted by Weisz, Sigman, Weiss, and Mosk (1993). They looked at African-American and Caucasian children in the United States, and also at Thai children and children from the Embu district of Kenya. The results are shown in Figure 16.1. Externalizing problems were most common

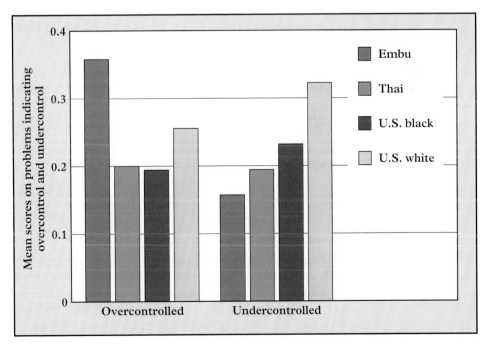

FIGURE 16.1 Average amounts of overcontrolled (internalizing) and undercontrolled (externalizing) behavior for Embu, Thai, African-American, and Caucasian-American children. After "Parent Reports of Behavioral and Emotional Problems Among Children in Kenya, Thailand, and the United States," by J. R. Weisz, M. Sigman, B. Weiss, and J. Mosk, 1993, *Child Development, 64,* 98–109.

among the Caucasian-American children, and internalizing problems were most common among the Embu. Across all the samples, boys were more likely than girls to show externalizing problems.

Duration of Emotional Disturbance over Time

Parents whose children show disturbed behavior are intensely interested in knowing whether emotional problems in childhood portend long-term difficulties. Do children "grow out of" emotional problems? Although many children have minor problems that do not endure, serious behavioral and emotional problems in childhood are likely to continue in later life. Problems that arise during the preschool years are less likely to persist over several years than problems that are manifested in the elementary school years; school-age children's emotional and behavioral disturbances have a moderately high probability of persisting (S. B. Campbell, 1983; M. Fischer, Rolf, Hasazi, & Cummings, 1984). However, even preschool children's disturbances should not be ignored on the grounds that they will eventually disappear; early intervention has a better probability of success than intervention after several years of difficulty.

Externalizing problems are particularly persistent over time. When children with these patterns were followed into adulthood, they had higher rates of antisocial behavior, illegal behavior, marital problems, and alcoholism than a control sample from the same neighborhood (Robins, 1966). Stability for externalizing symptoms is particularly high in a subgroup of children who have marked symptoms reported by several observers at several periods in time; occasional symptoms are less likely to recur (Moffitt, 1993). Internalizing problems also continue over time, but there is less evidence that they persist into adulthood, (S. B. Campbell, 1983; M. Fischer et al., 1984).

Effectiveness of Psychotherapy with Children

Do children and adolescents with problems get better when treated with psychotherapy? A very large number of studies have been done to evaluate the effectiveness of psychological treatment. Reviews combining the effects found in these therapy outcome studies using statistical techniques have shown clearly that therapy is indeed effective (Casey & Berman, 1985; Weisz, Weiss, Alicke, & Klotz, 1987; Weisz, Weiss, Han, Granger, & Morton, 1995). The difference between treated and untreated children seems large and significant, summed across studies varying widely in methodology and sample characteristics.

These reviews have also suggested some more specific conclusions and avenues for further investigation. Behavioral treatments—that is, those using techniques such as skills training, relaxation training, self-reinforcement, and modeling—have been found to be more effective than "traditional" therapies based on psychodynamic principles. The latter continue to be widely used, however. It is possible that they have not been properly evaluated; relatively few outcome studies have looked at such approaches. Also, behavioral approaches may be used particularly with problems that are responsive to these kinds of treatments.

Therapists have been found to be equally successful with problems of under- and overcontrol. Paraprofessionals have been found to obtain good treatment outcomes, at least in delivering the therapies they are generally trained to deliver; however, professional training seems especially helpful in treating problems of overcontrol.

PROBLEMS OF UNDERCONTROL

Attention Deficit Hyperactivity Disorder (ADHD)

Descriptions of young children who are physically restless, have great difficulty paying attention to tasks and following through on them, and who act impulsively, have appeared in the clinical literature for over a hundred years (D. M. Ross & Ross, 1982). A great variety of names have been attached to these children, including "hyperactive," "hyperkinetic," and suffering from "minimal brain dysfunction." Current definitions stress deficits in attention—along with poor impulse control and overactivity—in a syndrome called **attention deficit hyperactivity disorder**, or ADHD (Barkley, 1990). Controversy exists, however, as to whether attention deficit and hyperactivity are separable, although frequently co-occurring, symptoms rather than constituting a single problem. ADHD also frequently co-occurs with conduct disorder (discussed in the next section), but diagnosticians agree that the two syndromes can also each be observed alone.

ADHD probably occurs in about 3 to 5 percent of school-aged children, with males outnumbering females by ratios of at least 3:1, perhaps as high as 10:1 (Barkley, 1990). Lower prevalence rates are seen when only "pure" cases, unmixed with conduct disorder or other problems, are counted (Trites & Laprade, 1983). The problem is generally diagnosed by the age of 6 or 7 years, and symptoms may in fact be at their worst between the ages of 3 and 6 years, when parents are often deeply distressed by their children's defiant and noncompliant behavior (Mash & Johnston, 1983).

While referrals for the disorder may be caused in part by the fact that the symptoms are extremely annoying to adults, the disorder does not seem to be only a means of labeling children who are difficult. For instance, in the New Zealand community study we have already mentioned, diagnosis of attention deficit disorder was based on interviews with children as well as data from parents and teachers. At age 11, the prevalence of attention deficit disorder in the sample was 6.7 percent, with a sex ratio of 5.1 boys to every 1 girl; 85 percent of the children showed hyperactivity as well as attention problems and all of them had first shown problems before the age of 7 years (Moffitt, 1990a).

Academic and behavioral problems in children with ADHD have been found to persist through adolescence, but by adulthood many individuals are doing quite well, although perhaps not quite living up to their intellectual potential (Weiss, 1983). Better adjustment is seen when family environments remained positive and when symptoms of antisocial behavior (conduct disorder) did not appear (S. B. Campbell & Werry, 1986). In fact, the presence or absence of delinquency appears to be a key issue. Moffitt (1990a) reported that boys with attention deficit disorder but without delinquency (46 percent of the attention deficit cases in the New Zealand sample) did not show deficits in verbal IQ or reading, and they had only passing difficulty with antisocial behavior in early adolescence. However, the boys who showed both attention deficit disorder and delinquency did much worse, also showing difficulties in comparison with delinquents who did not suffer from attention deficit.

The causes of ADHD are still not well understood, although a vast number have been studied, including neurological, biochemical, social, and cognitive factors. Drug treatment may help in the short run but does not seem to improve the longer-term outlook; hence it should be considered very cautiously (Weiss, 1983). At present, efforts to maintain the family equilibrium and deal positively with the often disruptive behavior of the child seem the best prescription (S. B. Campbell, 1990). Positive family environments were much more common for the attention deficit children without delinquency than for those with delinquency in Moffitt's (1990a) study.

Conduct Disorders and Delinquency

The term **juvenile delinquent** is a legal phrase that refers to a young person, generally under 18 years of age, who engages in behavior that is punishable by law. Some delinquent acts—such as robbery, aggravated assault, rape, homicide, or illegal drug use—would also be considered crimes if they were committed by adults. Other delinquent acts are so-called **status offenses**—acts like curfew violations, truancy, "incorrigibility," running away, and underage drinking—that are illegal only when committed by young people. Given this fact, what is considered delinquent at one time and place may be lawful at another time or in another place.

Psychologists generally use the term **conduct disorder** to refer to children and adolescents who exhibit antisocial behavior, whether or not there are laws against it. Criteria for the diagnosis include committing at least three different antisocial acts over a six-month period, including stealing, arson, chronic truancy, destruction of property, or frequent physical fights. Using this definition, rather than the legal definition of delinquency, allows for the study of young children, whose troublesome behavior is unlikely to reach the attention of the judicial system. The category of conduct disorders is sometimes broken down further, to distinguish between individuals who commit antisocial behavior alone and those who act together with peers, for instance, in gangs (B. Martin & Hoffman, 1990). Conduct disorder and delinquency may overlap most clearly in the case of chronic antisocial behavior (D. R. Moore & Arthur, 1989).

There are obvious challenges in studying antisocial behavior. If one only studies people who come to the attention of the legal system, one cannot study younger children and one is studying a very biased sample of older children and adolescents. For instance, there is clear racial bias in decisions about arrest and prosecution in the United States (McCord, 1990). The alternative is to ask children and adolescents about their actions. However, even when promised confidentiality, individuals may not report accurately, due to lack of honesty about antisocial actions as well as to problems with memory for the actions and confusion regarding the exact meaning of questions (McCord, 1990).

Data from the legal system show that delinquency rates in the United States rose rapidly in the 1960s and 1970s. Rates flattened or even declined slightly in the early 1980s but increased again in the 1990s, a particularly disturbing trend in the case of violent crime (see Figure 16.2). Since 1960 the incidence of *serious* offenses by young people has been rising rapidly. In 1992, 30 percent of arrests for violent crimes in the United States were of individuals aged 14 or less (Wilkerson, 1994).

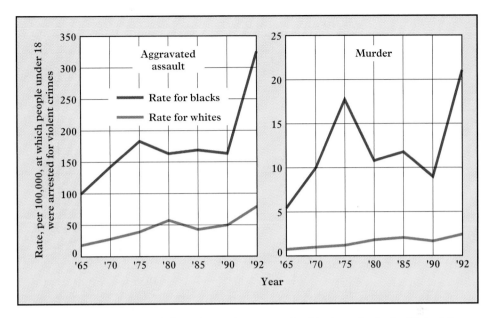

FIGURE 16.2 Historical trends for serious crimes committed by juveniles in the United States. From "Arrest Rates and Race," based on the FBI Uniform Crime Reports, from *The New York Times,* May 16, 1994. Copyright © 1994 by The New York Times Company. Reprinted by permission.

Similar trends are evident in other industrialized countries; using data from England, Figure 16.3 gives a vivid picture of how overall increases in crime in recent history are linked to increasing problems in adolescents and individuals in their 20s.

An important fact about delinquency is that a very large proportion of offenses are committed by a relatively small proportion of seriously antisocial individuals. For instance, in a study of 13,160 boys born in 1958 in Philadelphia, Tracy, Wolfgang, and Figlio (1990) found that 7.5 percent of the group were responsible for 61 percent of the total offenses, including 61 percent of homicides, 75 percent of rapes, and 65 percent of aggravated assaults. Other studies show the same phenomenon (e.g., Farrington, 1987).

There are clear sex differences in the incidence of recorded delinquency. Although the difference has declined both in the United States and in England, boys still outnumber girls in juvenile arrests, particularly for serious offenses (Farrington, 1987; Visher & Roth, 1986; Werner & Smith, 1982). For example, in 1990, girls under 18 were responsible for 72 percent fewer property offenses and 87 percent fewer violent offenses than boys under 18 (FBI Uniform Crime Reports, 1991). Sex ratios are lowest for offenses like theft and shoplifting. A number of factors may contribute to sex differences in delinquency. These include likelihood of gang membership; differences in aggressiveness and physical strength; and socialization differences, including less parental supervision of boys (Elliott, Hinzinga, & Ageton, 1985; Farrington, 1987).

A very large number of factors have been hypothesized to be associated with risk for delinquency. They include biological risk, individual personality, parental inadequacy, peer influence, and social and community factors (McCord, 1990). Each of these factors seems to contribute to the problem, although no one class of

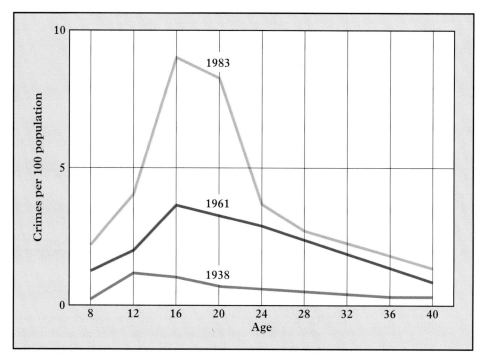

FIGURE 16.3 The relation between age and crime for English males in 1938, 1961, and 1983. From "Adolescence-Limited and Life-Course-Persistent Antisocial Behavior: A Developmental Taxonomy," by T. E. Moffitt, 1993, *Psychological Review, 100*, p. 692. Copyright © 1993 by American Psychology Association. Reprinted by permission.

variable taken alone accounts for the existence of conduct disorder and delinquency.

Biological risk includes genetic susceptibility and nongenetic factors, such as perinatal risk. There is some evidence for a role of genetics in delinquency, although the effects seem less marked than are genetic effects in adult criminality (DiLalla & Gottesman, 1991). Perinatal problems, such as prematurity and low birth weight, are also associated with delinquency, although primarily when the family is also poor and poorly functioning (Yoshikawa, 1994). A biological risk factor possibly caused by perinatal stress is neuropsychological problems. A comprehensive review by Moffitt (1990b) concludes that such problems are associated with delinquency, even in well-designed prospective studies (Denno, 1989).

There is also evidence linking delinquency to social and environmental variables. Impulsivity and risk taking are prospectively associated with later delinquency (McCord, 1990). Involvement with antisocial peers is closely tied to delinquency (e.g., Patterson & Dishion, 1985), and such involvement is predicted in turn by earlier academic failure and by peer rejection (Dishion, Patterson, Stoolmiller, & Skinner, 1991). Conflict between parents, inadequate discipline, and parental rejection increase the probability of delinquency (Loeber & Stouthamer-Loeber, 1986; McCord, 1990; Yoshikawa, 1994). Many of these risk factors are more common for children in families of low socioeconomic status, which may account for the association of socioeconomic status and delinquency. However, lower socioeconomic status is also generally associated with residence in neighborhoods where other community-level risk factors occur, such as overcrowding, unemployment among adults, and high rates of mobility. In addition, community violence may have both

BOX 16.1

AN INSIDE PERSPECTIVE ON DELINQUENT GANGS

There are a variety of theories and explanations for gang behavior. In a personal account of his involvement in gang activity in Los Angeles, Luis Rodriguez both chronicled the chaos and violence of his teen years and wrote a passionate book tracing responsibility for the social phenomenon to the economic inequality of society.

> Gangs are not alien powers. They begin as unstructured groupings, our children, who desire the same as any young person. Respect. A sense of belonging. Protection. The same things that the YMCA, Little League or the Boy Scouts want. It wasn't more than I wanted as a child.
>
> Gangs flourish when there's a lack of social recreation, decent education or employment. Today, many young people will never know what it is to work. They can only satisfy their needs through collective strength—against the

police, who hold the power of life and death, against poverty, against idleness, against their impotence in society.

> Without definitive solutions, it's easy to throw blame. For instance, politicians have recently targeted the so-called lack of family values.
>
> But "family" is a farce among the property-less and disenfranchised. Too many families are wrenched apart, as even children are forced to supplement meager incomes. Family can only really exist among those who can afford one. In an increasing number of homeless, poor, and working poor families, the things that people must do to survive undermines most family structures.

Source: From *Always Running: La Vida Loca, Gang Days in L.A.* (p. 250) by Luis T. Rodriguez, 1993, New York: Simon & Schuster.

---

direct and indirect effects in increasing the likelihood of antisocial acts by children and adolescents (Garbarino, Kostelny, & Dubrow, 1991). Box 16.1 contains a passionate accusation of social factors in causing delinquency.

We are left with an apparent overabundance of causal factors. A very long list of risks for the development of delinquency seems to tell us as little about the origins of delinquency as would a state of complete ignorance. Fortunately, recent discussions of delinquency and conduct disorder have delineated several ways in which more integrative and interesting approaches to the problem can be taken.

First, it is important to analyze the complex interactive effects of various risk factors. For instance, genetic and environmental effects have been shown to interact with each other, to be more than simply additive (see discussion in Chapter 2). For instance, Cadoret, Cain, and Crowe (1983) studied adopted children who had a genetic risk of antisocial behavior based on the history of their biological parents. They found that children in this genetically at-risk group were almost three times as likely to show adolescent antisocial behavior when they had poor adoptive environments. In another study, Caspi, Lynam, Moffitt, and Silva (1993) showed an interaction between biological risk and environment in one of the very few studies to look at delinquent behavior in girls. It is known that girls who undergo earlier puberty are at higher risk for deviant behavior, with the link apparently being that such girls tend to associate with older peers (Stattin & Magnusson, 1990). Caspi et al. showed that such effects occurred only for girls who attended mixed-sex schools in New Zealand, not for those who attended single-sex schools (a kind of school much more common and much less selective in New Zealand than in the United States). (See Figure 16.4.) Thus, association with older boys (an environmental variable) is key to the link between earlier puberty (a biological variable) and delinquency in girls.

Second, it may be important to distinguish two quite different kinds of individuals who show delinquent behavior in adolescence (Moffitt, 1993). There appear to be two kinds of individuals who commit delinquent acts in adolescence. One engages in antisocial acts beginning in early childhood and continuing persistently throughout their lives. There is evidence that these individuals are the ones characterized by biological vulnerabilities exacerbated by adverse environments. The other group engages in delinquent acts only during adolescence. Moffitt suggests that these individuals perceive antisocial behavior as adult, and they engage in antisocial acts in order to appear mature. As they actually grow into adulthood, however, they have less motivation to engage in such acts. There are practical implications of the distinction; prevention and treatment programs should be very different in the two cases.

Third, the fact that risk for antisocial behaviors is determined by a long list of interactive factors underlines the fact that no one prevention program or treatment package can be expected to work miracles. Yoshikawa (1994) stresses prevention as *cumulative;* he argues that interventions need to combine family support and early education efforts.

Efforts to treat delinquency have generally not shown encouraging results (Lorion, Tolan, & Wahler, 1987; Rutter & Giller, 1984; Sheldrick, 1985). Counseling and psychotherapy, transactional analysis, treatment in "therapeutic communi-

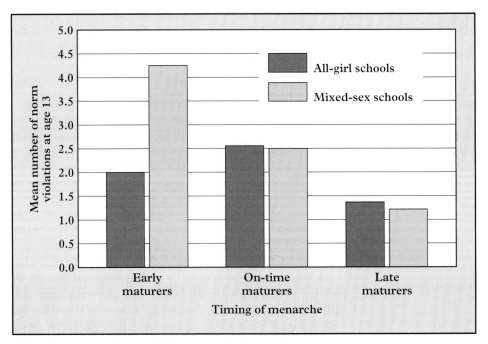

FIGURE 16.4 Norm violations for girls at age 13, as related to age at puberty and type of school. From "Unraveling Girls' Delinquency: Biological, Dispositional, and Contextual Contributions to Adolescent Misbehavior," by A. Caspi, D. Lynam, T. E. Moffitt, and P. A. Silva, 1993, *Developmental Psychology, 29,* pp. 19–30. Copyright © 1993 by American Psychology Association. Reprinted by permission.

ties," family casework, foster home placement, recreational programs, educational and vocational programs, youth service bureaus, and combinations of these and other approaches (e.g., health care, legal aid) have not had widespread success. Working with young people who already have serious problems may be doing too little, too late (M. W. Klein, 1979; Quay, 1987; Sechrest & Rosenblatt, 1987).

There is considerable evidence that imprisonment in traditional "correctional" institutions does little to solve the problem of delinquency. It subjects the young person to traumatic and embittering experiences, frequently including sexual and physical abuse, while providing little or no psychological, educational, or vocational help. Moreover, such institutions often serve as "finishing schools" for future criminals (Kaufman, 1979; Prescott, 1981; Wooden, 1976). Not surprisingly, reconviction rates among previously institutionalized youth generally run between 60 and 70 percent (Rutter & Giller, 1984).

Behavioral methods show some promise for the treatment of delinquency (Garrett, 1984, 1985; Quay, 1987; Rutter & Giller, 1984). In this approach, appropriate behavior is systematically rewarded, perhaps with tokens that can be exchanged for special privileges. Inappropriate behavior earns the person no reward and may have unpleasant consequences, such as a temporary loss of privileges. Behaviorial methods may be applied in an institutional setting such as a residential treatment center or correctional institution, in school or community programs, or in the family (Burchard & Harig, 1976; Kirigin, Wolf, Braukman, Fixsen, & Phillips, 1979; Rutter & Giller, 1984; I. G. Sarason, 1978; Snyder & Patterson, 1987).

Recent research findings have several implications. One is that in the long run prevention efforts may have more chance of success than intervention with individuals who already have problems. Such prevention efforts will need to include efforts to change the home environment and existing patterns of parent-child relationships through family support and early education (Yoshikawa, 1994). Another implication is that in most instances efforts to help the delinquent directly must be concerned with improving his or her social problem-solving skills and social competence generally, rather than just seeking to suppress deviant behavior (Rutter & Giller, 1984).

Substance Abuse

Until recently, American adults tended to view drug use as an isolated adolescent phenomenon and as specific to the use of drugs that are currently illegal. However, excessive drug use is increasingly being viewed as a major problem not only of adolescents and youth but also of society as a whole. In addition, serious attention is being paid to addictive substances such as alcohol, tobacco products, and prescription drugs. While these substances are legal, at least for certain age groups in certain circumstances, they can have grave physical and psychological consequences. Concern over their use is heightened by how common they are. Alcohol, cigarettes, and smokeless tobacco are the most frequent substances used by eighth- and tenth-graders in the United States. Even in twelfth grade, marijuana edges out smokeless tobacco for third place in frequency of use only by a single percentage point (L. D. Johnston, O'Malley, & Bachman, 1993).

Prevalence of Adolescent Drug Use. It is important to note that although far too many adolescents become substance abusers, the majority do not. Despite predictions in the late 1960s of an all-out epidemic of indiscriminate adolescent drug use that would spread to most young people, to date an epidemic of this magnitude has not occurred. Although use of alcohol, tobacco products, and marijuana is widespread among young people, other substances have never been used by more than one person in five in the United States (fewer in most other Western countries), and many occasional users appear to have quit, as indicated by the response "no use in the past year" (see Figure 16.5).

The overall rate of drug use by adolescents, which reached a peak in 1978 and 1979, declined from 1979 through 1992 (L. D. Johnston et al., 1993). For instance, use of marijuana within the past year, which had been rising steadily among high school students prior to 1978, stood at 22 percent in 1992, 29 percentage points below its high of 51 percent in 1979. Daily use dropped from 11 percent to 1.9 percent. Increases in peer disapproval of marijuana use—particularly steady use—and in the perceived risk associated with the drug may account for some of this decline (Bachman, Johnston, O'Malley, & Humphrey, 1988; Johnston, 1988). Decreases also occurred, of varying magnitudes and at varying time periods, in usage of most other illicit and prescription drugs, including barbiturates, tranquilizers, inhalants, and cocaine. Alcohol use has also declined. For instance, the incidence of occasional heavy drinking (five or more drinks in a row at some time within the past two weeks) dropped from 41 percent at its high in 1979 to 37 percent in the mid-1980s and to 28 percent in 1992.

There are more disturbing trends for tobacco. Cigarette smoking fell in the late 70s and early 80s, but this decline seems to have leveled off since 1984 and 10 percent of high school seniors still smoke a half pack of cigarettes or more per day (L. D. Johnston et al., 1993).

Substance Use vs. Abuse. In the minds of most people who work with adolescents, the young person in greatest danger is not the one who has occasionally had a few drinks or smoked marijuana with friends "for fun"; it is the adolescent or youth who repeatedly turns to drugs in order to cope with insecurity, stress, low self-esteem, feelings of rejection or alienation, or problems of daily living. In fact, Shedler and Block (1990) reported that individuals in a longitudinal study who had experimented with drugs without using them extensively scored *higher* on various indices of mental health than those who had never tried them, as well as higher than those individuals who had continued drug use. This finding indicates that experimentation alone is not necessarily a marker of future problems. Rather, failure to accomplish the important tasks of adolescence (e.g., learning to cope with stress, conflict, and frustration; developing cognitive, social, and vocational skills; establishing rewarding interpersonal relationships) because of repeated escapes into the world of drugs leaves the young person ill prepared to meet the demands of responsible adulthood.

Causes of Substance Abuse. Adolescents may try a drug simply because it is easily available and they are curious about it (L. D. Johnston & O'Malley, 1986; Johnston et al., 1987). But as we have just seen, understanding the causes of abuse is more important than understanding the causes of experimentation, because it is abuse that negatively affects development.

Peers are often said to play an important part in adolescent drug abuse (Brook, Lukoff, & Whiteman, 1980; Brunswick & Boyle, 1979; Elliott et al., 1985). Indeed, one of the best predictors of whether an adolescent will use a drug is use of that drug by friends, especially the young person's best friend (Jessor & Jessor, 1977; Kandel, 1980). However, because friends are selected by an individual, cause and effect relations are hard to disentangle.

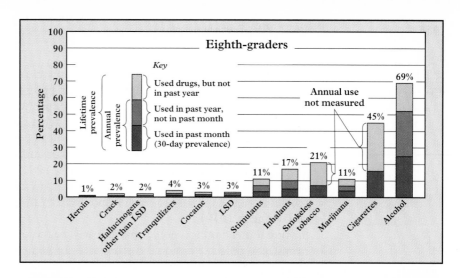

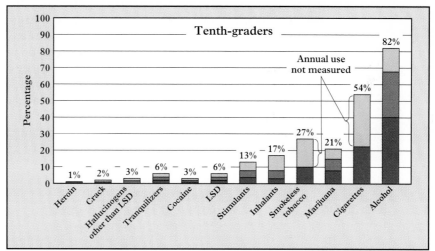

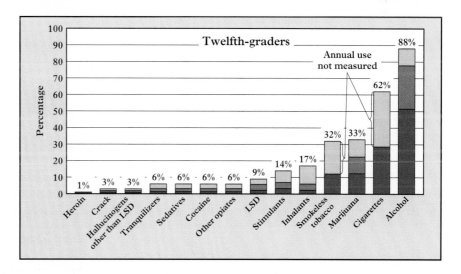

FIGURE 16.5 Prevalence and recency of drug use by eighth-, tenth-, and twelfth-graders in 1992. From *National Survey Results on Drug Use from Monitoring the Future Study, 1975–1992* (Vol. 1) (U.S. Department of Health and Human Services), by L. D. Johnston, P. M. O'Malley, and J. G. Bachman, 1993, Rockville, MD: National Institute on Drug Abuse. Copyright © 1993 by American Psychology Association. Reprinted by permission.

Whether adolescents become involved in serious drug use appears to depend a good deal on their relationships with their parents. For children of democratic, authoritative, accepting parents (especially those with relatively traditional values) who allow the gradual development of independence, the risk of serious drug involvement is generally low. For children whose parents have not been loving and who are either neglectful (overly permissive) or authoritarian and hostile, the risk of significant drug use is much greater (Barnes, 1984; Jessor, 1984; Kovach & Glickman, 1986). In such cases a young person may use drugs as a form of anger or rebellion—or simply to get some response from the parents as a sign that they care (J. J. Conger, 1979).

For other young people, particularly heavy multiple-drug users, reliance on drugs may reflect emotional disturbance. In some such cases we need to look to disturbances in family relationships during the course of development for clues to the young person's difficulties. Among adolescents in residential treatment centers and halfway houses for alcohol and drug users, common themes acknowledged both by staff members and by recovering users are feelings of parental rejection or indifference; lack of acceptance by peers; emotional isolation; and low self-esteem, which the young person attempts to conceal by appearing "cool" (Brook et al., 1980; J. J. Conger, 1979; Kandel, 1980).

Biological susceptibility may play a role in leading to substance abuse as well. There is evidence from studies of alcoholism that adolescent children of alcoholics may differ from children of nonalcoholics in how they metabolize alcohol and how they experience its effects, at points that predate any alcohol abuse by the children

The most commonly abused substance in the United States is alcohol.

themselves (McCord, 1990; Sher, 1991). There is also similar, but more preliminary, evidence regarding reactions to illegal drugs (McCord, 1990).

✿ PROBLEMS OF OVERCONTROL

In our opening vignette, the teacher was more concerned about her student with symptoms of undercontrol than with the student who showed symptoms of depression. There are many reasons for this state of affairs, which is typical for parents and teachers. Undercontrol poses more immediately pressing problems than overcontrol. In addition, until recently it has been common to think that children were too young to show true depression or that any anxieties they had were likely to disappear in the normal course of events. It is now recognized, however, that childhood anxiety and depression are real and troubling. It is important to identify and understand symptoms of anxiety and depression in children and adolescents.

Anxiety

Fears are common in childhood. Children from preschool through age 12 may have 5 to 11 fears of things such as dogs or the dark (Jersild & Holmes, 1935; Lapouse & Monk, 1959; Ollendick, 1983). In fact, common fears—such as fears of burglars or fire, fears of looking foolish, and fears of getting low grades—show constant rates of occurrence through the age of 18 years (Ollendick, Matson, & Helsel, 1985). Thus, it is important to distinguish between the child who has normal fears and anxieties and the child who is overanxious.

Overanxious children worry a great deal, over long periods of time, about unrealistic possibilities. They are difficult to reassure, may have many physical complaints, and may seem tense and find it hard to relax (S. M. Miller, Boyer, & Rodoletz, 1990). Almost 3 percent of children in one study of prevalence showed symptoms of this kind (Anderson et al., 1987). Children are at particular risk for anxiety problems if they have anxious parents (Turner, Beidel, & Costello, 1987).

There are substantial problems still to be addressed in standardizing diagnoses for childhood anxiety and conducting prospective studies to clarify risk factors and possible outcomes (Kendall et al., 1991; S. M. Miller, Boyer, et al., 1990). Treatments for children are, however, emerging. Kendall et al. advocate the use of a combination of cognitive-behavioral approaches, including modeling, role playing, and relaxation training.

Depression

Depressive disorders range from mild, temporary states of sadness, often in response to a specific life event, to severely disturbed conditions that may involve cognitive as well as affective disturbances (Emde, Harmon, & Good, 1986; Klerman, 1988; Shaffer, 1985). Until recently it was widely assumed that children and younger adolescents rarely exhibit depression (Klerman, 1988; Rutter, 1986). However, recent clinical and research studies have demonstrated that this is not the case. Both major and minor forms of depression have been found during childhood, puberty, and adolescence (Kovacs, Feinberg, Crouse-Novak, Paulauskas, & Finkelstein, 1984; Puig-Antich, 1986; Rutter, Izard, & Read, 1986).

Estimates of childhood depression vary widely across research studies (from 2 to 14 percent), but the number of children is never negligible (Stark, Rouse, & Livingston, 1991). Furthermore, investigators agree that depression shows marked increases from childhood to adolescence (Cantwell, 1990). This increase is especially large for girls, and depressive symptoms and outright depression are more frequent among girls than boys after puberty and throughout adult life (Pearce, 1982; Rutter, 1986; Weissman & Boyd, 1983).

The reasons for girls' special vulnerability to depression after puberty are still being debated. Nolen-Hoeksema and Girgus (1994) argue that, even prior to adolescence, girls have developed several attributes that make them more vulnerable to depression than boys. Girls are less assertive than boys, less dominant in group interactions, and more likely to deal with problems by brooding than with active coping. However, at this point in development, girls are not more subject to depression than boys. These authors suggest that, beginning in adolescence, sex-specific stress factors interact with preexisting vulnerabilities to create depressed mood. One specific stressor for girls and women, starting with puberty, is that they are more likely than boys to have worries about their body image, due to unrealistic cultural ideals regarding the female body. A second stressor for women after sexual maturity is that they have an increased likelihood—much greater than that of men—of suffering from forms of sexual abuse, including acquaintance rape. A third factor is that, as girls mature, they may experience pressure to conform to a restrictive social role some adults still consider appropriate for women. Such pressure may explain J. H. Block, Gjerde, and J. Block's (1991) finding that depressive symptoms are positively correlated with intelligence for girls but not for boys.

Depression in children is likely produced by many of the same factors associated with depression in adults, including high levels of stress and negative life events; impaired family communication patterns; maladaptive coping patterns; and attributions of problems and failures to the self, which creates feelings of helplessness (Compas, Ey, & Grant, 1993; Hammen, Burge, & Stansbury, 1990; S. M. Miller, Birnbaum, & Durbin, 1990; Stark et al., 1991). Neuroendocrine functioning may also be a factor in leading to depression (Compas et al., 1993). Without treatment, depressive problems are very likely to persist or—if they disappear for a time—to recur. Current approaches to treatment include a variety of interpersonal and cognitive-behavioral approaches (Mufson, Moreau, Weissman, & Klerman, 1993; Stark et al., 1991). Children and adolescents may be taught how to express their feelings, how to change their patterns of thinking about themselves and their problems, and how to deal with issues such as peer rejection.

Suicide

Suicide is rare in children and almost as infrequent among young adolescents. After that, however, the reported suicide rate increases rapidly, accounting for 11.3 deaths per 100,000 people in the 15–19-year age group, the third highest cause of death for that group (Garland & Zigler, 1993). Suicide is markedly higher for white males than for nonwhite males and females. There is a disturbing historical trend in adolescent suicide: rates have increased steadily since the 1960s, while suicide rates for the total population have held steady (see Figure 16.6). The increase is most apparent in the at-risk group of white males.

Females in the United States are more likely than males to use passive methods of suicide, such as ingestion of drugs or poisons, and less likely to use active meth-

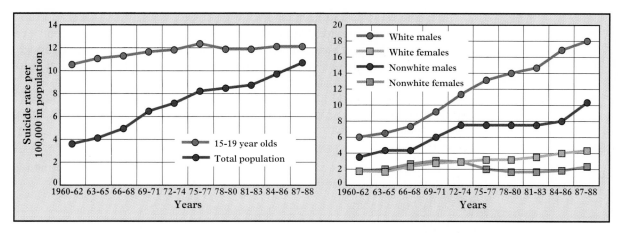

FIGURE 16.6 Historical trends in suicide rates in the United States. The top panel shows data for adolescents from 15 to 19 compared to data for the total population. The bottom panel shows data for 15- to 19-year-olds, according to race and gender. After "Adolescent Suicide Prevention: Current Research and Social Policy Implications," by A. F. Garland and E. Zigler, 1993, *American Psychologist, 48*, p. 170. Adapted with permission.

ods, such as shooting or hanging. Among both sexes, firearms or explosives account for the greatest number of completed suicides, whereas drugs or poisons account for the greatest number of attempted suicides. Although males outnumber females in completed suicides, attempted suicides are far more common among females (D. K. Curran, 1987; Holinger, 1978; Shaffer, 1986).

Reasons for Suicide Attempts. In considering attempts at suicide, it is important to distinguish between immediate precipitating factors and longer-term predisposing factors. Precipitating events may include the breakup or threatened breakup of a romance; pregnancy (real or imagined); school failure; conflicts with parents; rejection by a friend; being apprehended in a forbidden or delinquent act; loss of a parent or other loved person; and fear of serious illness or imminent mental breakdown (D. K. Curran, 1987; Jacobs, 1971; M. L. Miller, Chiles, & Barnes, 1982). On closer examination, however, it becomes clear that the individual's reaction to such events is generally the culmination of a series of difficulties. One study of 154 adolescents who had attempted suicide found that hopelessness, rather than depression resulting from immediate situations, was most often the critical factor (Wetzel, 1976).

Adolescents who attempt suicide frequently have a long history of escalating family instability and discord, and they show significant psychopathology (Garland & Zigler, 1993). They have reached a point at which they feel unable to communicate with their parents or turn to them for support. Early parental loss is also more common among suicidal adolescents (G. W. Brown, Harris, & Bifulco, 1986; D. K. Curran, 1987; Shaffer, 1986). Typically, suicidal adolescents have fewer close friends, but their relationships with them are much more intense: "Their relationships become supercharged with a degree of desperation and need that is often not shared by their friends and lovers" (D. K. Curran, 1987, p. 30).

Prediction of Suicide. There is a dangerous myth, not only among the public but also among some clinicians, that a person who talks about committing suicide will not do so. The tragic fact, however, is that many adolescents (and adults) who have threatened suicide and been ignored or dismissed as attention seekers do subsequently take their own lives. Moreover, in talking about suicide, adolescents are conveying a message that something is wrong and that they need help, even though they may not yet be seriously intent on suicide as the only remaining solution to their problems.

Talk of suicide should always be taken seriously (Parry-Jones, 1985; H. L. P. Resnick, 1980; Teicher, 1973). It is not easy to predict suicide, but there are a number of warning signals that can alert the careful observer to the possibility. They include the following:

1. A persistently depressed or despairing mood (or frantic activity alternating with intolerable boredom and listlessness).

2. Eating and sleeping disturbances.

3. Declining school performance.

4. Gradual social withdrawal and increasing isolation from others.

5. Breakdown in communication with parents or other important people in the young person's life.

6. A history of previous suicide attempts or involvement in accidents.

7. Seemingly reckless, self-destructive, and uncharacteristic behavior, such as serious drug or alcohol use, reckless driving, sexual acting out, delinquency, or running away.

A teenage suicide hot line.

Males are more likely than females to use guns in committing suicide.

8. Statements like "I wish I were dead" or "What is there to live for?"

9. Inquiries about the lethal properties of drugs, poisons, or weapons.

10. Unusually stressful events in the young person's life, such as school failure, breakup of a love affair, or loss of a loved one.

Eating Disorders

Many adolescents go through brief periods in which their weight deviates upward or downward from generally accepted norms. Once their growth has stabilized, most adolescents will correct their weight by regulating their diet; some, however, will not. In some cases, sustained overeating may lead to serious obesity (Rodin, 1985; Stunkard, 1980). In others, pathologically prolonged and extreme dieting may lead to serious, sometimes life-threatening degrees of weight loss. This latter condition, known as **anorexia nervosa**, is most likely to occur during adolescence and is far more common among females than among males (Bruch, 1973; P. E. Garfinkel & Garner, 1983; Herzog, 1988).

Both obese and anorexic young people often lack a clear sense of their own identity as separate and distinct individuals capable of setting and achieving their own goals. Anorexia is a particularly puzzling condition because the adolescent has such a distorted perception of her own body. Many anorexic females who appear to neutral observers as little more than an emaciated bundle of skin and bones continue to express concern about putting on too much weight. We still have much to learn about this condition, which, while relatively rare, seems to be increasing in frequency, especially among affluent youth. Biological factors (possibly an impairment of the functioning of the anterior pituitary gland at the base of the brain) may play some role, but psychological factors appear to be of primary importance.

Parents are often surprised by the onset of anorexia because their child has always seemed so "normal." As children, anorexic adolescents typically seemed almost "too good"—quiet, obedient, always dependable, eager to please. Most have been good students. When one looks more closely, however, the picture is not as bright. At least unconsciously, most anorexic young people feel that they have been exploited and prevented from leading their own lives and that they have been unable to form a strong personal identity. Perhaps in reaction, they are likely to display an obsessional need to be in control of every aspect of their life, particularly bodily functions. They may also feel incapable of meeting the demands of sexual maturity. Severe undereating, which can interrupt menstruation and make secondary sex characteristics less prominent, may be—at least unconsciously—a way to avoid growing up.

Studies of the parents of female anorexic adolescents indicate that the parents have frequently exerted such firm control and regulation during childhood that the girl had difficulty establishing a sense of identity and gaining confidence in her ability to make decisions for herself. These parents are also likely to have encouraged their children to become perfectionistic overachievers (S. Minuchin, Rosman, & Baker, 1978).

Still another eating disorder, **bulimia**, has shown a dramatic increase among female adolescents and young women (Herzog, 1988; Russell, 1985; Striegel-Moore, Silberstein, & Rodin, 1986). In this disorder, which combines elements of both anorexia and obesity, binge eating (gorging) alternates with forced purging through self-induced vomiting or laxative abuse. Although health is likely to be impaired by this disorder, often seriously, normal weight may be maintained, making the disorder more difficult to detect. Bulimic individuals characteristically are afraid that they will be unable to stop this eating pattern (which they recognize as abnormal). They typically report a depressed mood and self-deprecating thoughts following the eating binges. Nearly three-fourths acknowledge that their abnormal eating pattern has adverse effects on their physical health (C. Johnson, 1982; C. Johnson, Lewis, & Hagman, 1984).

Bulimic practices, as well as the condition of being greatly over- or underweight, can cause serious, sometimes life-threatening physiological problems. Specialized medical care is essential in such cases. Over the long term, however, skilled psychological treatment is important. And because disturbed parent-child relationships (including problems related to the development of independence and sexual maturation) typically play an important part in eating disorders, a well-designed therapeutic program for adolescents almost always requires active involvement on the part of the parents (S. Minuchin et al., 1978).

✿ MAJOR DISORDERS IN CHILDHOOD AND ADOLESCENCE

The disorders of under- and overcontrol that we have studied so far are problems that seem to be on a continuum with normal experience. We have all, at one time or another, felt anxious or depressed, shown inappropriate aggression, or done things for which we later feel regret. Other psychological problems, however, seem much more removed from everyday life. Normal people rarely hear voices or go through

Bulimia is an increasing problem among young women.

life without expressing any emotions. Normal children rarely fail to develop language and would rarely, if ever, spend their time staring for hours at their rhythmically moving fingers. In this section, we turn our attention to consider severe forms of psychopathology, sometimes called psychoses.

Autism

Autistic children have several kinds of severe symptoms, which cluster together to form the syndrome. First, they do not develop language normally, showing both extreme delay in learning and a variety of deviant learning patterns, such as the wholesale repetition of long memorized phrases and pronoun reversal (use of "I" to mean "you" and "you" to mean "I"). Second, they show rigid and unimaginative kinds of play, coupled with obsessions with certain kinds of objects (e.g., shiny rocks) and a rigid insistence on following certain rituals (e.g., always leaving toys in exactly the same position). Third, they show deviant patterns of social interaction, never developing normal attachments to their caretakers, and, indeed, averting their eyes from contact with others. Autism is manifest before the age of 3 years.

Autism occurs in 2 to 5 children out of 10,000 (Hertzig & Shapiro, 1990; Howlin & Yule, 1990). It is more frequent in boys than girls, with a ratio of about three boys to every one girl. Some improvement in symptoms occurs as the children get older, and about half eventually develop useful speech. However, only a small minority attain social independence at adulthood (see Box 16.2 for a personal

BOX 16.2

AN AUTISTIC CHILDHOOD

The world of the autistic child must be very different from that of the normal one, and people have long been fascinated by what it could be like. The following description of childhood experience is taken from a personal account written by an autistic woman who was able to use her intellectual skills to achieve a better degree of self-expression than is common with most autistics.

I discovered the air was full of spots. If you looked into nothingness, there were spots. People would walk by, obstructing my magical view of nothingness. I'd move past them. They'd gabble. My attention would be firmly set on my desire to lose myself in the spots, and I'd ignore the gabble, looking straight through this obstruction with a calm expression, soothed by being lost in the spots. . . .

My father catered to my fascination for small fancy things and shiny objects. He would bring me something different every week and would always build me up by asking me if I knew how special and magical these various bits and bobs were. I would sit on his knee, my eyes fastened to the object, listening to the story as though he were one of my story-telling records. In my head I would do the introduction: "This is an original little long-playing record, and I am your story-teller. We are going to begin now to read the story of . . . "

Source: From *Nobody Nowhere.* (pp. 3, 7) by Donna Williams, 1992, New York: Avon Books.

account of autism by one such individual, who is now able to write about her experiences). Better outcomes occur in children with higher IQs and those who develop language before the age of 5 years.

When originally described by the psychiatrist Leo Kanner in 1943, autism was attributed to deficient mothering. However, subsequent research does not support this hypothesis. Current investigation centers on biological theories. One reason for this focus comes from studies of twins. If one identical twin was autistic, in 36 percent to 100 percent of the cases studied, the other twin was autistic; the wide range is because different studies found different results. For nonidentical twins, the rate was from 0 percent to 36 percent (Rubenstein, Lotspeich, & Ciaranello, 1990), a rate lower than that for identical twins. However, no specific cause has as yet been discovered (Hertzig & Shapiro, 1990), although there are some interesting findings regarding abnormalities in certain parts of the brain (Rubenstein et al., 1990).

Adolescent Schizophrenia

Among adolescents, schizophrenia is by far the most frequently occurring psychotic disorder. Its incidence, though still relatively rare (under 1 percent) increases dramatically from age 15 onward and reaches a peak during late adolescence and early adulthood, leveling off when people approach 30 (Cancro, 1983; P. Graham & Rutter, 1985). Boys are more likely than girls to develop schizophrenia in childhood and adolescence; adult onset is more frequent among women than among men (Lewine, 1980). Like its adult counterpart, adolescent schizophrenia is characterized by disordered thinking; distortions of, or lack of contact with, reality; limited capacity for establishing meaningful relationships with others; and poor emotional control (P. Graham & Rutter, 1985; Steinberg, 1985; Weiner, 1970, 1980).

In its fully developed form, adolescent schizophrenia can usually be identified without much difficulty. Speech is likely to seem peculiar—stilted, overelaborate, disconnected, or even incoherent. Schizophrenics may make odd facial grimaces or movements; appear distracted, withdrawn, or confused; and show inappropriate emotional reactions—either failing to respond with appropriate feeling or overreacting in a poorly controlled fashion. Hallucinations—usually auditory and typically reflecting control by others (e.g., outside voices telling one what to do)—and intense, bizarre delusions may also be present (Steinberg, 1985).

Proper diagnosis may be difficult in the early stages of adolescent schizophrenia, partly because the symptoms may be far less obvious or dramatic than they will become later, and partly because some characteristics that might suggest incipient schizophrenia in adults are more likely to occur among nonschizophrenic as well as schizophrenic adolescents (Weiner, 1970, 1980). These include circumstantial thinking, abstract preoccupation, and conscious awareness of sexual and aggressive imagery, as well as ideas of reference (the belief that others are talking about one). All of these symptoms tend to occur more frequently among nonschizophrenic adolescents than among nonschizophrenic adults (Rutter, Graham, Chadwick, & Yule, 1976).

Causal Factors. Several generations ago it was believed that traumatic experiences in childhood are the primary determinants of schizophrenia (Steinberg, 1985). However, as you saw in Chapter 2, recent research indicates that biological and hereditary factors frequently play a major role in the development of this disorder. As noted previously, it may be more accurate to speak of inheriting an increased vulnerability to schizophrenia than of inheriting schizophrenia per se. Longitudinal studies have found that vulnerable individuals are more likely to develop schizophrenia or to suffer relapses after treatment if their families are characterized by high levels of stress, negative expressed emotions, and disturbed communication patterns (M. J. Goldstein, 1987; J. Marcus et al., 1987; Mednick et al., 1987; Tienari et al., 1987).

Prognosis. Among hospitalized adolescent schizophrenics "it can be anticipated that about one-quarter will recover, one-quarter will improve but suffer residual symptoms or occasional relapses, and the remaining 50 percent will make little or no progress and require continuing residential care" (Weiner &

Elkind, 1972, p. 220). In general, the older the adolescent is when schizophrenia appears, the better the prognosis is likely to be. Other favorable indications include sudden onset of the disturbance; clear-cut precipitating factors; above-average intelligence; previously good personal, academic, and social adjustment; and early response to treatment (Eggers, 1978; King & Pitman, 1971; Steinberg, 1985; Weiner, 1980). Finally, the outlook for improvement is better if the family is able to accept the disturbance and if there is adequate planning for future treatment and school, work, and living arrangements (M. J. Goldstein, 1987; C. E. Vaughn et al., 1982).

It is important to distinguish between brief psychotic episodes brought on as reactions to some crisis event and schizophrenia (American Psychiatric Association, 1987; Feinstein & Miller, 1979). Although during a reactive episode the individual may exhibit some psychotic symptoms, such as incoherence, disorganized associations or behavior, delusions, or hallucinations, these symptoms appear suddenly and are short-lived (lasting from a few hours to at most a couple of weeks). The psychotic symptoms typically appear immediately after a severe and recognizable "psychosocial stressor"—such as loss of a loved one or a life-threatening event—that would evoke significant symptoms of distress in almost anyone. Invariably there is emotional turmoil, manifested by rapid, generally depressed, and anxious mood swings. This disorder, which usually appears first in adolescence or young adulthood, may be followed by feelings of mild depression or loss of self-esteem. But with psychological assistance and support, the young person or adult may be expected to return fully to his or her previous level of functioning.

✷ SUMMARY

It is important to study problems in development within the context of an understanding of normal development. This perspective has been called developmental psychopathology. Study of this kind makes use of knowledge concerning the causes of normal development and the way in which normal development proceeds in order to understand what can cause children to develop less than optimally. The preferred method of study is the prospective longitudinal study, in which investigators can observe children as some develop well and others more poorly.

Emotional disturbance in childhood is defined as deviance from behavior that is usual for the child's age. The emotional problems of children fall into two broad categories: internalizing and externalizing syndromes. Internalizing syndromes include anxiety and depression; externalizing syndromes involve behavior that is hyperactive, aggressive, and/or delinquent. Externalizing problems are particularly persistent over time.

Psychotherapy is effective with most childhood disorders and can be administered by trained paraprofessionals as well as psychologists and psychiatrists. Behavioral treatment is generally superior to nonbehavioral forms, although the latter have not been well studied.

Children who have difficulty with attention and self-control, and who may have difficulty controlling their physical activity, are said to have attention deficit hyperactivity disorder (ADHD). This problem is more common among boys than girls. The cause is unknown and treatments are still being worked on. Drugs seem to help only in the short run, but careful management is the key for favorable long-term outcome.

The term *juvenile delinquent* refers to a young person who engages in behavior that is punishable by law. Such behavior includes status offenses that are illegal only when committed by young people. Boys outnumber girls in juvenile arrests, particularly for serious offenses. There are many factors that are associated with delinquency. As a group, delinquents score somewhat lower on IQ tests and show symptoms of neuropsychological problems. Delinquents are more likely than nondelinquents to be impulsive, defiant, and lacking in self-control. Within a social-class group, family relationships predict delinquency. Lax or overly strict discipline, usually involving physical punishment, and weak parental supervision are associated with delinquency. Given this multiplicity of causes, investigators are increasingly attempting to unravel the complex interactive effects of risk factors and to delineate subgroups of delinquents who differ substantially from one another. Efforts to treat delinquency have not been very successful, although behavioral methods show some promise. Imprisonment in correctional institutions exacerbates the problem. Prevention may represent a more promising approach than treatment of established problems.

Rates of substance abuse among American adolescents remain high, although they have been falling. Adolescents abuse drugs for a variety of reasons. These include peer pressure, poor parent-child relationships, desire to escape from the pressures of life, emotional disturbance, and alienation or societal rejection.

Problems of overcontrol are increasingly being given attention in childhood. Anxiety and depression are recognized as real problems, likely to persist if untreated. Substantial numbers of children are affected. Suicide is a problem that has been worsening recently; while uncommon in childhood, rates rise dramatically in adolescence. Another problem that becomes manifest in adolescence, especially among girls, is eating disorders, including anorexia and bulimia.

Major disorders of development include infantile autism, a profound developmental deviation manifest in the first years of life, and adolescent schizophrenia, which is basically an adult psychopathology, vulnerability for which begins in adolescence. Autistic children are delayed in developing language, have abnormal social relationships, and show impoverished and ritualistic play. The cause is likely to be biological, but no specific cause is known. Adolescent schizophrenia is characterized by disordered thinking.

REVIEW QUESTIONS

1. What are the main types of emotional disturbances experienced by children and adolescents?

2. What social and individual factors contribute to juvenile delinquency?

3. Briefly describe current trends in adolescent drug use.

4. Why do adolescents abuse drugs?

5. How is depression manifested during childhood and adolescence?

6. Why do adolescents attempt suicide? How can suicide attempts be predicted?

7. What kinds of eating disorders sometimes occur among adolescents?

8. What are the signs of infantile autism?

9. Why is it sometimes difficult to diagnose adolescent schizophrenia?

CRITICAL THINKING ABOUT THE CHAPTER

1. Have you or someone you know ever suffered from one of the problems described in this chapter? If so, write an account of the problem. Try to analyze what created the problem and what helped (or could help) to deal with it.

2. There are marked sex differences in many of the problems discussed in this chapter. Girls are more likely than boys to suffer from depression and eating disorders and to attempt suicide; boys are more likely than girls to have problems with attention deficit disorders and conduct disorders and to complete suicides. Discuss the factor or factors that you think may account for these sex differences. Are there any reasons to think that the sex ratios may change in the next decade?

KEY TERMS

- anorexia nervosa
- attention deficit hyperactivity disorder
- bulimia
- comorbidity
- conduct disorder
- developmental psychopathology
- externalizing problems
- infantile autism
- internalizing problems
- juvenile delinquent
- major developmental deviation
- prospective study
- schizophrenia
- status offense

SUGGESTED READINGS

Cicchetti, D., & Schneider-Rosen, K. (Eds.). (1984). *New directions in child development: Vol. 26. Childhood depression.* San Francisco: Jossey-Bass. Contains four papers on the developmental patterns and causes of childhood depression. Depression is discussed in relation to cognitive and social development. Relationships between maternal depression and children's emotional disturbance are described.

Curran, D. K. (1987). *Adolescent suicidal behavior.* Washington, DC: Hemisphere. This well-balanced, comprehensive discussion of the problem of adolescent suicidal behavior in contemporary society corrects a number of popular—and dangerous—misconceptions.

Johnston, L. D., O'Malley, P. M., & Bachman, J. G. (1993). *National Survey Results on Drug Use from Monitoring the Future Study, 1975–1992.* Ann Arbor, MI: Institute of Social Research, University of Michigan. Recent edition of a series, published annually since 1975, that shows national trends in drug use among high school seniors. (Senior authorship varies from year to year.)

Lewis, M., & Miller, S. M. (Eds.). (1990). *Handbook of developmental psychopathology.* New York: Plenum Press. Contains excellent reviews of a variety of issues in research in this area, together with current information on what is known about most psychological problems in childhood and adolescence.

Rutter, M., & Giller, H. (1984). *Juvenile delinquency: Trends and perspectives.* New York: Guilford. A clear, well-written summary and evaluation of research on the causes, prevention, and treatment of delinquency.

GLOSSARY

abilities The processes used in solving problems and dealing with new information.

accommodation The process of changing existing concepts in response to environmental demands. Compare **assimilation.**

achievement The amount a person has learned in a particular course or school subject.

achievement motivation An overall tendency to evaluate one's performance against standards of excellence, to strive for successful performance, and to experience pleasure contingent on successful performance.

adolescence The period of development that extends from puberty to adulthood.

adoption study Behavior genetics studies that involve studying the development of adopted children.

amniocentesis A procedure in which cells from the amniotic fluid are sampled to assess the presence of genetic problems in the fetus, as well as certain other developmental anomalies, including spinal cord defects.

amnion One of two fetal membranes surrounding the developing embryo. See also **chorion.**

amniotic fluid The liquid within the sac surrounding the developing embryo and fetus.

anal stage Freud's characterization of toddlerhood, emphasizing the energy bound up for the infant in activities involving the anus.

androgynous A term used to describe a person who combines feminine and masculine psychological qualities.

anorexia nervosa An eating disorder characterized by obsessive dieting, sometimes coupled with excessive exercise.

anoxia Lack of oxygen.

applied research Research designed to help parents, schools, and others who deal with children.

aptitude The ability to learn a new skill or to do well in some future learning situation.

assimilation The individual's efforts to deal with the environment by making it fit into his or her own existing structures. Compare **accomodation.**

attachment (1) An emotional relationship between an infant and a particular caregiver who is better able than anyone else to soothe the baby and whom the baby approaches for play and consolation. (2) Bowlby's idea of infancy, emphasizing the formation of an emotional bond between infants and caretakers.

attention deficit hyperactivity disorder (ADHD) A disorder characterized by problems in concentration, poor impulse control, and overactivity.

attributions Inferences about the causes of one's own or someone else's behavior.

auditory localization Knowing where something is from listening to a sound it emits.

authoritarian A term describing parents who are cold and demanding of mature behavior.

authoritative A term describing parents who are warm but also demanding of mature behavior.

autonomous A term used to refer to adults who seem free to recall childhood experiences and to discuss attachment issues in a coherent fashion.

autonomous standards Standards based on comparisons with one's own past performance.

autosomes Chromosomes that are possessed in equal measure by males and females.

avoidant attachment A pattern of insecure attachment in which infants seem not to use their caretakers for comfort.

axons The extensions of a neuron that send out messages. See also **dendrites.**

basic research Research intended to generate knowledge about the processes and sequences of development, even when there is no immediate social need for the knowledge.

behavior genetics The study of how genes affect complex behaviors and of how genetic effects interact with environmental ones.

bidirectionality A principle stating that a child's development is the product of the interaction between the child's own characteristics and those of the people who socialize the child.

bound morpheme A morpheme that cannot stand alone as a word but must be attached to another morpheme.

bulimia An eating disorder characterized by bingeing on food and then purging the food through self-induced vomiting or laxative abuse.

Caesarean section A surgical method of delivery involving an incision through the abdomen and uterus.

category A mental representation of the dimensions that are shared by a set of similar, but not identical, events.

child-directed language The simplified speech usually addressed to children who are learning language.

chorion One of two fetal membranes surrounding the developing embryo. See also **amnion.**

chorionic villus sampling A procedure in which cells from the placenta are sampled to assess the presence of genetic problems in the fetus.

chromosomes Particles within the cell that contain the individual's genetic inheritance; each cell contains twenty-three pairs of chromosomes.

class inclusion The ability to understand how classes are hierarchically related, in particular, to know that a subset can never have more members than the class of which it is a subset.

classical conditioning The establishment of a relationship between a neutral event and a biologically salient event through repeated presentation of the former before the latter.

comorbidity The situation in which an individual suffers from more than one diagnosable disorder at the same time.

competence The knowledge and skills that an individual possesses.

conditioning The learning of a relationship between two events or between an action and a subsequent event.

conduct disorder A disorder in which individuals commit repeated antisocial acts; there may or may not be laws against these actions.

conservation of number The ability to understand that the number of objects in a set does not change just because the objects are rearranged.

conservation of substance The ability to understand that the amount of a substance does not change just because its shape or configuration changes.

correlation A statistical measure of the relation or association between two characteristics.

critical period A time in life during which particular experiences are crucial for normal development.

cross-modal perception Using information gained in one sense modality to predict information from another modality; for example, knowing what something will feel like from looking at it.

crossing-over A process in which chromosomes exchange blocks of corresponding genetic material during meiosis.

cross-sectional investigation Research in which children of different ages are compared at one point in time.

crystallized abilities The knowledge a person has accumulated.

decentration The ability to focus attention on several attributes of an object or event simultaneously and to understand the relationships among dimensions or attributes.

dendrites The extensions of a neuron that receive messages. See also **axons.**

dependent variable In an experiment, the variable on which the investigator collects objective measurements.

development Orderly and relatively enduring changes over time in physical and neurological structures, thought processes, and behavior.

developmental psychopathology An approach to emotional problems that considers how they arise in the course of normal development.

dilation Opening of the cervix in preparation for birth.

dishabituation The process of recovering interest in a repeated stimulus when the stimulus is perceived to have changed. Compare **habituation.**

dismissing A term used to refer to adults who deny the importance of attachment.

disorganized attachment A pattern of insecure attachment in which infants show mixtures of avoidant and resistant attachment, sometimes mixed with signs of fear or confusion.

dizygotic (fraternal) twins Twins who develop from different ova that are fertilized at the same time.

DNA Deoxyribonucleic acid, molecular chains that encode genetic information.

dominant A term used to describe a gene whose effects will be expressed whenever it is present. Compare **recessive.**

ecology An environmental context considered as including not only an immediate situation but also the larger context of cultural groups, including neighborhoods, work settings, and ethnic and national identities.

ectoderm The outer layer of a developing embryo, which will give rise to the skin, hair, nails, parts of the teeth, the sensory cells, and the nervous system.

effacement Thinning and drawing up of the cervix in preparation for birth.

ego control The ability of the ego to control other impulses, resulting in self-control.

ego resilience An index of flexibility or adaptability.

embryonic stage The period of prenatal development that extends from the second to the eighth week and is characterized by cell differentiation as the major organs begin to develop.

emotion Changes in the brain and behavioral disposition that follow encounters with pain, deprivation, novelty, danger, sensory gratification, challenge, play, social interaction, or separation from a familiar person.

empathy The ability to appreciate the perceptions and feelings of others.

endoderm The inner layer of a developing embryo, which will give rise to the lining of the gastrointestinal tract, the respiratory system, and other internal organs.

equilibrium The state in which an individual is in cognitive balance, when it is possible to explain experience in terms of existing concepts.

equilibration The process of modifying concepts in a search for better explanation of experience and the achievement of equilibrium.

ethology An approach to the study of social development that emphasizes the presence of fixed action patterns in newborn animals and attempts to identify similar patterns in human infants.

experiment A method of study in which an investigator controls or manipulates a factor or variable in order to determine if it has a causal impact on another factor or variable.

externalizing problems Emotional disturbances that involve hyperactivity, poor behavior control, aggression, and delinquency.

extinction The process of eliminating undesired behavior by not reinforcing it.

fetal alcohol syndrome A condition linked to alcohol consumption by a pregnant woman, resulting in retarded physical and mental growth and physical malformations in her offspring.

fetal stage The period of prenatal development that extends from 8 weeks until delivery and is characterized mainly by growth.

field experiment An experiment in which people are observed in naturally occurring situations, often over relatively long periods of time.

first stage of labor The time during which the cervix becomes completely effaced and dilated.

fixed action patterns A term used in ethology to refer to stereotyped behavioral sequences occurring in response to environmental stimuli.

gender constancy A child's understanding that gender does not change.

gender identity Acceptance of one's basic biological nature as female or male.

genes Particles within the chromosomes that contain the instructions that cause an individual to develop a specific inherited trait.

genetic counseling A type of counseling in which an individual or a couple learn more about what their risks may be for having children with genetic problems, and what steps can be taken to identify or reduce the risks.

genotype An individual's genetic makeup.

germinal stage The period of prenatal development that extends from fertilization until implantation of the zygote in the wall of the uterus.

growth spurt The period of pubertal development in which growth in height and weight occurs at an accelerated rate.

habituation The process of losing interest in a repeated stimulus. Compare **dishabituation.**

high-amplitude sucking A technique in which infants' rate and intensity of sucking is measured in a situation in which sucking causes a stimulus to be heard or seen.

horizontal décalage The fact that apparently similar cognitive abilities, such as conservation of number and of mass, can appear at very different ages in the same child.

identification A process in which a person incorporates the characteristics and global behavior patterns of another person.

identity achievement The end product of successful identity exploration.

identity diffusion A prolonged period in which an individual is unable to develop a strong, clear sense of identity.

identity foreclosure A premature fixing of an individual's self-image that interferes with the development of other potentials and possibilities for self-definition.

imitation Behavior that selectively duplicates the behavior shown by a model; the act of copying specific behaviors of another person.

independent variable In an experiment, a variable that the investigator systematically changes.

induction Discipline through reasoning with children and pointing out to them the painful consequences of misbehavior.

inductive techniques Nonpunitive strategies for modifying a child's behavior by explaining the rationale for desired actions.

infantile autism A profound disturbance in normal development, beginning very early in life.

inhibition A term referring to a dimension of temperament. Inhibited children are shy, timid, and somewhat fearful; uninhibited children are outgoing and more adventurous.

insecure attachment A term referring to infants who do not show secure attachment. There are three identified types of insecure attachment: avoidant, resistant, and disorganized.

instrumental (operant) conditioning The establishment of a relationship between a response and a subsequent event (called a reinforcement) that increases the probability that the response will recur.

intelligence The capacity to learn and use the skills that are required for successful adaptation to the demands of one's culture and environment.

internalizing problems Emotional disturbances that involve excessive internal distress, anxiety, depression, social withdrawal, and self-deprecation.

juvenile delinquent A young person, generally under 18 years of age, who engages in behavior that is punishable by law.

learned helplessness The belief that one's successes do not reflect ability and that one's failures cannot be reversed by effort.

libido Freud's concept of biological energy.

long-term memory Knowledge that is potentially available for a long time, perhaps forever.

longitudinal investigation Research in which the same children are observed or tested at regular intervals over an extended period.

mainstreaming The integration of children with physical and mental handicaps into regular classrooms.

major developmental deviation Profound disturbances in the normal development of cognitive and social functioning; also called psychoses.

maturation A universal sequence of biological events occurring in the body and the brain that permits a psychological function to appear, provided that the infant is healthy and lives in an environment containing people and objects.

mean length of utterance The average number of morphemes in a single utterance; a measure of language development.

meiosis A process in which germ cells (from which sperm and ova are derived) divide to form cells whose nuclei contain half the number of chromosomes present in the parent cell.

menarche The onset of menstruation.

mesoderm The middle layer of a developing embryo, which will give rise to the inner layer of skin, the muscles, the skeleton, and the circulatory and excretory systems.

metamemory Knowledge about memory.

minimum sufficiency principle The idea that the best way to change behavior is through reinforcers that are just sufficient to produce the desired behavior.

mitosis A process in which a fertilized ovum divides and subdivides.

monozygotic (identical) twins Twins who develop from the same fertilized ovum.

moral realism According to Piaget, the moral reasoning of young children, emphasizing the role of authority.

moral relativism According to Piaget, the moral reasoning of older children and adolescents, emphasizing the idea that rules and laws are socially created.

moratorium A period of questioning and exploration during which an adolescent forms an identity.

Moro reflex A reflex in which a sudden stimulus, such as a loud noise, leads an infant's arms and legs to be spread and then come together.

morpheme The smallest unit of meaning in a language.

multifactorial A term used to describe traits that depend on more than one genetic or environmental factor.

myelination The buildup of fatty sheaths around the paths of nerve cells, increasing the speed and efficiency with which impulses are conducted.

negative feedback Information that would indicate to a child that some hypothesis formed about language is incorrect.

neuron A nerve cell.

nonshared environment The aspects of environment that may differ among children growing up in the same family, such as who their friends are.

object permanence The belief that objects continue to exist even when they are out of sight.

operation A manipulation of ideas that can be performed in reverse.

oral stage Freud's idea of infancy, emphasizing the energy bound up for the infant in activities involving the mouth.

overextension Use of a word by a child to apply to more instances than are considered correct in adult speech.

overregularization The use of a grammatical rule by a child in a situation in which the rule is not generally applied in adult speech.

perceived self-efficacy One's judgments of how well one can execute courses of action required to deal with prospective situations.

performance The demonstration of knowledge and skills in observable problem-solving situations.

permissive A term describing parents who are warm but who do not demand mature behavior.

phenotype How an individual actually appears or behaves.

phonemes The basic sounds that are combined to make words.

placenta The section of the uterine wall to which the embryo is attached.

placental barrier The ability of the placenta to prevent large substances and structures, such as blood cells, from flowing from fetus to mother, and vice versa.

play A voluntary, spontaneous activity that does not seem to have a real-world goal.

polygenetic inheritance A situation in which expression of a trait requires the presence of a number of genes.

pragmatics The relationship between the meaning of an utterance and the context in which the utterance is made.

preoccupied A term used to refer to adults who talk about early attachment experiences in a confused and often contradictory way.

primary reinforcer A term used in learning theory to refer to an event that satisfies biological needs. Compare **secondary reinforcer.**

prospective study Longitudinal study of the development of emotional problems in which a group of individuals, either unselected or identified as being at risk, are observed, starting before the point where problems are expected to appear.

puberty The initial phase of adolescence, in which the reproductive system matures and secondary sex characteristics develop.

reaction range The idea that individual development will occur within a certain specified array of possibilities.

recall memory Ability to retrieve an encoded stimulus when no relevant stimulus is present.

recessive A term used to describe a gene whose effects will be masked whenever a dominant gene for the same trait is present. Compare **dominant.**

recognition memory Ability to know that a physically present stimulus has been encountered before.

reinforcer A reward for desired behavior.

rejecting-neglecting A term describing parents who are cold and do not demand mature behavior.

releasers In ethology, the environmental stimuli that lead to the production of fixed action patterns.

resistant attachment A pattern of insecure attachment in which infants seek proximity to caretakers when distressed and yet resist comfort.

reversibility The state of affairs in which a sequence can be logically undone and returned to the starting point.

rooting reflex A reflex in which stroking a cheek causes a baby to turn its head in that direction and to try to suck.

schizophrenia A profound disturbance in thought and social interaction, usually beginning in adolescence or young adulthood after a period of apparently normal development.

second stage of labor The time during delivery in which the baby is pushed out.

secondary reinforcer A term used in learning theory to refer to an event associated with the satisfaction of biological needs that acquires reinforcement value as a result. Compare **primary reinforcer.**

secure attachment A pattern of infant attachment in which infants are able to use their caretakers as secure bases for exploration and to derive comfort from them when distressed.

self-awareness Awareness of one's own qualities, states, and abilities.

self-concept A set of ideas about oneself that is descriptive but not judgmental.

self-esteem One's evaluations of one's own qualities.

semantics The meanings of words.

sensorimotor period In Piaget's theory, the first stage of intellectual development, occupying the first 18 to 24 months of life and emphasizing infant exploration of the world through sensory and motoric endowment.

sensorimotor scheme A representation of a class of motor actions that attains a goal.

sensory memory Memory that vanishes within 1 second if it is not stored in short- or long-term memory.

seriation The ability to arrange objects according to some quantified dimension such as weight or size.

sex chromosomes Chromosomes that differ in males and females; normal females have two X chromosomes, while normal males have an X and a Y chromosome.

sex-role identity A feeling that one's interests, personality, and behavior conform to one's own definitions of femininity or masculinity.

sex typing The processes by which biological gender and its cultural associations are incorporated into the child's self-perceptions and behavior.

shared environment The aspects of environment that children growing up in the same family would have in common, such as parental educational level.

short-term memory Memory that holds information for a maximum of 30 seconds unless an effort is made to retain it.

social-comparison standards Standards based on comparisons with other people's performance.

social referencing A phenomenon in which a child looks to an adult for guidance as to what emotion or reaction to have in a situation.

socialization The process through which children acquire the behavior, skills, motives, values, beliefs, and standards that are characteristic, appropriate, and desirable in their culture.

sociometric techniques Methods in which researchers ask children about who they like and don't like in their peer group.

stages of development Steps in the growth of children which are qualitatively distinct from previous functioning and which occur in a fixed order.

stage of trust Erikson's conception of infancy, which emphasizes that interaction with caretakers is central and can lead infants to develop a sense of basic trust (or mistrust) about the world.

status offense An act that is illegal only when committed by young people.

stereopsis Depth information gained from the fact that the right and left eyes produce slightly different images of the same thing.

Strange Situation An experimental situation used to assess attachment in infants, in which a fixed sequence of caretaker departures and returns and stranger arrivals and departures occurs.

symbolic ability The ability to create and accept an arbitrary relationship between an object and an idea.

synapses Short-range connections among neurons.

syntax The grammatical rules that specify how words should be combined in sentences.

taxonomic assumption The hypothesis that, given a word, a child initially assumes that the appropriate grouping for that word is objects that are similar in kind rather than merely associated.

temperament An inborn bias favoring certain moods and reaction styles.

teratogen A substance or circumstance causing birth defects.

third stage of labor The time during delivery in which the placenta is pushed out.

transition The time during labor between the first and second stages.

transitivity The ability to reason about the ordering of objects and to draw inferences. For instance, if A > B and B > C, then A > C.

trophoblast The outer layer of a developing fertilized ovum.

twin study Behavior genetics studies that involve studying the development of twins.

umbilical cord The structure leading from the belly region of the embryo and fetus to the placenta.

unbound morpheme A morpheme which can stand alone as a word.

underextensions Use of a word by a child only in a more restricted set of circumstances than adults would use the word.

ultrasound scans A procedure in which the structure of the developing fetus can be visualized in order to determine if abnormalities exist.

viability The age at which a fetus is able to survive if born.

visual cliff An apparatus for studying an infant's reactions to depth. A runway rests on a sheet of glass, with a checked pattern directly under the glass on one side but a few feet below the glass on the other side.

visual preference A technique in which infants are shown two stimuli and looking time is measured to determine if one is looked at longer.

whole-object assumption The hypothesis that young children initially assume that an unfamiliar word labels a whole object, not a part of it, an attribute, or a particular circumstance.

zone of proximal development The range of activities just beyond a child's current abilities, which the child can deal with if offered support and structuring by an adult or a more skilled person.

zygote A fertilized ovum.

REFERENCES

Abel, E. L. (1980). Fetal alcohol syndrome: Behavioral teratology. *Psychological Bulletin, 87,* 29–50.

Achenbach, T. M. (1990). Conceptualization of developmental psychopathology. In M. Lewis, & S. M. Miller (Eds.), *Handbook of Developmental Psychopathology* (pp. 3–14). New York: Plenum.

Achenbach, T. M., & Edelbrock, C. S. (1981). Behavioral problems and competencies reported by parents of normal and disturbed children aged four through sixteen. *Monographs of the Society for Research in Child Development, 46*(Serial No. 188).

Achenbach, T. M., & Howell, C. T. (1993). Are American children's problems getting worse? A 13-year comparison. *Journal of the American Academy of Child and Adolescent Psychiatry, 32,* 1145–1154.

Adams, E. H., Gfroerer, J. C., & Rouse, B. A. (1989). Epidemiology of substance abuse including alcohol and cigarette smoking. *Annals of the New York Academy of Sciences* (Vol. 562). New York: New York Academy of Sciences.

Adams, G. R., Abraham, K. G., & Markstrom, C. A. (1987). The relations among identity development, self-consciousness, and self-focusing during middle and late adolescence. *Developmental Psychology, 23,* 292–297.

Ainsworth, M. D. S., Blehar, M. C., Waters, E., & Wall, S. (1978). *Patterns of attachment: A psychological study of the Strange Situation.* Hillsdale, NJ: Erlbaum.

Alan Guttmacher Institute. (1994). *Sex and America's teenagers.* New York: Alan Guttmacher Institute.

Alejandro-Wright, M. N. (1985). The child's conception of racial classification: A socio-cognitive developmental model. In M. B. Spencer, G. K. Brookins, & W. R. Allen (Eds.), *Beginnings: The social and affective development of black children* (pp. 185–200). Hillsdale, NJ: Erlbaum.

Allen, M. C. (1984). Developmental outcome and followup of the small-for-gestational-age infant. *Seminars in Perinatology, 8,* 123–133.

Allison, P. D., & Furstenberg, F. F. (1989). How marital dissolution affects children: Variations by age and sex. *Developmental Psychology, 25,* 540–549.

Almy, M., Monighan, P., Scales, B., & Van Hoorn, J. (1983). Recent research on playing: The perspective of the teacher. In L. Katz (Ed.), *Current topics in early childhood education* (Vol. 5). Norwood, NJ: Ablex.

American Psychiatric Association. (1987). *DSM III R: Diagnostic and statistical manual of mental disorders* (3rd rev. ed.). Washington, DC: American Psychiatric Association.

Ames, L. B. (1937). The sequential patterning of prone progression in the human infant. *Genetic Psychology Monographs, 19,* 409–460.

Anastasi, A. (1958). *Differential psychology* (3rd ed.). New York: Macmillan.

Anastasi, A. (1987). *Psychological testing* (6th ed.). New York: Macmillan.

Anderson, B. E. (1989). Effects of public day-care: A longitudinal study. *Child Development, 60,* 857–866.

Anderson, D. R., & Collins, P. A. (1988). *The impact on children's education: Television's influence on cognitive development.* Washington, DC: U.S. Department of Education.

Anderson, D. R., & Field, D. E. (1983). Children's attention to television: Implications for production. In M. Meyer (Ed.), *Children and the formal features of television.* Munich: K. G. Saur.

Anderson, D. R., & Lorch, E. P. (1983). Looking at television: Action or reaction? In J. Bryant & D. R. Anderson (Eds.), *Children's understanding of television: Research on attention and comprehension.* New York: Academic Press.

Anderson, D. R., Lorch, E. P., Field, D. E., & Sanders, J. (1981). The effects of TV program comprehensibility on preschool children's visual attention to television. *Child Development, 52,* 151–157.

Anderson, J. C., Williams, S., McGee, R., & Silva, P. A. (1987). DSM-3 disorders in preadolescent children. *Archives of General Psychiatry, 44,* 69–76.

Angier, N. (1994, May 17). The male of the species: Why is he needed? *The New York Times,* C12.

Anglin, J. M. (1977). *Word, object, and conceptual development.* New York: Norton.

Anglin, J. M. (1993). Vocabulary development: A morphological analysis. *Monographs of the Society for Research in Child Development, 58*(10, Serial No. 238).

Apgar, V., & Beck, J. (1974). *Is my baby all right?* New York: Pocket Books.

Applegate, J. L., Burke, J. A., Burleson, B. R., Delia, J. G., & Klein, S. L. (1983). Reflection-enhancing parental communication. In I. E. Sigel (Ed.), *Parental belief systems: The psychological consequences for children.* Hillsdale, NJ: Erlbaum.

Arend, R., Gove, F. L., & Sroufe, L. A. (1979). Continuity of individual adaptation from infancy to kindergarten: A predictive study of ego resiliency and curiosity in preschoolers. *Child Development, 50,* 950–959.

Aronfreed, J. (1968). *Conduct and conscience: The socialization of internalized control over behavior.* New York: Academic Press.

Aronson, E., Blaney, N., Stephan, C., Sikes, J., & Snapp, M. (1978). *The jigsaw classroom.* Beverly Hills, CA: Sage.

Asendorpf, J. (1991). Development in inhibited children's coping with unfamiliarity. *Child Development, 62,* 1460–1474.

Asher, S. R., & Hymel, S. (1981). Children's social competence in peer relations: Sociometric and behavioral assessment. In J. D. Wine & M. D. Smys (Eds.), *Social competence.* New York: Guilford.

Asher, S. R., & Renshaw, P. D. (1981). Children without friends: Social knowledge and social skill training. In S. R. Asher & J. M. Gottman (Eds.), *The development of children's friendships.* New York: Cambridge University Press.

Asher, S. R., Singleton, L. C., & Taylor, A. R. (1982). *Acceptance versus friendship: A longitudinal study of racial integration.* Paper presented at the annual meeting of the American Educational Research Association, New York.

Aviezer, O., van IJzendoorn, M. H., Sagi, A., Schuengel, C. (1994). "Children of the dream" revisited: 70 years of collective early child care in Israeli Kibbutzim. *Psychological Bulletin, 116,* 99–116.

Azar, B. (1994, May). Pregnancy prevention needs two-pronged effort. *APA Monitor,* pp. 24–25.

Azmitia, M., & Montgomery, R. (1993). Friendship, transactive dialogues, and the development of scientific reasoning. *Social Development, 2,* 202–221.

Babad, E., Bernieri, F., & Rosenthal, R. (1991). Students as judges of teachers' verbal and nonverbal behavior. *American Educational Research Journal, 28,* 211–234.

Babson, S. G., Pernoll, M. L., & Benda, G. I. (1980). *Diagnosis and management of the fetus and neonate at risk.* St. Louis: Mosby.

Bachman, J. G., Johnston, L. D., O'Malley, P. M., & Humphrey, R. H. (1988). Differentiating the effects of perceived risks, disapproval, and general life style factors. *Journal of Health and Social Behavior, 29,* 92–112.

Bachman, J. G., & Schulenberg, J. (1993). How part-time work intensity relates to drug use, problem behavior, time use and satisfaction among high school seniors: Are these consequences or merely correlates? *Developmental Psychology, 29,* 220–235.

Bacon, M. K., & Ashmore, R. D. (1986). A consideration of the cognitive activities of parents and their role in the socialization process. In R. D. Ashmore & D. M. Brodzinsky (Eds.), *Thinking about the family: Views of parents and children.* Hillsdale, NJ: Erlbaum.

Baillargeon, R., Spelke, E. S., & Wasserman, S. (1985). Object permanence in five-month-old infants. *Cognition, 20,* 191–208.

Bakermans-Kranenburg, M. J., & van IJzendoorn, M. H. (1993). A psychometric study of the Adult Attachment Interview: Reliability and discriminant validity. *Developmental Psychology, 29,* 870–879.

Ball, S., & Bogatz, G. A. (1970). *The first year of "Sesame Street": An evaluation.* Princeton, NJ: Educational Testing Service.

Bandura, A. (1981). Self-referent thought: A developmental analysis of self-efficacy. In J. H. Flavell & L. Ross (Eds.), *Social cognitive development: Frontiers and possible futures.* New York: Cambridge University Press.

Bandura, A. (1982). Self-efficacy mechanism in human agency. *American Psychologist, 37,* 122–147.

Bandura, A., & Mischel, W. (1965). Modification of self-imposed delay of reward through exposure to live and symbolic models. *Journal of Personality and Social Psychology, 2,* 698–705.

Bank, S., & Kahn, M. D. (1975). Sisterhood-brotherhood is powerful: Sibling subsystems and family therapy. *Family Process, 14,* 311–337.

Banks, M. S., Aslin, R. N., &. Letson, R. D. (1975). Sensitive period for the development of human binocular vision. *Science, 190,* 675–677.

Barkley, R. A. (1990). Attention deficit disorders: History, definition, and diagnosis. In M. Lewis & S. M. Miller (Eds.), *Handbook of developmental psychopathology* (pp. 65–75). New York: Plenum.

Barnes, G. M. (1984). Adolescent alcohol abuse and other problem behaviors: Their relationships and common parental influences. *Journal of Adolescence and Youth, 13,* 329–348.

Barnes, H., & Olson, D. H. (1985). Parent-child communication and the circumplex model. *Child Development, 56,* 438–447.

Barr, H. M., Streissguth, A. P., Darby, B. L., & Sampson, P. D. (1990). Prenatal exposure to alcohol, caffeine, tobacco, and aspirin: Effects on fine and gross motor performance in 4-year-old children. *Developmental Psychology, 26,* 339–348.

Bar-Tal, D. (1978). Attributional analysis of achievement-related behavior. *Review of Educational Research, 48,* 259–271.

Bar-Tal, D., & Raviv, A. (1979). Consistency of helping-behavior measures. *Child Development, 50,* 1235–1238.

Baruch, G. K., & Barnett, R. C. (1986). Fathers' participation in family work and children's sex-role attitudes. *Child Development, 57,* 1210–1223.

Bates, E., Bretherton, I., & Snyder, L. (1988). *From first words to grammar.* New York: Cambridge University Press.

Bates, E., Dale, P. S., & Thal, D. (1994). Individual differences and their implications for theories of language development. In P. Fletcher & B. MacWhinney (Eds.), *Handbook of child language.* Oxford: Basil Blackwell.

Bates, J. E. (1982). *Temperament as part of social relationships: Implications of perceived infant difficultness.* Paper presented at the International Conference on Infant Studies, Austin, Texas.

Bates, J. E., Marvinney, D., Kelly, T., Dodge, K. A., Bennett, D. S., & Pettit, G. S. (1994). Child-care history and kindergarten adjustment. *Developmental Psychology, 30,* 690–700.

Battaglia, F. C., & Simmons, A. (1978). The low-birthweight infant. In F. Falkner & J. Tanner (Eds.), *Human growth (Vol. 2): Postnatal growth* (pp. 507–556). New York: Plenum.

Bauer, P. J., & Fivush, R. (1992). Constructing event representations: Building on a foundation of variation and enabling relations. *Cognitive Development, 7,* 381–401.

Bauer, P. J., & Mandler, J. M. (1989). Taxonomies and triads: Conceptual organization in one- to two-year-olds. *Cognitive Psychology, 21,* 156–184.

Baumrind, D. (1967). Child care practices anteceding three patterns of preschool behavior. *Genetic Psychology Monographs, 75,* 43–88.

Baumrind, D. (1968). Authoritarian vs. authoritative control. *Adolescence, 3,* 255–272.

Baumrind, D. (1971). Harmonious parents and their preschool children. *Developmental Psychology, 4,* 99–102.

Baumrind, D. (1973). The development of instrumental competence through socialization. In A. D. Pick (Ed.), *Minnesota Symposia on Child Psychology* (Vol. 7). Minneapolis: University of Minnesota Press.

Baumrind, D. (1975). Early socialization and adolescent competence. In S. E. Dragastin & G. H. Elder, Jr. (Eds.), *Adolescence in the life cycle: Psychological change and social context.* New York: Wiley.

Baumrind, D. (1978). A dialectical materialist's perspective on knowing social reality. In W. Damon (Ed.), *New directions for child development: Moral development.* San Francisco: Jossey-Bass.

Baumrind, D. (1988). *Familial antecedents of social competence in middle childhood.* Unpublished manuscript.

Baumrind, D. (1991). Effective parenting during the early adolescent transition. In P. A. Cowan & E. M. Hetherington (Eds.), *Family transitions: Advanced in family research transition* (pp. 111–163). Hillsdale, NJ: LEA.

Baumrind, D. (1993). The average expectable environment is not good enough: A response to Scarr. *Child Development, 64,* 1299–1317.

Baydar, N., & Brooks-Gunn, J. (1991). Effects of maternal employment and child-care arrangements on preschoolers' cognitive and behavioral outcomes: Evidence from the children of the National Longitudinal Survey of Youth. *Developmental Psychology, 27,* 932–945.

Beach, F. A. (1977). Hormonal control of sex-related behavior. In F. A. Beach (Ed.), *Homosexuality in four perspectives* (pp. 247–267). Baltimore, MD: Johns Hopkins University Press.

Behrman, R. E., & Vaughn, V. C. (1987). *Nelson textbook of pediatrics.* Philadelphia: Saunders.

Bell, A. P., & Weinberg, M. S. (1978). *Homosexualities: A study of diversity among men and women.* New York: Simon & Schuster.

Bell, A. P., Weinberg, M. S., & Hammersmith, S. K. (1981). *Sexual preference: Its development in men and women.* Bloomington: Indiana University Press.

Bell, R. (1980). *Changing bodies, changing lives: A book for teens on sex and relationships.* New York: Random House.

Belsky, J. (1984). The determinants of parenting: A process model. *Child Development, 55,* 83–96.

Belsky, J. (1993). Etiology of child maltreatment: A developmental-ecological analysis. *Psychological Bulletin, 114,* 413–434.

Belsky, J., & Isabella, R. (1988). Maternal, infant, and social-contextual determinants of attachment security. In J. Belsky & T. Nezworski (Eds.), *Clinical implications of attachment* (pp. 41–94). Hillsdale, NJ: LEA

Belsky, J., Lerner, R. M., & Spanier, G. B. (1984). *The child in the family.* Reading, MA: Addison-Wesley.

Belsky, J., & Most, R. K. (1981). From exploration to play: A cross-sectional study of infant free play behavior. *Developmental Psychology, 17,* 630–639.

Belsky, J., & Rovine, M. (1987). Temperament and attachment security in the Strange Situation. *Child Development, 50,* 787–792.

Belsky, J., & Vondra, J. (1989). Lessons from child abuse: The determinants of parenting. In D. Cicchetti & V. Carlson (Eds.), *Child maltreatment: Theory and research on the causes and consequences of child abuse and neglect* (pp. 153–202). New York: Cambridge University Press.

Bem, S. L. (1974). The measurement of psychological androgyny. *Journal of Consulting and Clinical Psychology, 42,* 155–162.

Bem, S. L. (1981). Gender schema theory: A cognitive account of sex typing. *Psychological Review, 88,* 352–364.

Bem, S. L. (1983). Gender schema theory and its implications for child development: Raising gender-aschematic children in a gender-schematic society. *Signs, 8,* 598–616.

Bem, S. L. (1989). Genital knowledge and gender constancy in preschool children. *Child Development, 60,* 649–662.

Bender, B. G., Linden, M. G., & Robinson, A. (1987). Environmental and developmental risk in children with sex chromosome abnormalities. *Journal of the American Academy of Child and Adolescent Psychiatry, 26,* 499–503.

Benedict, H. (1979). Early lexical development: Comprehension and production. *Journal of Child Language, 6,* 183–200.

Berko, J. B. (1958). The child's learning of English morphology. *Word, 14,* 150–177.

Berndt, T. J. (1979). Developmental changes in conformity to peers and parents. *Developmental Psychology, 15,* 606–616.

Berndt, T. J. (1982). The features and effects of friendship in early adolescence. *Child Development, 53,* 1447–1460.

Berndt, T. J. (1993). Remarks at the plenary session of the Peer Relations. Society for Research in Child Development, Pre-Conference, New Orleans, LA.

Berndt, T. J., & Bulleit, T. N. (1985). Effects of sibling relationships on preschoolers' behavior at home and at school. *Developmental Psychology, 21,* 761–767.

Berndt, T. J., Hawkins, J. A., & Hoyle, S. G. (1986). Changes in friendship during a school year: Effects on children's and adolescents' impressions of friendship and sharing with friends. *Child Development, 57,* 1284–1297.

Berry, G., & Mitchell-Kernan, C. (Eds.). (1982). *Television and the socialization of the minority child.* New York: Academic Press.

Bersoff, D. N. (1981). Testing and the law. *American Psychologist, 36,* 1047–1056.

Bertenthal, B. I., Proffitt, D. R., & Cutting, J. E. (1984). Infant sensitivity to figural coherence and biomechanical motions. *Journal of Experimental Child Psychology, 37,* 213–230.

Bertenthal, B. I., Proffitt, D. R., Kramer, S. J., & Spetner, M. B. (1987). Infants' coding of kinetic displays varying relative coherence. *Developmental Psychology, 23,* 171–178.

Bertoncini, J., Bijelac-Babic, B., Jusczyk, P. W., Kennedy, L. J., & Mehler, J. (1988). An investigation of young infants' perceptual representations of speech sounds. *Journal of Experimental Psychology: General, 117,* 21–33.

Bhatia, V. P., Katiyar, G. P., & Apaswol, K. N. (1979). Effect of intrauterine nutritional deprivation on neuromotor behaviour of the newborn. *Acta Paediatrica Scandinavica, 68,* 561–573.

Bickerton, D. (1981). *Roots of language.* Ann Arbor, MI: Karoma.

Bierman, K. L., Smoot, D. L., & Aumiller, K. (1993). Characteristics of aggressive-rejected, aggressive (non-rejected), and rejected (nonaggressive) boys. *Child Development, 64,* 139–151.

Bigler, R. S. (1994). *The role of classification skill in moderating environmental influences on children's gender stereotyping.* Unpublished manuscript.

Bigler, R. S., & Liben, L. S. (1992). Cognitive mechanisms in children's gender stereotyping: Theoretical and educational implications of a cognitive-based intervention. *Child Development, 63,* 1351–1363.

Bijou, S., & Baer, D. (1961). *Child Development I: A systematic and empirical theory.* Englewood Cliffs, NJ: Prentice-Hall.

Bird, H. R., Canino, G., Rubio-Stipec, M., Gould, M. S., Ribera, S., Sesman, M., Woodbury, M., Huertas-Goldman, S., Pegan, A., Sanchez-Lacay, A., & Moscoso, M. (1988). Estimates of the prevalence of childhood maladjustment in a community survey in Puerto Rico. *Archives of General Psychiatry, 45,* 1120–1126.

Bishop, J. E. (1986, November 18). Genetic omen: Chromosome impairment linked to mental impairment raises abortion issue. *The Wall Street Journal,* pp. 1, 31.

Blasi, A. (1980). Bridging moral cognition and moral action: A critical review of the literature. *Psychological Bulletin, 88,* 1–45.

Blasi, A. (1983). Moral cognition and moral action: A theoretical perspective. *Developmental Review, 3,* 178–210.

Blass, E. M., Ganchrow, J. R., & Steiner, J. E. (1984). Classical conditioning in newborn humans 2–48 hours of age. *Infant Behavior and Development, 7,* 223–235.

Block, J., & Block, J. H. (1973). *Ego development and the provenance of thought: A longitudinal study of ego and cognitive development in young children.* (Progress report for National Institute of Mental Health).

Block, J., Gjerde, P. F., & Block, J. H. (1991). Personality antecedents of depressive tendencies in 18-year-olds: A prospective study. *Journal of Personality and Social Psychology, 60,* 726–738.

Block, J. H. (1984). *Sex role identity and ego development.* San Francisco: Jossey-Bass.

Block, J. H., & Block, J. (1980). The role of ego-control and ego-resiliency in the organization of behavior. In W. A. Collins (Ed.), *Minnesota Symposia on Child Psychology: Vol. 13. Development of cognition, affect, and social relations.* Hillsdale, NJ: Erlbaum.

Block, J. H., Block, J., & Gjerde, P. F. (1986). The personality of children prior to divorce: A prospective study. *Child Development, 57,* 827–840.

Bloom, L. (1973). *One word at a time: The use of single word utterances before syntax.* The Hague: Mouton.

Bloom, L., Hood, L., & Lightbown, P. (1974). Imitation in language development: If, when, and why. *Cognitive Psychology, 6,* 380–420.

Bloom, L., Lahey, L., Hood, L., Lifter, K., & Fiess, K. (1980). Complex sentences: Acquisition of syntactic connectives and the semantic relations they encode. *Journal of Child Language, 7,* 235–261.

Bloom, L., Rocissano, L., & Hood, L. (1976). Adult-child discourse: Developmental interaction between linguistic processing and linguistic knowledge. *Cognitive Psychology, 8,* 521–552.

Blum, E. J., Fields, B. C., Scharfman, H., & Silber, D. M. (1994). Development of symbolic play of deaf children aged 1 to 3. In A. Slade & D. P. Wolfe (Eds.), *Children at play: Clinical and developmental perspective.* New York: Oxford University Press.

Blyth, D. A., Simmons, R. G., Bulcroft, R., Felt, D., VanCleave, E. F., & Bush, D. M. (1981). The effects of physical development on self-image and satisfaction with body-image for early adolescent males. In R. G. Simmons (Ed.), *Research in Community and Mental Health, 2,* 43–73.

Bogatz, G. A., & Ball, S. (1971). *The second year of "Sesame Street": A continuing evaluation* (Vols. 1 & 2). Princeton, NJ: Educational Testing Service.

Bomba, P. C., & Siqueland, E. R. (1983). The nature and structure of infant form categories. *Journal of Experimental Child Psychology, 35,* 294–328.

Bornstein, M. H., Kessen, W., & Weiskopf, S. (1976). The categories of hue in infancy. *Science, 191,* 201–202.

Bouchard, T. J., Jr., & McGue, M. G. (1981). Familial studies of intelligence: A review. *Science, 212,* 1055–1059.

Bourne, E. (1978a). The state of research on ego identity: A review and appraisal (Part 1). *Journal of Youth and Adolescence, 7,* 223–251.

Bourne, E. (1978b). The state of research on ego identity: A review and appraisal (Part 2). *Journal of Youth and Adolescence, 7,* 371–392.

Bowerman, M. (1976). Semantic factors in the acquisition of rules for word use and sentence construction. In D. M. Morehead & A. E. Morehead (Eds.), *Normal and deficient child language* (pp. 99–179). Baltimore, MD: University Park Press.

Bowlby, J. (1969). *Attachment and loss.* New York: Basic Books.

Boxer, A. M., & Petersen, A. C. (1986). Pubertal change in a family context. In G. K. Leigh & G. W. Peterson (Eds.), *Adolescents in families* (pp. 73–103). Cincinnati: South-Western.

Boykin, A. W. (1983). Academic performance of Afro-American children. In I. Spence (Ed.), *Achievement and achievement motive.* San Francisco: W. Freeman.

Brackbill, Y. (1979). Obstetrical medication and infant behavior. In J. Osofsky (Ed.), *Handbook of infant development* (pp. 76–125). New York: Wiley.

Bradley, R. H., & Caldwell, B. (1984). The relation of infants' home environments to achievement test performance in first grade: A follow-up study. *Child Development, 55,* 803–809.

Bradley, R. H., Caldwell, B. M., & Elardo, R. (1977). Home environment, social class, and mental test performance. *Journal of Educational Psychology, 69,* 697–701.

Braine, M. D. S. (1963). The ontogeny of English phrase structures: The first phase. *Language, 39,* 1–13.

Brainerd, C. J. (Ed.). (1983). *Recent advances in cognitive-developmental theory: Progress in cognitive development research.* New York: Springer-Verlag.

Brandt, I. (1978). Growth dynamics of low-birth-weight infants with emphasis on the perinatal period. In F. Falkner & J. Tanner (Eds.), *Human growth: Vol. 2. Postnatal growth.* New York: Plenum.

Braungart, J. M., Fulker, D. W., & Plomin, R. (1992). Genetic mediation of the home environment during infancy: A sibling adoption study of the HOME. *Developmental Psychology, 28,* 1048–1055.

Brazelton, T. B., Nugent, J. K., & Lester, B. M. (1987). Neonatal behavioral assessment scale. In J. D. Osofsky (Ed.), *Handbook of infant development* (pp. 780–817). New York: Wiley.

Bregman, J. D., Dykens, E., Watson, M., Ort, S. I., & Leckman, J. F. (1987). Fragile-X syndrome: Variability of phenotypic expression. *Journal of the Academy of Child and Adolescent Psychiatry, 26,* 463–471.

Breitmayer, B. J., & Ramey, C. T. (1986). Biological nonoptionality and quality of postnatal environment as codeterminants of intellectual development. *Child Development, 57,* 1151–1165.

Brent, R. L., & Harris, M. I. (1976). Fogarty *International Center series on preventive medicine: Vol. 3. Prevention of embryonic, fetal, and perinatal disease.* Bethesda, MD: National Institute of Health.

Brittain, C. V. (1966). Age and sex of siblings and conformity toward parents versus peers in adolescence. *Child Development, 37,* 709–714.

Brittain, C. V. (1969). A comparison of rural and urban adolescents with respect to parent vs. peer compliance. *Adolescence, 13,* 59–68.

Broman, S. H., Nichols, P. L., & Kennedy, W. A. (1975). *Preschool IQ: Prenatal and early developmental correlates.* Hillsdale, NJ: Erlbaum.

Bronfenbrenner, U. (1979). *The ecology of human development: Experiments by nature and design.* Cambridge, MA: Harvard University Press.

Brook, J. S., Lukoff, J. F., & Whiteman, M. (1980). Initiation into adolescent marijuana use. *Journal of Genetic Psychology, 137,* 133–142.

Brooks-Gunn, J., & Chase-Lansdale, P. L. (1995). Adolescent parenthood. In M. H. Bornstein (Ed.), *Handbook of parenting* (Vol. 3). Hillsdale, NJ: LEA.

Brooks-Gunn, J., Klebanov, P. K., Liaw, F., & Spiker, D. (1993). Enhancing the development of low-birth-weight, premature infants: Changes in cognition and behavior over the first three years. *Child Development, 64,* 736–753.

Brooks-Gunn, J., & Ruble, D. N. (1982). The development of menstrual-related beliefs and behaviors during early adolescence. *Child Development, 53,* 1567–1577.

Brooks-Gunn, J., & Ruble, D. N. (1983). The experience of menarche from a developmental perspective. In J. Brooks-Gunn & A. C. Petersen (Eds.), *Girls at puberty: Biological and psychosocial perspectives* (pp. 155–177). New York: Plenum.

Brooks-Gunn, J., & Ruble, D. N. (1983). The experience of menarche from a developmental perspective. In J. Brooks-Gunn & A. C. Petersen (Eds.), *Girls at puberty: Biological, psychological, and social perspectives.* New York: Plenum.

Brown, A. L. (1975). The development of memory: Knowing, knowing about knowing, and knowing how to know. In H. W. Reese (Ed.), *Advances in child development and behavior* (Vol. 10). New York: Academic Press.

Brown, A. L., Bransford, J. D., Ferrara, R. A., & Campione, J. C. (1983). Learning, remembering, and understanding. In P. H. Mussen (Series Ed.), J. H.

Flavell, & E. M. Markman (Eds.), *Handbook of child psychology: Vol. 3. Cognitive development* (4th ed., pp. 77–166). New York: Wiley.

Brown, B. B. (1990). Peer groups and peer cultures. In S. S. Feldman & G. R. Elliott (Eds.), *At the threshold: The developing adolescent* (pp. 171–196). Cambridge, MA: Harvard University Press.

Brown, B. B., Mounts, N., Lamborn, S. D., & Steinberg, L. (1993). Parenting practices and peer group affiliation in adolescence. *Child Development, 64,* 467–482.

Brown, G. W., Harris, T. O., & Bifulco, A. (1986). Long-term effects early loss of parent. In M. Rutter, C. E. Izard, & P. B. Read (Eds.), *Depression in young people: Developmental and clinical perspectives* (pp. 251–296). New York: Guilford.

Brown, R. (1966). *Words and things.* Glencoe, IL: Free Press.

Brown, R. (1973). *A first language: The early stages.* Cambridge, MA: Harvard University Press.

Brown, R., & Hanlon, C. (1970). Deviational complexity and order of acquisition in child speech. In V. R. Hayes (Ed.), *Cognition and the development of language* (pp. 11–54). New York: Wiley.

Brown, W. T., Jenkins, E. C., Friedman, E., Brooks, J., Wisniewski, K., Raguthu, S., & French J. (1982). Autism is associated with the fragile X syndrome. *Journal of Autism and Developmental Disorders, 12,* 303–307.

Bruch, H. (1973). *Eating disorders.* New York: Basic Books.

Bruner, J. S. (1975). From communication to language: A psychological perspective. *Cognition, 3,* 255–287.

Bruner, J. S., Jolly, A., & Sylva, K. (1976). *Play: Its role in development and evolution.* London: Kenwood.

Brunswick, A. F., & Boyle, J. M. (1979). Patterns of drug involvement: Developmental and secular influences on age of initiation. *Youth and Society, 11,* 139–162.

Bryant, B., & Crockenberg, S. (1980). Correlates and discussion of prosocial behavior: A study of female siblings with their mothers. *Child Development, 51,* 529–544.

Buchanan, C. M., Eccles, J. S., & Becker, J. B. (1992). Are adolescents the victims of raging hormones? Evidence for activational effects of hormones on moods and behavior at adolescence. *Psychological Bulletin, 111,* 62–107.

Buchanan, C. M., Maccoby, E. E., & Dornbusch, S. M. (1991). Caught between parents: Adolescents' experience in divorced homes. *Child Development, 62,* 1008–1029.

Bukowski, W. M., Gauze, C., Hoza, B., & Newcomb, A. E. (1993). Difference and consistency between same-sex and other-sex peer relationships during early adolescence. *Developmental Psychology, 29,* 255–263.

Bukowski, W. M., & Hoza, B. (1989). Popularity and friendship: Issues in theory, measurement, and outcome. In T. Berndt & G. Ladd (Eds.), *Peer relationships in child development* (pp. 15–45). New York: Wiley.

Bullinger, A., & Chatillon, J. F. (1983). Recent theory and research of the Genevan school. In P. H. Mussen (Series Ed.), J. H. Flavell, & E. M. Markman (Eds.), *Handbook of child psychology: Vol. 3. Cognitive development* (4th ed., pp. 231–262). New York: Wiley.

Burchard, J. D., & Harig, P. T. (1976). Behavior modification and juvenile delinquency. In H. Leiternberg (Ed.), *Handbook of behavior modification and behavior therapy* (pp. 405–452). Englewood Cliffs, NJ: Prentice-Hall.

Burgess, R. L., & Conger, R. D. (1978). Family interaction in abusive, neglectful, and normal families. *Child Development, 49,* 1163–1173.

Burns, B., & Lipsitt, L. P. (1991). Behavioral factors in crib death: Toward an understanding of the sudden infant death syndrome. *Journal of Applied Developmental Psychology, 12,* 159–184.

Burt, M. R. (1986). Estimating the public costs of teenage childbearing. *Family Planning Perspectives, 18,* 221–226.

Buss, A. H., & Plomin, R. (1984). *Temperament: Early developing personality traits.* Hillsdale, NJ: Erlbaum.

Byrne, D., & Griffitt, W. B. (1966). A developmental investigation of the law of attraction. *Journal of Personality and Social Psychology, 4,* 699–702.

Cadoret, R. J., Cain, C. A., & Crowe, R. R. (1983). Evidence for gene-environment interaction in the development of adolescent antisocial behavior. *Behavior Genetics, 13,* 301–310.

Cairns, R. B. (1983). An evolutionary and developmental perspective on aggressive patterns. In C. Zahn-Waxler, E. M. Cummings, & R. Iannotti (Eds.), *Altruism and aggression.* New York: Cambridge University Press.

Calkins, S. D., & Fox, N. A. (1992). The relations among infant temperament, security of attachment, and behavioral inhibition at twenty-four months. *Child Development, 63,* 1456–1472.

Calvert, S. L., & Huston, A. C. (1987). Television and children's gender schemata. In L. Liben & M. Signorella (Eds.), *New directions for child development: Vol 38. Children's gender schemata: Origins and implications* (pp. 75–88). San Francisco: Jossey-Bass.

Campbell, S. (1979). Mother-infant interaction as a function of maternal ratings of temperament. *Child Psychiatry and Human Development, 10,* 67–76.

Campbell, S. B. (1983). Developmental perspectives on child psychopathology. In T. H. Ollendick & M. Hersen (Eds.), *Handbook of child psychopathology* (pp. 13–40). New York: Plenum.

Campbell, S. B. (1990). The socialization and social development of hyperactive children. In M. Lewis & S. M. Miller (Eds.), *Handbook of developmental psychopathology* (pp. 77–91). New York: Plenum.

Campbell, S. B., & Werry, J. S. (1986). Attention deficit disorder (hyperactivity). In H. C. Quay & J. S. Werry (Eds.), *Psychopathological disorders of childhood* (3rd ed., pp. 111–115). New York: Wiley.

Campos, J., Hiatt, S., Ramsay, D., Henderson, C., & Svejda, M. (1978). The emergence of fear on the visual cliff. In M. Lewis & L. Rosenblum (Eds.), *The origins of affect.* New York: Plenum.

Campos, J. J., Langer, A., & Krawitz, A. (1970). Cardiac responses on the visual cliff in prelocomotor human infants. *Science, 170,* 196–198.

Campos, R., Raffaelli, M., Ude, W., Greco, M., Ruff, A., Rolf, J., Autunes, C. M., Hasley, N., Greco, D., & Street Youth Study Group. (1994). Social networks and daily activities of street youth in Belo Horizonte, Brazil. *Child Development, 65,* 319–330.

Cancro, R. (1983). History and overview of schizophrenia. In H. I. Kaplan & B. J. Sadock (Eds.), *Comprehensive textbook of psychiatry* (Vol. 1, pp. 631–642). Baltimore: Williams and Wilkins.

Cann, A., & Newbern, S. R. (1984). Sex stereotype effects on children's picture recognition. *Child Development, 55,* 1085–1090.

Cantwell, D. P. (1990). Depression across the early life span. In M. Lewis & S. M. Miller (Eds.), *Handbook of developmental psychopathology* (pp. 293–309). New York: Plenum.

Caparulo, B., & Zigler, E. (1983). The effects of mainstreaming on success expectancy and imitation in mildly retarded children. *Peabody Journal of Education, 60,* 85–98.

Carey, S. & Bartlett, E. (1978). Acquiring a single new word. *Papers and Reports on Child Language Development* (No. 15, pp. 17–29). Department of Linguistics, Stanford University.

Carlson, V., Cicchetti, D., Barnett, D., & Braunwold, K. (1989). Disorganized/disoriented attachment relationships in maltreated infants. *Developmental Psychology, 25,* 525–531.

Carmichael, L. (1970). The onset and early development of behavior. In P. Mussen (Ed.), *Carmichael's manual of child psychology* (3rd ed., Vol. 1). New York: Wiley.

Carpenter, C. J. (1983). Activity structure and play: Implications for socialization. In M. B. Liss (Ed.), *Social and cognitive skills: Sex roles and children's play.* New York: Academic Press.

Carter, S. L., Osofsky, J. D., & Hann, D. M. (1991). Speaking for the baby: A therapeutic intervention with adolescent mothers and their infants. *Infant Mental Health Journal, 12,* 291–301.

Casey, R. J., & Berman, J. S. (1985). The outcome of psychotherapy with children. *Psychological Bulletin, 98,* 388–400.

Caspi, A., Elder, G. H., & Bem, D. J. (1988). Moving away from the world: Life-course patterns of shy children. *Developmental Psychology, 24*, 824–831.

Caspi, A., Lynam, D., Moffitt, T. E., & Silva, P. A. (1993). Unraveling girls' delinquency: Biological, dispositional, and contextual contributions to adolescent misbehavior. *Developmental Psychology, 29*, 19–30.

Caspi, A., & Moffitt, T. E. (1991). Individual differences are accentuated during periods of social changes: The sample case of girls at puberty. *Journal of Personality and Social Psychology, 61*, 157–168.

Cassese, J. (1993). The invisible bridge: Child abuse and the risk of HIV infection in childhood. *SIECUS Reports, 21*, 1–7.

Cassidy, J., Parke, R. D., Butkovsky, L., & Braungart, J. M. (1992). Family-peer connections: The roles of emotional expressiveness within the family and children's understanding of emotions. *Child Development, 63*, 603–618.

Catz, C., & Yaffe, S. J. (1978). Developmental pharmacology. In F. Falkner & J. M. Tanner (Eds.), *Human growth: Vol. 1. Principles and prenatal growth.* New York: Plenum.

Caudill, W., & Frost, L. A. (1973). A comparison of maternal care and infant behavior in Japanese-American, American, and Japanese families. In W. Lebra (Ed.), *Youth, socialization, and mental health.* Honolulu: University Press of Hawaii.

Cavior, N., & Dokecki, P. R. (1973). Physical attractiveness, perceived attitude similarity, and academic achievement as contributors to interpersonal attraction among adolescents. *Developmental Psychology, 9*, 44–54.

CDF Reports. (1988, January). Vol. 9, No. 8, p. 1.

Ceci, S. J. & Bruck, M. (1993). Suggestibility of the child eyewitness: A historical review and synthesis. *Psychological Bulletin, 113*, 403–439.

Centers for Disease Control and Prevention. (1991). Current tobacco, alcohol, marijuana and cocaine use among high school students—United States, 1990. *Morbidity and Mortality Weekly Reports, 40*, 659–663.

Challman, R. C. (1932). Factors influencing friendships among preschool children. *Child Development, 3*, 146–158.

Chandler, M. J. (1973). Egocentrism and antisocial behavior: The assessment and training of social perspective-taking skills. *Developmental Psychology, 9*, 326–332.

Chi, M. R. H. (1978). Knowledge structures and memory development. In R. Siegler (Ed.), *Children's thinking: What develops?* Hillsdale, NJ: Erlbaum.

Children's Defense Fund. (1987). *A children's defense budget.* Washington, DC: Children's Defense Fund.

Childs, C. P., & Greenfield, P. M. (1982). Informal modes of learning and teaching: The case of Zinacanteco weaving. In N. Warren (Ed.), *Advances in cross-cultural psychology* (Vol. 2). London: Academic Press.

Chilman, C. S. (1983). *Adolescent sexuality in a changing American society: Social and psychological perspectives* (2nd ed.). Washington, DC: U.S. Government Printing Office.

Chomsky, N. (1957). *Syntactic structures.* The Hague: Mouton.

Chomsky, N. (1959). Review. Skinner: Verbal behavior. *Language, 35*, 26–58.

Chudley, A. (1984). Behavior phenotype. In A. Chudley & G. Sutherland (Eds.), Conference Report: International Workshop on the Fragile X Syndrome and X-Linked Mental Retardation. *American Journal of Medical Genetics, 17*, 45–53.

Cicchetti, D., Beeghly, M., & Weiss-Perry, B. (1994). Symbolic development in children with Down syndrome and in children with autism: An organizational, developmental psychopathology perspective. In A. Slade & D. P. Wolfe (Eds.), *Children at play: Clinical and developmental perspective.* New York: Oxford University Press.

Clark, E. V. (1973). What's in a word? On the child's acquisition of semantics in his first language. In T. E. Moore (Ed.), *Cognitive development and the acquisition of language.* New York: Academic Press.

Clarke-Stewart, K. A., & Hevey, C. M. (1981). Longitudinal relations in repeated observations of mother-child interactions from 1 to 2 and one-half years. *Developmental Psychology, 17*, 127–145.

Clasen, D. R., & Brown, B. B. (1985). The multidimensionality of peer pressure in adolescence. *Journal of Youth and Adolescence, 14*, 451–468.

Clary, E. G., & Miller, J. (1986). Socialization and situational influences on sustained altruism. *Child Development, 57*, 1358–1369.

Clausen, J. A. (1975). The social meaning of differential physical and sexual maturation. In S. E. Dragastin & G. H. Elder, Jr. (Eds.), *Adolescence in the life cycle: Psychological change and social context.* New York: Wiley.

Cleary, T. A., Humphreys, L. G., Kendrick, S. A., & Wesman, A. (1975). Educational use of tests with disadvantaged students. *American Psychologist, 36*, 15–41.

Clingenpeel, W. G., & Segal, S. (1986). Stepparent-stepchild relationships and the psychological adjustment of children in stepmother and stepfather families. *Child Development, 57*, 474–484.

Cohen, D. J., Dibble, E., & Grawe, J. M. (1977). Fathers' and mothers' perceptions of children's personality. *Archives of General Psychiatry, 34*, 480–487.

Cohler, B. J., & Boxer, A. M. (1984). Settling into the world: Person, time and context in the middle-adult years. In D. Offer & M. Sabshin (Eds.), *Normality and the life cycle.* New York: Basic Books.

Cohn, J. F., & Tronick, E. Z. (1987). Mother-infant face-to-face interaction. *Developmental Psychology, 23,* 68–77.

Coie, J. D., & Cillessen, A. H. N. (1993). Peer rejection: Origins and effects on children's development. *Current Directions in Psychological Science, 2,* 89–92.

Coie, J. D., & Dodge, K. A. (1983). Continuities and changes in children's social status: A five-year longitudinal study. *Merrill-Palmer Quarterly, 29,* 261–282.

Colby, A., Kohlberg, L., Gibbs, J., & Lieberman, M. (1983). A longitudinal study of moral judgment. *Monographs of the Society for Research in Child Development, 48* (Serial No. 200).

Cole, N. S. (1981). Bias in testing. *American Psychologist, 36,* 1067–1077.

Cole, P. M., Barrett, K. C., & Zahn-Waxler, C. (1992). Emotion displays in two-year-olds during mishaps. *Child Development, 63,* 314–324.

Coleman, J. C. (1980). *The nature of adolescence.* London: Methuen.

Coles, R., & Stokes, G. (1985). *Sex and the American teenager.* New York: Harper & Row.

Coll, C. G., Kagan, J., & Reznick, S. (1984). Behavioral inhibition in young children. *Child Development, 55,* 1005–1019.

Colletta, N. D. (1983). At risk for depression: A study of young mothers. *Journal of Genetic Psychology, 142,* 301–310.

Colletta, N. D. (1981). *The influence of support systems on the maternal behavior of young mothers.* Paper presented at the meeting of the Society for Research in Child Development, Boston.

Collins, W. A. (1982). Cognitive processing in television viewing. In D. Pearl, L. Bouthilet, & J. Lazar (Eds.), *Television and behavior: Ten years of scientific progress and implications for the eighties.* Washington, DC: U.S. Government Printing Office.

Colombo, J. (1986). Recent studies in early auditory development. *Annals of Child Development, 3,* 53–96.

Compas, B. E., Ey, S., & Grant, K. E. (1993) Taxonomy, assessment, and diagnosis of depression during adolescence. *Psychological Bulletin, 114,* 323–344.

Conel, J. L. (1939–1963). *The postnatal development of the human cerebral cortex.* Cambridge, MA: Harvard University Press.

Conger, J. J. (1979). *Adolescence: Generation under pressure.* New York: Harper & Row.

Conger, J. J. (1987). Behavioral medicine and health psychology in a changing world. *Child Abuse and Neglect, 11,* 443–453.

Conger, J. J. (1988). Hostages to fortune: Youth, values, and the public interest. *American Psychologist, 43,* 291–300.

Conger, J. J., & Petersen, A. C. (1984). *Adolescence and youth: Psychological development in a changing world* (3rd ed.). New York: Harper & Row.

Conger, R., Burgess, R., & Barrett, C. (1979). Child abuse related to life change and perceptions of illness: Some preliminary findings. *Family Coordinator, 28,* 73–78.

Conger, R. D., Conger, K. J., Elder, G. H., Lorenz, F. O., Simons, R. L., Whitbeck, L. B. (1992). A family process model of economic hardship and adjustment of early adolescent boys. *Child Development, 63,* 526–541.

Conway, E., & Brackbill, Y. (1970). Delivery medication and infant outcomes: An empirical study. In W. A. Bowes, Y. Brackbill, E. Conway, & A. Steinschneider (Eds.), *Monographs of the Society for Research in Child Development, 35*(4), 24–34.

Cook, T. D., Appleton, H., Conner, R. F., Shaffer, A., Tabkin, C., & Weber, S. J. (1975). *"Sesame Street" revisited.* New York: Russell Sage.

Cooper, C. R. (1977, March). *Collaboration in children: Dyadic interaction skills in problem solving.* Paper presented at the biennial meeting of the Society for Research in Child Development, New Orleans.

Cooper, C. R., & Ayers-Lopez, S. (1985). Family and peer systems in early adolescence: New models of the role of relationships in development. *Journal of Early Adolescence, 5,* 9–21.

Cooper, C. R., & Grotevant, H. D. (1987). Gender issues in the interface of family experience and adolescents' friendship and dating identity. *Journal of Youth and Adolescence, 16,* 247–264.

Cooper, C. R., Grotevant, H. D., & Condon, S. M. (1983). Individuality and connectedness in the family as a context for adolescent identity formation and role-taking skill. In H. D. Grotevant & C. R. Cooper (Eds.), *Adolescent development in the family* (pp. 43–60). San Francisco: Jossey-Bass.

Cooper, H. M. (1979). Pygmalion grows up: A model for teacher expectation communication and performance influence. *Review of Educational Research, 49,* 389–410.

Coplan, R. J., Rubin, K. H., Fox N. A., Calkins, S. D., & Stewart, S. L. (1994). Being alone, playing alone, and acting alone: Distinguishing among reticence and passive and active solitude in young children. *Child Development, 65,* 120–137.

Corah, N. L., Anthony, E. J., Painter, P., Stern, J. A., & Thurston, D. (1965). Effects of perinatal anoxia after 7 years. *Psychological Monographs, 79,* 1–34.

Cordua, G. D., McGraw, K. O., & Drabman, R. S. (1979). Doctor or nurse: Children's perceptions of sex-typed occupations. *Child Development, 50,* 590–593.

Corsaro, W. (1981). Friendship in the nursery school: Social organization in a peer environment. In S. R. Asher & J. M. Gottman (Eds.), *The development of children's friendships.* Cambridge: Cambridge University Press.

Costanzo, P. R. (1970). Conformity development as a function of self-blame. *Journal of Personality and Social Psychology, 14,* 366–374.

Costanzo, P. R., Coie, J. D., Grumet, J. F., & Farnill, D. (1973). A reexamination of the effects of intent and consequence on children's moral judgments. *Child Development, 44,* 154–161.

Costanzo, P. R., & Shaw, M. E. (1966). Conformity as a function of age level. *Child Development, 37,* 967–975.

Costello, E. J. (1990). Child psychiatric epidemiology: Implications for clinical research and practice. In B. B. Lahey & H. E. Kazdin (Eds.), *Advances in Clinical Child Psychology* (Vol. 13, pp. 53–90). New York: Plenum.

Costello, E. J., Costello, A. J., Edelbrock, C., Burns, B. J., Dulcan, M. K., Brent, D., & Janiszewski, S. (1988). Psychiatric disorders in pediatric primary care: Prevalence and risk factors. *Archives of General Psychiatry, 45,* 1107–1116.

Costello, E. J., & Janiszewski, S. (1990). Who gets treated? Factors associated with referrals in children with psychiatric disorders. *Acta Psychologica Scandinavica, 81,* 523–529.

Cousins, J. H., Siegel, A. W., & Maxwell, S. E. (1983). Way finding and cognitive mapping in large-scale environments: A test of a developmental model. *Journal of Experimental Child Psychology, 35,* 1–20.

Covington, M., & Omelich, C. (1979). Effort: The double-edged sword in school achievement. *Journal of Educational Psychology, 71,* 169-182.

Cox, M. J., Owen, M. T., Lewis, J. M., & Henderson, V. K. (1989). Marriage, adult adjustment, and early parenting. *Child Development, 60,* 1015–1024.

Crandall, V. C. (1969). Sex differences in expectancy of intellectual and academic reinforcement. In C. P. Smith (Ed.), *Achievement-related motives in children* (pp. 11–45). New York: Russell Sage.

Crandall, V. C. (1978, August). *Expecting sex differences and sex differences in expectancies.* Paper presented at the annual meeting of the American Psychological Association, Toronto.

Cravioto, J., & DeLicardie, E. R. (1978). Nutrition, mental development, and learning. In F. Falkner & J. M. Tanner (Eds.), *Human growth: Vol. 3. Neurobiology and nutrition.* New York: Plenum.

Crockenberg, S. (1981). Infant irritability, mother responsiveness, and social support influences on the security of infant-mother attachment. *Child Development, 52,* 857–865.

Crockenberg, S. (1987). Predictors and correlates of anger toward and punitive control of toddlers by adolescent mothers. *Child Development, 58,* 964–975.

Crockett, L. J., & Petersen, A. C. (1987). Pubertal status and psychosocial development: Findings from the early adolescent study. In R. M. Lerner & T. T. Foch (Eds.), *Biological and psychosocial interactions in early adolescence: A life-span perspective* (pp. 173–188). Hillsdale, NJ: Erlbaum.

Cross, W. E., Jr. (1985). Black identity: Rediscovering the distinction between personal identity and reference group orientation. In M. B. Spencer, G. K. Brookins, & W. R. Allen (Eds.), *Beginnings: The social and affective development of black children* (pp. 155–172). Hillsdale, NJ: Erlbaum.

Culbertson, J. L., Krous, H. F., & Bendell, R. D. (1988). *Sudden infant death syndrome: Medical aspects and psychological management.* Baltimore: Johns Hopkins University Press.

Curran, D. K. (1987). *Adolescent suicidal behavior.* Washington, DC: Hemisphere Publishing Corporation.

Curran, J. W., Jaffee, H. W., Hardy, A. M., Morgan, W. M., Selik, R. M., Dondero, T. J., & Fareir, A. S. (1988). Epidemiology of HIV infection and AIDS in the United States. *Science, 239,* 610–616.

Curtiss, S. (1977). *Genie: A psycholinguistic study of a modern-day "wild-child."* New York: Academic Press.

Damon, W. (1977). *The social world of the child.* San Francisco: Jossey-Bass.

Damon, W. (1983). *Social and personality development.* New York: Norton.

Damon, W., & Hart, D. (1982). The development of self-understanding from infancy through adolescence. *Child Development, 53,* 841–864.

Darville, D., & Cheyne, J. A. (1981). *Sequential analysis of response to aggression: Age and sex effects.* Paper presented at the biennial meeting of the Society for Research in Child Development, Boston.

Darwin, C. (1963). *The origin of species.* New York: Washington Square Press. (Original work published 1859.)

David, A., DeVault, S., & Talmadge, M. (1961). Anxiety, pregnancy, and childbirth abnormalities. *Journal of Consulting Psychology, 25,* 74–77.

Davis, J. M., & Rovee-Collier, C. K. (1983). Alleviated forgetting of a learned contingency in eight-week-old infants. *Developmental Psychology, 19,* 353–365.

Davitz, J. R. (1955). Social perception and sociometric choice in children. *Journal of Abnormal and Social Psychology, 50,* 173–176.

Dawson, D. A. (1986). The effects of sex education on adolescent behavior. *Family Planning Perspectives, 18,* 162–170.

de la Cruz, F. (1985). Fragile X syndrome. *American Journal of Medical Genetics, 23,* 573–580.

de Villiers, P. A., & de Villiers, J. G. (1974). On this, that, and the other: Nonegocentrism in very young children. *Journal of Experimental Child Psychology, 18,* 438–447.

DeCasper, A. J., & Fifer, W. P. (1980). Of human bonding: Newborns prefer their mothers' voices. *Science, 208,* 1174–1176.

DeCasper, A. J., & Spence, M. J. (1986). Prenatal maternal speech influences newborns' perception of speech sounds. *Infant Behavior and Development, 9,* 133–150.

DeLoache, J. S. (1989). Young children's understanding of the correspondence between a scale model and a larger space. *Cognitive Development, 4,* 121–139.

Demetriou, A., Efklides, A., Papadaki, M., Papantoniou, G., & Economou, A. (1993). Structure and development of causal-experimental thought: From early adolescence to youth. *Developmental Psychology, 29,* 480–497.

Denno, D. J. (1989). *Biology, crime and violence: New evidence.* Cambridge: Cambridge University Press.

Diamond, A. (1985). Development of the ability to use recall to guide action, as indicated by infants' performance, on A $\bar{\text{B}}$. *Child Development, 56,* 868–883.

Diamond, A. (1990). Frontal lobe involvement in cognitive changes during the first year of life. In K. R. Gibson & A. C. Petersen (Eds.), *Brain maturation and cognitive development: Comparative and cross-cultural perspectives.* New York: Aldine de Gruyter.

Diamond, A. (1994). Phenylalanine levels of 6–10 mg/dl may not be as benign as once thought. *Acta Paediatrica, 83,* 89–91.

Diener, C. I., & Dweck, C. S. (1978). An analysis of learned helplessness: Continuous changes in performance, strategy, and achievement cognitions following failure. *Journal of Personality and Social Psychology, 36,* 451–462.

Diener, C. I., & Dweck, C. S. (1980). An analysis of learned helplessness: II. The processing of success. *Journal of Personality and Social Psychology, 39,* 940–952.

Dietz, W. H., Jr., & Gortmaker, S. L. (1985). Do we fatten our children at the television set? Obesity and television viewing in children and adolescents. *Pediatrics, 75,* 807–812.

DiLalla, L F., & Gottesman, I. I. (1991). Biological and genetic contributions to violence: Widom's untold tale. *Psychological Bulletin, 109,* 125–129.

Dishion, T. J., Patterson, G. R., Stoolmiller, M., & Skinner, M. L. (1991). Family, school, and behavioral antecedents to early adolescent involvement with antisocial peers. *Developmental Psychology, 27,* 172–180.

Dix, T. H., & Grusec, J. E. (1985). Parent attribution processes in the socialization of children. In I. E. Sigel (Ed.), *Parental belief systems: The psychological consequences for children.* Hillsdale, NJ: Erlbaum.

Dixon, J. (1994, April 12). Poverty rise reported for the very young. *Philadelphia Inquirer,* A9.

Dlugokinski, E. L., & Firestone, I. J. (1974). Other centeredness and susceptibility to charitable appeals: Effects of perceived discipline. *Developmental Psychology, 10,* 21–28.

Dobbing, J. (1976). The later development of central nervous system and its vulnerability. In A. V. Davison & J. Dobbing (Eds.), *Scientific foundations of pediatrics.* London: Heinemann.

Dodge, K. A. (1980). Social cognition and children's aggressive behavior. *Child Development, 51,* 162–170.

Dodge, K. A. (1985). A social information processing model of social competence in children. In M. Perlmutter (Ed.), *Minnesota Symposia on Child Psychology: Vol 18. Cognitive perspectives on children's social and behavioral development.* Hillsdale, NJ: Erlbaum.

Dodge, K. A. (1986). Social information-processing variables in the development of aggression and altruism in children. In C. Zahn-Waxler, E. M. Cummings, & R. Iannotti (Eds.), *Altruism and aggression: Biological and social original.* New York: Cambridge University Press.

Dodge, K. A. (1990). Developmental psychopathology in children of depressed mothers. *Developmental Psychology, 26,* 3–6.

Donaldson, M. (1978). *Children's minds.* New York: Norton.

Donovan, J. M. (1975). Ego identity status and interpersonal style. *Journal of Youth and Adolescence, 4,* 37–56.

Dore, J. (1979). Conversation and preschool language development. In P. Fletcher & M. Gorman (Eds.), *Language acquisition.* Cambridge: Cambridge University Press.

Dornbusch, S. M., Ritter, P. L., Leiderman, P. H., Roberts, D. F., & Fraleigh, M. J. (1987). The relation of parenting style to adolescent school performance. *Child Development, 58,* 1244–1257.

Dorr, A. (1986). *Television and children: A special medium for a special audience.* Beverly Hills, CA: Sage.

Douvan, E., & Adelson, J. (1966). *The adolescent experience.* New York: Wiley.

Drucker, M., & Block, G. (1992). *Rescuers: Portraits in moral courage in the Holocaust.* New York: Holmes & Meier.

Dudgeon, J. A. (1976). Infective causes of human malformations. *British Medical Bulletin, 32,* 77–83.

Duncan, G. J. (1984). *Years of poverty, years of plenty.* Ann Arbor, MI: Survey Research Center, University of Michigan.

Duncan, G. J., Brooks-Gunn, J., & Klebanov, P. K. (1994). Economic deprivation and early childhood development. *Child Development, 65,* 296–318.

Duncan, O. D., Featherman, D. L., & Duncan, B. (1972). *Socioeconomic background and achievement.* New York: Seminar Press.

Dunlap, D. W. (1994, October 18). Gay survey raises a new question. *The New York Times,* p. B8.

Dunn, J. (1983). Sibling relationships in early childhood. *Child Development, 54,* 787–811.

Dunn, J. (1988). *The beginning of social understanding.* Cambridge, MA: Harvard University Press.

Dunn, J., Brown, J., Slomkowski, C., Tesla, C., & Youngblade, L. (1991). Young children's understanding of other people's feelings and beliefs: Individual differences and their antecedents. *Child Development, 62,* 1352–1366.

Dunn, J., & Kendrick, C. (1979). Interaction between young siblings in the context of family relationships. In M. Lewis & L. A. Rosenblum (Eds.), *The child and its family.* New York: Plenum.

Dunn, J., & Kendrick, C. (1981). Social behavior of young siblings in the family context: Differences between same-sex and different-sex dyads. *Child Development, 52,* 1265–1273.

Dunn, J., & Kendrick, C. (1982). Siblings and their mothers: Developing relationships within the family. In M. C. Lamb & B. Sutton-Smith (Eds.), *Sibling relationships.* Hillsdale, NJ: Erlbaum.

Dunn, J., & Plomin, R. (1990). *Separate lives: Why siblings are so different.* New York: Basic Books.

Dunn, J., Slomkowski, C., & Beardsall, L. (1994). Sibling relationships from the preschool period through middle childhood and early adolescence. *Developmental Psychology, 30,* 315–324.

Dunphy, D. C. (1963). The social structure of urban adolescent peer groups. *Sociometry, 26,* 230–246.

Duyme, M. (1988). School success and social class: An adoption study. *Developmental Psychology, 24,* 203–209.

Dweck, C. S. (1975). The role of expectations and attributions in the alleviation of learned helplessness. *Journal of Personality and Social Psychology, 31,* 674-685.

Dweck, C. S., & Elliot, E. S. (1983). Achievement motivation. In P. H. Mussen (Series Ed.) & E. M. Hetherington (Eds.), *Handbook of child psychology: Vol. 4. Socialization, personality, and social development* (pp. 643–692). New York: Wiley.

Dweck, C. S., & Leggett, E. L. (1988). A social-cognitive approach to motivation and personality. *Psychological Review, 95,* 256–273.

Eccles, J. (1983). Expectancies, values, and academic behaviors. In J. T. Spence (Ed.), *Achievement and achievement motives* (pp. 75–146). San Francisco: Freeman.

Eccles, J., Adler, R., & Meece, J. L. (1984). Sex differences in achievement: A test of alternate theories. *Journal of Personality and Social Psychology, 46,* 26–43.

Eccles, J., & Harold, R. (1993). Parent-school involvement during the early adolescent years. *Teachers College Record, 94,* 568–587.

Edelman, M. W. (1987). *Families in peril: An agenda for social change.* Cambridge, MA: Harvard University Press.

Eder, R. A. (1990). Uncovering young children's psychological selves: Individual and developmental differences. *Child Development, 61,* 849–863.

Edwards, C. P. (1981). The development of moral reasoning in cross-cultural perspective. In R. H. Munroe, R. L. Munroe, & B. B. Whiting (Eds.), *Handbook of cross-cultural human development.* New York: Garland Press.

Egeland, B., Breitenbucher, M., & Rosenberg, D. (1980). Prospective study of the significance of life stress in the etiology of child abuse. *Journal of Consulting and Clinical Psychology, 48,* 195–205.

Egeland, B., Jacobvitz, D., & Papatola, K. (1987). Intergenerational continuity of abuse. In R. Gelles & J. Lancaster (Eds.), *Child abuse and neglect: Biosocial dimensions* (pp. 255–276). Chicago: Aldine.

Egeland, B., & Sroufe, L. A. (1981). Attachment and early maltreatment. *Child Development, 52,* 44–52.

Egeland, J. A., Gerhard, D. S., Pauls, D. L., Sussex, J. N., Kidd, K. K., Allen, C. R., Hostetter, A. N., & Housman, D. E. (1987). Bipolar affective disorders linked to DNA markers on chromosome 11. *Nature, 325,* 783–787.

Eggers, C. (1978). Course and prognosis of childhood schizophrenia. *Journal of Autism and Childhood Schizophrenia, 8,* 21–36.

Eifermann, R. R. (1970). Cooperativeness and egalitarianism in kibbutz children's games. *Human Relations, 23,* 579–587.

Eimas, P. D. (1975). Developmental studies of speech perception. In L. B. Cohen & P. Salapatek (Eds.), *Infant perception.* New York: Academic Press.

Eisenberg, N., & Miller, P. (1987). Empathy, sympathy, and altruism: Empirical and conceptual links. In N. Eisenberg & J. Strayer (Eds.), *Empathy and its development.* New York: Cambridge University Press.

Ekman, P., & Friesen, W. (1982). Felt, false, and miserable smiles. *Journal of Nonverbal Behavior, 6,* 238–252.

Elder, G. H., Jr. (1980). *Family structure and socialization.* New York: Arno Press.

Elder, G. H., Jr., & Caspi, A. (1988). Economic stress in lives: Developmental perspectives. *Journal of Social Issues, 44,* 25–46.

Elkind, D. (1968). Cognitive development in adolescence. In J. F. Adams (Ed.), *Understanding adolescence.* Boston: Allyn & Bacon.

Elliot, A. J. (1981). *Child language.* Cambridge: Cambridge University Press.

Elliott, D. S., Hinzinga, D., & Ageton, S. S. (1985). *Explaining delinquency and drug use.* Beverly Hills, CA: Sage.

Emde, R., Harmon, R., & Good, W. (1986). Depressive feelings in children: A transactional model of research. In M. Rutter, C. E. Izard, & P. B. Read (Eds.), *Depression in young people: Developmental and clinical perspectives* (pp. 135–162). New York: Guilford.

Emler, N. P., & Rushton, J. P. (1974). Cognitive-developmental factors in children's generosity. *British Journal of Social and Clinical Psychology, 13,* 277–281.

Emmerich, W. (1966). Continuity and stability in early social development: II. Teacher's ratings. *Child Development, 37,* 17–27.

Enright, R. D., Lapsley, D., & Shukla, D. (1979). Adolescent egocentrism in early and late adolescence. *Adolescence, 14,* 687–695.

Erikson, E. H. (1956). The problem of ego identity. *Journal of the American Psychoanalytic Association, 4,* 56–121.

Erikson, E. H. (1963). *Childhood and society* (2nd ed.). New York: Norton.

Erikson, E. H. (1968). *Identity: Youth and crisis.* New York: Norton.

Ernhart, C. B., Graham, F. K., & Thurston, D. (1960). Relationship of neonatal apnea to development at three years. *Archives of Neurology, 2,* 504–510.

Eron, L. D. (1987). The development of aggressive behavior from the perspective of a developing behaviorism. *American Psychologist, 42,* 435–442.

Eron, L. D., & Huesmann, L. R. (1984). The control of aggressive behavior by changes in attitudes, values and the conditions of learning. In R. J. Blanchard & C. Blanchard (Eds.), *Advances in the study of aggression* (Vol. 2). New York: Academic Press.

Eron, L. D., Walder, L. O., & Lefkowitz, M. M. (1971). *Learning of aggression in children.* Boston: Little, Brown.

Ervin-Tripp, S. M. (1972). Children's sociolinguistic competence and dialect diversity. In I. J. Gordon (Ed.), *Early childhood education* (The 71st Yearbook of the National Society for the Study of Education. Part II, pp. 123–160). Chicago: University of Chicago Press.

Ervin-Tripp, S. (1977). Wait for me, rollerskate. In C. Mitchell-Kernan & S. Ervin-Tripp (Eds.), *Child discourse.* New York: Academic Press.

Eskenzai, B. (1993). Caffeine during pregnancy: Grounds for concern? *Journal of American Medical Association, 270,* 2973–2974.

Estrada, P., Arsenio, W. F., Hess, R. D., & Holloway, S. D. (1987). Affective quality of the mother-child relationship: Longitudinal consequences for children's school-relevant cognitive functioning. *Developmental Psychology, 23,* 210–215.

Fagan, J. F. (1973). Infants' delayed recognition memory and forgetting. *Journal of Experimental Child Psychology, 16,* 424–450.

Fagan, J. F. (1990). The paired-comparison paradigm and infant intelligence. In A. Diamond (Ed.), *The development and neural bases of higher cognitive functions. Annals of the New York Academy of Sciences, 608,* 337–364.

Fagan, J. F., Yengo, L. A., Rovee-Collier, C. K., & Enright, M. K. (1981). Reactivation of a visual discrimination in early infancy. *Developmental Psychology, 17,* 266–274.

Fagot, B. I. (1974). Sex differences in toddlers' behavior and parental reaction. *Developmental Psychology, 10,* 554–558.

Fagot, B. I. (1977). Consequences of moderate cross-gender behavior in preschool children. *Child Development, 49,* 902–907.

Fagot, B. I., & Hagan, R. (1982). *Hitting in toddler groups: Correlates and continuity.* Paper presented at the annual meeting of the American Psychological Association, Washington, DC.

Falbo, T., & Polit, D. F. (1986). Quantitative review of the only child literature: Research evidence and theory development. *Psychological Bulletin, 100,* 176–189.

Falkner, F., & Tanner, J. M. (Eds.). (1978a). *Human growth: Vol. 1. Principles and prenatal growth.* New York: Plenum.

Falkner, F., & Tanner, J. M. (Eds.). (1978b). *Human growth: Vol. 2. Postnatal growth.* New York: Plenum.

Farrington, D. P. (1987). Epidemiology. In H. C. Quay (Ed.), *Handbook of juvenile delinquency* (pp. 33–61). New York: Wiley.

Fauber, R., Forehand, R., Thomas, A. M., & Wierson, M. (1990). A mediational model of the impact of marital conflict on adolescent adjustment in intact and divorced families: The role of disrupted parenting. *Child Development, 61,* 1112–1123.

Faust, M. S. (1960). Developmental maturity as a determinant in prestige of adolescent girls. *Child Development, 31,* 173–184.

Faust, M. S. (1977). Somatic development of adolescent girls. *Monographs of the Society for Research in Child Development, 42(1),* 1–90.

Faust, M. S. (1983). Alternative constructions of adolescence and growth. In J. Brooks-Gunn & A. C. Petersen (Eds.), *Girls at puberty: Biological, psychological, and social perspectives* (pp. 105–125). New York: Plenum.

FBI. (1991). *Uniform crime reports for the United States: 1990.* Washington, DC: U.S. Government Printing Office.

Feinstein, S. C., & Miller, D. (1979). Psychoses of adolescence. In J. D. Noshpitz (Ed.), *Basic handbook of child psychiatry: Vol. 2. Disturbances in development* (pp. 708–722). New York: Basic Books.

Feld, S., Rutland, D., & Gold, M. (1979). Developmental changes in achievement motivation. *Merrill-Palmer Quarterly, 25,* 43–60.

Feldman, D. H. (1986). *Nature's gambit: Child prodigies and the development of human potential.* New York: Basic Books.

Fennema, E., & Peterson, P. (1985). Autonomous learning behavior: A possible explanation of gender-related differences in mathematics. In L. C. Wilkinson & C. B. Marrett (Eds.), *Gender influences in classroom interaction* (pp. 17–36). Orlando: Academic Press.

Feshbach, N. D. (1978). Studies of empathic behavior in children. In B. A. Maher (Ed.), *Progress in experimental personality research* (Vol. 8). New York: Academic Press.

Field, T. M. (1991). Quality infant day-care and grade school behavior and performance. *Child Development, 62,* 863–870.

Fischer, M., Rolf, J. E., Hasazi, J. E., & Cummings, L. (1984). Follow-up of a preschool epidemiological sample: Cross-age continuities and predictions of later adjustment with internalizing and externalizing dimension of behavior. *Child Development, 55,* 137–150.

Fischman, J. (1994). Putting a new spin on the birth of human birth. *Science, 264,* 1082–1083.

Fisher, C. B. (1993, Winter). Integrating science and ethics in research with high-risk children and youth. *Social Policy Report: Society for Research in Child Development, 7(4).*

Flavell, J. H. (1963). *The developmental psychology of Jean Piaget.* Princeton, NJ: Van Nostrand.

Flavell, J. H. (1985). *Cognitive development* (2nd ed.). Englewood Cliffs, NJ: Prentice-Hall.

Flavell, J. H. (1986). The development of children's knowledge about the appearance-reality distinction. *American Psychologist, 41,* 418–425.

Floderus-Myrhed, B., Pedersen, N., & Rasmuson, I. (1980). Assessment of inheritability for personality, based on a short form of the Eysenck Personality Inventory: A study of 12,898 twin pairs. *Behavior Genetics, 10,* 153–162.

Forbes, G. B. (1978). Body composition in adolescence. In F. Falkner & J. M. Tanner (Eds.), *Human growth: Vol. 2. Postnatal growth.* New York: Plenum.

Forsterling, F. (1985). Attributional retraining: A review. *Psychological Bulletin, 98,* 495–512.

Fowler, A. E. (1990). Language abilities in children with Down syndrome: Evidence for a specific syntactic delay. In D. Cicchetti & M. Beeghley (Eds.), *Children with Down syndrome: A developmental perspective.* New York: Cambridge University Press.

Fox, N. A. (1991). If it's not left, it's right: Electroencephalograph asymmetry and the development of emotion. *American Psychologist, 46,* 863–872.

Fox, N. A. (1995). Of the way we were: Adult memories about attachment experiences and their role in determining infant-parent relationships: A commentary on van IJzendoorn. *Psychological Bulletin, 117,* 404–410.

Fox, N. A., & Davidson, R. J. (1988). Patterns of brain electrical activity during facial signs of emotion in 10-month-old infants. *Developmental Psychology, 24,* 230–236.

Fraiberg, S. (1975). The development of human attachments in infants blind from birth. *Merrill Palmer Quarterly, 21,* 325–334.

Fraiberg, S. (1977). *Insights from the blind.* New York: Basic Books.

Fraser, F. C., & Nora, J. J. (1986). *Genetics of man.* Philadelphia: Lea & Febiger.

Freedman, R., Adler, L. E., Baker, N., Waldo, M., & Mizner, G. (1987). Candidate for inherited neurobiological dysfunction in schizophrenia. *Somatic Cell and Molecular Genetics, 13,* 479–484.

Freud, S. (1964). *An outline of psychoanalysis* (Standard edition of the works of Sigmund Freud). London: Hogarth Press.

Fried, P. A., Watkinson, B., & Gray, R. (1992). A follow-up study of attentional behavior in 6-year-old children exposed prenatally to marijuana, cigarettes, and alcohol. *Neurotoxicology and Teratology, 14,* 299–311.

Friedrich, L. K., & Stein, A. H. (1973). Aggressive and prosocial television programs and the natural behavior of preschool children. *Monographs of the Society for Research in Child Development, 38*(4, Serial No. 151).

Fuller, J. L., & Clark, L. D. (1968). Genotype and behavioral vulnerability to isolation in dogs. *Journal of Comparative and Physiological Psychology, 66,* 151–156.

Furrow, D., Nelson, K., & Benedict, H. (1979). Mothers' speech to children and syntactic development: Some simple relationships. *Journal of Child Language, 6,* 423–442.

Furstenberg, F. F., Jr. (1976). Premarital pregnancy and marital instability. *Journal of Social Issues, 32,* 67–86.

Furstenberg, F. F., Jr., & Brooks-Gunn, J. (1986). Children of adolescent mothers: Physical, academic, and psychological outcomes. *Developmental Review, 6,* 224–251.

Furstenberg, F. F., Jr., Brooks-Gunn, J., & Morgan, S. P. (1987a). Adolescent fertility: Causes, consequences, and remedies. In L. Aiken & D. Mechanic (Eds.), *Applications of social science to clinical medicine and health policy.* New Brunswick, NJ: Rutgers University Press.

Furstenberg, F. F., Jr., Brooks-Gunn, J., & Morgan, S. P. (1987b). *Adolescent mothers in later life.* New York: Cambridge University Press.

Furstenberg, F. F., Jr., Nord, C. W., Peterson, J. L., & Zill, N. (1983). The life course of children of divorce:

Marital disruption and parental contact. *American Sociological Review, 48,* 656–668.

Gallistel, C. R., & Gelman, R. (1992). Preverbal and verbal counting and computation. *Cognition, 44,* 43–74.

Garbarino, J., Kostelny, K., & Dubrow, N. (1991). What children can tell us about living in danger. *American Psychologist, 46,* 376–383.

Garbarino, J., & Sherman, D. (1980). High-risk neighborhoods and high-risk families: The human ecology of child maltreatment. *Child Development, 51,* 188–198.

Gardner, H. (1983). *Frames of mind.* New York: Basic Books.

Garfinkel, I., & McLanahan, S. S. (1986). *Single mothers and their children: A new American dilemma.* Washington, DC: Urban Institutes Press.

Garfinkel, P. E., & Garner, D. M. (1983). *Anorexia nervosa: A multidimensional perspective.* New York: Brunner/Mazel.

Garland, A. F., & Zigler, E. (1993). Adolescent suicide prevention: Current research and social policy implications. *American Psychologist, 48,* 169–182.

Garn, S. M. (1980). Human growth. *Annual Review of Anthropology, 9,* 275–292.

Garrett, C. J. (1984). *Meta-analysis of the effects of institutional and community residential treatment on adjudicated delinquents.* Unpublished doctoral dissertation, University of Colorado, Boulder.

Garrett, C. J. (1985). Effects of residential treatment on adjudicated delinquents: A meta-analysis. *Journal of Research on Crime and Delinquency, 22,* 287–308.

Garrett, P., Ng'andu, N., & Ferron, J. (1994). Poverty experiences of young children and the quality of their home environments. *Child Development, 54,* 331–345.

Garvey, C. (1975). Requests and responses in children's speech. *Journal of Child Language, 2,* 41–63.

Garvey, C. (1977). *Play.* Cambridge, MA: Harvard University Press.

Garwood, S. G., & Allen, L. (1979). Self-concept and identified problem differences between pre- and postmenarcheal adolescents. *Journal of Clinical Psychology, 35,* 528–537.

Gelman, R., & Baillargeon, R. (1983). A review of some Piagetian concepts. In P. H. Mussen (Series Ed.), J. H. Flavell & E. M. Markman (Eds.), *Handbook of child psychology: Vol. 3. Cognitive development* (pp. 167-230). New York: Wiley.

Gelman, R., & Gallistel, C. R. (1978). *The child's understanding of number.* Cambridge, MA: Harvard University Press.

George, C., Kaplan, N., & Main, M. (1985). *Adult Attachment Interview.* Unpublished manuscript.

Gerson, R. P., & Damon, W. (1978). Moral understanding and children's conduct. In W. Damon (Ed.), *New directions for child development: Moral development.* San Francisco: Jossey-Bass.

Gesell, A., & Amatruda, C.S. (1941). *Developmental diagnosis: Normal and abnormal child development.* New York: Hoeber.

Gesell, A., Halverson, H. M., Thompson, H., Ilg, F. L., Costner, B. M., & Amatruda, C. S. (1940). *The first five years of life: A guide to the study of the preschool child.* New York: Harper & Row.

Gewirtz, J. L. (1965). The cause of infant smiling in four child-rearing environments in Israel. In B. M. Foss (Ed.), *Determinants of infant behavior* (Vol. 3). London: Metheun.

Gibson, E. J., & Walk, R. D. (1960). The "visual cliff." *Scientific American, 202,* 64–71.

Gilligan, C. (1977). In a different voice: Women's conceptions of self and of morality. *Harvard Educational Review, 47,* 481–517.

Gilligan, C. (1982). *In a different voice.* Cambridge, MA: Harvard University Press.

Gilligan, C., & Belenky, M. F. (1982). A naturalistic study of abortion decisions. In R. Selman & R. Yando (Eds.), *Clinical-developmental psychology.* San Francisco: Jossey-Bass.

Ginsburg, H. P., & Opper, S. (1979). *Piaget's theory of intellectual development* (2nd ed.). Englewood Cliffs, NJ: Prentice-Hall.

Ginsburg, H. P., & Russell, R. L. (1981). Social class and racial influences on early mathematical thinking. *Monographs of the Society for Research in Child Development, 46* (Serial No. 193).

Glick, P. C. (1984). Marriage, divorce, and living arrangements: Prospective changes. *Journal of Family Issues, 5,* 7–26.

Goethals, G. W., & Klos, D. S. (1976). *Experiencing youth: First-person accounts* (2nd ed.). Boston: Little, Brown.

Goldberg, W. A., & Easterbrooks, M. A. (1984). Role of marital quality in toddler development. *Developmental Psychology, 20,* 504–514.

Goldfarb, J. L., Mumford, D. M., Schum, D. A., Smith, P. B., Flowers, C., & Schum, D. (1977). An attempt to detect "pregnancy susceptibility" in indigent adolescent girls. *Journal of Youth and Adolescence, 6,* 127–144.

Goldsmith, H. H. (1983). Genetic influences on personality from infancy to adulthood. *Child Development, 54,* 331–355.

Goldsmith, H. H. (1984). Continuity of personality: A genetic perspective. In R. N. Emde & R. J. Harmon (Eds.), *The development of attachment and affiliative systems.* New York: Plenum.

Goldsmith, H. H., & Campos, J. J. (1982). Genetic influence on individual differences in emotionality. *Infant Behavior and Development, 5,* 99.

Goldsmith, H. H., & Gottesman, I. I. (1981). Origins of variation in behavioral style. *Child Development, 52,* 91–103.

Goldsmith, R., & Radin, N. (1987, April). *Objective versus subjective reality: The effects of job loss and financial stress on fathering behaviors.* Paper presented at the meeting of the Society for Research in Child Development, Baltimore.

Goldstein, A. (1981). *Psychological skill training.* New York: Pergamon.

Goldstein, K. M., Caputo, D. V., & Taub, H. B. (1976). The effects of perinatal complications on development at one year of age. *Child Development, 47,* 613–621.

Goldstein, M. J. (1987). The UCLA high-risk project, 1962–1986. *Schizophrenia Bulletin, 13,* 505–514.

Goldstein, M. J., Baker, B. L., & Jamison, K. R. (1980). *Abnormal psychology: Experiences, origins, and interventions.* Boston: Little, Brown.

Goleman, D. (1993, July 21). 'Expert' babies found to teach others. *The New York Times,* p. C10.

Golinkoff, R. M., Hirsh-Pasek, K., Bailey, L. M., & Wenger, N. R. (1992). Young children and adults use lexical principles to learn new nouns. *Developmental Psychology, 28,* 99–108.

Goodchilds, J. D., & Zellman, G. L. (1984). Sexual signaling and sexual aggression in adolescent relationships. In N. M. Malamuth & E. D. Donnerstein (Eds.), *Pornography and sexual aggression.* New York: Academic Press.

Goodnow, J. J. (1985). Change and variation in ideas about childhood and parenting. In I. E. Sigel (Ed.), *Parental belief systems: The psychological consequences for children.* Hillsdale, NJ: Erlbaum.

Gottesman, I. I., & Shields, J. (1982). *Schizophrenia: The enigmatic puzzle.* New York: Cambridge University Press.

Gottman, J. M. (1977). Toward a definition of social isolation in children. *Child Development, 48,* 513–517.

Gottman, J. M. (1983). How children become friends. *Monographs of the Society for Research in Child Development, 48*(Serial No. 201).

Graham, F. K., Matarazzo, R. G., & Caldwell, B. M. (1956). Behavioral differences between normal and traumatized newborns. *Psychological Monographs, 70*(5).

Graham, P., & Rutter, M. (1985). Adolescent disorders. In M. Rutter and L. Hersov (Eds.), *Child and adolescent psychiatry.* Oxford: Blackwell Scientific Publications.

Green, R. (1980). Homosexuality. In H. I. Kaplan, A. M. Freedman, & B. J. Sadock (Eds.), *Comprehensive textbook of psychiatry* (Vol. 2, 3rd ed., pp. 1762–1770). Baltimore: Williams and Wilkins.

Green, R. (1987). *The "sissy boy syndrome" and the development of homosexuality.* New Haven, CT: Yale University Press.

Greenberg, B. S. (1972). Children's reactions to TV blacks. *Journalism Quarterly, 49,* 5–14.

Greenberg, B. S. (1986). Minorities and the mass media. In J. Bryant and D. Zillmann (Eds.), *Perspectives on mass media effects* (pp. 165–188). Hillsdale, NJ: Erlbaum.

Greenberger, E., & Steinberg, L. (1986). *When teenagers work: The psychological and social costs of adolescent employment.* New York: Basic Books.

Greenough, W. J., Black, J. E., & Wallace, C. S. (1987). Experience and brain development. *Child Development, 58,* 539–555.

Greenspan, S. I., & Lieberman, A. F. (1994). A quantitative approach to the clinical assessment of 2-to-4-year olds. In A. Slade & D. P. Wolf (Eds.), *Children at Play: Clinical and developmental perspectives.* New York: Oxford University Press.

Greif, E. B., & Ulman, K. J. (1982). The psychological impact of menarche on early adolescent females: A review of the literature. *Child Development, 53,* 1413–1430.

Grossman, F. K., Eichler, L. S., Winikoff, S. A., & Associates. (1980). *Pregnancy, birth, and parenthood: Adaptations of mothers, fathers, and infants.* San Francisco: Jossey-Bass.

Grossmann, K., Grossmann, K. E., Huber, F., & Wartner, Y. (1981). German children's behavior toward their mothers at 12 months and their fathers at 18 months in the Ainsworth Strange Situation. *International Journal of Behavioral Development, 4,* 157–181.

Grotevant, H. D., & Cooper, C. R. (Eds.). (1983). *Adolescent development in the family.* San Francisco: Jossey-Bass.

Grotevant, H. D., & Cooper, C. R. (1985). Patterns of interaction in family relationships and the development of identity exploration in adolescence. *Child Development, 56,* 415–428.

Grubb, N., & Lazerson, M. (1988). *Broken promises: How Americans fail their children.* New York: Basic Books.

Gruendel, J. M. (1977). Referential extension in early language development. *Child Development, 48,* 1567–1576.

Grumbach, M. M. (1978). The central nervous system and the onset of puberty. In F. Falkner & J. M. Tanner (Eds.), *Human growth: Vol. 2. Postnatal growth.* New York: Plenum.

Grusec, J. E., & Goodnow, J. J. (1994). Impact of parental discipline methods on the child's internalization of values: A reconceptualization of current points of view. *Developmental Psychology, 30,* 4–19.

Grusec, J. E., & Pedersen, J. (1989). *Children's thinking about prosocial and moral behavior.* Paper presented at the biennial meeting of Society for Research in Child Development, Kansas City, KS.

Grusec, J. E., Saas-Kortsaak, P., & Simutis, Z. M. (1978). The role of example and moral exhortation in the training of altruism. *Child Development, 49,* 920–923.

Guidubaldi, J., Perry, J. D., & Cleminshaw, H. K. (1983). The legacy of parental divorce: A nationwide study of family status and selected mediating variables on children's academic and social competencies. *School Psychology Review, 2,* 148.

Guilford, J. P. (1979). *Cognitive psychology with a frame of reference.* San Diego: Edits Publishers.

Gunderon, V., & Sackett, G. P. (1982). Paternal effects on reproductive outcome and developmental risk. In M. E. Lamb & A. L. Brown (Eds.), *Advances in developmental psychology* (Vol. 2, pp. 85–124). New Jersey: LEA.

Gunnar, M. R., Leighton, K., & Peleaux, R. (1984). The effect of temporal predictability on the reactions of one-year-olds to potentially frightening toys. *Developmental Psychology, 20,* 449–458.

Gunter, N. C., & LaBarba, R. C. (1980). The consequences of adolescent childbearing on postnatal development. *International Journal of Behavioral Development, 3,* 191–214.

Gupta, D., Attanasio, A., & Raaf, S. (1975). Plasma estrogen and androgen concentrations in children during adolescence. *Journal of Clinical Endocrinology and Metabolism, 40,* 636–643.

Gustafson, G. E. (1984). Effects of the ability to locomote on infants' social and exploratory behaviors: An experimental study. *Developmental Psychology, 20,* 397–405.

Guttmacher, A. F., & Kaiser, J. H. (1986). *Pregnancy, birth, and family planning.* New York: New American Library.

Haan, N., Smith, B., & Block J. (1968). Moral reasoning of young adults. *Journal of Personality and Social Psychology, 10,* 183–201.

Hack, M. (1983). The sensorimotor development of the preterm infant. In A. A. Fanaroff, R. J. Martin, & J. R. Merkatz (Eds.), *Behrman's neonatal-perinatal medicine.* St. Louis: Mosby.

Haith, M. M. (1987). *Expectations and the gratuity of skill acquisition in early infancy.* Unpublished manuscript.

Haith, M. M. (1980). *Rules that babies look by.* Hillsdale, NJ: LEA.

Hall, V. C., & Kaye, D. B. (1980). Early patterns of cognitive development. *Monographs of the Society for Research in Child Development, 45*(Serial No. 184).

Halle, M. (1990). Phonology. In D. N. Osherson & H. Lasnik (Eds.), *Language: An invitation to cognitive science* (Vol. 1, pp. 43–68). Cambridge: MIT Press.

Hallinan, M. T., & Teixeira, R. A. (1987). Opportunities and constraints: Black-white differences in the formation of interracial friendships. *Child Development, 58,* 1358–1371.

Hamburg, D. A., & Trudeau, M. B. (1981). *Biobehavioral aspects of aggression.* New York: Alan R. Liss.

Hammen, C., Burge, D., & Stansbury, K. (1990). Relationship of mother and child variables to child outcomes in a high-risk sample: A causal modeling analysis. *Developmental Psychology, 26,* 24–30.

Hansen, R. D., & O'Leary, V. E. (1986). Sex-determined attributions. In V. E. O'Leary, R. K. Unger, & B. S. Wallston (Eds.), *Women, gender, and social psychology* (pp. 67–100). Hillsdale, NJ: Erlbaum.

Hanson, J. W. (1977). Unpublished paper, cited in A. Clarke-Stewart & S. Friedman (1982) *Child development: Infancy through adolescence* (p. 127). New York: Wiley.

Harlap, S., Kost, K., & Forrest, J. D. (1991). *Preventing pregnancy, protecting health: A new look at birth control choices in the United States.* New York: The Alan Guttmacher Institute.

Harlow, H. F., & Harlow, M. K. (1966). Learning to love. *American Scientist, 54,* 244–272.

Harlow, H. F., & Suomi, S. J. (1970). The nature of love—simplified. *American Psychologist, 25,* 161–168.

Harris, P. L., & Kavanaugh, R. D. (1993). Young children's understanding of pretense. *Monographs of the Society for Research in Child Development, 58*(1, Serial No. 231).

Harris, P. L., Kavanaugh, R. D., & Meredith, M. C. (1994). Young childrens' comprehension of pretend episodes: The integration of successive actions. *Child Development, 65,* 16–30.

Harrison, A., Serafica, F., & McAdoo, H. (1984). Ethnic families of color. In R. D. Parke (Ed.), *Review of child development research: Vol. 7. The family.* Chicago: University of Chicago Press.

Harter, S. (1983). Developmental perspectives on the self-system. In P. H. Mussen (Series Ed.) & E. M. Hetherington (Ed.), *Handbook of child psychology: Vol. 4. Socialization, personality, and social development* (4th ed., pp. 275–386). New York: Wiley.

Harter, S. (1985). Competence as a dimension of self-evaluation: Toward a comprehensive model of self-worth. In R. Leahy (Ed.), *The development of the self.* New York: Academic Press.

Harter, S. (1990). Self and identity development. In S. S. Feldman & G. R. Elliot (Eds.), *At the threshold: The developing adolescent* (pp. 352–387). Cambridge, MA: Harvard University Press.

Hartup, W. W. (1970). Peer interaction and social organization. In P. H. Mussen (Ed.), *Carmichael's manual of child psychology* (Vol. 2). New York: Wiley.

Hartup, W. W. (1974). Aggression in childhood: Developmental perspectives. *American Psychologist, 29,* 336–341.

Hartup, W. W. (1983). Peer relations. In P. H. Mussen (Series Ed.) & E. M. Hetherington (Ed.), *Handbook of child psychology: Vol. 4. Socialization, personality, and social development* (4th ed., pp. 103–196). New York: Wiley.

Hartup, W. W., Brady, J. E., & Newcomb, A. F. (1981). *Children's utilization of simultaneous sources of social information: Developmental perspectives.* Unpublished manuscript, University of Minnesota.

Haskins, R. (1985). Public school aggression among children with varying day-care experience. *Child Development, 56,* 689–703.

Hauser, S. T., Book, B. K., Houlihan, J., Powers, S., Weiss-Perry B., Follansbee, D., Jacobson, A. M., & Noam, G. G. (1987). Sex differences within the family: Studies of adolescent and parent family interactions. *Journal of Youth and Adolescence, 16,* 199–220.

Hauser, S. T., & Kasendorf, E. (1983). *Black and white identity formation.* Malabar, FL: Robert E. Krieger.

Hawkins, R. P. (1977). Behavioral analysis and early childhood education. In H. L. Hom & P. A. Robinson (Eds.), *Psychological processes in early education.* New York: Academic Press.

Hawley, T. L., & Disney, E. R. (1992). Crack's children: The consequences of maternal cocaine abuse. *Social Policy Report of the Society for Research in Child Development, 6,* 1–22.

Hay, D. F. (1979). Cooperative interactions and sharing among very young children and their parents. *Developmental Psychology, 15,* 647–653.

Hayes, C. D. (Ed.). (1987). *Risking the future: Adolescent sexuality, pregnancy, and childbearing* (Vol. 1). Washington, DC: National Academy Press.

Hayes, D. S. (1978). Cognitive bases for liking and disliking among preschool children. *Child Development, 49,* 906–909.

Hayes, D. S., & Casey, D. M. (1992). Young children and television: The retention of emotional reactions. *Child Development, 63,* 1423–1436.

Hearold, S. (1986). A synthesis of 1043 effects of television on social behavior. In G. Comstock (Ed.), *Public communication and behavior* (Vol. 1, pp. 66–133). New York: Academic Press.

Heibeck, T. H., & Markman, E. M. (1987). Word learning in children: An examination of fast mapping. *Child Development, 58,* 1021–1034.

Hermans, H. J. M., Ter Laak, J. J., & Maes, P. C. (1972). Achievement motivation and fear of failure in family and school. *Developmental Psychology, 6,* 520–528.

Hertzig, M. E., & Shapiro, T. (1990). Autism and pervasive developmental disorders. In M. Lewis & S. M. Miller (Eds.), *Handbook of developmental psychopathology* (pp. 385–395). New York: Plenum.

Herzog, D. P. (1988). Eating disorders. In A. M. Nicholi, Jr. (Ed.), *The new Harvard guide to psychiatry* (pp. 434–445). Cambridge, MA: Harvard University Press.

Hess, R. D., Holloway, S. D., Dickson, W. P., & Price, G. G. (1984). Maternal variables as predictors of children's school readiness and later achievement in vocabulary and mathematics in sixth grade. *Child Development, 55,* 1902–1912.

Hess, R. D., & McDevitt, T. M. (1984). Some cognitive consequences of maternal intervention techniques: A longitudinal study. *Child Development, 55,* 2017–2030.

Hetherington, E. M. (1967). The effects of familial variables on sex typing, on parent-child similarity, and on imitation in children. In J. P. Hill (Ed.), *Minnesota Symposia on Child Psychology* (Vol. 1). Minneapolis: University of Minnesota Press.

Hetherington, E. M. (1988). Parents, children, and siblings: Six years after divorce. In R. A. Hinde & J. Stevenson-Hinde (Eds.), *Relationships within families: Mutual Influences* (pp. 311–331). Oxford, England: Oxford University Press.

Hetherington, E. M. (1989). Coping with family transitions: Winners, losers, and survivors. *Child Development, 60,* 1–14.

Hetherington, E. M. (1991). Presidential address: Families, lies, and videotapes. *Journal of Research and Adolescence, 1,* 323–348.

Hetherington, E. M., Camara, K. A., & Featherman, D. L. (1983). Achievement and intellectual functioning of children from one-parent households. In J. T. Spence (Ed.), *Achievement and achievement motives.* San Francisco: Freeman.

Hetherington, E. M., Cox, M., & Cox, R. (1982). Effects of divorce on parents and children. In M. Lamb (Ed.), *Nontraditional families.* Hillsdale, NJ: LEA.

Hill, J. P. (1988). Adapting to menarche: Familial control and conflict. In M. R. Gunnar & W. A. Collins (Eds.), *Minnesota Symposia on Child Psychology* (pp. 43–77). Hillsdale, NJ: LEA.

Hill, K. T. (1980). Motivation, evaluation, and educational testing policy. In L. J. Fyans (Ed.), *Achievement motivation: Recent trends in theory and research* (pp. 34–95). New York: Plenum.

Hill, K. T., & Sarason, S. B. (1966). The relation of test anxiety and defensiveness to test and school performance over the elementary school years: A further longitudinal study. *Monographs of the Society for Research in Child Development, 31*(Serial No. 104).

Hirsch, H. V. B., & Spinelli, D. N. (1971). Modification of the distribution of receptive field orientation in cats by selective visual exposure during development. *Experimental Brain Research, 13,* 509–527.

Hirsh-Pasek, K., & Golinkoff, R. (in press). *The origins of grammar.* Cambridge, MA: MIT Press.

Hirsh-Pasek, K., & Golinkoff, R. M. (1993). Skeletal supports for grammatical learning: What infants bring to the language learning task. In C. Rovee-Collier & L. Lipsitt (Eds.), *Advances in Infancy Research, 8,* 299–338.

Hirsh-Pasek, K., Treiman, R., & Schneiderman, M. (1984). Brown and Hanlon revisited: Mothers' sensitivity to ungrammatical forms. *Journal of Child Languages, 11,* 81–88.

Hodapp, R. M., & Zigler, E. (1990). Applying the developmental perspective to individuals with Down syndrome. In D. Cicchetti & M. Beeghley (Eds.), *Children with Down syndrome: A developmental perspective.* New York: Cambridge University Press.

Hodgson, J. W., & Fischer, J. L. (1978). Sex differences in identity and intimacy development in college youth. *Journal of Youth and Adolescence, 7,* 333–352.

Hoffman, L. W. (1991). The influence of the family environment on personality: Accountability for sibling differences. *Psychological Bulletin, 110,* 187–203.

Hoffman, M. L. (1967). Moral internalization, parental power, and the nature of the parent-child interaction. *Developmental Psychology, 5,* 45–57.

Hoffman, M. L. (1970). Moral development. In P. Mussen (Ed.), *Carmichael's manual of child psychology* (Vol. 2, 3rd ed.). New York: Wiley.

Hoffman, M. L. (1975). Developmental synthesis of affect and cognition and its implications for altruistic motivation. *Developmental Psychology, 11,* 607–622.

Hoffman, M. L. (1981). Development of the motive to help others. In J. P. Rushton & R. M. Sorrentino (Eds.), *Altruism and helping.* Hillsdale, NJ: LEA.

Hoffman, M. L. (1983). Affective and cognitive processes in moral internalization. In E. T. Higgins, D. N. Ruble, & W. W. Hartup (Eds.), *Social cognition and social behavior: Developmental perspectives.* New York: Cambridge University Press.

Hoffman, M. L. (1988). Moral development. In M. H. Bornstein & M. E. Lamb (Eds.), *Developmental psychology: An advanced book* (2nd ed., pp. 497–548). Hillsdale, NJ: LEA.

Hoffman, M. L., & Saltzstein, H. D. (1967). Parent discipline and the child's moral development. *Journal of Personality and Social Psychology, 5,* 45–47.

Holinger, P. C. (1978). Adolescent suicide: An epidemiological study of recent trends. *American Journal of Psychiatry, 135,* 754–756.

Holmbeck, G. N., & Hill, J. P. (1991). Conflictive engagement, positive effect, and menarche in families with seventh-grade girls. *Child Development, 62,* 1030–1048.

Honzik, M. P., Macfarlane, J. W., & Allen, L. (1948). The stability of mental test performances between two and eighteen years. *Journal of Experimental Education, 17,* 309–324.

Hook, E. B. (1982). Epidemiology of Down syndrome. In S. H. Pueschel & J. E. Rynders (Eds.), *Advances in biomedicine and behavioral sciences.* Cambridge, MA: Ware Press.

Horn, J. M. (1968). Organization of abilities and the development of intelligence. *Psychological Review, 75,* 242–259.

Horn, J. M. (1983). The Texas adoption project: Adopted children and their intellectual resemblance to biological and adoptive parents. *Child Development, 54,* 268–275.

Hornick, J. P., Doran, L., & Crawford, S. H. (1979). Premarital contraceptive usage among male and female adolescents. *Family Coordinator, 28,* 181–190.

Horowitz, F. D. (1987). *Exploring developmental theories: Toward a structural/behavioral model of development.* Hillsdale, NJ: LEA.

Horowitz, F. D., & Paden, L. Y. (1973). The effectiveness of environmental intervention programs. In B. M. Caldwell & H. N. Ricciuti (Eds.), *Review of child development research* (Vol. 3). Chicago: University of Chicago Press.

Howes, C. (1987). Social competence with peers in young children: Developmental sequences. *Developmental Review, 7,* 252–272.

Howes, C. (1988a). Peer interaction of young children. *Monographs of the Society for Research in Child Development, 53*(1).

Howes, C. (1988b). Relations between early child care and schooling. *Developmental Psychology, 24,* 53–57.

Howes, C., Hamilton, C. E., & Matheson, C. C. (1994). Children's relationships with peers: Differential associations with aspects of the teacher-child relationship. *Child Development, 65,* 253–263.

Howes, C., Matheson, C. C., & Hamilton, C. E. (1994). Maternal, teacher, and child case history correlates of children's relationships with peers. *Child Development, 65,* 264–273.

Howes, C., Phillips, D. A., & Whitebook, M. (1992). Thresholds of quality: Implications for the social development of children in center-based child care. *Child Development, 63,* 449–460.

Howes, C., & Stewart, P. (1987). Child's play with adults, toys, and peers: An examination of family and child-care influences. *Developmental Psychology, 23,* 432–430.

Howes, C., & Wu, F. (1990). Peer interactions and friendships in an ethnically diverse school setting. *Child Development, 61,* 537–541.

Howlin, P., & Yule, W. (1990). Taxonomy of major disorders in childhood. In M. Lewis & S. M. Miller (Eds.), *Handbook of developmental psychopathology* (pp. 371–383). New York: Plenum.

Huesmann, L. R., & Eron, L. D. (Eds.) (1986). *Television and the aggressive child: A cross-national comparison.* Hillsdale, NJ: Erlbaum.

Huesmann, L. R., Eron, L. D., Lefkowitz, M. M., & Walder, L. O. (1984). The stability of aggression over time and generations. *Developmental Psychology, 20,* 1120–1134.

Huesmann, L. R., Lagerspetz, K., & Eron, L. D. (1984). Intervening variables in the television violence-aggression relation: Evidence from two countries. *Developmental Psychology, 20,* 746–775.

Hunt, C. E. (1991). Sudden infant death syndrome: The neurobehavioral perspective. *Journal of Applied Developmental Psychology, 12,* 185–188.

Hunt, M. (1974). *Sexual behavior in the 1970s.* Chicago: Playboy Press.

Hurston, Z. N. (1991). *Dust tracks on a road.* New York: Harper Perennial. (Original work published 1942.)

Huston, A., McLoyd, V. C., & Coll, C. G. (1994). Children and poverty: Issues in contemporary research. *Child Development, 65,* 274–282.

Huston, A. C. (1983). Sex typing. In P. H. Mussen (Series Ed.), & E. M. Hetherington (Ed.), *Handbook of child psychology: Vol. 4. Socialization, personality, and social development* (4th ed., pp. 387–467). New York: Wiley.

Huston, A. C. (1984). *Do adopted children resemble their biological parents more than their adoptive parents? No. A note on the study of behavioral genetics.* Unpublished manuscript, University of Kansas.

Huston, A. C., & Carpenter, C. J. (1985). Gender differences in preschool classrooms: The effects of sex-typed activity choices. In L. C. Wilkinson & C. B. Barett (Eds.), *Gender influences in classroom interaction* (pp. 143–166). New York: Academic Press.

Huston, A. C., Carpenter, C. J., Atwater, J. B., & Johnson, L. M. (1986). Gender, adult structuring of activities, and social behavior in middle childhood. *Child Development, 57,* 1200–1209.

Huston, A. C., & Wright, J. C. (1983). Children's processing of television: The informative functions of formal features. In J. Bryant & D. R. Anderson (Eds.), *Children's understanding of television: Research on attention and comprehension.* New York: Academic Press.

Huston, A. C., Wright, J. C., Rice, M. L., Kerkman, D., & St. Peters, M. (1990). Development of television viewing patterns in early childhood: A longitudinal investigation. *Developmental Psychology, 26,* 409–420.

Huston, T., & Ashmore, R. D. (1986). Women and men in personal relationships. In R. D. Ashmore & F. K. Del Boca (Eds.), *The social psychology of female-male relations.* Orlando: Academic Press.

Huston-Stein, A., Friedrich-Cofer, L., & Susman, E. J. (1977). The relation of classroom structure to social behavior, imaginative play, and self-regulation of economically disadvantaged children. *Child Development, 48,* 908–916.

Huttenlocher, J., Haight, W., Bryk, A., Seltzer, M., & Lyons, T. (1991). Early vocabulary growth: Relation to language input and gender. *Developmental Psychology, 27,* 236–248.

Huttenlocher, J., Jordan, N. C., & Levine, S. C. (1994). A mental model for early arithmetic. *Journal of Experimental Psychology: General, 123,* 284–296.

Huttenlocher, J., Newcombe, N., & Sandberg, E. H. (1994). The coding of spatial location in young children. *Cognitive Psychology, 27,* 115–147.

Huttenlocher, J., & Smiley, P. (1987). Early word meanings: The case of object names. *Cognitive Psychology, 19,* 63–89.

Huttenlocher, J., Smiley, P., & Charney, R. (1983). Emergence of action categories in the child: Evidence from verb meanings. *Psychological Review, 90,* 72–93.

Huttenlocher, P. R. (1984). Synapse elimination and plasticity in developing human cerebral cortex. *American Journal of Mental Deficiency, 88,* 488–496.

Huttenlocher, P. R. (1990). Morphometric study of human cerebral cortex development. *Neuropsychologia, 28,* 517–527.

Hyde, J. S., & Linn, M. C. (1988). Gender differences in verbal ability: A meta-analysis. *Psychological Bulletin, 104,* 53–69.

Hymel, S., Rubin, K. H., Rowden, L., & LeMare, L. (1990). Children's peer relationships: Longitudinal prediction of internalizing and externalizing problems from middle to late childhood. *Child Development, 61,* 2004–2021.

Iannotti, R. J. (1985). Naturalistic and structured assessments of prosocial behavior in preschool children: The influence of empathy and perspective taking. *Developmental Psychology, 21,* 46–55.

Illingworth, R. S. (1987). *The development of the infant and young child: Normal and abnormal.* Edinburgh: Churchill Livingstone.

Infante-Rivard, C., Fernandez, A., Gauthier, R., David, M., & Rivard, G. (1993). Fetal loss associated with caffeine intake before and during pregnancy. *Journal of American Medical Association, 270,* 2940–2943.

Ipsa, J. (1981). Social interactions among teachers, handicapped children, and nonhandicapped children in a mainstreamed preschool. *Journal of Applied Developmental Psychology, 1,* 231–250.

Isabella, R. A., & Belsky, J. (1991). Interactional synchrony and the origins of infant-mother attachment: A replication study. *Child Development, 62,* 373–384.

Izard, C. E. (1982). *Measuring emotions in infants and children.* New York: Cambridge University Press.

Izard, C. E., Hembree, E. A., Dougherty, L. M., & Spizzirri, C. C. (1983). Changes in two to nineteen month infants' facial expressions following acute pain. *Developmental Psychology, 19,* 418–426.

Jackson, J. F. (1993). Human behavioral genetics, Scarr's theory, and her views on interventions: A critical review and commentary on their implications for African American children. *Child Development, 64,* 1318–1332.

Jacobs, J. (1971). *Adolescent suicide.* New York: Wiley.

Jacobson, S. (1979). Matching behavior in the young infant. *Child Development, 50,* 425–431.

James, W. (1892/1961). *Psychology: The briefer course.* New York: Harper & Row.

Jenkins, J. (1992). Sibling relationships in disharmonious homes: Potential difficulties and protective effects. In F. Boer & J. Dunn (Eds.), *Children's sibling relationships* (pp. 125–138). Hillsdale, NJ: LEA.

Jensen, A. R. (1969). How much can we boost IQ and scholastic achievement? *Harvard Educational Review, 39,* 449–483.

Jersild, A. T., & Holmes, F. B. (1935). Children's fears. *Child Development Monograph* (No. 20).

Jessor, R. (1984). Adolescent development and behavioral health. In J. D. Matarazzo, S. M. Weiss, J. A. Herd, N. E. Miller, & S. M. Weiss (Eds.), *Behavioral health: A handbook of health enhancement and disease prevention* (pp. 69–90). New York: Wiley.

Jessor, R., & Jessor, S. L. (1977). *Problem behavior and psychosocial development: A longitudinal study of youth.* New York: Academic Press.

Joffe, J. M. (1969). *Prenatal determinants of behavior.* Oxford: Pergamon.

Johnson, B., & Moore, H. A. (1968). Injured children and their parents. *Children, 15,* 147–152.

Johnson, C. (1982). Anorexia nervosa and bulimia. In T. J. Coates, A. C. Petersen, & C. Perry (Eds.), *Adolescent health: Crossing the barriers.* New York: Academic Press.

Johnson, C., Lewis, C., & Hagman, J. (1984). The syndrome of bulimia. *Psychiatric Clinics of North American, 7,* 247–274.

Johnson, E. S., & Meade, A. C. (1987). Developmental patterns of spatial ability: An early sex difference. *Child Development, 58,* 725–740.

Johnson, J. S., & Newport, E. L. (1989). Critical period effects in second language learning: The influence of maturational state on the acquisition of English as a second language. *Cognitive Psychology, 21,* 60–99.

Johnson, W. F., Emde, R. N., Pannabecker, R., Stenberg, C., & Davis, M. (1982). Maternal perception of infant emotions from birth through 18 months. *Infant Behavior and Development, 5,* 313–322.

Johnston, F. E. (1978). Somatic growth of the infant and preschool child. In F. Falkner & J. M. Tanner (Eds.), *Human growth: Vol. 2. Postnatal growth.* New York: Plenum.

Johnston, J., & Ettema, J. S. (1982). *Positive images: Breaking stereotypes with children's television.* Beverly Hills, CA: Sage.

Johnston, L. D. (1988, January 13). *Summary of 1987 drug study results.* Press release available from News and Information Service, University of Michigan.

Johnston, L. D., & O'Malley, P. M. (1986). Why do the nation's students use drugs and alcohol? Self-reported reasons from nine national surveys. *The Journal of Drug Issues, 16,* 29–66.

Johnston, L. D., O'Malley, P. M., & Bachman, J. G. (1987). *American high school students and young adults, 1975–1986.* (U. S. Department of Health and Human Services). Washington, DC: National Institute on Drug Abuse. (DHHS Publication No. ADM 87-1535).

Johnston, L. D., O'Malley, P. M., & Bachman, J. G. (1993). *National survey results on drug use from Monitoring the Future Study, 1975–1992* (Vol. 1). (U.S. Department of Health and Human Services). Rockville, MD: National Institute on Drug Abuse.

Johnston, J. R., & Slobin, D. I. (1979). The development of locative expressions in English, Italian, Serbo-Croatian and Turkish. *Journal of Child Language, 6,* 529–545.

Jones, E. F., & Forrest, J. D. (1992). Contraceptive failure rates based on the 1988 National Survey of Family Growth. *Family Planning Perspectives, 24,* 12–19.

Jones, H. E. (1946). Environmental influence on moral development. In L. Carmichael (Ed.), *Manual of child psychology.* New York: Wiley.

Jones, H. E. (1954). The environment and mental development. In L. Carmichael (Ed.) *Manual of child psychology* (2nd ed.). New York: Wiley.

Jones, K. L., Smith, D. W., Ulleland, C. N., & Streissguth, A. P. (1973). Patterns of malformation of offspring of chronic alcoholic mothers. *Lancet, 1,* 1267–1271.

Jones, M. C. (1957). The later careers of boys who were early- or late-maturing. *Child Development, 28,* 113–128.

Kagan, J. (1981). *The second year.* Cambridge, MA: Harvard University Press.

Kagan, J. (1984). *The nature of the child.* New York: Basic Books.

Kagan, J., Kearsley, R., & Zelazo, P. (1978). *Infancy: Its place in human development.* Cambridge, MA : Harvard University Press.

Kagan, J., Klein, R. E., Finley, G. E., Rogoff, B., & Nolan, E. (1979). A cross-cultural study of cognitive development. *Monographs of the Society for Research in Child Development, 33*(4, Serial No. 120).

Kagan, J., & Moss, H. A. (1962). *Birth to maturity.* New York: Wiley.

Kagan, J., Reznick, J. S., Davies, J., Smith, J., Sigal, J., & Miyake, K. (1986). Selective memory and belief: A methodological suggestion. *International Journal of Behavioral Development, 9,* 205–218.

Kagan, J., Reznick, J. S., & Snidman, N. (1988). Biological bases of childhood shyness. *Science, 240,* 167–171.

Kagan, J., & Snidman, N. (1991). Infant predictors of inhibited and uninhibited profiles. *Psychological Science, 2,* 40–44.

Kail, R. (1988). Developmental functions for speeds of cognitive processes. *Journal of Experimental Child Psychology, 45,* 339–364.

Kamerman, S. B., Kahn, A. J., & Kingston, P. (1983). *Maternity policies and working women.* New York: Columbia University Press.

Kandel, D. B. (1978). Similarity in real-life adolescent friendship pairs. *Journal of Personality and Social Psychology, 36,* 306–312.

Kandel, D. B. (1980). Drug and drinking behavior among youth. *Annual Review of Sociology, 6,* 235–285.

Kaplan, H., & Dove, H. (1987). Infant development among the Ache of Eastern Paraguay. *Developmental Psychology, 23,* 190–198.

Karniol, R. (1978). Children's use of intention cues in evaluating behavior. *Psychological Bulletin, 85,* 76–85.

Kassebaum, N. L. (1994). Head Start: Only the best for America's children. *American Psychologist, 49,* 123–126.

Katchadourian, H. A. (1985). *Fundamentals of human sexuality* (4th ed.). New York: Holt, Rinehart, & Winston.

Katz, M., Keusch, G. T., & Mata, L. (1975). Malnutrition and infection during pregnancy: Determinants of growth and development of the child. *American Journal of Diseases of Children, 29,* 419–463.

Katz, P. A. (1976). The acquisition of racial attitudes in children. In P. A. Katz (Ed.), *Towards the elimination of racism.* New York: Pergamon.

Katz, P. A., & Ksansnak, K. R. (1994). Developmental aspects of gender role flexibility and traditionality in middle childhood and adolescence. *Developmental Psychology, 30,* 272–282.

Kaufman, I. R. (1979, October 14). Juvenile justice: A plea for reform. *New York Times Magazine,* pp. 42–60.

Kaufman, J., & Zigler, E. (1989). The intergenerational transmission of child abuse. In D. Cicchetti & V. Carlson (Eds.), *Child maltreatment: Theory and research on the causes and consequences of child abuse and neglect* (pp. 129–150). Cambridge, MA: Cambridge University Press.

Keating, D. P. (1975). Precocious cognitive development at the level of formal operations. *Child Development, 46,* 276–280.

Keating, D. P. (1980). Thinking processes in adolescence. In J. Adelson (Ed.), *Handbook of adolescent psychology.* New York: Wiley.

Keil, F. C. (1989). *Concepts, kinds, and cognitive development.* Cambridge, MA: MIT Press.

Kelley, K. (1979). Socialization factors in contraceptive attitudes: Roles of affective responses, parental attitudes, and sexual experience. *Journal of Sex Research, 15,* 6–20.

Kellman, P. J., & Spelke, E. S. (1983). Perception of partly occluded objects in infancy. *Cognitive Psychology, 15,* 483–524.

Kelsoe, J. R., Ginns, E. I., Egeland, J. A., Gerhard, D. S., et al. (1989). Re-evaluation of the linkage relationship between chromosome 11p loci and the gene for bipolar affective disorder in the Old Order Amish. *Nature, 342,* 238–243.

Kempe, R. S., & Kempe, C. H. (1978). *Child abuse.* Cambridge, MA: Harvard University Press.

Kendall, P. C., Chansky, T. E., Freidman, M., Kim, R., Kortlander, E., Sessa, F. M., & Siqueland, L. (1991). Treating anxiety disorders in children and adolescents. In P. C. Kendall (Ed.), *Child and adolescent therapy: Cognitive-behavioral procedures* (pp. 131–164). New York: Guilford Press.

Kendall-Tackett, K. A., Williams, L. M., & Finkelhor, D. (1993). Impact of sexual abuse on children: A review and synthesis of recent empirical studies. *Psychological Bulletin, 113,* 164–180.

Kendler, K. S., Gruenberg, A. M., & Strauss, J. S. (1981). An independent analysis of the Copenhagen sample of the Danish Adoption Study of Schizophrenia. I. The relationship between anxiety disorder and schizophrenia. *Archives of General Psychiatry, 38,* 937–977.

Kessler, S. S. (1975). Psychiatric genetics. In D. A. Hamburg & K. Brodie (Eds.), *American handbook of psychiatry: Vol. 6. New psychiatric frontiers.* New York: Basic Books.

Kessler, S. S. (1980). The genetics of schizophrenia: A review. *Schizophrenia Bulletin, 6,* 404–416.

Kety, S. S., Rosenthal, D., Wender, P. H., Schulsinger, F., & Jacobsen, B. (1975). Mental illness in the biological and adoptive families of adoptive individuals who have become schizophrenic: A preliminary report based on psychiatric interviews. In R. Fieve, D. Rosenthal, & H. Brill (Eds.), *Genetic research in psychiatry.* Baltimore: Johns Hopkins University Press.

Kety, S. S., Rosenthal, D., Wender, P. H., Schulsinger, F., & Jacobsen, B. (1978). The biological and adoptive families of adopted individuals who became schizophrenic: Prevalence of mental illness and other characteristics. In L. C. Wynne, R. L. Cromwell, & S. Matthysse (Eds.), *The nature of schizophrenia: New approaches to research and treatment.* New York: Wiley.

Kidman, C. (1993). Non-consensual sexual experience and HIV education: An educator's view. *SIECUS Report, 21,* 9–12.

Kiell, N. (1967). *The universal experience of adolescence.* Boston: Beacon.

King, L. J., & Pitman, G. D. (1971). A follow-up of 65 adolescent schizophrenic patients. *Diseases of the Nervous System, 32,* 328–334.

Kinsey, A. C., Pomeroy, W. B., & Martin, C. E. (1948). *Sexual behavior in the human male.* Philadelphia: Saunders.

Kinsey, A. C., Pomeroy, W. B., Martin, C. E., & Gebhard, P. H. (1953). *Sexual behavior in the human female.* Philadelphia: Saunders.

Kirby, D., Short, L., Collins, J., Rugg, D., Kolbe, L., Howard, M., Miller, B., Sonenstein, F., & Zabin, L. S. (1994). School-based programs to reduce sexual risk behaviors: A review of effectiveness. *Public Health Reports, 109,* 339–360.

Kirigin, K. A., Wolf, M. M., Braukman, C. J., Fixsen, D. L., & Phillips, E. L. (1979). A preliminary outcome evaluation. In J. S. Stumphauzer (Ed.), *Progress in behavior therapy with delinquents* (pp. 118–145). Springfield, IL: Chas C. Thomas.

Klaus, R. A., & Gray, S. W. (1968). The early training project for disadvantaged children: A report after five years. *Monographs of the Society for Research in Child Development, 33*(4, Serial No. 120).

Klebanoff, M. A., Gronbard, B. I., Kessel, S. S., & Berendes, H. W. (1984). Low birth weight across generations. *Journal of the American Medical Association, 252,* 2423–2427.

Klein, J. R., & Litt, I. F. (1984). Menarche and dysmenorrhea. In J. Brooks-Gunn & A. C. Petersen (Eds.), *Girls at puberty: Biological, psychological, and social perspectives.* New York: Plenum.

Klein, M. W. (1979). Deinstitutionalization and diversion of juvenile offenders: A litany of impediments. In N. Morris & M. Tonry (Eds.), *Crime and justice: An annual review of research* (Vol. 1, pp. 145–201). Chicago: University of Chicago.

Klerman, G. L. (1988). Depression and related disorders of mood (affective disorders). In A. M. Nicholi, Jr., (Ed.), *The new Harvard guide to psychiatry* (pp. 309–336). Cambridge, MA: Harvard University Press.

Kliegman, R. M., & King, K. C. (1983). Intrauterine growth retardation: Determinants of aberrant fetal growth. In A. A. Fanaroff, R. J. Martin, & J. R. Merkatz (Eds.), *Behrman's neonatal-perinatal medicine.* St. Louis: Mosby.

Kligman, D., Smyrl, R., & Emde, R. (1975). A non-intrusive longitudinal study of infant sleep. *Psychosomatic Medicine, 37,* 448–453.

Klinnert, M. D., Campos, J., Sorce, J. F., Emde, R. N., & Svejda, M. J. (1983). Social referencing. In P. Plutchik & H. Kellerman (Eds.), *The emotions in early development.* New York: Academic Press.

Knoblock, H., & Pasamanick, B. (1966). Prospective studies on the epidemiology of reproductive casualty: Methods, findings, and some implications. *Merrill-Palmer Quarterly of Behavior and Development, 12,* 27–43.

Koff, E., Rierdan, J., & Jacobson, S. (1981). The personal and interpersonal significance of menarche. *Journal of the American Academy of Child Psychiatry, 20,* 148–158.

Kohlberg, L. (1963). The development of children's orientations toward a moral order: I. Sequence in the development of human thought. *Vita Humana, 6,* 11–33.

Kohlberg, L. (1964). Development of moral character and moral ideology. In M. L. Hoffman & L. W. Hoffman (Eds.), *Review of child development research* (Vol. 1). New York: Russell Sage.

Kohlberg, L. (1966). A cognitive-developmental analysis of children's sex role concepts and attitudes. In E. E. Maccoby (Ed.), *The development of sex differences.* Stanford, CA: Stanford University Press.

Kohlberg, L. (1969). Stage and sequence: The cognitive-developmental approach to socialization. In D. A. Goslin (Ed.), *Handbook of socialization theory and research.* Chicago: Rand McNally.

Kohlberg, L. (1976). Moral stages and moralization: The cognitive-developmental approach. In T. Lickona (Ed.), *Moral development and behavior.* New York: Holt, Rinehart, and Winston.

Kohlberg, L. (1978). Revisions in the theory and practice of moral development. In W. Damon (Ed.), *Moral development: New directions for child development* (No. 2.). San Francisco: Jossey-Bass.

Kohlberg, L., & Gilligan, C. (1972). The adolescent as a philosopher: The discovery of the self in a postconventional world. In J. Kagan & R. Coles (Eds.), *12 to 16: Early adolescence.* New York: Norton.

Konopka, G. (1976). *Young girls: A portrait of adolescence.* Englewood Cliffs, NJ: Prentice-Hall.

Koop, C. E. (1986). *Surgeon General's report on acquired immune deficiency syndrome.* Washington, DC: U.S. Department of Health and Human Services.

Kopp, C. B., & McCall, R. B. (1982). Predicting later mental performance for normal, at-risk, and handicapped infants. In P. B. Baltes & O. G. Brim, Jr. (Eds.), *Life-span development and behavior* (Vol. 4, pp. 33–61). New York: Academic Press.

Kopp, C. B., & Parmelee, A. H. (1979). Prenatal and perinatal influences on infant behavior. In J. Osofsky (Ed.), *Handbook of infant development.* New York: Wiley.

Korner, A. F. (1987). Preventive intervention with high-risk newborns: Theoretical, conceptual, and methodological perspectives. In J. D. Osofsky (Ed.), *Handbook of infant development* (pp. 1006–1036). New York: Wiley.

Korones, S. B. (1986). *High risk newborn infants.* St. Louis: Mosby.

Kotelchuck, M., Schwartz, J., Anderka, M., & Finison, K. (1983). *1980 Massachusetts Special Supplemental Food Program for Women, Infants, and Children (WIC) evaluation project.* Prepublication manuscript.

Kovach, J. A., & Glickman, N. W. (1986). Levels and psychosocial correlates of adolescent drug use. *Journal of Youth and Adolescence, 15,* 61–78.

Kovacs, M., Feinberg, T. L., Crouse-Novak, M. A., Paulauskas, S. L., & Finkelstein, R. (1984). Depressive disorders in childhood. I.: A longitudinal prospective study of characteristics and recovery. *Archives of General Psychiatry, 41,* 229–237.

Kozol, J. (1988a). Rachel and her children: Homeless families in America. New York: Crown.

Kozol, J. (1988b). Heartbreak hotel. *Journal of Christian Nursing, 5,* 4–8.

Krebs, D., & Sturrup, B. (1982). Role-taking ability and altruistic behavior in elementary school children. *Journal of Moral Education, 11,* 94–100.

Kreutzer, M. A., Leonard, C., & Flavell, J. H. (1975). An interview study of children's knowledge about memory. *Monographs of the Society for Research in Child Development, 40*(1, Serial No. 159).

Kuczynski, L. (1983). Reasoning, prohibitions, and motivations for compliance. *Developmental Psychology, 19,* 126–134.

Kuczynski, L., Zahn-Waxler, C., & Radke-Yarrow, M. (1987). Development and content of imitation in the second and third year of life. *Developmental Psychology, 23,* 276–282.

Kuhl, P., & Meltzoff, A. (1982). The bimodal perception of speech in infancy. *Science, 218,* 1138–1141.

Kurdek, L. A., & Krile, D. (1982). A developmental analysis of the relation between peer acceptance and both interpersonal understanding and perceived social self-competence. *Child Development, 53,* 1485–1491.

Laboratory of Comparative Human Cognition (1983). Culture and cognitive development. In P. H. Mussen (Series Ed.) & W. Kessen (Ed.), *Handbook of child psychology: Vol. 1. History, theory, and methods* (pp. 295–358). New York: Wiley.

Labov, W. (1970). The logic of nonstandard English. In F. Williams (Ed.), *Language and poverty: Perspectives on a theme.* Chicago: Markham.

LaGasse, L. L., Gruber, C. P., & Lipsitt, L. P. (1989). The infantile expression of avidity in relation to later assessments of inhibition and attachment. In J. S. Reznick (Ed.), *Perspectives on behavioral inhibition* (pp. 159–176). Chicago: University of Chicago Press.

Lamb, M. E., Hwang, C. P., Frodi, A. M., & Frodi, M. (1982). Security of mother and father infant attachment and its relation to sociability with strangers in traditional and nontraditional Swedish families. *Infant Behavior and Development, 5,* 355–368.

Lamb, S. (1988). *The emergence of moral concern in the second year of life.* Unpublished doctoral dissertation, Harvard University, Cambridge, MA.

Lamborn, S. D., Mounts, N. S., Steinberg, L., & Dornbusch, S. M. (1991). Patterns of competence and adjustment among adolescents from authoritative, authoritarian, indulgent, and neglectful families. *Child Development, 62,* 1049–1065.

Landau, R., & Gleitman, L. (1985). *Language and experience.* Cambridge, MA: Harvard University Press.

Langlois, J. H., Roggman, L. A., Casey, R. J., Ritter, J. M., Rieser-Danner, L. A., & Jenkins, V. Y. (1987). Infant preference for attractive faces: Rudiments of a stereotype. *Developmental Psychology, 23,* 363–369.

Lapouse, R., & Monk, M. A. (1959). Fears and worries in a representative sample of children. *American Journal of Orthopsychiatry, 29,* 223–248.

Largo, R. H., & Schinzel, A. (1985). Developmental and behavioral disturbances in 13 boys with fragile-X syndrome. *European Journal of Pediatrics, 143,* 269–275.

Larson, L. E. (1972a). The influence of parents and peers during adolescence. *Journal of Marriage and the Family, 34,* 67–74.

Larson, L. E. (1972b). The relative influence of parent-adolescent affect in predicting the salience hierarchy among youth. *Pacific Sociological Review, 15,* 83–102.

Larson, R., & Richards, M. H. (1991). Daily companionship in late childhood and early adolescence: Changing developmental contexts. *Child Development, 62,* 284–300.

Laursen, B., & Collins, W. A. (1994). Interpersonal conflict during adolescence. *Psychological Bulletin, 115,* 197–209.

Lavine, L. O. (1982). Parental power as a potential influence on girls: Career choice. *Child Development, 53,* 658–661.

LaVoi, J. C. (1973). Punishment and adolescent self-control. *Developmental Psychology, 8,* 16–24.

Lawton, T. A. (1992). *Maternal cocaine addiction: Correlates and consequences.* Unpublished doctoral dissertation, University of Michigan, Ann Arbor, MI.

Lazar, I., & Darlington, R. (1982). Lasting effects of early education: A report from the Consortium of Longitudinal Studies. *Monographs of the Society for Research in Child Development, 33*(Serial No. 120).

Lee, V. E., Brooks-Gunn, J., & Schnur, E. (1988). Does Head Start work? A 1-year follow-up comparison of disadvantaged children attending Head Start, no preschool, and other preschool programs. *Developmental Psychology, 24,* 210–222.

Lefkowitz, M. M., Eron, L. D., Walder, L. O., & Huesmann, L. R. (1977). *Growing up to be violent.* New York: Pergamon.

Leibold, S. R. (1988). Infant life on a monitor: Family implications. In P. W. Power, A. E. Dell, & M. B. Gibbons (Eds.), *Family interventions throughout chronic illness and disability* (pp. 60–73). New York: Springer.

Leiman, B. (1978, August). *Affective empathy and subsequent altruism in kindergartners and first graders.* Paper presented at the meeting of the American Psychological Association, Toronto.

LeMare, L. J., & Rubin, K. H. (1987). Perspective taking and peer interaction: Structural and developmental analyses. *Child Development, 58,* 306–315.

Lemish, D., & Rice, M. L. (1986). Television as a talking picture book: A prop for language acquisition. *Journal of Child Language, 13,* 251–274.

Lempers, J. C., Flavell, E. R., & Flavell, J. H. (1978). The development in very young children of tacit knowledge concerning visual perception. *Genetic Psychology Monographs, 95,* 3–53.

Lempert, H. (1984). Topic: A starting point for syntax. *Monographs of the Society for Research in Child Development, 49*(Serial No. 208).

Lennon, R., Eisenberg, N., & Carroll, J. (1986). The relation between nonverbal indices of sympathy and preschoolers' prosocial behavior. *Journal of Applied Developmental Psychology, 7,* 219–224.

Lepper, M. R. (1981). Intrinsic and extrinsic motivation in children: Detrimental effects of superfluous social controls. In W. A. Collins (Ed.), *Minnesota Symposia on Child Psychology* (Vol. 14). Hillsdale, NJ: LEA.

Lepper, M. R. (1983). Social control processes, attributions of motivation, and the internalization of social values. In E. T. Higgins, D. N. Ruble, & W. W. Hartup (Eds.), *Social cognition and social behavior: Developmental perspectives.* New York: Cambridge University Press.

Lerner, R. M. (1991). Changing organism-context relations as the basic process of development: A developmental contextual perspective. *Developmental Psychology, 27,* 27–32.

Lerner, R. M., & Knapp, J. R. (1975). Actual and perceived intrafamilial attitudes of late adolescents and their parents. *Journal of Youth and Adolescence, 4,* 17–36.

Lerner, R. M., & Lerner, J. (1977). Effects of age, sex, and physical attractiveness on child-peer relations, academic performance, and elementary school adjustment. *Developmental Psychology, 13,* 585–590.

Lesser, G. S., & Kandel, D. (1969). Parent-adolescent relationships and adolescent independence in the United States and Denmark. *Journal of Marriage and the Family, 31,* 348–358.

Lester, B. M., Corwin, M. J., Sepkoski, C., Seifer, R., Pencker, M., McLaughlin, S., & Golub, H. L. (1991). Neurobehavioral syndromes in cocaine-exposed newborn infants. *Child Development, 62,* 694–705.

Leung, E. H. L., & Rheingold, H. L. (1981). Development of pointing as a social gesture. *Developmental Psychology, 17,* 215–220.

Levine, L. E. (1983). Mine: Self definitions in two year old boys. *Developmental Psychology, 19,* 544–549.

Levitt, M. J., Guacci-Franco, N., & Levitt, J. L. (1993). Convoys of social support in childhood and early adolescence: Structure and function. *Developmental Psychology, 29,* 811–818.

Levy-Shiff, R. (1982). Effects of father absence on young children in mother-headed families. *Child Development, 53,* 1400–1405.

Lewine, R. R. J. (1980). Sex differences in age of symptom onset and first hospitalization in schizophrenia. *American Journal of Orthopsychiatry, 50,* 316–322.

Lewis, M. (1990). Challenges to the study of developmental psychopathology. In M. Lewis & S. M. Miller (eds.), *The handbook of developmental psychopathology* (pp. 29–40). New York: Plenum.

Lewis, M., & Brooks-Gunn, J. (1979). *Social cognition and the acquisition of self.* New York: Plenum.

Liben, L. S., & Downs, R. M. (1989). Understanding maps as symbols: The development of map concepts in children. In H. Reese (Ed.), *Advances in child development and behavior* (Vol. 22, pp. 145–201). New York: Academic Press.

Liben, L. S., & Signorella, M. L. (Eds.). (1987). *New directions for child development: Vol. 38. Children's gender schemata.* San Francisco: Jossey-Bass.

Liebert, R. M., & Baron, R. A. (1972). Some immediate effects of televised violence on children's behavior. *Developmental Psychology, 6,* 469–475.

Liebert, R. M., & Sprafkin, J. (1988). *The early window: Effects of television on children and youth* (3rd ed.). New York: Pergamon.

Linn, M. C., & Petersen, A. C. (1985). Emergence and characterization of sex differences in spatial ability: A meta-analysis. *Child Development, 56,* 1479–1498.

Linn, S., Reznick, J. S., Kagan, J., & Hans, S. (1982). Salience of visual patterns in the human infant. *Developmental Psychology, 18,* 651–657.

Lippsitt, L. P. (1977). Taste in human neonates: Its effects on sucking and heart rate. In J. M. Weiffenbach (Ed.), *Taste and development: The genesis of sweet preference.* Washington, DC: U.S. Government Printing Office.

Little, G. A. (1987). The fetus at risk. In R. A. Hekelman, S. Blatman, S. B. Friedman, N. M. Nelson, & H. M. Seidel (Eds.), *Primary pediatric care* (pp. 397–410). St. Louis: Mosby.

Livesley, W. J., & Bromley, D. B. (1973). *Person perception in childhood and adolescence.* London: Wiley.

Livson, N., & Peskin, H. (1980). Perspectives on adolescence from longitudinal research. In J. Adelson (Ed.), *Handbook of adolescent psychology* (pp. 47–98). New York: Wiley.

Loeber, R., & Stouthamer-Loeber, M. (1986). Family factors as correlates and predictors of juvenile conduct problems and delinquency. In M. Tonry & N. Morris (Eds.), *Crime and justice: An annual review of research* (Vol 7., pp. 29–150). Chicago: University of Chicago Press.

Loehlin, J. C., & Nichols, R. C. (1976). *Heredity, environment, and personality.* Austin: University of Texas Press.

Loftus, E. (1993). The reality of repressed memories. *American Psychologist, 48,* 518–537.

Londerville, S., & Main, M. (1981). Security of attachment and compliance in maternal training methods in the second year of life. *Developmental Psychology, 17,* 289–299.

London, P. (1970). The rescuers: Motivational hypotheses about Christians who saved Jews from the Nazis. In J. Macaulay & L. Berkowitz (Eds.), *Altruism and helping behavior.* New York: Academic Press.

Lorenz, K. Z. (1981). *The foundations of ethology.* New York: Springer-Verlag.

Lorion, R. P., Tolan, P. H., & Wahler, R. G. (1987). Prevention. In H. C. Quay (Ed.), *Handbook of juvenile delinquency* (pp. 383–416). New York: Wiley.

Lubchenco, L. O. (1976). *The high risk of infants.* Philadelphia: Saunders.

Lubchenco, L. O., Searls, D. T., & Brazie, J. F. (1972). Neonatal mortality rate: Relationship to birth weight and gestational age. *Journal of Pediatrics, 81,* 814–822.

Lytton, H. (1977). Do parents create, or respond to, differences in twins? *Developmental Psychology, 13,* 456–459.

Maccoby, E. E. (1984). Middle childhood in the context of the family. In W. A. Collins (Ed.), *Development during middle childhood: The years from six to twelve.* Washington, DC: National Academy Press.

Maccoby, E. E., & Jacklin, C. N. (1974). *The psychology of sex differences.* Stanford, CA: Stanford University Press.

Maccoby, E. E., & Jacklin, C. N. (1980). Sex differences in aggression: A rejoinder and reprise. *Child Development, 51,* 964–980.

Maccoby, E. E., & Martin, J. A. (1983). Socialization in the context of the family: Parent-child interaction. In P. H. Mussen (Series Ed.) & E. M. Hetherington (Ed.), *Handbook of child psychology: Vol. 4. Socialization, personality and social behavior* (4th ed., pp. 1–102). New York: Wiley.

Maccoby, E. E., Snow, M. E., & Jacklin, C. N. (1984). Children's dispositions and mother-child interactions at 12 and 18 months: A short-term longitudinal study. *Developmental Psychology, 20,* 459–472.

Macfarlane, A. (1975). *Olfaction in the development of social preferences in the human neonate. CIBA Foundation Symposium 33: Parent-infant interaction.* Amsterdam: Elsevier.

Madden, J., Payne, R., & Miller, S. (1986). Maternal cocaine abuse and effects on the newborn. *Pediatrics, 77,* 209–211.

Madsen, M. C. (1967). Cooperative and competitive motivation of children in three Mexican sub-cultures. *Psychological Reports, 20,* 1307–1320.

Madsen, M. C., & Shapira, A. (1970). Cooperative and competitive behavior of urban Afro-American, Anglo-American, Mexican-American, and Mexican village children. *Developmental Psychology, 3,* 16–20.

Magsud, M. (1979). Resolution of moral dilemmas by Nigerian secondary school pupils. *Journal of Moral Education, 7,* 40–49.

Main, M., & George, C. (1979). Social interaction of young abused children: Approach, avoidance, and aggression. *Child Development, 50,* 306–318.

Main, M., & Hesse, E. (1990). Parents' unresolved traumatic experiences are related to infant disorganized attachment status: Is frightened and/or frightening parental behavior the linking mechanism? In M. T. Greenberg, D. Cicchetti, & E. M. Cummings (Eds.), *Attachment in the preschool years: Theory, research and intervention* (pp. 161–182). Chicago: University of Chicago Press.

Main, M., Kaplan, N., & Cassidy, J. (1985). Security in infancy, childhood, and adulthood: A move to the level of representation. In I. Bretherton & E. Waters (Eds.), *Monographs of the Society for Research in Child Development, 50* (No. 1–2).

Main, M., & Solomon, J. (1986). Discovery of an insecure-disorganized/disoriented attachment pattern. In T. B. Brazelton & M. W. Yogmen (Eds.), *Affective development in infancy.* New Jersey: Ablex Publishing.

Main, M., & Solomon, J. (1990). Procedures for identifying infants as disorganized/disoriented during the Ainsworth Strange Situation. In M. T. Greenberg, D. Cicchetti, & E. M. Cummings (Eds.), *Attachment in the preschool years: Theory, research, and intervention* (pp. 121–160). Chicago: University of Chicago Press.

Main, M., Weston, D. R., & Wakeling, S. (1979). *"Concerned attention" to crying of an adult actor in infancy.* Paper presented at the meeting of the Society for Research in Child Development, San Francisco.

Mandler, J. M., & McDonough, L. (1995). Long term recall of event sequence in infancy. *Journal of Experimental Child Psychology, 59,* 457–474.

Marcia, J. E. (1980). Identity in adolescence. In J. Adelson (Ed.), *Handbook of adolescent psychology.* New York: Wiley.

Marcia, J. E., & Friedman, M. L. (1970). Ego identity status in college women. *Journal of Personality, 38,* 249–263.

Marcus, G. F., Pinker, S., Ullman, M., Hollander, M., Rosen, T. J., & Xu, F. (1992). Overregularization in language acquisition. *Monographs of the Society for Research in Child Development, 57*(4, Serial No. 228).

Marcus, J., Hans, S. L., Nagler, S., Auerbach, J. G., Mirsky, A. P., & Aubrey, A. (1987). Review of the NIMH Israel Kibbutz-city study and the Jerusalem infant development study. *Schizophrenia Bulletin, 13,* 425–438.

Markman, E. M., & Hutchinson, J. E. (1984). Children's sensitivity to constraints on word meaning: Taxonomic vs. thematic relations. *Cognitive Psychology, 16,* 1–27.

Marsh, H. W. (1985). Age and sex effects in multiple dimensions of preadolescent self-concept: A replication and extension. *Australian Journal of Psychology, 37,* 167–179.

Marsh, H. W., Smith, I. D., & Barnes, J. (1985). Multidimensional self-concepts: Relations with sex and academic achievement. *Journal of Educational Psychology, 77,* 581–596.

Marshall, W. A. (1978). Puberty. In F. Falkner & J. M. Tanner (Eds.), *Human growth: Vol. 2. Postnatal growth.* New York: Plenum.

Marshall, W. A., & Tanner, J. M. (1970). Variations in the pattern of pubertal changes in boys. *Archives of Disease in Childhood, 45,* 13.

Marsiglio, W., & Mott, F. L. (1986). The impact of sex education on sexual activity, contraceptive use and premarital pregnancy among American teenagers. *Family Planning Perspectives, 18,* 151–162.

Martin, B. (1975). Parent-child relations. In F. D. Horowitz, E. M. Hetherington, S. Scarr-Salapatek, & G. M. Siegel (Eds.), *Review of child development research* (Vol. 4). Chicago: University of Chicago Press.

Martin, B., & Hoffman, J. A. (1990). Conduct disorders. In M. Lewis & S. M. Miller (Eds.), *Handbook of developmental psychopathology* (pp. 109–117). New York: Plenum.

Martin, C. L., & Halverson, C. F., Jr. (1981). A schematic processing model of sex typing and stereotyping in children. *Child Development, 52,* 1119–1134.

Mash, E. J., & Johnston, C. A. (1982). A comparison of the mother-child interactions of younger and older hyperactive and normal children. *Child Development, 53,* 1371–1381.

Mash, E. J., & Johnston, C. (1983). Parental perceptions of child behavior problems, parenting self-esteem, and mothers' reported stress in younger and older hyperactive and normal children. *Journal of Consulting and Clinical Psychology, 51,* 68–99.

Mash, E. J., Johnston, C., & Kovitz, K. A. (1983). A comparison of the mother-child interactions of physically abused and non-abused children during play and task situations. *Journal of Clinical Child Psychology, 12,* 337–346.

Masten, A. S., Morison, P., & Pellegrini, D. S. (1985). A devised class play method of peer assessment. *Developmental Psychology, 21,* 523–533.

Matas, L., Arend, R. A., & Sroufe, L. A. (1978). Continuity of adaptation in the second year: The relationship between quality of attachment and later competence. *Child Development, 49,* 547–556.

Matheny, A. P., Jr. (1983). A longitudinal twin study of stability of components from Bayley's Infant Behavior Record. *Child Development, 54,* 356–360.

Matheny, A. P., Jr., Wilson, R. S., Dolan, A. B., & Krantz, J. Z. (1981). Behavior contrasts in twinships: Stability and patterns of differences in childhood. *Child Development, 52,* 579–588.

McCall, R. B. (1983). Environmental effects on intelligence: The forgotten realm of discontinuous nonshared within–family factors. *Child Development, 54,* 408–415.

McCall, R. B., Appelbaum, M. I., & Hogarty, P. S. (1973). Developmental changes in mental performance. *Monographs of the Society for Research in Child Development, 38*(3, Serial No. 150).

McCall, R. B., & Carriger, M. S. (1993). A meta-analysis of infant habituation and recognition memory performance as predictors of later IQ. *Child Development, 64,* 57–79.

McCartney, K., Scarr, S., Phillips, D., & Grajek, S. (1985). Day care as intervention: Comparisons of varying quality programs. *Journal of Applied Developmental Psychology, 6,* 247–260.

McCord, J. (1990). Problem behavior. In S. S. Feldman & G. R. Elliott (Eds.), *At the threshold: The developing adolescent* (pp. 414–430). Cambridge, MA: Harvard University Press.

McGuire, W. J., McGuire, C. V., Child, P., & Fujioka, T. (1978). Salience of ethnicity in the spontaneous self-concept as a function of one's ethnic distinctiveness in a social environment. *Journal of Personality and Social Psychology, 36,* 511–520.

McLoyd, V. C. (1989). Socialization and development in a changing economy: The effects of paternal job and income loss on children. *American Psychologist, 44,* 293–302.

McLoyd, V. C., Jayaratne, T. E., Ceballo, R., & Borquez, J. (1994). Unemployment and work interruption among African American single mothers: Effects on parenting and adolescent socioemotional functioning. *Child Development, 65,* 562–589.

Mednick, S. A., Parnas, J., & Schulsinger, F. (1987). The Copenhagen high-risk project, 1962–1986. *Schizophrenia Bulletin, 13,* 485–495.

Medrich, E. A., Rosen, J., Rubin, V., & Buckley, S. (1982). *The serious business of growing up: A study of children's lives outside of school.* Berkeley: University of California Press.

Meltzoff, A. N. (1988). Infant imitations and memory: Nine-month-olds in immediate and deferred tests. *Child Development, 59,* 217–225.

Meltzoff, A. N., & Borton, R. W. (1979). Intermodal matching by human neonates. *Nature, 282,* 403–404.

Meltzoff, A. N., & Moore, M. K. (1977). Imitation of facial and manual gestures by human neonates. *Science, 198,* 75–78.

Menken, J. (1980). The health and demographic consequence of adolescent pregnancy and childbearing. In C. Chilman (Ed.), *Adolescent pregnancy and childbearing: Findings from research.* Washington, DC: U.S. Department of Health and Human Services.

Mervis, C. B. (1987). Child-basic object categories and early lexical development. In U. Neisser (Ed.), *Concepts and conceptual development: Ecological and intellectual factors in categorization* (pp. 201–233). New York: Cambridge University Press.

Messaris, P., & Hornik, R. C. (1983). Work status, television exposure, and educational outcomes. In C. D. Hayes & S. B. Kamerman (Eds.), *Children of working parents: Experiences and outcomes* (pp. 44–72). Washington, DC: National Academy Press.

Metcoff, J. (1978). Association of fetal growth with maternal nutrition. In F. Falkner & J. M. Tanner (Eds.), *Human growth: Vol. 1. Principles and prenatal growth.* New York: Plenum.

Millar, W. S., & Watson, J. S. (1979). The effect of delayed feedback on infant learning reexamined. *Child Development, 50,* 747–751.

Miller, B. C., & Moore, K. A. (1990). Adolescent sexual behavior, pregnancy, and parenting: Research through the 1980s. *Journal of Marriage and the Family, 52,* 1025–1044.

Miller, M. L., Chiles, J. A., & Barnes, V. E. (1982). Suicide attempters within a delinquent population. *Journal of Consulting and Clinical Psychology, 50,* 490–498.

Miller, P. H., Haynes, V. F., DeMarie-Dreblow, D., & Woody-Ramsey, J. (1986). Children's strategies for gathering information in three tasks. *Child Development, 57,* 1429–1439.

Miller, S. M., Birnbaum, A., & Durbin, D. (1990). Etiological perspectives on depression in childhood. In M. Lewis & S. M. Miller (Eds.), *Handbook of developmental psychopathology* (pp. 311–325). New York: Plenum.

Miller, S. M., Boyer, B. A., & Rodoletz, M. (1990). Anxiety in children: Nature and development. In M. Lewis & S. M. Miller (Eds.), *Handbook of developmental psychopathology* (pp. 191–207). New York: Plenum.

Minton, C., Kagan, J., & Levine, J. A. (1971). Maternal control and obedience in the two-year-old. *Child Development, 42,* 1873–1894.

Minuchin, P. (1985). Families and individual development: Provocations from the field of family therapy. *Child Development, 56,* 289–302.

Minuchin, P. P., & Shapiro, E. K. (1983). The school as a context for social development. In P. H. Mussen (Series Ed.) & E. M. Hetherington (Ed.), *Handbook of child psychology: Vol. 4. Socialization, personality and social development* (4th ed., pp. 197–274). New York: Wiley.

Minuchin, S., Rosman, B. L., & Baker, L. (1978). *Psychosomatic families: Anorexia nervosa in context.* Cambridge, MA: Harvard University Press.

Mischel, W. (1966). Theory and research on the antecedents of self-imposed delay of reward. In B. A. Maher (Ed.), *Progress in experimental personality research* (Vol. 3). New York: Academic Press.

Mischel, W. (1968). *Personality and assessment.* New York: Wiley.

Mischel, W. (1970). Sex typing and socialization. In P. H. Mussen (Ed.), *Carmichael's manual of child psychology* (Vol. 2, 3rd ed). New York: Wiley.

Mischel, W. (1974). Processes in the delay of gratification. In L. Berkowitz (Ed.), *Advances in experimental social psychology* (Vol. 7). New York: Academic Press.

Mischel, W., & Ebbesen, E. B. (1970). Attention in delay of gratification. *Journal of Personality and Social Psychology, 16,* 329–337.

Mischel, W., & Metzner, R. (1962). Effects of attention to symbolically presented rewards upon self-control. *Journal of Abnormal and Social Psychology, 64,* 425–431.

Mischel, W., & Patterson, C. J. (1978). Effective plans for self-control in children. In W. A. Collins (Ed.), *Minnesota Symposia on Child Psychology* (Vol. 11, pp. 199–230). Hillsdale, NJ: Erlbaum.

Mishkin, M., & Appenzeller, T. (1987). The anatomy of memory. *Scientific American, 256,* 80–89.

Moffitt, T. E. (1990a). Juvenile delinquency and attention deficit disorder: Boys' developmental trajectories from age 3 to age 15. *Child Development, 61,* 893–910.

Moffitt, T. E. (1990b). The neuropsychology of juvenile delinquency: A critical review. In M. Tonry & N. Morris (Eds.), *Crime and justice: A review of research* (Vol. 12, pp. 99–169). Chicago: University of Chicago Press.

Moffitt, T. E. (1993). Adolescence-limited and life-course-persistent antisocial behavior: A developmental taxonomy. *Psychological Review, 100,* 674–701.

Moffitt, T. E., Caspi, A., Belsky, J., & Silva, P. A. (1992). Childhood experience and the onset of menarche: A test of a sociobiological model. *Child Development, 63,* 47–58.

Moir, J. (1974). Egocentrism and the emergence of conventional morality in preadolescent girls. *Child Development, 45,* 299–304.

Mondell, S., & Tyler, F. (1981). Parental competence and styles of problem solving/play behavior with children. *Developmental Psychology, 17,* 73–78.

Monighan-Nourot, P., Scales, B., Van Hoorn, J., with Almy, M. (1987). *Looking at children's play: A bridge between theory and practice.* New York: Teachers College Press.

Moore, B. S., & Eisenberg, N. (1984). The development of altruism. In G. Whitehurst (Ed.), *Annals of child development* (pp. 107–174). Greenwich, CT: JAI Press.

Moore, D. R., & Arthur, J. L. (1989). Juvenile delinquency. In T. H. Ollendick & M. Herson (Eds.), *Handbook of child psychopathology* (2nd ed., pp. 197–217). New York : Plenum.

Moore, E. G. J. (1986). Family socialization and the IQ test performance of traditionally and transracially adopted black children. *Developmental Psychology, 22,* 317–326.

Moore, K. A., Nord, C. W., & Peterson, J. L. (1989). Nonvoluntary sexual activity among adolescents. *Family Planning Perspectives, 21,* 110–114.

Moore, K. L. (1982). *The developing human: Clinically oriented embryology* (3rd ed.). Philadelphia: Saunders.

Morelli, G. A., Rogoff, B., Oppenheim, D., & Goldsmith, D. (1992). Cultural variation in infants' sleeping arrangements: Questions of independence. *Developmental Psychology, 28,* 604–613.

Morgan, J. L., & Travis, L. L. (1989). Limits on negative information in language input. *Journal of Child Language, 16,* 531–552.

Morgan, M., & Gross, L. (1982). Television and educational achievement and aspiration. In D. Pearl, J. Bouthilet, & J. Lazar (Eds.), *Television and behavior: Ten years of scientific progress and implications for the eighties* (Vol. 2). Washington, DC: U.S. Government Printing Office.

Morison, P., & Masten, A. S. (1991). Peer reputation in middle childhood as a predictor of adaptation in adolescence: A seven-year follow-up. *Child Development, 62,* 991–1007.

Morrison, D. M. (1985). Adolescent contraceptive behavior: A review. *Psychological Bulletin, 98,* 538–568.

Moss, H. A., & Susman, E. J. (1980). Longitudinal study of personality development. In O. G. Brim & J. Kagan (Eds.), *Constancy and change in human development.* Cambridge, MA: Harvard University Press.

Mueller, E., & Brenner, J. (1977). The origin of social skills in interaction among play group toddlers. *Child Development, 48,* 854–861.

Mufson, L., Moreau, D., Weissman, M. M., & Klerman, G. L. (1993). *Interpersonal psychotherapy for depressed adolescents.* New York: Guilford Press.

Muir, D., Abraham, W., Forbes, B., & Harris, L. (1979). The ontogenesis of an auditory localization response from birth to four months of age. *Canadian Journal of Psychology, 33,* 320–333.

Munsinger, H. (1975). Children's resemblance to their biological and adopting parents in two ethnic groups. *Behavior Genetics, 5,* 239–254.

Murray, J. P., & Kippax, S. (1978). Children's social behavior in three towns with differing television experience. *Journal of Communication, 28,* 19–29.

Mussen, P. H., & Jones, M. C. (1957). Self-conceptions, motivations, and interpersonal attitudes of late and early maturing boys. *Child Development, 28,* 243–256.

Myers, B. J. (1982). Early intervention using the Brazelton training with middle-class mothers and fathers of newborns. *Child Development, 53,* 462–471.

National Academy of Sciences (1989). *Recommended dietary allowances.* Washington, DC: National Academy of Sciences.

National Commission on Youth. (1980). *The transition to adulthood: A bridge too long.* New York: Westview Press.

Neimark, E. D. (1975a). Intellectual development during adolescence. In F. D. Horowitz (Ed.), *Review of child development research* (Vol. 4). Chicago: University of Chicago Press.

Neimark, E. D. (1975b). Longitudinal development of formal operations thought. *Genetic Psychology Monographs, 91,* 171–225.

Nelson, K. (1975). Individual differences in early semantic and syntax development. In D. Aaronson & R. W. Rieber (Eds.), *Developmental psycholinguistics and communication disorders. Annals of the New York Academy of Science, 263,* 132–139.

Newcomb, A. F., & Bagwell, C. L. (1995). Children's friendship relations: A meta-analytic review. *Psychological Bulletin, 117,* 306–347.

Newcomb, A. F., Bukowski, W. M., & Pattee, L. (1993). Children's peer relations: A meta-analytic review of popular, rejected, neglected, controversial, and average sociometric status. *Psychological Bulletin, 113,* 99–128.

Newcombe, N. (1982). Sex-related differences in spatial ability: Problems and gaps in current approaches. In M. Potegal (Ed.), *Spatial abilities: Developmental and physiological foundations.* New York: Academic Press.

Newcombe, N., & Dubas, J. S. (1992). A longitudinal study of predictors of spatial ability in adolescent females. *Child Development, 63,* 37–46.

Newcombe, N., & Huttenlocher, J. (1992). Children's early ability to solve perspective-taking problems. *Developmental Psychology, 28,* 635–643.

Newcombe, N., & Lerner, J. C. (1982). Britain between the wars: The historical context of Bowlby's theory of attachment. *Psychiatry, 45,* 1–12.

Newcombe, N., & Zaslow, M. (1981). Hints and question directives in the speech of 2½-year-old children to adults. *Discourse Processes, 4,* 239–252.

Newport, E. (1991). Contrasting conceptions of the critical period for language. In S. Carey & R. Gelman (Eds.), *The epigenesis of mind: Essays on biology and cognition* (pp. 111–130). Hillsdale, NJ: Erlbaum.

Newport, E. L., Gleitman, H., & Gleitman, L. R. (1977). Mother, I'd rather do it myself: Some effects and noneffects of maternal speech style. In C. E. Snow & C. A. Ferguson (Eds.), *Talking to children.* Cambridge: Cambridge University Press.

Nezworski, T., Tolan, W. J., & Belsky, J. (1988). Intervention in insecure infant attachment. In J. Belsky & T. Nezworski (Eds.), *Clinical implications on attachment* (pp. 352–386). Hillsdale, NJ: LEA.

Nicholls, J. G. (1978). The development of the concepts of effort and ability, perception of academic attainment, and the understanding that difficult tasks require more ability. *Child Development, 49,* 800–814.

Nicholls, J. G., & Miller, A. T. (1985). Differentiation of the concepts of luck and skill. *Developmental Psychology, 21,* 76–82.

Nilsson, L., Furuhjelm, M., Ingelman-Sundberg, A., & Wirsen, C. (1981). *A child is born.* New York: Dell (Delacorte Press).

Ninio, A., & Bruner, J. (1976). *The achievement and antecedents of labelling.* Unpublished paper, Hebrew University, Jerusalem.

Nisan, M., & Kohlberg, L. (1982). Universality and variation in moral judgment: A longitudinal and cross-sectional study in Turkey. *Child Development, 53,* 865–876.

Nolen-Hoeksema, S., & Girgus, J. S. (1994). The emergence of gender differences in depression during adolescence. *Psychological Bulletin, 115,* 424–443.

Nucci, L., & Nucci, M. (1982). Children's social interactions in the context of moral and conventional transgressions. *Child Development, 53,* 865–876.

Nucci, L., & Turiel, E. (1978). Social interactions and the development of social concepts in preschool children. *Child Development, 49,* 400–407.

Nurnberger, J. I., & Gershon, E. S. (1981). Genetics of affective disorders. In E. Friedman (Ed.), *Depression and antidepressants: Implications for courses and treatment.* New York: Raven.

O'Brien, M., & Huston, A. C. (1985). Development of sex-typed play behavior in toddlers. *Developmental Psychology, 21,* 866–871.

Oden, S., & Asher, S. F. (1977). Coaching children in social skills for friendship making. *Child Development, 48,* 95–506.

Offord, D. R., Boyle, M. H., Szatmari, P., Rae-Grant, N. I., Links, P. S., Cadman, D. T., Byles, J. A., Crawford, J. W., Monroe Blum, H., Byrne, C., Thomas, H., Woodward, C. (1987). Ontario Child Health Study: 2. Six month prevalence of disorders and rates of service utilization. *Archives of General Psychiatry, 44,* 832–836.

Ollendick, T. H. (1983). Reliability and validity of the Revised Fear Survey Schedule for Children (FSSC-R). *Behavior Research and Therapy, 21,* 685–692.

Ollendick, T. H., Matson, J. L., & Helsel, W. J. (1985). Fears in children and adolescents: Normative data. *Behavior Research and Therapy, 23,* 465–467.

Olweus, D. (1979). Stability of aggressive reaction patterns in males: A review. *Psychological Bulletin, 86,* 852–875.

Olweus, D. (1980). Familial and temperamental determinants of aggressive behavior in adolescent boys: A causal analysis. *Developmental Psychology, 16,* 644–660.

Orlofsky, J. L. (1978). Identity formation, achievement, and fear of success in college men and women. *Journal of Youth and Adolescence, 7,* 49–62.

Orlofsky, J. L., Marcia, J., & Lesser, I. (1973). Ego identity status and the intimacy versus isolation crisis of young adulthood. *Journal of Personality and Social Psychology, 27,* 211–219.

O'Rourke, D. H., Gottesman, I. I., Suarez, B. K., Rice, J., & Reich, T. (1982). Refutation of the general single-locus model for the etiology of schizophrenia. *American Journal of Human Genetics, 34,* 630–649.

Ostrea, E. M., Jr., Brady, M., Gause, S., Raymundo, A. L., & Stevens, M. (1992). Drug screening of newborns by meconium analysis: A large-scale, prospective, epidemiologic study. *Pediatrics, 89,* 107–113.

Overton, W. F., Byrnes, J. P., & O'Brien, D. P. (1985). Developmental and individual differences in conditional reasoning: The role of contradiction training and cognitive style. *Developmental Psychology, 21,* 692–701.

Overton, W. F., Ward, S. L., Noveck, I., Black, J., & O'Brien, D. P. (1987). Form and content in the development of deductive reasoning. *Developmental Psychology, 23,* 22–30.

Ozer, D. J. (1987). Personality, intelligence, and spatial visualization: Correlates of mental rotations test performance. *Journal of Personality and Social Psychology, 53,* 129–134.

Page, D. C., Mosher, R., Simpson, E. M., Fisher, E. M. C., Mardon, G., Pollack, J., McGillivray, B., de la Chapelle, A., & Brown, L. G. (1987). The sex-determining region of the human chromosome encodes a finger protein. *Cell, 51,* 1091–1094.

Page, E. W., Villee, C. A., & Villee, D. B. (1981). *Human reproduction: Essentials of reproductive and perinatal medicine* (3rd ed.). Philadelphia: Saunders.

Paikoff, R. L., & Brooks-Gunn, J. (1991). Do parent-child relationships change during puberty? *Psychological Bulletin, 110,* 47–66.

Paikoff, R. L., Brooks-Gunn, J., & Carlton-Ford, S. (1991). Effect of reproductive status changes on family functioning and well-being of mothers and daughters. *Journal of Early Adolescence, 11,* 201–220.

Papousek, H. (1967). Experimental studies of appetitional behavior in human newborns and infants. In H. W. Stevenson & H. L. Rheingold (Eds.), *Early Behavior.* New York: Wiley.

Paris, S. G., Newman, R. S., & McVey, K. A. (1982). Learning the functional significance of mnemonic actions: A microgenetic study of strategy acquisition. *Journal of Experimental Child Psychology, 34,* 490–509.

Parke, R. D. (1977). Punishment in children: Effects, side effects, and alternative strategies. In H. L. Hom & P. A. Robinson (Eds.), *Psychological processes in early education.* New York: Academic Press.

Parke, R. D., Berkowitz, L., Leyens, J. P., West, S., & Sebastian, R. J. (1977). Some effects of violent and nonviolent movies on the behavior of juvenile delinquents. In L. Berkowitz (Ed.), *Advances in experimental social psychology* (Vol. 10). New York: Academic Press.

Parke, R. D., & Collmer, C. W. (1975). Child abuse: An interdisciplinary analysis. In E. M. Hetherington, J. W. Hagen, R. Kron, & A. H. Stein (Eds.), *Review of child development research* (Vol. 5). Chicago: University of Chicago Press.

Parke, R. D., & Slaby, R. G. (1983). The development of aggression. In P. H. Mussen (Series Ed.) & E. M. Hetherington (Ed.), *Handbook of child psychology: Vol. 4. Socialization, personality, and social development* (4th ed., pp. 547–642). New York: Wiley.

Parke, R. D., & Tinsley, B. R. (1981). The father's role in infancy: Determinants of involvement in caregiving and play. In M. E. Lamb (Ed.), *The role of the father in child development.* New York: Wiley.

Parker, J. G., & Asher, S. R. (1987). Peer relation and later personal adjustment: Are low-income children at risk? *Psychological Bulletin, 102,* 357–389.

Parry-Jones, W. L. L. (1985). Adolescent disturbance. In M. Rutter & L. Hersov (Eds.), *Child and adolescent psychiatry: Modern approaches* (2nd ed., pp. 584–598). Oxford: Blackwell Scientific Publications.

Parsons, J. E., Adler, T. F., & Kaczala, C. M. (1982). Socialization of achievement attitudes and beliefs: Parental influences. *Child Development, 53,* 310–321.

Pastor, D. L. (1981). The quality of mother-infant attachment and its relationship to toddlers' initial sociability with peers. *Developmental Psychology, 17,* 326–335.

Patterson, G. R. (1976). The aggressive child: Victim and architect of a coercive system. In L. A. Hamerlynck, L. C. Handy, & E. J. Mash (Eds.), *Behavior modification and families: I. Theory and research.* New York: Brunner/Mazel.

Patterson, G. R. (1980). The unacknowledged victims. *Monographs of the Society for Research in Child Development, 45*(5, Serial No. 18b).

Patterson, G. R. (1982). *Coercive family process.* Eugene, OR: Castalia Press.

Patterson, G. R., & Dishion, T. J. (1985). Contributions of families and peers to delinquency. *Criminology, 23,* 63–79.

Payne, F. (1980). Children's prosocial conduct in structured situations and as viewed by others. *Child Development, 51,* 1252–1259.

Pea, R. D. (1980). The development of negation in early child language. In D. R. Olson (Ed.), *The social foundations of language and thought: Essays in honor of Jerome S. Bruner.* New York: Norton.

Pearce, J. (1982, March). Personal communication (cited in Graham, P., & Rutter, M. Adolescent disorders). In M. Rutter & L. Hersov (Eds.), *Child and adolescent psychiatry: Modern approaches* (pp. 351–367). Oxford: Blackwell Scientific Publications.

Peevers, B. H., & Secord, P. F. (1973). Developmental changes in attribution of descriptive concepts to persons. *Journal of Personality and Social Psychology, 27,* 120–128.

Pellegrini, A. D. (1985). Social-cognitive aspects of children's play: The effects of age, gender, and activity centers. *Journal of Applied Developmental Psychology, 6,* 129–140.

Penner, S. G. (1987). Parental responses to grammatical and ungrammatical child utterances. *Child Development, 58,* 376–384.

Pepler, D. J., Abramovitch, R., & Corter, C. (1981). Sibling interaction in the home: A longitudinal study. *Child Development, 52,* 1344–1347.

Perner, J., Ruffman, T., & Leekam, S. R. (1994). Theory of mind is contagious: You catch it from your sibs. *Child Development, 65,* 1228–1238.

Peskin, H. (1967). Pubertal onset and ego functioning. *Journal of Abnormal Psychology, 72,* 1–15.

Peskin, H. (1973). Influence of the developmental schedule of puberty on learning and ego functioning. *Journal of Youth and Adolescence, 2,* 273–290.

Petersen, A. C. (1988). Adolescent development. *Annual review of psychology, 39,* 583–608.

Peterson, L., & Brown, D. (1994). Integrating child injury and abuse-neglect research: Common histories, etiologies, and solutions. *Psychological Bulletin, 116,* 293–315.

Petitto, L. (1983). *From gesture to symbol.* Unpublished doctoral dissertation, Harvard University.

Petitto, L. A., & Marentette, P. F. (1991). Babbling in the manual mode: Evidence for the ontogeny of language. *Science, 251,* 1493–1496.

Phillips, D. A. (1987). Socialization of perceived academic competence among highly competent children. *Child Development, 58,* 1308–1320.

Phillips, D. A., McCartney, K., & Scarr, S. (1987). Child-care quality and children's social development. *Developmental Psychology, 23,* 537–543.

Phillips, L. D. (1991). *Ethnic self-identification in biethnic adolescents: Familial influences, psychological adjustment, and distress symptomology.* Unpublished master's thesis. Penn State University, University Park, PA.

Piaget, J. (1926). *The language and thought of the child.* London: Routledge & Kegan Paul.

Piaget, J. (1965). *The moral judgment of the child.* New York: Free Press. (Original work published 1932)

Piaget, J. (1951). *Play, dreams, and imitation in childhood.* New York: Norton.

Pinker, S. (1979). Formal models of language learning. *Cognition, 7,* 217–283.

Pinker, S. (1994). *The language instinct.* New York: W. Morrow & Co.

Pinon, M. F., Huston, A. C., & Wright, J. C. (1989). Family ecology and child characteristics that predict young children's educational television viewing. *Child Development, 60,* 846–856.

Plato. (1953). *The dialogues of Plato (Vol. 4): Laws* (4th ed.). In B. Jewett (Trans.). Oxford: Clarendon Press.

Plomin, R. (1986). *Development, genetics, and psychology.* Hillsdale, NJ: Erlbaum.

Plomin, R., & Daniels, D. (1987). Why are children in the same family so different from one another? *Behavioral and Brain Sciences, 10,* 1–16.

Plomin, R., & DeFries, J. C. (1985). A parent-offspring adoption study of cognitive abilities in early childhood. *Intelligence, 9,* 341–356.

Plomin, R., & Foch, T. T. (1980). A twin study of objectively assessed personality in childhood. *Journal of Personality and Social Psychology, 39,* 680–688.

Plomin, R., Willerman, L., & Loehlin, J. C. (1976). Resemblance in appearance and the equal environments assumption in twin studies of personality. *Behavior Genetics, 6,* 43–52.

Pollitt, E., Gorman, K. S., Engle, P. L., Martorell, R., & Rivera, J. (1993). Early supplementary feeding and cognition: Effects over two decades. *Monographs of the Society for Research in Child Development, 58*(7, Serial No. 235).

Potts, R., Huston, A. C., & Wright, J. C. (1986). The effects of television form and violent content on boys' attention and social behavior. *Journal of Experimental Child Psychology, 41,* 1–17.

Powell, G. J. (1973). *Black Monday's children: A study of the effects of school desegregation on self-concepts of Southern children.* Englewood Cliffs, NJ: Prentice-Hall.

Powell, G. J. (1985). Self-concepts among Afro-American students in racially isolated minority schools: Some regional differences. *Journal of the American Academy of Child Psychiatry, 24,* 142–149.

Powlishta, K. K., Serbin, L. A., Doyle, A., & White, D. R. (1994). Gender, ethnic, and body type biases: The generality of prejudice in childhood. *Developmental Psychology, 30,* 526–536.

Prescott, P. S. (1981). *The child savers.* New York: Knopf.

Pressley, M. (1979). Increasing children's self-control through cognitive intervention. *Review of Educational Research, 49,* 319–370.

Puig-Antich, J. (1986). Psychobiological markers: Effects of age and puberty. In M. Rutter, C. E. Izard, & P. B. Read (Eds.), *Depression in young people: Developmental and clinical perspectives* (pp. 341–382). New York: Guilford.

Putallaz, M. (1987). Maternal behavior and children's sociometric status. *Child Development, 58,* 324–340.

Quay, H. C. (1987). Institutional treatment. In H. C. Quay (Ed.), *Handbook of juvenile delinquency* (pp. 244–265). New York: Wiley.

Quindlen, A. (1988). *Living out loud.* New York: Random House.

Quinton, D., & Rutter, M. (1985). Parenting behavior of mothers raised "in care." In R. Nicol (Ed.), *Longitudinal studies in child psychology and psychiatry* (pp. 157–201). Chichester: Wiley.

Radke-Yarrow, M., Cummings, E. M., Kuczynski, L., & Chapman, M. (1985). Patterns of attachment in two- and three-year-olds in normal families and families with parental depression. *Child Development, 56,* 884–893.

Radke-Yarrow, M., & Zahn-Waxler, C. (1984). Roots, motives, and patterns in children's prosocial behavior. In E. Staub, D. Bar-Tal, J. Karylowski, & J. Reykowski (Eds.), *Development and maintenance of prosocial behavior: International perspectives on positive development.* New York: Plenum.

Radke-Yarrow, M., Zahn-Waxler, C., & Chapman, M. (1983). Children's prosocial dispositions and behavior. In P. H. Mussen (Series Ed.) & E. M. Hetherington (Ed.), *Handbook of child psychology: Vol. 4. Socialization, personality and social development* (4th ed., pp. 469–546). New York: Wiley.

Rakic, P. (1977). Prenatal development of the visual system in rhesus monkey. *Philosophical Transactions of the Royal Society of London, Series B, 278,* 245–260.

Ramey, C. T., Yeates, K. O., & Short, E. J. (1984). The plasticity of intellectual development: Insights from preventive intervention. *Child Development, 55,* 1913–1925.

Reed, E. W. (1975). Genetic anomalies in development. In F. D. Horowitz (Ed.), *Review of child development research* (Vol. 4). Chicago: University of Chicago Press.

Renshaw, P. D., & Asher, S. R. (1983). Children's goals and strategies for social interaction. *Merrill-Palmer Quarterly, 29,* 353–374.

Reschly, D. J. (1981). Psychological testing in educational classification and placement. *American Psychologist, 36,* 1094–1102.

Rescorla, R. A. (1988). Behavioral studies of Pavlovian conditioning. *Annual Review of Neuroscience, 11,* 329–352.

Resnick, H. L. P. (1980). Suicide. In H. I. Kaplan, A. M. Freedman, & B. J. Sadock (Eds.), *Comprehensive textbook of psychiatry* (Vol. 2, pp. 2085–2097). Baltimore: Williams & Wilkins.

Resnick, S. M., Berenbaum, S. A., Gottesman, I. I., & Bouchard, T. J., Jr. (1986). Early hormonal influences on cognitive functioning in congenital adrenal hyperplasia. *Developmental Psychology, 22,* 191–198.

Rest, J. R. (1983). Morality. In P. H. Mussen (Series Ed.), J. Flavell, & E. Markman (Eds.), *Handbook of child psychology: Vol. 3. Cognitive development* (4th ed., pp. 556–629). New York: Wiley.

Rest, J. R. (1986). *Moral development: Advances in research and theory.* New York: Praeger.

Reznick, J. S. (1990). Visual preference as a Test of Infant Word Comprehension. *Applied Psycholinguistics, 11,* 145–165.

Rheingold, H. L., Hay, D. F., & West, M. J. (1976). Sharing in the second year of life. *Child Development, 47,* 1148–1158.

Rholes, W. S., Blackwell, J., Jordan, C., & Walters, C. (1980). A developmental study of learned helplessness. *Developmental Psychology, 16,* 616–624.

Rice, M. E., & Grusec, J. E. (1975). Saying and doing: Effects on observer performance. *Journal of Personality and Social Psychology, 32,* 584–593.

Rice, M. L., Huston, A. C., Wright, J. C., & Truglio, R. (1988). *Words from Sesame Street: Learning vocabulary while viewing.* Unpublished manuscript, Center for Research on the Influences of Television on Children, University of Kansas, KS.

Richman, N., Graham, P., & Stevenson, J. (1982). *Preschool to school: A behavioral study.* London: Academic Press.

Richmond, J. B. (1982, November). *Health needs of young children.* Paper presented at the John D. and Catherine MacArthur Foundation conference on child care: Growth-fostering environments for young children, Chicago.

Riese, M. A. (1987). Temperament stability between the neonatal period and 24 months. *Developmental Psychology, 23,* 216–221.

Ritchie, D., Price, V., & Roberts, D. F. (1987). Television, reading, and reading achievement: A reappraisal. *Communication Research, 14,* 292–315.

Robins, L. (1966). *Deviant children grow up: A sociological and psychiatric study of sociopathic personality.* Baltimore: Williams & Wilkins.

Roche, A. F. (1978). Bone growth and maturation. In F. Falkner & J. M. Tanner (Eds.), *Human growth: Vol. 2. Postnatal growth.* New York: Plenum.

Rodin, J. (1985). Insulin levels, hunger, and food intake: An example of feedback loops in body weight regulation. *Health Psychology, 4,* 1–24.

Rodning, C., Beckwith, L., & Howard, J. (1989). Prenatal exposure to drugs and its influence on attachment. *Annals of the New York Academy of Sciences, 562,* 352–354. New York: New York Academy of Sciences.

Rodning, C., Beckwith, L., & Howard, J. (1991). Quality of attachment and home environments in children prenatally exposed to PCP and cocaine. *Development and Psychopathology, 3,* 351–366.

Roff, M., Sells, S., & Golden, M. (1972). *Social adjustment and personality development in children.* Minneapolis: University of Minnesota Press.

Roffwarg, H. P., Muzio, J. N, & Dement, W. C. (1966). Ontogenetic development of the human sleep dream cycle. *Science, 152,* 604–619.

Rogoff, B. (1990). *Apprenticeship in thinking.* New York: Oxford University Press.

Rosenberg, M. (1985). Identity: Summary. In M. B. Spencer, G. K. Brookins, & W. R. Allen (Eds.), *Beginnings: The social and affective development of black children* (pp. 231–236). Hillsdale, NJ: LEA.

Rosenhan, D. (1969). Some origins of concern for others. In P. Mussen, J. Langer, & M. Covington (Eds.), *Trends and issues in developmental psychology.* New York: Holt, Rinehart, and Winston.

Rosenthal, D. (1970). *Genetic theory and abnormal behavior.* New York: McGraw-Hill.

Rosenthal, D., Wender, P., Kety, S., Welner, J., & Schulsinger, F. (1971). The adopted-away offspring of schizophrenics. *American Journal of Psychiatry, 128,* 307–311.

Rosenthal, R. (1976). *Experimenter effects in behavioral research* (2nd ed.). New York: Irvington.

Rosenthal, R., & Jacobson, L. (1968). *Pygmalion in the classroom: Teacher expectation and pupils' intellectual development.* New York: Holt, Rinehart, and Winston.

Ross, D. M., & Ross, S. A. (1982). *Hyperactivity: Current issues, research, and theory* (2nd ed.). New York: Wiley.

Ross, R. J. (1973). Some empirical parameters of formal thinking. *Journal of Youth and Adolescence, 2,* 167–177.

Rothbart, M. K., & Derryberry, D. (1981). Development of individual differences in temperament. In M. E. Lamb & A. L. Brown (Eds.), *Advances in developmental psychology* (Vol. 1). Hillsdale, NJ: Erlbaum.

Rovee-Collier, C. K., Sullivan, M., Enright, M., Lucas, D., & Fagen, J. (1980). Reactivation of infant memory. *Science, 208,* 1159–1161.

Rubenstein, J. L. R., Lotspeich, L., & Ciaranello, R. D. (1990). The neurobiology of developmental disorders. In B. B. Lahey & A. E. Kazdin (Eds.), *Advances in clinical child psychology* (pp. 1–52). New York: Plenum.

Rubin, K. H., & Asendorpf, J. (1993). Social withdrawal, inhibition, and shyness in childhood: Conceptual and definitional issues. In K. H. Rubin & J. Asendorpf (Eds.), *Social withdrawal, inhibition, and shyness in children.* Hillsdale, NJ: LEA.

Rubin, K. H., Fein, G. G., & Vandenberg, B. (1983). Play. In P. H. Mussen (Series Ed.) & E. M. Hetherington (Ed.), *Handbook of child psychology: Vol. 4. Socialization, personality, and social development* (4th ed., pp. 693–774). New York: Wiley.

Rubin, K. H., & Mills, R. S. (1988). The many faces of social isolation in childhood. *Journal of Counselling and Clinical Psychology, 56,* 916–924.

Rubin, S. (1980). *It's not too late for a baby: For women and men over 35.* Englewood Cliffs, NJ: Prentice Hall.

Rubin, Z. (1980). *Children's friendship.* Cambridge, MA: Harvard University Press.

Ruble, D. N., Boggiano, A. K., Feldman, N. S., & Loebl, J. H. (1980). Developmental analysis of the role of social comparison in self-evaluation. *Developmental Psychology, 16,* 105–115.

Ruble, D. N., & Brooks-Gunn, J. (1982). The experience of menarche. *Child Development, 53,* 1557–1566.

Ruble, D. N., Parsons, J. E., & Ross, J. (1976). Self-evaluative responses of children in an achievement setting. *Child Development, 47,* 990–997.

Rugh, R., & Shettles, L. B. (1971). *From conception to birth: The drama of life's beginnings.* New York: Harper & Row.

Rushton, J. P. (1975). Generosity in children: Immediate and long term effects of modeling, preaching, and moral judgment. *Journal of Personality and Social Psychology, 31,* 459–466.

Rushton, J. P., & Weiner, J. (1975). Altruism and cognitive development in children. *British Journal of Social and Clinical Psychology, 14,* 341–349.

Russell, G. F. M. (1985). Anorexia and bulimia nervosa. In M. Rutter & L. Hersov (Eds.), *Child and adolescent psychiatry: Modern approaches* (pp. 625–637). Oxford: Blackwell Scientific Publications.

Rutter, M. (1979). Maternal deprivation, 1972–1978: New findings, new concepts, new approaches. *Child Development, 50,* 283–305.

Rutter, M. (1980). *Changing youth in a changing society: Patterns of adolescent development and disorder.* Cambridge, MA: Harvard University Press.

Rutter, M. (1986). The developmental psychopathology of depression. In M. Rutter, C. E. Izard, & P. B. Read (Eds.), *Depression in young people: Developmental and clinical perspectives* (pp. 3–30). New York: Guilford.

Rutter, M. (1989). Isle of Wight revisited: Twenty-five years of child psychiatric epidemiology. *Journal of the American Academy of Child and Adolescent Psychiatry, 28,* 633–653.

Rutter, M., & Giller, H. (1984). *Juvenile delinquency: Trends and perspectives.* New York: Guilford.

Rutter, M., Graham, P., Chadwick, O. F. D., & Yule, W. (1976). Adolescent turmoil: Fact or fiction? *Journal of Child Psychology and Psychiatry, 17,* 35–56.

Rutter, M., Izard, C. E., & Read, P. B. (Eds.). (1986). *Depression in young people: Developmental and clinical perspectives.* New York: Guilford Press.

Rutter, M., Quinton, D., & Hill, J. (1990). Adult outcome of institute-reared children: Males and females compared. In L. N. Robins & M. Rutter (Eds.), *Straight and devious pathways from childhood to adulthood* (pp. 135–157). Cambridge: Cambridge University Press.

Sackett, G. P., Ruppenthal, G. C., Fahrenbruch, C. E., Holm, R. A., & Greenough, W. T. (1981). Social isolation rearing effects in monkeys vary with genotype. *Developmental Psychology, 17,* 313.

Sagi, A., Lamb, M. E., & Gardner, W. (1986). Relations between Strange Situation behavior and stranger sociability among infants in Israeli kibbutzim. *Infant Behavior and Development, 9,* 271–282.

Sagotsky, G., Patterson, C. J., & Lepper, M. R. (1978). Training children's self-control: A field experiment in self-monitoring and goal-setting in the classroom. *Journal of Experimental Psychology, 25,* 242–253.

Salomon, G. (1977). Effects of encouraging Israeli mothers to co-observe "Sesame Street" with their five-year-olds. *Child Development, 48,* 1146–1151.

Salomon, G. (1979). *Interaction of media, cognition, and learning.* San Francisco: Jossey-Bass.

Salomon, G. (1983). Television watching and mental effort: A social psychological view. In J. Bryant & D. R. Anderson (Eds.), *Children's understanding of television: Research on attention and comprehension* (pp. 181–198). New York: Academic Press.

Sameroff, A. M., & Zax, M. (1973). Perinatal characteristics of the offspring of schizophrenic women. *Journal of Nervous and Mental Diseases, 157,* 191–199.

Sandoval, J., & Millie, M. P. W. (1980). Accuracy of judgments of WISC-R item difficulty for minority groups. *Journal of Consulting and Clinical Psychology, 48,* 249–253.

Sanson, A., Prior, M., Garino, E., Oberkaid, F., & Sewell, J. (1987). The structure of infant temperament. *Infant Behavior and Development, 10,* 97–104.

Santrock, J. W. (1975). Father absence, perceived maternal behavior, and moral development in boys. *Child Development, 46,* 753–757.

Santrock, J. W. (1987). *Adolescence: An introduction* (3rd ed.). Dubuque, IA: Wm. C. Brown.

Santrock, J. W., & Warshak, R. A. (1979). Father custody and social development in boys and girls. *Journal of Social Issues, 35,* 112–135.

Santrock, J. W., Warshak, R., Lindbergh, C., & Meadows, L. (1982). Children's and parents' observed social behavior in stepfather families. *Child Development, 53,* 472–480.

Sarason, I. G. (1978). A cognitive social learning approach to juvenile delinquency. In R. Hare & D. Schalling (Eds.), *Psychopathic behavior: Approaches to research* (pp. 299–317). New York: Wiley.

Sarason, S. B., Hill, K. T., & Zimbardo, P. C. (1964). A longitudinal study of the relation of test anxiety to performance on intelligence and achievement tests. *Monographs of the Society for Research in Child Development, 29* (No. 7).

Savin-Williams, R. C., & Berndt, T. J. (1990). Friendship and peer relations. In S. S. Feldman & G. R. Elliot (Eds.), *At the threshold: The developing adolescent* (pp. 277–307). Cambridge, MA: Harvard University Press.

Scarr, S. (1981). *Race, social class, and individual differences in IQ.* Hillsdale, NJ: LEA.

Scarr, S. (1992). Developmental theories for the 1990's: Development and individual differences. *Child Development, 63,* 1–19.

Scarr, S., Caparulo, B. K., Ferdman, B. M., Tower, R. B., & Caplan, J. (1983). Developmental status and school achievements of minority and non-minority children from birth to 18 years in a British Midlands town. *British Journal of Developmental Psychology, 1,* 31–48.

Scarr, S., & Carter-Saltzman, L. (1979). Twin method: Defense of a critical assumption. *Behavior Genetics, 9,* 527–542.

Scarr, S., & Eisenberg, M. (1993). Child care research: Issues, perspectives, and results. *Annual Review of Psychology, 44,* 613–644.

Scarr, S., & Kidd, K. K. (1983). Developmental behavior genetics. In P. H. Mussen (Series Ed.), M. Haith, & J. Campos (Eds.), *Handbook of child psychology: Vol. 2. Infancy and developmental psychobiology* (pp. 345–435). New York: Wiley.

Scarr, S., & McCartney, K. (1983). How people make their own environments: A theory of genotype and environment effects. *Child Development, 54,* 424–435.

Scarr, S., & Weinberg, R. A. (1976). IQ test performance of black children adopted by white families. *American Psychologist, 31,* 726–739.

Scheirer, M. A., & Kraut, R. E. (1979). Increasing educational achievement via self-concept change. *Review of Educational Research, 49,* 131–150.

Scheper-Hughes, N. (1985). Culture, scarcity, and maternal thinking: Maternal detachment and infant survival in a Brazilian shantytown. *Ethos, 13,* 291–317.

Schiff, M., Duyme, M., Dumaret, A., Stewart, J., Tomkiewicz, S., & Feingold, J. (1978). Intellectual status of working-class children adopted early into upper-middle-class families. *Science, 200,* 1503–1504.

Schiff, M., Duyme, M., Dumaret, A., & Tomkiewicz, S. (1982). How much could we boost scholastic achievement and IQ scores: A direct answer from a French adoption study. *Cognition, 12,* 165–196.

Schindler, P. J., Moely, B. E., & Frank, A. L. (1987). Time in day care and social participation of young children. *Developmental Psychology, 23,* 255–261.

Schneider, M. L. (1992). The effect of mild stress during pregnancy on birthweight and neuromotor maturation in rhesus monkey infants. *Infant Behavior and Development, 15,* 389–403.

Schomberg, S. F. (1978). Moral judgment development and freshmen year experiences. *Dissertation Abstracts International, 39,* 3482A (University Microfilms no. 7823960).

Schorr, L. B. (1988). *Within our reach: Breaking the cycle of disadvantage and despair.* New York: Double-day/Anchor.

Schunk, D. H., & Cox, P. D. (1986). Strategy training and attributional feedback with learning disabled students. *Journal of Educational Psychology, 78,* 201–209.

Schwartz, D., Dodge, K. A., & Coie, J. D. (1993). The emergence of chronic peer victimization in boys' play groups. *Child Development, 64,* 1755–1772.

Schwarz, J. C., Schrager, J. B., & Lyons, A. E. (1983). Delay of gratification by preschoolers: Evidence for the validity of the choice paradigm. *Child Development, 54,* 620–625.

Schweder, R., Turiel, E., & Much, N. (1981). The moral intuitions of the child. In J. H. Flavell & L. Ross (Eds.), *Social cognitive development: Frontiers and possible futures.* New York: Cambridge University Press.

Scott-Jones, D. (1991). Adolescent child bearing: Risks and resilience. *Education and Urban Society, 24,* 53–64.

Sears, R. R., Maccoby, E. E., & Levin, H. (1957). *Patterns of child rearing.* New York: Harper & Row.

Sebald, H., & White, B. (1980). Teenagers divided reference groups: Uneven alignment with parents and peers. *Adolescence, 15,* 579–984.

Sechrest, L., & Rosenblatt, A. (1987). Research methods. In H. C. Quay (Ed.), *Handbook of juvenile delinquency* (pp. 417–450). New York: Wiley.

Seitz, V., & Apfel, N. H. (1994). Parent-focused intervention: Diffusion effects on siblings. *Child Development, 65,* 677–683.

Selfe, L. (1977). *Nadia: A case of extraordinary drawing ability in an autistic child.* New York: Academic Press.

Selman, R. L. (1976a). Social cognitive understanding: A guide to educational and clinical practice. In T. Likona (Ed.), *Moral development and behavior: Theory, research, and social issues.* New York: Holt, Rinehart and Winston.

Selman, R. L. (1976b). Toward a structural analysis of developing interpersonal relations concepts: Research with normal and disturbed preadolescents. In A. D. Pick (Ed.), *Minnesota Symposia on Child Psychology* (Vol. 10). Minneapolis: University of Minnesota Press.

Selman, R. L. (1980). *The growth of interpersonal understanding.* New York: Academic Press.

Selman, R. L. (1981). The child as a friendship philosopher. In S. R. Asher & J. M. Gottman (Eds.), *The development of children's friendships.* New York: Cambridge University Press.

Semba, R. D., Miotti, P. G., Chiphangwi, J. D., Saah, A. J., Canner, J. K., Dallabetta, G. A., & Hoover, D. R. (1994). Maternal vitamin A deficiency and mother-to-child transmission of HIV-1. *Lancet, 343,* 1593–1597.

Serafica, F. C. (1990). Peer relations of children with Down syndrome. In D. Cicchetti & M. Beeghley (Eds.), *Children with Down syndrome: A developmental perspective.* New York: Cambridge University Press.

Serbin, L. A., Powlishta, K. K., & Gulko, J. (1993). Sex roles, status, and the need for social change. *Monographs of the Society for Research in Child Development, 58*(2, Serial No. 232), 93–95.

Serbin, L. A., & Sprafkin, C. (1986). The salience of gender and the process of sex typing in three- to seven-year-old children. *Child Development, 57*, 1188–1199.

Sex education and sex related behavior (1986). *Family Planning Perspectives, 18*, 150–192.

Shaffer, D. (1985). Depression, mania, and suicidal acts. In M. Rutter & L. Hersov (Eds.), *Child and adolescent psychiatry: Modern approaches* (2nd ed., pp. 698–719). Oxford: Blackwell Scientific Publications.

Shaffer, D. (1986). In M. Rutter, C. E. Izard, & P. B. Read (Eds.), *Child and adolescent psychiatry: Modern approaches* (pp. 283–396). New York: Guilford.

Shantz, C. U. (1983). Social cognition. In P. H. Mussen (Series Ed.), J. H. Flavell, & E. M. Markman (Eds.), *Handbook of child psychology: Vol. 3. Cognitive development* (4th ed., pp. 495–555). New York: Wiley.

Shapira, A., & Madsen, M. C. (1970). Cooperation and competitive behavior of urban Afro-American, Anglo-American, Mexican-American, and Mexican village children. *Developmental Psychology, 3*, 16–20.

Shapira, A., & Madsen, M. C. (1974). Between- and within-group cooperation and competition among Kibbutz and non-Kibbutz children. *Developmental Psychology, 10*, 140–145.

Shatz, M., & Gelman, R. (1973). The development of communication skills: Modifications in the speech of young children as a function of the listener. *Monographs of the Society for Research in Child Development, 38*(Serial No. 152).

Shedler, J., & Block, J. (1990). Adolescent drug use and psychological health: A longitudinal inquiry. *American Psychologist, 45*, 612–630.

Sheldrick, C. (1985). Treatment of delinquents. In M. Rutter & L. Hersov (Eds.), *Child and adolescent psychiatry: Modern approaches* (pp. 743–752). Oxford: Blackwell Scientific Publications.

Sher, K. J. (1991). *Children of alcoholics: A critical appraisal of theory and research.* Chicago: University of Chicago Press.

Shibley-Hyde, J., & Linn, M. C. (1986). *The psychology of gender: Advances through meta-analysis.* Baltimore: Johns Hopkins University Press.

Shimojo, S., Bauer, J., O'Connel, K. M., & Held, R. (1986). Pre-stereoptic binocular vision in infants. *Visual Research, 26*, 501–510.

Shiono, H. H., Klebanoff, M. A., Gronbard, B. I., Berendes, H. W., & Rhoads, G. G. (1986). Birth weight among women of different ethnic groups. *Journal of the American Medical Association, 255*, 48–52.

Shure, M. B., & DiGeronimo, T. F. (1994). *Raising a thinking child.* New York: Henry Holt.

Shurkin, J. N. (1992). *Terman's kids: The groundbreaking study of how the gifted grow up.* Boston: Little, Brown.

Shweder, R., & Bourne, E. J. (1984). Does the concept of the person vary cross-culturally? In R. A. Shweder & R. A. LeVine (Eds.), *Cultural theory: Essays on mind, self, and emotion.* Cambridge: Cambridge University Press.

Siegel, L. S. (1979). Infant perceptual, cognitive, and motor behaviors as predictors of subsequent cognitive and language development. *Canadian Journal of Psychology, 33*, 382–392.

Siegler, R. S. (1983). Information processing approaches to development. In P. H. Mussen (Series Ed.) & W. Kessen (Ed.), *Handbook of child psychology: Vol. 1. History, theory, and methods* (pp. 129–212). New York: Wiley.

Siegler, R. S. (1986). Unities across domains in children's strategy choices. In M. Perlmutter (Ed.), *The Minnesota Symposia on Child Psychology: Vol. 19. Perspectives on intellectual development* (pp. 1–48). Hillsdale, NJ: LEA.

Siegler, R. S. (1991). *Children's thinking* (2nd ed.). Englewood Cliffs, NJ: Prentice-Hall.

Sigel, I. E. (1986). Reflections on the belief-behavior connection: Lessons learned from a research program on parental belief systems and teaching strategies. In R. D. Ashmore & D. M. Brodzinsky (Eds.), *Thinking about the family: Views of parents and children.* Hillsdale, NJ: LEA.

Sigel, I. E., McGillicuddy-DeLisi, A. V., & Goodnow, J. J. (Eds.). (1992). *Parental belief systems: The psychological consequences for children* (2nd ed.). Hillsdale, NJ: LEA.

Signorella, M. L., & Liben, L. S. (1984). Recall and reconstruction of gender-related pictures: Effects of attitude, task difficulty, and age. *Child Development, 55*, 393–405.

Simmons, R. G., Blyth, D. A., & McKinney, K. L. (1983). The social and psychological effects of puberty on white females. In J. Brooks-Gunn & A. C. Petersen (Eds.), *Girls at puberty: Biological and psychological perspectives* (pp. 229–272). New York: Plenum.

Simmons, R. G., Blyth, D. A., VanCleave, E., & Bush, D. (1979). Entry into early adolescence: The impact of school structure, puberty, and early dating on self-esteem. *American Sociological Review, 44*, 948–967.

Simmons, R. G., Burgeson, R., Carlton-Ford, S., & Blyth, D. A. (1987). The impact of cumulative change in early adolescence. *Child Development, 58*, 1220–1234.

Simmons, R. G., & Rosenberg, F. (1975). Sex, sex roles, and self-image. *Journal of Youth and Adolescence, 4*, 229–258.

Simons, R. L., Lorenz, F. O., Wu, C., & Conger, R. D. (1993). Social network and marital support as mediators and moderators of the impact of stress and depression on parental behavior. *Developmental Psychology, 29,* 368–381.

Singleton, L. C., & Asher, S. R. (1979). Racial integration and children's peer preferences: An investigation of developmental and cohort differences. *Child Development, 50,* 936–941.

Skinner, B. F. (1938). *The behavior of organisms: An experimental analysis.* New York: Appleton-Century-Crofts.

Skodak, M., & Skeels, H. M. (1949). A final follow-up of one hundred adopted children. *Journal of Genetic Psychology, 75,* 85–125.

Slade, A., & Wolf, D. P. (1994). *Children at play: Clinical and developmental perspective.* New York: Oxford University Press.

Slater, A., Morison, V., & Rose, D. (1983). Perception of shape by the newborn baby. *British Journal of Developmental Psychology, 1,* 135–142.

Slater, A., Morison, V., & Rose, D. (1984). Habituation in the newborn. *Infant Behavior and Development, 7,* 183–200.

Slavin, R. E. (1987). Developmental and motivational perspectives on cooperative learning: A reconciliation. *Child Development, 58,* 1161–1167.

Slobin, D. I. (1971). *Psycholinguistics.* Glenview, IL: Scott, Foresman.

Slomkowski, L. L., & Dunn, J. (1992). Arguments and relationships within the family: Differences in young children's dispute with mother and sibling. *Developmental Psychology, 28,* 919–924.

Smetana, J. (1981). Preschool children's conceptions of moral and social rules. *Child Development, 52,* 1333–1336.

Smetana, J. (1988) Adolescents' and parents' conceptions of parental authority. *Child Development, 59,* 321–335.

Smetana, J., & Asquith, P. (1994). Adolescents' and parents' conceptions of parental authority and personal autonomy. *Child Development, 65,* 1147–1162.

Smith, I. M., & Bryson, S. E. (1994). Imitation and action in autism: A critical review. *Psychological Bulletin, 116,* 259–273.

Smith, P. K. (1977). Social and fantasy play in young children. In B. Tizard & D. Marvey (Eds.), *Biology of play.* London: William Heinemann Medical Books.

Smith, P. K. (1982). Does play matter? *Behavioral and Brain Sciences, 5,* 139–184.

Smith, P. K., & Connolly, K. J. (1980). *The ecology of preschool behavior.* Cambridge: Cambridge University Press.

Smith, S. R. (1975). Religion and the conception of youth in seventeenth-century England. *History of Childhood Quarterly: The Journal of Psychohistory, 2,* 493–516.

Smith, T. A. (1988). A methodological review of sexual behavior questions on the 1988 and 1989 GSS. *GSS Methodological Reports* (No. 65). Chicago: National Opinion Research Center.

Smoking and health: A report of the Surgeon General. (1979). (DHEW Publication No. [PHS] 79-50066, U.S. Department of Health, Education and Welfare.) Washington, DC: U.S. Government Printing Office.

Snow, C. E. (1974). *Mother's speech and research: An overview.* Paper presented at the Conference on Language Input and Acquisition, Boston.

Snyder, J., & Patterson, G. (1987). Family interaction and delinquent behavior. In H. C. Quay (Ed.), *Handbook of juvenile delinquency* (pp. 216–243). New York: Wiley.

Society for Research in Child Development. (1973, Winter). Ethical standards for research with children. *SRCD Newsletter,* 3–4.

Society for Research in Child Development. (1993). Ethical standards for research with children. In *Directory of members* (pp. 337–338). Ann Arbor, MI: Society for Research in Child Development.

Sokolov, J. L. (1993). A logical contingency analysis of the fine-tuning hypothesis. *Developmental Psychology, 29,* 1008–1023.

Sonenstein, F. L., Pleck, J. H., & Ku, L. C. (1989). Sexual activity, condom use, and AIDS awareness among adolescent males. *Family Planning Perspectives, 21,* 152–158.

Sontag, L. W. (1944). War and fetal maternal relationship. *Marriage and Family Living, 6,* 1–5.

Sontag, L. W., Baker, C. T., & Nelson, V. L. (1958). Mental growth and personality: A longitudinal study. *Monographs of the Society for Research in Child Development, 23*(Serial No. 68).

Sorensen, R. C. (1973). *Adolescent sexuality in contemporary America: Personal values and sexual behavior ages 13–19.* New York: Abrams.

Spence, J. T., & Helmreich, R. L. (1978). *Masculinity and femininity: Their psychological dimensions, correlates, and antecedents.* Austin: University of Texas Press.

Spencer, M. B. (1983). Children's cultural values and parental child rearing strategies. *Developmental Review, 3,* 351–370.

Spickelmier, J. L. (1983). *College experience and moral judgment development.* Doctoral dissertation. Minneapolis: University of Minnesota Press.

Spivack, G., & Shure, M. B. (1976). *Social adjustment of young children: A cognitive approach to solving real-life problems.* San Francisco, CA: Jossey-Bass.

Sroufe, L. A., & Wunsch, J. P. (1972). The development of laughter in the first year of life. *Child Development, 43,* 1326–1344.

St. Clair, S., & Day, H. D. (1979). Ego identity status and values among high school females. *Journal of Youth and Adolescence, 8,* 317–326.

St. Peters, M., Fitch, M., Huston, A. C., Wright, J. C., & Eakins, D. J. (1991). Television and families: What do young children watch with their parents? *Child Development, 62,* 1409–1423.

Standley, K. (1979). Personal communication. Cited in Y. Brackbill. Obstetrical medication and infant behavior. In J. Osofsky (Ed.), *Handbook of infant development.* New York: Wiley.

Stark, K. D., Rouse, L. W., & Livingston, R. (1991). Treatment of depression during childhood and adolescence: Cognitive-behavioral procedures for the individual and family. In P. C. Kendall (Ed.), *Child and adolescent therapy: Cognitive-behavioral procedures* (pp. 165–206). New York: Guilford Press.

Starkey, P., & Cooper, R. S. (1980). Perception of numbers by human infants. *Science, 210,* 1033–1035.

Stattin, H., & Magnussen, D. (1990). *Pubertal maturation in female development.* Hillsdale, NJ: LEA.

Stein, A. H., & Bailey, M. M. (1973). The socialization of achievement orientation in females. *Psychological Bulletin, 80,* 345–366.

Stein, A. H., & Friedrich, L. K. (1975). Impact of television on children and youth. In E. M. Hetherington (Ed.), *Review of child development research* (Vol. 5, pp. 183–256). Chicago: University of Chicago Press.

Steinberg, L. (1977). *A longitudinal study of physical growth, intellectual growth, and family interaction in early adolescence.* Unpublished doctoral dissertation, Cornell University.

Steinberg, L. (1981). Transformation in family relations at puberty. *Developmental Psychology, 17,* 833–840.

Steinberg, L. (1985). Psychotic and other severe disorders in adolescence. In M. Rutter & L. Hersov (Eds.), *Child and adolescent psychiatry: Modern approaches* (2nd ed., pp. 567–583). Oxford: Blackwell Scientific Publications.

Steinberg, L. (1988). Reciprocal relation between parent-child distance and pubertal maturation. *Developmental Psychology, 24,* 122–128

Steinberg, L. (1990). Autonomy, conflict, and harmony in the family relationship. In S. S. Feldman & G. R. Elliot (Eds.), *At the threshold: The developing adolescent* (pp. 255–276). Cambridge, MA: Harvard University Press.

Steinberg, L., Catalano, R., & Dooley, D. (1981). Economic antecedents of child abuse and neglect. *Child Development, 52,* 975–985.

Steinberg, L., & Dornbusch, S. M. (1991). Negative correlates of part-time employment during adolescence: Replication and elaboration. *Developmental Psychology, 27,* 304–313.

Steinberg, L., Dornbusch, S. M., & Brown, B. B. (1992). Ethnic differences in adolescent achievement: An ecological perspective. *American Psychologist, 47,* 723–729.

Steinberg, L., Elmen, J. D., & Mounts, N. S. (1989). Authoritative parenting, psychosocial maturity, and academic success among adolescents. *Child Development, 60,* 1424–1436.

Steinberg, L., Fegley, S., & Dornbusch, S. M. (1993). Negative impact of part-time work on adolescent adjustment: Evidence from a longitudinal study. *Developmental Psychology, 29,* 171–180.

Steinberg, L., & Hill, J. P. (1978). Patterns of family interaction as a function of age, the onset of puberty, and formal thinking. *Developmental Psychology, 14,* 683–684.

Steinberg, L., Lamborn, S. D., Dornbusch, S. M., & Darling, N. (1992). Impact of parenting practices on adolescent achievement: Authoritative parenting, school involvement, and encouragement to succeed. *Child Development, 63,* 1266–1281.

Steinberg, L., Mounts, N. S., Lamborn, S. D., & Dornbusch, S. M. (1991). Authoritative parenting and adolescent adjustment across varied ecological niches. *Journal of Research on Adolescence, 1,* 19–36.

Steinberg, L., & Silverberg, S. B. (1986). The vicissitudes of autonomy in early adolescence. *Child Development, 57,* 841–851.

Steiner, J. (1979). Human facial expressions in response to taste and smell stimulation. In H. Reese & L. Lipsitt (Eds.), *Advances in child development and behavior* (Vol. 13). New York: Academic Press.

Stenberg, C., & Campos, J. J. (1983). The development of the expression of anger in human infants. In M. Lewis & C. Saarni (Eds.), *The socialization of affect.* New York: Plenum.

Sternberg, R. J. (Ed.). (1984). *Mechanisms of cognitive development.* New York: W. H. Freeman.

Sternberg, R. J. (1985). *Beyond IQ: A triarchic theory of human intelligence.* Cambridge: Cambridge University Press.

Sternberg, R. J., & Suben, J. G. (1986). The socialization of intelligence. In M. Perlmutter (Ed.), *Minnesota Symposia on Child Psychology: Vol 19. Perspectives on intellectual development* (pp. 201–236). Hillsdale, NJ: LEA.

Stevenson, H. W., Parker, T., Wilkinson, A., Bonnaveaux, B., & Gonzalez, M. (1978). Schooling environment and cognitive development: A cross cultural study. *Monographs of the Society for Research in Child Development, 43* (Serial No. 175).

Stevenson, H. W., Stigler, J. W., Lee, S., Lucker, G. W., Kitamura, S., & Hsu, C. (1985). Cognitive performance and academic achievement of Japanese, Chinese, and American children. *Child Development, 56,* 718–734.

Stewart, R. B. (1983). Sibling attachment relationships: Child-infant interactions in the strange situation. *Developmental Psychology, 19,* 191–199.

Stigler, J. W., Lee, S., & Stevenson, H. W. (1987). Mathematics classrooms in Japan, Taiwan, and the United States. *Child Development, 58,* 1272–1285.

Stilwell, R. (1983). *Social relationships in primary school children as seen by children, mothers, and teachers.* Unpublished doctoral thesis, University of Cambridge.

Stoneman, Z., Cantrell, M. L., & Hoover-Dempsey, K. (1983). The association between play materials and social behavior in a mainstreamed preschool: A naturalistic investigation. *Journal of Applied Developmental Psychology, 4,* 163–174.

Strauss, M. S., & Curtis, L. E. (1981). Infant perception of numerosity. *Child Development, 52,* 1146–1152.

Strayer, F. F., Waring, S., & Rushton, J. P. (1979). Social constraints on naturally occurring preschool altruism. *Ethology and Sociobiology, 1,* 3–11.

Streissguth, A. P., Barr, H. M., & Martin, D. C. (1983). Maternal alcohol use and neonatal habituation assessed with the Brazelton Scale. *Child Development, 43,* 1109–1118.

Streissguth, A. P., Martin, D. C., Barr, H. M., Sondman, B. M., Kirchner, G. L., & Darby, B. L. (1984). Intrauterine alcohol and nicotine exposure: Attention and reaction time in 4-year-old children. *Developmental Psychology, 20,* 533–541.

Striegel-Moore, R. H., Silberstein, L. R., & Rodin, J. (1986). Toward an understanding of risk factors for bulimia. *American Psychologist, 41,* 246–263.

Stunkard, A. J. (1980). Obesity. In H. I. Kaplan, A. M. Freedman, & B. J. Sadock (Eds.), *Comprehensive textbook of psychiatry* (Vol. 2, 3rd ed., pp. 1872–1882). Baltimore: Williams & Wilkins.

Sullivan, H. S. (1953). *The interpersonal theory of psychiatry.* New York: Norton.

Super, C. M. (1976). Environmental effects on motor development: The case of African infant precocity. *Developmental Medicine and Child Neurology, 18,* 561–567.

Surbey, M. K. (1990). Family composition, stress, and human menarche. In T. E. Ziegler & F. B. Bercovitch (Eds.), *Socioendocrinology of primate reproduction* (p. 11–32). New York: Wiley-Liss.

Sutton-Smith, B., & Rosenberg, B. G. (1970). *The sibling.* New York: Holt, Rinehart, and Winston.

Sylva, K., Bruner, J. S., & Genova, P. (1976). The role of play in the problem solving of children three to seven years old. In J. S. Bruner, A. Jolly, & K. Sylva (Eds.), *Play: Its role in development and evolution.* London: Kenwood.

Takanishi, R., & DeLeon, P. H. (1994). A Head Start for the twenty-first century. *American Psychologist, 49,* 120–122.

Tanner, J. M. (1969). Growth and endocrinology of the adolescent. In J. L. Gardner (Ed.), *Endocrine and genetic diseases of childhood.* Philadelphia: W. B. Saunders.

Tanner, J. M. (1970). Physical growth. In P. H. Mussen (Ed.), *Carmichael's manual of child psychology* (Vol. 2, 3rd ed.). New York: Wiley.

Tanner, J. M. (1971). Sequence, tempo, and individual variation in the growth and development of boys and girls aged twelve to sixteen. *Daedalus, 100,* 907–930.

Taylor, A. R., Asher, S. R., & Williams, G. A. (1987). The social adaptation of mainstreamed mildly retarded children. *Child Development, 58,* 1321–1334.

Taylor, M. (1988). Conceptual perspective taking: Children's ability to distinguish what they know from what they see. *Child Development, 59,* 703–718.

Teasdale, T., & Owen, K. (1985). Heredity and familial environment in intelligence and educational level—A sibling study. *Nature, 309,* 620–622.

Teicher, J. (1973). A solution to the chronic problem of living: Adolescent attempted suicide. In J. C. Schoolar (Ed.), *Current issues in adolescent psychiatry.* New York: Brunner/Mazel.

Tellegen, A., Lykken, D. T., Bouchard, T. J., & Wilcox, K. J., Segal, N. L., & Rich. S. (1988). Personality similarity in twins reared apart and together. *Journal of Personality and Social Psychology, 54,* 1031–1039.

Terman, L. M., & Merrill, M. A. (1973). *Stanford-Binet Intelligence Scale: Manual for the third revision of Form L-M.* Boston, MA: Houghton Mifflin.

Thase, M. E. (1988). The relationship between Down syndrome and Alzheimer's disease. In L. Nadel (Ed.), *The psychobiology of Down syndrome* (pp. 345–374). Cambridge, MA: MIT Press.

Thomas, A., & Chess, S. (1977). *Temperament and development.* New York: Brunner/Mazel.

Thomas, A., Chess, S., & Birch, H. G. (1968). *Temperament and behavior disorders in children.* New York: New York University Press.

Thomas, N. G., & Berk, L. E. (1981). Effects of school environments on the development of young children's creativity. *Child Development, 52,* 1153–1162.

Thompson, J. R., & Chapman, R. S. (1977). Who is "Daddy" revisited: The status of two-year olds' overextended words in use and comprehension. *Journal of Child Language, 4,* 359–375.

Thompson, L. E., Detterman, D. K., & Plomin, R. (1991). Associations between cognitive abilities and scholastic achievement: Genetic overlap but environmental differences. *Psychological Science, 2,* 158–165.

Thompson, R. A., Lamb, M. E., & Estes, D. (1982). Stability of mother-infant attachment and its relationship to changing life circumstances in an unselected middle-class sample. *Child Development, 53,* 144–148.

Thompson, V. D. (1974). Family size: Implicit policies

and assumed psychological outcomes. *Journal of Social Issues, 30,* 93–124.

Thorndike, R. L., Hagen, E. P., & Sattler, J. M. (1986). *The Stanford-Binet Intelligence Scale: Fourth edition. Guide for administering and scoring.* Chicago: Riverside Publishing.

Tienari, P., Sorri, A., Lahti, I., Naarla, M., Wahlberg, J. M., Pohjola, J., & Wynne, L. C. (1987). Genetic and psychosocial factors in schizophrenia: The Finnish adoptive family study. *Schizophrenia Bulletin, 13,* 477–484.

Tinbergen, N. (1951). *The study of instinct.* Oxford: Oxford University Press.

Tobin-Richards, M., Boxer, A., & Petersen, A. C. (1984). The psychological impact of pubertal change: Sex differences in perceptions of self during early adolescence. In J. Brooks-Gunn & A. C. Petersen (Eds.), *Girls at puberty: Biological, psychological, and social perspectives.* New York: Plenum.

Toder, N. L., & Marcia, J. E. (1973). Ego identity status and response to conformity pressure in college women. *Journal of Personality and Social Psychology, 26,* 287–294.

Tomasello, M., Kruger, A. C., & Ratner, H. H. (1993). Cultural learning. *Brain and Behavior Sciences, 16,* 495–552.

Tomlinson-Keasey, C., & Keasey, C. B. (1974). The mediating role of cognitive development in moral judgment. *Child Development, 45,* 291–298.

Toner, I. J., Moore, L. P., & Emmons, B. A. (1980). The effect of being labeled on subsequent self-control in children. *Child Development, 51,* 618–621.

Torgersen, A. M., & Kringlen, E. (1978). Genetic aspects of temperamental differences in infants: A study of same-sexed twins. *Journal of the American Academy of Child Psychiatry, 17,* 433–444.

Tracy, P. E., Wolfgang, M. E., & Figlio, R. M. (1990). *Delinquency careers in two birth cohorts.* New York: Plenum.

Travis, J. (1993). Helping premature lungs breathe easier. *Science, 261,* 426.

Treaster, J. B. (1993, February 16). For children of cocaine, fresh reasons for hope. *The New York Times,* pp. A1, B12.

Trickett, P. K., & Kuczynski, L. (1986). Children's misbehaviors and parental discipline strategies in abusive and nonabusive families. *Developmental Psychology, 22,* 115–123.

Trites, R. L., & LaPrade, K. (1983). Evidence for an independent syndrome of hyperactivity. *Journal of Child Psychology and Psychiatry and Allied Disciplines, 24,* 573–586.

Troiden, R. R. (1989). The formation of homosexual identities. *Journal of Homosexuality, 17,* 43–73.

Tronick, E. Z., Morelli, G. A., & Ivey, P. K. (1992). The Efe forager infant and toddler's pattern of social rela-tionships: Multiple and simultaneous. *Developmental Psychology, 28,* 568–577.

Turiel, E. (1983). Interaction and development in social cognition. In E. T. Higgins, D. N. Ruble, W. W. Hartup (Eds.), *Social cognition and social development.* New York: Cambridge University Press.

Turiel, E., Edwards, C. P., & Kohlberg, L. (1978). Moral development in Turkish children, adolescents, and young adults. *Journal of Cross-Cultural Psychology, 9,* 75–86.

Turner, S. M., Beidel, D. C., & Costello, A. A. (1987). Psychopathology in the offspring of anxiety disorders patients. *Journal of Consulting and Clinical Psychology, 55,* 229–235.

Udry, J. R., & Cliquet, R. L. (1982). A cross-cultural examination of the relationship between ages at menarche, marriage, and first birth. *Demography, 19,* 53–93.

Ugurel-Semin, R. (1952). Moral behavior and moral judgment of children. *Journal of Abnormal and Social Psychology, 47,* 463–474.

UNICEF. (1989). *Annual Report.* New York: UNICEF.

U.S. Bureau of the Census. (1987). *Statistical abstract of the United States, 1988.* Washington, DC: U.S. Government Printing Office.

U.S. Bureau of the Census. (1992). Households, families, and children: A 30 year perspective. *Current Population Reports* (Series P23, No. 181). Washington, DC: U.S. Government Printing Office.

U.S. Commission on Civil Rights. (1977). *Window dressing on the set: Women and minorities on television.* Washington, DC: U.S. Government Printing Office.

Valkenburg, P. M., & van der Voort, T. H. A. (1994). Influence of TV on daydreaming and creative imagination: A review of research. *Psychological Bulletin, 116,* 316–339.

van den Boom, D. C., & Hoeksma, J. B. (1994). The effect of infant irritability on mother-infant interaction: A growth-curve analysis. *Developmental Psychology, 30,* 581–590.

Van Doorninck, W. J., Caldwell, B. M., Wright, C., & Frankenburg, W. K. (1981). The relationship between 12-month home stimulation and school achievement. *Child Development, 52,* 1080–1083.

van IJzendoorn, M. H. (1995). Adult attachment representations, parental responsiveness, and infant attachment: A meta-analysis on the predictive validity of the Adult Attachment Interview. *Psychological Bulletin.*

van IJzendoorn, M. H., Goldberg, S., Kroonenberg, P. M., & Frenkel, O. J. (1992). The relative effects of maternal and child problems on the quality of attachment: A meta-analysis of attachment in clinical samples. *Child Development, 63,* 840–858.

van IJzendoorn, M. H., & Kroonenberg, P. M. (1988). Cross-cultural patterns of attachment: A meta-analysis of the Strange Situation. *Child Development, 59,* 147–156.

Vandell, D. L., & Corasaniti, M. A. (1990). Child care and the family: Complex contributors to child development. In K. McCartney (Ed.), *New Directions for Child Development: Vol 49. Child care and maternal employment: A social ecology approach* (pp. 23–37). San Francisco: Jossey-Bass.

Vandell, D. L., Henderson, V. K., & Wilson, K. S. (1988). A longitudinal study of children with day-care experiences of varying quality. *Child Development, 59,* 1286–1292.

Vandenberg, S. G., Singer, S. M., & Pauls, D. L. (1986). *The heredity of behavior disorders in adults and children.* New York: Plenum.

Vaughn, B. E., Kopp, C. B., & Krakow, J. B. (1984). The emergence and consolidation of self-control from eighteen to thirty months of age: Normative trends and individual differences. *Child Development, 55,* 990–1004.

Vaughn, C. E., Snyder, K. S., Freeman, W., Jones, S., Falloon, T. R. A., & Libeman, R. P. (1982). Family factors in schizophrenia relapse. *Schizophrenia Bulletin, 8,* 425–428.

Velez, C. N., Johnson, J., &. Cohen, P. (1989). The children in the community project: A longitudinal analysis of selected risk factors for childhood psychopathology. *Journal of the American Academy of Child and Adolescent Psychiatry, 28,* 861–864.

Veroff, J. (1969). Social comparison and the development of achievement motivation. In C. P. Smith (Ed.), *Achievement-related motives in children.* New York: Russell Sage.

Visher, C. A., & Roth, J. A. (1986). Participation in criminal careers. In A. Blumstein, J. Cohen, J. A. Roth, & C. A. Visher (Eds.), *Criminal careers and "career criminals"* (Vol. 1, pp. 211–291). Washington, DC: National Academy Press.

Vollmer, F. (1986). The relationship between expectancy and academic achievement—How can it be explained? *British Journal of Educational Psychology, 56,* 64–74.

Vorhees, C. V., & Mollnow, E. (1987). Behavioral teratogenesis: Long-term influences on behavior from early exposure to environmental agents. In J. D. Osofsky (Ed.), *Handbook of infant development* (pp. 913–971). New York: Wiley.

Voorhies, T. M., & Vanucci, R. C. (1984). Perinatal cerebral hypoxia-ischemia: Diagnosis and management. In H. B. Sarnot (Ed.), *Topics in neonatal neurology.* New York: Grune & Stratton.

Vorster, J. (1974). *Mother's speech to children: Some methodological considerations.* Publications of the Institute for General Linguistics (No. 8). Amsterdam: U.S. Department of Amsterdam.

Vuchinich, S., Hetherington, E. M., Vuchinich, R. A., & Clingempeel, W. G. (1991). Parent-child interaction and gender differences in early adolescents' adaptation to stepfamilies. *Developmental Psychology, 27,* 618–626.

Wachs, T. D. (1979). Proximal experience and early cognitive intellectual development: The physical environment. *Merrill-Palmer Quarterly, 25,* 3–41.

Wagner, S., Winner, E., Cicchetti, D., & Gardner, H. (1981). Metaphorical mapping in human infants. *Child Development, 52,* 728–731.

Walker, E., & Emory, E. (1985). Commentary: Interpretive bias and behavioral genetic research. *Child Development, 56,* 775–778.

Walker, L. J. (1984). Sex differences in development of moral reasoning: A critical review. *Child Development, 55,* 677–691.

Wallerstein, J. S., & Kelly, J. B. (1980). *Surviving the breakup: How children and parents cope with divorce.* New York: Basic Books.

Ward, S. L., & Overton, W. F. (1990) Semantic familiarity, relevance, and the development of deductive reasoning. *Developmental Psychology, 26,* 488–493.

Wartella, E., & Hunter, L. (1983). Children and the formats of television advertising. In M. Meyer (Ed.), *Children and the formal features of television* (pp. 144–165). Munich: K. G. Saur.

Waterman, A. S., & Waterman, C. K. (1974). A longitudinal study of changes in ego identity status during the freshman to the senior year in college. *Developmental Psychology, 10,* 387–392.

Waters, E., Wippman, J., & Sroufe, L. A. (1979). Attachment, positive affect, and competence in the peer group. *Child Development, 50,* 821–829.

Watson, J. B. (1928). *Psychological care of infant and child.* New York: Norton.

Watson, J. B. (1967). *Behaviorism.* Chicago: University of Chicago Press. (Originally work published 1930)

Watson, J. D., & Crick, F. H. C. (1953). Molecular structure of nucleic acids: A structure for deoxyribose nucleic acid. *Nature, 171,* 737–738.

Waxman, S., & Gelman, R. (1986). Preschoolers' use of superordinate relations in classification and language. *Cognitive Development, 1,* 139–156.

Webb, T. P., Bundey, S. E., Thake, A. I., & Todd, J. (1986). Population incidence and segregation ratios in the Martin-Bell Syndrome. *American Journal of Medical Genetics, 23,* 573–580.

Weiner, I. B. (1970). *Psychological disturbance in adolescence.* New York: Wiley.

Weiner, I. B. (1980). Psychopathology in adolescence. In J. Adelson (Ed.), *Handbook of adolescent psychology* (pp. 447–471). New York: Wiley.

Weiner, I. B., & Elkind, D. (1972). *Child development: A core approach.* New York: Wiley.

Weinmann, L. L., & Newcombe, N. (1990). Relational aspects of identity: Late adolescents' perceptions of their relationships with parents. *Journal of Experimental Child Psychology, 50,* 357–369.

Weinraub, M., Clemens, L. P., Sockloff, A., Ethridge, T., Gracely, E., & Myers, B. (1984). The development of sex role stereotypes in the third year: Relationships to gender labeling, gender identity, sex-typed toy preference, and family characteristics. *Child Development, 55,* 1493–1503.

Weinraub, M., & Gringlas, M. B. (1995). Single parenthood. In M. H. Bornstein (Ed.), *Handbook of parenting* (Vol. III). Hillsdale, NJ: LEA.

Weinraub, M., & Wolf, B. M. (1983). Effects of stress and social supports on mother-child interactions in single and two-parent families. *Child Development, 54,* 1297–1311.

Weiss, G. (1983). Long-term outcome: Findings, concepts, and practical implications. In M. Rutter (Ed.), *Developmental neuropsychiatry* (pp. 422–436). New York: Guilford.

Weissman, M. M., & Boyd, J. H. (1983). Affective disorders: Epidemiology. In H. I. Kaplan & B. J. Sadock (Eds.), *Comprehensive textbook of psychiatry* (Vol. I, pp. 764–768). Baltimore: Williams and Wilkins.

Weissman, M. M., Gershon, E. S., Kidd, K. K., Brusoff, B. A., Leckman, J. F., Dibble, E., Hamovit, J., Thompson, W. D., Pauls, D. L., & Guroff, J. J. (1984). Psychiatric disorders in the relatives of probands with affective disorders. *Archives of General Psychiatry, 41,* 13–21.

Weisz, J. R., Sigman, M., Weiss, B., & Mosk, J. (1993). Parent reports of behavioral and emotional problems among children in Kenya, Thailand and the United States. *Child Development, 64,* 98–109.

Weisz, J. R., Weiss, B., Alicke, M. D., & Klotz, M. L. (1987). Effectiveness of psychotherapy with children and adolescents: A meta-analysis for clinicians. *Journal of Consulting and Clinical Psychology, 55,* 542–549.

Weisz, J. R., Weiss, B., Han, S. S., Granger, D. A., & Morton, T. (1995). Effects of psychotherapy with children and adolescents revisited: A meta-analysis of treatment outcome studies. *Psychological Bulletin, 117,* 450–468.

Wellman, H. M. (1990). *Children's theories of mind.* Massachusetts: MIT Press.

Werker, J. F., & Tees, R. C. (1984). Cross-language speech perception: Evidence for a perceptual reorganization during the first year of life. *Infant Behavior and Development, 7,* 49–64.

Werner, E. E. (1979). *Cross-cultural child development.* Monterey, CA: Brooks-Cole.

Werner, E. E., & Smith, R. S. (1982). *Vulnerable but invincible.* New York: McGraw-Hill.

Werner, J. S., & Perlmutter, M. (1979). Development of visual memory in infants. In H. W. Reese & L. P. Lipsitt (Eds.), *Advances in Child Development and Behavior* (Vol. 14, pp. 1–56). New York: Academic Press.

Wertsch, J., McNamee, G. D., McLane, J. B., & Budwig, N. A. (1980). The adult-child dyad as a problem solving system. *Child Development, 51,* 1215–1221.

Weston, D., & Turiel, E. (1980). Act-rule relations: Children's concepts of social rules. *Developmental Psychology, 16,* 417–424.

Wetzel, R. (1976). Hopelessness, depression, and suicide intent. *Archives of General Psychiatry, 33,* 1069–1073.

Whaley, L. F. (1974). *Understanding inherited disorders.* St. Louis: Mosby.

White, C. B., Bushnell, W., & Regnemer, J. L. (1978). Moral development in Bahamian school children: A three-year examination of Kohlberg's stages of cognitive development. *Developmental Psychology, 14,* 58–65.

Whitebook, M., Howes, C., & Phillips, D. A. (1990). Who cares? Child care teachers and the quality of care in America. *The national child care staffing study.* Oakland: Child Care Employee Project.

Whiting, B. B., & Whiting, J. W. M. (1973). Altruistic and egotistic behavior in six cultures. In L. Nader & T. W. Maretzki (Eds.), *Cultural illness and health: Essays in human adaptation.* Washington, DC: American Anthropological Association.

Whiting, B. B., & Whiting, J. W. M. (1975). *Children of six cultures: A psychocultural analysis.* Cambridge, MA: Harvard University Press.

Wilkerson, I. (1994, May 16). 2 Boys, a debt, a gun, a victim: The face of violence. *The New York Times,* A1/A14.

Wilks, J. (1986). The relative importance of parents and friends in adolescent decision making. *Journal of Youth and Adolescence, 15,* 323–334.

Willerman, L. (1979). Effects of families on intellectual development. *American psychologist, 34,* 923–929.

Williams, P. A., Haertel, E. H., Walberg, H. J., & Haertel, G. D. (1982). The impact of leisure-time television on school learning: A research synthesis. *American Educational Research Journal, 19,* 19–50.

Williams, T. M. (Ed.). (1986). *The impact of television: A natural experiment involving three towns.* New York: Academic Press.

Wilson, M. N., & Saft, E. W. (1993). Child maltreatment in the African-American community. In I. E. Sigel (Series Ed.), D. Cicchetti, & S. L. Toth (Eds.), *Advances in applied developmental psychology: Vol 8. Child abuse, child development, and social policy* (pp. 213–248). Norwood, NJ: Ablex.

Wilson, R. S. (1985). Risk and resilience in early mental development. *Developmental Psychology, 21,* 795–805.

Wilson, R. S., & Harpring, E. B. (1972). Mental and motor development in infant twins. *Developmental Psychology, 7,* 277–287.

Winn, M. (1987). *Unplugging the plug-in drug.* New York: Penguin.

Winokur, G. (1975). Heredity in the affective disorders.

In E. Anthony & T. Benedek (Eds.), *Depression in human existence.* Boston: Little, Brown.

Wolff, P. H. (1987). *The development of behavioral states and the expression of emotions in early infancy.* Chicago: University of Chicago Press.

Wooden, K. (1976). *Keeping in the playtime of others.* New York: McGraw-Hill.

Worobey, J. & Belsky, J. (1982). Employing the Brazelton scale to influence mothering: An experimental comparison of three strategies. *Developmental Psychology, 18,* 736–743.

Wynn, K. (1990). Children's understanding of counting. *Cognition, 36,* 155–193.

Wynn, K. (1992). Addition and subtraction by human infants. *Nature, 358,* 749–750.

Wynne, L. C., Singer, M. T., Bartko, J.J., & Toohey, M. (1976). Schizophrenics and their families: Recent research on parental communication. In J. M. Tanner (Ed.), *Psychiatric research: The widening perspective.* New York: International Universities Press.

Yando, R., Seitz, V., & Zigler, E. (1978). *Imitation in developmental perspective.* Hillsdale, NJ: LEA.

Yarrow, M. R., Scott, P. M., & Waxler, C. Z. (1973). Learning concern for others. *Developmental Psychology, 8,* 240–260.

Yoshikawa, H. (1994). Prevention as cumulative protection: Effects of early family support and education on chronic delinquency and its risks. *Psychological Bulletin, 115,* 28–54.

Younger, B. A., & Cohen, L. B. (1983). Infant perception of correlations among attributes. *Child Development, 54,* 858–869.

Youniss, J. (1980). *Parents and peers in social development: A Sullivan-Piaget perspective.* Chicago: University of Chicago Press.

Youniss, J. (1983). Social construction of adolescence by adolescents and parents. In H. D. Grotevant & C. R. Cooper (Eds.), *Adolescent development in the family* (pp. 93–109). San Francisco: Jossey-Bass.

Youniss, J., & Ketterlinus, R. D. (1987). Communication and connectedness in mother- and father-adolescent relationships. *Journal of Youth and Adolescence, 16,* 265–280.

Youniss, J., & Smollar, J. (1985). *Adolescent relations with mothers, fathers, and friends.* Chicago: University of Chicago Press.

Zabin, L. S., Kantner, J. F., & Zelnik, M. (1979). The risk of adolescent pregnancy in the first months of intercourse. *Family Planning Perspectives, 11,* 215–222.

Zahn-Waxler, C., & Chapman, M. (1982). Immediate antecedents of caretakers' methods of discipline. *Child Psychiatry and Human Development, 12,* 179–192.

Zahn-Waxler, C., Kochanska, G., Krupnick, J., & McKnew, D. (1990). Patterns of guilt in children of depressed and well mothers. *Developmental Psychology, 26,* 51–59.

Zahn-Waxler, C., & Radke-Yarrow, M. (1990). The origin of empathetic concern. *Motivation and Emotion, 14,* 107–130.

Zahn-Waxler, C., Radke-Yarrow, M., & King, R. A. (1979). Child rearing and children's pro-social initiation toward victims of distress. *Child Development, 50,* 319–330.

Zelazo, P., Zelazo, N, & Kolb, S. (1972). "Walking" in the newborn. *Science, 176,* 314–315.

Zigler, E. (1980). Controlling child abuse: Do we have the knowledge and/or the will? In G. Gerbner, C. J. Ross, & E. Zigler (Eds.), *Child abuse: An agenda for action.* New York: Oxford University Press.

Zigler, E., & Styfco, S. J. (1993). Using research and theory to justify and inform Head Start expansion. *Society of the Research of Child Development Social Policy Report, 7* (2).

Zigler, E., & Valentine, J. (Eds.). (1979). *Project Head Start: A legacy of the war on poverty.* New York: Free Press.

Zillmann, D., Williams, B. R., Bryant, J., Boynton, K. R., & Wolf, M. A. (1980). Acquisition of information from educational television programs as a function of differentially paced humorous inserts. *Journal of Educational Psychology, 72,* 170–180.

PHOTO CREDITS

Unless otherwise acknowledged, all photographs are the property of Scott, Foresman and Company. Page abbreviations are as follows: T (top), B (bottom), L (left), C (center), R (right).

NAME INDEX

SUBJECT INDEX